THE PEOPLE'S LAW REVIEW

Editor:	Ralph Warner
Associate Editors:	David Brown, Katherine M. Galvin, Peter Jan Honigsberg, Toni Ihara
Assistant Editors:	Stephanie Harolde, Keija Kimura, Steven T. Murray
Illustrators:	Linda Allison, Hope Emerson Winslow
Book Design:	Toni Ihara, Hope Emerson Winslow

A NOLO PRESS BOOK

ADDISON-WESLEY PUBLISHING COMPANY

Reading, Massachusetts
Menlo Park, California • London • Amsterdam • Don Mills, Ontario • Sydney

Library of Congress Cataloging in Publication Data

Main entry under title:

The People's law review.

  Includes index.
  1. Law—United States—Popular works. I. Warner,
Ralph E.
KF387.P46   349.73   80-18475
ISBN 0-201-08306-X

Reproduced by Addison-Wesley from camera-ready copy supplied by the authors.

Copyright © 1980 by Addison-Wesley Publishing Company, Inc.
Philippines copyright © 1980 by Addison-Wesley Publishing Company, Inc.

ISBN 0-201-08306-X
ABCDEFGHIJ-DO-89876543210

★

To Our Readers

We hope that this book will be of assistance to you and your family. Although it is not primarily a "how-to-do-it" book, there are several sections which do contain specific suggestions and instructions on how to accomplish legal tasks. Many knowledgeable people have reviewed these materials and many of their suggestions for change and clarification have been included. But advice, no matter how well-intentioned, does not always bring the desired results. So, here are some qualifications. If you have retained a lawyer, and his or her advice is contrary to that given here, follow your lawyer's suggestions; the individual characteristics of your problem can better be considered by a person in possession of all the facts. Also, laws and procedures vary considerably from one state to the next. It is impossible to guarantee that the information and advice contained here will be completely accurate for your particular location. It's your responsibility to check local rules and procedures before following advice given here. You should also be aware that this book was printed in the summer of 1980 and that laws and legal procedures are subject to change. And finally, we call your attention to this general disclaimer: of necessity, neither the editors, authors, nor publishers of this book make any guarantees regarding the outcome or the uses to which this material is put. Thank you and good luck!

★

Thank You

Many talented people have contributed to this book. We are particularly grateful to our book scouts who alerted us to regional people's law materials: Doe Coover, Brian Crockett, Ann Dilworth, Bee Pladsen, Cecil Stewart and Trudie Warner.

To acknowledge by name everyone who contributed ideas, insights and constructive criticism to this project would require a forest of paper—so in the interests of conservation, we offer instead a hearty and collective thank you to all of you who helped with this publication. However, we would particularly like to acknowledge the special assistance of Karen Brown, Shirley Fogarino, Stewart Miller, Della Rice, Linda Roberts, Ray Shonholtz, Kathy Sullivan and Paul Wahrhaftig.

We wish also to thank Stephanie Harolde for the many nights and weekends spent on manuscript preparation and copy editing. And finally, a special thanks to Steve Murray at Berkeley's Accent & Alphabet, who did a fine and dedicated job of setting the type.

Table of Contents

★

About Nolo Press

This book was created by Nolo Press in Berkeley, California. Nolo consists of a group of friends (some lawyers, some not) who have come to see much of what passes for the practice of law as meaningless mumbo-jumbo and needless paper-shuffling designed by lawyers to mystify and confuse. Since 1971, Nolo has published more than a dozen books designed to give ordinary people access to their legal system, and in doing so, it has become one of the principal energy centers of the self-help law movement.

Introduction

This book is about eliminating the need for lawyers. Here, we gather resources and ideas that point to ways in which access to everyday law and the resolution of common disputes can be opened to all. We happily concede that we are biased in favor of the idea that all citizens should be encouraged to actively participate in the legal decisions that touch their lives. We are convinced that the average person is competent to represent herself or himself, and that the right to do so must again become a cornerstone of our democracy.

The idea that there can be law without lawyers is at least as old as recorded history. In this country, people's law was well established before the first angry gunfire in 1775 turned colonies into country. Even a hundred years ago, when our great-grandparents lived on farms or in small towns, and lawyers were modest fellows who could read and write a little better than average and owned a fireproof box, most folks still had some chance to participate in the legal decisions that affected their lives. How these country lawyers metamorphosed into armies of ambitious grey-flanneled hustlers determined to run every aspect of our lives, while traveling first-class all the way, is a longer story than we have time to chronicle here. But it is important for each of us to face the fact that lawyer-dominance is a product of a society that preaches the value of finishing first no matter what the cost, and of the American ethic which holds that going 75 miles an hour is dandy as long as you don't get caught. Or to put it another way, it is our greed and fear that have put those crowds of esquires on the tops of every tall building in town.

If lawyers, whose tight grip now controls every nook and cranny of our legal system, were even doing an adequate job, there would be little reason for this book. Manifestly, they are not. Our legislatures are dominated by lawyers who cynically place the interests of their "profession" before those of the electorate. Our laws themselves are deliberately made complex and unintelligible and our courts are designed to be expensive, constipated and purposefully intimidating to the non-lawyer. The situation has become so bad that, when most people face a legal problem, the best they can do is to shrug their shoulders and hope that it will go away.

But rather than dwell on all the negative aspects of American legal institutions, our goal is to communicate a sense of the excitement that comes with understanding legal rules and procedures and representing oneself in court. Whether this means that you learn how to do your own divorce, get a poem copyrighted, or force the landlord to stop interfering with your privacy, is not as important as the fact that, by taking charge of your own legal problem, you will have become a more powerful and creative person. If there is a central premise to this book, it is that there is no such thing as "abstract" justice that can be dispensed by a black-robed judge (who is, of course, nothing more than a lawyer, sitting on a wooden pedestal at the end of a drafty room), but that justice for all can only be a product of participation by all.

When we first thought about putting together information on the self-help law movement, we considered all sorts of possibilities, from doing a catalogue of people's law materials and groups, to showing how computers can be used to speed us toward the day when there will be genuine popular participation in our legal system. Along the way, we considered creating materials which provide practical information on how to deal with the existing laws and courts, as well as the value of exploring how other societies deal with law and lawyers. And then there were those of us who wished to do a book on mediation as an alternative to our adversary system; others expressed the view that, before we talk about fundamental changes in our legal institutions, it is necessary to understand the history and philosophical underpinnings of our law. Each one of these subjects is in itself so large as to be beyond our

1

power to fully deal with. Nevertheless, in the end we decided to take them all on. We thought that with a little luck we could put together a potpourri of people's law and then stand back and look for those spontaneous connections that lead to new and exciting insights.

None of the editors of this book has ever done anything like this before, and we have had a genuinely exciting time inventing as we have gone along.

When we began, we all thought we knew a lot about self-help law and how ordinary folks could make it a part of their lives. As our publication date drew near, though, we deepened our understanding to the point that we realized that we knew (and know) very little. Indeed, we wouldn't be the least surprised if some of your ideas are better than some of ours. If so, what can we say except—welcome to the people's law movement.

Berkeley, California
Summer, 1980

Ralph Warner

★ A note to—and about—lawyers ★

In these pages lawyers tend to be pictured (rather regularly) as ogres. Indeed, we do have a considerable bias against the profession as a whole and what we feel is its negative power in our society. That said, let us say too that we know many wonderful, concerned people who happen to be lawyers. Come to think of it, many of the people who worked on this book are lawyers who have abandoned their "professional" role while holding on to a love for the law. Oh, and one more thing: the self-help law movement has not yet developed the information and resources to help you solve all of your legal problems. There are times when you will need the information and assistance that a lawyer can provide. But we hope you will not see a lawyer until you have legally researched a problem as much as possible on your own so that you can relate to your lawyer as your advisor, and not your master. Remember, the Latin root of the word "client" is "to hear," "to obey."

PART I

Law: Where We Have Been, Where We Are Going, & Other Ways to Get There

When we think about the deficiencies of our existing legal system, it's easy to accept the broad outline of the way things are done and to try to improve them by tinkering with details. For example, we might push for procedures to streamline divorce, but not take time to ask why we entrust the details of our domestic lives to the courts in the first place.

So, before we get down to the nitty-gritty of particular laws, procedures, and courts, let's take a few minutes to get a little perspective. It is important to realize that the regulation of human conduct has been handled very differently in various ages and parts of our planet. Thus, there seems to be no reason to be in awe of some grand absolute called THE LAW because no such thing exists. In actuality, law is a relative concept, changing with time and circumstance.

St. Yves is from Brittany
A lawyer but not a thief
Such a thing is beyond belief

*A popular rhyme about a 14th
century lawyer who was made a saint
because he represented the poor.*

People's Law: A Return to Self-Reliance

by Mort Rieber

One of the most exciting things we learned while preparing this book was that there was once an active, vibrant people's law movement in the United States. Having worked with self-help law for years, it is amazing that we didn't know this. But lawyers chanting the mantra of their union—that "a man who represents himself has a fool for a client"—have so hidden our tradition of legal self-reliance, that it has never occurred to most of us that their absolute control of our legal system is a recent phenomenon.

We live in an age in which we are constantly reminded how much we need experts to help us deal with even the simplest aspects of everyday life. From our earliest days in the schoolroom, we have been taught to rely not on our own abilities, but on the expertise of the specialist. Reinforced by advertising that extolls the virtues of the professional, even in such relatively uncomplicated matters as carpet cleaning and dog grooming, it is not surprising that the vast majority of the public is convinced that only an obstetrician can deliver a baby and only a lawyer can draw up a will form.

This ubiquitous reliance on experts is a relatively new phenomenon in the history of our nation. Not more than 100 years ago the majority of the population lived in rural areas, often a considerable distance from cities and shops. As a matter of necessity, people learned, from an early age, to be self-reliant. Soap and candle making, leather tanning, housebuilding, metal forging, weaving, and a multitude of other skills were common knowledge in most households.

Surprisingly enough, it was not only home and farm skills that were common knowledge. By 1879, John Wells had published his newly revised edition of *Every Man His Own Lawyer*. This book was sold as "a complete guide in all matters of law and business negotiations for every State of the Union. With legal forms for drawing the necessary papers, and full instructions for proceeding, without legal assistance, in suits and business transactions of every description." Apparently, the popularity of this book was widespread. In the introduction, the author states "The original edition of this work was prepared and presented to the public many years ago and was received with great favor, *attaining a larger scale, it is believed, than any work published within its time*" [italics added]. He goes on to say that hundreds of thousands of copies of the former editions were sold.

Layman's Law was nothing new. It was part of a tradition that went back to colonial times. Eldon Revare James, in his *A List of Legal Treatises Printed in the British Colonies and the American States Before 1801*, came to the conclusion that:

> In the hundred years between the publication in 1687 of William Penn's gleanings from Lord Coke and the issuance of the American editions of Buller's *Nisi Pruis* and Gilbert's *Evidence* in 1788, not a single book that could be called a treatise intended for the use of professional lawyers was published in the British Colonies and American States. All of the books within this period which by any stretch of definition might be regarded as legal treatises were for the use of laymen.

As early as 1784, another book entitled *Everyman His Own Lawyer* was in its ninth edition. Published in London as a comprehensive guide to both civil and criminal law, it was divided into seven sections covering the following diverse topics:

I. Of Actions and Remedies, Writs, Process, Arrest, and Bail.
II. Of Courts, Attorneys and Solicitors therein, Juries, Witnesses, Trials, Executions, etc.
III. Of Estates and Property in Lands and Goods, and how acquired; Ancestors, Heirs, Executors and Administrators.
IV. Of the Laws relating to Marriage, Bastardy, Infants, Idiots, Lunaticks.
V. Of the Liberty of the Subject, *Magna Charta*, and *Habeas Corpus* Act, and other statutes.
VI. Of the King and his Prerogative, the Queen and Prince, Peers, Judges, Sheriffs, Coroners, Justices of Peace, Constables, etc.

VII. Of publick Offences, Treason, Murder, Felony, Burglary, Robbery, Rape, Sodomy, Forgery, Perjury, etc. And their punishment.

In addition to dealing with almost every aspect of law, the book also promised that "All of (the topics) so plainly treated that all manner of persons may be particularly acquainted with our laws and statutes, concerning civil and criminal affairs, and know how to defend themselves and their estates and fortunes, in all cases whatsoever."

Today, many critics have referred to the unnecessary expense inherent in our legal system.

> Much has been recently done, to simplify and harmonise the system of practice in the courts; something has been gained in point of expedition; but little, if anything, in the reduction of the *expense* of bringing and defending actions. Useless proceedings are still required, apparently for no other purpose than to extract money from pockets of the unfortunate suitors. Forms, the pretenses for which have been long exploded, are pertinaciously adhered to, merely because they are productive of emolument to the retainers of the courts; — and while this is the case, legal proceedings will remain characterised by an uncertainty of result, a loss of time, and a ruinous expense, which should induce every one to learn as effectually as possible to guard against a seduction into its labyrinths, or, if entangled in them, to make the most easy and expeditious escape.

Lest one think that this criticism of the legal establishment is a relatively recent phenomenon, this statement appeared in Thomas Wooler's preface to *Every Man His Own Attorney*, published in 1845.

Although lawyers command respect of the nearly exclusive access to the world of legal affairs, it would not be unfair to say that this respect is granted rather grudgingly. The public's disdain for lawyers dates back at least to biblical times. "Woe unto you, lawyers for ye have taken away the key of knowledge: ye entered not in yourselves, and them that were entering in ye hindered." (Luke 11:52) Biblical criticism was not directed just at lawyers. Even then, the judicial system itself came under attack when Jesus warned "Agree with thine adversary quickly, whiles thou art in the way with him: lest at any time the adversary deliver thee to the judge, and the judge deliver thee to the officer, and thou be cast in

EVERY · MAN

HIS OWN ATTORNEY:

COMPRISING THE

Law of Landlord and Tenant,

THE BANKRUPT AND INSOLVENT LAWS,

The Law of Debtor and Creditor,

WITH INSTRUCTIONS TO COMMENCE AND DEFEND ACTIONS IN PERSON, THE AMOUNT OF COSTS, OFFICERS' FEES, &c.

THE LAW OF WILLS,

THE LAWS OF CRIMINAL JURISPRUDENCE, &c. &c.

WITH
AN APPENDIX,

CONTAINING ALL THE MODERN ALTERATIONS IN PRACTICE.

A NEW EDITION, REVISED, CORRECTED AND ENLARGED,

BY THOMAS JONATHAN WOOLER, Esq.

London:

PUBLISHED BY TALLIS & Co. 2, NORTHAMPTON SQUARE,
AND SOLD BY G. VIRTUE, 26, IVY LANE.

prison." (Matthew 5:25)

Early lay guides to law recognized the dangers of a system which was structured so that one had to depend upon professional counsel to protect one's vital interests. Distrusting lawyer's motives, Wooler in 1845 saw the necessity for educating the public for their own protection.

> When attorneys are employed, they must be paid; and their charges are not always regulated either by their abilities, or their services to a client, but by their own desire to make as much as they can. This evil can only be remedied by making their clients well informed on common subjects, and able to see what course they are taking in matters of more intricacy.

Coming out of a self-reliant pioneering tradition, how did we ever get into a situation where we do not trust our own judgment and abilities on matters which are so important in our everyday life? In her carefully documented analysis of the rise of professionalism, especially in the last century, Magali Larson[1] writes of the monopoly of competence created by professionals to protect their special status within society.

The visible professions which have a clear monopoly of competence—and not only a monopoly of practice—have *authority* over a kind of knowledge that is important for every man's life. The gap in competence between professionals and laymen, institutionalized by the monopolies of training and certification, ipso facto sets *every* professional apart: he belongs to a privileged society of "knowers," which the public tends to identify with its elite spokesmen. The "mysteries" interpreted by the individual professional have been named and partially revealed to the public before he comes in. It is a rare individual who can challenge by himself the whole image of a field and the social construction of an aspect of reality in which professional elites are particularly active and influential.

Institutionalized education, which plays a major role in perpetuating the myth of the average citizen's incompetence, has established the paradox that, along with an almost complete eradication of illiteracy, there is an equally thorough dependency on experts and specialists. As many critics of our educational system have pointed out, the main function of our schools is certification rather than education, and so the special interests of the certifiers become closely tied to the interests of those certified; so much so, that these two interest groups conspire to structure society in such a way that they maintain their monopolistic control.

The material and ideological importance of the educational system for both the consolidation of professions and the reproduction of the social order cannot be overemphasized. (Larson, p. 239)

NEW REVISED EDITION.

WELLS'

EVERY MAN HIS OWN LAWYER

AND

Business Form Book.

A COMPLETE GUIDE IN ALL MATTERS OF LAW AND BUSINESS NEGOTIATIONS,

FOR EVERY STATE IN THE UNION.

WITH LEGAL FORMS FOR DRAWING THE NECESSARY PAPERS, AND FULL INSTRUCTIONS FOR PROCEEDING, WITHOUT LEGAL ASSISTANCE, IN SUITS AND BUSINESS TRANSACTIONS OF EVERY DESCRIPTION.

BY

JOHN G. WELLS,

AUTHOR OF "ILLUSTRATED NATIONAL HAND-BOOK," "ARMY AND NAVY HANDY BOOK," "CHICAGO AS IT WAS AND IS," ETC., ETC.

With a Portrait of the Author.

NEW YORK:

JOHN G. WELLS, 729 BROADWAY.

ROBERT MACOY, 4 BARCLAY STREET.

Our legal system, which is based on precedence, has served to further mystify and sanctify the lawyer's job. De Tocqueville, writing in the mid 1800's, observed:

> The absolute need of legal aid that is felt in England and in the United States, and the high opinion that is entertained of the ability of the legal profession, tend to separate it more and more from the people and to erect it into a distinct class. The French lawyer is simply a man extensively acquainted with the statutes of his country: but the English or American lawyer resembles the hierophants of Egypt, for like them he is the sole interpreter of an occult science. (de Tocqueville, *Democracy*, p. 287.)

Considering the fact that the percentage of lawyers in the U.S. House of Representatives and Senate has varied from 55 to 75% in recent decades (with similar figures in state legislatures), it is not surprising to see that the cumbersome nature of our system of justice continues to exclude most of us from access to it without placing our complete trust in the hands of an attorney.

The trend towards mystification of competence brought about by the enormous growth of professionalism has resulted in a subtle form of disenfranchisement of the person. Writing about the effects of this process, Theodore Roszak[2] states "Mystification is aggression upon the spiritual autonomy of others; it is inevitably a depersonalizing assertion of hierarchial status based on the assumption that there is an authority somewhere that has the right to assign and enforce identities."

Over the past few years, there has been a growing awareness of the sacredness of each individual human being's uniqueness and competence. This desire to know and understand ourselves is reflected in the many faceted experiments in self-realization that can be seen in the new therapies — roughly categorized under the heading of Human Potential Movement — as well as the ever increasing number of liberation movements (women, gays, Native Americans, etc.) and the growing interest in spiritual development. Increasingly, and along many different paths, there is a dawning of consciousness that proclaims to self and others "I matter, I am special, I am competent." This attitude naturally leads to a desire to take charge of one's life and is the antithesis of an attitude of chronic dependence upon experts and professionals.

As a Saturday visit to the local home improvement center or automotive parts supermarket will demonstrate, more and more people are trying out their abilities in areas which are so essential for everyday living, yet are almost completely ignored by conventional schooling. Understandably, the urge to demonstrate one's competence will manifest first in those areas which are concrete and relatively simple to understand. But along with this, many are testing their new found confidence in their abilities by taking charge of more complex matters in their life, such as health maintenance, and legal matters. The growing popularity of self-help law books is testimony to the fact that people are reasserting their right to take care of their own affairs, as part of the process of self-discovery.

1. Larson, Magali S., *The Rise of Professionalism — A Sociological Analysis*, University of California Press. Berkeley, 1977.
2. Roszak, Theodore, *Person/Planet: The Creative Disintegration of Industrial Society*. Anchor Press/Doubleday. New York, 1979.

Mort Rieber is an itinerant psychology teacher who lives in the country and spends much of his time raising children and vegetables.

"Justice" As Ordeal

by Anne Strick

We often hear the Anglo-American adversary system of dispute-resolution praised by lawyers and judges as being the best ever devised to get at the truth. In this review we will present another view—that the adversary system itself is perhaps the most negative aspect of our dispute-resolution process. But before we get into this, we thought it would be fun to understand some of the origins of the idea that justice could be arrived at through a sort of judicial battle. The following piece is excerpted from Anne Strick's wonderful book Injustice For All—How Our Adversary System of Law Victimizes Us and Subverts True Justice *(more about this book in Part 5).*

Once upon a time, before written laws, judges, and courts, the administration of justice in disputed cases was inexpensive and direct. If evidence was inadequate or too evenly balanced, or an issue sufficiently hotly contested, the accused was made to undergo some physical peril. His survival or demise was interpreted as the verdict upon him of the all-knowing gods. Did he live? Ah, innocent. Oh, he died? Guilty, obviously! That tidy episode was trial, judgment, and punishment in one. Such was judicial ordeal.

That technique did not stand alone in early Western legal procedure. From area to area, era to era, people to people, it existed in varying prominence alongside other judicial methods. Disputes between individuals were commonly settled by fines, or the measured physical retaliation of injury for injury; while exile and death might be solutions for broader antisocial crime. But where decision was difficult—where information was lacking, where culpability was unclear, where accused denied a charge or litigants were backed by equally bellicose family groups so that feud threatened, ordeal was usually the resort. Clan chiefs, feudal lords, or kings handed the problem, with a sigh, up to heaven via ordeal.

There were a variety of ordeals. The commonest were those of water, fire, food, and poison; of oath and trial by battle. All shared a single premise: belief that the best way to end a controversy was to place at least one of the disputants in grave danger and thus force the omniscient spirits to take sides in rescue. "Right" would manifest itself in minimum of injury—or survival. Ordeal contributed largely to the first fruition of Western legal ideas.[1] More particularly, it is the spiritual parent of our adversary legal approach.

Our concept of "equal justice" was no part of that early legal model. Though the gods rescued him who was "right"—he was generally right who was deity's friend. Culpability, in other words, was relative to status. For although anyone might be subject to ordeal, it was preeminently the weak who were called upon to furnish such proof of worthy origin, and thereby of a right to life and safety. Aliens, outsiders, and particularly women and children were most often that "discarded class."

Thus, a frequent case in the legends is that of the woman whose illicit pregnancy reveals her misconduct. Though pariah if she had introduced into her group of relatives a child of lesser blood, she was praised if she had been intimate with a scion of the gods. But she must prove her claim of a celestial visitor. That proof would consist in the god's rescuing her and their child from mortal danger: from drowning at sea, for example, in one variation of water ordeal. In the legends—he ofttimes did. To know a god (one way or another) was useful indeed.

The ordeals of fire, food, and poison similarly required the accused to demonstrate the solicitude of some all-powerful spirit. In ordeal of fire, a man might be made to walk over glowing coals, thrust his hand into boiling water or oil, or hold a red-hot iron. Guilt or innocence rested upon the degree of injury sustained—as judged by the medicine man. In ordeal of food, an accused might be made to swallow bread or cheese over which prayers, subject sometimes only to the presiding priest's imagination, had been incanted. If, throat constricted in

Winslow

terror, the victim was unable to swallow, he was promptly held guilty and condemned. With poison, the result depended somewhat on the accused's constitution, but perhaps more on the motives of that infinitely influential medicine man—priest who mixed the dose.

Peril, then, was the essence of ordeal. And exculpation (in practice if not in theory) was very much a matter of high birth, sheer luck, or sufficient clout with heaven's representative, the friendly neighborhood shaman.

Political motives, however, eventually began to alter notions both of the gods and of the justice they dispensed. Morality entered the picture in a formal sense. Nations declared their wars just, looked to their gods for victory, and considered virtuous those deities who granted that success and who had, at the same time, often become associated with governments in "lawgiving." As the gods came to represent virtue, the meaning of divine judgment in judicial ordeal changed formally, too. That "judgment of God" was now seen as heavenly ruling on the moral justice of the claim, rather than lineage or status of the claimant. According to that judgment, the omniscient beings would never forsake the innocent; never permit the wrong to triumph.

In other words: high connection and lucky chance might still be "right"—but they were now called "justice." Our adversary ethic still calls them justice today.

In one form of another, an oath always accompanied ordeal. Here and there it came to be a kind of ordeal in itself. Such oath was a self-curse (or "conditional curse") calling down upon the perjurer heaven's vengeance. For instance, "If faithful, may much good come unto me; if false, may evil come in place of good."

Skillful perjury, however, soon became a hallmark of the judicial sophisticate. ("Sophistication," defines Webster's: ". . . misrepresentation or falsification in argument . . .") As early as 1000 B.C., in Greece, it was considered "meritorious to be skillful in profiting as much from the false oath as from a theft. . . ." Five hundred years later, the rhetoricians and sophists served as a "manual of perjury" at the service of the litigant. The object was to preserve the letter of the oath, while evading its spirit.

For example: A sly fellow, accused of refusing to restore a sum of money held in trust, hid the money in the hollow of his staff. Just before taking the oath of innocence, he handed the staff to the plaintiff to hold. Thus we could "truly" swear he had delivered the funds to the plaintiff—and yet keep it all, "even the favor of the gods!" Or, goes another tale, a man who stole a fish in a market slipped it into another's basket and swore with clear conscience that he "had it not, nor knew of any other person who took it." And then there was the judge who, technically faithful to his judicial oath, cast his own vote for the death of a guilty friend on trial—but persuaded his two colleagues to vote for acquittal.

It was against this state of affairs that Plato inveighed: ". . . the law, if intelligently framed, should not require the oath from either party . . . we cannot for a moment doubt that perhaps a half of our citizens are perjurers, who nevertheless do not hesitate to sit at table with the rest nor to associate with them in public assembly and private homes. . . ." Plato was not heeded.

Eventually Christianity, attempting to add sanctity, brought the oath into church. There the defendant was made to swear innocence with hand upon the altar or some heavily blessed relic. When perjury persisted, the number of altars requisite was multiplied. The Anglo-Saxons, for instance, in certain cases allowed the plaintiff to substantiate his charge in four churches, while the defendant could rebut by swearing an oath of denial in twelve. When such altar-arithmetic got out of hand, emphasis shifted to relics as means of perjury control. This led to an increasingly complex religio-legal account-juggling. For example, perjury on a consecrated cross required three times the penance requisite for perjury on an unconsecrated one; but seven times the penance was necessary to absolve perjury if the oath had been taken on an altar with relics. If, however, no priest had officiated at the original ceremony, the false swearer was home free—the oath void and perjury without penalty![2]

Nevertheless, neither churchly sanctity, altar, nor relic deterred the determined. Over one thousand years after Plato, complaints still rose. About A.D. 700, a section of the Burgundian code deplored, "Many we find, are so depraved, that they do not hesitate to offer an oath upon things uncertain, and to commit perjury upon things unknown to them."

It has been suggested that this plague of perjury accounted for the rise of that most famous of ordeals, trial by battle. Unlike the false oath, whose evil consequence might not immediately fall, battle brought down prompt and dramatically unequivocal divine retribution upon the perjurer. Certainly Charlemagne in the eighth century post-Christ (some 1,100 years after Plato's plaint) considered battle a practical remedy for the prevalence of perjury and certainly, too, outraged litigants increasingly took the law into their own hands and settled matters with violence; while the authorities, in order to maintain some semblance of control, began to structure rules for conduct of the carnage.

In any case, judicial battle was a bilateral ordeal: one to which both sides had to submit. And, however it developed, ordeal appears to be a Western ancestral institution. "Trial by battle," says Holdsworth, "is almost universally found among the barbarian tribes from whom the nations of modern Europe trace their descent. . . . It was accompanied by a belief that Providence will give victory to the right. Christianity merely transferred this appeal from the heathen deities to the God of Battles." Another historian suggests, ". . . the Church found in [ordeal] a powerful instrument to enforce her authority, and to acquire influence over the rugged nature of her indocile converts." In other words, religion's blessing helped institutionalize Battle as an acceptable legal technique in the Western world.

Oddly, the Anglo-Saxons seem to have been almost the only people who did not initially pos-

sess the ordeal of battle. But in 1066, William the Bastard (son of Robert the Devil) brought trial by battle to England. Here, with the conquerors' backing, it took fast hold, superseding those other ordeals that were native custom, and lending itself increasingly to the "advantage of the turbulent and unscrupulous."

Explains Lea, ". . . The strong and the bold are apt to be the ruling spirits in all ages, and were emphatically so in those periods of scarcely curbed violence. . . . It is no wonder, therefore, that means were readily found for extending the jurisdiction of the wager of battle as widely as possible. . . ." In Europe as well as England, one of the most fruitful expedients was the custom of challenging witnesses. If, for instance, your case were going badly, you simply challenged an inconvenient witness to defend his veracity. If your swordsmanship was good, this generally took care of both the witness and the case. Such tactics quickly became a favorite method of escaping legal condemnation. Witnesses, in fact, were finally required to come into court armed—and to have their weapons blessed on the altar before giving testimony. One of the Frisian tribes actually enshrined in legal code a handy variation of this technique: A man, if unable to disprove an accusation of homicide against himself, was permitted to *transfer the charge to anyone else he wished*; and then decide the question between himself and the hapless bystander, by combat!

Eventually, no dispute existed that might not be submitted to the decision of sword or club. Between the 10th and 13th centuries, judicial battle was so integral a part of the ordinary law, civil as well as criminal, employed habitually in the most everyday affairs, that only infants, women, ecclesiastics, and those over sixty could avoid it. (The guardians of women and minors, however, were required to give battle in their behalf.) Anyone suffering certain physical disabilities might likewise decline. But such disabilities were codified with the utmost nicety: the loss of molar teeth, for instance, did not permit disqualification; while the absence of incisors, considered important weapons, did.

Nor did even death assure escape. A North German law provided that the dead, when prosecuted, might appear in the lists by substitute. A Scottish law firmly ordered that if the accused should die before the appointed time, his body must be brought to the battlefield, "for no man can essoin [excuse] himself by death."

Women, though usually exempt from compulsory combat, were permitted to fight if they wished. This was now and then regulated with tender care. Under a German law, "The chances between such unequal adversaries were adjusted by placing the man up to the navel in a pit three feet wide, tying his left hand behind his back, and arming him only with a club, while his fair opponent had the free use of her limbs and was furnished with a stone as large as a fist... fastened in a piece of stuff...." Not everywhere, however, was such fastidious adjustment made. The Frankish kingdoms of the East reserved a special atrocity for women, or at least for those who preferred to hire champions to fight for them. When a woman's champion was defeated, she was promptly burned to death no matter what the crime for which the combat occurred. This was one of the numerous instances in medieval law of "the injustice applied habitually to the weaker sex."

Defeat, then, generally involved a triple risk: loss of the suit, possible death on the field, or—if the loser survived—conviction of perjury often punishable by death or dismemberment. A vanquished combatant was classified with perjurers, false witnesses, and other infamous persons.

Nevertheless, persons exempt from combat still sometimes wished to contest a matter. Champions, again, were their means to battle. In theory, the champion was a witness, "swearing" through arms to the justice of the disputant's case. But in practice he was often simply a hireling-fighter. Gradually, toward the 12th and 13th centuries, the ablebodied too began to seek ways of appointing substitutes. One such way turned to advantage the custom of challenging witnesses, and at the same time affirmed the contradictory duality of witness-champion. The litigant would hire, ostensibly to testify but actually to disrupt, "some truculent bravo who swore unscrupulously" and whose false evidence would bring down upon him the wrath of the adverse party. The bravo, forced out of court at sword's point, would then turn and in one swoop demolish the adverse litigant and the litigation, too. Eventually a class of professional champions arose. These were permanently retained by landowners, churches, and sometimes entire communities—all

wanting, of course, the best fighters money could buy.

Through such devices the profession of champion became before long almost synonymous with "false witness." That synonymity was in fact often demanded by the legal codes themselves, which required the champion to assume the position of someone who had witnessed the action at issue. In England and Normandy, for example, this curious legal fiction required the plaintiff's champion to swear that he had heard and seen the matters alleged in the claim; while the adverse champion dutifully swore the opposite.

Thus, ultimately, the exigencies of bilateral judicial ordeal created a kind of schizophrenic ethic. That legal ethic caught the professional battler between conflicting obligations: to the appearance of truth on one hand, and the practice of deception on the other. Both were his duties. They still are.

When the champion lost, however, he suffered heavily. Publicly revealed as a liar, he became a scapegoat for the community's complicity in his deceit. Thus, while the losing principal in criminal cases might possibly escape with a fine or imprisonment, the hired ruffian was hanged, or at best lost a hand or foot, as punishment for perjury. "With such risks to be encountered, it is no wonder that the trade of champion offered few attractions to honest men who could keep body and soul together in any other way." Indeed, champions came to be classed with the "... vilest criminals, and with the unhappy females who exposed their charms for sale ... the extraordinary anomaly was exhibited of seeking to learn the truth in affairs of the highest moment by a solemn appeal to God, through the instrumentality of those who were already considered as convicts of the worst kind. ..."

Finally, in Western Europe judicial battle was

> ... so skillfully interwoven through the whole system of jurisprudence that no one could feel secure that he might not, as plaintiff, defendant or witness, be called upon to protect his estate or his life either by his own right hand or by the club of some professional and possibly treacherous bravo. This organized violence assumed for itself the sanction of a religion of love and peace, and human intelligence seemed too much blunted to recognize the contradiction.

It was not until 1819 that trial by battle was (with belated official rectitude) officially outlawed in England.

(Because of space considerations, many footnotes have been deleted. See *Injustice For All* for complete listing of footnotes.)

1. Gustave Glotz, in Albert Kocourek and John Wigmore, *The Evolution of Law*. Boston, Little Brown, 1915 vol. 2, p. 610.
2. Henry C. Lea, *Superstition and Force*. New York, Haskell House, 1971, pp. 100–1.
3. Henry C. Lea, in *Law and Warfare*, edited by Paul Bohannon. Garden City, N.Y., Natural History Press, 1967, p. 236.

Anne Strick has made an intensive study of our system of law over the past seven years, both here and abroad. Since the publication of Injustice For All, *she has become recognized as one of the most active voices for opening up our legal system to allow participation by all.*

The Backdrop of Our Legal Institutions

by Michael E. Tigar
with the assistance of Madeleine R. Levy

Our ideas about law go way back in time, before we even learned to scratch messages in the sand and paint them on the walls of caves. Perhaps it's even fair to say that some legal principles—such as those having to do with territory—are older than man. Mike Tigar and Madeleine Levy pick up the story with Rome and give us a good overview of man's western legal traditions that form so much of the basis for the way we see law and dispute-resolution today. This article is excerpted from Chapter 2 of Law and the Rise of Capitalism, *which is entitled "The Backdrop of the New Legal Institutions." (This book is reviewed in Part 5.)*

The systems of law designed by and for the bourgeoisie take elements from, and look for authority to, six different bodies of legal thought:

1. **Roman law:** which developed forms of legal relationships designed to accommodate and to further commerce with all parts of the Empire.

2. **Feudal, or seigneurial, law:** those rules defining the relationships which characterized the personal feudal tie between a lord and his vassals.

3. **Canon law:** the legal rules of the Western Roman Catholic Church, which claimed varying but always considerable amounts of control over the very secular business of trade.

4. **Royal law:** rules that manifest the consolidating influence of those who forced the creation of the first modern states, and of whom the bourgeoisie

5. **Law merchant:** rules derived from Roman law but adapted over the centuries to the needs of those whose business was business.

6. **Natural law:** the bourgeois claim, developed fully in the seventeenth century though portended earlier, that the combination of rules which best served free commerce was eternally true, in accord with God's plan, and self-evidently wise.

Roman Law

By 1000 A.D. the Western Roman Empire had been gone six hundred years, but people in Western Europe still walked on roads that dated from Augustus Caesar's time—the first century A.D. The ruins of Roman cities, Roman harbors, and Roman churches dotted the landscape. The well-educated merchant—and his lawyer—was taught that in the wake of the Roman conquest had come Roman laws and Roman commerce, including the freedom to buy and sell by means of enforceable contracts. For the Church, and for those temporal lords who also aspired to universal overlordship, the Roman Empire provided a conscious organizational model.

The Roman legal system was created between the fifth century B.C. and the second century A.D. To shroud the law's origins in mystery and to invest it with the sanction of tradition, Roman jurisprudents purported to derive every important legal principle from the Twelve Tables. This concise collection of laws, difficult to reconstruct but of undoubted authenticity, was drawn up around 450 B.C. under the Roman Republic. The Tables outline only the simplest of legal principles concerning property, family law, and citizenship, and they are characterized by reliance upon magic and ritual.

In the Twelve Tables we first see the emergence of legal ideas of debt, contract, and civil wrong. These ideas turn up later in countless medieval charters and customals (written collections of customs). Early Romans, like some others in societies organized on a clan basis, dealt with murder or injury of a kinsperson by revenge upon the murderer's kinfolk. An early step away from this violent solution for the Romans was the "composition," a payment in money or goods to the victim's kin, accompanied by a solemn ceremony acknowledging the obligation to pay. It seems probable that the earliest Roman compositions took the form described in the Twelve Tables as *nexum*. *Nexum* was the bond created between a debtor and creditor by the former's promise to subject himself to the latter until the debt was paid. By the time of the Twelve Tables, the device was used to create a lien between any creditor and any debtor, no matter how the debt arose.

Bonds persisted in all their original vigor long past the time when the debtors — *nexi* — had forgotten the origins of the law that bound them to their creditors. The distinctly Roman customs of southern France yielded contracts such as one of 1362 in which Jaciel of Grasse, a moneylender, required that his debtor, in the event of nonpayment, come from Nice (thirty-five miles away) and live in Grasse to work under Jaciel's direction until the debt was paid. Municipal records show that Jaciel actually enforced this *hostagium* clause and obtained a court order requiring his debtor to lodge in the Grasse prison.

Early Roman procedure for the enforcement of claims was also laden with formalism. The plaintiff was required to fit his claim into a precise form and to speak the required words exactly to the magistrate. Non-Romans were, by the Twelve Tables, rightless, without capacity to make contracts, to own property, or to bring an action to enforce debts or obligations.

With colonization on the shores of the Mediterranean in the third and second centuries B.C. came a great expansion of trade, and with it the need for a more comprehensive legal system. A legal system that gave rights only to Romans could not serve for commerce with non-Romans. And even in local transactions, rules devised for an agricultural economy did not encompass the interests of the great merchants, whose wealth was increasing at the expense of small peasants and artisans.

For Roman merchants, a new magistracy, the praetorship, was created in 367 B.C. with power to issue an annual edict stating the claims the courts would recognize in suits between Romans. At about the same time, treaties ceded commercial rights to some non-Romans.

In 243 B.C. a *praetor peregrinus* was appointed to supervise the trial of cases involving non-Romans; by this action, Roman law took the step which is repeatedly and romantically referred to in the ideology of merchants for the next two thousand years. The former *praetor* took the name *praetor urbanus*, and his edicts were founded upon the existing law, the *jus civile*; in the words of Gaius, the leading Roman jurist of the first century A.D., the *jus civile* was "the law which a people establishes for itself [as] particular to it, . . . as being the special law of the civitas." The *praetor peregrinus*, on the other hand, purported to fashion and apply the *jus gentium* — in Gaius' words, "the law that natural reason establishes among all mankind [which] is followed by all peoples alike."

To regard Roman legal concepts as applicable to "all peoples" was not so formidable a conceit. Between 280 B.C. and the destruction of Carthage in the Third Punic War in 146 B.C., Rome had forcibly conquered most of the lands bordering on the Mediterranean. A village-based agricultural economy was rapidly being replaced by the class structure of the Empire, in which the dominant figures were traders, bankers, merchants, landowners, and the military power which protected their interests. The labor force which fueled this system was slave or half-free, recruited mainly from the conquered and colonized peoples. Adoption of the term *jus gentium* reflected the conquest by the new Roman ruling class of its foreign and domestic enemies.

This "law of all peoples" was not, however, purely the product of Roman jurists, imposed by Roman might; it bears traces of those civilizations in the West with which the Romans first traded and which they first colonized.

By the time the *praetor peregrinus* was established, Roman law already recognized *unilateral* binding promises: X could promise (*stipulatio*) Y to deliver some goods on a certain day, and for breach of that promise the law would provide a remedy. A contract to do a thing in the future is called executory, and underlies all modern commercial transactions. Prior to this, Roman law, like early Anglo-Saxon law and other early legal systems, had recognized only *executed* contracts, those that involved face-to-face dealings, with an exchange of the property concerned at the moment the deal was made and according to a prescribed form. Recognition of unilateral, binding, executory promises was one step toward freedom of commerce, for it gave merchants greater flexibility in commercial dealings.

The next step was recognition of *bilateral* executory contracts, including those encompassing complex, long-term business associations. The *jus gentium* ratified and elaborated bilateral contracts regarding sale, hiring, deposit, and partnership, as well as commercial concept of fiduciary relations—those of special trust and confidence. The distinction between the unilateral binding promise and the bilateral contract with obligations on both sides is of great importance. The unilateral binding obligation was created by the person *assuming* the obligation—to deliver goods, to pay money, and so on—by repeating a set speech that was essential to the validity and enforceability of the promise. If the promisor failed to perform, the beneficiary of the promise could sue to enforce the deal or collect damages for non-performance. Such a contract seldom reflects the reality of even the simplest commercial transaction, for usually one party promises to deliver and the other promises to pay on condition the goods arrive and are in satisfactory condition. If a legal system admits only unilateral promises, these two obligations must be assumed separately, and separate lawsuits are required for the enforcement of each promise.

To the Romans medieval lawyers owed the concept—which has continued to present times—of the corporation as a fictitious artificial person, entitled to buy, sell, and enforce its claims in the courts. Corporate organization permitted a pooling of interests and therefore an accumulation of capital far greater than in an individual enterprise or a partnership. The distinction was this: a partnership, formed by the agreement of its members, remained in the law's eyes an amalgam of individual rights and duties. To sue the partnership and get a court judgment enforceable against its members' assets one had to bring all the partners before the court. And if the partnership itself came to court, it had in general to have sued in the name of all its members. A corporation, however, swallows up the identities of its shareholder-owners in the common, artificial personality of itself, and is sued and sues, has rights and obligations, on its "own" account.

The other striking feature of the corporation, in the form it began to take in the medieval period, is that shareholders or members were not obligated beyond the amount they put in for their shares—the notion of "limited liability." A wealthy individual could put a part of his or her wealth in a corporation and not risk—if the corporation failed—invasion of the balance of his or her personal fortune to pay the

insolvent corporation's debts. It is doubtful that the corporation existed in this form for business enterprises in Rome, and there was great resistance many centuries later to general recognition of the limited-liability principle in Western Europe, but medieval bourgeois ideologists could look back to the words of a leading third-century Roman jurist, Ulpian. Ulpian wrote: "*Si quid universitati debetur, singalis non debetur;· nec quod debet universitalis singali debet*"—roughly, the property and debts of a corporate body are not the property and debts of each individual member. The corporate character of institutions as diverse as a company of merchants, a medieval city, and the entire Roman Catholic Church led to Ulpian's words being perhaps the most commented-upon in all Roman jurisprudence.

The naming of the *praetor peregrinus* was one of those devices by which a rising class without power to sweep away old institutions is able to create new ones alongside the old to serve its special needs. The old form, created to serve an earlier and different set of social relations, is then more quickly emptied of the substance it once contained. Thus the Roman *jus civile* retained the fiction that it carried forward the principles of the Twelve Tables and the legislation of the Republic, while being progressively over-whelmed by the *jus gentium*, tool of the newly rich and powerful merchants. By 150 B.C., procedure before the *praetor urbanus* had become the same as that before the *praetor peregrinus*.

In about 150 A.D. there began the prolific pro-duction of Roman legal writing that was to become the basis of medieval knowledge of Roman law. These writings, by emperors and legal scholars, grew progressively more arid and decadent as the Western Roman Empire drew to a close. Periodically, these great outpourings were codified, excerpted, and arranged by subject matter. The best-known, most complete, and to the medieval bourgeoisie most influential codification was the *Corpus Juris Civilis*, compiled under the direction of the Eastern Roman emperor Justinian in the sixth century A.D.

Justinian's codification performed the signal serv-ice of sorting through the thousands of imperial edicts and legal treatises, eliminating contradiction by choosing the practice or rule which was current in 533, and systematizing the whole under titles corresponding to the areas of law: contracts, prop-erty, family law, procedure, crimes, and so on. Most of the sources from which the *Corpus Juris* is taken are lost: we know of them only from its pages.

Justinian was, however, an Eastern emperor, sit-ting at Constantinople. His work does not appear to have influenced commercial practice in Western Europe until the eleventh century. This is not to say that Roman legal concepts did not survive, although there was little commercial life in most of Western Europe which would have called for their use; they subsisted in local customs, canonical practice, and in such works as a partial codification, the *Lex Romana Visigothorum* of about 506 A.D., attrib-uted to the Visigoth leader Alaric II, who had a power base in Spain. The monasteries remained centers of Roman law and Latin learning. At the same time, there is no question that with the death of commercial life attendant upon the fall of the Western Empire in 476 A.D., the technical, artfully constructed precepts of Roman classical law, and the structure for applying them, fell into disuse.

Feudal Law
On August 11, 1789, the French National Assem-bly, in the first flush of revolutionary victory, de-creed that it "totally abolishes the feudal regime."

The draftsmen of the Code Napoleon, fourteen years later, spoke of the "many vestiges of the feudal regime which still covered the surface of France," and which the Code laid to rest. Yet for some eight hundred years a good number of merchants had lived and even prospered in the midst of this feudal regime. Why was it suddenly found necessary to destroy it at whatever cost? It is important to exam-ine some aspects of feudal society in order to under-stand the merchants' centuries-long oscillation between accommodation and rebellion.

Even at its high point, in the first three centuries A.D., the Roman commercial and military empire contained the contradictions that were to bring it down. Slave labor undercut free labor, throwing artisans and small farmers out of work to roam the cities and create foci of unrest. The revolutionary doctrines of the young Christian church spread dis-affection among the lower classes and spurred the authorities to brutal repression of its adherents. On the borders of the Empire, groups driven out of Central Europe by the advancing Huns added to the administrative problems of an increasingly overbur-dened and expensive bureaucracy. Communica-tion, the ability to protect the wealthy, and the security of commerce began to diminish in the third century A.D., and with them went the prosperity of the Empire.

For the large latifundia in the area closest to Rome, one solution to the labor problem was to rent out part of the latifundist's domain to freemen or slaves, exacting rent in kind in the form of an obli-gation to toil on that part of the domain reserved for the latifundist's personal use and profit. On the borders of the Empire, to help keep the invaders at bay, free Romans were given land and the status of *coloni*, under the supervision of a landlord with governmental authority. Wherever possible, the invaders were bought off by being invited into fed-eration with the Empire. The *federati* were given land to till, swore an oath to defend the Empire, and adapted their social organization to the system prac-ticed by the latifundists and the *coloni*, but they were allowed to maintain their own laws in disputes within the group.

The "fall" of the Western Empire in 476 was only the last step in the process of disintegration. Epis-copal and archespiscopal cities as well as Roman administrative centers survived; but large regions occupied by latifundists, *coloni*, and *federati* became autonomous, professing only nominal allegiance to the distant Eastern emperor in Constantinople. The need for survival and military defense, the lack of a Roman governmental presence and of the Roman legions, made possible and necessary a manorial system in which one finds the origins of what later writers were to term feudalism.

In places not under Roman rule, such as in Scotland, Ireland, Scandinavia, and Germany, surviving records indicate that feudal forms were developing as well, adapting the needs for food and defense to local social organization.

Throughout Europe in this period, particularly in Germany and southern France, there were farmers and peasants who were neither Romans nor *coloni* and *federati*, but who had in the past looked to Roman officials as their governors. Possessors of plots of various sizes, called *allods*, they were swept into the feudal system by the need for protection or by force.

In the part of Europe once ruled from Rome, therefore, feudalism represented the retreat into the manor and village of a ruling class deprived of protection by a decayed and dying imperial government. Elsewhere, it was a change from a pastoral, nomadic, and war-directed existence to a more stable agricultural life (although still warlike enough).

At the root of the feudal relation was the act of homage, supplemented from the time of Charlemagne (ninth century) by the oath of fealty. Two men, one stronger (the lord), the other weaker (the vassal), face one another. As the French historian Marc Bloch describes it, the latter

> puts his hands together and places them, thus joined, between the hands of the other man — a plain symbol of submission, the significance of which was sometimes further emphasized by a kneeling posture. At the same time, the person proferring his hands utters a few words — a very short declaration — by which he acknowledges himself to be the "man" of the person facing him. Then chief and subordinate kiss each other on the mouth, symbolizing accord and friendship. Such were the gestures, very simple ones — eminently fitted to make an impression on minds so sensitive to visible things — which served to cement one of the strongest social bonds known in the feudal era.

The essence of the feudal relation was this personal nexus, originally enduring only for the life-time of the vassal, and later extended to the vassal's heirs in the male line. For the vassal held the land he tilled, and virtually all his movable possessions, "of" his lord. The oath-bound relation of dominance and subordination, from the tiller to his lord, and through the latter's pledge of homage to some more powerful seigneur, consituted a system often described by its ideologists in pyramidal, symmetrical terms. Death and mayhem were common enough in feudal society, and retribution swift and vengeful. But violence offered to one's lord was a special sort of misdeed.

Few lived outside the feudal system. The Church participated, as feudal lord. Local priests were attached to a village or manor. Those who did not were few — pilgrims, wandering friars, itinerant merchants, troubadours, and other social outcasts.

If we look at a map of Western Europe in about 800, manorial society predominates. Trade slowed to a trickle of luxury goods. Manors were self-sufficient entities, and commerce mainly local. Inside the manor the quality of life was regulated by the lord's administrators and by his seigneurial court. The lord's power, and that of his court, included everything of concern to his vassals.

By the eleventh century, Western Europe was under the rule of a patchwork system of local customs, influenced in varying degrees by Roman law. In Germany, the Low Countries, and the northern two-thirds of what is now France, the old customs furnished the basis of law, although a few legislative decrees of territorial overlords may have been acknowledged. England, despite its Roman occupation, had never been brought into the Roman legal orbit. A feudal system of land tenure was functioning at the time of the Norman Conquest, but English law after 1066 was heavily infused by northern French — more precisely, Norman — customary law.

Southern France, Italy, and non-Moorish Iberia retained nominal allegiance to Roman law, but the contracts and other writings of the period display ignorance of Roman legal principles, and the feudal legal relation was, of course, not regulated by Roman law.

In all of these regions, procedure in the secular feudal courts was uniformly slow, arbitrary, and unfair to the lower orders of society. It was characterized by reliance upon an oral tradition of custom maintained by the lord and his officers and judges. An inquest might be held to determine the content of the customary law, with a sort of jury whose members were called "inquestors," *coutumiers*, or (by a French ordinance of 1270) *turbiers*. The presence of such persons may have provided some protection, but it also multiplied the opportunity for fraud and bribery.

The life of the tiller in this millieu was regulated by the round of feudal obligations. The family worked on the lord's domain, tilled its own plot, obtained its necessities from the manor, and had the right to use common and waste land. (This last right would assume great importance in the centuries to come.) The family was obliged to provide troops or provisions for the lord's armed retinue. It was bound to the land, and could not sell either the land or most movable goods, or transmit them to a future generation, or marry, or trade, without the consent of the lord and perhaps the payment of a tax. The lord had obligations, too, and in years of bad harvest his storehouses were to be open to ensure that his vassals did not starve. The legal system was a world apart, run by men who spoke *"Moult bele: le Latin,"* and who knew words, as one French custumnal says, which the ordinary man does not understand though they be spoken in French.

Such a social system did not need a law of commerce. The "great towns" were little more than large fortified villages, great in southern Europe only because a greater lord than any other in the region resided there, and great in the north — where lords lived in the countryside — because a bishop or archibishop had his seat there. Trade between the years 500 and 1000 consisted of goods for the ruling class: silks, spices, jewelry, and other items light in weight so that a small caravan could carry merchandise of a great total value over land routes from the Orient.

Under pressure from artisans and petty traders in the feudal hierarchy, and from traveling merchants who acknowledged no direct feudal tie, lords were forced beginning in the twelfth century to codify and regularize the chaotic and uncertain body of customs they administered.

The noble class began reluctantly to accept some merchant practices, at least if the lord of the manor could make money through tolls and taxes. Provisions in many collections of local customs regulated merchant dealings, providing a market area and an occasional market fair within which exchange could regularly occur, monitored by the lord's men. In 1283 in Beauvais, the fine was five sous for beating up a fellow-citizen, but it increased to sixty sous of

GRAIN TAX, SALT TAX, WINE TAX... DON'T ASK ME WHAT'S NEXT, ASK THE GOOD LORD...

the citizen was in or on the way to the market.

Putting the *coutumes* in writing, originally authorized by an *ordonnance* of St. Louis in the thirteenth century but systematically undertaken only much later, was a sign of the consolidation of feudal rule and of the emergence of a king or prince at the head of the feudal hierarchy in a particular region. The study of the *coutumes* signaled the rise within the feudal system of a social stratum of lawyers, whose special task it was to discover, study, and state the law.

Canon Law and the Roman Catholic Church

By the beginning of the fifth century the Papacy was holding together what remained of the dismembered Empire. The primacy of Rome in the Western Church was established by Pope Innocent I (402 –417); by the accession of Leo I (the Great) in 440 the Pope's temporal authority around Rome had become considerable. Little more than one hundred years had passed since Catholicism had been legalized by the Empire in the Edict of Milan (313).

The Church's claim to temporal hegemony was betokened by Pope Leo's crowning, on Christmas Day 800, of Charlemagne as Emperor of the Holy Roman Empire. The Empire, built by exaction of homage from lesser lords, had little claim to be holy, and no claim at all to be Roman. Within a few years after Charlemagne's death in 814, it had also ceased to be an empire.

The Pope's claim to have placed Charlemagne in the line of Roman emperors rested upon two of the Church's dominant ideas. The first of these myths was that the Roman Empire had been prophesied in Scripture, as the last of the four kingdoms to reign before the final conquest of God's armies and the Last Judgment.

Second, the Church ideologically and organizationally reflected feudal society, at once exacting loyalty from its myriad sovereignties and providing their ideological foundation.

As it expanded its temporal power and gained new converts, the Church built an ideology which saw in the pyramid of feudal obligation, with the husbandmen as tillers at its base, a parallel to its own pyramidal organization, with the tillers as the mass of faithful.

The Church's law claimed jurisdiction coterminous with the Church's concerns. The ecclesiastical courts coveted the power to decide all disputes involving the welfare of souls, and pressed the secular courts to apply canon law to all such disputes as well. The conflicting claims of secular and canon-law courts is a recurrent issue in the eleventh through the fourteenth centuries. By contract, too, as we have seen, the Church's tribunals might be chosen as forums for purely secular disputes. The Church's libraries and monasteries were centers of learning and study of Roman law texts.

And the church had power, even when it did not have troops to enforce its will. It was a feudal overlord: from early in the feudal age, prelates had accepted the homage of tillers, knights, and petty nobles, and added to its wealth through property left it by the wealthy and pious. The secular courts could inflict death, but the ecclesiastical tribunal could ex-communicate and thereby condemn souls. The Church's centralization and temporal authority reached their apogee during the Crusades. Renewal of interest in Roman legal learning progressed with the Church's fortunes, taking a qualitative leap in the reign of Pope Gregory VII (1073-85), the "merchant Pope." The Catholic Church was the state church of the emerging Western European monarchs and other feudal overlords, excepting only the remaining Moorish holdings on the Iberian peninsula.

The beginnings of royal centralization and the return of trade spurred economic growth. The tillers and producers produced more than enough to support the manorial economy and the reviving cities, and their temporal and spiritual masters could expect more of the surplus to fund their own activities.

A part of the economic surplus was channeled to lawyers and legal researchers. Pope Gregory VII, with the support of the merchants whose favor he courted, founded a law school at Bologna which began to reassemble the texts of Justinian, great portions of which were rediscovered on a Florentine manuscript. The words of Justinian were invested with Papal authority, and upon these "ruins of that heathen power" the structure of canon law was erected. At the same time, scholars of the Church's own internal law collected laws, decrees, opinions, and rulings of Church authority.

But the Church, having saved the texts of the old Roman law, and having claimed to inherit the mantle of the old Roman Empire, found itself too easily embarrassed by the interpretations of Roman law made by able lawyers in the service of merchants or the secular state. The Roman texts as interpreted by the canonists, and the Church's own decrees, texts, and opinions were legislated into primacy: the study of civil (that is, Roman) law was forbidden to monks in 1180 and to priests in 1219; in 1234 Henry III ordered the sheriffs of London to close the schools of civil law.

Throughout the Middle Ages, canon lawyers struggled with the problem of reviving trade. We have seen that Roman law, which underlay much of canon law, was solicitous of the interest of merchants. For the canonists, however, a central problem was resolution of the Roman texts with the Church's moral teaching. A religion which began as the faith of persecuted victims of commercial Roman civilization had for centuries maintained that being a merchant was suspect if not immoral. That this same Church should also claim to inherit Roman law was, during all of capitalism's rise, the weakest point in the armor of the Church intellectual.

One aspect of the problem was that it was difficult for the Church to sanction a legal system built upon the ideal of "law" in the sense of highly structured rules for administration by a rigid system of secular and ecclesiastical courts. Saint Paul, in the First Epistle to the Corinthians, had preached charity instead of justice and had recommended resort to arbitration by a pastor, or by friends, as being far preferable to litigation. Saint Augustine said the same. It was not until the twelfth century that the dilemma was resolved. By then the revival of the Roman law had become an important aspect of the Church's consolidation of secular and churchly authority, and the Church abandoned any pretense of creating an apostolic community of the faithful. St. Thomas Aquinas defended this decision; he argued that Roman law, like the works of Aristotle and certain other pre-Christian writings, was based upon reason, and was therefore independent of religious belief.

The Church maintained that it cared for the soul, and defined its claims for temporal power as well as its decisions in particular cases upon that concern. In the law of crimes, for example, the Church revived the extensive and, for the times, enlightened

Roman law about the element of intent in criminal justice: a person could not be punished for committing a crime unless that person had the capacity to choose between good and evil and had in fact chosen evil. Imprisonment, the Church taught, might be preferable to capital punishment, as giving the offender a chance to reflect on his or her wrong. In the midst of legal systems dominated by customary practices of vengeance and blood feuds, this was an innovative spirit.

Procedure in canon-law courts was more regular and predictable than in the arbitrary feudal tribunals. Written demands and defenses were normal practice much earlier than in secular tribunals, and written records of testimony and judgments were similarly more common in ecclesiastical courts. The Christian courts even permitted cross-examination.

But the written procedure of the ecclesiastical trial was not universally approved. Some critics regarded it as dangerous. Forged documents, charters, and donations abounded, and charges of fraud and chicanery were often leveled against ecclesiastical judges. The detailed and extensive written contracts favored by merchants, particularly in the south of France and in Italy, may have been designed as a response to fears of perjury or fraud in court, and to avoid any question as to what was actually agreed upon.

After centuries of thinking of oaths as sacrilege and blasphemy, the Church accepted in the eleventh century the view that testimony under oath was the most satisfactory means to find out the truth. The oath insured divine retribution for the mendacious. Resolving disputes by sworn testimony was surely more rational than trial by battle and trial by ordeal. The Church also encouraged the search for other means of determining the truth. In criminal matters, this view led be a grotesque logic to torture as being the best means to induce the accused to tell all.

Merchants, in their contracts, often designated an ecclesiastical court as the forum for any eventual dispute. And once the Church had sanctioned the oath, it was used to seal bargains as well and thus gave the canon-law courts jurisdiction over a breach of contract whether or not the parties had chosen to have the dispute judged there.

Canon law adopted in large measure the Roman

law of contracts, again with singular emphasis upon the moral element of bargain. For the Church's lawyers, the oath of fealty was a prime example of a binding and godly contract. Unilateral binding promises of all kinds, even those for which the promisor received nothing in return and which were therefore invalid under most secular legal systems, could be enforced under canon law.

Many historians have discussed canon law of the Middle Ages as though its only concern with business was the problem of usury—lending money at interest. Such narrowness of vision is unfortunate and ill-informed. The Papacy itself, not to mention the thousands of churchly overlords of lesser rank, was a creditor and debtor of the rising merchant class. And Roman law, revived in clerical garb, proved ready to abandon earlier positions when the revival of trade demanded it.

More legal talent was spent in devising means around the prohibitions on usury than in drafting their terms, particularly as the Church's position as creditor grew. The Church was especially likely to tolerate evasion on the part of the wealthy, since it stood to benefit when they succeeded in business. R.H. Tawney, in *Religion and the Rise of Capitalism*, remarks upon the history of the canon-law codes' prohibition on usury:

> The ingenuity with which professional opinion elaborated the code was itself a proof that considerable business—and fees—were the result of it, for lawyers do not serve God for naught. The canonists who had a bad reputation with the laity, were not, to put it mildly, more innocent than other lawyers in the gentle art of making business. The Italians, in particular, as was natural in the financial capital of Europe, made the pace, and Italian canonists performed prodigies of legal ingenuity.

Skillful evasion was preferable to direct disobedience, for the latter risked one's soul. The rising merchant class was weak enough and harassed enough without facing the threat of eternal damnation, which seemed to that age real enough. The Church had the power to excommunicate, as well as the power to burn at the stake, but burning was reserved for heretics; the doctrinal deviations of merchants were treated rather more kindly.

The canon-law courts, then, often decided disputes about trade and commerce, as well as matters more obviously related to salvation. With the demise of the personality of laws, each forum—feudal, religious, royal—applied its own rules. Not uncommonly, more favorable law and a more propitious procedure might await a litigant in one court than in another. When trade had developed to the point that large-scale "fairs" were held for sale and exchange, and port cities became international trading centers, this problem was solved by the merchants establishing their own courts. But earlier on, the choice of forum was crucial, and it remained of no small importance.

The Church was an omnipresent force in European financial and legal development. As the largest landowner in Europe, it was committed to the defense of feudalism and with all its authority aided in the suppression of the peasant revolts which swept Europe. Those who wished to restore the image of a communal, apostolic church it denounced as heretics or shut up in monasteries.

The Church recognized clearly that free trade conducted by those who were vassals to no one, or vassals only in a technical sense, was profoundly corrosive of social stability. If ancient doctrine taught that trade was sin, the new political reality taught that traders threatened the feudal system. Yet the Church could not ignore the great wealth that trade accumulated, for only by tapping that wealth could ecclesiastical rulers build cathedrals and universities and live in the style to which they had become accustomed. And so, it sought to bring commerce within its universal system of theology, morals, and law. Within that system dwelt the Church's claim to have revived Roman law.

The Church translated Roman "natural reason" into "natural law" and set up God rather than the common consent of humanity as the arbiter of that law. But God rarely spoke directly to human beings; the casuistry of the canon lawyers put this divinely sanctioned law to practical secular use. The Church required good faith and equity in dealing; the emerging capitalists took over these terms and claimed that they meant the good faith and equity that a merchant would show according to the custom of the marketplace. If "honor among men" is the maxim, but thieves make the rules, then "honor among thieves" is the rule in practice. The Church tolerated only the "just price" and required payment of the "just wage," but if feudal bonds were destroyed or weakened and the forces of a market were at work, "just" could easily mean "what the market will bear."

Royal Law

> For every king is a sort of fountain, from which a constant shower of benefits or injuries rains down upon the whole population.

Thomas More's characterization of a king's power, though written in 1516 to begin a sharp attack on kingship, was typical of thought in the late Middle Ages. The idea of royal power, and in particular of the absolute power to make laws and enforce them, began to develop in the eleventh century. Throughout this period, relations between monarchy and merchants were more often than not cordial, for the aims of both were often served by the same policies of consolidation.

Imagine the merchant of 1150 or so, criss-crossing Europe from Italy to the Low Countries, buying and selling. With a few other merchants, his caravan is equipped for travel and fighting. Private wars of vengeance and conquest make the journey dangerous, and danger is redoubled by knightly brigandage.

In addition to outlaw knights, the merchant faced roads in disrepair, the wide Roman highways and bridges having long ago fallen into ruin. And, as he passed across the country, he was likely to be met with a hundred demands for tolls and taxes from petty local seigneurs. For his physical safety and that of his goods, every traveling merchant was a fighter. Merchants and artisans in the cities had also to fight for their right to practice their occupations and engage in trade.

Little wonder, then, that this class of traders came to rely upon powerful overlords and protectors. The Italian cities could amass fortunes and navies large enough to wrest control of Mediterranean trades from the Arabs; a smaller prince, duke, or duchess could concede merchant privileges to a city within his or her domain; an archbishop ruling an ancient city could sponsor trade within its walls; but the larger territorial overlords—the kings—were the longest-term, firmest, and richest friends the merchants had.

The kings united their lesser nobles behind the Crusades and won control of important trading centers in the Eastern Mediterranean. They began to insist that the roads be kept up. The power to legislate, fallen into disuse since the ninth century, was revived in order to establish systems of national law and national courts. Royal legislation forbade private war, with varying success but with unvarying purposefulness. The cities, originally a product of bourgeois revolt and noble concessions, were brought under royal control and patronage. Merchant dealings were regulated in order to protect citizens against competition from foreigners and to enhance foreign-exchange revenues; the foreign policy of monarchs included establishing consuls abroad to protect the merchants. For the merchant, the king could be an important ally; for the king, the merchant could be an important means of raising money, and of ensuring a surplus of gold in the balance of international payments. For, though the mechanism of international trade was not well understood until the seventeenth century, the importance of a net surplus of gold was perceived early on.

There is a crucial distinction between unified royal power and the feudal system it first led and then helped break down. The feudal relationship rested upon personal homage, and combined in one person or institution the roles of owner and landlord, chief military defender, and law-giver. With its immediate personal possession of the land, this may be contrasted with the notion of the state as a separate, *sovereign* entity, with only a distant, regulatory interest in the land.

In the thirteenth century legal writers begin to speak of kings as "sovereign," and to ascribe to them the authority attributed to emperors in Roman law. Ulpian's maxim, "What pleases the king must be taken for law," appears in Beaumanoir as a dictum of customary law—without attribution of its source—and Beaumanoir's discussion of sovereignty is among the first recognitions in France of a new sort of state power.

It is in England, however, that we gain the clearest idea of the fundamental notion of royal law and its relation to the demands of the rising merchant class. William, bastard Duke of Normandy, relying on a dynastic claim to the throne of England, crossed the Channel in 1066 and established the first modern state in Europe. On William's death his French possessions became less important, but the consolidation of central power in England, and its extension to Wales, Scotland, and Ireland in succeeding centuries, is remarkable.

With the power to govern, reinforced immediately by requiring all lesser nobles to take an oath to the kind as their feudal overlord and they as tenants of his land—that is, of all England—came the power to pass laws governing the entire kingdom. To enforce these laws, royal officials took the place of local feudal officials, beginning the separation of landlordism from state power. Royal courts were armed with the power to dispense the king's justice, and they began by upholding the forcible dispossession of many nobles who had adhered to the cause of William's rival.

With this, feudal barriers to trade were struck down, though several centuries more were needed before the royal courts fashioned and applied laws which at all resembled eighteenth-century notions of contracts, property, and procedure.

A merchant and artisan class arose largely in the towns, which began to grow separately from the manorial economy during the reign of King John (1199–1216). Over a period of centuries the town burgesses established themselves on land nominally in the hands of feudal barons, but in reality increasingly controlled by the Crown and its officers. In the thirteenth century a "town" was considered to be all its inhabitants with equal status, but later the centralization of wealth and power in the hands of a few merchants and employers led to a separation of the "town"—the legal entity governed by these wealthy people—from the totality of the residents.

Other courts that looked for their law to mercantile custom were established with the crown's blessing. When, for example, the crown authorized a trading fair, drawing merchants from many countries, it also authorized a "fair court" to settle disputes arising between merchants at the fair. In the great Channel cities—Dover, Hastings, Hythe, Romney, and Sandwich—special courts of marine and merchant law were established by port officials under royal auspices.

Basic principles of marine and merchant law—which came to the same thing in a country so dependent upon sea commerce—made great inroads upon common law, although the takeover was not completed until the bloody and tumultuous social upheavals of the seventeenth century.

The English pattern was repeated, with variations, elsewhere: an alliance between crown and merchants, the latter supporting the legislative and judicial power of the former in order to obtain uniform laws favorable to trade throughout a large area. The merchant repaid this debt by paying taxes and customs duties and in many cases by making huge loans to the crown to carry on military policy abroad. These military policies might in turn—and usually did—benefit the merchants at home.

Royal aspirations toward territorial control coincided with the needs of merchants for a unified trading area. The ensuing alliance was a crucial factor in both the lawmaking of the rising bourgeois class and in the progress from merchant to industrial economies. This alliance was never consistently peaceful, for with the crown's help went crown control, whether in the form of the "state capitalism" of the English Tudors, or the heavy taxation imposed by the French Bourbons. These measures either angered the unprotected, who moved outside the royal sphere of special protection to build positions of power from which to bring down the royally sponsored system of privilege, or weighed upon the rising class as a whole, fomenting angry discontent and spawning the teaching that good government governs little in the field of financial affairs.

Law Merchant

Differing legal systems for different classes did not seem odd in the Middle Ages—no more so than differing systems erected upon different territorial bases. Nobles had extra rights; churchmen had their own set of privileges. The word "privilege" appears with great frequency in custumnals, charters, and lawbooks, and usually denotes access to a special court or the right to a special favorable rule of law.

It should not surprise us, therefore, to find that merchants had law of their own, brought back into Europe with the rebirth of trade. The "law merchant" was a form of international law, whose fundamental elements were the ease with which it permitted binding contracts, its stress on security of contracts, and the variety of devices it contained for establishing, transmitting, and receiving credit.

Throughout the Middle Ages, the application of merchant law to disputes about trade spread through the royal courts, the ecclesiastical courts, and even the feudal seigneurial courts. For the international merchant and trader, the law merchant was indispensable. The law merchant was, at least in theory, uniformly applied to dealings between merchants of every nation. As such, it promoted the consciousness of the bourgeois that he was a member of a class.

Perhaps the clearest analogy is to the present-day law of admiralty. If a Dutch and an English ship collide on the high seas and lawsuits result, any court—English, Dutch, or other—will apply the law of admiralty, a body of international law which is customary where not modified by treaty. This law determines matters from rules of the seaways, to rights of seamen to ownership of cargo, to the rules of jettison in the event of shipboard crisis. The very universality of this law encourages the reference of maritime disputes to special arbitration tribunals, rather than to courts whose judges may or may not be experts in the complexities of admiralty. These same features characterized the law merchant.

In 1622 the English courts were willing to summon merchants to testify about their customs and help the court to resolve a dispute. By late in the eighteenth century, Lord Mansfield said for the Court of King's Bench that the traders' law was not a special, unusual customary law, but was known to and would be applied by all of His Majesty's judges: "The law merchant is the law of the land."

Natural Law

"Natural law," as the term came to be used by the bourgeoisie, meant divine sanction for using force and violence in a certain way. The idea that natural law might mean something different from the Roman Catholic claim of divine sanction for its own laws goes back to the communal urban uprisings of the eleventh and twelfth centuries; when a number of revolutionaries in cities across Europe banded together to establish the right to trade within a certain area, they bound themselves by a communal oath. Invoking the name of God, they pledged that they would stand together as a single body. This rudimentary claim for divine sanction is the beginning of the bourgeois, *burgens*, burgess ideal of natural law, in opposition to that of the Church and feudal hierarchy.

The self-conscious development of a secularized natural law begins somewhat later, however. In the sixteenth century at Bourges, a group under the leadership of Cujas began to reinterpret the Roman texts in light of "humanism" and under the influ-

ence of Renaissance philosophy. At the same time, Calvin and his followers at Geneva sought to establish an ecclesiastical state which brought the Vulgate Gospel and the pursuit of wealth into harmony with one another. The radical Protestants who followed, in Geneva, in France, in the Low Countries, and in England, refined and developed the notion of a self-evident order of the universe which mandated freedom of contract and property.

In the 1600s and 1700s, a succession of writers united this form of natural law with the principles of Roman commercial law. There were, from the sixteenth century on, prodigious efforts to state and justify a legal system which would accommodate the needs of a prosperous and strong merchant class. These efforts looked backward to old customs and, more often, to "rediscovered" Roman law. They looked forward to the liquidation of feudal obligations and to the creation of civil societies based on freedom of contract and of property. And they laid the basis for the waves of legislation to assure these ends which accompanied and were necessary to further the bourgeois revolutions.

The blend of history with ideology was evident and powerful; the class whose interests these writers represented meant to take power, and were already— or were soon to be—convinced of the historical necessity for doing so. Yet this blend reflects the truth that revolutions do not do away with all old institutions, but keep two kinds of rules derived from the past: those which reflect concessions wrested by the now-victorious class from the old regime, and those which reassure the populace that nothing too drastic has been done. After the people have done their work in ousting the old regime by force of arms, the new regime has need of rules to force the people to return to their homes and stop fighting before the revolution endangers the interests of the newly dominant class.

★ ★ ★

Michael E. Tigar is a lawyer. He tries to live according to the following bit of doggerel:

Sanctus Yvo erat brito
Advocatus et non latro:
Res miranda populo!

Madeleine R. Levy, a graduate of the State University of New York at Buffalo and Georgetown University Law Center, is now a lawyer with the Attorney General's Office of the State of Alaska.

A Window and a Mirror:
Law Without Lawyers

by Victor H. Li

Perhaps the best way to see how tightly our ideas about law are tied to our history and culture is to step outside both. China, with a legal system that has a strong bias against lawyers, is a wonderful place to look. Anyone who has read Robert Van Gulick's wonderful detective stories about Judge Dee, the legendary seventh century Chinese magistrate and detective, knows well that the rules and etiquette surrounding Chinese law and legal procedure were already well developed when the inventors of our common law tradition were still running about their little island hitting each other over the head with sticks. The following article is excerpted from Law Without Lawyers, A comparative View of Law in China and the United States. *We heartily recommend the entire book, which is published by the Stanford Alumni Association, Stanford University, Stanford, California.*

In 1974 a benchmark in the American legal system was passed: The number of lawyers in this country reached 400,000 [Eds note: The figure in 1980 is more like 500,000.] We should pause on that figure for a while because it is truly astounding. Four hundred thousand lawyers means that approximately one person out of every 500 in our population is a lawyer. Since most law school graduates are at least 24 years old, and if we arbitrarily define an adult as a person over the age of 24, then approximately one out of every 250 adults is a lawyer. Further, since until recently very few women were in the legal profession, approximately one in 125 adult males is a lawyer! The ratio would become even smaller if one corrected to find the number of lawyers in the population of adult white males between the ages of 24 and 65.

Equally striking is another benchmark involving personnel that was also surpassed in 1974: The number of law students in the United States reached 100,000. Clearly, our national trend is toward having an even larger percentage of the population function as lawyers in the future.

The arithmetic alone is overwhelming, but it is not only a question of numbers. In addition to sheer quantity, lawyers hold many of the key positions in government, the economy, and society in general. To the extent that income and the market mechanism are a reflection of value or importance, lawyers are obviously one of the key components of American society.

If one looks at the same personnel questions for China, a vastly different picture develops. The largest number of lawyers ever claimed by China was 3,500 (in 1956), or slightly fewer than the number of lawyers practicing in the city of Oakland, California. And even these ceased practicing law in the Western sense of the term after the late 1950s. This number is somewhat inaccurate. I would estimate the number of law school graduates in China to be about 10,000 or a little higher. In addition, there are an unknown number of people who have received on-the-job training in legal-type work, perhaps supplemented by more formal short-term, in-service training. Nevertheless, however one adjusts for these figures, there is still a glaring difference between the number of lawyers in the United States and in China. China, a country with four times our population, has only 1 to 2 percent of the number of lawyers in the United States. The difference can also be seen in the number of law students. At present there are three or four law schools operating in China; the Law Department of Peking University, probably the largest of these, has a total student body of only about 200.

The consequences of not having a large cadre of legal specialists are important. On a very simple level, *even if* China wanted to adopt American legal theory and structure, the Chinese legal system would function very differently since it would be staffed by a few thousand instead of 400,000 specialists. Conversely, as China has only a few thousand legal specialists, it should not and would not think of constructing a complex legal system (such as exists in the United States) which requires the services of a very large number of professionally trained people.

With so few legal specialists, the Chinese legal system must, of necessity, be simple in structure, method, and content so that relatively untrained people or even members of the general public can play an active role in the legal process. But the emphasis on simplicity goes beyond this. The Chinese maintain that law *ought* to be simple: How is law to serve the masses if the masses cannot readily understand or easily use the law? This may be making a virtue of necessity, but I think it goes much deeper. The underlying principle is that law *should* be, and indeed *must* be, broadly based rather than the special province of a group of elite professionals. In that way, law becomes a tool by which the masses can carry out their wishes, rather than a set of rules for the use of the legal profession alone.

We obviously part ways with the Chinese on this point. The differences are partly historical. Over the centuries we have developed a body of legal institutions and practices and a cadre of legal professionals. Even if we wanted to get rid of them at this point, we would be unable to. In addition, there is also a philosophical difference. We seem less fearful of the consequences of elitism. Indeed, we may feel that a system of elitism based on knowledge and skill is a desirable thing; also we may doubt the ability of the masses to manage their own affairs.

A Comparative View

Going beyond the simple level, what can we learn from examining the legal systems of two societies, one using a large number of legal specialists and the other apparently managing to have law without lawyers? The making of such comparisons is a healthy thing to do since it gives us a means of measuring another society while at the same time it forces us to examine our own values and measures. But comparisons must be carried out very carefully so that we end up weighing equal or similar things against each other rather than trying to match apples against oranges.

Comparative law has been an important method of study for two centuries, yet with a few notable exceptions it is still an intellectually underdeveloped area. In the usual course, scholars look at the legal system of another society and find whole institutions or small tidbits that may surprise, dismay, or amuse. On occasion, we might come across an idea worth copying. Yet what this kind of study does not produce is a thorough understanding of how law operates in the context of the historical development and present political/economic conditions of that society. From a different perspective, these studies often do not adequately investigate the question of whether there are legal concepts, institutions, and methods that remain valid and useful independent of the specific conditions of any particular society.

Historically, and to an extent even now, a principal method of comparative legal studies has been the following: One examines one's own legal system and identifies its most important and fundamental characteristics. These might include the presumption of innocence, right to counsel, judicial independence, or even trial by jury. Each person can make his list according to his own beliefs and preferences. A "comparative" study is made by seeing how many of the items on this list also appear in the foreign legal system. Depending on the extent of congruence, the foreign system is graded from "good" to "bad," or, in more correct historical terms, from "civilized" to "uncivilized." Societies falling in the first category are treated as equals, while those falling in the second category are denied participation or allowed only partial participation in the international community. In order to become a full participant, the foreign society must upgrade or "modernize" its legal system. Since the measure for acceptability was the list of fundamental characteristics described above, and since for international law purposes the measuring was done by Western states, modernization usually meant Westernization.

Universal Law?

This manner of making comparisons does not stem merely from cultural chauvinism or intellectual laziness, although these factors do play an important role. More positively, there is a tendency on the part of many people, laymen and lawyers alike, to think of law as Law. That is, there is a certain logic and rationale to how a legal system ought to operate that

gives law, or rather Law, a substance and existence that is independent of its connections to any particular society. This belief derives in large part from law's early close association both with religion and with Natural Law philosophy, which held that certain basic concepts and principles are applicable to all mankind. Thus, our own legal system, for all its imperfections, still contains the basic elements of Law. If we can identify the fundamental characteristics of our own legal system, such as the presumption of innocence or of judicial independence, we are likely also to have identified the fundamental characteristics of Law. Consequently, the fundamental characteristics of our legal system are valid criteria for measuring the quality and worthiness of a foreign legal system.

The elevating of law to Law is not necessarily undesirable. In particular, it assists in ensuring compliance. But this approach should not be carried over to comparative legal studies. It does not seem to me, or at least it has not been shown to me, that there is a single law, the fundamental characteristics of which are the same for all societies. On the contrary, I think that law is a social mechanism that helps society function in a harmonious and efficient manner. The precise content and manner of operation of this mechanism is determined by the needs, problems, resources, cultural preferences, and historical development of a particular society. Since these factors may vary greatly from society to society, one would also expect that law (or its equivalent) would correspondingly vary, both in content and in style, from society to society. Thus, one might expect the French and German legal systems to be somewhat different but not very different, while there should be enormous differences between the legal systems of Europe and China.

What the method of comparison described above accomplishes is to measure the degree of similarity between two societies. It does not tell us much about how the foreign legal system operates or whether the foreign methods, different though they are, might be well suited for the conditions and needs of that society.

I am not suggesting that we are incapable of making value judgments about another society because each society can be judged only on its own terms. The use of torture, for example, should be generally condemned. What I am saying is that even if we assume the fundamental characteristics of our legal system to be "good" and "civilized," it does not necessarily follow that a foreign legal system which is different from ours is therefore "bad" or "uncivilized." It may be different and still properly serve the needs of that society.

The Rule of Law

By way of illustration, the historical development of law in China has taken a path very different from that of the West and consequently has produced some very different results. The concept of the "rule of law" is one of the philosophic and political cornerstones of Western society. Yet in China, this term was used in a critical or derisive way, at least until the end of the 19th century. In traditional Confucian terms, a ruler should govern by means of *virtue* rather than *law*. That is, through a painstaking process of socialization and education, the people first learn and then internalize the rules of proper behavior. Only when a person is an extreme recalcitrant or when the educational system has broken down would it be necessary to use the severe sanctions of law. If society is functioning harmoniously, law is something to be avoided—even feared. Thus, a ruler who governs by the "rule of law" is admitting the loss of virtue and the breakdown of the system of education. (I should note that other philosophical schools in traditional China, particularly the Legalists, did not view law in such an unfavorable light.)

Two quotations from Chinese and English sources highlight the difference concerning the rule of law. In the 6th century B.C., a Confucian scholar criticized the promulgation of an early criminal code:

> The ancient kings taught the people the principles of sincerity, urged them on by their own exemplary conduct, instructed them in what was most important, called for their services in a spirit of harmony, came before them in a spirit of reverence, met exigencies with vigor, and made their decisions with firmness. . . . In this way the people could be successfully dealt with, and misery and disorder be prevented from arising.
>
> When the people know what the exact laws are, they do not stand in awe of their superiors. They also come to have a contentious spirit and make their appeal to the literal words, hoping peradventure to be successful in their argument. They can no longer be managed.

The argument is that more laws do not make for a better and more harmonious society. On the con-trary, the emphasis on law makes people more litigious and loophole-happy, and also diverts attention away from the more important work of moral education. Compare this view with a "Western" attitude toward law expressed by Sir Thomas More in Robert Bolt's play, *A Man For All Seasons*:

> And when the last law was down, and the devil turned round on you—where would you hide, Roper, the laws all being flat? This country's planted thick with laws from coast to coast—man's laws, not God's—and if you cut them down—and you're just the man to do it—d'you really think you could stand upright in the winds that would blow then?

A Quest for Functional Equivalents

In addition to raising questions about the role of law in different societies, the use of a comparative approach presents several other more subtle, though no less serious, problems. By using our own legal system as the starting point, we necessarily look for those things in the foreign legal system that are considered important in our own. The courts, for example, occupy a crucial position in our legal system. Under our governmental system the courts act as the final arbiters of disputes and ultimate interpreters of the law. In addition, the public visibility of the courts and even the emphasis on case law in legal education add to the prominence of the courts.

But in China, traditionally, the court was a place to be feared and avoided. Even today, the courts in China do very little. Much of the work of controlling antisocial behavior is handled at the peer group level or through administrative sanctions; industrial and interenterprise disputes are resolved by administrative agencies and tribunals; and except for dwellings and minor personal effects, there is little private property to disagree over. This leaves the courts only two general categories of cases—contested divorces and very serious criminal cases. Given these limited functions, it would be a mistake to focus a great deal of attention on the Chinese courts and to draw conclusions about the entire legal system on the basis of observations made about the courts. Conversely, major concerns about the courts in our system, such as judicial independence or judicial activism, are of far less importance in China.

Perhaps the most striking example of having to look in unexpected places to find functional equivalents in the American and Chinese legal systems concerns the body of statutory, judicial, and other legal materials. The Stanford Law Library, for example, contains over a quarter of a million volumes of legal materials that describe, often in excruciating detail, the legal rules and institutions that govern our conduct. In China, the total number of volumes of statutory material, judicial decisions, legal treatises, and the like published since 1949 would not fill a small bookcase. Does this mean that there are no laws or rules in China? Hardly so. To draw such a conclusion from the fact that China lacks the expected quantity of what we consider the usual legal materials would be another example of reaching the wrong answer because we asked the wrong question in the first place.

Instead, we have to look elsewhere for the means by which legal norms are communicated. The mass media, such as the *People's Daily*, play a major role in this regard. A Chinese newspaper, unlike an American newspaper, is not a chronicle of daily events but rather a means by which messages are sent from the center to the intermediate levels and then to the bottommost levels. These messages urge particular types of conduct — criticize revisionism, carry out the principle of self-reliance, etc. — and also lay down some general guidelines on how this work should be carried out. Good consequences ensue for those who carry out these urgings, and less pleasant consequences follow for those who do not. Is this law? No, not in the sense that we are accustomed to; among other things, it lacks the precision and the use of legal institutions and mechanisms that we regard as part of law. And yet it does lay down norms of conduct, norms backed by the enforcement mechanism described later in the book.

The Reach of Law

The use of our own legal system as a starting point for inquiry not only focuses our attention on certain matters, but also turns our attention away from others. At the simplest level, in thinking about our own legal system we associate particular institutions and activities with law. Thus, in the area of criminal law, some of the obvious avenues of inquiry concern search and seizure, arrest, bail, plea bargaining, trial, sentencing, and imprisonment. Yet, as will be seen, these are not the areas of primary importance in the Chinese criminal process. Most of the crucial actions and decisions take place at the peer group

level, sometimes with the participation of a local patrolman. Only an extremely small proportion of the cases involving antisocial or criminal conduct ever reach the level of arrest, much less the subsequent steps. By focusing on these latter steps, we would miss the great bulk of the actual Chinese "criminal law" system.

More fundamentally, when we define what is law in the American system, we are also defining what is *not* law. The determination of what a legal matter is centers around considerations concerning who the actors are (policemen, lawyers, etc.), which institutions are involved (legislature, governmental agency), and what forms and mechanisms are used (contract, will). This leaves out very large parts of human activity. In the area of criminal law and the control of antisocial conduct, for example, childhood and adult socialization processes, religious influences, and education are generally excluded, even though they are far more important factors in forming and controlling conduct than criminal codes and policemen. And indeed, these "nonlegal" areas are the most important aspects of Chinese "criminal law."

Along a somewhat different line, criminal law in our system consists basically of prohibitions against certain severe or extreme kinds of conduct: don't rob banks, don't assault your neighbor, and so forth. Transgressions of these rules lead to a clearly identifiable procedure for determining liability which is handled by designated legal officials and institutions. The entire process is stigmatized as "criminal." In China, however, it is difficult to distinguish between the manner in which a "criminal" matter — as opposed to a social, moral, or political matter — is handled, or between the kinds of sanctions imposed. Thus, a person who punches his neighbor might be treated to very much the same peer group criticism and pressure as one who is lazy at work, neglectful of his children, or unenthusiastic in the study of Marxism-Leninism. The point to be noted is that because the criminal process operates differently in the two societies, matters considered outside the scope of law in the United States may be very much to the heart of the matter in China.

Victor H. Li came to the United States from his native China in 1947 at the age of six. He received a Doctorate of Jurisprudence from Harvard Law School and currently teaches courses on Chinese law and international law at Stanford Law School.

Law in Post-Revolutionary Cuba

by Katherine M. Galvin

It's one thing to look at how a society outside the Western tradition of law deals with law without lawyers, it's quite another to examine the struggles of a western country to fashion a legal system which truly involves ordinary people in the decisions that affect their lives. Post-revolutionary Cuba offers one of the best examples of a society trying to do this. Rather than present a scholarly treatise on Cuban law, we thought it would be more interesting to have Kathy Galvin, one of our crew here at Nolo Press and a dedicated socialist, note some of her personal impressions of the ways Cuba is dealing with law and the delivery of legal services.

In November 1978, I had the opportunity to meet with Cuban lawyers, judges, and legislators, as well as factory workers, students, farmers, fishermen and housewives. I was in Cuba as part of a National Lawyers Guild delegation and had a chance to see many areas of post-revolutionary Cuban life. I returned home more than a little inspired by the people I met and the stories of the changes in their lives since the revolution. One person who left me with a lasting impression was a miner who worked in a copper mine in Pinar del Rio, a province located in the western part of the island. After a tour of the mine, we talked with some of the workers who informed us that great efforts were being made to achieve a level of sixth grade education for all 811 workers. Before the revolution, they explained, not one miner had received more than six months of education. In the course of this explanation, we noticed a lot of glances being exchanged and much elbowing of ribs. Finally one of the miners, a huge black man, modestly informed us that at the time of the revolution he had been illiterate. Now he was in law school and intended to continue his work in the mines only as a lawyer, not a miner. His story itself was a remarkable example of the transformation of Cuban society. But what was more moving, were the proud and beaming expressions on the faces of his fellow workers.

These beaming faces reflect the new attitude Cubans are taking toward law, lawyers, and the whole legal system. This attitude has been gaining momentum since 1977. At that time, a process of institutionalization was begun to structurally redefine every aspect of the nation's legal system to reflect the class perspective which the Cubans have adhered to for the last 21 years. During the initial stages of constructing a socialist society, the development of a new legal system was a low priority in the face of a 75% unemployment rate, a level of illiteracy of 29% (only 5% of the population had a sixth-grade education or higher), and an average life span of 54 years. Dealing with these problems, at the same time that Cuba was suffering the impact of mass emigration (the loss of most technicians and half of their lawyers and doctors), was an essential first step. And remember, it was a first step that had to be taken in the face of a military aggression and crippling economic blockade from the United States, a blockade which continues today.

One early legal innovation was the People's Tribunal. These "courts" were run by lay judges elected by the people, and dealt with a wide range of both criminal and civil matters. There was a particular effort in these people's tribunals to resolve disputes in a non-penal way, although the judges did have power to impose sentences. The people's tribunals were one vehicle that aided the Cubans in developing rules and procedures which have now begun to be incorporated in legal institutions and laws. It must be remembered that the "law" in Cuba is a calculated reflection of its socialist experience, and a concerted attempt to protect and foster the interests of workers. Their legal system is in contrast to ours, which I view as a tool of the corporate interests who rule this country to further their own interests and oppress those of everyone else.

Evaluating the Cuban legal system is much like evaluating any other legal system, in that careful examination should be made both of the substance of the law, as well as the manner in which it is administered. If the content of a law is unfair, no amount of procedural protections can produce a just result. For example, if in the United States draft counseling were to be made a felony, conviction and imprisonment for such a crime would not be fair merely because a person was found guilty by an unbiased judge. It is also important to trace the process of how laws are made. In the draft situation, this would mean evaluating whose interests are served and whose harmed, should draft counseling be made a felony. We would also want to focus on the type of people who would enact such a law, how the law was enforced and who did the enforcing. Obviously, no amount of protections like those contained in the Bill of Rights would be meaningful if they were enforced sporadically, unfairly, or not at all.

Laws
The laws which Cuban revolutionary society inherited were a reflection of the colonial interests of Spain and the imperialist interests of the United States. An initial task for the new socialist society, therefore, was to revise all laws comprehensively to reflect as accurately as possible the needs of a socialist society. To date, this has been a huge undertaking, including both revisions to the Constitution, as well as to the Criminal Procedure Code, the Civil and Administrative Procedure Code, the Family Code, the Youth and Children Code, and the Penal Code.

The new Constitution is not only a statement of socialist objectives, but more importantly, it provides the means to encourage direct popular parficipation in the government. The new Penal Code includes a list of crimes committed by public officials, as an example of the socialist notion that crimes should be characterized as injuries to the social body. In addition, prohibitions of official abuse of power against individuals or their homes appear in several places. Finally, the Penal Code contains many provisions protecting the rights of the individual, such as the right to free counsel and a provision for the release of the accused if there is no bail hearing within 72 hours of arrest.

The Family Code may be the most innovative in the world. The rights and duties between husband and wife are illustrative:

> Marriage is established with equal rights and duties for both parties... spouses must live together, be loyal, considerate, respectful and mutually helpful to each other... Both parties have the right to practice their profession or skill and it is their duty to help each other and to cooperate in this direction and to study or improve their knowledge.

Perhaps more impressive than the content of these codes, was the process of codification. In the United States, the legislative process usually begins with one or several men, generally lawyers, drafting laws in isolation (except to the extent that "experts" are consulted). The proposed legislation is then rejected or adopted by lawmakers, after having been furiously lobbied by professionals who represent various interests, many of which have almost unlimiting financing. The lawmakers are mostly white, middle-aged men—for the most part lawyers—who were successful in an election in which perhaps 30% of the voters participated. So much for Popular participation in our democratic process.

In Cuba, after a lengthy drafting process, legislation is circulated and actively debated not only in the legislative assemblies but also in countless meetings of trade unions, student organizations, Committees for the Defense of the Revolution (CDR), Cuban Women's Federation (FMC), farmer organizations, etc. For instance, we were told by a representative of the Poder Popular (the legislature) that in 1976 a draft resolution of the Constitution was discussed by over six million Cubans. From these discussions, there were more than 12,800 suggestions for changes to the original draft. As a result of these suggestions, 2,400 amendments were made, and explanations given as to why each suggestion was either formulated into an amendment or rejected. The final draft was overwhelmingly approved in a referendum in which 97% of the voters participated.

This process of public participation not only helps to demystify the law, it is also a useful educational tool. For example, one of the most hotly debated provisions of the Family Code was the requirement that husband and wife would be equally responsible for the care and upbringing of their children and for the housework.[1] The fact that one spouse contributes all the financial support to the family does not prejudice his or her duty to cooperate equally with childcare or housework. Given the nature of most husband-wife relationships, compliance with such a provision would certainly alter many marriages, and as a result, many Cuban men — and even some women — objected. After hours of grassroots discussion, this provision was eventually adopted, reflecting new and evolving ideas about the family and the role of women and men in a traditionally male-dominated society. Although the enactment of the law does not ensure the end of machismo, or the full participation of men with the housework, it does create a public awareness of the need for equality and its official sanction as an important value in a socialist society. As one woman put it, "Now at least my husband washes the clothes, even though he still refuses to hang them up on the line, where he would be in view of the neighbors."

I KNOW I HUNG OUT THE WASH LAST SATURDAY, BUT HERNANDEZ WASN'T HOME...

Dispute Resolution

The People's Tribunals, established in 1965, were abolished in February, 1978 as part of the reorganization of the judicial system. However, lay judges still sit in all the tribunals — municipal, provincial,

and national; and in the municipal court, they comprise the majority. Lay judges are nominated by workers in the workplaces, or by neighbors in the local Committees for Defense of Revolutions (CDR's), and then elected by the assembly corresponding to the level of the court on which they sit. They serve two non-consecutive months each year for two years and receive the same salary they would have received at their usual work. The other ten months of each year, they work at their normal jobs. Retired persons and unemployed persons (usually housewives) are also elected as lay judges and continue to receive their normal pensions or governmental assistance. Lay judges receive training and can be re-elected indefinitely. The fact that they only serve as part-time judges, and continue to work, encourages them to be more sensitive to people's everyday problems.

Professional judges are also elected by the appropriate legislative assembly after nominations from workers, parties, and community organizations are submitted to the Minister of Justice. These professional judges are generally lawyers and differ from lay judges by virtue of their technical training and experience. Both professional and lay judges can be recalled both for conduct unbecoming a judge *outside* the courtroom (drunkness, criminal behavior, etc.), as well as for conduct *in* the courtroom — by the assemblies who elected them.

In contrast, virtually all judges in the United States are lawyers. This seems to be the only qualification — even intelligence and legal competence are not usually considered relevant. Not even at the Small Claims Court level are there lay judges. Furthermore, the majority of U.S. judges, whether elected or appointed, are white male lawyers who are financially comfortable and tend to share the attitudes and interests of the wealthy. Most have little practical experience with the day-to-day realities of the people whose lives they rule, resulting in decision-making that is neither compassionate nor fair. Moreover, in the United States, to remove a judge is extremely difficult and removal is almost never the result of his or her conduct on the bench.

Cuba has also developed a mechanism to resolve disputes at the work place. These labor tribunals are composed of workers elected to handle the grievances and disputes of other workers. For instance, there is a regulation which prohibits a miner from working in any area which he considers to be unsafe. If he violates this safety rule, he is subject to a hearing before the labor tribunal.

A third area where disputes are commonly resolved is the Committee for the Defense of the Revolution (CDR). CDR's are local mass organizations which exist in all neighborhoods. Their duties include mobilizing people for volunteer work, planting trees, improving the appearance of the neighborhood, coordinating vaccinations and blood donations, coordinating recycling, directing political study, and facilitating participation in the government. They are also responsible for sorting out neighborhood problems, and dealing with husbands who abuse their wives.

Lawyers

In January 1959, out of a population of 5.5 million Cubans, there were 6,000 doctors and 6,000 lawyers. Within a short time, half of each group left the country. In 1978, with a population of 9.5 million, there were 12,000 doctors but only 2,600 lawyers. These statistics reflect the fact that the Cuban government placed a higher priority on the provision of health care than legal services. Now, because of the 1977 institutionalization and a trend toward societal stabilization, there is a movement to educate more lawyers. In 1978, there were 3,500 students in the six Cuban law schools.

Legal education in Cuba stands in marked contrast to the training of lawyers in the United States. Curriculum in Cuban law schools is directed towards producing a politically conscious cadre of legal professionals. In addition to familiar law courses such as contracts, criminal law, etc., a significant portion of the five-year curriculum includes courses such as political economy, history of the labor movement in the Cuban Revolution, and theory of state and law. In addition, students spend two months each year in a law office as part of their training.

Students may enroll in the full-time program or in a workers' program. The workers' program, in which the miner I talked with was enrolled, is designed for people to attend school twice every fifteen days. The curriculum is the same for both full and part-time students, but the part-time students (workers) do much of their study on an independent basis. Full-time students are provided with

stipends for their living expenses or, in some instances, receive a salary from their former work place. For example, workers can decide collectively to provide one of their colleagues the opportunity to pursue legal education on a full-time basis. Law school itself—including books, tuition, and all fees —like all education in Cuba, is free.

In the United States, most people are motivated to pursue a career in law because of their expectation of a substantial income and considerable power and prestige. They also expect to influence legislation and in general to direct the course of society. In Cuba, these particular incentives do not exist for several reasons. First, there is less elitism, since ordinary people are heavily involved in legal and legislative decision-making. In addition, despite the growing importance of legal technicians in the present phase of institutionalizing the Cuban state, a state lawyer makes less money than a miner, many factory workers, and even taxi drivers. A beginning lawyer in a private practice "bufete" will always make less than the secretary in the office.

The private practice of law as we know it doesn't really exist in Cuba. Instead, they have a national system of law collectives known as bufetes. There are 62 bufetes in the country, ten of which are located in the city of Havana. The one we visited —the largest in the country—had sixty lawyers and reminded me of an old, run-down legal services office. We met with the director, a woman lawyer, and ten of the other staff lawyers. Most of them had practiced law prior to the revolution and described their pre-revolution lawyering experiences to us. They said that corruption was so rampant then, it was common practice for rich lawyers to pay the police to alter their reports, and for lawyers to keep lists of the judges' birthdates in order to give them birthday presents. We were even told of lawyers making direct payoffs to judges—sometimes in open court. Lawyers like those in the bufete, who represented leftists, labor agitators, student militants, etc., made very little money and were harassed as much as their clients.

Today, all lawyers belong to a union and receive salaries set by a national organization of bufete lawyers. There is a minimum salary which increases gradually to a maximum level. A female lawyer is entitled to maternity leave—six weeks before and six weeks following delivery—as are all other workers.

A Cuban who is charged with a crime has the right to counsel at the moment of arrest, as well as equal access to representation in any civil case. He or she selects a lawyer from a bufete, or if he has no preference, is assigned a lawyer by the bufete director. Clients are charged fees according to the category of the case, and only when there is an actual case. Legal advice is free. If a client cannot afford the cost of the service, he pays nothing; there is no sliding scale.

If the client is dissatisfied with the representation he is receiving from an individual lawyer, he can always request that another lawyer be assigned to the case. Lawyers handle the standard fare—divorce and other family cases, wills, and criminal cases. Conspicuously absent are eviction cases, since no one can be evicted. Cases are also taken against the state on behalf of individuals who may have been harmed or mistreated by a bureaucratic agency, or whose interests have been damaged as a result of a law.

Conclusion

In Cuba, I witnessed many problems which are endemic to any poor, developing country, but which, in this case, are aggravated by the continuing blockade imposed by the United States. Goods are unavailable or rationed, both medical supplies and housing are severely limited, and public transportation is abominable. I heard remarks about women and gay people that suggested that traditional male and homophobic attitudes will suffer a slow and painful death. Not all Cubans are satisfied with their society, as was evidenced by the migration of many in the spring of 1980.

But I was constantly impressed by the incredible strides made by the Cuban people in such a short period of time. While there I came to accept as normal that all education is free; that all health care is free; that no one is evicted from his or her home; that a primary goal is achieving employment for every man and every woman; and that every child is decently clothed. It was only when I returned to the cold Boston winter and found my clients being put

out on the streets, families without any resources being denied food stamps, and homes being foreclosed because the owner was unable to pay a hospital bill past due, that I realized many of the differences between Cuban society and our own.

Within this framework, I am therefore cautiously supportive of this new era of legal institutionalization. Ten years ago I naively went into law believing it to be an instrument of social change. Instead, I discovered that it is more often a barrier to change. But the Cuban lawyers with whom we met were dedicated to using law as a tool to achieve socialist goals. And the major changes undergone in Cuban law reflect those goals. Finally, I believe the new emphasis on law will not impede the ongoing process, because of the majority participation of the populace in the legislative process, the presence of lay people in the various tribunals, an increased awareness of the law, and the fact that these new laws are understandable, reflect the experience of the Cuban people, and thus make sense. This process will continue as long as the Cuban people follow the declaration set out in the preamble of their own Constitution:

> We declare our will that the law of laws of the Republic be guided by the following strong desire of Jose Martí at last achieved:
> 'I want the fundamental law of our Republic to be the tribute of Cubans to the full dignity of man.'

---

1. If a husband has not done his share of the housework, he is not considered to have committed a "crime," but his wife can base her divorce complaint on his negligence.

Kathy Galvin is a dropped-out lawyer from Boston/ Cambridge, where she practiced law for the past five years—mostly in the areas of tenant rights, women's rights and welfare rights. Like Annie Hall and Joanna Kramer, she came to Berkeley, California to find herself and mellow out. She holds some hope of finding Kathy one of these days, and in the meantime practices her "mellowing" at Nolo Press. She is also an active member of the National Lawyers Guild.

The Creation of Legal Dependency:
Law School in a Nutshell

by Michael Lowy and Craig Haney

We have taken a look at our own legal roots as well as the legal traditions of other cultures. With this historical/comparative perspective we can gain a clearer, more objective picture of the American Legal System as it exists today. But what about the individuals who make up this system? Who is your common garden-variety lawyer? To fully understand the species we must first scrutinize the ritual metamorphosis that each prospective candidate must undergo. Law school is the process whereby citizens from every race, creed, color, gender, size and background are turned into lawyers. It is awesome what transitions are accomplished in these three short years.

> ...They come into these sacred halls of which you have become the yearling priests. They stink of laity. They must be cleansed, they must be quickly cleansed, or all of us will be profaned. Gird up your loins, then, my beloved, and descend into the pools; in each left hand a pot of legal germicidal soap, each right fist brandishing a foot-long brush of dialectic. Seize these new woolly lambs and scrub them for the law...
>
> —*Karl Llewellyn*
> The Bramblebush *(1930)*

We may be among the few people who went to law school hoping not to get "hooked" on law. We do not know if we succeeded. If we did it is only because we came to law school with a partial immunity to the condition. Graduate education (in anthropology and psychology) and several years studying the legal system critically, as scholars, gave us an alternative perspective with which we could understand and analyze what was happening to us and our classmates. Indeed, we attended law school in part to *understand* the cultural and psychological assumptions embedded in the process of legal education.

As social scientists we were struck by the extent to which law and law school was consciously, explicitly, and vehemently anti–social science. To create legal dependency among its acolytes, legal education weans them away from all competing sources of understanding. Many law professors savagely attack and purge alternative explanations of human behavior. Control over students, many of whom were social science majors in college, is established quickly. This control is accomplished by depriving students of their familiar models of social problems and hence their familiar solutions. This deprivation is not based on an adequate critique of these models or on a demonstration that the solutions they imply are unworkable. They are dismissed with what soon becomes the most damning indictment of all—they are simply "non-legal."

The results of this process are tragic and profound. Legal "junkies" are set loose upon society looking for a fix. Their influence is pervasive, extending far beyond the courts, into business and government. Dependency upon the legal model in this society is so pronounced that many promising social change programs or efforts are either crushed or co-opted by law and legalism. We believe that a careful examination of legal education and the legalistic frame of mind it creates will lead analysts to an abiding pessimism about the use of law as an instrument of progressive social change. We think so, not—as some of our colleagues believe—because law is primarily "derivative" and therefore impotent; rather because so many of those who operate and staff our legal system have been made intellectually dependent upon a view of truth, justice, and human behavior that serves to maintain the status quo. Our purpose in writing this essay is to describe the basis of this legal dependency. We hope that from this description prospective law students as well as other non-lawyers will gain some insight into the conceptual world inhabited by most lawyers.

Thinking Like A Lawyer: The Road to Salvation

Legal education begins with a well-orchestrated campaign to destabilize, disorient, and intimidate its recruits. The process begins immediately. Students are assigned cases to read with little or no guidance as to what they are to focus on. Even though some of these initial cases are quite brief, students invariably spend hours trying to make sense out of what is essentially a foreign language (legalese). Initial comprehension is virtually impossible.

The resulting confusion and disorientation is particularly traumatic to a group of typical law students whose verbal prowess has been previously unquestioned. The reaction of the professors to student distress is a key to understanding the creation of legal dependency. Rather than explaining or empathizing with the difficulty of the task and the inexperience of the beginners, the professors demand competence and many humiliate those students who do not quickly appear to master the new language. As one of our professors succinctly put it: "In order to be a lawyer, you have to sound like you know what you're talking about." For those who adopted this point of view, stopped trying to make sense out of what they were reading in terms of their previous models of reality, and began aping their teachers, control was quickly established.

Students are humbled by this abrupt and painful transition. They are made to feel inadequate in their encounters with the seemingly vast, even mysterious, complexities of the law. It is important to recognize that the complexity resides as much in the way law is taught and presented, as it does in the material itself. Textbooks are no more than collections of cases in which no basic principles are summarized or underscored. The cases are presented in no discernable order—an 1840 Massachusetts case follows one 1957 in California and an 1803 English case. (Imagine what this does to the development of an historical or sociopolitical analysis of law.) The opinions are not written to be understood, least of all by students. Some of them have been selected precisely because they are such bad examples of logic and reasoning. And these are not clearly distinguished from the good ones. The opinions continuously introduce terms and concepts that are nowhere defined.

To anyone who looks closely at the process of legal education, it is hard to avoid the conclusion that the resulting confusion is intentionally created. It is also hard to avoid the conclusion that if law were taught the way many other academic subjects

are—with a pedagogical concern for clarity and organization—law school would take no more than one year. (Bar review courses, in which most of the three-year curriculum is taught, adopt precisely these strategies and take only six weeks.)

Confronted with this maze of confusing and poorly presented information coupled with the intimidating and competitive atmosphere of law school, many students lose their confidence, and with it their willingness and ability to challenge. Vision and perspective are too often sacrificed as well. Since they cannot really fathom the depths of the law, or perceive its boundaries, their gaze can hardly transcend it. Many give up any hope of changing or improving law and instead seek only to understand or master it. By the time they are comfortable enough with the intellectual content of the law school curriculum, it is too late. They have taken its categories as their own. The initial confusion of law school leads to helplessness, helplessness to vulnerability. From this purgatory of confusion, intimidation, and self-doubt, "thinking like a lawyer" is offered as the only salvation.

Legal Librarianship

For some who remain obdurate, their introduction to the law library becomes a turning point in their struggle to remain independent. In many ways, the law library is a remarkable and efficient information storage and retrieval system. It is also intimidating and frightening. The first assignments, again largely in the absence of adequate preparation or instruction, set students to work on finding a case about a particular and very specific kind of human problem. The exercise is remarkable in several respects. Again, a simple task such as looking up information in a library becomes, for those used to accomplishing such tasks in minutes, a labor of many hours.

Secondly, but more profound for the issue of legal dependency, the student is led into the seemingly endless world of appellate case law. After marvelling at the range of this monument to the common law, students are left with the impression that the decided cases contain within them the answers to every conceivable human problem. Not only does each issue appear to have been carefully and exactly defined, but a range of alternative, seemingly exhaustive answers have been given by courts from different centuries and different jurisdictions. The social science and humanistic approaches to problem-solving are nowhere to be found here and soon begin to pale in comparison to the accumulated wisdom of many centuries of the "English-speaking people."

Moreover, what the courts have said about these problems is *all* that comes to matter. Here the students are introduced to and immersed in the historically conservative and fundamentally authoritarian nature of legal argument and decision. Current problems are solved on the basis of decisions made by past courts who are "higher" authorities in our hierarchically arranged system of law. *Who* has solved these problems is what matters; the quality and cogency of their logic, the range and validity of the factual record on which their opinion was based, the bias and prejudice that may have informed their decision, the historical and even geographical idiosyncrasies that may render their opinion obsolete, irrelevant, unjust are largely ignored. These cases come to define the range and domain of legal reasoning. They set the limits of legal problem-solving, indeed, of legal thought itself. But who are these judges? From what narrow socioeconomic and intellectual backgrounds do they come? How have these remarkably similar backgrounds influenced their decisions? What do they *really* know about the people and situations affected by their decisions? These questions go unasked and unanswered.

Because of the students' initial helplessness in the face of foreign and confusing legal reasoning, these opinions appear to contain not only wisdom but a mysterious, awesome logic capable of being fathomed by only the greatest of minds (an image fostered by the tone and symbolism of law school classrooms and decor). By the time students have achieved enough familiarity with the foreign language of law (again, offered without benefit of glossary or dictionary), that mysterious logic has become their own—not to be objectively examined or critiqued, but rather to be skillfully and adeptly employed in legal discourse and debate with one's fellow, fledgling lawyers. A virtual stranglehold on the legal imagination is thus insured after only a few short months in law school.

Hard Cases, Bad Law, and Law School

Those who relish the movies of Italian film director Federico Fellini would love the typical law school classroom. The collection of human oddities and tragedies typically presented in case material is wondrous to behold. This technique—using "hard cases," those that are at the fringes of (or beyond) our capacity to understand or interpret logically—diverts student attention away from the reality of the everyday. No matter that most criminal cases involve poor young people who are accused of robbery or burglary—the criminal law class focuses on ax-murdering somnambulists. Forget that industrial pollution and occupational health hazards are everyday phenomena, the law school class focuses on exploding bottles and bizarre coincidences.

In a seemingly unending parade of statistically insignificant occurrences, the student's theories for explaining and understanding human behavior are severely tested. The belief that life is infinitely complex and that no one can know the perversity that lurks within the hearts of man is engendered. The perfect compatibility of these legal beliefs with a laissez-faire world view that eschews social planning and government regulation in favor of the "invisible hand," of course, is nowhere noted or discussed.

For the remaining recalcitrant few, it is often the "hard case" that converts them to the legal model. For example, consider the case of *Riss v. City of New York*, 22 NY 2nd 579 (1968), and the way it was presented in class. The facts, although unusual, are straightforward. Ms. Riss sought police protection from her former suitor when he threatened to harm her after she had rejected him. The police declined to provide her protection, claiming that they had inadequate resources to protect every citizen who had been threatened. The jilted suitor carried out his threats by hiring a third person to throw lye in Ms. Riss's face, causing permanent damage to her vision.

The injured party's lawsuit against the police was dismissed, the court stating that it lacked the power to allocate police resources (which it decided was a legislative or executive function). Class discussion of this case focused upon the alleged policy reasons behind the decisions and a general theme of minimal court involvement developed. However, not once were students encouraged to examine the myriad of empirical questions on which any real policy analysis must rest: Just how many threats were there in this city? What do we know about the likelihood of such threats being carried out? What else were the police doing? Who was getting protection? How have other jurisdictions handled the situation? Without answers to these questions, and thus with no general factual context for the case, no real policy analysis could proceed. Nonetheless, the incomplete and idiosyncratic facts of this case were used as a basis for developing a general attitude of judicial restraint—the idea that judges should refrain from deciding certain kinds of issues that other branches of government could control.

Then a quite unusual situation developed. Ordinarily, law professors never talk about the consequences or aftermath of policies and rules that are decided in the cases. The implementation or impact of appellate case law is apparently beyond their control or interest. However, the torts professor did comment on the consequences of the Riss case, a few days after its initial class discussion. After serving many years in prison, the jilted suitor, Mr. Pugash, was released and *married* Ms. Riss. Incredible!! The class was upset by this outcome. We were confused. Clearly, if this outcome was possible, who could really say what was right or better or proper for other human beings? The lesson was dramatic—who really knows? Who can predict human behavior? As a lawyer, all you are required to do is provide a mechanism—the legal process—for understanding human behavior.

Why was this the only case in which we learned

the outcome for the participants? Why not the outcome or consequences in the hundreds of thousands of typical cases in which the results are far more predictable? This focus on the unusual or exceptional event undermines any sweeping critique of what exists in favor of a more "pragmatic" concession to the status quo. To accommodate the most improbable, we ignore the normative and important. A rejection of social science data and methods is essential to this process.

The Strawman Has Tremendous Clout
On occasion, law professors lead their students down the "ugly path" of social-science reasoning. Their distortions, otherwise known as strawmen, turn out to have tremendous vitality and power. Consider the following discussion from a criminal law class, on the necessity of dealing with one case at a time, and not allowing the defenses of "poverty," "situation" or "culture." The question at issue was why social-science data is generally not admitted in defense of alleged criminals. The professor used the following argument. Since much statistical evidence is available to support the fact that more than half of all felony arrests in the U.S. are made on minority males between the ages of 17 and 35, the data could be used to "solve" the crime problem —by incarcerating all minority males between those ages! Using this strawman argument, the professor went on to explain that for this reason, we need the criminal law with all its built-in safeguards, to focus only on the individual, and to protect the constitutional rights of the individual. Notwithstanding the fact that few people have *ever* proposed misusing such statistics in this fashion, we were invited to believe that the individuation of the crime problem was what kept hordes of ill-intentioned social scientists from depriving us all of our constitutional rights to be treated as unique human beings.

It is important to realize how skillfully the professor had set up the strawman. First of all, he entirely skirted the issue of a differential arrest rate for minority males in this country. The first question a criminal law school class might want to examine is why only certain people get arrested for certain crimes? Instead the entire class focused on "crime in the streets, not in the suites" (to borrow a phrase from Ralph Nader), not realizing at all that they had narrowed the definition of crime in this analysis.

Moreover, the most ubiquitous crimes in this country are victimless—drug offenses, prostitution, public drunkenness, vagrancy—but they receive barely
a mention in the typical law school class. And,
focusing on the strawman himself, the professor had
missed an excellent opportunity to highlight an area
in need of legal research and change. Rather than
scaring neophytes about the negative uses to which
such data can be put, why not use this information
positively and begin to examine the causes of crime
and how (if at all) criminal law can be used (or
modified) to change such patterns? Such is the
power of the strawman that none of these issues
surfaced during the discussion.

Indeed most of the class did come away from the
discussion fearful of the use to which social-science
data could be put and committed—in theory—to a
constitutional defense of each and every criminal
defendant, free of statistical or causal "determinist"
analysis. Never mind all the social-science evidence
showing that the criminal defense attorneys who
would raise these constitutional protections on
behalf of their poor and minority clients are so over-
worked and compromised by the adversary system
that in almost 90% of the cases they bargain for
guilty pleas without ever so much as raising a single
constitutional objection. Never mind the social-
science evidence that the poverty and discrimination
experienced by the defendant class gives them so
much more reason to commit crime and makes the
"even-handed" application of law inherently dis-
criminatory. Never mind the social-science evidence that these people are more likely to be
suspected, arrested, prosecuted, and incarcerated
because of their race and social class.

Be grateful instead for a system of "due process"
that *could* guarantee that constitutional rights are
upheld in the course of this endemic and well-
documented more *basic* mistreatment. Indeed, it is
this system, and this system of education, that makes
lawyers the exclusive guardians of our rights and
empowers them to make policy decisions in our
society only *after* it has convinced them that limited
legal rights are all that matter, and creates a dependency on narrow, often illusory, legal formulas in
our society as well as in its lawyers.

**The Adversary System: Don't Be a Boor,
Who Really Knows the Truth?**

It's very hard when you get to law school to maintain the ideals you have because you learn so
quickly that nothing you believed in is absolute.
There are really two sides or fifty sides to every
question.

Student comment
Stanford Law School
Board of Visitors Report,
1975–76

The adversary system rests upon a procedural notion
of truth. Literal truth is the secondary (and by no
means necessary) outcome of a fair, balanced,
adversarial process. Of course, the system cannot
function without the existence of two sides to an
issue—two sides close enough together but far
enough apart so that a "real" conflict exists, yet
sufficiently "balanced" so that "experts" (lawyers
and judges) are needed to solve the dilemma. Law
students in this system are taught to accept unques-
tioningly certain fundamental assumptions (perhaps
the most important of which are the rules of the
adversary game itself), but to become intensely dis-
putatious about literally *everything* else.

For the adversary system to operate, then, there
must be conflict or the *appearance* of conflict. In
order to operate within the adversary system, the
neophyte law student adds at least three new expressions to his or her vocabulary: "There is a colorable
legal argument...," "It's a close question...," and
"But on the other hand...." At the same time, the
student is warned against the use of certain words in
legal writing: " 'We,' 'I,' 'believe,' and 'think' should
be avoided altogether in legal discourse," a one of
our second-term legal writing instructors told his
class. This terminology and these habits of speaking
and writing are the surface manifestations of a much
deeper set of changes in thinking and feeling that
legal education effects.

Law students ar constantly *assigned* points of view
to advocate or defend. In classroom discussion, in
moot court exercises, and in all-important final
examinations students are given one side of an issue
and evaluated on the basis of how well they present
their assumed positions. The consummate legal
skill, they are taught, is to be able to argue *both* sides
of an issue *equally* well. And even within a single
position or point of view, flexibility is the touch-
stone. An advocate must be able to instantly change
direction or alter the basis of an argument as the
court indicates displeasure with the preferred rea-

soning or justification. The psychological consequences of this indiscriminate role-playing and constant shifting of opinion and position are nowhere discussed.

Students are chided to "unpack" the overstuffed conceptual baggage of "justice" and "fairness." Apparently, terms like "economic efficiency" come neatly packed in luggage whose design is so compact that it cannot be improved upon. Whatever cannot be quantified (or perceived by the largely upper- or middle-class students in a tangible way) cannot become part of the cost-benefit analysis urged upon them. Intangibles like "justice" and "truth" are quickly dismissed as sophomoric concerns, too imponderable to become part of any "bottom-line" calculation. Risk, in these terms, is always calculated as loss from the status quo, rather than foregone opportunities to achieve the possible or what might have been. Coupled with the hierarchical and historical nature of legal decision-making, this obsession with risk instills a strongly conservative bias in many students. Creativity is discounted and caution rules.

Despite disclaimers to the contrary, of course, values *are* taught in law school classrooms. Indeed, as we have tried to show, a powerful set of biases is introduced into legal thinking, albeit implicitly and with little or no awareness or discussion. It is a pedagogy that teaches as much by what it does not say as by what it does. It is the kind of pedagogy, for example, that allows professors in administrative law to make fun of environmentalists who challenged the standing requirements in federal courts so they could sue on behalf of fish and trees, but to mock them in seemingly "neutral" fashion. The professor sarcastically and righteously bellowed, amidst much student laughter, "who really represents the fish?" His implied condemnation centered on the "hold-up" value of such cases—his suggestion that environmentalists could use their standing to "extort" millions of dollars from large corporations. Did the professor really not know that the courts regularly appoint guardians to represent minors and the mentally disabled? Did he not know that a corporation is a legal fiction—clearly less alive than fish or trees? Who represents the *corporations*? Of course, we did not need to ask.

And even when the law seems to openly embrace certain noble values, the structure of legal education

can act to subvert them. In a book entitled *Persons and Masks of the Law* (1976), for example, John Noonan has written very persuasively about the law's lack of real concern with *persons*, despite its expressed devotion to upholding the rights of individuals. Instead, his analysis shows that persons function in law as "masks," acting as a cover for the real determinants of decisions rather than a personalizing reality in legal opinions. This professional myopia originates in law school, where no time is spent discussing *who* the parties are in the cases that are examined or what the real consequences of judicial decisions are for the parties who brought the lawsuit. Instead, people and their problems are used as nothing more than vehicles for the illustration of abstract legal principles.

Legal fictions can render reality impotent and unimportant. When facts are surrendered up to legal definitions that bear little relationship to the events they supposedly describe, a kind of epistemological anarchy reigns. In this arena victory goes to whomever persuades best. Of course, the ability and resources to marshall persuasive arguments are not evenly distributed in our society. Once again, the powerful and wealthy, and the status quo, are the beneficiaries of the law's neutral principles. In the "value-free" world of legal neutrality, law students are not encouraged to take the inherent biases of law and legal education into account. If they were, perhaps they would soon realize that the methodology of law is not so much a powerful method as it is often merely the method of the powerful.

Michael J. Lowy has been the director of the Northern California Public Interest Research Group at Santa Clara University since 1979. He holds a Ph.D. in Anthropology from the University of California, Berkeley and a J.D. from Stanford Law School.

Craig Haney currently teaches psychology and law at the University of California at Santa Cruz. He received a Ph.D. and a J.D. from Stanford University.

Mediation: Reducing Dependence on Lawyers and Courts to Achieve Justice

by Gary Friedman

We have all seen so many judicial dramas on film, it is no wonder that we imagine all courtrooms to be presided over by a facsimile of the late Charles Laughton, with a tortured Henry Fonda in the witness box, and a stocky E.G. Marshall or Raymond Burr pacing back and forth before the jury, formulating his hard-edged questions as he glares over his shoulders at the witness. Indeed, the adversary system of arriving at truth is so deeply ingrained in our consciousness that, until recently, our court system was rarely questioned. Just as we learned as children that "God is on our side" and that democracy is the best of all possible systems, we have accepted that, Sacco and Vanzetti aside, the truth will out in an American courtroom. But can we be so sure? If we ignore the programming we received from our high school civics teachers, is it reasonable to expect that the truth will reveal itself when lawyers assume outrageously extreme positions and then try to prove those positions in verbal courtroom jousts ruled by stylized and often archaic procedures? And is there another way to solve disputes that seems more reasonable? Perhaps so. Please read on.

It's a familiar story to most people who have had to hire a lawyer. A no-win situation. Legal fees are likely to run higher than the fiscal returns you stand to gain from winning your case, and the dispute will probably take so long to resolve that winning won't be worth the effort—especially if you consider the bitterness and anger that typically accompany the fight. Either way, you're going to end up feeling like you've lost, even when your lawyer tells you that you've won.

As a lawyer facing these realities every day, I grew tired of participating in a system that appears to be blatantly insensitive to the people it was designed to serve. And out of that frustration, I thrashed about for another way to practice law. I didn't subscribe to those postures most lawyers assume almost automatically, such as winning at any cost, and I was no longer ready to assume the worst and plunge into the fray with an arsenal of hostility, aggressiveness, and intimidation directed at the soft underbelly of my opponent. Yet, knowing what I wanted to avoid was easier than conceiving a more constructive way to relate to law. After much mental confusion and anguish, I realized that what I wanted was to use law to bring together people with disputes and help them create an agreement that they could both feel good about. Gradually, and at first only with clients who were friends, I began to mediate disputes rather than counselling people to fight it out in expensive court battles. And soon it became clear that the mediation approach not only made me feel positive about my career, but was also an efficient way to solve disputes. Now I have complete confidence in the mediation process as a preferable way for many, if not most, people to work out their legal disputes. The results of my work have been encouraging, sometimes dramatically so, with a few disappointments and a fair share of mistakes. Here are a couple of examples:

Three years ago a couple decided that they wanted me to mediate their divorce. Within three one and a half hour sessions they reached an agreement on all issues necessary to draw up a written agreement. But at the last moment, the man got cold feet and refused to sign, claiming that he had been advised by another lawyer that he could do much better if he hired him as his advocate. Two years and over $20,000 in legal fees later, the couple reappeared in my office and signed the agreement I had originally drawn up.

At first I was self-conscious about being a "mediator" and not exclusively a "fighter." But gradually I have become more willing to come out of the closet and express my confidence in mediation. Now I make the mediation option available to every client who walks into my office, whereas in the past I would suggest the possibility of mediation quite tentatively. Fortunately, one early client was willing to

accept my tentative offer to mediate rather than liti-
gate. He was the father of a twenty-one year old
woman and originally wanted to hire me to have his
daughter declared legally incompetent to manage
her life. The idea was to deny the daughter money
from a trust fund set up for her by a deceased grandmother, so that it would not be available to buy
drugs and liquor. When the father and I carefully
examined the negative effect that his "winning" the
case might have on his daughter, I suggested to him
that it might be preferable for me to act as a mediator between him and his daughter, rather than as his
lawyer. I met with the daughter and described the
mediation process; she was willing to participate.
Five sessions later, she and her father came to an
agreement that she would seek therapeutic help,
keep track of her finances, and go to school, if he
would agree not to interfere with her life. The agreement is still in effect, has been honored by both
father and daughter, and has been jointly modified
twice over the years. The father is satisfied that the
daughter has "straightened out" and the daughter
feels that she and her father have enjoyed a positive
relationship for the first time in her life.

It is no surprise to me that more and more people
decide that hiring a lawyer to represent them as part
of the traditional adversary process is simply too
expensive, time-consuming, mystifying and alien-
ating. Many people are also unwilling to accept the
feeling of powerlessness and helplessness that comes
from having set legal wheels in motion and then
realizing that these wheels have acquired an impetus
of their own—one that is often far removed from
the original concerns of the person who started them
rolling. All too often small disputes seem to escalate
almost automatically into legal wars marked by
aggressiveness, righteousness, and hostility whenever lawyers are involved.

Mediation represents a positive way to slow down
the process of hostility-escalation and gap-widening
that usually accompanies a dispute. Where the
parties to the dispute have need of a continuing
relationship (i.e. neighbors, parents and children,
businessmen, friends, tenants and landlords), it is
particularly important to have avenues of resolving
differences that don't further separate them. The
presence of a neutral third person—the mediator
—becomes both a symbolic and real recognition of
the larger community—a community that partici-

pates with the disputants on an equal footing, rather
than sitting in judgment and holding up one party as
being right and the other wrong.

The two most essential elements of a mediation
are, first, the presence of a neutral third party who
has no power to decide the dispute and does not
represent either or both of the individuals, and
second, the willingness of the disputants to enter
into mediation.

Working together with the mediator, the parties
establish mutually agreeable ground rules to govern
their discussions. The goal is to reach a solution
which is satisfactory to all of the participants. Once
an agreement is reached, the role of the mediator
(my usual role) is to reduce the agreement to
writing, have it reviewed by the parties, and, if
desired, by their lawyers, and then to have it signed
by the parties. Once signed, with or without a lawyer's review, it represents a valid contract with all of
the usual rights and remedies.

Differences Between Mediation and Typical Legal Representation

Mediation can be seen, not as a competing alternative to legal representation, but as a way to solve a
dispute before it escalates into a full-scale battle.
The simplest most direct way of settling an argument is for the two people who disagree to sit down
and work out their differences. When this process is
not successful, people typically turn to a lawyer to
help them prevail against the other person, who
then in turn also hires a lawyer. When this happens,
the lawyers typically either negotiate an agreement
acceptable to the parties or submit their dispute to a
judge or jury to decide. Mediation represents
another alternative—an often overlooked opportunity to solve the dispute before it has escalated to the
state where people feel that lawyers and courts are
required to resolve it.

The parties themselves determine both the mediation method, as well as the specific ends they seek.
The advantages to a successful mediation process are
numerous. Since the parties have played such a central role in resolving their differences, the chances of
their living up to their agreement are much greater
than when the decision has been either reached
through coercion of "handed down" by a court.
Although lip service is often paid to the client's right
to make ultimate choices when represented by a

lawyer in a formal adversary proceeding, the legal process is often so foreign to non-lawyers, that undue deference is given to the lawyer's opinion.

The role of law itself is also different in the mediation setting as compared to situations where lawyers are in charge. The parties in a mediation are free to determine how the law shall be used in resolving their differences. In a court setting, the law tends to become the "property" of the judge and to a lesser extent, the "lawyers." Only in a mediation setting can the parties to the dispute make their own rules.

One of the things I like best about mediation is that there are no losers. In adversary representation, the process is structured for one party to win and the other to lose. When the mediation process works, both parties feel like winners for having worked through their difficulties together. All of the effort of the mediation is directed toward bringing the parties together, rather than dividing them further from each other by identifying one as right and the other as wrong.

But it's important to remember that mediations do not take place in a vacuum. They exist in the context of our adversary legal system and our political and economic systems, and the possibility of threat or resort to the courts always lurks behind the process of mediation. And the adversary approach is certainly not limited to the legal system. Indeed, aggressiveness and open competition are deeply ingrained in our culture, from the base of our economic system of capitalism to the way we are raised by our parents. Even when we decide that we want to act in a cooperative, mutually respectful way, it is often difficult to prevent our aggressive conditioning (our need to survive) from getting in the way. Succeeding at doing this is what mediation is all about. Mediation should not be confused with arbitration. In arbitration, the arbitrator acts as a judge; thus the decision-making process is taken out of the hands of the parties just as it is in court.

Disputes That Qualify for Mediation

Any dispute can be mediated provided *all* of the parties are willing to pursue the process. Since the process depends so heavily on the willingness of the parties to freely enter the mediation, coercion of any kind tends to be counterproductive. A basic premise of mediation is that any agreement which is unacceptable to one or more of the parties is considered

as bad, or worse, than no agreement at all. Although it is impossible to screen out all pressures felt by mediation participants in coming to an agreement, it is basic that all parties must be engaging in the mediation because they want to, not because they feel pressured by others to do it.

The question of timing is also important in determining if mediation is appropriate. A dispute can be so charged with intense feelings that the parties are unwilling or simply not ready to deal directly with each other. I remember one couple who came to me to mediate their divorce at a time when they were both so upset and angry that they weren't capable of having the perspective necessary to make a good agreement. Still, they were clear enough to realize that they didn't want to hire lawyers and drag what was left of their relationship through the judicial mire. I suggested that they agree to take a couple of months as an official cooling-off period and then come back and give mediation a try. Two months later they came back and reached an agreement on all issues in one two-hour session.

I have successfully mediated disputes in many different areas of law, including divorcing couples, landlord-tenant, neighbors in dispute, partnership, internal business problems, real-estate, employer-employee and medical malpractice. I believe that, ideally, it is even possible to mediate in the area of criminal law, although I have serious reservations about how much can be accomplished today, given society's present orientation toward punishment. Let me give you an example of a mediation approach involving a minor dispute that I think could have much wider application. A client came to me after having been arrested for assaulting a young boy by dousing him with water. The boy had been continually annoying the entire neighborhood by riding his motorcycle without a muffler in the middle of the night. I suggested to the prosecutor that, instead of proceeding to court, he and I sit down with the victim, my client, and a group of concerned neighbors without acting as adversaries. He was willing to give it a try. I made it clear to my client that I would not be acting as his representative, and that the prosecutor and I would be there to facilitate the discussion; he was amenable. The case was resolved in one three-hour discussion resulting in an agreement between all of the parties. The boy agreed to restrict his motorcycle riding to an area that did not disturb the neighbors, and the neighbors and my client agreed to pay for his medical bills, in return for the dismissal of all criminal charges against my client.

The mediation was successful in the above example because everyone was willing to mediate in good faith. There can be problems with mediation in criminal cases, however. The pressure of a criminal charge in the event no agreement is reached, operates as an obvious coercive factor that can lead to poor settlements.

Who Should Mediate?

Since the mediation process so heavily depends on a non-hierarchical relationship between the parties and the mediator for its success, the problems of domination and distance which have permeated the professions (especially law) have led some to believe that it is not wise to develop a professional class of mediators. It is certainly true that, as a lawyer, I have found it necessary to "untrain" myself in certain ways. The heavy emphasis in legal training on aggressiveness, automatic escalation of disputes, righteousness, competition, and so on, all get in the way of successful mediation. But I have found that the ability to clarify complex situations, organize and cut to the heart of a matter—which I also learned in law school—are an invaluable aid to

mediation. I do think that a mediator's interpersonal skills and the understanding of human nature emphasized in the social sciences, including psychotherapy, are at least as valuable as skills in legal analysis. It may be that a system which allows for the cooperation of lay and professional mediators will work well, but in the final analysis, the choice of a mediator should be based primarily on the parties' trust in the mediator as a person. Success as a mediator depends heavily upon personal qualities, the ability to create a positive climate where the deeply held personal values of the disputants can be recognized and expressed. The mediator's ability to create such a climate is based on his or her own ability to identify and act on values that support the mediation process.

What Happens in a Mediation?

At the heart of a successful mediation is an understanding between the parties and the mediator. Establishing a good initial agreement avoids many problems which can short-circuit the mediation. The role that I usually agree to take with the participants is to keep the parties to the agenda they set. I ask clarifying questions, give feedback to the parties on their behavior, point out miscommunications, and make suggestions for possible resolution when the parties seem stuck. Some mediations are highly structured, with time-controlled opportunities to speak out and rebut. I favor a more flexible, informal format.

Here are some of the other rules that I have worked out with participants in many different mediations.

Representation: I make it clear from the beginning that my goal is to remain neutral and that I will not act as an advocate for either party. I also make it explicit that, in the event the mediation does not end in agreement, I will not act in any way with, or for, either party in the future.

Presence of Others in the Mediation: Often, one or more parties to a mediation will want to include other persons in the proceeding, perhaps because they have relevant first-hand information to contribute, or because they are somehow affected by the dispute. Sometimes experts in the area around which the dispute is centering are invited. At other times people are invited to provide emotional support during the mediation process. I have found that the presence of these people is rarely disruptive as long as the parties to the mediation have agreed on that person's presence, and it is clear to the person that he or she is not there to represent either party.

Confidentiality: There are at least two views concerning confidentiality with regard to conversations between the mediator and one of the parties in the absence of the other party. On occasion a situation arises where we all agree that it would be helpful for me to talk with one of the parties privately—either by phone or in person. I naturally hold all conversations between myself and the parties in confidence from the outside world. However, I make it clear to all parties that I will not hold what one tells me in the absence of the other(s) in confidence from the other(s). The reason I do this is that I believe that my possession of a "secret" can change the equal relationship between the three of us, and become a way of manipulating me into losing my impartiality.

Use of Information Disclosed by the Parties: I ask the parties to agree that, in the event the mediation does not end in agreement, they will not use information disclosed by the other in a later court proceeding. In California and some other states, if the parties agree that the mediation is a settlement discussion, information disclosed is inadmissible as evidence in any later adversary proceeding. This minimizes the risks of participating in the mediation, and confirms a spirit of cooperation between the parties.

Disclosure: Since neither party has coercive power to be certain that the other person is disclosing all relevant information, I ask the parties to agree that they will disclose all relevant information voluntarily, and that any agreement they come to is based on their mutual reliance on this agreement. This means that in the event that it is later discovered by one of the parties that he or she has been lied to, or an important fact has been intentionally omitted, the agreement is invalidated.

Cost: The cost of mediation varies widely from free community mediation centers to fees in excess of $100 per hour for teams of private mediators. A fee of $40–$50 per hour as the top of a sliding scale is about average for individual mediators. In the final analysis, it is almost always cheaper to mediate than to try to solve the problem through conventional litigation.

Time: Sessions usually range from one to two hours, subject to the stamina of the parties, and their schedules. My experience is that, if no agreement is within sight after three or four sessions, the prospects for eventual agreement are dim. My longest mediation took eighteen hours, the shortest, a half-hour.

My highest priority in a mediation is for the disputants to come to an agreement that they believe to be fair. In the overwhelming majority of cases, I do not express my opinion about the fairness of the agreement, even though I am usually satisfied that fairness has been achieved. My understanding with the parties is this: I will accept as wide a range of agreement between them as possible, but where I am convinced that either a court would not accept the agreement, or that the agreement is grossly unfair, I will express my opinion. If I object to a settlement for one of these reasons, and the parties still want to go on with the agreement, I will resign as mediator. In practice, this has never happened, but there have been times when I have expressed my opinion. In one such situation, I was mediating with two business partners who were trying to dissolve their partnership. I had the strong impression that the person who initiated the dissolution felt guilty and in order to assuage this guilt, was willing to pay an exorbitant amount to the other. I indicated my feeling that the agreement they were on the verge of coming to seemed grossly unfair to me. After listening to my explanation, the parties re-evaluated their positions, and the resulting agreement seemed more equitable to all of us.

Objecting to a settlement is extremely sensitive, as it has the potential for my acting as a judge, with the parties deferring to me. However, I believe that as mediators, we cannot pretend that we are value-free, even in situations where it is desirable to keep our beliefs from intruding.

Other Risks and Problems in Mediation
One risk that a party runs in entering a mediation is that he or she might agree to a settlement that would

be less desirable than could be obtained in court. It is also possible to accept a settlement that a lawyer might advise against, or that the party feels is unfair but was coerced into accepting. The most troublesome area for the mediator occurs when one party seems to be taking advantage of the other through pressure, manipulation, or power-tactics, or where a party is so desirous of ending a conflict that he or she is willing to agree to almost anything. Where the mediator observes this dynamic, it is important to find a way to redress the imbalance without having the mediator act as an advocate for one party.

I encountered this sort of problem in the course of mediating a post-divorce dispute concerning property division and the parents' relationship to the children. The ex-husband was obviously being pushed into a corner by his ex-wife. When I verbalized my observation, the ex-husband said that he had felt badgered by his ex-wife all of their married life, and that was why he had left the marriage. The ex-wife did not fully agree with my observation. Nevertheless, it was apparent to me that if this pattern persisted throughout the mediation, there would either be no agreement at all or the ex-husband would feel that he had lost. Finally, the ex-husband said that he did not feel strong enough to deal directly with his ex-wife at this point in his life, and that he wanted to stop the mediation. Again, I saw that not every dispute can be successfully mediated.

Where a mediation "fails," the time and expense of the mediation are not necessarily wasted. The impact of the parties having met with one another directly and having faced a problem together, can often have an important catalyzing effect in helping the parties come to terms with each other in the future. For example, the couple described just above eventually hired lawyers to represent them, but quickly came to an agreement once the ex-husband made it clear that he would not continue to repeat the "put-upon" pattern of the marriage. Acknowledging that he could not deal directly with his ex-wife, helped him to see more clearly what he needed to do.

Enforceability and Modification

As with any agreement between parties, circumstance can arise that call for a change in the understanding they've made. Where the parties agree, this presents no difficulty; the change can simply modify the existing agreement, with all of the enforceability of any agreement between two people. Where the parties disagree about the change, mediation can be utilized again to resolve the issue. Once people have come to an agreement through mediation, the benefits they have received from using the process initially often encourage them to use it again should the need arise. My experience in mediating agreements for the past several years is that no party has had to resort to court action to change or enforce an agreement reached through mediation. Some parties have felt a need to have an agreement reviewed by lawyers before signing it, feeling that by so doing, the agreement would be more enforceable. My own view is that where the parties have been on equal footing, as in the mediation, any agreement they arrive at should have the same force as an agreement negotiated by lawyers.

The Future of Mediation: Implications for the Society as a Whole

The growth of mediation as a way of settling disputes has enormous implications for our legal system and for society as a whole. In a world where alienation and isolation are increasingly common, and where many of us believe that survival depends on defeating others with whom we share our planet, we tend to orient our lives toward self-preservation and protection from each other. Yet the more isolated and fearful we become, the more apparent it is that our survival depends on the active cooperation of all members of our community, state, nation and planet.

Mediation is one way of making direct and immediate contact with others in a manner that allows us to resolve disputes and, at the same time, experience being part of a larger community. The mediation approach does not divide the world into winners and losers, or better or worse people. It allows individuals to shift away from a parochial approach towards a broader perspective of themselves in relation to others, with less of the hard-edged competitive anger that is almost always present in the adversary legal system. It is no accident that mediation is becoming popular at a time when the world-wide community is becoming increasingly aware of the need for cooperative efforts. Mediation allows us to reorient ourselves so as to recognize that we are part of, rather than separate from, those around us, and to see our own immediate community as part of a larger community. Mediation is a device that allows people to work together in a world which obviously needs such an approach if there is to be any hope of meeting everyone's needs. Finally, through mediation we can appreciate the points of view of others with whom we disagree, and participate in a healthy process which, if adopted on a wider scale, can be one part of the transformation that must take place if we are to continue to live peacefully and productively on this planet.

Gary Friedman has a private practice in law emphasizing mediation in Mill Valley, California. He teaches mediation at the New College of Law in San Francisco and is an adjunct lecturer in law at Golden Gate Law School. For the last three years, he has acted as the lawyer consultant to the Project for the Study and Application of Humanistic Education in Law, a nationwide effort to place a concern for the human principles and values which are the essence of law at the forefront of legal education and the profession of law.

Computers and the Law:
Self-Help Through High Tech
— a discussion between Howard Anawalt,
Hugh Treanor, Toni Ihara and Ralph Warner

We tend too often to think of THE LAW and JUSTICE as OMNIPOTENT and maybe even MAJESTIC. It's often hard to remember that our laws are really no more than an agreed-upon set of rules that come in handy when we want the landlord to fix the roof, or a former spouse to pay child support. Perhaps we feel powerless when dealing with legal concepts because we have been systematically denied information about how they work. Indeed, much of the early stages of the self-help law movement has involved reducing LAW to law, by publishing the information necessary for people to understand their own legal affairs.

So far, the job of liberating law from lawyers has been only marginally successful. Much of the reason for this is that the self-help movement has concentrated on publishing as a way of disseminating legal information, and the majority of people aren't comfortable getting information from books. This leads us to the idea that a better way to liberate legal information from "professionals" may be just around the next computer terminal. Why not program a computer with information on a number of common legal problems (divorce, wills, auto accidents, landlord-tenant, etc.) so that non-lawyers can quickly and cheaply gain access to necessary information? The computer would have a screen (just like TV, Mom!) and a printer capable of turning out completed forms, contracts, letters, etc. And, at least logically, there is nothing to say that the computer would have to live in a lawyer's office — how about putting it in a public library, or a people's law center?

To find out if our interesting idea was also a practical one, we invited Howard Anawalt, a law teacher with an inquisitive mind, and experience using computers in teaching law, to chair a discussion. Howard recruited Hugh Treanor, a computer *industry pro who has worked with legal data bases. Together they sat down with Ralph Warner and Toni Ihara at Berkeley's China Station restaurant to talk about whether high tech can be helpful in taking the "capitals" out of THE LAW. Properly fortified with MSG, they all retired to the Nolo Press office and taped the following:*

HA: We've gathered to discuss whether or not computers can deliver direct legal assistance to people with legal problems. For example, suppose a person has a leaky roof at the same time that rent is due the landlord — is there some way that a person could go down to a computerized legal center and get some ready information? Hugh, do you think that's a possibility in the near future?

HT: I think that some simple legal problems like the one you describe are soluble with a computer. The computer can ask the person some questions about the problem at hand and make some recommendations as to the recourses that are available. However, I think that it is also necessary to understand that it is difficult for an uninitiated person to use the computer directly. For most people, there is going to have to be some intervention on the part of a paralegal or someone who understands both the law and the computer to get good information.

HA: What is the problem with using the computer directly?

HT: The best analogy that I can come up with is giving somebody who has only seen an automatic transmission the keys to a car with a stick shift and saying "Go out and drive it." To use the car to get from here to there, you need to know how the car works. Someone who uses a computer for the first time is dealing with a machine — a dumb machine — and they're going to need some help. Some people

49

may master the computer on their own, but generally speaking, someone without computer experience has a lot of problems dealing with computers.

HA: That's my impression too. A computer is a very powerful means of giving information very rapidly to someone who has a problem such as a leaky roof or who has to get started on a divorce. But handbooks such as the ones written here at Nolo Press, and which have been so very successful, may be better. They allow a person to look through a whole book that has all sorts of information, diagrams, and charts. The computer isn't as good at giving a person a feeling of understanding an entire problem.

RW: One reason why I'm so interested in computers is that there are a whole lot of people who don't relate to information out of books, but who need the practical legal information. How are they going to get it? One way is to participate in the revolution in information-delivery that computers offer. Everybody is buying computer toys these days and getting used to getting information on printouts, screens, etc. I don't see why you can't adapt simple computer functions to legal information—it's being done in the health field by the Kaiser Foundation and others. What I would imagine would be a programmer, say on the landlord/tenant situation, who has a certain sophistication about how the routine sorts of problems are likely to develop and could develop a program that would actually lead people to the information that they need. Now, I am no computer expert, so I don't know if my terms are right, but I imagine a tenant going to the computer, sitting down, and seeing a screen that had a list of legal categories—one of which would be landlord/tenant, or maybe Tenants' Rights. He or she would push a button coded to one of these and the next thing to flash on the screen would be a list of sub-categories such as "failure to pay rent," "uninhabitable conditions," "invasion of privacy," etc. The process would continue until the computer arrived at the appropriate sub-heading—say "subleasing" —then the detailed information necessary to solve the problem would appear on the screen or printout.

HA: It seems to me that what you describe, Ralph, is a real possibility. One thing that would have to be achieved is to be sure that the information stored in that computer covered the six or eight, say up to

twenty most common problem areas. Also, as with any good handbook, there would have to be the understanding that if you go beyond a certain level of complexity, you'd better call for help. I guess one of the big advantages of this sort of approach has to be a real cost reduction. Once you get a good program, you could deliver a lot of legal information to a lot of people at a low cost. But I do think that it's important for the computer to be made available as part of a system that includes somebody with some legal knowledge, who will actually operate the computer for the client. I think you've got to have that.

RW: I don't have any problem with having a person to help with the computer. I do have a problem, though, if the computer can only be run by lawyers and be made available in law offices. This defeats the whole idea of using the computer as an alternative to lawyers. Right now there are a couple of systems—Lexis and Westlaw—that are designed just for lawyers. To me, they're systems that are controlled by lawyers for lawyers and are closed to the general public in much the same way that a law library is pretty unintelligible to someone who may be intelligent but who hasn't broken the code. My idea is that you should be able to go into an office on the streetcorner where someone would help you run the machine to fill out your divorce papers, get information on an adoption, or whatever else. I look forward to the day that these machines would be in a public library or a similar setting and be available to everyone at low cost.

HA: But isn't what we are talking about at this stage really just substituting a computer and a television screen for a handbook? We're not really thinking about trying to get the computer to go beyond that and be analytical.

HT: I think that's true. We're suggesting that the computer is an alternative way to deliver the kind of information that might be in a self-help law bankruptcy book, not as a replacement for it. There are certain people who do very well with books and there are certain people who do very well with computers. For my part, if I were to choose between using a handbook or a computer for a legal problem, I'd probably use a handbook. But that's based on my experience with machines and my experience with books.

RW: Let's take divorce, for an example—it's the

area in which there is the most self-help experience. In California between 30 and 40% of divorce filings are In Pro Per with most of the people using handbooks. It would not be terribly difficult, would it, to put some sort of information on how to fill in each blank into a computer tied to a printer? And when you got done, the machine would print out all of your papers and then you'd just have to file them. What do you think?

HT: That's no problem. That's what I meant when I said that the computer is just another medium for delivering the same information. But the point is, it's just a medium. The fact that the computer can type out the data and your name and all the rest is no great technical achievement. With the handbook you can take the forms out of the back of the book and fill them in with a ballpoint pen and it accomplishes the same end.

RW: Is there some way the average non-lawyer could use the computer in a more sophisticated way?

HA: Maybe so, but let's not lose sight of what is easy for the computer to do. I think that it is really very useful for a computer to produce filled-out forms in a divorce proceeding. An even more obvious example would be incorporation papers. Not only do you have to fill in blanks to do a corporation, but you have to prepare pages and pages of boilerplate clauses from scratch. It's just standard language, and the computer with a printer can handle it easily.

TI: The truth is that so much of what affects most people, of a legal nature, is just rote procedure. To solve a problem you go from Step A to Step P, or whatever. That's the way our society filters out legal problems so that they can be handled quickly. Even though individual people may have more complex situations, they are usually reduced by the system to fit the procedures that have been evolved to handle them.

RW: In part, that's because the courts are starting to mechanize—to handle all of their paperwork with machines. They have all these blanks and forms to muck about with. Maybe if we can just plug our machines into their machines, we can do away with going to court at all.

HA: That's all very true, and in an odd way it gets

back to the history of the common law system. Originally common problems were all done by forms. Now we are returning to forms. If the trend continues with standard papers, standard divorce forms, etc., it seems to me that a form of the computer can be used readily by people directly. But what that is, is really the function of a word processor; it's not a sophisticated gadget at all. You only need a very small memory device which is hooked up to an electric typewriter so it can do the job of simply reproducing this material very, very fast. And that, very clearly, can be delivered more or less directly to people at a very low cost and a minimum of intervention by attorneys. Furthermore, I'd just like to mention one additional thing in regard to attorneys, since I am one, and I enjoy the work that I do. I think that computers need not be a threatening prospect to the legal profession. Many simple things should be handled by people themselves.

RW: Oops, you're stating an ideal that self-help law shouldn't be threatening to lawyers. But even the Nolo handbooks have been threatening to at least certain parts of the legal profession. Over the years, we've received a lot of complaints, criticisms, and abuse from lawyers who felt, quite frankly, that millions and millions of dollars in divorce and other fees were being taken away by our books.

HT: My feeling on that is that a lot of lawyers are afraid of the financial impact needlessly because very often the people who use the kits don't have the money to pay for expensive lawyers in the first place. The thing that I want to get back to is something that was said earlier. I think if lawyers participated in the process of making this computer system or word-processing system work, that they might be less scared or threatened by it. What I'm referring to is the earlier remark that you needed a programmer with a practical knowledge of the law in the particular area, so that a layperson could use it to get really helpful answers. That is exactly what you don't want. What you really want is some lawyers to sit down and go through the process that they go through in their heads whenever a client comes in. With simpler problems, within four or five minutes the skilled legal person should be able to sort out what has to be done, what forms have to be filled out, and what things the client has to do. All of the information that is stored in that lawyer's head should be put into the computer to solve that problem in the same fashion.

TI: I don't think I completely agree. Lawyers are brought up in our adversary system. They make money out of conflict and in keeping problems going, rather than in solving them, so I don't have basic confidence in the mind-set that an attorney uses to work out a problem. In a divorce, for example, often what happens is that one person's attorney suggests all the possible rights and remedies to his or her client, while the other spouse's lawyer picks out the best case for his side. By choosing the extremes, it is often easy to get a fight going which lasts until the money runs out. I think one of the wonderful things about self-help law has been—at least with many divorce cases—that the fact that it's simpler not to fight—to avoid conflict—encourages people to compromise. So I don't think I would be happy having a computer reason like a lawyer.

HT: I think we should point out one difficulty in using a computer to solve legal problems. That is, where do you draw the line on what the computer can do? Once you start getting into levels of complexity beyond the areas we have discussed, you get into problems with more and more alternatives. That's when you start getting into the controversial part of using a computer to do law. Suppose you get

into a divorce case where an attorney, even one with the best intentions in the world, is going to have to spend two hours, or three hours, or maybe even a day, discussing various alternatives. You're simply into an area that would be very difficult to reduce to a solution by computer.

RW: One thing that a computer can do easily and that has been a terrific problem for Nolo and for doing any law books, whether for lawyers or lay people, is that with a computer it's easy to update the data base. Half the books in the law libraries are out of date, or you have to get recent information from advance sheets, or pocket parts, or a convoluted procedure known as Shepardizing. And even so, you're always paranoid—whether you're a lawyer or a layperson—that you haven't found some crucial decision that happened ten days ago. With the proper kind of data base maintenance, a computer could be as up-to-date as fifteen minutes ago.

HA: Yes, that kind of reliability and self-confidence, by delivering up-to-date information practically instantaneously, would be a big advantage.

RW: Oh, one thing more. My experience with Nolo has been that as fast as we put out a book on a new subject, people call up and ask for books on three more. Lawyers ask us, "Haven't you run out of all the subjects now that you've done fifteen books?" at the same time that people are clamoring for more. So I have a feeling that once the twenty most common problems are done and the computer system works, there's going to be popular demand for an enormous number of additional materials. Writers are going to want materials on doing contracts with their publishers, and artists with their art galleries, and all sorts of small businesses with their employees, and so on. Maybe it's because I'm the least sophisticated person here when it comes to computers that I'm so optimistic.

HA: Yes, and that brings me back to what I said about the lawyers a moment ago. I think there are lawyers who will welcome a modification of their professional role, and that people having access to good information will strengthen their role as advisors and keep costs to the client at a minimum. I don't think that all the lawyers are scared about letting routine stuff go and reserving their creativity for harder cases. But I do think that self-help efforts should not make everyone feel that they should have to become their own plumber, their own roofer, their own painter, their own artist, or attorney, or anything else. Self-help law can get carried too far, so that people feel guilty going to ask for some help after looking at a handbook. It's one of the points I would bear in mind with respect to a computerized law office in the future—a little human help isn't going to undermine the self-help aspect. There's one other thing that Hugh said that I would like to comment on, and that is about complex problems. Presently, computers are not particularly good at posing questions—they will parrot back answers to questions that are already programmed into them, but not a lot more. But there does appear to be some capability in the software programming area that is going to make computers more flexible in terms of their capacity to pose questions to people who are dealing with them in the future. If that becomes more of a practical reality, then surely a computer could take a much greater role in direct communication with a person with a legal problem. It's not that the computer could think, but it could possibly associate concepts in a way that would get at important questions other than those that have been posed.

RW: You mean you're imagining somebody coming in and saying, "I want to change my name," and the computer asking, "Your first name or your last name?"

HA: Well, I'm trying to imagine a situation where the person comes in and mentions that they have a divorce problem, when in fact what they're dealing with is a child-custody problem. If the computer is only as good as the questions it's asked, it will be very limited. But if it could get at peoples' real concerns, even though they didn't phrase exactly the right questions, it would be more exciting.

HT: It reminds me of something one of my professors said when I was going to school, which was that the problem perceived by the client was very often not the real problem in the first place. And computers take literally the problem presented to them, instead of going beyond that. But I think that's way down the road. My feeling is that in order to get to that level, you have to solve routine problems and get the machine accepted by the public and by the professionals. Before you get complicated, you have to demonstrate success with easy problems.

Howard C. Anawalt is a professor of law at the University of Santa Clara, teaching constitutional law, communication law and torts. He has practiced law privately and for the government, and that practice has included work in criminal and commercial law, and civil rights.

Hugh Treanor works in the computer industry. He has worked with legal data bases in support of anti-trust cases. He is currently working with large technical data bases.

Where Do We Go From Here?

by Ralph Warner

It's fun to stretch our minds to reflect on how they used to solve legal problems in Rome, how they solve them today in China, and how computers may turn our system of dispute resolution on its head tomorrow. But now it's time to be a little more grounded and look at some inexpensive and easy steps we can take to immediately improve the average person's ability to deal with everyday disputes. Almost inevitably, this leads us to Small Claims Court.

It's easy to criticize the existing legal system— almost everyone knows that it's on the rocks. The $250-a-day experts with their degrees, titles and well-funded consulting companies have studied the problem to death with no positive results. And this is hardly surprising, since most of the experts involved in the studies and in the resulting decisions are lawyers who, at bottom, are unable to understand a problem of which they are so thoroughly a part.

But instead of my lecturing you about all the things that are wrong at the local courthouse, let's sit down at the kitchen table with a pot of tea and a bowl of raspberries and see if we can't design a better system. After all, this republic was founded by ordinary people taking things into their own hands— they had to because most of the governor, judge and lawyer-types were quite comfortable in England, thank you. And don't forget that we have already agreed that the present legal structure doesn't work, so we obviously have nothing to lose by making our own suggestions. Hey, leave a few raspberries for me, and why don't you jot down a few of your own ideas as we go along so that this becomes a two-way communication.

Before we get to specific suggestions for change, let's take a brief look around to see where we are starting from. As a society, we obviously have a fixation with trying to solve problems by suing one

another. Nowhere in the world do people come close to being as litigious as we do. The result of this love of lawsuits, or perhaps its cause—it's one of those chicken and egg problems—is the fact that, whenever we get into any sort of spat with anyone, or even think that we might get into one in the future, we run to a lawyer.[1] It's gotten so bad that people who suffer an injury have been known to call their lawyer before their doctor. But there is an odd paradox here. At the same time that we tolerate vast numbers of lawyers eating at the top end of our societal trough and are more and more likely to use them, public opinion polls tell us that our respect for lawyers has fallen so that we rate their trustworthiness below that of used-car salespeople, undertakers and loan sharks. It's as if the less we respect lawyers, the more we use them. Perhaps we're afraid that if we don't sue first, someone will get the jump on us. If you eat one more of those raspberries, I'll see you in court.

Have you ever thought about how people solved their disputes in other ages? Let's pretend for a moment that we are members of a society of deer hunters in an age when such things were still possible.[2] One fine fall morning we both set out, bow in hand, you to the east and I to the west. Before long, you hit a high cliff and turn north. My way is blocked by a swift river, and I too turn north. Gradually the topography of the area results in our coming close together without realizing it. Suddenly, a great stag jumps from the underbrush. By this time we are standing on opposite sides of the clearing. We both pull back our arrows and let fly. Our arrows pierce the deer's heart from opposite sides, seemingly at the same instant.

For a moment we stand frozen, each surprised by the presence of the other. Then we realize what has happened and that we have a problem. To whom does the deer belong? We carry the carcass back to the village, each unwilling to surrender our claim to the other. After the deer is gutted and hung, we go to speak to the chief of our group who convenes a council of elders to meet late in the afternoon. Each of us has his say as to what happened. The deer carcass is examined. Anyone else who has knowledge of our dispute is invited to speak. Tribal customs (laws) are consulted, our credibility is weighed, and a decision is made — in time for dinner.

Now, let's ask ourselves what would happen today, if you and I simultaneously shot a deer (instead of each other) on the first day of hunting season and were unable to agree to whom it belonged. Assuming we didn't fight it out on the spot, but wanted the dispute resolved by "proper" legal procedures, lawyers would have to be consulted, court papers filed and responded to, a court appearance scheduled, words spoken in legalese, and a formal court decision written and issued. All of this for a deer that would have long since rotted away unless it had been put in cold storage. If the deer had been frozen, the storage costs would have to be added to court costs and attorney fees which all together would surely add up to a lot more than the value of the deer. Oh well, next time we had better go hunting at McDonald's where everything is delivered safely wrapped in plastic.

Seriously, what were the differences between the ways that the two societies resolved the problem of who owned the deer? The so-called primitive one did a better job, but why? Obviously because their solution was in proportion to the problem, while today we make the solution process so cumbersome and expensive that it dwarfs most disputes. The hunting society handled the disagreement quickly, cheaply and, most importantly, with a process that allowed the disputing parties to participate in and understand what was going on.[3] Simple, you say. Why then can't our dispute resolution procedure achieve even one of these goals? In large measure, because lawyers have vested financial and psychic interests in the present cumbersome way of doing things and have neither the motivation nor the perspective to make changes.

But isn't my view a bit radical? Isn't there something uniquely valuable about the great sweep of the common law down through the ages? Doesn't the majestic black-robed judge sitting on his throne mumbling esoteric nonsense somehow guarantee that God is in heaven, the republic safe, and that "justice will be done"? Not necessarily. History is arbitrary — our dispute resolution mechanisms could have developed in a number of ways. If our

present system worked well, imposing it on the future would make sense. As, in fact, it hardly works at all, continuing it is silly. Those who get quite misty-eyed recounting the history, traditions and time-tested forms behind our present ways of doing things are almost always people that benefit by their continuance. Consider, too, that in North America we have no pure legal tradition, having borrowed large hunks of our jurisprudence from England, Spain, France, Holland, and Germany, as well as from various Native American cultures, Rome of 2000 years ago, and feudal and ecclesiastical traditions.

OK, granted that there have been legal systems that worked better than ours, and granted that at least some change is overdue, what should we do? Lots of things. Neighborhood systems, mediation centers, arbitration and other non-judicial problem-solving mechanisms offer considerable promise; but perhaps the most significant reform would be to expand Small Claims Court. Like the system followed by the deer hunters, but unlike the vast majority of our legal system, Small Claims Court is simple, fast and cheap, and allows for the direct participation of the disputing parties. Never mind

that up to now Small Claims Court has been tolerated as a way to keep lawyers' offices clear of penny-
ante people with penny-ante disputes. It's there, it
works, and we can expand it to play a meaningful
role in our lives.

As it is presently set up, Small Claims Court has
several disadvantages. First, the amount that can be
sued for is ridiculously low. Second, the court only
has the power to make judgments that can be satisfied by the payment of money damages.[4] Third, in
many states courts have the reputation of being
extensions of collection agencies, where bill collectors and their lawyers can quickly and cheaply
record judgments on behalf of cut-rate jewelry stores
and credit dentists. Fourth, many kinds of cases,
such as divorces, adoptions, probates, name
changes, etc., aren't permitted.

Why not start our effort to improve things by
doing away with these disadvantages? Let's raise the
maximum amount that can be sued for to $10,000.[5]
I would like to suggest $20,000, but perhaps we
should take one step at a time to limit attorney
opposition. An increase to $10,000 would be a
significant reform—allowing tens of thousands of
disputes to be removed from our formal legal system. One logical reason to pick $10,000 is that
people can't afford amounts below this. To illustrate, let's take a situation where Randy the carpen-
ter agrees to do $20,000 worth of rehabilitation to
Al's home. When the work is completed, an argument develops about whether the work was done
properly according to the agreement. Al pays Randy
$15,000, leaving $5,000 in dispute. Randy goes to
his lawyer, and Al to his. Each has several preliminary conferences after which the lawyers exchange
several letters and telephone calls. Eventually, a
lawsuit is filed and answered, a court date is obtained many months in the future and then changed
several times, and, finally, a two-hour trial is held.
Randy's lawyer bills him $1,255 (25 hours × $50
per hour) and Al's charges $960 (24 hours × $40 per
hour), for a total fee of $2,215. The dispute takes
eleven months to be decided. In the end, Randy is
awarded $3,500 of the $5,000.

This is a typical case with a typical solution.
Between them, the lawyers collected almost half of
the amount in dispute and took most of a year to
arrive at a solution that very likely left both Randy
and Al frustrated. Don't you think that Randy and

Al would have preferred presenting their case in
Small Claims Court where it would have been
heard and decided in a month? Of course, either of
them could have done worse arguing the case himself, but remember, when the legal fees are taken
into consideration, the loser would have had to do a
lot worse before he was out-of-pocket any money.
Randy recovered $3,500 with a lawyer, but after
subtracting the $1,255 lawyer fee, his net gain was
only $2,245. Al ended up paying $4,460 ($3,500 for
the judgment and $960 for his attorney). Thus, if a
Small Claims Court judge had awarded Randy any
amount from $2,246 to $4,459, both men would
have done better than they did with lawyers. Of
course, if this sort of case were permitted in Small
Claims Court, there would be two big losers. Can it
be a coincidence that lawyers (through their control
of every state legislature) make sure that Small
Claims maximums are kept as low as possible?

The second great barrier to bringing cases in
Small Claims Court is the fact that, with minor
exceptions, the court is limited to making money
judgments.[6] Think back for a moment to our problems with the twice-shot deer. How does the award
of money make sense in this situation? In Small
Claims Court, the Indian who didn't end up with
the carcass would have had to sue the other for the
fair market value of the deer. What nonsense—if
we are going to have a dispute resolution procedure,
why not permit a broad range of solutions, such as
the deer being cut in half, or the deer going to one
hunter and six ducks going to the other in compensation, or maybe even the deer going to the person
who needed it most. Using an example more common at the end of the 20th century, why not allow a
Small Claims Court judge to order an apartment be
cleaned, a garage repainted, or a car properly fixed,
instead of simply telling one person to pay X dollars
to the other? One advantage of this sort of flexibility
is that more judgments would be meaningful.
Under our present system, tens of thousands of
judgments can't be collected because the loser has
no obvious source of income. We need to get away
from the notion that people who are broke have
neither rights nor responsibilities. All people need
both.

Lawyers and judges often contend that it would be
impossible to enforce judgments granted under a
more flexible approach. Perhaps some would be

hard to keep track of. Certainly it might require some experimentation to find out what types of judgments will work and which will not; however, since it is often impossible to collect a judgment under the present system, it can't hurt to try some alternatives.

Now let's do something to deal with "collection agency" reputations of Small Claims Courts. Many states have already made considerable progress in this direction by limiting use of the court to people (including businesses) suing on their own claims. This means that lawyers and collection agencies are not permitted, and this is a reform that should be quickly adopted by the majority of states that have not yet done so. Unfortunately, barring lawyers and collection agencies does nothing to stop big organizations such as the telephone company or a large department store from using the court to routinely enforce their own judgments. Many people feel that large institutions such as these should be restricted because their bill collection activities tend to dominate individual claims. I don't agree. As obnoxious as it is to have a large business getting numerous judgments in Small Claims Court, it's more obnoxious to have them do the same thing in formal court, where costs for lawyers, filing fees, etc., are passed on to the debtor, and where the archaic procedures make it almost impossible for the debtor to represent himself. However, I do favor charging higher small claims filing fees to large-volume users, and spending the money to increase education as to how to defend oneself in Small Claims Court.

The fourth big change that I propose, and the one that would truly make over our court system, involves expanding the types of cases that can be heard in Small Claims. Why not be brave and take the 20 most common legal problems and adopt simplified procedures enabling all of them to be handled by the people themselves without lawyers? Why not open up our courthouses to the average person, who, after all, pays the bills?

To accomplish this democratization of our dispute resolution procedures, I suggest dividing Small Claims Court into several separate divisions, each one responsible for a broad area of common concern. For example, there would be a landlord-tenant and a domestic relations division.[7] Each division would have the authority to consider a broad range of problems and solutions falling within its area of concern. Today, if you have a claim against your landlord (or he against you) for money damages, you can use Small Claims only if the claim is under the dollar limit. If you want a roof fixed, a tenant evicted, or to protect your privacy, etc., most Small Claims Courts can't help you. The Canadian province of British Columbia has already put all landlord-tenant disputes in what amounts to a Small Claims format, easily and cheaply available to both landlord and tenant. Why can't we?

A domestic relations Small Claims Court could include simplified procedures to help people handle their own uncontested divorces, adoptions, name changes, guardianships, etc., safely and cheaply. And why not? Even with considerable hostility from lawyers and court personnel, over 20% of the divorces in California are already handled without a lawyer. When I suggest that people should be encouraged to handle their own domestic problems in a Small Claims type of forum, I'm not advocating that sensible safeguards be dropped. For example, if a divorce involves children, you would want to have someone trained in the field carefully examine the parents' plans for custody, visitation and support to see that they are reasonable.

Without going into detail, I suggest that if we took lawyers out of our domestic relations courts, we would save not only millions of dollars and hours, but more importantly, we would lighten the heavy burden of hostility and anxiety that the parties must now bear. Our present system, in which parents and children become clients to a "hired gun" (the lawyer), is a bad one. By definition, the client role is weak and the gunfighter role strong. This imbalance commonly results in lawyers making critical decisions, affecting the clients' lives, sometimes obviously, sometimes subtly. All too often these decisions benefit the lawyer and his bank balance to the detriment of both the client's psyche and pocketbook. The lawyer, after all, is paid more to fight, or at least to pretend to fight, than to compromise. I have seen dozens of situations where lawyers have played on people's worst instincts (paranoia, greed, ego, one-upmanship) to fan nasty little disagreements into flaming battles. Perhaps mercifully, the

battles normally last only as long as the lawyers' bills
are paid.[8]

I could list a number of other areas of law that
could be converted to a Small Claims approach
(auto accidents, simple probates, perhaps even some
criminal cases), but I am sure you get the point. We
must take control of the decision-making processes
that affect our lives. We must make ourselves welcome in our own courts and legislatures. We must
stop looking at ourselves as clients and start taking
responsibility for our own legal decisions.

Let's assume now that no matter what the obstacles, we are going to expand drastically the role of
Small Claims Court. In the process of so doing, we
will need to make a number of changes in the way
the court now operates. It will be a good opportunity
to throw out a number of existing procedures that
owe more to history than to common sense. Here
are a few ideas:

1. Before people present their dispute for resolution as part of a court proceeding, they should be
encouraged to talk it over among themselves. This
seems to be basic common sense, but a face-to-face
meeting to find out if a compromise is possible isn't
part of the present system. A meeting could occur at
the courthouse or, perhaps, at a less intimidating
location in the community, as a regular part of every
case. A number of experimental mediation projects
are now in operation around the country and it
would be wise to draw on their experiences to set up
procedures most conducive to people making their
own settlements.

2. Let's make our court one of truly easy access.
This means holding weekend and evening sessions.
This is being done now experimentally in a few
areas, but should be routinely available everywhere.
When court is held at 9 a.m. on weekdays, it often
costs more in lost job time for all the principals and
witnesses to show up than the case is worth. Why
too do we routinely hold Small Claims Court at
intimidating and often dangerous downtown locations when it would be often as easy to hold it in
neighborhoods where people live?

3. Let's get the judge out of his black robe and off
his throne. There is a part of all of us that loves the
drama involved in seeing our magistrate sitting on
high like the king of England, but I am convinced
by my own brief experience as a "pro tem" judge
that this is counterproductive. We would have a lot

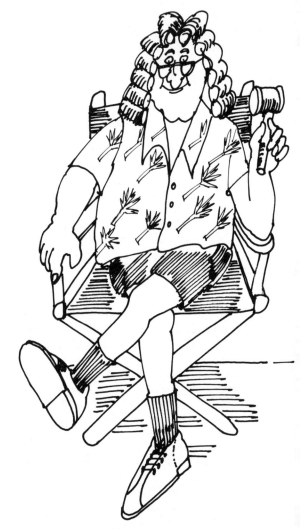

less confrontation, and a lot more willingness to
compromise, if we got rid of some of the drama.

4. While we're making changes, let's make a big
one—let's throw out the adversary system. It contributes a great deal to posturing and obfuscation
and little to arriving at a dispute resolution process
that everyone can live with. We must move toward
systems of mediation and arbitration in which, instead of a traditional judge, we have someone whose
role is to facilitate the parties arriving at their own
solution—deciding it for them only if they arrive at
a hopeless impasse. Big business, big labor, and
increasingly even lawyers are coming to realize that
arbitration and mediation are good ways to solve

problems. What I have in mind is something like this: All the parties to the dispute would sit down at a table with the Small Claims employee (let's drop the word "judge"). This person would be trained for the job, but would not normally be a lawyer. The court employee would help the parties search for areas of agreement and possible compromise and then help them define any areas still in dispute.

I don't mean to suggest that the changes I propose in this short chapter are the only ones necessary. If we are going to put the majority of our routine legal work in Small Claims, it will require turning our dispute resolution process on its head. Legal information must be stored and decoded so that it is available to the average person. Clerk's offices, and the other support systems surrounding our courts, must be expanded and geared to serve the non-lawyer. Legal forms must be translated from "legalese" into English.

Let's illustrate how things might change by looking at a case I recently saw argued in a Northern California Small Claims Court. One party to the dispute (let's call her Sally) arranged fishing charters for business and club groups. The other (let's call him Ben) owned several fishing boats. Sally often hired Ben's boats for her charters. Their relationship was of long standing and had been profitable to both. However, as the fishing charter business grew, both Sally and Ben began to enlarge their operations. Sally got a boat or two of her own and Ben began getting into the charter booking business. Eventually they stepped on one another's toes and their friendly relationship was replaced by tension and arguments. One day a blow-up occurred over some inconsequential detail, phones were slammed down, and Sally and Ben each swore never to do business with the other again.

Before the day of the final fight, Sally had organized two charters on Ben's boat. These were to have taken place a week after the phones were slammed down. For reasons unconnected with the argument, the charters were cancelled by the clubs that had organized them. Ben had about a week's notice of cancellation. He also had $400 in deposits that Sally had paid him. He refused to refund the deposits. Sally sued him in Small Claims Court for $500 ($400 for the charter fee and $100 for general inconvenience).

Testimony in court made it clear that charters were commonly cancelled and were often replaced by others booked at the last minute. Ben and Sally had signed a "Standard Marine Charter Agreement" because it was required by the Coast Guard, although they had never in the past paid attention to its terms. They had always worked out sensible adjustments on a situation-by-situation basis, depending on whether substitute charters were available and whether the club or business cancelling had paid money up front, etc.

When Ben and Sally first presented their arguments about the $500, it seemed that they were not too far apart as to what would be a fair compromise. Unfortunately, the adversary nature of the court system encouraged each to overstate his (her) case and to dredge up all sorts of irrelevant side issues. "What about the times you overloaded my boat?" Ben demanded. "How about those holidays when you price-gouged me?" Sally replied. As the arguments went back and forth, each person got angrier and angrier and was less and less able to listen to the other.

The result was that after an hour of testimony the judge was left with a confused mish-mash of custom, habit, maritime charter contracts, promises made or not made, past performance, etc. No decision that he arrived at was likely to be accepted by both Ben and Sally as being fair. Indeed, unless he gave one or the other everything he or she requested, both of them would surely feel cheated. That is not to say that the hearing was all bad — some good things did occur. The dispute was presented quickly and cheaply, and each person got to have his or her say and blow off some steam. All of these things would have been impossible in our formal court system. However, if Small Claims Court could be changed along the lines suggested above, a better result might have been reached.

Suppose that instead of a formal courtroom approach Ben and Sally are first encouraged to sit down and talk the dispute out. If this fails, then the next step is to sit down in a non-courtroom setting with a court employee who is trained as a mediator and whose purpose is to help Ben and Sally arrive at a fair compromise — a compromise which might provide a foundation for Ben and Sally to continue to work together in the future. Only if compromise is impossible would there be recourse to more formal proceedings. I am convinced that Ben and Sally would have worked out a compromise at the first or second stage.

One final point. Today lawyers are still trying to plug the holes in the rotten dike of our present legal system. Tomorrow the dike will burst and many of our present ways of doing things will be washed into the history books. Small Claims Court will survive the deluge and will expand. The danger is that lawyers will try to control Small Claims Court so that their attitudes and prejudices dominate it as they have dominated every other mechanism our society has to resolve disputes. To allow this to happen is to destroy much of the value of expanding Small Claims Courts. And don't minimize the danger. Claiming to be interested in consumer reform, lawyers are already serving in the role of mediators, arbitrators and legal advisors in Small Claims Courts in several areas of the country. This is now being done on a voluntary basis, but you can expect an effort to have it institutionalized soon. It is all too likely that under the guise of trying to protect us from ourselves, an effort will also be made to have everyone see a lawyer as part of the Small Claims procedure. Remember, it is our lawyer-dominated state legislature that makes Small Claims rules, and our lawyer-dominated judiciary that carries them out.

---

1. There are close to a half a million lawyers in the United States. New York City alone has more than 40,000. *The New York Times* recently reported that many lawyers are charging $25 for each six minutes of their time. In San Francisco during working hours, one out of every three hundred people is a lawyer.

The county of Los Angeles has more judges than the country of France. There are approximately 500,000 lawyers in the U.S. (population 225 million) and only 10,000 lawyers in China (population 1 billion).
2. Anthropologists will, I hope, accept this little fable as just that.
3. In a criminal case (if one hunter had attacked and injured the other) you would also want to think about restitution (making whole) to the injured person and perhaps to his dependents.
4. California and a few other states are beginning to allow judges to make some decisions that don't involve the payment of money. This is a step in the right direction.
5. While most states limit Small Claims jurisdiction to $750 (California) or $1,000 (New York), there are exceptions. For example, the United States Tax Court has a very successful Small Claims procedure which allows claims up to $5,000.
6. Some states allow judgments to include several types of equitable relief, such as recision, restitution and specific performance, but this sort of relief is limited in scope and rarely used.
7. There is nothing new about the idea of dividing a court by subject matter. This is already done in our formal trial courts and works well.
8. In an interesting article entitled "Valuable Deficiencies: A Service Economy Needs People in Need," in the Fall 1977 *Co-Evolution Quarterly*, John McKnight points out that "the Latin root of the word 'client' is a verb which translates 'to hear', 'to obey'."

Ralph Warner used to practice law. Finally, realizing that the American system of delivering legal services is institutionally corrupt (and that being a lawyer wasn't really much fun), he began writing legal self-help books and articles. When no one would publish them, he joined with some friends and started Nolo Press.

PART II
Self-Help Law:
How To Do It

It's all well and good to talk about reforming our courts, streamlining our laws, and insisting on improved legal services from our professional elite; but unfortunately, recognizing that we have a problem and even lobbying for constructive legislative change doesn't bring positive results. Too many people benefit from the status quo for there to be any real hope that the legal system will clean up its own act. In considering the reasons for lawyer rip-offs in areas as diverse as probate, personal injury, divorce, and bankruptcy, remember that all levels of government, including our legislatures, are dripping with lawyers.

But even though our legal establishment reacts to proposals to reform itself as if these proposals were a new strain of influenza, change is occurring simply because ordinary folks are bypassing lawyers and learning how to handle their own legal problems. "Pro per" (pro se) representation is on the rise in all types of legal actions, especially when it comes to handling such routine legal problems as divorce, landlord-tenant actions, adoptions, changes of name, incorporations, etc. But it's one thing to want to handle your own legal problems and another to do it efficiently. Before anyone (lawyer or non-lawyer) can sensibly handle his or her own legal affairs, he or she must have access to reliable information. In Part VI of this Review, we provide you with a catalogue of the best written self-help law materials available. Here we look at a dozen common areas of self-help in detail.

" . . . As a litigant, I should dread a lawsuit beyond almost anything short of sickness and death."

—*Judge Learned Hand*

An Introduction to Legal Research

by Peter Jan Honigsberg

As long as lawyers keep us ignorant of the workings of the law, we remain dependent on lawyers. In fact, the Latin root of the word "client" means "to hear" and "to obey." By gaining knowledge about the law, we gain power over our own lives. Unfortunately, however, there are so many laws and procedures that most of us can hope to know only a small fraction of them. Indeed, one of the most important skills that law students learn is how lawyers stall for time when asked a difficult question. The idea is to look wise, mutter a few monosyllables of Latin-sounding nonsense and get the client out of your office. Then you look up the answer, call the client back again, and charge $50 to $100 per hour for your time. The only real skill involved is knowing how to use law books so that you get the right answer quickly. But why can't anyone use these books? Why must you hire a lawyer to tell you what you can easily read yourself? Because legal information is indexed and stored according to a code which baffles all but the initiated. Thus, the lawyer is able to charge you a bundle because he or she knows the code and you don't. Peter Jan Honigsberg, the author of Cluing Into Legal Research, *is an expert at helping people break this code. Here he outlines some of the first practical steps in solving a typical legal problem. His book is separately reviewed in Part VI, below.*

Suppose your hot water heater is broken. You call the landlord. She says that someone will be out to fix it "right away." A week later, you're still taking cold showers. Your rent is due but you don't feel like paying it until the repairs are made. Nor do you want to move. What should you do?

Well, you could contact an attorney, or a tenant union/counseling group. Or you could check on the law yourself.[1] Researching the law isn't all that difficult. If it were, many lawyers wouldn't be practicing. Lawyers cannot possibly know about all areas of the law. They know a little about some and less about others. But they know — or should know —

how to find the law. And with a little work on your part, you'll find you can do much of the same.

Let's take our non-functioning water heater as an example and see how we might go about researching it. We'll assume this takes place in California. But no matter where you live, the process is basically the same. And since law libraries in every state should have a copy of the California books we'll be using, you can follow along with us.

First: Where do we start?
Law libraries can be found in law schools, federal, state, city and county courthouses, and county bar libraries. College libraries may also have some of the basic sets of law books, but they usually aren't complete. In Boston the public library has some. This may be true of other large city libraries. Friendly legal services offices, neighborhood law offices or public interest law firms may allow you to use their libraries.

Second: Review the problem. What exactly do you want to know?
In our example, we do not want to pay the rent until the landlord makes repairs on the heater. Can we do that?

A useful way to outline the situation is to think of some key words — words which when looked up in indexes of various legal sourcebooks will lead you to the proper textual material. You might want to chart it out something like this:

People	Landlord, tenant, lessor, lessee
Subject	Rent, repairs, apartment, dwelling
Legal Theory[2]	
Remedy Sought[2]	

Third: Look up several of your key words in the index of a legal sourcebook
Your first question is undoubtedly, "What is a legal

sourcebook?"Well, there are many different kinds of books which discuss the law, and we'll review some of them later on in this article. But since many people feel that the best place to begin your research is in a set of codes or statutes, we'll begin there.

Statutes are the acts or laws passed by a state legislature or Congress. State statutes are arranged by subject in different volumes. Sometimes they are referred to as "codes," general laws," "state laws" or "revised statutes." Basically just ask the librarian where the state laws are. Each state has at least one set of statutes; California has three. Two are commercially published — Deerings and West — the third is officially authorized by the state. It's usually better to use a commercially published edition, since it will also include "annotations." Annotations are notes of cases and other commentary which have dealth with, interpreted, or referred to the particular statutes.

For this example, we'll use the West Annotated California Codes. We start by looking up several of our key words in the index volumes. It's always advisable to look up more than one word. Appropriate helpful material can often be indexed in several places, and the first section you find, though helpful, may not be all there is. Moreover, the indexer may have thought in an entirely different pattern than you did, and a word that seems eminently suitable to you may not have been to the indexer.

The first word we'll check out is "Tenant." Looking it up in the index volumes to West Annotated California Codes, we see:

"Tenants — Landlord and Tenant generally, this index."

So we turn to the volume including "Landlord and Tenant." A long list of words follows this general heading. Looking down the list, we find "Rent." Under it is listed:

"Deduction upon repairs by lessee, limit CC 1942."

Below we see the word "Repairs." Under it is:

CC 1941.
Tenant CC 1929
Rent Reduction Limit, CC 1942

Next we check the supplement or "pocket part" in the back of the book. This is crucial. Law is always changing, and the supplement keeps the edition up-to-date. Be sure to always check to see whether there is a supplement to any legal sourcebook you use and make sure that it is current.

The supplement under "Rent" has nothing on repairs and deduction. The section under "Repairs" has:

Untenantable, defined CC 1941.1
Waiver, lessor's rights CC 1942.1

Well, our research uncovers some possibilities. But we'll need to check them out, since indexes can always be misleading.

Winslow

"CC" is an abbreviation for the California Civil Code. (You can always ask a librarian when you come up against a problem in location or abbreviation.)

Looking up Section 1941 in the Civil Code and then checking in the supplement to see whether any later changes have occurred, we find that the lessor is required to make the dwelling fit for occupancy. Section 1941.1 adds that if the dwelling lacks any of the following, it is deemed "untenantable." Paragraph (c) refers to maintaining a system of hot and cold running water in good working order.

§ 1941.1 Untenantable dwellings

A dwelling shall be deemed untenantable for purposes of Section 1941 if it substantially lacks any of the following affirmative standard characteristics:

(a) Effective waterproofing and weather protection of roof and exterior walls, including unbroken windows and doors.

(b) Plumbing or gas facilities which conformed to applicable law in effect at the time of installation, maintained in good working order.

(c) A water supply approved under applicable law, which is under the control of the tenant, capable of producing hot and cold running water, or a system which is under the control of the landlord, which produces hot and cold running water, furnished to appropriate fixtures, and connected to a sewage disposal system approved under applicable law.

(d) Heating facilities which conformed with applicable law at the time of installation, maintained in good working order.

(e) Electrical lighting, with wiring and electrical equipment which conformed with applicable law at the time of installation, maintained in good working order.

(f) Building, grounds and appurtenances at the time of the commencement of the lease or rental agreement in every part clean, sanitary, and free from all accumulations of debris, filth, rubbish, garbage, rodents and vermin, and all areas under control of the landlord kept in every part clean, sanitary, and free from all accumulations of debris, filth, rubbish, garbage, rodents, and vermin.

(g) An adequate number of appropriate receptacles for garbage and rubbish, in clean condition and good repair at the time of the commencement of the lease or rental agreement, with the landlord providing appropriate serviceable receptacles thereafter, and being responsible for the clean condition and good repair of such receptacles under his control.

(h) Floors, stairways, and railings maintained in good repair.

(Added by Stats.1970, c. 1280, p. 2314, § 1. Amended by Stats.1979, c. 307, p. —, § 1.)

Section 1941.2 requires the tenant to keep her/his side of the bargain, i.e., to keep the place in good condition.

§ 1941.2 Tenant's affirmative obligations

(a) No duty on the part of the * * * landlord to repair a dilapidation shall arise under Section 1941 or 1942 if the * * * tenant is in substantial violation of any of the following affirmative obligations, provided the tenant's violation contributes substantially to the existence of the dilapidation or interferes substantially with the landlord's obligation under Section 1941 to effect the necessary repairs:

(1) To keep that part of the premises which he occupies and uses clean and sanitary as the condition of the premises permits.

(2) To dispose from his dwelling unit of all rubbish, garbage and other waste, in a clean and sanitary manner.

(3) To properly use and operate all electrical, gas and plumbing fixtures and keep them as clean and sanitary as their condition permits.

(4) Not to permit any person on the premises, with his permission, to willfully or wantonly destroy, deface, damage, impair or remove any part of the structure or dwelling unit or the facilities, equipment, or appurtenances thereto, nor himself do any such thing.

(5) To occupy the premises as his abode, utilizing portions thereof for living, sleeping, cooking or dining purposes only which were respectively designed or intended to be used for such occupancies.

(b) Paragraphs (1) and (2) of subdivision (a) shall not apply if the * * * landlord has expressly agreed in writing to perform the act or acts mentioned therein.

(Added by Stats.1970, c. 1280, p. 2315, § 2. Amended by Stats.1979, c. 307, p. —, § 2.)

Section 1942 allows the tenant to make repairs him/herself and deduct the cost from the rent if the landlord does not make the repairs within a reasonable time after having been given notice.[3] However, the law limits the deduction of the cost of the repair to one month's rent.

So you call the heating company and find out that the heater is too old to be worth repairing and that a new one will cost $1000. Your rent is $300. This law isn't going to help you much. Now what?

Well, let's check the annotations under this statute. Maybe there is a case which deals with a similar problem. Do you have another possible remedy?

Under "½. In general," we see a note explaining that the "repair and deduct" statute (CC 1941 and 42) was only intended for "minor repairs" and does not prevent establishing a "warranty of habitability" (similar to any other kind of warranty) on residential leases. The case they cite for this proposition is *Green v. Superior Court*, 10 C.3d 616, 111 Cal. Rptr. 704, 517 P.2d 1168 (1974). This may be helpful. But, since we can never be sure what the note is really saying until we read the actual decision, we need to look up this case.

§ 1942. **Repairs by tenant; rent deduction or vacation of premises; presumption; limit; nonavailability of remedy; additional remedy**

(a) If within a reasonable time after written or oral notice to the * * * landlord or his agent, as defined in subdivision (a) of Section 1962, of dilapidations rendering the premises untenantable which * * * the landlord ought to repair, * * * the landlord neglects to do so, the * * * tenant may repair the same himself where the cost of such repairs does not require an expenditure * * * more than one month's rent of the premises and deduct the expenses of such repairs from the rent when due, or the * * * tenant may vacate the premises, in which case * * * the tenant shall be discharged from further payment of rent, or performance of other conditions as of the date of vacating the premises. This remedy shall not be available to the * * * tenant more than * * * twice in any 12-month period.

(b) For the purposes of this section, if a * * * tenant acts to repair and deduct after the 30th day following notice, he is presumed to have acted after a reasonable time. The presumption established by this subdivision is a rebuttable presumption affecting the burden of producing evidence and shall not be construed to prevent a tenant from repairing and deducting after a shorter notice if all the circumstances require shorter notice.

(c) The tenant's remedy under subdivision (a) shall not be available if the condition was caused by the violation of Section 1929 or 1941.2.

(d) The remedy provided by this section is in addition to any other remedy provided by this chapter, the rental agreement, or other applicable statutory or common law.

(Amended by Stats.1970, c. 1280, p. 2315, § 3; Stats.1979, c. 307, p. —, § 3.)

Supplementary Index to Notes

In general ½
Damages 10
Retaliatory eviction 9.2
Warranty of habitability 5.5

½. In general

"Repair and deduct" remedy of this section authorizing tenant, after giving reasonable notice of "dilapidations" to his landlord, either to quit premises without further liability for rent or to repair the dilapidations himself and to deduct cost of such repairs, up to one month's rent, from his rent was intended only to encompass relatively minor dilapidations in leased premises and was not designed as viable solution in serious instances of deterioration when cost of repairs are at all significant and remedy does not preclude warranty of habitability being implied by law in residential leases. Green v. Superior Court of City and County of San Francisco (1974) 111 Cal.Rptr. 704, 517 P.2d 1168, 10 C.3d 616.

1. Covenant to repair

Obligation of landlord to repair leased premises cannot be shifted to tenant, where landlord and tenant have expressly bargained to contrary as material part of consideration for lease. Groh v. Kover's Bull Pen, Inc. (1963) 34 Cal.Rptr. 637, 221 C.A.2d 611.

Agreement, consisting of exchange of letters, between landlords and tenants who took over occupancy of premises formerly leased to partnership of which he was member upon dissolution of partnership, properly construed, did not bind tenant as to clauses of lease between landlords and former partners exculpating landlords from liability for negligence, and including waiver of landlords' obligations under this section and § 1941. Fields v. City of Oakland (1956) 291 P.2d 145, 137 C.A.2d 602.

The numbers and letters following the name of the case are "citations" to the case. They are a shorthand key to the books known as "reporters" which contain the cases. "10 C.3d 616" means that the case can be found in Volume 10 of the California Reports third edition at page 616. The same case can also be found in Volume 11 of the California Reporter at page 704, and in Volume 517 of the Pacific Reporter second edition at page 1168. (Most cases are only reported in one or two reporters.)

The opening notes to the case usually summarize what the "holding" or ultimate decision is in the case. Sometimes the notes are misleading though, so it is important to read the whole decision. In *Green v. Superior Court*, the author, Justice Tobriner of the California Supreme Court, recognizes that the times have changed. The law used to require a tenant to pay the rent even if the landlord hadn't made the repairs. But that rule says the court was a product of an outdated agrarian society and has no relation to the social and legal realities of urban housing conditions today. The court proceeds to recognize an "implied warranty of habitability" guaranteeing each tenant a minimum level of health and safety in her/his home. Accordingly, the law now states that the tenant shall have the right to withhold his/her rent when the landlord does not make the necessary repairs to keep the dwelling "habitable." This case expands the law, going beyond Section 1942 of the Civil Code which is useful for only relatively minor repairs.

What affects the habitability of the dwelling? The Supreme Court refers to the housing codes for assistance in defining standards on what is habitable and what materially affects health and safety. Civil Code Section 1941.1 (c) referring to lack of hot water as making a tenancy "untenantable" also helps guide us.

So *Green* says that we can withhold our rent until the landlord repairs the water heater, and we have a defense if the landlord tries to evict us for not paying our rent as long as the repairs aren't made.[4]

Finally: How else might we have found this case?

There are several other sources we could have checked.

Legal Encyclopedias: These sets of books discuss the law from A to Z. There are encyclopedias covering the entire country. About fifteen states including California also have local encyclopedias (these are obviously preferable since they are more specific). (Check with your local librarian to see whether your state has one.) Encyclopedias will footnote the discussion with reference to some of the relevant cases and statutes.

If we had decided to research this problem using an encyclopedia, here's how we might have gone about it.

There are two California legal encyclopedias— *Witkin's Summary of California Law* and *California Jurisprudence* (abbreviated as *Cal. Jur.*, and now in its third edition—hence *Cal. Jur. 3rd*). Many people prefer *Witkin's*, but since most law libraries are more likely to have *Cal. Jur. 3rd*, we'll work with it.

Two separate indexes will get you into the textual material. One is the General Index. The other is at the end of each volume. (The set is arranged alphabetically by subject.)

At the time of this writing, the General Index is referenced to the second edition of *Cal. Jur.* (presumably a new set of indexes for the third edition will soon be published). We'll need to look in the supplement slipped into the back of the General Index Volumes for reference to the third edition.

The Landlord-Tenant Section in the supplement says: "Consult this index topic in back of Volume 42 Cal. Jur. 3rd."

Searching through the Landlord-Tenant Index of Volume 42, we find the subtopic, "Rent." Among its subheadings is "Repairs." Under "Repairs" it reads:

> deduction of costs of repairs from rent 105, 108, 111–113.
> liability for rent affected by breach of covenant to repair 153, 155.

In Section 105 of the text, reference is made to Civil Code (CC) Sections 1941 and 1942 (the "repair and deduct" statutes discussed above). Section 108 seems to be right on point. It explains that the landlord may no longer refuse to maintain the dwelling in a habitable condition. There is now an "implied warranty of habitability." *Green v. Superior Court* and *Hinson v. Delis* (a similar case) are cited in the footnotes as authority for this statement. The author also notes that Section 1942 of the Civil Code is not meant to be the only remedy for the tenant when a landlord fails to make repairs. "[A] tenant may withhold rent when a landlord breaches his "implied warranty of habitability." The reader is referred to Section 155 in the text.

Section 155 repeats the sentence we have just quoted above, and cites the *Hinson* case as authority. For some peculiar reason, *Green* is not mentioned here in the footnotes. Perhaps this part was written before *Green* was decided (since the *Hinson* case came first). Or perhaps one person wrote this section and another person wrote Section 108, and no one reviewed the two for inconsistencies. [5]

Checking out the other sections in the text, we see that Section 111 refers to your rights under Civil Code Section 1942. A footnote to Section 153 points out that *Green* has changed the law.

Now you need to check the supplement to this volume. Looking up the sections we found useful, we see that Sections 108, 111, and 155 all refer to a discussion on the warranty of habitability. The citation is to "66 CLR 37." In the front of each volume, there is a list of abbreviations. "CLR" is *Cal. Jur.*'s shorthand for *California Law Review*. Thus, Volume 66 of the *California Law Review* at page 37 may contain additional information and commentary on the subject. (Law reviews are briefly described below.)

Of course, assuming you had started out your research with this encyclopedia, you now need to look up the statutes (Civil Code Sections 1941 and 1942) and the cases (*Green* and *Hinson*) which were cited in the text. Never rely on the encyclopedia's text alone. Encyclopedias are not the law, they are just commentary on it. The text may not be accurate. Always check out the cases and statutes yourself.

Treatises: These cover one area of the law thoroughly. An up-to-date California treatise on landlord-tenant law would be a fine source.

Digests: There are collections of case notes (similar to annotations) organized by subject. There is no discussion as in an encyclopedia or treatise. Digests are usually so packed with case notes, that it is often difficult to ferret out the best cases without wasting a lot of time looking up each case to see whether the case is really as useful as the note seems to imply.

Law Reviews: These periodicals keep abreast of the law with articles by professors, lawyers, and law students. The *Index to Legal Periodicals* will lead you into the articles, but it is not a thorough index.

There are several other sourcebooks you can use at different times. These include horn books (treatises condensed into one-volume student editions), practice and procedure books (when you're taking your case to court), form books (examples of legal forms), and looseleaf materials (largely for federal material). A librarian can direct you to these as well as any others. There are also several books explaining legal research techniques and materials — check the card catalog.

Finally, there are many legal books now designed especially for the layperson, and written in a clear, readable style. They often explain the law to you a lot better than the more obtuse legal texts. In fact, these books have become so popular and acceptable that many lawyers (more than you might at first imagine) purchase these books themselves for a review of the law. There are legal books for laypersons in almost every field. The section in the back of this book reviews many of them.

---

1. Checking on the law yourself would be useful even if you hire an attorney. You won't feel like you're in the dark on your own case. Some lawyers would even be willing to charge you less because you've done some of the research.
2. As you get more sophisticated, you may want to consider these as well. But since we're just beginning here, we'll concentrate on the people and subject categories. In nearly every situation, you can find all you need to know by just using these top two terms thoroughly.
3. Certainly, a week of no hot water is "reasonable" time.
4. Many states have similar decisions establishing a warranty of habitability.
5. This is why it is always important to check several sections in the text — not just leap upon the first one you find. Trust yourself, not others, when doing research.

Peter Jan Honigsberg is the author of Cluing Into Legal Research.

Name Changes: A Rare Situation Where Law Is Easier Than You Might Think

by David Brown

Day after day, in courthouses all over the country, lawyers are filing petitions with law clerks and asking judges to approve their clients' change of name. How ludicrous that we should have to pay hundreds of dollars in lawyer and court fees and then go before a judge to humbly beg permission to change our name. We may soon need a lawyer if we buy a puppy and want to change her name from Millicent Fenwick IV to Pooch! But there is some hope at least in the area of name changes. In this article, David Brown shows how through the Usage method — simply using a new name — you can legally change your name without time-consuming and expensive court procedures.

Yesterday you were Willard Worms or Frieda Frump; tomorrow and for the rest of your life you can be Steven Sharp or Angela de L'Amour. How? Just do it! You don't need to go to court, or even to see a lawyer.

The law regarding name changes is a rare oasis in the vast desert of lawyers, courts, and judges. If ever there was an area of law where a lawyer is almost never required, this is it.

The legal tradition in the United States and Canada derives much from the "common law" of England. According to this system, whenever a legal problem isn't covered by a federal or state constitutional provision or statute, the "common law" — that which has customarily occurred in the past and has been sanctioned by published court decisions — takes over. And since, historically, there was no provision in England which governed name changes, an ordinary John Smith could decide to change his name to Ian Invincible, with no need to file reams of legal forms with dour-faced clerks, or to attend a hearing in a large, drafty room, accompanied by a bored lawyer mumbling esoteric nonsense to a be-wigged magistrate. The United States continued the English tradition by developing its own common law, and for the most part, we still follow this com-

mon sense tradition.

Many Americans don't realize that changing a name is so easy. Indeed, there is a common misconception that lawyers and courts must be involved in some mysterious mumbo-jumbo in order for the Willards and Friedas of this world to choose new names. But the simple fact is that changing one's name by the "Usage" method — using the new name exclusively — is *just as legal* as going to court and having a judge rubber-stamp the new name.

The requirements of the Usage method are:

1. That your new name be used *exclusively* and *consistently* in your daily affairs. If you use a name only in certain situations, i.e., for writing, acting, business, etc., you have not legally changed your name; and

2. That the new name not be used for fraudulent purposes, such as trying to escape payment of debts.

Usage is not the only way to change a name — it can also be accomplished by a court petition. But, if Usage name changes are just as legal, why bother with the expense, delay, and trouble of going to court to get a judge to approve the change? Because most people, including bureaucrats and administrators, both in business and in government agencies, are ignorant (or suspicious) of the validity of the Usage name change. They will often give you a difficult time until they see something "official" and "in writing" establishing your new name. Explaining that the Usage method is perfectly legal will often help, but it can become pretty tiresome after the innumerable repetitions you will undoubtedly be called upon to give, day in and day out, in this supposedly "free" society of ours. It is at this juncture that you may begin to ask if it isn't easier to humor the bureaucrats at the motor vehicles department, the registrar of voters, the banks, the credit card companies, the insurance and utility companies, the social security and passport offices, etc. by going to court and getting that "official" validation.

The decision is up to you. The courts of most states have held that a court petition procedure to change a name *supplements*, but does not replace, the common law right to change one's name by Usage. What do I recommend? I think it's just a question of whether you prefer the one major inconvenience of going to court, or the many minor inconveniences you will suffer each time you have to convince another bureaucrat that you have been true to the letter of the law in your Usage name change.

Forbidden Names

In addition to the requirement that the new name be used exclusively and consistently, and without fraudulent intent, there are some restrictions on your choice of a name. You cannot, for instance, adopt a new name if your taking it in any way interferes with the rights of another person (or persons). This generally means that you cannot take the name of a famous person. To illustrate, a number of years ago, an aspiring actor with an exceptional talent for impersonation petitioned a court to have his name changed to "Peter Lorie." The court refused to approve the petition because the more well-established film star, Peter Lorre, showed up at the hearing to protest.

However, the fact that you cannot take a famous name, with or without fraudulent attempt, does not necessarily mean that you cannot assume a name that someone else is already using. For example, you could change your name to Clark Klark, even if the name belonged to one or more members of your community — unless this person was so well-known there (a mayor, or some other prominent "pillar of the community") that the use of the name would infringe on his/her/their rights, or appear to be an attempt to capitalize on the new name.

A common fraudulent intent in name changes is to escape payment of debts. In fact, a name change doesn't accomplish this at all, except to the extent that it sometimes makes it harder for the creditor to find you. A name change to avoid payment of debts is not legal. But neither must you wait to pay off your debts before changing your name — whether by Usage or court petition. As long as you continue to honor your debts, you can change your name whenever you choose. And only if there are strong indications of intent to avoid debts by "disappearance," would the legal validity of a Usage-change name be questioned, or the granting of a court-approved name change be denied.

In one reported case, a man who had previously declared bankruptcy petitioned the court for a change of name and was granted court approval. According to the court, the fact that the man had declared bankruptcy wasn't enough to imply fraud-

ulent intent. After all, bankruptcy had already allowed him to discharge certain debts legally, and the fact that the name change request may have been motivated by a desire to escape the "stigma" of bankruptcy was not a reason to deny it.

Several interesting cases involving petitions for name changes have been noted. One case involved a Michael Dengler, who petitioned a Minnesota court for approval to change his name to "1069"—a number which he argued "symbolized my interrelationship with society, and conceptually reflects my personal and philosophical identity." The court would not approve the request, arguing that the use of a number for a name was "an abject dehumanization and totalitarian deprivation of dignified human privacy." The Minnesota Supreme Court upheld the refusal to grant the change of name, but added, "that is not to say that the appellant may not, if he chooses, apply for the same name, using words instead of numerals, i.e., 'Ten Sixty-Nine' or 'One Zero Six Nine.' Nothing we here decide would prevent the court from approving a name change fashioned in this manner."

Another case was noted involving Andrew Jones, a resident of Southern California, who petitioned a Los Angeles court to change his name to "Jesus Christ." The court clerk—perhaps in an effort to stall for time—made a diligent attempt to determine if this name change would infringe on the rights of anyone in the greater Los Angeles community. He found a Jesus Witness Christ living in East Los Angeles, and a Jesus J. Christ in Santa Monica. The clerk concluded that since Christ is a not-uncommon German last name, and Jesus is a common name in the Mexican-American community,

there seemed to be no showing of fraud or infringement of rights and the name change should be granted.

Women, Married Names, and Birth (Maiden) Names [1]

If you still have reservations about the legality of the Usage method, consider the person in your life who probably used it most successfully—your mother! Chances are that your mother took your father's last name as soon as they were married. And despite the popular misconception that the law "requires" the wife to assume her husband's last name, in most states this is not the case at all.

There are four guidelines which relate to women changing their names upon marriage:

1. *Marriage does not in and of itself change a woman's last name to that of her husband.* She must take affirmative steps to change it—by Usage.

2. *A woman is not required by law to adopt her husband's last name.* [2] *It is done only because of social custom.*

3. *The only way a married woman can "legally" take her husband's name is by Usage.* (Whether she does it willingly or because she believes the law

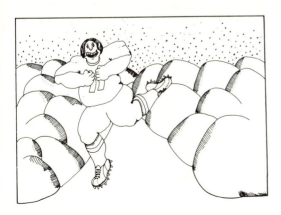

compels her, the Usage change is still legal.)

4. *A woman who marries and wants to keep her birth name need do NOTHING other than continue to use it exclusively.*

So, the vast majority of name changes in this country occur as a result of women assuming the last name of their husband through Usage. (It says something about early English and American notions of marriage that both a man's wife and his slave customarily took his surname.)

The tradition has perpetuated itself in this way:

1. Most married women take their husband's surnames;

2. Women see this and assume it is a requirement of the law;

3. When they marry they assume (incorrectly) that their surnames automatically change;

4. Consequently, they begin to use their husband's surname in the belief that the surname is already legally theirs;

5. Because of Usage, the husbands' surnames *do* become the legal surnames of the wives.

A woman does have a choice whether or not to take her husband's surname (or any other surname —including a hyphenated wife-husband surname), and more and more women are opting to continue to use their own birth name. Nor is there anything to prevent the husband from legally adopting his wife's surname by Usage. This was occasionally done in England when the wife's family name was more prominent than that of the husband. Imagine the benefits accruing to a [John] Jones who marries a [Ruth] Rockefeller and adopts her last name.

It is increasingly common for women who have used their husband's surnames for many years to re-adopt their birth names. Again, they can go to court or make the change through Usage. This is true, regardless of whether the woman is married, separated, or divorced. In no case is the husband's permission required, although in the past, some obnoxious judges have been known to ask married women if their husbands approved of the change.

Of course, changing back to your birth name after years of using your husband's surname will entail notifying all the businesses and government agencies with which you deal. It is similar to the process you went through when you originally took your husband's name, but this time it will be harder since you will—at least in the eyes of some—be bucking

social custom. Keep in mind, though, that you may reassume your birth name *legally* simply through the Usage method. You can look any bureaucrat in the eye and say, "I have legally changed my name from Jane Hisname to Jane Myname."

Many women find that the disadvantages of the Usage method far outweigh its advantages. People's reluctance to see a married woman go by her birth name, and the general ignorance about the Usage method, create difficulties which are eased when you can wave an "official" piece of paper signed by a judge. And although court approval is not required for a name change, there is one situation in which a woman will probably prefer to ask for court sanction, and that is when she is already involved in a divorce proceeding in the courts. In California, New York, Massachusetts and many other states, the divorce decree may, if the woman so requests, order that a woman be restored to her birth or former name. Given our over-priced legal system, this is a bargain—one filing fee for both a divorce and a name change, which, if sought separately, would require two different fees.

Court-Approved Change of Name — A Few Minor Advantages

I have said that both court-approved and Usage name changes are legal. This is true, but there are a few slight advantages in some states for court-approved changes. Some states will provide you with an "official amendment" to your birth certificate. This is useful in dealing with government agencies which require birth certificates for identification and are pretty strict about accepting anything else. As married women have learned, not having a birth certificate which matches one's current name isn't a major problem; still, if you get a court-approved change of name, mailing a certified copy of the decree to the Registrar of Vital Statistics in your state of birth will often suffice to get your birth certificate amended (depending, of course, on the laws of that state). It is easier to get an amendment if you live in — and therefore change your name in — the state where you were born, so that the court decree is from a court of the same state in which your birth certificate is on file. But even if you don't, your birth state registrar is supposed to give "full faith and credit" to the name-change decree of courts of other states. Getting an "amendment" to your birth certificate is not the same as getting a completely new birth certificate. The amendment is simply another piece of paper which is "legally stapled" to your birth certificate and filed in the same place. New birth certificates are generally not obtainable. When granted, they are usually given only to adopted minor children, individuals who didn't have the right father listed on the original birth certificate, and victims of typographical errors ("John Nose," who should have been listed as "John Rose").

Another slight advantage of a court-approved name change over a Usage-obtained one has to do with passports. With the court-approval method, you simply take a certified copy of the decree of change of name to the passport office, and you'll be issued a new passport exclusively in your new name. But if your new name is acquired by Usage, you can't get a new passport in the new name until you've used that name for at least two years.[3] Even then, you need notarized statements from two witnesses to this effect, and the passport is then listed in both the new and former names — unless you've used the new name for at least ten years.[4] These rules are relaxed a little for women whose Usage change of name has to do with going from a husband's surname to her birth name. In this instance, only one notarized affidavit is required and only your new name is listed on the passport. However, a woman who continues to use her birth name after marriage still has to fill out an affidavit and present identification to that effect.

Finally, a minor's name change must be approved through the courts. The Usage method is not available until the age of majority in his or her state of residence. Minors' names are most commonly changed when their parents divorce and the mother remarries, taking her husband's surname (by Usage only — remember?). The only way to have the child's legal surname reflect that of the mother and stepfather is for the mother to file a name-change petition in court for the child. Two things about this court-approved name change for minors should be remembered:

1. A court-approved name change for a minor has nothing to do with a step-parent adoption; does not alter the stepfather's legal relationship (almost none) with the child; and does not terminate the natural father's duties (of support) or rights (of visitation); and

2. The consent of the child's natural father must be obtained unless he has abandoned his parental duties.

How to Do It by Usage

The instructions "just use your new name" (or "keep your birth name") are deceptively simple. Legal acceptance is not the same as social acceptance. Here's how to change your name by one Usage method:

1. Tell the Post Office to list both your former and new names. (If you just list your new name, you might not get all your mail.)

2. Re-register to vote; you can do this by postcard, and you'll eventually receive a voter registration stub with your new name.

3. Write simple letters (Xerox copies if you wish) or send out announcement cards saying "I have legally changed my name from _____ to _____ ," to the following places:
   a. utilities (gas, electric, and telephone companies)
   b. insurance companies
   c. credit card companies
   d. other creditors
   e. schools and colleges

4. Go to your bank, savings and loan, and/or credit union, and sign new signature cards. Also, see if you can get new personalized checks printed solely in your new name.

5. Armed with some identification in your new name, go to your state's motor vehicles bureau and try to get them to issue a new driver's license and auto registration bearing your new name. Some states are more flexible about this than others. California simply requires that you sign a statement saying you've had a "legal name change" — which is true even if obtained by Usage. If the clerk hassles you because s/he is ignorant of the legality of the Usage method, demand to speak to his or her superior. Keep going up the ladder until you get results. Be firm!

6. Go to your Social Security office and ask to fill out the OAAN-7003 form ("Request for Change in Social Security Records"). You'll need a driver's license or a voter registration card as identification.

This isn't a complete list, of course, and the people and agencies that have to be contacted will, of course, vary for each individual. However, a voter registration card, credit cards, checks, social security card, and driver's license, all imprinted with your new name, will put you well on the way to acceptance of that new name.

As to married women who wish to keep their birth name, they need do nothing, in most states, except to keep on using the birth name. If someone tries to change your name for you, be firm. One way to keep such unauthorized name changers in line is to keep separate bank and credit card accounts in your own name—federal and some states' credit laws guarantee you the right to be free from discrimination as a result of changing your name. As long as you have your birth name on your checks, businesses will respect your right to be called by a different name (it's called "the power of the purse").

How to Do It by Court Petition

The court-approved name change procedure is somewhat similar to an uncontested divorce in a no-fault divorce state and is obtained in much the same manner. You file some papers with the court, and give sufficient notice to interested parties to allow them to contest it if they wish. A few weeks later you go to a court hearing and the judge rubber-stamps your request. The details will run something like this:

1. Prepare the initial papers: a "Petition for Change of Name" and an "Order to Show Cause." This is usually done on line-numbered legal paper having the following information: your former and proposed new names, date and place of birth, and reason for the change. The "Order to Show Cause" is a sort of notice-to-the-world, to be published in the legal section of a local newspaper, that you are seeking the change.

2. The above papers are then taken to the county courthouse for the county in which you live and filed with the clerk. The clerk collects a filing fee from you and gives you a court date which will be entered on your copy of the "Order to Show Cause."

3. A copy of the "Order to Show Cause" is either posted in a public place, or in some states is taken down to a local legal newspaper (or a regular newspaper with a legal notices section) for "Service by Publication." This notice—complete with court date, time, and place—is for anyone who might want to come and object to your change of name.

4. On the date set for the court hearing, you go to court and wait for your case to be called; after presenting a little speech to the judge (who may ask a few questions), the name change is usually granted. The judge signs a decree you've prepared; you file it with the clerk and send a copy to the state registrar of vital statistics.

Or to Put It Another Way!

It is of chief importance, in the law of change of name,
that whether Usage or by court, it's legal all the same.
If the name by which you're called now is not the proper sort,
despite all that they've told you, you needn't go to court.
Of a new name the requirement, which won't cost you a dime,
is to use the name exclusively, and that means all the time.

But alas there is a limit on the name that you can use;
you don't have total freedom your newfound name to choose.
The courts have now decided you cannot use the name
of certain well-known persons who have acquired fame.
Neither can you choose a name for purposes of fraud,
nor can you pick a number, not an even nor an odd.

A woman getting married, on our part of the earth,
may through continued usage retain her name of birth.
And whether married or divorced, legality won't lack
for women with their husband's names to take their birth names back.
In summary, the name by which you've wanted to be known
may instantly be taken, and now used as your own.

---

1. The use of the word "maiden" in reference to a woman's given name can be justly criticized as sexist. A more neutral term is "birth name," which I prefer and use consistently throughout this article.
2. A few southern and border states, including Alabama, have passed court decisions requiring a woman to use her husband's last name. This was approved by the U.S. Supreme Court. See *Fobush v. Wallace*, 341 F.Supp. 317 (1971) affirmed 415 U.S. 970 (1972).
3. This may cause you incredible hassles if you go overseas during this two-year period. Your passport will have one name and much of your other I.D. may have another. Try explaining American common law to a suspicious Chilean customs officer.
4. However, a woman on our Nolo Press staff who took a new first name three years ago had no problem recently in San Francisco getting a passport in her new name only. The Passport Office said that, because she was retaining her former first name (as her new middle name), they could authorize her passport without having notarized statements or any other supplementary evidence of her name change.

Dave Brown is part of the Nolo Press community. He has assumed the editorship of How To Change Your Name, *California Edition, since our friend David Loeb's untimely death, and is presently at work on a book on how to fight traffic tickets. In his spare time, he works as a chemist, goes to law school, and terrorizes local judges with motions to change venue.*

Search & Seizure: What the Police Can and Cannot Do

by N. Robert Stoll

The first people's laws to be adopted by the new republic known as the United States of America were the Bill of Rights. It is sad that today most Americans don't know what these rights are—and if they see them out of context, usually consider them to be overly radical. After the First Amendment protection of freedom of religion, speech, assembly and press, the Fourth Amendment, which guarantees the right to be secure from unreasonable searches and seizures, may be the most important. Here N. Robert Stoll gives us an excellent rundown on what this freedom really means. We also appreciate the contribution of Laura Graser in reviewing this material and updating it where necessary.

Generally, the police have no right to make unreasonable searches of citizens and their property or to seize their property. As we shall see, when a search is planned by police officers, a search warrant issued by a judge is normally required. Most searches, however, are unplanned and therefore, warrantless. To be legal, however, warrantless searches must fall within specified categories of areas where there are exceptions to the warrant requirement. These are discussed in section C of this chapter.

A.   What Is A Search?

A search, in the constitutional sense, not only includes the investigation of a citizen's home, books, and papers, but also includes such things as fingernail scrapings, wiretapping, and electronic eavesdropping. Broadly speaking, a search takes place whenever a citizen's privacy is invaded in the course of a governmental criminal investigation.

B.   What Is An Unreasonable Search?

The right of a citizen to his or her privacy is important, and it is the aim of our constitutions (both state and federal) to protect this right. However, while our state and federal constitutions prohibit unreasonable searches and seizures, the term "reasonable" is open to various interpretations. Thus each case depends on the particular circumstances related to it. Seemingly slight differences in the facts and circumstances are important when determining whether or not a search or seizure is lawful. Nevertheless, there are guidelines that the courts use when deciding whether or not a search is reasonable. (We shall look at these guidelines in the next section of this chapter.)

You should note that constitutional prohibitions against unreasonable searches and seizures only apply to the various governments' agents and officers. In other words, the constitutional requirements regarding searches and seizures do not cover a private citizen who conducts what would otherwise be an unconstitutional search or seizure. Furthermore, items seized by a private citizen's search, which would be unconstitutional if the search were conducted by police, would be admissible as evidence in a trial.

On the other hand, an unreasonable search by a private citizen who is acting as an agent of the government (such as a government-paid informant or private investigator) is unconstitutional, and anything obtained as a result of such a search or seizure could not be used as evidence in a subsequent trial. Courts have determined that planned warrantless searches of air cargo by air employees, acting pursuant to a plan with state and federal police officials, are unconstitutional searches by government "agents," and marijuana which is found in such searches and is unlawfully seized is therefore inadmissible as evidence in a trial against the persons shipping the "air cargo."

C. When Can There Be A Search Without A Warrant?

Although, under both federal and state constitutions, police may not make "unreasonable" searches or seizures and must have search warrants before they can search citizens' homes or property, there are three major exceptions to this rule:

- There is no "search" and no need for a warrant if the incriminating evidence that is seized is in plain view of the police officer.
- No warrant is necessary if the citizen being searched consents to the search or seizure.
- No warrant is required if there are so-called "exigent" (special) circumstances.

1. When are items in "plain view"?

Marijuana plants growing in a garden and visible from the street are considered to be in "plain view," and a police officer observing the plants from the street can seize the plants without a warrant. On the other hand, if the police officer had to trespass onto private property in order to observe the plants, and the officer did not have consent to enter the private property, it would be illegal for him to seize the plants without a warrant. The officer must have a lawful right to be where he is, and the matter seized must be plainly visible from that location.

2. If there is no warrant, who can give consent? What is consent?

The person who has a lawful right of possession of the item or area being searched must give his or her consent, if there is no search warrant. Thus, a houseguest cannot give proper consent to the police to search a house unless he has authority from the homeowner to give such consent. Moreover, normally the owner of an apartment house or hotel cannot give lawful consent to the police to search the premises occupied by his or her tenants.

The consent must be given voluntarily in order to be lawful. You may feel threatened or coerced into giving consent by the mere presence of the police at your doorway; however, you do not need to give your consent. Of course, the question of whether or not your consent is voluntary would be viewed in the light of your particular case. The courts have ruled that consent to search was lawfully given even though the occupants did not know they could refuse to let the police enter their premises without warrants.

If you do consent to a search when there is no warrant, that search (to be legal) is limited to the scope of your consent. In other words, if you consent to a search of your living room, the police cannot legally search the rest of your home. Furthermore, if you allow the police to search your home on Tuesday, your consent does not mean that they can also search your home on Wednesday.

3. What are "exigent" (special) circumstances?

Generally speaking, the courts have permitted searches without warrants if any of the following situations apply:

- The search is incident to a lawful arrest.
- The search takes place while the police are in "hot pursuit" of a suspect.
- It is an "inventory search." (I shall explain this term shortly.)
- In certain situations, automobiles are subject to lawful searches.

(a) Searches incident to a lawful arrest

If you, as a suspect, are lawfully arrested you—as well as the area *immediately* around you—may be searched without a search warrant. Such searches are called "searches incident to an arrest." The law permits such searches primarily for two reasons. First, your privacy has already been lawfully invaded by the arrest (assuming the arrest is lawful). If the police search you when they lawfully arrest you, they are not considered to be making any significant further intrusions upon your privacy. Second, arresting officers obviously have an interest in their own safety. Therefore, they do not need a warrant to search you (the suspect) for weapons or to search the area *immediately* within your reach. On the other hand, an arresting officer cannot use the "search incident to an arrest" right as a pretext to dispense with a warrant in order to search a wider area or to further and unnecessarily invade your privacy.

For example, if a man is sitting on his bed when he is arrested, the officer can search his clothing, as well as the area beneath the pillows and blankets that might be within the arrested man's reach. However, if the police officer has no search warrant, any search that extends beyond the immediate area of the arrested suspect is illegal. Thus, the officer could not lawfully search the remainder of the house without a warrant. Furthermore, the police officer could not lawfully search a locked briefcase even if it were next to the arrested person on the bed. In the case of the search of the briefcase, there would be an invasion of privacy further than just that involved with arresting the man on the bed. And, there would not be *reasonable* fear by the arresting officer for his or her safety since it would be difficult if not impossible for the arrested person to extract a weapon from a locked briefcase.

(b) Suppose the police are in hot pursuit of a suspect?

A police officer in hot pursuit of a suspect has a limited right to search without a warrant. In one well-known case, the police chased an armed suspect into his house. In this instance, the police were legally entitled to search the rooms through which the suspect fled in order to look for his weapons. As in other circumstances in which courts permit warrantless searches, it was not practical to require the issuance of a search warrant if reasonable precautions were to be taken for the officer's safety.

(c) Inventory searches

Courts have permitted "inventory searches" in order to protect the police from charges of losing property and also to protect the police from any danger that may be hidden inside property taken into custody. Inventory searches are common, even though there may be no probable cause to believe that property inventoried contains a weapon or proof of a crime. Once again, however, this "exigent circumstance" (of an inventory) cannot be used as a pretext by the police for dispensing with a search warrant when it would be practical for the police to obtain one.

For instance, a locked briefcase or sealed container taken into custody could not normally be lawfully searched without a search warrant. In order to "inventory" the briefcase or sealed container all the police would need to do is record "one locked briefcase" or "one sealed container"; it would not be necessary for them to list or inventory all of the contents of the briefcase or sealed container. If the

police were concerned that contraband or proof of a crime were contained in a briefcase or sealed container, the police would be required to apply to a judge for a search warrant.

(d) When may automobiles be searched?

Automobiles are frequently subjected to lawful searches, even though there may be no search warrant. If you, as a suspect, are lawfully arrested in your car, the car may be searched on the grounds that it is a search "incident to the arrest," or the police may make an inventory search if the car is then impounded. [The police may not search a closed container, such as a suitcase, found inside an automobile until the police get a warrant for the container.]

Cars stopped for mere traffic violations have also been lawfully searched when the traffic officer, while writing a ticket to the motorist, observes illegal material in plain view.

While police officers would not normally have a right to search motorists or their cars when stopping drivers for a traffic infraction, they may lawfully do so *if* they have *reasonable* grounds for fearing for their safety. For instance, if motorists who are stopped for traffic violations make suspicious, furtive gestures as if they were hiding weapons, officers may have a right to search the motorists and their vehicles.

Because it takes time to obtain a search warrant and because a motor vehicle is so mobile, the courts have been less stringent in requiring the police to have search warrants when searching automobiles, *if* the police officers have *good reason* to believe that there is illegal material or evidence of a crime in the automobile.

On the other hand, a police officer cannot lawfully search a car and its occupants stopped for a mere traffic infraction, simply because it is part of the officer's "routine." The federal and state constitutions outlaw such unreasonable "routines."

The constitutional prohibitions against unreasonable searches and seizures are mainly concerned with a citizen's personal privacy and the privacy of one's papers and home. Since automobiles and automobile travel are heavily regulated as a public activity, some courts have reasoned that one cannot expect the same sort of privacy with regard to one's automobile. Nevertheless, the U.S. Supreme Court has not permitted warrantless searches of automobiles simply because they are automobiles. In one well-known case, the U.S. Supreme Court ruled it was illegal for police to search without a warrant an automobile parked in a suspect's driveway; the automobile was not being used by the suspect, and there was plenty of opportunity for the police to obtain a search warrant to inspect the contents of the automobile.

D.   When May You Be Stopped and Frisked?

A police officer has the right to stop you on the street briefly and make *reasonable* inquiries. The inquiries must be reasonable (for example, "Why are you here at this time of night?"). The officer's stopping you *briefly* is not regarded as a seizure. However, if you are detained from leaving for an extended period of time, you are being seized and you are, therefore, entitled to certain constitutional rights.

1. Reasons for frisking people

You may be frisked by an officer *if* he reasonably believes that his safety or that of others is in danger. For instance, suppose an officer sees a suspicious looking person at an odd hour of night lurking around the doors of a bank that is closed. The officer may stop the person, request identification, and ask why he or she is standing there. If the officer observes a bulge in the suspect's pocket and the suspect makes a quick movement toward the bulge, the officer may frisk that person to determine if the bulge is a weapon. A lawful frisk consists of *only* a patdown, unless, during the patdown, the officer feels something that he reasonably believes is a weapon; in that case, the officer may then reach into the suspect's pocket and remove the weapon or item causing the bulge.

2. What may the officer seize during a frisk?

If the frisk is lawful (because it is reasonably related to the safety of the officer or others), anything the officer finds as the result of the frisk may be lawfully seized and, if the material is being possessed illegally, the officer can then arrest the suspect for possession of the material. In our example, if the officer reasonably believes that a bulge in the suspect's pocket was a weapon and, upon removing it, discovered that it was a package of illegal narcotics rather than a weapon, the officer could seize the narcotics

and arrest the suspect for possession of narcotics.

3. When is a frisk illegal?

A frisk is illegal if it is overly intensive or if the frisk is not reasonably related to the safety of the officer or others. An officer cannot lawfully frisk a suspect if the officer has no reasonable basis to believe that the suspect is armed. Moreover, an officer cannot lawfully search a suspect's car as part of a frisk simply because the suspect happens to be leaning against the car at the time the suspect is stopped and questioned by the police officer.

Note: Be diplomatic.

It is always a good policy to try to be polite to police officers, even when they don't reciprocate your politeness and even if they proceed without legal justification. Nothing can be gained by being impolite, sarcastic or abusive. If the police act improperly in making an arrest or search or seizure, that issue is reviewable by a judge. Judges are not impressed by defendants who are abusive or impolite. They are impressed, however, by defendants who maintain their composure and manners, even in the face of police misconduct. Police misconduct will be even more apparent if it cannot be shown that the defendants acted abusively themselves.

If you are faced with police misconduct, the best procedure is to identify (by badge number or name, if possible) all police officers involved and all witnesses to the misconduct. Identification of the wrongdoers, as well as witnesses to the wrongdoing, will be important when a judge later reviews the misconduct. It is difficult to identify these individuals if you are yourself embroiled in abusive conduct. In short, if you are the victim of police misconduct, keep your cool!

E. All About Search Warrants

The police have a legal right to search you if they have a search warrant. A search warrant is issued by a judge. For the warrant to be lawful, it must be based upon an affidavit or affidavits establishing "probable cause" for the search or seizure. The affidavits are usually written by police officers, frequently by officers working "under cover."

1. The affidavit must contain facts establishing "probable cause."

"Probable cause" means that there are grounds to believe that a crime has been committed and that property subject to seizure is at a designated location.

For example, an undercover agent making an affidavit offers a sworn statement that citizen X has, on several occasions, and within that last 24 hours purchased illegal drugs at specified premises (Apartment XYZ—ABC Street, Any City). From this statement a judge could reasonably conclude that there are, in all probabality, illegal drugs at these premises—and so there would be probable cause to issue a warrant for these premises.

The affidavit must state *facts:* asserted conclusions of illegality alone are not enough. For example, to apply for a warrant to search for illegal drugs, the officer must state in his affidavit that he observed illegal narcotics or that he has been informed by a reliable informant that illegal narcotics are located on certain premises. If the affidavit relies upon a "reliable informant" for the facts, the basis for believing that the informant is, in fact, reliable, must also be stated in the affidavit.

Mere conclusions or assertions of suspicions made by an officer making the affidavit do *not* constitute probable cause. Therefore, it is not enough for an officer to make a statement that he "has cause to suspect and does believe that illegal narcotics are illegally possessed at a location," because the officer did not state *the facts* on which he based his suspicion.

Suppose an officer is making a statement based upon facts that he has received from an informant. The following affidavit *would establish* probable cause.

Sample #1
Affidavit Proving Probable Cause

A confidential informant has told me that he has purchased illegal narcotics from John Smith at 123 Main Street on several occasions and within the last 24 hours. I believe this informant to be reliable because he has always given me reliable information over the last three years—information which has led to the arrest and conviction of eight narcotics dealers. I also believe his information is reliable in this case because I have examined the telephone listing for John Smith and found it to be 123 Main Street. I have also had the premises of 123 Main Street under surveillance and have seen numerous persons entering, and a short time later, leaving the premises, which appear to be a single-family residence; in my experience as a narcotics officer, such traffic is consistent with narcotics dealings.

This statement does *not* establish probable cause.

Sample #2
Affidavit Having No Factual Basis

I believe narcotics are at 123 Main Street because a confidential reliable informant tells me narcotics are now there.

Time is also important when an officer is establishing probable cause for a warrant. There may be narcotics at a certain place on one date, but that does not mean that there are narcotics still there a month later.

Final Note: It is not necessary to review the affidavit for a search warrant at the time the police enter the premises with the search warrant. Review of the adequacy of the affidavit can properly only occur before a judge at a later date.

2. The requirements of search warrants

A search warrant is intended to be a protection against "general warrants." The purpose of a search warrant is to limit the discretion of the police as to where, when and whom to search.

A search warrant must describe the place to be searched and the thing or person to be seized. An apartment or hotel room must be specifically identified; a search warrant is too broad in its description if it provides for the search of an entire apartment block. To identify a vehicle sufficiently, however, the officer only has to describe the correct license plate number or the operator and make of the car. If a search warrant allows officers to search a particular person, that person must be specifically named or described.

Any material that is to be seized can be described somewhat more broadly. Descriptions such as "a quantity of heroin", "burglary tools" and "narcotics paraphernalia" have been found by courts to be adequate descriptions of the material that may be seized.

In most states a search warrant can be utilized by the police only during daylight hours, unless the search warrant specifically provides otherwise by a judge. Nevertheless, in most instances, a judge does give permission in the search warrant for the police to use the search warrant at any time during the day or night.

A search warrant is void if it is not utilized within the dates proscribed by the judge when he or she signs it. For instance, in issuing a search warrant, a judge may provide that the warrant may be used, "at any time within seven days from the date of issue." If the police attempted to utilize the search warrant more than seven days after its issue, their search would not be lawful.

3. What do search warrants allow?
A warrant issued to search "the residence at so-and-so address," would permit a search of the garage, shed, and other related buildings. It would also permit the search of vehicles parked on the property.

During a lawful search with a warrant, any evidence of illegality that the police discover can be seized, even if they find items that are not named in the warrant. Since the police are lawfully on the premises (because they have a warrant) they may lawfully seize illegal items in plain view.

4. Do the police have to announce themselves?
Before entering a house with a search warrant, the police must first knock and announce their authority

and purpose, unless doing so would be too dangerous. The police may have to surprise the occupants if they have good reason to believe the occupants of the premises to be searched have firearms. In such an instance, the police do not have to "knock and announce," since if they do so, they may be met by gunfire.

Some courts have permitted the police to dispense with the "knock and announce" requirement if the police reasonably believe that occupants of the premises could easily and quickly destroy evidence or contraband if the police were to announce themselves before entering the premises.

5. Do the police have to show you the warrant?
In many states, the police do not have to show the search warrant to the owner of the premises to be searched, nor are the police required to read it to the owner prior to entering the premises.

F. Search and Seizure Under the Customs Laws
Usually, a search warrant is required for a search; otherwise one of the exceptions to the rule regarding search warrants must apply. Normally, there must be a reasonable factual basis for believing that something criminal is occurring or is about to occur. On

the other hand, warrantless border searches are permitted and can be used on mere suspicion without any reliable factual basis.

1. The officials' powers

Customs officials are authorized to check the identity of persons coming into this country. They are also authorized to search at the border for illegal material (such as narcotics) and for goods that require duty payments.

Whenever you cross the border, this is, in itself, sufficient grounds for border officials to search everything—ships, cars, trucks, envelopes, baggage, purses, wallets and similar items. Stopping and frisking entrants is commonplace and legal. If you are crossing the border, officials can even require you to strip so that they can search your body. Border "strip searches" have been upheld as lawful in cases where officials were simply suspicious because the person crossing the border was acting nervously.

2. How far within the border can officials search you?

Courts have permitted border searches without the normal constitutional requirements or warrants within 100 miles of the border. However, these cases have typically involved people whom the officials reasonably believed to have crossed the border illegally shortly before being stopped and searched.

A border search may occur hundreds of miles within the United States if that is the point of entry of the person searched. For instance, a traveller flying nonstop from London to Omaha could be subjected to a border search at Omaha.

3. Can mail be searched?

Some courts have permitted any suspicious looking mail entering this country to be searched by postal officials without a search warrant. Others have permitted such searches if the mail is not sent first class within this country. These court decisions are controversial, however. All courts agree that first class mail sent within the United States can only be searched if there is a warrant or if one of the exceptions to the search warrant requirement applies.

4. What happens when you are boarding an airplane?

When you board an airplane, the normal rules regarding search and seizure do not apply. Because we have had so many skyjackings, airlines have developed much tighter security precautions. The courts have approved of these search and seizure techniques on the basis that if you purchase an airline ticket, you are consenting to being searched.

However, there are certain procedures that the airport security personnel must follow. These procedures are designed to limit, as much as is reasonably possible, intrusions upon the traveller's privacy.

Suppose you are a passenger. Before you board the airplane, you are first surveyed by a magnetometer, which detects unusual concentrations of metal. If the magnetometer is "triggered," you can then voluntarily show the air security personnel any metal objects you may possess, and you are again surveyed by the magnetometer. However, if the magnetometer continues to detect unusual concentrations of metal, you may be questioned.

If your answers make the security personnel suspicious, or if your "profile" matches that of known hijackers, the officers can insist on frisking you or patting you down if you still want to board the airplane. If, while they are frisking you, they detect a suspicious "bulge," that "bulge" may be searched. However, at any time, you have the right to avoid the frisk or the search by choosing not to board the aircraft.

G. Seizure Under Income Tax Laws

The government may subpoena certain tax or business records if they are related to a civil (that is, a noncriminal) tax investigation. In such situations, a search warrant is not necessary. As with administrative inspections or searches, however, this tax authority cannot be used as a mere subterfuge to permit a warrantless search if the primary purpose is really a criminal investigation of the person being subpoenaed. Furthermore, you can stop a tax subpoena by taking court action.

The government may also lawfully seize, without a search warrant (or the necessity for the constitutional exceptions to a search warrant) items upon which there are tax liens. If, in carrying out the tax lien, the government comes across illegally possessed items, these can also be seized.

H. Searches Under Drunk Driving Laws

In all states it is illegal to operate a motor vehicle while you are under the influence of intoxicating liquor or drugs. In some states the operation of a motor vehicle with a blood alcohol content of a specified level (usually 0.15 of 1%) is, itself, a crime, even if the driver's operation of the vehicle is not affected by his or her blood/alcohol level.

If you are given a breath, urine, or blood test to determine intoxication, you are technically being searched. However, an officer does not need a search warrant. The law considers that if you are operating a vehicle on a public road you are automatically, by implication, consenting to an alcohol/drug test of your blood, urine, saliva, or breath. Nevertheless, the police officer must have reasonable grounds for believing that you are intoxicated. The officer must also first place you under arrest. In many states the officer must also tell you the consequences of refusing to be tested and tell you that you have a right (at your own expense) to have the tests administered by a qualified doctor, nurse, or technician.

You, as the driver, can always refuse to be tested. However, if you refuse to submit to such a test after your arrest for drunk driving, you will automatically have your driving privileges suspended for a specified period (usually three to six months).

I. Electronic Eavesdropping and Wiretapping

A conversation either on the phone or face-to-face, in which the participants reasonably believe that they are talking privately cannot lawfully be "bugged" by government officers, unless those officers meet constitutional requirements for searches and seizures. Thus, in a famous case in 1967, the United States Supreme Court ruled that police officers should have obtained a search warrant before wiretapping a public phone booth that the police knew was used by a defendant for private confiden-

tial communications. Similarly, search warrants are necessary before officers can "bug" a room in which the occupants believe that their conversations are private.

On the other hand, in some cases in which defendants have revealed confidences to persons to whom the police have attached eavesdropping devices, these procedures have been regarded as reasonable. In such situations, the people who were "wired" could reveal their conversations to others, anyway. Thus, the conversations would not be private. Similarly, telephone conversations can be monitored if either party to the conversations consents.

Electronic eavesdropping or wiretapping warrants — as with other search warrants — must be specific. They should specify whose conversations are to be overheard, the location of the eavesdropping device, and they should be limited to fixed times. Finally, the officer should notify the person who was tapped after the tap is over, or else the warrant must specify why such notification should not be given.

In 1968, Congress passed the Omnibus Crime Control and Safe Streets Act which, among other things, provides very strict requirements regarding wiretapping. The Act applies to state as well as federal law enforcement officials and forbids wiretapping, except that which is authorized by court order. Material obtained from an illegal wiretap may not be used as evidence on a subsequent trial. However, the police can go to the telephone company and install a pen register, which is a device which records what numbers you dial.

N. Robert Stoll is an attorney in Portland, Oregon. He is a former employee of criminal defense lawyer F. Lee Bailey, and past president of the Oregon Association of Criminal Defense lawyers.

How to Organize a Business as a Small Time Operator

by Bernard Kamoroff

It is the bright and shining dream of many Americans to own their own business. There is something in our national soul that just doesn't like, or trust, international conglomerates and cartels. But unfortunately, starting a business seems to mean that you have to deal with yards and yards of legal red tape. And it's hard enough to get the money together to start a little enterprise without simultaneously having to support a small army of lawyers and accountants to do the paperwork. But perhaps there is a better way—maybe you can learn to handle many of these legal details yourself. Bernard (Bear) Kamoroff thought so, and wrote a book entitled Small Time Operator *to explain how. A man of principle, Bear refused a number of generous offers to sell his book to big publishers, and instead, started his own publishing company. Nine printings and approximately 100,000 copies later, Bear is happy to report that his ideas work. Here we reprint a portion of his book that speaks to the various legal ways a small business can be organized. (*Small Time Operator *is separately reviewed in Part VI of this book.)*

Legally, a small business is simple to set up. A sole proprietorship or a partnership is legally created by (1) declaring yourself/selves to be in business and (2) doing it. After that, unfortunately, things aren't so simple. There are important legal and personal responsibilities you should be aware of before you get all tangled up in your new venture.

Sole Proprietorship: The Traditional One Person Business

A one person business or a business operated by a husband and wife is known as a "sole proprietorship." There are over 12½ million small businesses in this country, and most of them are sole proprietorships. This form of business has flourished over

the years because of the opportunities it offers to be boss, run the business, make the decisions and keep the profits. A sole proprietorship is the easiest form of business to start up, and despite all the regulations, is the least regulated of all businesses.

You, the owner of the business, the sole proprietor, are your own man or woman. You make or break your business, which may sound singularly appealing to those of you instilled with the entrepreneurial, pioneering spirit. But you also have sole responsibility as well as sole control. You and your sole proprietorship are one and the same in the eyes of the law. Any debts or obligations of the business are the personal responsibility of the owner. Damages from any lawsuits brought against the business can be exacted from the personal assets of the owner. You should be fully aware of these legal aspects of the sole proprietorship. If you get your business into legal trouble or too far into debt, not only could you lose your business, you could lose your shirt.

The owner of a sole proprietorship cannot hire herself as an employee. This is a point of law often misunderstood by new business people. You may withdraw from the business (i.e. pay yourself) as much or as little money as you want but this "draw" is not a wage, you do not pay payroll taxes on it and you cannot deduct the withdrawal as a business expense. The profit of your business, which is computed without regard to your personal draws, is your "wage" and must be included on your personal income tax return. If your business made a $10,000 profit last year, you personally owe taxes on $10,000. Even if you only withdrew $5,000 from the business, you still must pay taxes on $10,000. And if you withdrew $15,000, you still pay taxes only on $10,000. The sole proprietorship itself does not file income tax returns or pay income taxes.

Partnerships

Partnerships offer opportunities often not available

to the one person business: more capital, more skills and ideas, the extra energy generated when two or more people are working together. Partnerships are the traditional meeting ground of the "idea" person and the "money" person. Having a partner can relieve the sole proprietor pressures of having to do everything yourself; and, at last, you can take a little vacation without having to shut down the business.

Partnerships have their drawbacks as well. The independence and sole decision making that only the sole proprietor has must now be shared; there is more paperwork; inter-personal relations with your partner or partners may require both time and tact. Most important, the legal consequences of having one or more partners can be serious.

A partnership, like a sole proprietorship, is legally inseparable from the owners, the partners. Individual partners can be held responsible for financial debts and legal obligations of the partnership. The most important legal aspect of a general partnership is that all partners can be held personally liable for the acts of any one partner acting on partnership business. If your partner, representing the business, goes to the bank and borrows $5,000, you can be personally responsible to repay the debt, even if you didn't sign the papers yourself, even if you didn't know about the loan. In a more serious situation, if your partner gets into legal trouble while on partnership business, you may also be in legal trouble.

Like sole proprietors, partners cannot be employees of their partnerships. A partner's compensation is his or her share of the profits, taxable to the individual partners.

Partnerships must file a partnership income tax return, although the partnership itself pays no taxes.

Death or withdrawal of one partner or the addition of a new partner legally terminates a partnership. The business need not be liquidated, however; a new partnership agreement can be made. The original partnership agreement can include provisions for continuation of a partnership.

A partnership agreement is an "understanding" between partners as to how the business will be conducted. Many partnership agreements are nothing more than a handshake and a "Let's do it;" and often such agreements turn out to be more of a *mis*understanding than anything else. A written partnership agreement is not required by law, but it is something no partnership should be without. It reduces the possibilities of misunderstanding and future problems.

A written partnership agreement should be signed by all the partners and should specify:

1. What the business is and what are its goals. Be succinct: you should be able to pin this down in one paragraph. A simple, *written* statement of business goals is the first and most important step in any partnership agreement. If partners do not agree on the basics, the partnership is doomed from the start.

2. How much each partner will contribute—in cash, in property and in labor. There are no federal laws requiring partners to make equal or simultaneous contributions.

3. How each partner will share in the profits and losses. The easiest and most common arrangement is an equal division of profits between partners. You may wish, however, to provide for an unequal division of profits to compensate for differences in time or money contributed or for differences in ability and experience of the different partners.

4. Procedures for withdrawal of funds and payments of profits—how much and when. Such an understanding will prevent situations in which one partner can arbitrarily withdraw substantial amounts of money from the partnership. There is no federal law requiring partners to make equal or simultaneous withdrawals.

5. Provisions for continuing the business if one partner dies or wants out. A pre-arranged agreement to buy out the partner or bring in a new partner can prevent the shut down of the business.

6. You may also want a clause specifying the financial and legal powers of each partner. Such a clause will not relieve any partner of partnership obligations entered into by other partners; it only reduces the possibility of future problems.

The type of partnership just described is known as a "general" partnership and is by far the most common form of partnership. A "limited" partnership is a refinement of the general partnership concept. Limited partnerships allow investors to become partners without assuming unlimited liability. Limited partners usually risk only their investment in the business. There still must be at least one general partner in a limited partnership with full legal and financial responsibility.

Limited partnerships are subject to much greater government scrutiny than general partnerships.

Most states require limited partnerships to be registered with the county or the state; the Internal Revenue Service has special income tax rules for limited partnerships.

You, Incorporated: A Corporation Primer

The corporation is truly a misunderstood animal. People, even business people, have more misconceptions about corporations than about any other form of business. Some small time operations will benefit by incorporating; most will not. But in order for you to make an intelligent choice between "You" and "You, Incorporated" you will need a basic understanding of what a corporation is and what can and cannot be accomplished by incorporating.

A corporation is... just another business. The basic day to day operations, the management, the bookkeeping are virtually no different from the operations of an unincorporated business. A corporation can be as tiny as the tiniest unincorporated business; it can be loose and easy and very personal. Just as there are grey-suits-and-elevators corporations, there are blue-jeans-and-pure-funk corporations.

A corporation is just another business... but the rules of the game are different. The two main differences between corporations and other businesses are the tax laws and the laws governing liability.

Corporate Myth Number One: You're going to lower your taxes by incorporating. Not so. The fact is that most small businesses will not save tax money by incorporating. Corporate profits are taxed *twice*:

once as corporate income and again when distributed to the shareholders (owners) as dividends. In contrast, the profits from your unincorporated sole proprietorship or partnership are taxable only to you, the owner; the business itself pays no tax. So even though corporate tax rates are in some cases lower than individual tax rates, the effective corporate tax rate because of the double taxation is always higher. Small corporations do have a few ways to reduce the combined corporation and shareholder taxes but none will result in taxes lower than those paid by an unincorporated business.

Rules regarding liability are also different for corporations. These liability rules, which offer protection to the owners of corporations from lawsuits and creditors, are the most convincing reason—and, I feel, the only reason—for you to consider incorporating your small business.

A corporation is recognized by law as a "legal entity," which means that the business is legally separate from its owners. If your corporation does not pay its debts, the creditors usually cannot get their money from your personal, non-business assets. In most cases you will not be personally liable for lawsuits brought against your corporation.

High-risk businesses, even very small ones, often incorporate solely to protect the owners from personal loss. Businesses borrowing a lot of "risk" capital often fall in this category; businesses with a more than average likelihood of being sued—such as security businesses and manufacturers of potentially dangerous products—also incorporate for the

MELROSE SAFE CO.

Winslow

liability protection offered. Partnerships often incorporate to protect individual partners against possible lawsuit and losses resulting from the action of other partners.

Limited corporate liability, however, is not "blanket" or all encompassing. Officers of a corporation (in a small corporation, the officers are the owners) can be personally liabile for claims against their corporations in some situations. A corporation will not shield you from personal liability that you normally should be responsible for, such as not having car insurance or acting with gross negligence. Professionals such as doctors cannot hide behind corporations to protect themselves from malpractice suits. And as to financial commitments, any bank lending money to a small corporation will require the stockholders or officers to co-sign as personal guarantors of the loan.

Incorporating a business eliminates most of the legal and tax complications of a change in ownership. Sale of stock or death of a shareholder will not end the business; the same corporation can continue in business with new shareholders. By comparison, a sole proprietorship ceases to exist when the owner closes the business or dies; a partnership ceases to exist when one partner quits or dies. Of course, a sole proprietorship or a partnership can be sold or otherwise acquired by new owners. But the result, legally, is a new business requiring new records, new valuation of assets and liabilities, new business licenses, etc.

A corporation is the only form of business which can hire its owners as employees. Corporations can pay their owner/employees a wage and even offer company paid fringe benefits such as health insurance. Employees' wages, including those of owner/employees, are deductible expenses of the business. Expenses reduce profits, which means lower income taxes for the corporation. The wages, of course, are taxable to the owner/employee as personal income. But unlike regular corporate profits which are taxable to the corporation and again to the owners, wages paid to owner/employees are not subject to the double taxation. Any fringe benefits paid to owner/employees are also tax deductible expenses of the corporation. There is even a greater tax savings with company paid fringe benefits because the fringe benefits are not taxable to the employees at all.

Corporations are allowed to retain undistributed profits within the company and not pay the profits out to the owners. Though the corporation must pay income tax on these "retained earnings," as they are called, the owners do not have to pay the "double" or second tax because the profits have not been paid out to them. Retained earnings can be reinvested in the business, distributed to the shareholders at a later date or retained indefinitely by the company. An unincorporated business can also retain the profits in the business, but the owners must pay income tax on the profits whether distributed to them or not.

Small Business (Subchapter S) Corporations

There is a form of corporation different from the type just described. It is sort of a hybrid between a traditional corporation and a partnership, with some of the advantages of both.

The Small Business Corporation (known in the trade as "Subchapter S" or the "Sub S" corporation) has the same basic structure as a regular corporation and offers the same limited liability protection to the stockholders. The Sub S corporation, however, pays no corporate income tax. Like a partnership, all the profits of the Sub S corporation pass through to the owners who are taxed at their regular individual rates.

There are two main advantages to the Sub S corporation. The first and most obvious is the elimination of the double taxation. The other advantage is due to some complex tax laws which allow current business losses to be carried back to prior years to offset prior years' taxes, bringing immediate tax refunds. Any business, corporation or otherwise, can avail itself of operating loss carryback laws. But if a corporation is brand new and sustains a loss, there are no prior years to carry the loss back to. In the case of a Sub S corporation the loss passes through to the stockholders, and they in turn can carry the loss back to their personal prior years' returns even though the business did not exist then. Losses of a regular corporation (or any other business) that cannot be carried back can be carried forward to offset future years' earnings, but the business must wait a full year or more to get the refund.

Only "closely held" corporations—those having ten or fewer stockholders—can elect to become Subchapter S corporations. There are special and very stringent requirements as to who may be a stockholder, how profits are to be distributed, how and when the election to go Sub S must be made. Sub S corporations are penalized heavily by the IRS if they fail to file timely reports or follow the proper (and lengthy) procedures demanded of them. According to one IRS agent who specializes in Subchapter S corporations, "Ninety percent of all Sub S audits end right there—the failure to file the report on time. One day can make all the difference in the world." Also, some states do not recognize the Sub S status and tax these businesses as regular corporations. Lastly, owner/employees of Sub S corporations are not allowed all of the fringe benefits available to owner/employees of regular corporations.

Steps to Incorporating a Business

The states, not the federal government, license corporations. The requirements vary greatly from state to state as do the fees, which can run from $10 in some states to as high as $2,500 in others. And unless you are willing and able to study all the incorporating laws, which can get complicated, and file all the necessary forms yourself, add another $200 to $400 for a lawyer's assistance.

Generally, the first and most important step in the required incorporation procedures is the preparation of a "certificate" or "articles" of incorporation. This document usually must show the following information:

1. The proposed name of the corporation.

2. The purposes for which the corporation is formed. In some states the wording of this section can be critical and if improperly worded can severely limit the type of business you can conduct.

3. Names and addresses of incorporators.

4. Location of the principal office of the corporation. Most small corporations obtain their charter from the state in which the greater part of their business is conducted.

5. The names of subscribers (future shareholders) and the number of shares to which each subscribes. This is known as a "limited offering" of stock. Corporate stock is issued either as a "limited offering" or as a "public offering." Most small corpora-

tions make limited offerings of stock, with each shareholder individually named in the articles of incorporation.

6. The type and maximum amount of capital stock to be issued. Stock is typically classed as "common" or "preferred." Holders of preferred stock generally have prior or preferred claim on corporate assets over common stockholders.

7. Capital required at time of incorporation. This is another important decision and requires a knowledge of corporate "equity," which is comprised of "stated capital" and "paid in surplus." "Stated capital" is basically an amount of money that belongs to the corporation and cannot be paid out to stockholders until the corporation is liquidated. All corporations must have some stated capital. Some states specify the dollar minimum; some states require the corporation to bank the stated capital in cash. Since stated capital is money with only limited use, most corporations try to keep stated capital as small as possible. "Paid in surplus" is money in excess of stated capital and generally is not restricted.

In some states, one person can incorporate a business. Most states, however, require three. But be it a one person corporation or a huge conglomerate, if you are going to incorporate you must play the corporate game entirely. You must hold meetings and keep written minutes of the meetings. Your corporation must have stockholders who elect directors (you must have directors) who are a policy making and overseeing group. The directors appoint officers (that's right, you must have officers) who run the business. Officers in turn hire employees, who do the work. In a small corporation, one person often wears all four hats: stockholder, director, officer and employee.

Bear Kamaroff is a C.P.A. who can rarely be coaxed out of his home in the Northern California woods except to play music. He is presently working on a book about the legal and practical aspects of running a collective business.

The Living Lease
by Michael Phillips

Landlord-tenant relationships are frequently bad. Indeed, they probably haven't improved much since the first caveperson charged six duck eggs and a brontosaurus bone in exchange for letting someone occupy the unused back portion of his or her cave. Most books on the subject are either militantly pro-landlord or pro-tenant. Rarely is there an attempt at creative thinking in the area of landlord-tenant relationships. Michael Phillips' book is one of those rare—and we think, successful—attempts.

Could cities look significantly different with just a minor social change? I think so. More than 60% of all housing units in cities are rentals. It's hard to make capital improvements in a place, or really upgrade your home, if the consequence is being kicked out or having your rent raised. Not to mention the unreasonable horror of being evicted from your "home" to make room for your landlord's cousin. If tenants had leases that gave them security similar to ownership, wouldn't that have an effect on the way cities look?

The Living Lease has many of the qualities of a conventional business lease where both parties are fairly equal. Rent increases are based on open books, improvements are depreciated over their lifetime, and termination of the lease requires increasing notice and increasing compensation to the tenant as the years go on.

1. Purpose of the Lease
A person who rents a "living space" is entitled to have as much emotional and legal security in connection with his/her living space as a person who "owns" his/her own living space. Upon that belief this lease is drawn up between Michael Phillips, the owner of 62 Stanton Street, and Don Sachs, tenant of the downstairs apartment at 62 Stanton Street.

2. Term: How Long This Lease Will Last
From this date _____ forward this lease shall be in effect so long as Don Sachs is alive, and so long as all other provisions of this lease are met. This lease ceases with Don Sachs' death or as provided under Termination in Section 4. However, this lease continues in force as an obligation of the estate of Michael Phillips in the event of his death except as noted in other provisions of this agreement.

Rates: The Rental Rate for This Living Space
Rent is $150.00 per month, for the space described in attachment A, payable in advance on the first day of every month.

A) *Deposit:* A deposit of $150.00 shall be made at the beginning of this lease and shall be returned to Don Sachs upon termination (a) if the rental space is in a clean condition, or (b) if it is unclean the cost of hiring a person to clean it and return it to the original condition shall be deducted from the deposit; however, if four years shall pass from this date the deposit shall be refunded to Don Sachs.

B) *Change in rental rate:* The landlord shall be able to raise or lower the rent at any time with 30 days' notice in writing to Don Sachs if he can demonstrate a real sustained change in the cost of providing the living space.

C) *Demonstrating a change in expenses:* Shall consist of a comparison of all present costs associated with the rental space (such as utilities, property tax, mortgage interest, maintenance) and the new costs in effect. On a percentage of space used basis, the actual dollar costs (or savings) can be passed on to Don in monthly rent. This comparison shall be in writing. If Don protests the change in rates, he shall nevertheless pay it along with the regular monthly rent payments, and any difference determined by arbitration shall be returned to Don.

(Example: Rent in 1980 is $200 per month, and all associated costs are $108 at that time; in 1984 Michael Phillips notifies Don that costs are averaging $128 per month and in 30 days the rent will go up to $220.) Don Sachs shall have the right to see the documents and costs involved once a year upon request and Michael has 30 days to prepare them. Rental rates shall go down in a similar manner, if costs go down.

4. Termination: How This Agreement Shall Be Ended

The form of termination and the conditions of termination shall change with the length of time the agreement has been in force. The following table describes the relationship between termination and the length of occupancy.

Years of Occupany	Amount of termination notice to be given	Settlement	Reasons needed for Termination
0 to ½ yr	30 days	None	Any reason, including whim or intuition
½ to 2 yrs	60 days	None	Any genuine reason, given in good faith, in writing, concerning the relationship of the two parties involved
Beg. of 3d yr to end of 10th yr	1 mo. for every year of occupancy, OR	Basic 2 mos rent + ½ mo rent for ea. year of occupancy greater than 3 yrs (i.e., 7 yrs occupancy = a 4 mo rent settlement)	Same
Beg. of 11th yr to death of Don Sachs	1 year's notice + settlement	1 month's rent for ea. year's occupancy up to 25 years	Only on sale of property, violation of agreement or death of Michael Phillips

NOTE: Rent is calculated from the average of the prior 12 months' rent.

5. Capital Improvements: Painting and Fixing Up

Any "capital" improvements made by Don Sachs must be approved by Michael Phillips in advance if they are to meet the provisions of this clause. Michael's approval is not subject to arbitration. An improvement will be valued at cost (excluding free labor) and a rapid depreciation schedule shall be agreed upon. If termination of this agreement occurs before the end of depreciation, Don shall be reimbursed for the balance of the depreciation. Example: A new formica sink top is installed at a cost of $120. Normal life is figured at 7 years, but rapid depreciation is 4 years. Don leaves after three years, he gets back $30.

6. Occupancy, Privacy, and Neighborliness

The "living space" shall be occupied by no more than two persons except for guests. Should a guest stay more than one month, each successive month shall require the permission of Michael in writing.

Don shall be entitled to as much privacy as possible. Michael shall have access to Don's living space after giving 24 hours' notice, except in emergencies where immediate access is necessary to repair damage, or cope with a serious problem of an emergency nature.

Neighborliness shall constitute a very important provision of this agreement. Neither Michael nor Don shall make any loud, excessive, or undue noise at any time; nor shall either create any other such nuisance including those related to smell or sound, unless it is by agreement with the other party in advance. Both parties shall try to operate in this provision under good will; if restraint is not satisfactory after 3 years, specific written provisions shall be added.

7. Arbitration: Settling Disagreements

A) In the event of a disagreement both parties shall present their cases to an arbitrator. The arbitrator shall be _____. The parties agree to abide by the arbitrator's decision.

B) If the named arbitrator must be replaced for any reason, he or she shall name a replacement. If for any reason this is not done and the parties cannot agree on a replacement, the American Arbitration Society can be used (and the rules used will be those of the S.F. American Arbitration Society or its successor). Each year $25 shall be available from rent to pay for arbitration (not cumulative); once this is used up, the next two issues of arbitration shall be paid for equally by both parties; in any subsequent arbitration issues occurring in any one year the arbitrator shall determine who pays the cost of arbitration.

8. Tax Law Changes

Any changes in the federal, state, or local tax structure that have direct implications for the cost of owning or maintaining this living space shall be considered under section 3(C) in calculating costs.

9. Non-Transferable

This agreement is not transferable to any other party except by the agreement of both parties in writing. (This paragraph prohibits subleasing.)

10. Insurance and Security

Neither party shall be responsible for the insurance protection of the other party. Both parties shall act to provide personal and property security for the other party insofar as is reasonable, including the installation of security equipment (costs to be covered under Section 5).

11. Maintenance

The living space shall be maintained at all times by Michael in the condition in which the space was rented and shall meet all code requirements in force at the time of the agreement.

12. Miscellaneous Provisions

A) In the event of property destruction such as fire or earthquake where damage exceeds 20% of the value of the house, Michael shall decide whether to rebuild the house.

B) Neither party shall violate zoning provisions or other ordinances regulating the property except by mutual agreement.

C) In the event of bankruptcy of either party the termination provisions of Section 4 can be invoked by the non-bankrupt party.

Estate Planning — Why Bother?

by Denis Clifford

Some people relate to their own death by planning for its consequences in minute detail. They imagine that by becoming as familiar as possible with all of its implications, they gain power over it — or at least, glean an understanding of what it's all about. Others refuse to think about their death at all — including its practical consequences to those around them. People in the former group may know much of what is written here, while those in the second category will have already stopped reading. Denis Clifford writes for the majority of us who are somewhere in the middle. We really do want to know how to ensure that our property will go to our loved ones rather than to lawyers and tax collectors, but we want to be told gently.

"Estate Planning," my editor decreed — "just a short, good piece, 2000–4000 words." (And already 18 are gone.) That's surely not enough space to cover any aspect in depth, nor to give some how-to-do-it-yourself specifics. Perhaps it's just enough space to pass along that little knowledge which is reputed to be a dangerous thing. What to do? Attack from both ends: offer some general thoughts on why "estate planning" exists, using probate as an example of how expensive things can become without planning; then some quick suggestions of money-saving estate planning methods you can do yourself, without lawyers. The message: you can do-it-yourself, and it's a sensible thing to do.

Before we get to the larger area of estate planning, let's take a quick look at probate and probate avoidance, if for no other reason than to convince you that they are only a part of a good estate plan. Every society has some means for transferring the property of a person who dies. After all, it can't just be allowed to sit there and wait for whoever grabs it first. While there are scores of different ways a person can pass his or her possessions to the next generation, few are as cumbersome, lawyer-ridden, time-consuming and expensive as the American system of wills, probate and death taxes. In the United States, the overwhelming majority of property transferred by a will must go through probate.

By now, most people sense there's something wrong with the way "probate" works; indeed, the very word has acquired an evil ring. Well, they're right. Probate is pretty outrageous — an institutionalized lawyer's rip-off that's gone on far too long. Perhaps the saddest part of the whole mess is that the American legal establishment has convinced itself — if no one else — that probate is essential for the preservation of society, and thus fights all suggestions for any kind of change.

When someone dies, his or her assets have to be identified and gathered, all debts (including death taxes) paid, and the remaining property distributed to inheritors. As you might have noticed, there's nothing in this list that sounds particularly complicated. The work is tedious, but basically clerical. However, for almost all property transferred by a will, American law requires this record-keeping to be run through probate court, with numerous legal forms, court appearances, and rubber-stamp judicial approval of each step of the process. Probate work is lucrative for lawyers. This is because their fees are often based on the value of the estate, not the hours the lawyer (or more realistically, his or her secretary and staff) has worked.

The lawyer-court procedure is required in all probate cases even though there is no hint of any conflict. Many lawyers love to prattle on about the glories of the "adversary system," but they don't dwell on it when attempting to justify probate, because in the overwhelming majority of probate cases there aren't any adversaries. There's simply no need for depositions, motions, cross-examination, the hearsay rule, august judges in black robes, court reporters, and all the rest of the courtly fol-de-rol. Most of the time it's simply a matter of seeing that great Aunt Jane's old house and furniture are sold and the proceeds divided between her children and grandchildren, all of whom like and respect one another.

So why are lawyers involved in probate? Many lawyers seem to act as if some natural law decrees that they must profit when there is a death. The truth is more prosaic—they got involved as the result of a historical accident. In medieval England —a culture which had a genuine passion for intricate, ceremonial legal proceedings—land was power and the inheritance of land of direct concern to the king. The transfer of land after a person's death was done through the king's courts, inappropriately called "common law" courts. By contrast, the transfer of other types of property (money, animals, and other personal possessions) had much less political significance, was handled through either an ecclesiastical process or in equity courts, both of which required much less formality. When the United States broke with crazy old George the Third and became independent, it adopted the "common law" court system for the settlement of all disputes. This meant that we ended up with lawyer-ridden probate procedures not only for the transfer of land, but also for personal property. Even though this increased complexity made little sense, the system obviously benefited lawyers, and they have managed to keep probate procedures costly, technical and time-consuming ever since.

No other Western country has a will-probate system nearly as lawyer-ridden as ours—a fact which comes as a shock to many probate lawyers. England no longer requires lawyers and court proceedings for many probates. In 1926 (not exactly last week), that island adopted a simplified probate procedure. After a death there, the person named in the will as the executor traces the dead person's assets and debts, and files an accounting with the tax authorities who appraise the property and assess any death taxes due. Then the executor applies for a "general grant of probate" at a court administrative office, which provides assistance on any technical transfer problems. If the papers are in order, as they normally are in routine cases, the grant of probate can be issued in as little as seven days. The executor insures that all debts are paid, and distributes the remaining property to inheritors. Lawyers are not involved at all, unless a lawyer happens to be named as executor, or if some conflict develops such as a challenge to the validity of the will, a contested creditor's claim, etc.

In civil law countries (most of Europe), probate is even simpler. Wills are presented to a notary (a quasi-judicial official) when they are first prepared and are largely free from attack. Upon death, the dead person's "universal successor" (named in the will and similar to an executor) performs the probate functions without any judicial or direct administrative supervision. In the rare case of conflict, the dispute is handled like any other legal proceeding. Meanwhile, our probate system creaks on, taking months or years, and thousands of dollars in legal fees, to accomplish what is accomplished elsewhere quickly and cheaply.

Aside from writing your legislators (many of them lawyers) to demand probate reform (don't hold your breath), what can you do to escape high probate costs? You can take advantage of certain conventional legal methods that allow you to transfer your property outside of probate. While none of these is either dangerous or complicated, each method does require some planning and work. Is it worth the bother? That's obviously up to you, but many people can achieve large savings with a minimum of effort. Incidentally, if you do *no* planning at all, your property will pass under the "intestate" laws, to specific blood relations, as set out by state law. This is called dying "intestate" and probate of all your property will be required. Dying "intestate" makes little sense if you've gone to the trouble of acquiring property. Why have thousands of dollars consumed in probate fees that could otherwise go to people, causes, or institutions you care for?

There are several methods you can use to avoid probate, including:

Revocable intervivos trusts, (commonly called a "living trust"). This is a paper device by which you legally transfer specified assets to a trust. You are the trustee, retain complete control over the transferred property, and can revoke the trust whenever you so decide. When you die, the beneficiary of the trust (whom you name) quickly receives the property outside of probate.

"Joint Tenancy." Owning property "in joint tenancy" or "as Joint Tenants" gives the other joint tenant(s) an automatic right of survivorship. By using these magic legal words, the surviving joint tenant(s) receive the share of the deceased joint owner with no need to go through probate.

Gifts. Property that has been transferred to another prior to death obviously doesn't go through probate.

"Totten trust." Sometimes called a "savings book trust," this is no more than a simple revocable trust that can be opened in minutes by completing standard forms at any bank, savings and loan, or credit union. For example, "John Adams in trust for John Quincy Adams." When John dies, John Quincy receives the money outside of probate. But as long as John is alive, the money is his and John Quincy has no right to it.

Each of these methods has its own advantages, complexities and drawbacks. There is no one right way for everyone to transfer property. For example, intervivos trusts are legal entities, and paperwork is required—a taxpayer I.D. number obtained, trust records maintained, sometimes tax returns filed. With joint tenancy, one possible drawback is that any joint tenant can sell his or her half interest in the jointly owned property at any time—and the person setting up the joint tenancy can't prevent it. Gifts obviously involve the loss of legal ownership over the property given and, if you give someone more than $3,000 per year, render you liable for gift taxes. "Totten trusts" are easy and have no real drawback so far as they go—no paperwork is required after the account is open, and you have complete control over the account while you live —but they can be used only for cash, not other assets.

Which method, or methods, of probate avoidance make most sense for you? Should you transfer all your property outside of probate, or is it desirable to leave a will, even though that would require probate of some of your property? As soon as you ask questions like these, you enter the field of estate planning. To answer them wisely, you should understand all of the possible uses of a will, the pros and cons of each method of probate avoidance, and how tax planning can save you a bundle. In short, you should make a comprehensive estate plan.

Estate planning is a broad field. As I've said, probate avoidance is one important component of it, but by no means the only one. People with estates up to $500,000 can sensibly do a great deal of their own planning. Once an estate plan is made, you may want the security of having your plan reviewed by a lawyer. Doing it this way will cost you far less than if you just dump everything into the lawyer's lap in the beginning.

A sensible estate plan covers (at least) the following:

- Arranging for disposition of your body'
- Making a plan to distribute your property;
- Deciding if you want a will and preparing one if you do;
- Minimizing or avoiding probate;
- Minimizing or avoiding death taxes.

IN SOUTHERN MELANESIA THE HOUSES, FISHING NETS AND OTHER POSSESIONS OF A PERSON WHO HAS DIED ARE DESTROYED. EVEN THE CROPS AND FIELDS ARE PUT TO THE TORCH.

All of this can become complicated, but it doesn't have to be nearly as forbidding as professionals make it seem. The first thing that you need to do is to get good information. There are several books that claim to help non-lawyers with estate planning. As the author of one,[1] there's a chance that I'm biased against others. But even allowing for this, it's fair to say that many are written by established lawyers and adopt a "you-must-have-a-lawyer-do-it-all philosophy." A good test of any how-to-plan-your-own-estate materials is to check what is said about probate. If the book attempts to justify or rationalize our present probate system, be wary. Also, look for specific how-to-do-it methods — forms, rules, etc. — not just vague general advice. Each state has its own laws on probate, death taxes, etc. so you will want to find materials and rules for your own state. Of particular interest are the "how-to-do-it" books written for lawyers. (They never teach the practical stuff in law school.) Most states have these books and they can be found in local law libraries, law schools, etc.

While I don't have space to give you the mechanics necessary for actually planning your estate, I can offer a few tips (not to be confused with definitive legal advice).

IN POLAND THE ESTATE IS SETTLED ON THE EIGHTH DAY AFTER THE FUNERAL. THE SOUL OF THE DEPARTED IS FELT TO BE WATCHING WHICH DOESN'T NECESSARILY PREVENT SQUABBLES AMONG THE HEIRS

■ Commercial funerals can be very expensive — often the third most expensive life-time purchase (after house and car). The best examination of the commercial funeral business is Jessica Mitford's *The American Way of Death*, a fascinating look at the unique (many think grotesque) development of commercial funeral parlors, undertakers, embalming, "grief therapy," etc.

■ There are many alternatives to commercial funeral parlors, including funeral societies, cremation, donation of your body to medical school, or body parts to transplant banks. The need for body parts — heart, kidney, ears, eyes, even knees — is great and growing.

■ Probate can, as I've said, be avoided, or probate fees greatly reduced, through the common sense application of several devices such as joint tenancy, totten trusts, etc.

■ A will is often advisable even though most property is transferred outside of probate. A will that covers most normal situations and desires can be readily drafted by a non-lawyer. There are a few technical legal requirements you must check for in your own state's law, but not as many as you might think. Generally, your will should be typed (handwritten wills are legal in some states, but are not recommended except for very small estates), and must clearly state that it is your will. In addition, the finished product must be dated, signed by you, and be witnessed (in some states only two witnesses are required). In most states, that's about it.

■ If your "taxable" estate — basically the value of all you own, whether it's transferred by probate or other methods — is less than $175,625, your estate won't owe any federal estate taxes. If your estate is worth more than $175,625, there are several ways you can significantly reduce federal estate taxes although not as many as you'd hope. Major ways of reducing federal estate taxes include:

■ Making gifts (check the rules here first. Aside from gift taxes, gifts must be made at least three years before death or they are automatically disallowed for federal estate tax purposes).

---

1. *Planning Your Estate with Wills, Probate, Trusts & Taxes,* California Edition, Nolo Press; soon to be available in Texas and other states, published by Addison-Wesley. (See review in part VI of this book for more information — ed.)

■ Transfers of life insurance so the insured is not the legal owner (if transferred as a gift, the usual case, it must be given at least three years before death).

■ Use of federal estate tax exemptions, particularly the "Marital deduction," primarily useful for leaving property to a surviving spouse in non-community property states.

■ Certain trusts, particularly "generation skipping transfers," i.e. trusts where a grandparent leaves money in trust for his or her grandchildren, with only the income of the trust to go to his children.

■ State death tax rules vary considerably from state to state. Nevada is the only state that doesn't have any. In general, state death taxes must be paid on smaller estates than federal taxes, but the taxes themselves are not as steep.

Oops—almost out of space. These suggestions will, I hope, indicate that you, and your inheritors, can benefit substantially if you do some estate planning. One final note—why do we allow inherited wealth at all? Or, to reverse the question, why do we tax inherited wealth at all? Clearly, there is no "natural law" at work here. As a society we make decisions about money, including inherited wealth, and these decisions become the underpinning for all the complexities of estate planning. If we don't like what's going on, we can make different decisions. For example, the 1976 Federal Tax Reform Act was designed, according to its drafters, to eliminate the loop-holes the very rich had used for years to pass on the bulk of their wealth free of estate taxes. Before 1977 (when the Act became law), property left in a "generation skipping trust" escaped death taxes entirely on the middle generation. Thus, pre-1977 if you left property in trust for your grandchild with

the income to go to your child during her life, there would be no death taxes when your child died. The '76 Tax Reform Act limited that tax exemption to $250,000 per child—if you have three kids who each have two kids, you can transfer a total of $750,000 to the grandchildren tax free by these trusts. But any amount over $250,000 per child (it makes no difference how many grandchildren there are) is taxed at the federal death tax rates, whether a trust is used or not.

Not being rich myself, or in line to inherit millions, I'm all for taxing millionaire inheritors. Why should some rich loafer live off the sweat of his parents' brow while the rest of us work? Without going into the intricacies of the 1976 Tax Reform Act, let me state that on paper it looks good. I've heard that it was written after Nelson Rockefeller—up for Vice-President at the time—was grilled intensively by Congressional staffers to unearth all the tricks his family used to preserve its wealth. There are those who think the '76 Tax Reform Act was truly—if very quietly—a radical measure, and will lead to greater economic equality in the United States. Perhaps so, but on the basis of no evidence at all (I don't have millionaire clients), I suspect that big money will find a way to buy itself "legal" loopholes as it usually does. In fact, I'm prepared to bet that the '76 Tax Reform Act will not produce radical results. Any takers? Anybody know if it's working or not?

Denis Clifford is the author of Planning Your Estate with Wills, Probate, Trusts and Taxes, *one of the most successful self-help law books ever published. He lives in Berkeley, California, where, among other things, he makes beautiful stained glass windows.*

Living Together Contracts

by Toni Ihara

Had Lee and Michele Marvin followed the simple advice Toni Ihara gives in "Living Together Contracts," they might have avoided ten years (so far) of litigation. If you need an example of just how out-of-control our legal system is—though you probably have several of your own—remember that the Marvins' lawsuit has now lasted three years longer than they actually lived together.

Changing times, the industrial and sexual revolutions, and a healthy dose of pragmatism have produced a social climate that has nurtured a kaleidoscope of personal relationships that defy all the old labels. There are couples living together who want to be treated as if they were married; there are couples living together precisely because they *don't* want to be treated as if they were married and there are married couples who would just as soon not have the marriage laws of the state apply to them. To be or not to be married? As more and more people decide on relationships that vary from the old "until death do us part" norm, the legal consequences become more and more curious. Every state has a stack of laws governing the rights and obligations of the married. For the first three-quarters of this century, people who lived together without benefit of a license lived in a virtual legal vacuum. And then, along came Lee and Michelle Marvin, that peculiarly unattractive couple who dragged their egos and paranoia across our T.V screens and ended forever the notion that living together was simple.

In December of 1976, the California Supreme Court rendered a decision in the *Marvin* case that made hundreds of thousands of unmarried couples sit up and take notice. Here was one of the most influential courts in the country decreeing that when an unmarried couple separated, the court would not only uphold written contracts agreed upon by the couple, but would also recognize oral and implied contracts. And that wasn't all, the Court went on to say that if fairness so dictated, it would enforce a whole battery of equitable remedies.

Well, the *Marvin* case and its progeny have filled the once blissful legal void that used to govern the relationships of unmarried couples, and the ensuing muddy legalisms are confusing to everyone—everyone, that is, but the lawyers who, not surprisingly, are the only people who clearly gain by this new legal trend to oversee and administer the lives of unmarried couples. After all, who else can allege the terms of implied contracts and attempt to prove the facts of an agreement which had "pooled" possessions?

What becomes evident to any unmarried couple who has paid attention to the unsavory court battle between the Marvins is the need to order their lives in a way that will avoid ending their relationship in a similar manner. But what exactly must be done? Happily, the solution is simpler than you might expect. At a practical level, every unmarried couple should sit down as early as possible and articulate their expectations and understandings about property and finances and whatever else is important to them. When they arrive at a clear understanding, it should then be written down in the form of a contract. It doesn't matter whether the couple is straight or gay. In most states, as long as an agreement involves property and doesn't mention "sexual services" (why should it?), indications are that the reasoning of the *Marvin* case will be applied to contracts between gay and lesbian couples as well.

Contracts? Yuck! Your brow furrows as visions of fine-print, standard form documents leap to mind. You are justifiably apprehensive at the prospect of a contract because it is likely that all of your prior experiences have been negative and one-sided. Automobile contracts, insurance contracts, bank loans, leases—all come complete with incomprehensible jargon and inalterable clauses, with your only input being a signature on the dotted line. Whoever heard of anyone calling up General Motors and saying "Hey General, how about a little extension of that one year warranty?"

Fortunately, living together agreements are different. You are free to design your agreement to say exactly what you want, in words that you can understand. And, there is nothing illegal about writing a contract in simple English. "Wherefores" and "pursuants" have to do with lawyers' institutional need to confuse issues, not with contracts themselves. Legally, a contract need be no more than your promise to do something in exchange for someone else's promise to do something in return. And while contracts can be oral, writing down your expectations is a good way to record your shared recollection and is the best way to avoid paranoia and stay out of court. Given our adversary domestic relations system, any money or property that exists at the start of a court fight almost always gets consumed by the lawyers. In the end, personal disputes can only be solved well by the people involved.

But before you can actually draw up an agreement, you must have given adequate thought to the nature of the contract you wish to make. There is as wide a variety of possible economic arrangements as there are different sorts of people. Indeed, the fact that you do have the freedom and flexibility to sensibly order your life in the way you want, free from the traditional institutional rules of marriage, is one of the reasons why living together has become so popular. Many people who live together want to keep their property (or most of it) separate, while others operate on the assumption that what belongs to one belongs to both. A couple may choose to pool a part, but not all, of their earnings, or form a partnership, or hold property as joint tenants, or

compensate one person for services of benefit to the other, or agree to any of countless other plans. Living together agreements can also include anything relevant to the living together arrangement, including division of housework, whether or not to have children, and in the case of separation, who would have custody of the children. Sometimes there are provisions about who should feed the cat and water the plants. However, agreements are normally only enforceable in court when they concern real and personal property. Provisions relating to children will only be enforced by a court if the court, in its independent judgment, believes that the contract terms are in the best interest of the children. Provisions having to do with personal conduct are not enforceable because courts don't want to be in the business of telling you or your friend to dust more often or to stop squeezing the toothpaste in the middle.

Here are examples of two of the simplest kinds of property agreements—one to keep things together, and one to keep things separate.

★☆★☆★☆★☆★☆★☆★☆★

Toni Ihara is the author (with Ralph Warner) of The Living Together Kit, *published by the Fawcett Publishing Company. She is one of the original members of the Nolo Press Collective and has written a number of books and articles on self-help law. She is a lawyer, but doesn't practice—preferring, she says, "to be an honest woman."*

Sample Agreement (Together)

Jennifer LeBlanc and Dennis Jacobs agree as follows:

1) That they have been living together and plan to do so indefinitely;

2) That all property earned or acquired by either Jennifer or Dennis prior to their living together belongs absolutely to the person earning or acquiring it [an itemization can be attached to this agreement];

3) That while they are living together, all income and property earned and accumulated by either Jennifer or Dennis, whether real or personal, belongs in equal shares to both and that should they separate, all accumulated property shall be divided equally;

4) That should either Dennis or Jennifer inherit or be given property, it belongs absolutely to the person receiving the gift or inheritance;

5) That the separate property of either Dennis or Jennifer covered in paragraphs 2 and 4 of this agreement can become the separate property of the other or the joint property

of both, only under the terms of a written agreement;

6) That should Jennifer and Dennis separate, neither has claim for property or support except as set out in paragraph 3.

Date _____   _____
                                  Jennifer LeBlanc

Date _____   _____
                                  Dennis Jacobs

Sample Agreement (Separate)

Marlene Petrocelli and Winthrop Marsh agree as follows:

1) That they have been living together and plan to do so indefinitely;

2) That all property whether real or personal owned by either Marlene or Winthrop as of the date of this agreement shall remain the separate property of the title holder [if there is a large amount of property you will want to include an itemization];

3) That Marlene and Winthrop will share their love and good energy, but they agree that the income of each, and any accumulations of property traceable to that income, belong absolutely to the person who earns the money. Any joint purchases shall be made under the terms of paragraph 7 below;

4) That in the event of separation neither Marlene nor Winthrop has a claim upon the other for any money or property for any reason unless there is a subsequent written agreement to the contrary under paragraph 7;

5) That Marlene and Winthrop shall each use his/her own name and will maintain his/her own bank accounts, credit accounts, etc.;

6) That the monthly expenses for rent, food, household utilities and upkeep, and joint recreation shall be shared equally;

7) That if, in the future, any joint purchases are made (such as a house, car, boat, etc.) the joint ownership of each specific item will be reflected on the title slip to the property, or by use of a separate written agreement which shall be signed and dated. Joint agreements to purchase or own property shall only cover the property specifically set out in the agreement and shall in no way create an implication that other property is jointly owned;

8) That property owned now, or acquired in the future, as the separate property of either Marlene or Winthrop, can only become the separate property of the other, or Marlene and Winthrop's joint property under the terms of a written agreement signed by the person whose property is to be reclassified;

9) That this agreement replaces any and all prior agreements whether written or oral, and can only be added to or changed by a subsequent written agreement.

Date _____   _____
                                  Marlene Petrocelli

Date _____   _____
                                  Winthrop Marsh

Crash = Cash: How to Handle Your Own Automobile Accident Claim

by Jeffrey Carter

There is probably no area of the law where lawyers receive more money for doing less work than in the auto-collision field. Commonly, a lawyer takes from 25 to 50% of each settlement, with 33% being about average. Lawyers argue that they are entitled to such whopping percentages because they take cases on a contingency fee arrangement basis—that is, they don't get paid if there is no recovery. But what they don't say is that they won't even touch cases that look like losers, and thus are overpaid most of the time. In recent years, there have been attempts at reform in the auto accident recovery area, since many people have come to realize that a large portion (about 25%) of the high auto insurance premiums we pay finds its way into the pockets of lawyers. "No-fault" auto insurance is one such reform scheme. But like most efforts to cut back lawyer fees, it has met with fierce opposition by the organized Bar. For example, here is part of a recent letter sent to lawyers by The Association of Trial Lawyers of America:

> *Dear Colleague:*
>
> *Without exaggeration, I can tell you that your support is sorely and urgently needed. We are leading the battle against restrictive tort [read auto accident] reform measures being proposed in legislatures across the land, and we need your help.*
>
> *We need you to help raise our collective voice in the controversies over legal specialization, regulation of attorney's fees, mandatory arbitration of medical malpractice claims, and no-fault insurance, just to name a few of the many issues which threaten to undermine our system of justice [bracketed material added].*

Personal injury, or P.I., law is one of the most familiar, if not infamous, fields of law practice in the eyes of the American public. Spectacular accidents and severe injuries, followed by highly publicized jury trials, huge monetary awards to victims, high attorney's fees—all these get substantial press coverage. And then there are the recent exposés of rings of lawyers, doctors and other conspirators who manufacture accidents and present fraudulent claims against insurance companies. It's not a pretty picture and has led to law reform efforts in many states to pass "no-fault" auto insurance plans.[1] But as "no-fault" insurance has thus far only been adopted in a minority of states, I will focus here on traditional "tort" liability rules which are in force in California, New York, and most other areas of the country.

The vast majority of claims made by accident victims are legitimate within the rules of the Anglo-Saxon American system of jurisprudence which provides for compensation in money to those injured as a result of someone else's negligence. In this article, I will attempt to explain this system and how you, as an automobile accident victim (theoretical, I hope), can most effectively make a claim against the insurance company of the person who has caused the accident, WITHOUT A LAWYER. To this end, we will go through a scenario, step by step, which is based on a "typical" rear-end collision in which the victim has suffered the even more typical "whiplash" injury.[2] If the injuries you have sustained are more serious, or are of a prolonged duration, or if you haven't settled your case and it is nearing one year[3] since the accident, it is extremely advisable to consult an attorney.

The Accident

Priscilla Innocenti, on her way home from her job, stops at a red light. Shortly thereafter, a car, owned and driven by David Whitless, crashes into the rear of Priscilla's car. The impact throws Priscilla forward and backward in her seat. (Fortunately, her fastened seat belt prevents her from hitting the windshield.)

Immediately After the Accident

Priscilla and David, though considerably shaken, are able to get out of their cars. The two exchange names, addresses, telephone numbers, car license numbers, and the names of their respective insurance companies. One of them calls the local police department. The cars are left in their accident positions. In addition to studying the accident scene and obtaining their names, addresses, etc., the police officer asks both Priscilla and David to describe their versions of the accident so that he can complete his report. A copy of this report will be available from the police department in written form within a few days at a cost of a few dollars. In this accident, there is no argument about fault, as David agrees that the accident was caused when he turned his head to stare at a perfectly maintained pink Edsel.[4]

Shortly Thereafter

Since Priscilla has her own "collision" coverage, she notifies her insurance company of the car's location. The company will send an appraiser to view the damage and, if reparable, will pay for the repair, less the "deductible" amount which Priscilla is obligated to pay. Later, Priscilla will demand the amount of her "deductible" from David's insurance company. She is also entitled to be compensated for the "loss of use" of her car. Thus, if it is going to take three weeks to repair Priscilla's car, her automobile rental costs for those weeks should be reimbursed by David's insurance company.

If Priscilla didn't have collision insurance, then she would have to get two estimates for repairs and send them to David's insurance carrier. Probably, David's company would then send Priscilla a check for the lower of the two.[5] If Priscilla's car was totalled, David's insurance company will offer to pay her the pre-accident market value of her car.

After she has called her insurance company, Priscilla notices increasing discomfort in her neck and back and goes to the local emergency room for an examination. X-rays are taken and no broken bones are found. The injury is diagnosed as "cervical and dorsal strain," or "whiplash" injury. The emergency room physician prescribes a cervical collar and tells Priscilla that if her symptoms continue or get worse, she should consult her physician. Over the next 24 hours, her symptoms do get worse—pain and stiffness increase. To Priscilla, "whiplash" is no longer a cartoon image of dozens of cervical collars cluttering an attorney's reception room.

The Day (or Two) After

Priscilla visits her family doctor. The diagnosis remains the same—cervical and dorsal strain. Her doctor prescribes treatment in the form of physical therapy. The doctor further advises her not to work for two weeks and recommends bedrest.

The initial contact with David's insurance company may occur within several days of the accident. If she hasn't heard from David's company after a few days, Priscilla should contact them. During these initial encounters, adjusters have been known to urge a quick (and cheap) settlement of a claim. Priscilla should tell the adjuster gently but firmly that she will notify the adjuster when she has finished medical treatment and recovered from her injuries. (Remember that neither Priscilla's insurance agent nor her insurance company have anything to do with her claim against David. Her company will only pay Priscilla to the extent of the coverage she has purchased and it will defend her if a claim is brought by David.) Priscilla has no obligation to engage in lengthy discourse with David's adjuster. In fact she could request that if David's adjuster has any questions for her, that they be submitted to her in writing. This will give Priscilla time to reflect upon the questions rather than feeling pressured.

The Next Few Weeks

Priscilla takes hot baths, rests frequently and has physical therapy several times per week. In addition, she keeps a regular diary, noting her condition (mental, as well as physical), what she is able and unable to do, etc. Gradually, Priscilla's condition improves. Physical therapy, which she was receiving three or four times a week, is now down to once or twice a week.

Twelve Weeks (or six, or nine, or sixteen, or however long it takes)

Priscilla reports to her doctor that she feels much better; therapy is discontinued. Priscilla requests that her doctor prepare a written report which includes her medical history related to the accident, diagnosis of the injuries, the course of treatment, and prognosis. She may have to pay a fee for this report, which can range from $25 to $100. (This fee is not covered by her insurance, nor should it be included as part of her medical bills which she submits to David's company.) Priscilla also obtains copies of the medical records from the hospital emergency room, as well as copies of all the medical bills related to her injuries (the emergency room, doctor, physical therapist, sales receipts for medication, cervical collar, etc.).

If Priscilla is covered by her own insurance policy for medical bills, she should submit her bills to her company for payment. Note, however, that virtually all automobile insurance companies offering medical coverage require that they be reimbursed if a claim is settled. Therefore, if Priscilla has other medical insurance—such as Blue Cross, Blue Shield, etc. — she should submit her claim to them, since she is usually not obligated to reimburse them if she receives any settlement money.

In addition to gathering medical information, Priscilla obtains a letter from her employer stating the days that she was absent from work and the resulting salary loss because of her injuries. Even if she has not lost actual wages because of accumulated sick pay or vacation pay, she is still entitled to compensation for that time. She should also document the property damage done to her car, if she has not already settled this aspect of her claim. By this time, Priscilla should have set up a neat file system in which she will keep photocopies of her documentation, letters, etc.

Once all this material has been obtained, Priscilla is ready to prepare her "settlement memorandum." This is simply a several-page narrative describing the accident, the injuries, course of treatment, and the interference with her life and work. (Priscilla will be able to be quite specific because she can quote passages from her diary.) It also includes a paragraph describing her job and the time and wages lost, as well as material documenting the repairs that were necessary to put her car back on the road, and concludes with a specific monetary demand for settlement. (A sample "settlement memorandum" follows the article.)

Settlement Talks

After the adjuster has received Priscilla's settlement package, he/she will review the material and evaluate the claim. This may take from a few days to a few weeks. Sometimes, the adjuster will want to review the medical records of the treating physician, and will send Priscilla an authorization for her signature so that these records may be obtained. In order to protect her privacy, Priscilla can write on the face of the authorization that the records to be provided are limited to those related to the accident of such-and-such date. After the evaluation is completed, the adjuster will call Priscilla to commence negotiations. If a few weeks pass without her hearing anything, Priscilla should call the claims adjuster.

The discussion Priscilla has with the claims adjuster may go something like this:

CA: "Well, let's see here—the property damage to your vehicle was only $350, and was minimal to our insured. The impact was apparently not very great and doesn't seem to justify the amount of treatment you received. And your injury was diagnosed as a moderate cervical strain. I think that your demand is too high, but I am prepared to offer you $X."

PI: "Listen, I don't think that because the damage to my car was only $350, that this is any indication that I was not thrown about quite severely when Mr. Whitless hit me. I went to a doctor immediately and she was the one who diagnosed my injury and prescribed treatment. And it was also she who agreed with me that I could stop the treatment when I felt I'd improved. You know I am not asking for a million dollars, but *I* was the one who received the injury, suffered the pain, lost a considerable amount of money, and missed opportunities for my career advancement. I think you have all of that information in the memo I sent you. In any case, your offer is not commensurate with all that I went through."

At some point in the conversation, Priscilla might say:

PI: "Okay, my original demand was a little high. We all know how bargaining takes place. I'll lower my demand to $X" [$300, $500, or $750 less than her opening].

The adjuster may, during this conversation, revise his original upward. She can continue haggling at this point, or she could say:

"Let's think it over and I'll get back to you in a few days."

The conversations could continue for a round or two more.

When an adjuster prefaces an offer by saying that it is the final offer, this may or may not actually be the case. The decision to accept the offer is one based on what is in the realm of fair and reasonable, as well as what a case similar to yours generally settles for in your area.

What Is a Fair and Reasonable Settlement?

Whiplash injury settlements can range from $500 to $7,500 or more. The average is usually found in the $1,500 to $4,500 range. To these amounts would be added the total wages lost by the victim. As there is often a bit of negotiation concerning the final settlement amount, a person normally makes a demand in excess of the amount he or she is willing to accept — perhaps one and a half to two times the figure he or she has in mind.

The offer made by the insurance company will vary from company to company, from adjuster to adjuster, and from region to region. The yardstick is generally derived from jury verdicts in the area. (San Francisco juries award larger sums 'than Omaha, Nebraska juries.) The insurance company offers usually fall between 2½ to 5 times the total medical billing, with the wage loss and any damage to the vehicle, if not already paid, added on.

These figures are somewhat arbitrary. After all, how much is it worth to feel crummy for two to three months and have virtually every aspect of one's life interrupted for this period of time? Ten dollars per day? Twenty dollars? One hundred dollars? What can I tell you except that on the average, the settlement ranges stated above are accurate.

In order to determine what is a reasonable settlement in your area, you may wish to consult with an attorney who specializes in plaintiff's personal injury cases (a lawyer who specializes in defense work represents insurance companies). You can do this by arranging for a consultation to review your case. Be sure to get the fee ($50 should be enough) set in advance and be sure that the attorney is supportive of the idea that you are representing yourself.

There are obviously many variations which could take place in the above hypothetical discussion — too many to attempt to anticipate and elaborate in this article. You should remember to be relaxed and amicable.

Adjusters for the insurance companies can be human. While representing their company's interests, they are, in the majority of cases, not trying to trick you. It is their job to settle claims. You should not feel pressured into accepting an offer — mull it over for several days. Often, their "top offer" may not be the top offer. Not infrequently, over time, offers will gradually increase. If, after the negotiation with the insurance company, you are dissatisfied with their offer, you may again consider consulting with an attorney and possibly making arrangements for him or her to carry on from this point. If this is done, there should be a clear understanding that the attorney fee will be derived only from the amount in excess of what you have already been offered.

For example, suppose Priscilla requests $4,000 (four times the amount of the $1,000 medical bill). The insurance company offers her only $2,100. At this point, she hires an attorney with the understanding that he or she will get paid ⅓ of any recovery over $2,100. If the lawyer gets the insurance company to raise the offer to $3,000, he or she would get $300 and Priscilla $2,700. This is substantially better than if she had a lawyer handle the entire case. In that situation, she would have received $2,000 and the lawyer $1,000.

When Priscilla has agreed on a settlement sum, the insurance company will prepare a draft (like a check) for that amount and will require that she sign a "release," which releases both the insurance company and David Whitless from any future claim relating to this accident.

Conclusion

If you have approached your claim methodically, more or less as outlined by this article, it is likely that you will be able to settle the claim for a reasonable amount. There are really no tricks or totally unexpected pitfalls to undermine your claim, or somehow make it worth millions, either. If you get lost, you can always consult an attorney. As a final caution, if your claim hasn't settled and you are a month or two from the expiration of the statute of limitations, you should see an attorney.

---

1. "No-fault" insurance laws have been passed in several states. The details vary greatly. If you are in a "no-fault" state, you should check your state law carefully. Basically, "no-fault" means that, regardless of who has "caused" the accident, an insured driver who suffers injury, and/or whose car is damaged, receives compensation from his or her own insurance company. This compensation is for out-of-pocket expenses and does not include damages for pain and suffering. However, some states have adopted modified "no-fault" laws that do allow collection for pain and suffering in some circumstances.
2. Whiplash injury is defined as a "cervical, lumbar, dorsal strain and/or sprain; often referred to as 'soft tissue' injury."
3. In most states, a lawsuit must be filed against the defendant (the culprit) within one year of the date of the accident, or else a claim will be barred by the Statute of Limitations. The fact that you are negotiating with the insurance company does not extend the time limit.

4. There isn't much space to discuss rules of negligence (fault) in detail here. Most states follow a comparative negligence system which would find that if a person were 50% at fault, his/her claim would be reduced by 50%. A recent California Appellate Court decision held that if party A was 70% at fault, she would be able to collect 30% of her loss from party B's insurance company; while party B would be able to collect 70% of her loss from party A's company. Note, however, that some states still follow the old contributory negligence rules which state that, if a person's negligence contributes to the accident even in a very minimal way, he or she cannot recover at all, even if the other person was significantly more at fault. If you want to do some research on this point, see *The Negligence Case—Comparative Fault*. Woods, Lawyers Co-operative Publishing Co. (1978 with 1980 Supplement).
5. Sometimes the insurance company will want the damage estimated by its own appraiser.

Jeffrey Carter practices law in Berkeley, California. He was one of the pioneers in establishing pro per tenants' rights clinics and has extensive experience in the personal injury field. And what is perhaps most important—Jeffrey plays trombone in the latin-punk dance band, the East Bay Mud. (For bookings call (415) 848-4752.)

---

8 December 1980

Jess Triet
Claim Representative
No State Insurance
P.O. Box 5421
Berkeley, CA 94701

               Re: Priscilla Innocenti
                   Your insured: David Whitless
                   Your File: 43ZM5900
                   Date/Loss: 6/23/80

Dear Mr. Triet:

Enclosed please find medical reports and bills, wage loss verification, and a settlement memorandum outlining the facts of the case and stating a demand figure. After having had an opportunity to review these materials, and at your earliest convenience, please call me so that we may discuss settlement.

                   Very truly yours,

                   Priscilla Innocenti

Settlement Memorandum – Priscilla Innocenti

Facts of Accident:

On June 23, 1980, I was stopped for a light at the intersection of Van Ness and Clay in San Francisco. My car was behind one other car when the car driven by David Whitless crashed into the rear of my auto, pushing it into the car in front.

Injuries and Discussion:

1. Cervical, lumbar, and thoracic strain and sprain.
2. Nausea.
3. Traumatic depression.

The force of the impact threw me forward and backward. Shortly afterward, I began feeling somewhat dissociated and nauseous. These symptoms persisted for a few days. Within twenty-four hours, I began developing pain and stiffness in my neck and back and I sought medical attention from my physician, Dr. Susan C. Monahan. I began a course of physical therapy at Central Hospital, which continued through July 31, 1980. As this treatment had certain beneficial effects but not others, I sought additional treatment from David Ross, D.C., which continued through September 2, 1980. Copies of Dr. Monahan's and Dr. Ross's reports and billings are attached to this memorandum. The treatments I received had a beneficial effect so that by mid-September I was able to resume most of my pre-accident level of activities. However, it was not until the end of October that I felt fully recovered from the injuries I sustained.

I am an extremely active person, aspiring to become a professional actress. I have worked with several theater groups including the Berkeley Shakespeare Festival and the Oakland Ensemble Theatre. As part of my daily routine, I would do calisthenics and run 2½ miles. Twice weekly I participate in two-hour Afro-Haitian dance classes. These activities were completely interrupted for approximately two months after the accident. In fact, on July 2, I noted in my diary that the physical therapist at Central told me that I should do no running or swimming for two months. This forced inactivity caused me great concern since I was unable to audition for roles (virtually all the auditions required various postures and movements which I was unable to perform).

I noted in my diary on July 4 that doing minimal/necessary errands exhausted me and caused pain in my neck and back, requiring me to lie down and rest for an hour or more thereafter. A July 7 entry:

Jess Triet, Settlement Memo   8 December 1980
Re: Priscilla Innocenti   Page two

I have been quite depressed as my neck aches as soon as I try to be the least bit active. I have auditions coming up and I'm afraid I won't be able to manage them. My neck is feeling worse today but hopefully it's only a phase. I can't carry anything, including my purse.

On July 11, I noticed that being upright for prolonged periods made me nauseous. Similar entries continue through mid-September, though gradually I noted improvement in my condition.

In my opinion, the psychological ramifications of my injuries and resulting inactivity should not be underestimated. Were I lethargic and relatively sedentary, several months of requisite passivity could perhaps be viewed as a minor inconvenience. However, a physically active lifestyle was and is central to my existence and the three-month interruption was extremely disturbing for me, a fact which can be seen throughout my diary of this period.

Wage Loss:
At the time of the accident, I was employed regularly by the Oakland Model's Agency (see attached wage loss verification letter) an average of twelve hours per week, at an average salary of $5.35 per hour. This work required me to sit, stand, and assume various postures for three-hour periods. Due to my injuries, I was unable to perform this work from the date of the accident until September 21, 1980. Total wage loss was as follows:

12 hours per week @ $5.35 × 13 weeks = $834.60

There is an additional item of wage loss, which, though not precisely determinable, must be taken into consideration, and that is the setback to my career as an actress. I was, during this period, unable to audition for parts and to perform and to keep in shape, which is mandatory in the performing arts. The financial effect is difficult to measure, yet this three-month involuntary hiatus is a factor to be weighed.

Medical Specials:

Susan Monahan, M.D.		$ 62.00
Central Hospital		1002.00
David Ross, D.C.		200.00
	TOTAL	$1264.00

Conclusion and Demand:
My life and vocational pursuits were virtually suspended for a three-month period due to the injuries sustained in the automobile accident caused by your insured. Based on the above facts and discussion, I, Priscilla Innocenti, demand settlement of my case in an amount of SEVEN THOUSAND FIVE HUNDRED DOLLARS ($7,500.00).

Very truly yours,

Priscilla Innocenti

Breaking Out of the Age Trap

by Edith Manley

When we were putting the People's Law Review *together, an unsolicited article slipped through the Nolo mail slot. Edith Manley had heard Ralph Warner and Toni Ihara of Nolo on San Francisco radio station KGO talking about doing your own law and wondered if we would be interested in her material on age discrimination and how to fight it. We hadn't thought much about the subject before, but thanks to Edith we started to and immediately decided to include her material here. Edith's article was followed by another serendipitous occurrence—D.J. Soviero, a San Francisco lawyer with much experience in age discrimination disputes, happened along just as we realized that none of us knew enough about the field to provide Edith with editorial assistance. D.J. made a number of excellent suggestions and pointed out that this was one area of law that, if it doesn't interest you now, almost surely will later!*

How many times have you heard it? "Nobody'll hire an old duffer like me; after all, I'm 53." "I think I could get that promotion if I just didn't have these bags under my eyes... I wonder if I could get a loan for a facelift?" "Laid off after 35 years on the job, there goes my pension. I guess I'll have to take odd jobs until I can get Social Security."

What is this anyway? Age discrimination, that's what it is. This discrimination is not new—it goes back years in American business and government. Employers want the dynamic young Turk, the svelte 23-year-old secretary, or at least, the experienced 31-year-old with a "great future." Managers make points of hiring and promoting younger and younger "tigers" who present an image of energy, modernism and, above all, youth, youth, youth. What is likewise pervasive is the idea that employees over 40 are tired out, sagging, slow to change, resistant to new techniques and likely to have a heart attack any day.

The victim of age discrimination isn't just the displaced homemaker, the widow or divorcee who has devoted a lifetime to home and family and is left with neither a steady income nor the skills necessary to earn one. It is also the machinist, 23 years on the job, whose company merges with another, resulting in a "retrenchment" or "consolidation" situation. What this means is that our 23-year veteran gets the ax and a 30-year old gets promoted. And what about that patient woman in the accounting department who has been studying for her degree at night for the past six years? When the job of accounting supervisor comes up, does she get the job? Not likely. Even though she knows every inch of the company's financial picture, she has gray hair and a "mature figure" and thus is passed over. And then there is the 45-year old who has been on the production line for 26 years. His doctor has told him that he has late-onset diabetes and he asks for a transfer to another less physically demanding job. The request is refused because the other department doesn't really want an older man with a health problem. "Stick it out for another four years on the line, at which time you can take an early retirement" (at a fraction of his salary), our man is told, and so he too experiences the bitter taste of age discrimination.

One brutal theme dominates each of these stories. Skilled, mature, experienced workers are being kicked around, ignored, passed over and put out to pasture because of their age. And sadly these older Americans often think that the fault is theirs—that there is something wrong with being 42 or 53 or 57. Older workers are ashamed of something they can't help; ashamed of something that's going to happen to all of us. Even more distressing is that many people who are unfairly passed over don't even get angry. Instead, they blame themselves—"I'm over 40, what else can I expect?"

Age discrimination has been called the "last, the lowest and the least of the equal employment civil rights." It will end only when it becomes too embarrassing and too costly for employers to continue it. And it's so sadly unnecessary, because employers need older workers. In test after test older workers have proved to be at least as adaptable as younger persons in learning new skills; they have less absenteeism and, in general, a greater devotion to that "work ethic" so prized by employers. It is expected that by the year 2000 there will be an increase of 22.1 million Americans over age 45. If you couple this with a declining birth rate, you get a picture of the future with fewer and fewer younger workers. So logically it would seem that employers, both public and private, should jump at the chance to hire, re-hire, train, and re-train and promote their over-40 workers. But, it just doesn't happen. Instead, employers give excuses on top of excuses in a frantic effort to justify not utilizing older workers.

But things are looking up—there is now a federal law forbidding age discrimination—the Age Discrimination in Employment Act (ADEA). It is proving to be an effective weapon with which to fight age discrimination. If you are a worker (or a job applicant) over 40, you are covered.

Briefly, the ADEA protects workers, ages 40 to 70, from arbitrary age discrimination in hiring, discharge pay, promotions, fringe benefits and other aspects of employment. The law applies to private employers of 20 or more workers; federal, state and local governments; employment agencies serving several employers; and most labor organizations of 25 or more members, including those that operate hiring halls or recruit workers for employers. The ADEA is administered by the Equal Employment Opportunity Commission (EEOC) which also has the duty of investigating complaints of discrimination based on race and sex.

You should also be aware that 42 states have laws prohibiting age discrimination. These are usually administered by agencies known variously as Civil or Human Rights Commissions, Commissions Against Discrimination, or Fair Employment Practices Commissions. But the state laws vary tremendously in effectiveness. Some states have age discrimination laws with real teeth; they are usually linked with tough race and sex bias state laws. But others have laws that are little more than wishy-washy statements which disapprove of age discrimination. Contact your state agency and carefully read its information packet. If it turns out that your state has a weak, ineffective age bias law, ignore the state agency and file your complaint directly with the EEOC. If a state or federal agency can't or won't help you, you have the right to bring a private lawsuit. I talk more about this later.

Okay, now let's assume that you are convinced that you are being discriminated against. You genuinely believe that with your work record and qualifications, you would be treated more favorably if you were younger. What do you do? Well, if you are considering making a complaint, you must do it correctly. In general, personnel departments know all about ADEA and they won't make the mistake of announcing that they don't hire, or promote, people over a certain age. If you want to prove that you are a victim of age discrimination, you must first do your homework. Here are some suggestions.

Start with a SELF-APPRAISAL. Ask yourself if you are being discriminated against primarily because of your age. Write down a self-evaluation.

1. Have you abused sick leave? Become careless over the years? Taken too many Mondays and Fridays off?

2. What are your relationships with co-workers and supervisors? If you're a troublemaker, management has probably noticed.

3. Most important, how good are your skills? Have you kept abreast of new regulations, new processes, new techniques? Do you express an unwillingness to do some job because "That isn't the way we used to do it," or worse, show an attitude of meekness, insecurity, lack of self-esteem?

If you're presently unemployed, you can apply this same checklist with some minor modifications. It's important to remember that "unfair treatment by your employer" is not the same as "illegal treatment." But it's important to remember something else too—don't be too tough on yourself. You don't have to be perfect to deserve good treatment. If you can do the job as well, or better, than younger workers, you deserve to be treated accordingly.

Let's say you've come through the SELF-

APPRAISAL pretty well, and you firmly believe you've been discriminated against because of your age. How do you prove it? Use your common sense and ask around. Who got the new job? Who got the promotion? Use your eyes and ears. Ask discreet questions. Look for patterns. Is this company known in the community and/or by other employees, to hire and promote only young people? Employment statistics can often be of great help. What is the age composition of your work force? Do your co-workers get hired young and leave as they get older? In one recorded case, 60% of the terminations were employees 50 years of age and over, even though only 29% of the work force was that age. In another, of the 35 people hired as tellers, all were under 40. In fact, only three tellers were over 30. Statistical patterns aren't absolute proof, but they would add weight to your total argument that age was a factor in your situation.

Now, you've done your self-appraisal and you've asked around about the job, and you are convinced that you are a victim of age discrimination. What next?

1. Keep a file. *Start documenting your case.* Keep a copy of every single document that could possibly relate to your situation. If you're a mess at keeping records, have your spouse or a good friend help you. *It's very important.*

2. Write a letter to the company/agency asking why you have been rejected for the job or promotion or transfer. Ask for a written response and put it in your file.

3. Keep a diary. Enter every date, incident, phone conversation, comments and the names of all persons involved. This diary will be very important later, when you explain to a disinterested third party

what the sequence of events was. You should also include in your diary basic scuttlebutt about age — that is, how it is viewed and treated in your company. For example, if the grapevine says B.B. didn't get the sales manager's job because of his age, write it down even though you don't know B.B. at all.

Your diary might look something like this:

Aug. 14: Applied for promotion to Clerical Supervisor. Self-Appraisal okay.

Aug. 21: Informed by personnel (phone call) that N. Jones got the job. Asked G.J. about N. Jones — came to company four years ago. I've been here 14 years.

Aug. 27: S.L. works in that department. Says N. Jones is 26 years old and came to the company after seeing a job announcement that promised fast promotion for "recent graduates."

Sept. 3: Wrote a letter to personnel asking why I was rejected for this position. Copy in file.

Sept. 8: Phone call from C. Smith in personnel. "They don't give out that kind of information."

Sept. 15: Phone call from friend, L. Davis. Says three new people hired yesterday. All under 30. Doctor has put me on tranquilizers. Can't sleep nights.

Oct. 17: Received letter from personnel signed L. Johnson.

Well, you get the idea. All these occurrences can help prove to an investigator that there is a pattern of age discrimination even though management will flatly deny it.

Where Do We Go from Here?

If after all these preliminary steps — the application, the rejection, the self-analysis, request for reasons for refusal, the diary — you are absolutely convinced that you are a victim of age discrimination, then you should be burning with rage. It's not fair, it's not legal and you don't have to tolerate it.

You're ready to make your complaint — but it's not easy. If you make a fuss and lose the job you have, it will be hard to find another at your age. Isn't that the basic problem? Age discrimination again. But hang in there. Retaliation for fighting age discrimination under the ADEA can also be illegal. If you've got a good case, pursue it; the law's on your side.

Go about your complaint in the proper way. Most legal and government complaint mechanisms require that you exhaust all administrative channels before a formal charge is made. The place to start complaining is within your company. To do this, look up your company's personnel policies. Somewhere you'll find a section on discrimination. Follow the procedures exactly. Put your complaint in writing. If you are unsure of how to do this, have a friend help. Complaints usually have to be made within a certain time limit after the discrimination occurs. Pay close attention to this limit. If you are covered by a union contract, file a grievance with your union too.

Once you have made your complaint under your company's personnel policy, the die is cast. From now on you must hang tough. Be prepared for the atmosphere at work to turn decidedly chilly. Be sure that your job performance is excellent.

Getting the Government Into the Act

At the same time that you file an internal personnel complaint and a union grievance, write a letter of complaint (the "charge") to the Equal Employment Opportunities Commission of the federal government. They are in the phone book under "U.S. Government Offices." If you are in a remote area, write to the EEOC in Washington, D.C. for the address of your nearest regional EEOC office. Your charge letter doesn't have to be fancy, but it must tell some facts about your situation. Here your self analysis and diary will be invaluable. Often it is not difficult to know the exact date of the discrimination; it is the date you were fired, or notified you would not be hired. But if the discrimination is of the continuing sort—not being promoted, not receiving the same benefits as younger workers, etc., there is no one date of discrimination. You will want to file as soon as circumstances demonstrate there is a good likelihood that you are in fact experiencing discrimination because of your age. Charges filed with the EEOC should be made within 180 days of the violation.

As I mentioned above, many states also have laws barring age discrimination, and procedures to enforce these laws. States *without* laws providing protection from age discrimination are Alabama, Arkansas, Kansas, Mississippi, Missouri, Tennessee, Vermont, Virginia, and Wyoming. And since there is usually a time limit for filing a complaint with a state agency, check on this and then keep

within its limits. If you file with both the state agency and the EEOC, the agency you filed with first will handle the matter, except that a charge made originally to EEOC will be referred to the state agency for information purposes. But if you intend to file a lawsuit (and you should not discount this possibility), you *must* file with *both* the state agency (if there is one in your state) and EEOC.

Shortly after you have filed your written charge, and EEOC employee will arrange a personal interview. Keep the interview businesslike and don't get emotional. The specialist is interested in the facts and how they apply to federal law. It is here that your diary will be most useful. Make a short outline of the sequence of events, including not only your own situation, but the names and situations of others in your company. Bring it along to the interview together with any written material you can find, such as company memos, job announcements, relevent letters, your employment evaluations, etc. to back up your allegations. Also, bring your own performance evaluations and other helpful documentation to the interview. One general area of employer personnel policy you should be particularly careful to check out involves the common employer practice of terminating or "squeezing out" employees before their pension rights vest. Common ways of doing this involve putting older employees into physically demanding jobs over their objections, or promoting them into jobs that they don't want and can't handle. In both situations, the employee is eventually forced out for poor job performance.

Try A Little Consciousness Raising

Well, you've come this far and you never thought you'd have the nerve, did you? Perhaps now it's time (or even past time) to get some support. The complaint process that you are embarked on can work for other over-40 year old workers in your company or your community. Try talking to some of your older friends on the job. If you've been victim of age bias, other workers probably have too. See if you can't form a network of support among the older workers. Encourage others to file EEOC complaints. You may be surprised and shocked to learn that most older workers know nothing about age discrimination laws. Make it your mission to tell them and to allay their fears about the complaint process. When

you spread the word, be discreet about it. In other words, do it on your time, not on company time.

What to Expect from an EEOC Complaint

What's the worst that can happen as a result of your complaint? You may lose—that's what. Keep in mind that if the employer has a "bona fide occupational qualification" related to age regarding the particular position that you want, and can prove it, you will lose. You already know that you *can* be discharged or refused hire because of a bad performance record, and company "discrimination" won't help. These negative comments are given not to discourage you but to insist that you keep a realistic attitude toward the whole process of complaint. You're not in this thing unless you're over 40 years old, and let's hope that your 40 and more years have given you the maturity of knowing that not everyone in this world loves you and that there is a big difference between justice and the law.

The process of handling an age discrimination charge through EEOC or the state agency begins with conciliation. Once the agency has interviewed you and has otained all possible information, the specialist assigned to the case writes up the facts and sends a registered letter to the employer informing him that a complaint has been filed. A conciliation meeting is arranged between the EEOC specialist, the employer representative, and you. This procedure offers a quick and easy way to achieve a settlement and complaints are often settled at this stage,

especially in the "open and shut" situation (the foreman said to you in front of witnesses who would testify, "I'll never hire that guy . . . he's too old.")

Employers often want to settle disputes at the conciliation phase. They don't want the hassle and expense of drawn-out investigation by federal and state government. If your dispute is unique—that is, the company can re-hire or promote you without setting a broad (and expensive) precedent—they are particularly likely to do so. But if your action will open the door, or they perceive it will open the door, to a whole class or group of people being hired, re-hired, or promoted, and it's going to cost lots of money, your employer will be less likely to settle easily. If you are offered a settlement, be sure that it's one you can live with.

If conciliation fails, EEOC will conduct an investigation. Generally, employers dread these investigations because they may reveal a widespread pattern of discrimination. The discovery and remedy of such a pattern is very costly since it requires a complete overhaul of employment practices to bring the company into line with federal and state guidelines. If EEOC finds serious abuses of ADEA in your situation, it will probably refer the matter to federal attorneys for litigation. The federal attorneys may not accept the case. If they do bring it to court, they probably believe you have a strong, legally defensible action. In this case, the lawsuit will be in your name, but you will have the full weight and investigatory power of the U.S. Government behind you.

Should You Get A Lawyer?

ADEA gives you the right to sue the company/agency directly, but you must file a charge with the EEOC within 180 days of the discrimination and must have contacted the appropriate state agency first. After 60 days from the date the charge has been filed, you may file your own lawsuit. This is different from having the government sue for you. It's your case and you have the right to trial by jury. Direct lawsuits have been instituted in a number of cases. If you have the resources, it's probably a good idea.

The results of age discrimination lawsuits filed by individuals, have been mixed; some have gone in favor of the company; some have resulted in favorable verdicts for the plaintiff (victim). Remember, if you get a lawyer, you are facing a full-fledged legal action with all the expense and time involved. Some attorneys will offer you a contingency arrangement; that is, you will agree to pay the attorney some percentage of actual and liquidated damages assessed if you win your suit. This sort of arrangement is particularly likely if you are part of a large group who have all been discriminated against in a similar fashion. But attorneys' fees are only part of the story in an ADEA suit. You must also pay the costs of investigation. This legal investigation is called "discovery." It involves obtaining personnel records and researching them to discover ages of persons in specific classifications, ages of those promoted, originally hired, etc. Depositions (testimony transcribed outside the courtroom) from various persons, such as co-workers, supervisors, personnel representatives, are needed.

The courts have specifically ruled that punitive damages may not be given in ADEA suits. Thus, if you file suit and win, you will recover lost pay and benefits if any, plus any monies you would have received if you hadn't been discriminated against in promotions, job classifications, etc. ADEA lawsuits can get you a new job, or an old job back, or a promotion, but they will probably not get you a bundle of easy money. There is no recovery for "pain and suffering" even though you've had plenty of both.

Is It Worth It?

As you can see, fighting for your rights can be a time-consuming affair from the initial charge until some resolution is reached. It also involves real commitment on your part and some hard decisions; whether to file with your own state's agency or the EEOC, whether to get a private attorney or not. But the over-40 worker has *no* other recourse but these complaint procedures, at least until there is some turnaround in public attitudes.

So the final word is this—make it your personal mission to do some outreach and political action to remedy this national injustice. The problem of age discrimination in employment demands affirmative action programs similar to those of the race and sex bias laws. This will not come about without public pressure and vigorous enforcement by EEOC of all complaints.

Edith Manley holds a Master's Degree in Public Administration and has made a special study of age discrimination in employment. She is interested in hearing from those who have been victims of age bias in employment, since she would like to form a national network to combat this practice. Contact her at P.O. Box 6358, Hayward, CA 94540.

Paying With Plastic:
Protect Yourself With a Letter

by Howard Anawalt

When we talk about self-help law, it's easy to imagine ourselves striding Perry Mason–like into a courtroom to vindicate our cause. In reality, of course, even lawyers get almost nothing done in courts, where the rules are obscure, cumbersome, and carefully designed to turn molehills into mountains. Lawyers—when they aren't simply trying to run up their bill—solve most everything by phone or letter. Knowing how to negotiate, how to write a good letter, what to say and who to say it to, are all important skills, both for the lawyer and the person who wishes to represent himself or herself in court. Here Howard Anawalt demonstrates how simple it is to protect our rights in one of the most common problem areas that affect us—credit card billing. It's almost disappointing that there isn't more to handling a legal problem, isn't it?

Every purchase you make these days is a personal confrontation with inflation. And the chances are good that you frequently pay with "plastic." Plastic is certainly convenient, but can be expensive if you pay over time. The use of credit cards also involves certain hazards, such as errors in billing. Knowing how to deal with this sort of problem involves "doing your own law" at its most basic and practical level.

It is important for credit card users to know their rights. Many of these rights come from a federal regulation called "Regulation Z." The creditor himself is required by federal law to give you a statement of your rights which is often labeled "In Case of Errors or Inquiries About Your Bill." Such a statement must be delivered to you prior to your first transaction with the card. Some creditors also print the statement on the back of their periodic bills. The statement is required to be an accurate rendition of the requirements of the Truth in Lending Regulations—Regulation Z.

The credit card account is an "open-end credit" account. The monthly statements which you receive from the bank or other creditor are typically too complicated to read or comprehend. Depending on your own bent, you may either go over your statement carefully, or scarcely at all. Whatever your personal habits, it is a good idea to look over a statement carefully, at least once.

Once in a while you may discover an error in your account. If this happens, you must *write a simple note to the creditor*; you must do this promptly if you want to preserve your rights. Refer to your monthly statement or your original contract for the requirements of Regulation Z. The following guidelines may also be helpful to you:

The Requirements of Your Protest Letter or Note:

1. Make sure it is in *writing*. (Keep a copy for yourself. A phone call may help, but it is the *written note* that protects your rights.)

2. Include your *name, account number*, and *address*.

3. Describe the *error*. (The description does not have to be lengthy.)

4. Briefly describe *why* you think it is an error.

5. Send the letter to the *address given* by the creditor. (Important: Check this address on the notice of the rights form from the creditor.)

6. The letter is usually required to be on a *separate piece* of paper from the bill. Do not just scribble on your bill and toss it in the mail—it will vent your feelings, but will not protect your rights.

7. Observe the *time limits*. These are stated in the notice of rights—"Mail it as soon as you can, but in any case, early enough to reach the creditor within 60 days after the bill was mailed to you."

A Sample Letter

Writing a letter which complies with the regulations is relatively easy. It can be short and handwritten. Here is a sample:

Sunshine National Bank
P.O. Box 27
Los Arboles, CA 95751

Ladies and Gentlemen:

I discovered an error in my bill for February 20, 1980. (Susan Jones, 21 Broad St., Los Arboles, CA, Master Charge #407-92171-218-419.) My check book shows that I made a payment to you of $29.00 on January 10, 1980 and it has not been credited on my bill.

I would really appreciate it if you would look into this and correct it for me. I hope to hear from you soon.

Susan Jones

The essential information in this note is stated in about 40 words. The last paragraph is not essential, but it makes things more comfortable for everyone involved if inquiries are made in a polite and friendly way.

The creditor must either correct the billing error or acknowledge the note within 30 days of receiving it. If the correction is not made within the first 30 days, the creditor has another 60 days to either correct the bill or explain why he believes the bill was correct. The creditor is not permitted to have either an attorney or collection agency take any action or report you to a credit bureau until the source of the error is determined. Furthermore, if the creditor does not follow the rules, he is not allowed to collect the first $50 of the disputed amount, even if the bill turns out to be correct. The creditor *is* permitted to continue sending you the regular statements of your account.

In Case of Poor Goods or Services
(15 U.S.C. 1661i)

There is a second situation in which writing a letter can protect your rights as a credit card user. Let us say you purchase a stereo set from a local merchant, using your credit card. According to the arrangement you've made with the merchant, the set is

delivered to your house the following day—but it doesn't work. One of the merchant's service personnel comes by and makes some adjustments and the set now works—but very poorly. If your efforts to get the matter straightened out with the merchant appear to have failed (it is a good idea to "document" these efforts), you can write to the bank or credit card issuer and preserve your right not to have to pay for defective merchandise. The following information should be included in your letter to the credit card issuer:

1. The name of the retailer
2. The date of purchase
3. The amount involved
4. The kind of goods or service(s) purchased (in this case, a stereo set)

5. The nature of your defense to the claim for payment (that the stereo does not work)
6. The efforts which you have taken to resolve the matter with the merchant.

Your letter might look like this:

---

211 Unity Lane
Fairfax, Texas

August 20, 1980

Big State Bank
1 State Plaza
San Angelo, Texas

Re: MasterCard Account #123456

Dear People:

I just received my MasterCard bill for August 14, 1980 (copy enclosed). Item three on the bill is $345.00 for a stereo which I purchased at Bill's Stereo in San Angelo on July 12, 1980.

When I got the stereo home, it worked poorly, and was unable to maintain a consistent tone. I called Bill's Stereo Shop and they sent a repair person to my home. While the adjustment improved things somewhat, the stereo still works very poorly and doesn't sound as good as my $19.95 portable radio. I have repeatedly asked Bill's to either fix or replace the set. To date they have done neither.

Therefore, please be informed that under the terms of 15 U.S.C. 1661i, I am refusing to pay for the stereo. I am sending you the balance of my bill.

Thank you for your consideration.

Sincerely,

Robert Von Gulick

If you do not write a letter, you will ordinarily be considered liable to the credit card issuer for the cost of the stereo.

The right to preserve defenses has some limits. If the card is issued by a third party, such as a bank (MasterCard, Visa) or a company (American Express or Carte Blanche), you can protest and withhold payment only where the value of the goods or service(s) sold exceeds $50 and where the transaction is local—that is, the purchase is made within your state or within 100 miles of the address which you have most recently supplied to the bank or other credit card issuer.[1] However, if the seller of the goods is owned and operated by the creditor/credit card company (a department store, gas company, or airline) or if the creditor mailed you an advertisement for the item, there are no limitations to your rights based on the amount of the purchase or the distance from your home. You can refuse to pay simply by notifying the credit card company as outlined above.

Remember, you have the right to withhold payment for a defective stereo or other types of defective goods and services. You may find yourself in conflict with the merchant who sold you the merchandise, or with the bank, but at least you will not have to initiate the action in order to get your money back. This is a very valuable right and one which you should use when you feel genuinely aggrieved. As with any strong remedy, you will want to use it in good faith — with usually means that you have tried to work things out with the merchant first.

A credit card does not have the legend "In God We Trust" engraved on it, but it has many of the advantages and risks of using cash, and requires your careful attention. The basic concept of "plastic" or "electronic" money is moving rapidly into new areas of our economy. For example, banks now offer direct payment and direct deposit arrangements, as well as banking withdrawal cards like "Versatel" and the "Express Banking Card." Errors are bound to occur in systems like these, just as they do in cash transactions. Be prepared to deal with an error. It takes literally only a few minutes, a few words, and a postage stamp.

----

1. Consumer Credit Protection Act, Section 170, 15 U.S.C. 1661i

Howard C. Anawalt is a professor of law at the University of Santa Clara, teaching constitutional law, communication law and torts. He has practiced law privately and for the government, and that practice has included work in criminal and commercial law, and civil rights.

Breaking Up:
Self-Help for Gay/Lesbian Couples
by Hayden Curry and Denis Clifford

Handling your own legal affairs, while usually a positive experience, is not, as a rule, an absolute necessity. For example, if you try to work out a settlement with your landlord and fail, you can always hire a lawyer and file formal court papers. But suppose you find yourself with a legal problem for which there is no established court or administrative procedure? Being in this position might be a bit scary. Certainly, if there is no possibility of getting help from the regular legal system, you have to take self-help law more seriously. If you are a gay/lesbian couple, you face that situation everyday. You can't get married or divorced, and your very right to exist is not acknowledged by much of the legal establishment. Unfortunately, despite the obvious need for it, there has been very little solid self-help legal information available for gay/lesbian couples. Finally, this vacuum has been filled with the publication of A Legal Guide for Gay/Lesbian Couples by Hayden Curry and Denis Clifford, an excerpt from which we include here.

1. Emotional Considerations

Splitting up with your lover is never easy and legal rules can't assist you much with the grief, pain, anger and sense of loss which will usually accompany your separation. Legal problems, such as who owns what, are rarely the real core of the separation experience, although we all know that fights over property can become a way for former friends to take out their frustrations on each other. Unfortunately, property disputes can degenerate into bitterness, and poison a relationship so that a separating couple ends up becoming enemies rather than maintaining a friendly relationship. To avoid this, we offer some practical advice on the settlement of your economic

affairs. But first, here are some observations about what's really involved in a separation.

The break-up of a couple, especially one which has been together for a while, is normally seen as a sad event, though it may well be a healthy step for the people involved. The very language used to describe the ending of a relationship can contribute to creating bitterness, rather than understanding. Breaking-up is often described as a "failure," while a relationship that lasts is called "successful." To us, it seems a peculiar notion that the duration of a relationship should determine its worth. In fact, the very idea that the concepts of "success" and "failure" are applied to love in the first place, strikes us as crazy. We were impressed with E.M. Forster's description (from "What I Believe," in *Two Cheers for Democracy*) of the man who always views the world in terms of winning and losing:

> He fails with a completeness which no artist and no lover can experience, because with them the process of creation is itself an achievement, whereas with him the only possible achievement is success.

Love is complete in itself; it isn't a struggle toward some end product. What matters in a break-up is not "what do I have to show for my one–five–or fifteen years with you?" but rather, the preservation of whatever positive remains from living together and loving one another during those years. And even if in retrospect that time looks bleak and insincere, nothing good can be salvaged from it by being mean or nasty during the separation process. We know that this all sounds obvious, but still, it is worth remembering and it does put property disputes in perspective.

2. If You Want an Expensive Nasty Fight — Hire a Lawyer

Gay/Lesbian couples who write a living-together agreement while they are feeling good about each other will be in a favorable position to end their relationship without hassles as long as both are willing to abide by the agreement in good faith. In our experience, most couples with agreements do follow them conscientiously. But what happens if you and your lover don't have a contract? Basically, you have two choices—you can be reasonable and reach an agreement over property distribution, or you can engage in all-out legal warfare. If you choose (or are dragged into) a lawsuit, lawyers will love you for the fees you'll generate. A full-scale court battle between former lovers over property will be expensive—there is likely to be lots of legal research, depositions, interrogatories, motions, a trial, etc. And all the while the lawyer's meter is running at $75 to $150 an hour. Also, the fact that you're litigating in a developing area of the law means that no one can predict results with certainty. Some judges may be hostile to the very existence of gay/lesbian couples, while other judges may be sympathetic and find the legal issues interesting. Whatever the result, both you and your former lover will lose money, time, and what remains of your good feelings for each other.

So, how can this craziness be avoided? By coming to your own compromise settlement of any property

disputes and then committing your settlement to writing. In most situations, you can do this yourselves without recourse to lawyers, although if there is a considerable amount of property involved, you may want to have your work checked by a sympathetic attorney when it's complete.

3. Practical Things to Do When Splitting Up

It is always advisable to keep your bank accounts and credit cards separate. However, if your friend's finances have been intertwined with yours, you need to untwine them as soon as possible after separation. This means that you should promptly terminate all joint charge accounts. We've heard several horror stories about people who were stuck with large bills when their ex-lovers charged up a fortune on joint credit cards. Notify not only credit card companies, but any other stores or business people who might extend credit to the two of you—the grocer, the hardware store folk, the lumberyard, etc.

Cancellation of joint credit accounts can usually be accomplished by a phone call, but it's wise to follow up that call with a confirming letter, keeping a carbon for your own records. We know of people who've run an announcement in the local paper saying they will not be responsible for the debts of their ex-partner, but usually these announcements have no legal effect, and seem rather excessive in any case.

A reminder: You are not responsible for your partner's debts unless you co-signed for the debt, or credit was extended based on a "reasonable reliance" that both of you would be responsible for payment. However, if you have joint or shared debts, the creditor can hold either of you responsible for the whole debt. This means that as soon as possible, the two of you should decide on an allocation of your joint debts. Once you've reached your agreement, you can ask the creditors if they would be willing to put each debt in one person's name only. Most of the time they won't do this, as good business sense dictates that it's better to have two people responsible for a debt than one. So, realistically, you probably have to trust your ex-partner to pay off his or her share of your joint debts. If he or she fails to do this and you end up being stuck for more than your share, you can sue your ex-friend, but of course this won't help if he or she is living in the south of France.

4. Separation Agreements

The sooner a separating couple can make a detailed agreement, the less chance there is for misunderstanding. This doesn't mean that "cooling off" for a short period of time isn't helpful if lots of pain or anger makes communication difficult at first. At times, seeking the counsel of level-headed friends can also be a good way to begin making a good separation agreement. But sooner or later you're going to have to come to grips with the division of your property if you don't want to wind up in court, and, if you've been together for a while, you will probably need a more precise agreement than just an "I'll-take-my-stuff-and-you-take-yours." One effective method of initiating the agreement process is for the two of you to list all the major pieces of property you both own. Then identify each item as being either shared property, the separate property of one of you, or property of which ownership is disputed. Make a similar list for your debts. And remember, when feelings are raw, generosity often works wonders, and a wise person will go a little more than half-way to arrive at a compromise.

Here are some work-sheets you can use to make these lists, and some examples of how to use them.

Property Division – Worksheet

I. A. Separate Property

    1. Owned by (name): _____

       (itemize) _____

       _____

    2. Owned by (name): _____

       (itemize) _____

       _____

B. Separate Debts

    1. Owed by (name): _____

       (itemize) _____

       _____

    2. Owed by (name): _____

       (itemize) _____

       _____

II. A. Shared Property

Item	Market Value	Owed	Equity*

                  TOTAL EQUITY $ _____

* Add percentage of each person's equity interest if property is owned in unequal shares.

B. Shared Debts

Amount   Owed to:

Total Owed: $ _____

III. Disputed Items

Item	Value	Owed	Equity	Reason disputed

The best way to use these worksheets is to start by concentrating on what you can both agree to, putting off potential disputes until later. When there is a dispute as to the ownership of an item, simply list that under "Disputed Property" and go on.

Example:

III. Disputed Items

Item	Value	Owed	Equity	Reason disputed
Silverware	$800	-0-	$800	Mark says his mother gave the silver to him and he should have it all. Alfred says it was a joint gift so he should get half.
Truck	$1,400	$400	$1,000	Alfred says he paid the $400 down payment to buy the truck, so he should get it. Mark says he contributed to ½ the insurance and ½ of 10 payments, so he wants 2/5 interest.
Garbo, the cat				Mark and Alfred both love her and want her.

etc.

If you were able to place all of your assets in either the "separate property" category or the "shared property" category, you are ready for distribution. Obviously, each person keeps his or her separate property. Your shared property should be divided 50-50, unless you agree that there is unequal ownership of some or all of it. Of course, you can horse-trade and bargain if you want. If disputes remain, we suggest—indeed, we urge—you to resolve them by arbitration or mediation. (Ed. note: How to do this is covered in detail by the authors in their book *Gay and Together: A Legal Guide for Gay/Lesbian Couples.*)

When you have reached agreement on the distribution of all of your property, it's time to write it down. Here is a sample agreement that can be used, or modified to fit your circumstances.

Separation Agreement of
_____ and _____

We have agreed to go our separate ways, and to divide our property as specified in this agreement. This is a final division of all of our property and can only be changed or amended by both of us, in writing.

I. Property
A) We have agreed to divide all of our property as follows: We agree that the following is the separate property of _____ and (s)he is the sole owner of each item:
1.
2.
3.
etc.

B) We agree that the following property is the separate property of _____ and (s)he is the sole owner of each item:
1.
2.
3.
etc.

C) We agree that we will both retain (share) ownership of the following property:
1.
2.
3.
etc.

(add any specifics on this—e.g., "Mike will make the payments on the truck and his percentage of ownership will be increased by _____," etc.)

II. Debts
We have divided our joint debts. Each of us is solely responsible for the debts listed below under his/her name. Should the person listed fail to make a payment on a debt, and the other person ends up making the payment, the person making the payment may sue the person listed for all costs and expenses incurred, including reasonable legal fees necessary

to enforce this agreement.
    A) Debts which will be solely assumed by _____.

        Creditor   Amount Owed
    1.
    2.
    3.
    etc.

Note: You can add as many additional clauses to your separation agreement as you need or desire. Our preference is to keep these agreements as short and succinct as possible. But do be sure you cover all your financial matters in that agreement. If you are going to continue shared ownership of a home or a boat, or other large item, specify the exact terms you've agreed upon. If there is a "buy-out" provision—common in the case of shared real estate—specify all the terms and conditions of that buy-out.

Support Agreements

It's conceivable, but not likely, that a court could order one member of a separating gay or lesbian couple to pay support to the other. However, if a couple has drafted a living-together agreement that provides for support, it is our belief that most courts will enforce it. If one member of a gay/lesbian couple has fulfilled a role similar to that of the traditional wife—economically dependent, at home, caring for the children—and the other member has been the sole income provider for some time, support for the quasi-wife seems fair. In these circumstances, two people might want to include a support provision in their agreement. Here is a sample:[1]

---

1. The contract is phrased in terms of each person relinquishing all legal claims not because we're encouraging paranoia about lawsuits, but because of the technical rules of contracts. Each side to a valid contract must provide something of value—called "consideration" in legalese. Acts already performed are normally not valid consideration. However, a promise not to sue in the future over past acts is valid consideration.

Sample Agreement

Alfred Gwyne and Mark Jones have decided to separate and live apart from this date on. For the past seven years, they have lived together; Mark has not been employed during that time and has provided many household services for Alfred.

It is hereby agreed that Alfred shall pay Mark the sum of $200 a month for one year, commencing December 1, 1980, with the payments to be made on the first of each month. These payments are to help Mark during his transition following the parties' separation, and to assist him while he seeks gainful employment. In exchange, Mark hereby relinquishes all other claims he may have against Alfred for money or support for his services to Alfred during the time they lived together.

Dated: _____   _____

                                     Alfred Gwynne

                                     _____

                                     Mark Jones

Hayden Curry and Denis Clifford are partners along with Mervin Cherrin in an Oakland, California law firm and have been friends for years. As a part of writing this book, they have done extensive legal work involving gay and lesbian couples. Hayden likes to be described as a "pirate" or a "poet," and also renovates old houses and teaches hypnosis. Denis, in answer to the question "What do you do?" stated that he is a "soldier of fortune." When he grows up, he wants to be a play-making guard for the Golden State Warriors.

Bargain Basement Justice: Representing Yourself in Small Claims Court

by Ralph Warner

In the early part of the twentieth century, Small Claims Courts were established as part of a reform effort designed to give ordinary folks access to law. The development of these courts owed much of its philosophical underpinning to a successful conciliation court procedure established in Norway in 1795 by a royal edict whose preamble stated:

> *Inasmuch as it has come to our notice that the peasants and other loyal, good and true subjects in our dominion are incited to quarrel about trifling things by dishonest lawyers who generally get their clutches on their unsuspecting clients till they have robbed them of their property, we have, in our fatherly wisdom and for the protection of our loyal subjects, evolved a form of law of procedure designed to abate and check this monstrous evil.*

What else is new?

Looking back at my years in law school, I can't think of a single mention of Small Claims Court. Perhaps this isn't surprising when you remember that fundamentally law school doesn't exist to train people in law, but in making money, and lawyers don't even get to take out their wallets when people handle their own problems. But despite the fact that lawyers

have little economic motive to encourage self-help law, the idea that non-lawyers can represent themselves in Small Claims Court has been around long enough that it still surprises me that not one of my learned professors hit on it with even a glancing blow.

Even after law school when I was working as a legal aid lawyer in the late 1960s, I had no clear idea how Small Claims Court worked. Oh, occasionally I would refer people with small disputes there (mostly as a way to get them out of my office), but I had never been there myself. I still believed—as most lawyers believe to this day—that Small Claims Court wasn't a legitimate part of our legal system, but rather a place where people were sent when their dispute wasn't important enough to be handled by a "professional," and they didn't have enough sense to go home and forget about it. Oddly, I continued to hold to this narrow view even though I was becoming, day by day, more fed up with, and cynical about, our formal legal system. I could see that people were paying a great deal of money to get very little of either law or justice, but it never occurred to me that I was walking past one good solution to our increasingly time-consuming, contentious and expensive way of doing things every time I hurried through the courthouse.

Then, one morning in the spring of 1973, I found myself in a local courthouse with fifteen minutes to kill. I had already drunk three cups of coffee and read all about how the San Francisco Giants were sure to have a great year, so I wandered into the only court in session and sat down. It was Small Claims, and had I not been wearing my overly tight, pointy-toed cowboy boots (I always wore them when I appeared in court because they made me feel tough), I would probably have walked out. Fortunately, I sat and witnessed what turned out to be a special moment of revelation—one that has fundamentally affected my life.

From the first case, I was amazed at what I saw. People were competently handling their own legal problems—doing with little apparent difficulty what I had been repeatedly taught was dangerous and foolish for anyone but a lawyer to handle. In less than fifteen minutes a tenant presented a case involving a landlord's failure to return a deposit and a gardener convinced the judge that the tire company which was suing him on an unpaid bill should only get part of its claim because the tires wore out too soon. Perhaps this doesn't sound remarkable, but in the formal legal courts across the hall, these two cases could easily have used up half a day, not to mention the fees of four lawyers at $30 per hour (this was 1973, remember).

But it was the third dispute that really stands out in my mind. It involved two conservatively dressed men, European by birth and older than this century, arguing over buttons. The plaintiff was a tailor, the defendant his customer. The customer, a small round man with white hair whose accent was German, refused to pay for a two-button suit the tailor had made, emphatically insisting that never in his 79 years had he worn a suit with less than three buttons. The tailor, a thin bald fellow whose English and gesticulations had a Southern European flavor, replied with equal fervor that at no time had he ever made one with more than two.

The argument grew heated as the men tried to out yell one another. When the judge asked to see the coat, they both moved toward the bench, each clutching a sleeve. Then a wonderful thing happened—the tailor forgot where he was and commenced shouting in Italian. The frustrated customer replied in German. The judge finally gave up his battle to keep a straight face and laughed along with everyone else in the courtroom. The two men paused as if interrupted in a dream, looked around, and themselves began to chuckle. They had said everything there was to say in every possible language, and now they were ready to sit down.

I never learned the outcome of the dispute because I had to hurry across the hall to argue a case on behalf of a client who was paying me well to defend him in a pot bust prosecution. But as I tried to convince the judge that my client thought that a couple of bags of marijuana were oregano (you can probably guess how that argument came out), I kept thinking—Why am I here? Why doesn't my pot-smoking friend just stand on his own hind legs and tell his own story? He might not do any better than I am, but at the very least he would be taking responsibility for his own life while he saved himself my attorney fee.

My discovery of Small Claims Court coincided with the beginning of my serious work on self-help law materials with Nolo Press, which at that time had published only *How To Do Your Own Divorce* and *The California Tenants Handbook*, which I had written with Myron Moskovitz and Charles Sherman. Immediately, I thought of working on Small Claims Court materials. Other commitments intervened but eventually they were completed and I had the time to spend a few months hanging out at Small Claims Court; I was able to serve for a few days as a Berkeley, California Small Claims Court judge (pro tem). On the basis of this experience, I wrote and published, *Everybody's Guide to Small Claims Court* which has now appeared in four editions.

The more time I have spent working on Small Claims Court materials, the more excited I have become. As the years passed and lawyer fees went up, at the same time that client service and satisfaction declined, it became more obvious that our formal legal system was on the skids. Small Claims Courts have begun to emerge as one of the main hopes for restructuring our dispute resolution system along lines that are fair, efficient, cheap and open to all. But enough philosophy—let's take a look at how Small Claims Court works.

Small Claims Courts are located throughout the country, and while procedures are established by state law, differences between Small Claims Court from one state to another tend to be of detail rather than substance. Perhaps the major problem with Small Claims Courts, as they are presently organized, is that the amounts for which you can sue are far too low, with a $750–$1000 maximum as typical in the more populous states (see chart). But to counterbalance this one easily correctable disadvantage, there are many advantages. In Small Claims Court, disputes are heard relatively quickly. There are no complicated rules of evidence or convoluted language, and perhaps most important, people are encouraged to represent themselves without needing to pay a lawyer more than the dispute is worth.

Usually a Small Claims Court case begins when a person feels genuinely ripped off. The plumber charged a lot of money, but didn't unplug the drain. The new stove won't turn on properly. The car mechanic installed a Datsun carburetor in your Toyota. Or perhaps the friendly, affable landlady started playing now-you-see-me, now-you-don't games when you contacted her about getting your

security deposit returned. Whatever the cause, you feel a genuine sense of grievance and need to do something about it.

Your first step is to take a deep breath, or put another way, to slow down enough so that you can ask yourself some basic questions before you run to the court house and start filing papers. Begin with this one. Are the results you are likely to achieve by starting a law suit in proportion to, or greater than, the effort you will have to expend? This question may be answered individually, and different people in the identical circumstance may answer it differently. But there are several obvious points that everyone will want to consider. Important among these are:

1. Do you have a good legal case? Did the person or organization whom you are thinking of suing clearly breach some duty that caused you a loss or injury? Often this is an easy question to answer (you lend someone money and they fail to pay you back). But sometimes it's not so easy (you are bitten but not seriously by a dog when you enter a person's fenced yard to try and sell them a new model carrot peeler).

2. Can you prove your case? Do you have witnesses, documents, photographs, a damaged piece of machinery, estimates or whatever will be necessary to convince the judge that you are right?

3. Can you recover if you win? If the person you are suing is working, has a business, a bank account that you know about or has other tangible property that is not exempt under state exemption laws, you can collect. If not, you may be better off not to sue in the first place. As my canny Irish grandmother used to say, "No one ever got to live in the big house on the hill by throwing a good dime after a bad quarter."

OK, let's assume that you have a good case, can prove it, and are pretty sure you will have no difficulty collecting if you win even if your opponent refuses to pay voluntarily. How do you start?

A. Familiarize yourself with your local Small Claims Court rules.

You need to understand the maximum amount you can sue for in your state, how court papers are served (often this can be done by certified mail), where you can sue (usually in the area where the defendant lives and/or does business, but commonly at other locations, too), what the filing fee is (it usually ranges from $2.00 to $10.00), etc. The court clerk should be able to supply you with this information.

Let's look at an example of a potential Small Claims suit. Assume that you live in California where, in most areas of the state, the maximum amount you can sue for in Small Claims is $750 (you can sue for $1,500 in a few experimental judicial districts). You have a dispute with John's Car Repair Shop for $1,200 because they ruined the engine and transmission on your pick-up truck while they were supposed to be reconditioning it. Can you bring this case into Small Claims Court? Yes, but to do so you would have to waive all claims to the amount over the $750 maximum and limit your suit to that amount. But wouldn't it be silly to give up your claim to $450? Probably not, when you consider how much it would cost to hire a lawyer to file in regular court. But before you decide to go ahead and file suit against John's Car Repair Shop for the $750, you had better procede with caution. Because in most states you often can't collect a judgment against a business in the name it commonly uses (there are a few exceptions, including New York). To collect you must sue and get a judgment in the name(s) of the business owner(s). For example, John's Car Repair Shop might be owned by Pablo Garcia or the Winifred Wilson Corporation,

and to get a valid judgment, you would have to sue in the correct name of the owner. You can find ownership information by checking with the local tax and license authorities.

B. Attempting to Compromise Your Case

Assume that you have a pretty good understanding of your local court rules, that you have a solid case and are pretty certain that you can recover when you win. Are you ready to file? Not quite. Most Small Claims Courts have a rule requiring that a written demand be made on the opposing party before a case is filed in court. Most states simply require reasonable notice, and some allow you to make your demand orally. But even where an oral demand is okay, it's better to make it in writing. Be brief, but review all the facts in a non-hostile way. It's absolutely essential to adopt a reasonable tone. If your attempt to settle the case fails, you will be able to present the demand letter to the judge as part of your case and you don't want to come across as an angry yo-yo. The fact that you make a compromise offer —say to settle an $800 dispute for $600—doesn't mean that you are limited to suing for $600 if the compromise is rejected. You can still sue for the original amount.

Here is a sample demand letter:

January 1, 1981

Jennifer Tenant
111 Sacramento Street
Palos Verdes, CA 91234

Dear Jennifer:

As you will recall, you moved into my house at 61 Spring Street, Los Angeles, California, on August 1, 1980, agreeing to pay me $450 per month rent on the first of each month. On November 29 you suddenly moved out, having given me no advance notice whatsoever.

I was unable to get a tenant to replace you (although I tried every way I could and asked you for help) until January 1, 1981. This means that I am short $450 (December rent) for the room you occupied. If necessary, I will take this dispute to court because, as you know, I am on a very tight budget. I hope that this isn't necessary and that we can arrive at a sensible compromise. I have tried to call you with no success. Perhaps you can give me a call in the next week to talk this over.

Sincerely,

Patricia Landperson

C. Preparing Your Case

Most Small Claims cases are won or lost before any-one puts a foot in the courtroom. Eloquence in argument is fine, but it's no substitute for good prep-aration. This generally means gathering together pictures, letters, estimates and other tangible evi-dence that a judge can rely on to rule in your favor. Let's look at how a typical case should be prepared:

Tillie Tenant decides to move out of the cottage that she rents from Louise Landlord on a month-to-month tenancy. Tillie gives a proper, written 30-day notice, pays her rent through the last day of her tenancy, cleans up the cottage thoroughly and moves. A few weeks pass and she doesn't receive her $400 in cleaning and security deposits. After writing Louise asking for the money and being put off with a lot of vague excuses about dirty and damaged condi-tions, Tillie files suit for $400 in Small Claims Court. (In many states, including Texas, Illinois, and California, Tillie could also sue for punitive damages if deposits are withheld by a landlord in bad faith. In Massachusetts, Tillie could sue for three times her deposit simply if the landlord didn't return it to her within 30 days.) If Tillie shows up in court and explains her problem to the judge without any evidence to back it up, she is almost guaranteed to lose. Why? Because human nature being what it is, Louise is likely to present an entirely different story, and the judge will have nothing but Tillie's contra-dicted word on which to base a judgment in her favor. As judges tend to be property owners, they are often more likely to believe a landlord than a tenant. But what sort of evidence should Tillie bring? As many of the following as possible:

- Cancelled check or receipt for the deposits;
- Photos of the apartment at the time she moved in

showing any dirt or damage already existing;
- Photos of the apartment upon moving out, show-ing clean conditions;
- Receipts for cleaning supplies used in the final clean-up;
- A copy of the written lease or rental agreement, if any;
- Copies of correspondence with the landlord ask-ing for her money and outlining her position;
- One, or preferably two, witnesses who were familiar with the property and saw it after Tillie cleaned it up. People who actually helped with the clean-up are always particularly effective as witnesses.

D. Presenting Your Case in Court

Okay—the big day finally arrives. There you are, all combed and curried, waiting for the judge to call your case. When he finally does, you stand, square your shoulders like Raymond Burr, clear your throat like Charles Laughton, and launch into a brilliant and irrefutable argument à la E.G. Marshall, or perhaps Henry Fonda. Right? No, wrong! You are suffering from the most common and debilitating ailment to afflict the Small Claims Court user. It's called "Movieitis," and while your chances of eventual recovery are excellent, your case is very likely to die in the process.

Cases that should be easily won are lost every day because otherwise sensible people march around the courtroom antagonizing everyone with comic opera imitations of their celluloid heroes. Don't assume that you are immune. Movieitis is a subtle disease and people often don't realize they have it. Ask yourself a few self-diagnostic questions. Have you watched courtroom scenes on T.V. or in the movies? Have you ever imagined that you were one of the actor-lawyers? How many real life courtroom experiences have you had in contrast to your movie and T.V. set courtroom experiences?

There are only two simple rules by which to present your case successfully: be prepared and be yourself. You need no fancy clothes, fancy airs or fancy language. In most courtrooms, you simply stand behind an ordinary table facing the judge and explain your version of the facts. If you want the judge to examine letters, documents, or pictures, hand them to the court clerk who will pass them along. Witnesses should be introduced to the judge and will be allowed briefly to have their say. Never read your testimony—reading is simply too boring. But it is sometimes helpful to list the main points that you want to make on a 3″ x 5″ index card that you can glance at if you get flustered. Above all, be thorough but brief. Judges are a little like donkeys —load them down too heavily and they are likely to lie down and go to sleep.

Now, let's pick up our drama of Tillie and Louise and see how it might be presented in court.

Clerk: "Tillie Tenant and Louise Landlord. Please step forward."

Judge: "Good morning. Please tell me your version of the facts. Ms. Tenant."

Tillie Tenant: "I moved into the cottage at 1700 Walnut Street in the Spring of 1978. I paid Louise Landlord my first and last months' rent which totaled $400. I also paid her $400 in deposits. The deposits were divided, $200 for cleaning and $200 for damage. Here is a copy of the rental agreement (hands it to the clerk) which specifically states that these deposits [as well as copies of my cancelled checks showing that the money was paid] are to be returned to me if the apartment is left clean and undamaged.

When I moved into 1700 Walnut, it was a mess. It's a nice little cottage, but the people who lived there before me were sloppy. The stove was filthy, as was the bathroom, the refrigerator, the floors and just about everything else. In addition, the walls hadn't been painted in years. But I needed a place and this was the best available, so I moved in despite the mess. I painted the whole place—everything. Louise Landlord gave me the paint, but I did all of the work. And I cleaned the place thoroughly, too. It took me three days. I like to live in a clean house.

Here are some pictures of what the place looked like when I moved in (hands photos to clerk who gives them to the judge). Here is a second set of photos which were taken after I moved out and cleaned up (again hands pictures to clerk). Your Honor, I think these pictures clearly show that the place was clean when I moved out. I also have receipts (hands to clerk) for cleaning supplies and a rug shampooer that I used during the clean-up. They total $28.25. I also have brought two people who saw the place the day I left and can tell you what it looked like."

Judge: (looking at one of the witnesses) "Do you have some personal knowledge of what this cottage looked like?"

John DeBono: "Yes, I helped Tillie move in and move out. I simply don't understand what the landlady is fussing about. The place was a smelly mess when she moved in, and it was spotless when Tillie moved out."

Judge: (addressing the second witness) "Do you have something to add?"

Puna Prince: "I never saw 1700 Walnut when Tillie moved in because I didn't know her then. But I did help her pack and clean up when she moved out. I can tell you that the windows were washed, the floor waxed and the oven cleaned, because I did it. And I can tell you that the rest of the cottage was clean, too, because I saw it."

Judge: "Ms. Landlord, do you want to present your position?"

Louise Landlord: "Your Honor, I am not here to argue about whether the place was clean or not. Maybe it was cleaner when Tillie Tenant moved out than when she moved in. The reason I withheld the deposits is that the walls were all painted odd, bright colors and I have had to paint them all over. Here are some color pictures of the walls taken just after Tillie Tenant moved out. They show several pink, light blue and purple rainbows, and dancing hedgehogs, six birds apparently laughing, a purple dog, and several unicorns of various sizes. I ask you, your Honor, how was I going to rent that place with a purple bulldog painted on the living room wall, especially with an orange butterfly on his nose? It cost me more than $300 to have the place painted over white."

Judge: (looks at the pictures and gives up trying to keep a straight face, which is okay as everyone in the courtroom is laughing except Louise Landlord) "Let me ask a few questions. Was it true that the place needed a new coat of paint when you moved in, Ms. Tenant?"

Tillie Tenant: "Yes."

Judge: "Do you agree, Ms. Landlord?"

Louise Landlord: "Yes, that's why I paid the paint bills, although I never would have if we had known about that bulldog, not to mention the rainbows."

Judge: "How much did the paint cost?"

Louise Landlord: "$95."

Judge: "I normally send decisions by mail, but today I am going to explain what I have decided. First, the apartment needed repainting anyway, Ms. Landlord, so I am not going to give you any credit for paying to have the work done. However, Ms. Tenant, even though the place looks quite—shall I say, cheerful—decorated with its assorted wildlife, Ms. Landlord does have a point in that you went a little beyond what is reasonable. Therefore, I feel that it's unfair to make her pay for paint twice. My judgment is this: The $95 for the paint that was given to Ms. Tenant is subtracted from the $400 deposits. This means that Louise Landlord owes Tillie Tenant $305 plus court costs of $4.00.

LANDLORDS NOTE: I focus here on a deposit case from the tenant's point of view. This is because tenants are the ones who initiate this sort of case, not because I believe tenants are always right—I don't. Landlords too, though, should gain by carefully reading the list of evidence that is helpful in court. Often the best witness for a landlord is the new tenant who has just moved in. This person is likely to feel that the place isn't as clean as did the person who moved out.

E.   Collecting When You Win

As I indicated above, thought should be given as to whether a judgment can be collected before a case is filed, and cases shouldn't be filed against people who have no resources with which to pay. But what happens if you sue a solvent business or individual (now called the "judgment debtor") and they simply won't pay out of simple cussedness? I go into this in detail in *Everybody's Guide to Small Claims Court*. Here there is space for only a few brief reminders. In most states you can order a sheriff or marshall to:

1. Attach the person's wages, if he or she works and you know where;

2. Attach most types of bank accounts, if you know where the judgment debtor banks;

3. Take the money out of the cash register at a business (called a till tap);

4. File a lien against real property, if you know where it is located. In a few states a portion of the equity in a person's dwelling house is exempted from attachment under state homestead laws, but usually filing a lien against rent property will result in eventual collection;

5. Attach any particularly valuable objects of personal property, such as an expensive car or boat in which the debtor has enough ownership equity to cover your debt. But before you try to have personal property attached, be sure you understand what personal property is exempt from attachment under the debtor protection laws of your state.

Ralph Warner is the author of Everybody's Guide to Small Claims Court, *published by Nolo Press (California Edition) and The Addison-Wesley Publishing Company (50-State Edition).*

Writers & the Law

by Jane Shay Lynch

In the process of putting the Review Section (Part VI) of this book together, we collected about 700 books. People were continually coming through the office trying to "borrow" one or another of them and we found ourselves constantly defending our laboriously collected hoard until Dave Brown could review them. The book which required the most vigilant protection was Law and the Arts, Art and the Law, *a publication of the Lawyers for the Creative Arts, in Chicago. This shouldn't have surprised us, as many of our friends are involved in writing and publishing and had only a hazy notion of how the recently enacted copyright law changes affected them. We all benefited from reading Jane Shay Lynch's article and wanted to pass it along to you. After all, "for every two people reading a book, there are three writing one!"*

What is a copyright?

A copyright is a governmental grant, an acknowledgment that original writings are owned by the author. A copyright is the legal recognition of the special "property rights" in an author's work.

What kinds of writing does a copyright protect?

Copyright protection is available for almost all writing—books, short stories, magazine articles, newspaper columns, poetry, plays, screenplays, and songs. Both fictional and nonfictional works are covered, and copyright protection is even available for such writings as an index, a master's thesis, a map, even an original directory, such as the phone book, or a name and address guide to vegetarian restaurants.

What is not protected? In the language of the copyright law, "words and short phrases" are not. A catchy slogan, a clever word—if you are using these

in business as a brand name for a product, or as the name of your musical group or other business, protection for the single word or short slogan may be available under the *trademark* laws, but not the copyright laws.

What else is not protected? Lists of ingredients are not, hence, the major part of most recipes. Does this mean that you have no protection if you write a cooking article or cookbook? No, because your article or book as a whole presumably contains more text than a string of ingredients, affording you a basis for copyright protection.

The same principle applies to chemical formulae, and to math problems. Copyright law won't allow these to be removed from the "public domain," so an individual equation, such as $E = mc^2$, even if developed today under the new copyright act, would not be protected under the copyright laws. However, your math book or chemistry text would contain far more than a string of formulae or equations, and would, as a whole, be protected.

Computer programs—software—is an area where copyright laws are up in the air. Right now, software is not adequately protected under the copyright laws, but this situation may soon change. However, depending on the circumstances, protection is sometimes available under the "common law" of unfair competition and trade secrets.

Will a copyright protect my idea?

No! A copyright protects the specific way that you develop, detail and express your idea in writing. That is, if you have an idea for an article about nuclear-powered musical instruments of the future, you can't obtain protection for your *concept*. Anyone can use your idea, and can write, copyright and publish his or her own article about nuclear-powered musical instruments of the future.

However, if somebody else wants to write an article dealing with the same subject or idea of *your* copyrighted article, that second somebody had better not lift sentences or paragraphs from your article, and had better not even paraphrase your article, or parts of it, because that would be copyright infringement.

It is also possible to enter written agreements with your workers and clients forbidding unauthorized use of your program. Such contracts are in the nature of trade secret agreements and are generally enforceable.

How original must my writing be to gain copyright protection?

Not very! The Copyright Office does not make an extensive examination of the substance of your work, because what you are keeping from the public domain is your way of expressing a concept, which concept anyone is entitled to use in his or her own

words. That is, your "monopoly" does not work a serious hardship on the public, so your work does not have to pass serious muster to earn its copyright protection. Obviously, if your work was primarily copied from a public domain work and you find yourself holding a certificate of copyright registration nonetheless, an "infringer" you seek to sue over the matter can raise a public domain defense, despite your registration.

How different does something have to be from a copyrighted work in order not to infringe?

Substantially different! Rumors—all false—abound that "a ten per cent change" is sufficient, or that changing the main character from, say, Carl to Carla is sufficient or that relocating the action from San Francisco to Rio will protect against infringement. Such rumors are wrong, wrong, wrong.

The legal test of whether someone has copied your work is whether there is "substantial similarity" between the allegedly infringing work and your copyrighted one. Under the "substantial similarity" test, have people been found liable for copyright infringement if "all" they've done is paraphrase? Yes! Paraphrasing, under the copyright laws, is still plagiarism—infringement of copyright.

As we have discussed, an idea (or as the courts put it, a "mere naked idea") is not protectable. But what if there are already four thousand seventy-two articles on your chosen theme of, say, the conspiracy theory of the Kennedy assassination? Isn't your way of expressing yourself with respect to this idea going to collide with a previous copyrighted piece?

In some sense, yes, but you are entitled to write about the incident, using all of the facts you need to do so. Obviously, you are not required to change Jackie's name to Judy, or to move the murder site to Tacoma just to avoid duplication of these facts in a prior work. The law favors "independent creation." If it is clear that you have not copied or paraphrased the other articles, you'll not be penalized for redundancy!

Does "independent creation" mean that if you should *unconsciously* come too close to a copyrighted work, you're off the hook due to your good faith? No, especially if the copyright owner can prove that you've had access to the copyrighted work.

The case against George Harrison is a good example of an *innocent* infringer being found liable for copyright infringement. You may remember that Harrison's "My Sweet Lord" was charged to be an infringement of "He's So Fine," the song made popular by the Chiffons. The court concluded that it was likely that Harrison had *subconsciously* copied the work, despite all good intentions.

How about written fiction? If an idea can't be protected, can a plot? No, *if* you view a plot as merely the most pared-down skeleton, without detail or characterization or development, such as "boy meets girl, boy moves to big city, and urban/financial crisis occurs which causes boy to realize the small-town life is the good life, boy goes back to girl, who (a) has married another, or (b) has otherwise made a new life for herself."

But if your plot goes like this: "Boy (Fred) is a marine biologist. Girl (Julia) is a veterinarian, specializing in rare fish. Boy & girl live in resort town under the shadow of a UFO, causing boy to move to Nashville, etc.," or if your plot goes into Fred's family history, and Julia's bout with scarlet fever, and contains flashback episodes of the two with their respective fish, studying while the UFO hovers above the aquarium, then there is a difference. The difference is development, progression, specifics. The more developed a plot, the more willing a court will be to recognize that more than a "mere naked idea" has been stolen.

What if my work depends upon a prior work— let's say I want to write a play based on the "Doonesbury" cartoon strip, or *Hamlet*?

The right to adapt a work into another medium or form belongs to the copyright owner, as does the right to translate into another language. Naturally, the copyright owner is entitled to give or to sell you permission to make the adaptation. We're all aware that authors will often sell movie rights, for example. These adaptations are known as "derivative works."

Let us say you do get written permission from an author to write and produce your play based on his or her work. Can your particular adaptation be protected by copyright? Yes! Sometimes part of your agreement with the author of the "underlying work"—the first, or original version—is that you provide that the author is to own the copyright in your version. If your agreement does not so provide, then you own the copyright in your version.

Now, as to *Hamlet*, let us say you want to make a modern version, pointing out the day's ills, but using the basic characterization of the original. This you may do freely. Why? Shakespeare's work is in the public domain. Just make sure you've not copied from someone else's—current and copyrighted—modern version of *Hamlet*. And yes, your new version, insofar as it's original, is copyrightable, and you may protect it from infringement.

But what about "fair use"?

Fair use, as defined by Marybeth Peters, senior attorney/advisor to the Copyright Office, "allows copying without permission from, or payment to, the copyright owner where the use is reasonable and not harmful to the rights of the copyright owner." However, what is "reasonable" and "not harmful" is not necessarily determined by your personal beliefs.

Fair use is one of the most nebulous, tricky areas of the Copyright Law, since the same conduct is viewed differently depending on *who* is taking the copyrighted material from *where*, and to *what end*!

For example, your use of chunks of material from a copyrighted work, properly credited to the copyright owner, might be "fair use" in your doctoral thesis. But your use of the exact same chunk of quoted material, even if credited to the copyright owner, could get you into hot water if it is included in your article for the *Chicago Tribune*.

Why? In determining "fair use" the courts look to the "purpose and character of the use, including whether such use is of commercial nature, or for educational purposes."

In the example above, the use on a Broadway stage of a line or two from "Doonesbury" would probably *not* be excused as "fair use." On the other hand, use of half a dozen of the lines in a high-school play might well be excused as fair use. But, when you quote without permission, there are no guarantees, and the law of fair use operates on a continuum. That is, in our example, fifty lines, even in the high-school class play, would likely exceed the bounds of fair use.

Because of the ill-defined, continuum nature of fair use, there is no rule advising how many words you may quote before crossing the border from fair to unfair use. Again, you could quote more in a thesis than in a *Cosmopolitan* magazine feature. But in addition to the type of piece you've prepared, and the number of words you've quoted, fair use depends upon the percentage of quoted material in relation to the work as a whole from which the quote was taken. That is, if you used half of a two-hundred-word copyrighted article you're on shakier ground than if you'd used one hundred "borrowed" words from a 20,000-word book.

Another factor is timeliness. If you've had 6 months' lead time, you're expected to have had the opportunity to contact the copyright owner whose work you'd like to quote. If your article is due at the printers in two days, however, and you want to add a quoted sentence or two from somebody's article published this morning, the courts may conclude that your failure to obtain permission for use of the small quote was reasonable.

Does attributing the quoted portion to the author relieve you of liability for copyright infringement? No, but the reverse—*omitting* the author credit—may well make your copying appear to be intentional plagiarism, so that the equitable defense of fair use won't apply. Fair is fair. Also, as a practical matter, a quoted author is less likely to feel ripped off if properly credited, and, accordingly, is less likely to sue you.

We are discussing lawsuits because "fair use" does not automatically prevent an irate author or publisher from suing you and/or your publisher for copyright infringement with respect to the quoted material. Fair use merely permits you a defense—an excuse—to tell the judge if suit is filed.

How about parody—how can I evoke the original without infringing on it?

Naturally, your parody of someone else's copyrighted work is, in a sense, a fanciful paraphrase of it. As even paraphrasing is forbidden by the copyright laws, how can you spoof on another's work? The courts have, over the years, recognized parody as a legitimate art form, and have carved out certain "gut reaction" fair use exceptions to the infringement laws. The courts often cite that a parody is permitted to "recall and conjure up the original," but must add a contribution of its own.

When is this a problem? When there are aspects of unfair competition involved, or serious disparagement of another's copyrighted work.

That is, if the parody is such that the public might actually think the original author created it, the author may have a valid claim against the parodist. Sometimes, the very artistry of a parody is in its line-by-line adherence to the original. But this the courts have found unacceptable. An example from the comic book genre illustrates that point. Recently, after a court battle lasting some five years, and resulting in several court opinions, a group of cartoonists, The Air Pirates, were found liable for copyright infringement for their comic book showing Walt Disney characters enjoying sex and drugs. The Court was impressed with the argument of The Air Pirates that the beauty of their parody was in the near-duplication of the Disney works parodied. Argued the parodists, a less precise rendition would have destroyed the humor. Nevertheless, the Court concluded that, despite no intention on the part of the authors to have anyone believe the comic book came from Disney Studios, the copying disparaged the work, and it came too close to the copyrighted drawings.

If your parody involves a *product* rather than a literary piece, you may run into "unfair competition" problems, as the makers of the board game ANTIMONOPOLY learned when they were sued for trademark infringement of, and unfair competition with, MONOPOLY.

Also related is the spoof which, while not copyright infringement, is viewed as sufficiently damaging to the "spoof-ee" to warrant judicial relief. An example is the recent decision enjoining further distribution of the skin flick, "Debbie Does Dallas," in which actresses in uniforms resembling those of the Dallas Cowboys Cheerleaders were portrayed in the style to which that film genre is accustomed. In that case, the judge defined parody and satire, and concluded that *this* film did not pass muster:

> A parody is a work in which the language or style of another work is closely imitated or mimicked for comic effect or ridicule. A satire is a work which holds up the vices or shortcomings of an individual or institution to ridicule or derision, usually with an intent to stimulate change; the use of wit, irony or sarcasm for the purpose of exposing and discrediting vice or folly.
>
> In the present case, there is no content, by way of story line or otherwise, which could conceivably place the movie "Debbie Does Dallas" within any definition of parody or satire. The purpose of the

movie has nothing to do with humor; it has nothing to do with a commentary, either by ridicule or otherwise, upon the Dallas Cowboys Cheerleaders. There is basically nothing to the movie "Debbie Does Dallas" except a series of depictions of sex acts. The other phases of the movie — the dialogue and the "narrative" — are simply momentary and artificial settings for the depiction of the sex acts. *Dallas Cowboys Cheerleaders, Inc. v. Pussycat Cinema, Ltd.*, 201 U.S.P.Q. 740, 749 (S.D.N.Y. 1979).

The context in which your parody appears is also important. A short piece in a magazine spoofing a popular book would be more acceptable and less likely to be viewed as an infringement than would a *book* spoofing the book you've chosen as your subject of parody.

Are there special fair use guidelines for teachers and librarians who frequently photocopy copyrighted works?

The National Commission on New Technological Uses (CONTU), with the assistance of educators and librarians, has developed certain guidelines which the courts respect, as to what constitutes "fair use" for teachers and librarians.

If you are a teacher or librarian — or an author concerned with what legitimate "fair use" copying may be made by schools and libraries of your work — write or telephone the copyright office, requesting brochures with respect to these teacher/librarian fair use guidelines.

Briefly, "fair use" cannot be a substitute for the purchase of available works, except in the case of single articles or cartoons or in a genuine emergency, and it is not an emergency if a school or library simply cannot afford to buy the work it is photocopying. If a teacher finds a timely article, he or she can photocopy one copy for each student in the class per term, but cannot re-use the article the next term (because by then there will have been enough time to get permission of the copyright owner). Also, the school or school department cannot select the copyrighted piece to be shared under the "fair use" doctrine — an individual teacher must make this decision. Once the school administration or a department head gets involved, fair use ceases to be fair.

Well, what if my play is not based on "Doones-

bury," but features a few backdrops using the "Doonesbury" strips, or has a few of the characters sitting around and reading from the copyrighted comic strip?

Get permission! You are speaking here of a type of *collective work*, one which incorporates the work of others.

Generally, the same rules apply as for the "derivative" work, or adaptation. That is, if the work you incorporate in your own story, article or play is the copyrighted work of another, permission is necessary. If your characters are reading from Shakespeare, or the Bible, then you do not need permission to include these works. As with the derivative work, your new work is protectable under the copyright laws. If your collective work includes material in the public domain, the public domain sections will still be in the public domain, but the "new matter" of your work will be fully protected.

What about personal letters? My friend has become a candidate for President, and I want to publish a book of letters he wrote to me in 1968 when he was on acid.

The copyright in personal correspondence belongs to the person who wrote the letter, even, without a copyright notice, and even if there was no indication that your correspondent meant to "reserve all rights" in them!

This principle was used with great success by an individual who won a copyright infringement suit against the government for stealing his mail, and "publishing" it — circulating it to the CIA and others.

How do I protect an anthology?

An anthology is a common type of collective work. If you are preparing, say, an anthology of essays about pizza, you will need to obtain the prior permission of each copyright proprietor or owner of the articles you want to use.

Your collection of essays will then be the subject of a fresh copyright in your own name. This copyright protection will be limited but is likely to prohibit others from using all the same pizza articles in the same order, with no additional articles, in a subsequent anthology, even if the second anthology author also has permission from each of the essayists.

Your right to protect an anthology is not absolute

when your selections are the tried-and-true obvious ones for an anthology in your genre. If you are preparing an anthology of modern American fiction, for example, you will be permitted to use many of the same stories, and in generally the same order, as other anthologies dealing with the same topic, even though the other anthologies are copyrighted as a unit. How to protect your own collection? The best way is to have careful text "linking" the succession of pieces. By creating a distinguishable new work, you'll enhance your scope of copyright protection.

How do I get a copyright?

If you write it, you've got it.

Under the new copyright law, you obtain copyright protection under the federal laws the instant you have completed your work. Without more. Without a copyright notice. Without publishing the work. Without registering the work in Washington.

The minute you put down your pencil, you pick up your copyright automatically, and whether you know it or not!

Then what is a copyright notice for?

Under the old copyright law, if a work was published without proper notice, it went into the public domain. That is, with very rare exceptions, the old law took away copyright protection if a work was disseminated without a copyright notice, even by accident, or even if the work had the copyright notice on the wrong page. Under the old law, you could even write "this article is copyrighted to the author" on your piece, and could lose all your rights anyway, because such a statement is not a proper copyright notice.

While the copyright notion no longer has this life-giving and life-preserving significance, the new law still requires that your copyright notice appear on your published works. However, if you slip up, your work is *not* thrust into the public domain as a result. Rather, you have five years to put out a reprint bearing the correct notice. Also, the new law doesn't specify, as did the old one, a proper location for the notice. Any area where the notice can be readily seen is sufficient under the new law. The first page of your article, the title page of your book, would be reasonable.

Under the new law, if you see a relatively recent work without a copyright notice, how can you tell if it's in the public domain? You can't—or, more accurately, it isn't. Under the new law, lack of a copyright notice tells you *nothing* about the copyright status of a work created after Jan. 1, 1978. The copyright notice is desirable as a "no trespassing" sign to would-be infringers, warning that you know your rights.

Now, what is a proper copyright notice? The following is:

© 1980 Charles Maxson

This notice is sufficient to ensure protection in most countries. If you want protection in Latin America as well, add the following to your notice: "All Rights Reserved." The word "copyright" can, at your option, be added to the notice as an "extra strength" warning:

Copyright © Your name, 19__ [1]

If the work is a collective work and contains earlier material, or is adapted from an earlier work, it is sufficient to include the year date you completed this collective or derivative work. However, in a collective work such as an anthology, each separately copyrighted article or story should ideally include its own copyright notice on the first page of each such article or story, and again on the inside front cover or credits section of the collective work.

For the purposes of copyright protection, what is your name?
Seriously, under the old law, protection was lost because the copyright notice was in the name of a made-up entity that the author thought was amusing, or the copyright notice had only the initials, not the name, of the owner. The new law is less harsh, because the "wrong" name can be corrected on subsequent editions. Still, if you are not well-known

by your initials, use your last name, or the pseudonym by which you are well-known, in the copyright notice.

What is copyright registration and why is it important?
Copyright registration is the government's acknowledgment of your claim to copyright. A record is made of the fact of your copyright, a number is assigned, and a certificate bearing that number is issued to you. The registration does not confer copyright status upon your work. Your mere creation of the work did that automatically under the new copyright law.

There is some public confusion as to the nature of copyright registration. People sometimes say they've "taken out" a copyright. Actually, they've *registered* their already existing copyrights, whether or not they realize it.

Registration is *not* required for your copyright to be valid. However, registration triggers some very important protections and is, therefore, desirable.

First, copyright registration is a prerequisite to bringing a lawsuit against the infringer of your copyrighted work. But it *is* permissible to obtain the copyright registration the day before you file suit, even though you knew of the infringement a year before you applied for registration!

Second, early registration can mean a big difference in the amount of damages (money) you'll be awarded if you win an infringement suit. If the copyright in your work was registered *before* the infringement began, you'll be entitled to opt for "statutory damages," an amount often larger than the "actual damages" you'd be restricted to if your copyright was not registered at the time of the infringement. Also, you're far more likely to be awarded the dollar amount of your attorney's fees and costs, in addition to your damage award, if your work was registered when the infringement took place.

Third—and this is especially important with respect to *unpublished* manuscripts—your certificate of copyright registration is "prima facie" evidence of copyright ownership and validity. That is, your certificate is the best evidence possible if there

---

1. Year date in which you completed the work.

is any question concerning the date you created your work. This can be crucial if you want to establish that a publisher ripped off your unpublished manuscript.

Fourth, in the event that some other author wants to learn how to contact you, to get permission to quote your work in, say, a book, your registration provides your mailing address and the Copyright Office will provide a copy of your certificate to such persons.

Incidentally, the new copyright act is one of the few laws that has been written "bisexually" so that the author is referred to as "he or she" throughout the entire statute.

How do I register my copyright in a book, game, story, article, play or other written work?

First, obtain copyright form TX (or GPX, if you are an individual—not a corporation—seeking annual registration of all your published works for the previous year, as discussed below) from the Copyright Office, by writing:

> United States Copyright Office
> Library of Congress
> Washington, D.C. 20559

The forms include detailed line-by-line instructions.

In addition, the Copyright Office will at your request send you brochures concerning copyright registration of the type or writing you're interested in.

Also, the Copyright Office has a "hot line" telephone service to help you complete its forms and to provide related, but not legal, advice.

I write so many things that if I had to spend the $10 registration fee on each unpublished work, I'd go broke. Any break in the law?

Yes! If your works are arguably related in theme, you can register a number of them as a "collective work," like an anthology. Poetry, short stories, short opinion pieces and the like lend themselves to this type of registration.

How about my published works, can I group them too?

Yes! The new law gives a break to noncorporate freelancers who are published so regularly that the $10 fee would represent a hardship. If you have even a few pieces a year published, you are entitled to obtain a "group registration" at the end of twelve months, which will cover all of your published works for that period. The form to request from the Copyright Office is GX, and they'll send you instructions for its use, as well.

What is a "common law copyright"?

Extinct! Under the old law, a literary work could not be protected by the federal Copyright Act until it had been "published with proper notice." Accordingly, if your manuscript was ripped off you had to prove that you had never authorized "publication without notice." If you had made your manuscript widely available, and it bore no proper copyright notice, this was occasionally an adequate defense to an infringer under the old system.

The phrase "common law" simply means that there is no state or federal piece of *legislation*—statute—regulating the situation (e.g., "common law" spouse). Now, the federal Copyright Act has abolished "common law" with respect to copyrights, and has *included* unpublished works in the federal statute.

What does this mean to you? For one thing, it means you are entitled to register your copyright in an unpublished manuscript, poem, or whatever.

The advantage of registering an *unpublished* work is that it is "prima facie" evidence of your creation of the work on the day indicated on the registration. That is, if you send in your manuscript to a motion picture company that, without your consent, uses your script in its next movie, how are you going to be able to prove that *your* creation came *first*? By registering your copyright before, or around the same time, that you send your manuscript around. That way, the Library of Congress has the evidence —and so do you.

Before it was possible to register an unpublished manuscript, writers sometimes sent themselves copies of their work by registered mail, to secure a postmark date as "evidence." Contrary to popular belief, there is *no* law specifying that this is satisfactory evidence. Far better is to take advantage of the new law, and have the federal evidence of earlier creation that the new law gives you.

To register a manuscript in an unpublished work, use form TX, as you would for a published work, and read the directions applicable to an "unpublished work" (called "Space 3: Creation and Publication").

How can I protect myself if I send my idea to a magazine, book publisher or motion picture company?

Remember, *ideas* per se are not protectable. And remember, to be more than an idea, a plot has to be fleshed out, with much detail, character development and so on.

Your best protection is not to send a page or two "idea." Rather, prepare a tightly developed long scene or section.

It is a fact of life that almost no book publisher, or television or motion picture studio, will purchase "over-the-transom" unsolicited manuscripts, unless you have an agent.

They don't have to—they get enough manuscripts from agents with whom they've dealt and who have proven themselves to be sources of potentially usable material.

Magazine publishers generally *will* look at, and purchase, unsolicited works.

In any event, your best protection is to have a piece that is developed enough so that you are not merely sending off an "idea."

Back up your ownership by protecting your unpublished manuscript with a federal registration, which is prima facie evidence of your ownership, a copy of your manuscript being safely date-stamped and lodged with the Library of Congress.

Send your script or article registered mail, return receipt requested, so that there can be no question but that the publisher or studio had access to your manuscript. Send a cover letter with your work, explaining that you are submitting the work for possible purchase.

And do use your copyright notice (and the registration number of your unpublished work, if you have a registration) on the first page of the work.

When I sell a freelance article to a magazine, do I give up all further rights to my article?

No. You sell only one-time use with respect to your unsolicited freelance work which is purchased by a magazine or newspaper publisher.

How about a commissioned article?

A commissioned article—one where the publisher (or its editor) asks you to write a piece about a specific topic—can fall under the category of a work made for hire.

A "work made for hire" is a legal fiction which assumes that the person commissioning the work is the author and copyright owner. When you do an article which is viewed as a work made for hire, you have sold all rights, and own nothing more. You may not even reprint the article in an anthology of your own work for a different publisher without permission of the publisher to whom you sold your "work made for hire."

Why? A work made for hire is like a work made by an employee for an employer. The publisher's skill arguably goes into the topic selection, the shaping of the article, and the like, and the publisher is entitled to all rights.

How do you know if your work is a "work made for hire"? Because you sign a brief agreement to that effect. That is, the new copyright law is very clear that the piece is a "work made for hire" and the words "work made for hire" must be used.

Some publishers are now sending their regular freelancers what amounts to form letters stating "all work you do for us now will be viewed as works made for hire." Is this binding? Possibly not, because the law specifies that both publisher and author must sign the agreement. To date, the issue hasn't been litigated. The other tricky issue? What if you get a check which is stamped on the back with words to this effect: "By endorsing this check, the Author agrees that he/she has sold a work made for hire, and has agreed to release all further rights in the work." In a sense, if you endorse, both parties have signed the agreement, with the publisher's signature appearing on the front of the check. While this point has never been litigated to an outcome under the new law, it is possible that simply crossing out the "agreement" and endorsing the check will eliminate the problem, and this has been done by some writers with success, as the bank will usually process the check, and the cancelled check won't be sent to the editor or publisher, but to an accounting department, unnoticed by the publisher powers that be.

Who owns the copyright in articles I write as part of my employment?

Your employer. Your articles are viewed as "works made for hire." Elsewhere, as we have discussed, "works made for hire" agreements must be made in writing, signed by the author and the purchaser. **This is not the case where you are employed by the company that publishes your work.**

If you are an employee in the usual sense of the term, your employer is even considered the *author* of your work for purposes of copyright registration.

When is the situation not so clearcut? If you sometimes freelance for your employer, but sometimes have a salary. Or, if you are given an office and the use of a typewriter, but are only paid on a "per article" basis. In these grayer areas, it is always a good idea to have a brief statement in writing from your publisher or other employer indicating who is to own what rights. Otherwise, you may find yourself liable for copyright infringement by including *your own* writing in your future works, or you may be surprised to find that your employer—not you— owns the movie rights to the long article you slaved over!

I just sold an article to a magazine and the editors cut and changed it to the point where I am embarrassed to have my name on it. Do I have any rights?

Yes and no. European countries have long recognized this problem, and have laws acknowledging the "moral right," that is, the right of one who has created the work, to have it free from mutilation by its purchaser, or subsequent purchasers.

Our laws do not recognize the "moral right" as such. However, there have been several court case precedents in recent years suggesting a trend may yet emerge to recognize the "moral right" under certain extreme circumstances.

Otto Preminger won such a suit when one of his motion pictures was "seriously injured"—cut and edited in the extreme. Terry Gilliam, writer of the television show "Monty Python's Flying Circus," won another case here in the United States because in 1975 his work was seriously altered by ABC.

These precedents have some things in common. Neither court based its decision on any "moral right" but instead found other ways to handle the problem. Also, the creators of the works in question

were already well-known for their success with similar works, so that the possibility of damage to their careers was more real than speculative.

Accordingly, a new author is not likely to be given protection analogous to the moral right, while an established author might be.

It is occasionally possible to enter an agreement with a publisher that you have the right to okay or veto editorial changes in your work, but, realistically, unless you are a very hot property indeed, most publishers don't care to bind themselves in this way.

What are some of the points my lawyer or literary agent will be looking for in my book publishing contract?

Virtually all book publishers use some kind of standard, printed contract. Many publishers have updated their contracts to make them less "one-sided," and more attuned to writers' rights. However, some standard pitfalls remain in some contracts, and your lawyer or agent will be looking for the following:

1. **Who owns the copyright?** It is *always* preferable to own the copyright in your own work. With fiction, the publisher generally expects the author to own her own copyright. But with respect to certain nonfiction works, especially textbooks or treatises, some publishers take advantage of the writer's "publish or perish" anxieties to try to own the copyright.

2. **The publisher must publish the work or turn the rights back to the author.** Your contract should include a provision requiring the publisher to publish the work within a certain time period— 12 months is usually viewed as reasonable, after which the author has the right to terminate the contract and find another publisher. There is no practical way to force a publisher to publish your book. The next best thing is to make sure you can get the rights back to your own book if the publisher does *not* publish the book within a certain, specified time. That is, unless your contract permits you to terminate for failure of the publisher to publish, you are still barred from selling that work to another publisher. For example, let's say you have written a textbook on the aesthetics of roller disco and have entered into a contract with a publisher who realizes that the market is flooded with such books, and decides not to come out with yours. Everything has gone smoothly, you've been paid your advance, your manuscript was delivered on time, but you

suspect your publisher is waiting until the year 2000 to publish your work as a nostalgic look at 1979. All of a sudden, another publisher calls and says they'd love to publish your book. Can you sell it? Yes, *if* your contract includes a provision of the type we've discussed. Otherwise, no.

3. **How much is the advance, and can I keep it if the book isn't published?** An "advance" is just that — an advance against your future royalties. While a first-time author won't have much luck trying to negotiate for a higher royalty rate, s/he may well be able to negotiate for a higher *advance* on royalties. Publishers are more reasonable about increasing the advance payment if they understand you will have to make sizable out-of-pocket expenses for travel, research, and the like in connection with the book. (Some writers are able to have the publisher agree to expend a certain amount toward such preliminaries.)

How much can you keep if the publisher decides your manuscript is not satisfactory? This depends upon the wording of your contract. Often, an advance under $5,000 will be payable to the author by "halves," ½ upon signing of the contract, and the next ½ upon timely delivery of a *satisfactory* manuscript. Larger advances are payable in thirds, or even fourths. Sometimes the first payment is larger than the rest. Some contracts provide that at least some of the advance is "nonrefundable." That is, come what may, you don't pay it back. Try to have your contract negotiated so that you are never in a position of paying money *back* unless you completely default in delivery of the manuscript. That is, limit the publisher's financial clout so that, should your timely-delivered manuscript be unsatisfactory, the final payment need not be made to you, but you need not reimburse your publisher.

Make sure that your contract explains what happens to monies "advanced from royalties" that your publishers make for illustrations, indexes, or the like in case the contract is terminated. That is, sometimes a publisher will agree to write the check for a large expense involved in your book — say, paying for a technical illustrator — with the sum to be considered an additional advance on your royalties. If you or the publisher should terminate the contract for one of the reasons permitted by the contract, make sure you and your publisher have agreed as to what happens to the drawings, and that you are not

liable for repayment of the illustration expenses.

4. **Indemnification and "Hold Harmless" clauses:** Virtually every contract provides for some kind of representation that the author has not infringed the copyright of another, that the manuscript is not libelous, pornographic, and the like.

These representations are backed up by clauses making the author responsible for payment of the publisher's legal fees, money damages, and other costs should trouble arise. It is most important to have your attorney negotiate to limit your liability. You should not have to be responsible for payment of the publisher's lawyer from the moment a spurious accusation letter is sent to your publisher.

As to pornography, *you* don't control the places your book will be sold — your publisher does. And as pornography is defined differently in different areas of the country, it is your publisher's decision where to sell your work which is likely to result in trouble. Accordingly, it would not be fair to require you to foot the bill for your publisher's legal bills in this regard.

Similarly, because your publisher is, or should be, acquainted with the libel laws, and has chosen to publish your manuscript, he or she should share in the risk of a dispute based on libel. It would be reasonable for you to indemnify your publisher for your negligence in not researching your facts, or for your deliberate libels. But your publisher had the option of having questionable material edited from your manuscript, and, if s/he did not exercise that option, it is not your fault.

As to copyright infringement, it is harder to convince a publisher that s/he should share in the responsibility. However, copyright complaints are occasionally made in situations where an author did *not* copy. To some extent, such "nuisance" claims are a business risk the publisher should share. It is sometimes possible to negotiate a contract to limit your liability to the amount of your advance, for example, or, at your option, to the amount of future royalties, so that you are not stuck with a bill for $50,000 for your publisher's legal fees on a book that earned you $9,000.

5. **Rights and permissions:** Related to indemnification, this clause deals with whether you — or your publisher — are responsible for securing written permission from authors whose work will be quoted in your book.

Ideally, this should be handled by the publisher, at the publisher's sole expense, with the publisher bearing full responsibility for properly securing all rights and permissions. The worst possible contract has the author undertaking the work of contacting the quoted authors, with the author being responsible for paying the authors for their permission. Generally, a first-time author can negotiate at least a compromise between the two extremes.

6. **Revisions of subsequent editions:** Particularly if your book is a nonfiction text, revised editions may be necessary. In this case, your lawyer will want to make sure that *you* have the right to prepare the revised editions, and that you are paid fairly for your work. Many standard contracts provide that if you do not prepare the revised editions at a time, and in a manner acceptable to the publisher, the publisher has the right to hire another writer to do so. Worse, these contracts provide that the monies paid by the publisher to the other writer will be subtracted from your future royalties. It is possible to revise such a contract so that you alone will prepare revised editions, and it is possible to make sure that you will receive an advance payment for your revision work. Incidentally, the publisher will sometimes try to have your revision advance limited to the amount of the initial advance on the first, unrevised edition. If your book is popular enough to be revised, and, most likely, sold at a higher cover price, you should receive a larger advance than you did at the time the success of the book was not known.

7. **Your right to write:** Many contracts have a provision whereby you are asked to agree not to write and sell other manuscripts on the same topic as your book. Some contracts modify this provision by stating that you are prohibited from writing other books and articles "which may interfere with sales of" the book under contract. Such modifications are often not strong enough to protect you. If you are in a "publish or perish" situation, or are known as an authority in a certain field, you certainly do not want to restrict your right to publish other manuscripts, and your lawyer or agent should be able to delete, or limit, such provisions before you sign the publishing contract.

8. **Option to publish:** Many authors get excited when they see clauses in their publishing contracts indicating that the publisher has an option to publish the author's next book. *Beware!* This does not in any way help the author to have his or her next book published. It is strictly to the benefit of the publisher, and can harm the author. What the provision means is that the publisher has the right to keep you from finding a better publisher for your next book, from negotiating with a new publisher for higher royalties, a bigger advance, and the like. If your publisher hasn't made much effort to promote your book, you don't want to be stuck with that publisher on your next book.

How are such contractual provisions sometimes modified to everyone's satisfaction? You may contract to give the publisher a right of "first refusal" competitive with terms you've been offered by another publisher. That is, you'll be entitled to submit your next manuscript to other publishers, and if one of them offers you a better deal than your present publisher, your present publisher is obligated to match that deal with respect to your second book. If he or she does *not* offer the same deal, then you're entitled to enter a contract with that second publisher.

9. **Royalties not to be held to bail out publisher:** Some contracts provide that, should you have more than one book with the same publisher, the publisher has the right to withhold royalties on your successful work(s) to pay itself back for any losses it sustained with respect to your less successful work(s). This is absolutely unfair to the author, because the publisher is the one who made the business decision to purchase the unsuccessful work, and must bear the risk. Your lawyer or agent should eliminate contractual provisions requiring your subsidization of your less successful works.

These and other pitfalls can often be eliminated, or modified, from the publishing contract your publisher has submitted to you for signature. *When?* Before you sign the contract! That is, such modifications must be made before the contract is "executed," because the publisher has no obligation whatsoever to modify the contract after you've sent him or her your signed agreement!

Jane Shay Lynch is an attorney specializing in the areas of copyright, trademark and unfair competition law, with the Chicago law firm Kegan, Kegan & Berman. Lynch's other publications include The Women's Guide to Legal Rights, *Contemporary Books Inc.*, Chicago, 1979. She serves on the board of directors of Lawyers for the Creative Arts, a Chicago organization providing free legal services to artists, and arts organizations.

The Sun and the Law

by Steve Weissman

There is always much fun and excitement involved in pioneering any new area of human endeavor. But hovering immediately behind the people with vision and creativity are others who are looking for the money to be made and the positions of power to be secured. Not surprisingly, lawyers tend to be on the money-grabbing end of things, and while they sometimes provide a real service by inventing new legal devices which unfetter progressive forces (such as the corporate form of ownership), all too often they emphasize legal uncertainties in an effort to milk private advantage from someone else's innovation. But what's worse than attorneys' greed is the fact that they have been trained in a system which carefully perpetuates the absurd notion that the dilemmas of the future can be solved by applying the lessons of the past. Somehow, the obvious fact that new fields of human endeavor necessitate new approaches to law is completely ignored in American legal training. The field of solar energy is a good example. Here lawyers still use the property concepts of medieval England (easements, covenants, proscriptive rights, etc.), instead of properly acknowledging that in this energy-depleted age, everyone must have access to the sun.

Including this article in the People's Law Review *is a bit of an experiment. It has meant expanding the idea of self-help law to include areas of public policy, legislation, etc. But why not? If the people of this globe don't quickly learn to handle their energy needs more efficiently, much of the need for self-help law in other areas will become academic. Also, since the policy makers of our government and other legal establishments don't seem to be doing a very good job, isn't it time some ordinary folks got involved?*

You're feeling grubby and tired and you want to soak in a nice hot bath. You give the faucet a twist, and steaming hot water begins to cascade into the tub. Here is a recipe for that hot bathwater, courtesy of your local utility company:

1. Build a pump capable of drawing oil out of the ground in a field somewhere in the Middle East.
2. Carry that oil by pipeline to a coastal community.
3. Ship the oil across the ocean by tanker.
4. Deliver the oil to a refinery where it is processed into fuel oil.
5. Deliver the fuel to a power plant where it can be burned to heat a boiler to several hundred degrees and drive a turbine which generates electricity.
6. Transmit the electricity over high voltage lines, through substations and smaller distribution lines all the way to your home.
7. Use the electricity to warm up a little coil at the bottom of a water-heating tank in order to raise the temperature of the water about 30 to 60 degrees Fahrenheit.
8. Take a bath.

Here is an alternative recipe:

1. Run water through a solar collector located outside of the house, either on the roof or in the yard.
2. Take a bath.

There was a time in America when lots of people used the alternative recipe. Before the first world war, solar power was cheap and available, whereas electricity was expensive, and for much of rural America, hard to get. Even as late as the 1920s, thousands of solar collectors could be seen on rooftops in Southern California and Florida. Thereafter, electricity and gas became so cheap and available that solar heaters appeared to be impractical and unnecessary. Now, we have turned full circle. The cost of gas and electricity is climbing at a frightening pace. Our reliance on Middle Eastern petroleum may have unacceptable and perhaps even catastrophic political consequences. And we now realize that nuclear power is not the universal cure-all.

So why isn't everyone rushing out to buy solar energy devices? For a lot of reasons: lack of trust, lack of money, lack of interest. For most of us it is still easier to let the old water heater cook up the bath water one more time than it is to put thought and money into the purchase of an unfamiliar new contraption. And this is sad because individual effort is the key to increased use of solar energy devices. So how can we use the law and government to coax people into giving the sun a chance? Since, at least in theory, our lawmakers and government work for us, what can you and I do to encourage our legislators and courts to make the use of solar devices more attractive? In a few far-sighted places, some creative answers to these questions are starting to surface. But it is up to us to insist that these creative solutions are adopted everywhere. Let's look at some ideas that seem to have merit.

Solar Energy Access
Suppose you decide to remodel your kitchen by adding a greenhouse-type window system which will allow the sun to warm the house. Or suppose that you decide to place a collector system on your roof to provide hot water. How can you be sure that your next-door neighbor won't convert his ranch house to a fifteen-story condominium that casts a giant shadow on your hopes for energy independence? You can't, unless there is either a law or private agreement that protects you. An agreement between neighbors can establish a privilege, or "easement," which obliges your neighbor not to interfere. This agreement may be termed a "covenant" since only your neighbor is making a promise in return for something you have already done for him or her. Usually these "covenants" are said to "run with the

land," i.e., to pass on to subsequent neighbors. If sun access is made a part of statutory law, it is usually found in zoning ordinances or building codes.

Because the right to develop property is held in high regard in the United States, landowners have not traditionally been allowed to agree to easements or restrictions that would guarantee access to the sun. In old England, access to light and air was considered to be fair game for easements. It was called the "Doctrine of Ancient Lights," which held that if continued access to sunlight had been experienced by a landowner for an uninterrupted period of time, adjacent landowners could not obstruct that access. Makes a lot of sense, doesn't it? But in the United States, where bigger and taller has long been our most important product, this doctrine has not been applied under the theory that the right to develop land is a superior right to that of sun access. Fortunately, this is beginning to change. A number of states have now recognized the right of neighbors to create solar easements to protect one another. If you participate in such an agreement, it is important to know how to describe your right to access. The preferred manner of description varies from state to state. Some states require a written description of angles of exposure. Some allow for seasonal adjustments. Others simply allow the homeowners to make their agreement according to the time sunlight is expected to hit a particular spot. It is also extremely important to know whether you can pass on your right to sunlight access when you sell your home, as well as the obligation that would accrue to the buyer of your neighbor's house.

Unfortunately, agreements among neighbors do not always promote solar energy use. Historically, local ordinances and homeowners' agreements have been used to restrict or prohibit external alterations of residences. Often this means that solar collectors, greenhouses, and other positive changes are prohibited. In these cases, the right to control land use clashes with the right to solar energy implementation. One can try to overcome such limitations by fighting for an exemption from the law, or by trying to change it. At least one state has amended its statutes to provide a more comprehensive solution. California Civil Code Section 714 states that no zoning-type restriction or covenant will be allowed if it interferes with the use of a solar-energy system

"... except reasonable restrictions" which "do not significantly increase the cost of the sytsem or significantly decrease its efficiency, or which allow for an alternate system of cost and efficiency." Hawaii has a general rule that provides protection for solar collectors in situations where it does not lead to undue hardship for other property owners.

As I mentioned briefly above, a law guaranteeing sunlight access is usually in the form of local zoning ordinances, and can also restrict building heights and setbacks. In short, energy efficiency can become a major component of the planning of all new construction.

Creative attempts to maintain access to sunlight include a New Mexico statute (based on a long-standing water-rights concept) which provides that the first property owner to install a solar system maintains a right to sunlight access which is superior to that of his neighbors. Another concept with particular applicability to areas of high population density would create transferable development rights. Potential developers would be denied the right to construct a building which blocks the sun in one area in exchange for the right to develop other land. This idea has been used successfully to preserve historical property in Chicago and New York.

Finally, law can be used to actively encourage everyone to use solar energy. One way to do this is to revise building codes to require the use of both passive housing designs and active solar systems. For example, Santa Barbara and several other California counties require active solar water heaters in many newly-constructed homes. Building codes can also be used to control the quality of solar energy installations by setting workmanship and performance standards.

Tax Breaks

The U.S. seems to be in the middle of a medium-sized tax revolution. California's Proposition 13, and its siblings around the rest of the country, are changing the way governments are financed. Windfall profits taxes on oil and other energy resources can be seen as an attempt to develop new ways of paying the public bills. There is also an increased recognition that a government which uses its tax power to encourage the development of nuclear and coal power plants should also do something for its citizens who are trying to reach some form of energy

independence.

In the past few years, the federal government and a majority of the states have changed their tax rules to encourage individuals to purchase solar energy–related equipment. In addition, laws have been passed in over half the states to allow for property tax exemptions for home improvement investments which are directed toward the use of solar energy. Some states also apply a lower-than-normal sales tax on solar energy devices, while a handful offer tax breaks for companies which use solar energy systems.

But perhaps the most enticing tax incentives are tax deductions and credits. Deductions, which are now available in states such as Arkansas, Colorado, Idaho, and Montana, allow a solar system purchaser to subtract at least part of the cost of the solar system from his or her income before taxes are computed. Tax credits, which are also offered in at least a dozen states including Alaska, California, North Carolina, Vermont, and Wisconsin, allow a certain proportion of the cost of the solar system to be subtracted directly from the amount of state income tax owed. (California is the most enthusiastic, offering a 55% credit.) Most important (due to the size of its income tax take), the federal government also offers a tax credit for 40% of the cost of solar energy installations.

It is important to check with your state tax office to see which types of benefits are available in your area. Not only do different states have different tax breaks, but they often depend on the type of construction involved. Benefits may differ for houses versus apartments, and commercial or industrial versus residential or recreational (swimming pools). Some states allow residential applications for any purpose; others won't let tax benefits apply to the heating of a swimming pool or a spa. Some states place a limit on the dollar amount of the exemption or the number of years during which it can be applied. Others set quality standards for the systems being used. Also, a few states differentiate between active solar devices and passive (building design) applications, as does the federal tax credit.

Utility Companies As Energy Advisors

A portion of Jimmy Carter's National Energy Act of 1978 addressed the role that utility companies can play in promoting conservation and solar energy use. By March 1, 1981, each gas utility that sells more than 10 billion cubic feet of gas and every electric utility that sells more than 750 million kWh (kilowatt-hours) must announce to their customers the availability of a home energy audit service under the Residential Conservation Service program. An "energy audit" sounds like a complicated review of homeowners' record books; instead, it simply means that, upon request, the utility will send a representative out to a customer's home. The auditor will then suggest the types of home improvements that would result in economically favorable energy savings for the homeowner. Lists of qualified suppliers, installers and lenders will be provided upon request. The utility companies must also help arrange for loans and installations. Because federal law leaves this requirement vague, the types of arrangements available will vary from state to state. Insuring that utility companies enthusiastically comply with this program is an area in which much public involvement is needed.

Utility Companies As Lenders

It's difficult for solar energy devices such as water heaters to compete with conventional energy sources because of the high initial costs. Although costs even out—or more than even out—over the years, solar heating systems are expensive at the outset. For many builders and home buyers, it seems preferable to have small payments over the years (as with normal utility service) than to lay out big bucks for a solar device at the beginning, even if it will result in eventual savings. The lesson in this is

that, to be competitive, an initial purchase of a solar energy system must be made almost as easy as paying a utility bill. Although the tax credits and deductions discussed above are available, many feel that these alone are not enough to make a solar installation attractive.

Some states and their utility companies have considered using utility money to soften the financial blow to a consumer interested in buying a solar energy device. The Tennessee Valley Authority has made low-interest solar loans available to its customers. California utilities are setting up a program to provide no-interest, long-term loans for about 200,000 solar water heater purchases over a three-year period. The Rhode Island Division of Public Utilities has been considering a rental program under which the utility would own and maintain the water heater and customers would make small lease payments to cover all program costs, plus profits.

The rationale behind requiring the use of utility funds to promote solar installations is that, up to a point, it is less costly to invest in a means of cutting down future energy demand than it is to invest in new energy supplies. Therefore, a utility expenditure which leads to an economical reduction in energy demand is a prudent investment. The next logical step would be to require the utility to pay the entire cost of the solar device where it can be shown that the overall cost of putting a solar system on someone's house or apartment is less than the cost of providing conventional energy. Such investments are being tried as part of a California financing program.

Do-It-Yourself Utilities

Normally, when we refer to public utilities, we really mean privately-owned utility corporations that are regulated by the state and are obligated to provide service to a segment of the public. But there are utilities which are owned by the people they serve. These are called municipal utilities. In either case, utilities are burdened by all sorts of conflicting interests that can lead to poor decisions when it comes to emphasizing solar priorities. But perhaps there is another way—people in a community or city could decide to establish their own municipal *solar* utility that would have as its sole purpose the promotion of solar energy use.

The City of Santa Clara, California, has done just

that. It has established a municipal solar utility to promote the use of solar swimming-pool heaters. The utility owns and maintains the pool heating equipment and leases it to the pool owner at a cost of about $30 per month, to be paid only during the six months of spring and summer. The participating owner must also pay an initial service connection fee of about $300 to cover labor and materials. After ten years, the solar system belongs to the building owner. The big incentive for this approach is that rental charges have tended to be 20–30% less than the cost of the natural gas needed to perform the same task.

This is a small example, but it does demonstrate that people can decide to work together to promote solar energy development. Peg Curran Gardels, a representative for the Eastern Solar Utilization Network (a regional office of the U.S. Department of Energy) explains,

> The concept of a municipal solar utility is a flexible one. It can provide loans to consumers to enable them to purchase solar energy equipment for their homes. It can make loans available to solar businesses to help them get organized. The solar utility can get into solar business itself, manufacturing or installing solar equipment, which can be particularly useful for multi-family dwellings. And its activities needn't be limited to direct solar applications. Conservation, small-scale community wind

development, recycling and waste recovery, and methane generation can be considered as well.

And Tomorrow?
If we are to make a quick transition to the solar age, many other changes in the law will be necessary. For example, at-home generation of electricity through the use of solar cells and wind machines will soon be commonplace. At certain times in the day, a homeowner will have a surplus. By the creative use of law, utilities can be ordered to buy this excess energy and thus the economics of making one's own electricity will be greatly improved (e.g., the utility buys it from you at night when you don't need it and sells it to a farmer or factory owner who has been encouraged by a price discount to operate his other equipment at off-peak hours).

There is a great need for people to become involved with solar law issues if we are to guarantee that our laws facilitate the development of solar energy and do not deny us either individual or national energy independence.

Steve Weissman is an environmental and energy lawyer with the California Public Utilities Commission which is developing the most energetic conservation/solar energy program in the country.

Additional Thoughts
by Ira Lee Birnbaum and Charles Galvin, Jr.

In the above article Steve Weissman suggests that using law to promote the use of solar energy is in the best long-run interests of utility companies because such expenditures would be less costly than investing in equipment to generate new sources of energy. In his words, "it is less costly to invest in a means of cutting down future energy demand [by the use of solar energy] than it is to invest in new energy supplies." This is certainly true. But the utility companies would also benefit from the use of solar energy in the short run. In order to satisfy peak demand (generally between the hours of 10 a.m. and 8 p.m.), utility companies find it necessary to use their least efficient generators. This period of highest utilization coincides with the optimal hours of solar utilization. The widespread use of solar energy during peak hours would allow utility companies to minimize the use of their least efficient equipment, resulting in lower operating costs for the utility which would, in turn, benefit all of its customers — even those who don't use solar energy.

The Tennessee Valley Authority is one generator of electricity that has recognized the value of solar power to its own power sytem and to its customers who use solar energy. The T.V.A. has calculated the monetary value of each individual solar water heater, passive solar home, wood stove, etc., and offers this amount to customers — usually in the form of subsidized low-interest loans — as an incentive to purchase solar devices. T.V.A.'s residential solar program consists of five areas — water heaters, passive solar new homes, passive solar improvements of existing homes, modular solar homes (factory-built but not mobile), and wood heaters. T.V.A.'s original approval of these residential program areas was contingent upon a demonstration — through computer simulation — that they will pay for themselves and thus benefit T.V.A.

T.V.A. is unique because it is a federally-owned utility serving parts of seven states. But for the same reasons that the T.V.A. finds it in its own economic interest to promote solar energy, other utilities could likewise profit. Careful regulation by state Public Utility Commissions could encourage all utilities to pass along to their customers the savings associated with solar power. As noted, such savings include both the benefits of each particular solar unit as well as the lower overall utility operating costs. Moreover, if utilities were required by law to pass along solar-related savings to their customers, the public would recognize that the use of solar energy saves them money. This recognition would dispel the claim made by many utility companies that solar energy, by reducing the revenues available to utilities, costs their customers money.

Utilities, by virtue of the capital they have at hand and the monthly billing of customers, are in an excellent position to accelerate the conversion towards a solar America. However, care must be taken to limit the "domain" of the utility companies. For example, proposals which advocate that the utility companies be the *owners* of solar equipment while we, as customers, be its *renters*, are unacceptable. After all, many people see solar energy as a way to escape the tyranny of utilities. The law must be made to encourage options other than a continued reliance on utilities. Nor should the utility companies be permitted to corner the market on solar technology. To do so would stifle private enterprise in the solar field, as well as the cost reductions which should accompany competition among private firms. Furthermore, utility monopolization would tend to freeze the state of solar technology at the *status quo* and eliminate the innovation and experimentation which is so necessary if we are to become a solar society.

Charles Galvin, Jr. and Ira Lee Birnbaum work in the solar energy field. Both contributed to Towards A Solar America, *a technological and institutional assessment of on-site solar development in the United States sponsored by the Department of Energy (DOE). This report, which discusses in more detail many of the issues presented here, can be obtained from the Office of Advanced Energy System Studies, U.S. Department of Energy, Washington, D.C. 20585, Attn: Ron White.*

PART III

In Pro Per

While most of our legal establishment continues to act as if people are slightly daft if they aren't delighted to contribute $75 or so an hour to the support of a lawyer whenever a court appearance is necessary, as we have demonstrated in the previous section, it is perfectly legal to represent yourself. In this section we want to present some stories by and about people who have done just that.

One of the wonderful things about the self-help law movement is that ordinary people are discovering that appearing "In Pro Per," and helping others to do so, is fun. And self-representation isn't limited to filing for a divorce or bankruptcy these days. Many non-lawyers are involving themselves in writing legislation, teaching others how to negotiate with landlords or creditors, and assisting people in representing themselves in all sorts of court and administrative hearings. As someone said to us the other day, "This whole movement to open up our legal system to people can really be described with one word — 'democracy.' "

Not everyone believes that a rotten court system is a bad thing. David Hapgood in his interesting book, *The Average Man Fights Back*, reports the following statement by the Chinese Emperor K'ang Hsi:

> ... lawsuits would tend to increase to a frightening extent if people were not afraid of the tribunals and if they felt confident of always finding in them ready and perfect justice... I desire therefore that those who have recourse to the tribunals should be treated without pity and in such a manner that they shall be disgusted with law and tremble to appear before a magistrate.

The Wave Project

by Jolene Jacobs

Jolene Jacobs has administered a self-help divorce office for seven years. Thus far she has aided more than 3,000 people to do their own divorce. In 1973, when she opened her first office in San Jose, California, she charged $45 for her services. Now, working in San Francisco, she charges $75 to prepare divorce papers. By using $60 as her average fee, it is easy to compute that Jolene has charged the people she has helped a total of about $180,000. To put this amount in perspective—suppose each of her clients had seen a lawyer and paid an average fee of $400. The total bill would have been $1,200,000. We don't mean to suggest that the only advantage that Jolene Jacobs and other self-help divorce counselors provide is low cost. As Jolene discusses here, there are a number of other excellent reasons to act as one's own lawyer. Nevertheless, the fact that lawyers have priced themselves out of the market is one good reason to handle simple legal actions without them.

Growing up in the 1950s, I remember sitting in front of the TV, staring at the weekly procession of ordinary folks spitting and wailing at each other on Hollywood's real-life trauma drama—"Divorce Court." Although the media tend to make everything larger than life, it was true enough that before "no-fault" marriage dissolutions, divorce in the courtroom was almost as nasty as divorce on TV. It was, quite simply, a state-decreed battle. One spouse was required to accuse the other of one or more crimes against the marriage. Physical brutality, adultery, or incurable insanity would do, but you had to choose. Even friendly mutual separation usually ended in a court fight, given this morally judgmental adversary scheme.

Until the early 1970s, divorce meant that someone had to be proved to be at fault and often that someone had to pay dearly in property or support. It was a system that encouraged conflict and under which no one really benefited, except the lawyers. These self-appointed guardians of society charged heavy monetary and emotional tolls to their hapless victims, who then had the privilege of being led through the legal maze. Part of the reason why lawyers could charge so much was that they ran the only stores in town. If you wanted a divorce, you went to a lawyer and paid prices that were fixed through the bar association's fee-fixing committees.

Then, suddenly, in 1970 it all changed. California became one of the first states to adopt a no-fault system under which a spouse who wanted a divorce needed only to say the magic words "irreconcilable differences" and the marriage was dissolved. Under the new law, "divorces" became "dissolutions," and if there was basic agreement on questions of property division, child custody and support, only one spouse had to go through the court process. The best feature of no-fault divorce was that neither party had to be found to be "wrong" and that each was entitled to half the property of the marriage (California is a community property state), regardless of the grounds for the divorce. And there was another terrific benefit too—all of the paperwork was reduced to simple fill-in forms.

With these reforms, it began to occur to a few people that perhaps lawyers were no longer necessary to fill in the forms. Charles "Ed" Sherman, an ex–Legal Aid lawyer who had done scores of divorces for people who were unable to afford a conventional lawyer, was one of the first to perceive this breakthrough. Now that the forms had been translated out of their legal jargon and into garden-variety English, it was possible for people to handle their own divorces. In 1971, Sherman wrote and published *How to Do Your Own Divorce in California*, a concise, well-written paperback book which explained what divorce meant when dealing with property, custody and support. But perhaps more importantly, Ed explained how to fill in every blank in every form; how to file and serve the papers; and what to say at the hearing. In short, the book provided all the instructions, information and forms that were necessary for a layperson to handle the dissolution of his or her marriage. It is fair to say that *How to Do Your Own Divorce in California*, which has now sold over a quarter of a million copies and has been widely imitated in other states, started a revolution, a revolution that continues to move divorce out of the hands of lawyers and into the hands of people.

Predictably, the publication of Sherman's book outraged the official legal community. They called press conferences and ranted and raved at how dangerous it was for non-lawyers to attempt their own divorces with a book that cost only $4.95. With the help of the media, their warnings were broadcast across California. But their hysteria only served to call attention to the existence of the book and to alert people to the fact that an alternative existed. Moreover, public distrust of lawyers and official bar associations was already running so high that these warnings turned the book into a best seller. This process was aided, of course, by the fact that the statements by the bar associations were essentially lies. In truth, the book worked.

In the early seventies, there was also resistance to self-help divorce from the court system. Judges and clerks were often hostile to people who chose to represent themselves. Several judges refused to let people present their cases without a lawyer, and a great many others were as unpleasant and uncooperative as possible when people appeared "in pro per."[1] One clerk in San Jose had a sign on her counter restricting her services to "lawyers and clerks only." Other clerks were impatient with people who were representing themselves because the people

weren't quite sure what they were supposed to say and do. In all fairness, clerks did have to worry about lawyers watching over their shoulder to make sure that they weren't giving out legal advice. Even supplying information about whether or not a certain form was available, or on what date papers could be filed, could, and did, lead to complaints by paranoid lawyers that clerks were practicing law, thus placing their job in jeopardy. I think that lawyers, judges, and clerks hoped that, if they made things difficult and unpleasant enough, people would just give up and get a lawyer.

All of them (especially judges, who were at the top of the heap) had a vested interest in the *status quo*—it wouldn't do anything for their prestige as "professionals" if people could get a divorce as easily as a driver's license. But the legal establishment hadn't reckoned yet with Ed Sherman. Ed, along with Ralph Warner, the co-founder of Nolo Press in Berkeley, California, responded by attacking lawyers where it hurt the most—in the pocketbook. They set up what they called "the Wave Project," in which they trained para-legals to run their own businesses, to assist people with the legal red tape and paperwork of divorce. Think of it this way—if using the *How to Do Your Own Divorce in California* book was equivalent to riding a 10-speed bike, and having a lawyer handle your divorce was comparable to riding in a Rolls Royce, then utilizing the services of a Wave Project counselor can be seen as being the equivalent of getting about in a Volkswagen "Bug."

And this is where I came in. I had just graduated from college, where I had been inspired by Nader's Raiders and much of the rest of the consumer rights movement. But this was 1973 and the world wasn't full of jobs for consumer advocates. Then I heard about the Wave Project. I went to Berkeley in search of more information, learned how the project was organized, what potential problems there might be with the bar association and district attorneys, and when and where I could open an office. I was excited, but admittedly a little fearful of embarking on such a new and unexplored profession—especially since Ed and Ralph kept warning me that they couldn't guarantee that I wouldn't be prosecuted and sent to jail.

After some thought, I decided that the opportunity to train as a Wave Project counselor outweighed

the risks. Within a few weeks I was being trained alongside 12 other prospective counselors. We met in the living room of Ed and Ralph's brown-shingle house in Berkeley. We had already studied the "divorce" book individually and would now be spending the next week, a full eight hours a day, learning how to use the divorce forms and the court system. We were all pretty overwhelmed at first. There seemed to be so many forms and steps involved. We reviewed the material repeatedly, and gradually we came to see that our job was not impossible. By the end of the training, we all had a clear understanding of the paperwork involved in the divorce process. We knew we could help people as long as we weren't arrested.

Opening an office was the next big step. Mine was to be set up in San Jose and I was very definitely on my own. Ralph and Ed were so overwhelmed with setting up some sort of central structure that they provided no help. I drove around San Jose to familiarize myself with the area and to check for possible office locations. I had never had a business before, so I talked to many people to find out who did what and where in the community. I decided on the older downtown area, as it offered good bus transportation, proximity to the courthouse, lower rent, and boasted a number of similar community service agencies. Everyone I talked to was surprised by, but supportive of, the concept of the office.

Finally, I had an office, a phone, and some new contacts. The next step was to place an ad in the local newspaper. The woman who took the classified ads was hesitant. She had recently had a bad experience with a man who had placed an ad for a boat crew and then assaulted the women interviewees while at sea. As a result she felt a personal responsibility for future announcements and was skeptical about placing our ad. She had never heard of a self-help divorce clinic and didn't know if it was legitimate or not. Finally I convinced her and she accepted the ad.

Please keep in mind that prior to this time, I had no experience with or knowledge of advertising, public relations, or organizing a small business. Nor had I ever considered doing any of these things. I had never before been in the position of "selling" an idea, let alone convincing people that I could competently provide services normally provided by a "professional." Everything I did was a new experience.

All the newly-trained Wave Project counselors were setting up offices throughout the state, and all of us were nervous about out first customers. Would we remember everything we had learned in training, or would it all mysteriously vanish? My own first customer was not from San Jose, but from Salinas — about 50 miles south. Today, thousands of divorces later, I can clearly remember setting up that first appointment, the interminable waiting, and the arrival. The customer's name was Paul. He had seen the ad in the papers and couldn't believe he could get a divorce for $55 plus the county fee ($46). At that time, the office — a long, narrow room with a window at one end — consisted of a typewriter and two wooden boxes. One box was for the customer to sit on, and the other was for my typewriter. I sat on the floor. The office did not look established or permanent, but the price I offered was at least $300 less than an attorney, so Paul was willing to give me a try. We sat down as best we could, going through the book together and filling out the forms. It was a little tense and slow at first, but then things speeded up and we went through the paperwork just fine.

The newspaper ad generated business for a while, but the ad was later cancelled. Evidently, the paper's legal department (no doubt prompted by complaints from lawyers) issued an opinion that it was illegal to advertise anything concerning divorce. Ed and Ralph had warned us that the newspapers would eventually learn of the existence of an old California law (Penal Code Section 159a, enacted around 1890), which made it a misdemeanor to "advertise, print, publish, to distribute or circulate any circular, pamphlet, card, handbill, printed notice, book, newspaper or notice of any kind, offering to procure, to aid in procuring or obtaining any divorce. . . ." I understand that this code section originally had provisions aimed at the restrictions of information about birth-control and abortion as well. Obviously Section 159a was a reflection of a repressive social policy toward women, which advocated big families and no divorce. Wave Project counselors in other cities also encountered this law. None of us could understand how it could be illegal for us to offer information about divorce since divorce itself was a completely legal activity. It was astounding to me that there could be a law which said that giving a person written information about divorce was illegal

because it might encourage them to get one. What about the constitutionally guaranteed right of "freedom of speech," and the public's right to information?

But with my ad out of the newspaper, I had to develop other outreach skills. I sent out large mailings, made countless visits to agencies, and spoke to community groups. Because of Section 159a, passing out printed material on divorce always made me nervous, but I did it anyway. All of this was time-consuming, but with no access to media advertising, there was no other way to inform the public of our existence. But then an odd thing happened — although newspapers wouldn't take our ads, they began to write feature stories about us. What irony! We couldn't buy an ad, but we were controversial and so became news. Lots of potential clients read about our services in the feature stories and business grew.

Gradually, the Wave Project and other self-help divorce clinics began to make a significant dent in the incomes of lawyers all across the state. During some months, I would help more than 40 people do their own divorce. Other offices did even more business. Prior to our efforts, there had been two unquestioned taboos in the legal community: 1) you couldn't advertise prices (ungentlemanly competition among lawyers), and 2) you had to stick to the "minimum fee schedule" (no hidden meaning in that term!). So, it was an ironic turn of events when the same lawyers who had used the advertising issue to suppress our business were now demanding the right to advertise and lower their fees in order to recapture the clients who were coming to us. In San Jose, the president of the local bar association was actually quoted in a newspaper article as saying that lawyers needed to advertise in order to compete with the Pro Per divorce clinics. He added that lawyers just can't watch millions of dollars in divorce fees slip through their fingers without putting up a fight! When I read that, I really felt as if I had accomplished something positive.

One of the biggest legal hassles we were to face involved the legal community's charge that we were practicing law without a license. Traditionally, lawyers have defined that term so narrowly that "unauthorized practice" can be interpreted to include giving people such simple information as the fact that it takes six months to get a final decree of divorce in California. Of course, telling someone that he or she can turn right on a red light is also giving legal advice, but no one is going to be charged with unauthorized practice of the law in this situation because no lawyers fees are being lost.

Finally, the threat of prosecution for unauthorized practice became a reality. By 1975, the Wave Project had about 26 offices, and all of us were experiencing close scrutiny by local district attorneys and bar associations. The state legislature had their collective eye on us too. Most of the investigations that occurred began with a phone call. The investigator would pose as a potential client and proceed to try to trick the divorce counselor into giving legal advice. If the investigator felt there was sufficient reason to pursue to case, he would send in a "plant" to pose as a customer. Usually the plant would carry a hidden tape recorder. Some counselors had experiences that would have fit nicely into a grade-C detective movie, and all of us began to learn to distinguish clients from the D.A.'s investigators. A few counselors who were too trusting found themselves facing criminal charges. But sometimes the investigations backfired. In Santa Clara County, where I worked, an investigator called after his investigation to say that he had been impressed with the quality of the work we were doing. Several months later he called again, this time to ask if he might get a job with the Wave Project.

In the meantime, the California Bar Association was going after Ed Sherman for setting up the Wave Project. They subpoenaed several of us, as well as several of our customers, to a bar disciplinary hearing. I thought it was outrageous that the bar association, which is really only a professional trade association like the American Medical Association or a plumber's union, had the power to subpoena us under the jurisdiction of the Superior Court. I thought about not showing up until I discovered that failure to appear would result in my being found in contempt of court and subject to arrest. How Ed beat the Bar Association is another story, but suffice it to say that his suggestion to them that *they* were the ones who needed discipline and his offer to send them his license to practice if they would send him a stamped, self-addressed envelope, definitely threw them off balance!

Let me digress for a moment. Beyond the legal establishment's attempts to control access to legal information and services, my biggest philosophical disagreement with lawyers concerns their argument that people shouldn't represent themselves because they are not capable of making their own decisions. Only attorneys can make good decisions, so their reasoning goes, and the average layperson is somehow emotionally and mentally incapable of doing as well. I have watched and assisted almost 3,000 people who have handled their own divorces over the past seven years. It's my experience that most people know what they want to do when they come to my office and have often reached those decisions by mutual agreements with their spouses. Unfortunately, however, lots of people who are perfectly capable of making good decisions find it difficult to do so because they lack reliable information. Information is the key, and traditionally lawyers have been highly successful in withholding it, disclosing only small bits of it in exchange for large sums of money. As a society, we must change this. People have a right to the information they need to make their own decisions.

Many times I see situations in which one spouse (usually the wife), who has always been financially dependent on the other, has no idea what the total family income is. Even if she does have this information, she may feel uncomfortable asking for half of the marital assets, though by law they belong to her already. This type of situation often develops because neither spouse clearly understands the rules of property division. I honestly believe that most people would like to arrive at a separation in as easy and fair a manner as possible. That they sometimes fail is commonly because they are confused about what the law is. Overcoming this information problem is often a significant event in people's lives.

I have noticed time after time that when people competently handle the details of their own divorces — as opposed to handing over their lives to paid "legal experts" trained in the adversary system — they come out of the experience with a real sense of personal power and achievement. They also avoid the typical lawyer attitude that the longer a fight can be prolonged, the higher the fees that can be charged. Doing their own divorce can be a particularly dramatic breakthrough for some women who feel they are finally taking charge of their lives. One woman wrote to me about her experience handling her own court hearing:

They called my name and I went up to be both petitioner and lawyer in one . . . I made eye contact with the judge and began . . . my voice sounded clear, strong, definite, and I kept imagining myself as Jane Fonda there. I did it and I felt great, uplifted . . . a liberated woman.

But back to the Wave Project. The trials and confrontations of the beginning years served the positive purpose of bonding us together. We all felt a group identity. We made decisions as a group, did group advertising, had common business practices and policy. We held quarterly statewide meetings and frequent regional meetings. The group meetings were particularly important to those who worked in more isolated parts of California. We learned practical skills — how to start and maintain a small business, and how to do advertising and media work. It was important to us that we were working for the benefit of many people and not just ourselves, and that the work was socially useful.

Also, we formed a mutual defense fund. Each office contributed an amount of money per month that was based on the number of cases which had been initiated that month. The fund gave us a sense of contributing to each other's welfare, a feeling that if the D.A. in one county was particularly troublesome, one person wouldn't have to bear those legal costs alone. Also, we felt that money spent on legal costs would benefit not only ourselves but everyone throughout the state who hoped to do their own divorces. It is possible that this is another reason why we had fewer legal hassles. We were a statewide organization with the resources of the whole group available to us. Some of us were threatened by local D.A.s and we were able to give each other financial and emotional support. Other people trying to do what we were doing without support were routinely forced out of busines by lawyer-instigated harassment. They just didn't have the resources needed for a prolonged battle.

I don't mean to suggest that everything related to the Wave Project was easy and successful. There were problems with central administration. Ralph and Ed transferred their involvement in the Wave Project to the development of Nolo Press, and others took over the central office function, causing some difficulties. In several of the offices, work was not of the highest quality, and sometimes there were disagreements among the counselors as to how statewide policy should be coordinated. In short, as with any human endeavor, there were definitely times when our frustrations outnumbered our satisfactions.

But perhaps the one overriding reason for our eventual success, and the thing that continues to make the difficulties bearable, is the fact that we fulfill a real need. There are thousands of people who cannot afford the price of a traditional divorce and we provide a low cost, high-quality, non-lawyer alternative.

Times have changed for the better since I opened my office seven years ago. Self-representation in divorce proceedings has risen from an almost nonexistent 0.02% to 30–40% of all divorces done in the state of California. It has been both encouraging and personally satisfying to observe the self-help divorce movement cut into a wasteful, overly expensive, lawyer-dominated industry that has both encouraged dependence and monopolized information and services for way too long.

NOTE: The Wave Project has been renamed and is now known as Divorce Centers of California, Inc. For a complete listing of all these centers see *How to Do Your Own Divorce in California* by Charles Sherman (Nolo Press).

---

1. In many areas of the country, the term "pro se" is used.

Jolene Jacobs runs the Divorce Center of California office (formerly Wave Project) in San Francisco, CA. Her response to our request for information was: "There is nothing in my life suitable to print. I'm trying to get it together. I have a nice boyfriend, house and job — is that enough?"

Street Law: Delancey Street's Training in Social Survival Skills

by Carol Kizziah and Mimi Silbert

In this interview by Carol Kizziah, Mimi Silbert, co-president of San Francisco's Delancey Street Foundation, talks to us in some detail about Delancey Street's residence program—its history, its philosophy, and how it actually functions. Delancey Street concerns itself with an area of law that many of us take for granted—basic survival skills. Many of the drug addicts, alcoholics and prostitutes who enter its doors do not have the skills to cope with the world around them. Somehow they never learned—or perhaps they lost—the ability to deal with employers, bureaucrats, banks, courts, police, and all the others around whom life in modern society revolves. It's not so much that the people who come to Delancey Street are criminals that sets them apart from the rest of us (aren't we all?), but that they are caught. And don't underestimate the value of knowing how to cope with your surroundings, for the person who can successfully navigate through life will tie one on and wake up in her or his own bed. The person who can't navigate wakes up in the drunk tank. So, "right on!" Delancey Street—we need more programs which recognize the importance of teaching people the basic coping skills necessary for survival.

Much has been written about Delancey Street since it was first established as a residential program for drug addicts, alcoholics, prostitutes and criminal offenders on January 1, 1971, which is clearly a tribute to a program which has succeeded in a field where failure is the norm. Delancey Street traces its beginnings to an ex-con who invited a few junkies to stay in his apartment with the intention of helping them kick their heroin habits, and is today acknowledged to be a unique self-help program which has served over 3,000 people. Over 85% of Delancey Street's residents have been heroin addicts for an average of ten years; over 60% are poly-drug abusers; over 40% are alcoholics. (These statistics total over 100% because they reflect multiple abuse among residents.) Most residents have served an average of seven years in prison and have returned to prison three and four times. Some residents are referred by the courts and others come in off the street. Delancey Street's major operations are in San Francisco, California, but a new program has recently been established in New Mexico at the urging of that state's mental health and corrections officials. Delancey Street is a voluntary program, but acceptance into the program is conditional upon a two-year minimum commitment. Residents are not permitted to use any drugs or alcohol at any time. Delancey Street is a totally integrated program, serving Blacks, Anglos, Latinos, Asians, men, women, young and old.

The first step in the residential program is to remove the individual from his or her habitual life circumstance. The resident moves from an apparently criminogenic subculture into a tightly structured community where a complete process of re-education begins. The first area of re-education is in academic skills. Every Delancey Street resident is tutored in reading, writing and mathematics until he or she receives a high-school equivalency certificate. (Though not all Delancey Street residents were high-school dropouts.) Residents are then encouraged to enroll in courses through regular community resources. There are currently more than 100 residents in local colleges and professional schools.

The second area of re-education is in vocational training. Delancey Street maintains nine training schools which are also the businesses by which the Foundation earns its living. These include a restaurant, a catering business, a moving and trucking school, terrarium and sand-painting production and sales, speciality advertising sales, antique car restoration, outdoor Christmas tree lots, and a print shop. Every resident begins his vocational training in the kitchen and then goes on to receive training in three areas: physical labor, sales, and desk work. Once residents have reached a required level of competence and have developed strong work habits, they are expected to choose a career and then seek additional training in that field.

The last phase of vocational training is employment in the community, where residents must work successfully for six months prior to graduating from Delancey Street. Over three-fourths of Delancey Street's graduates are currently working in the community in occupations as varied as a deputy sheriff, a mortician, real estate brokers and advertising executives, truckers who own their own companies, engineers, medical and dental technicians, and lawyers.

The ex-con who founded Delancey Street is John Maher. Born in New York City's South Bronx, he was an addict by the age of 12 and had left school by the eighth grade. By the time Maher was 19, he had earned a substantial reputation on New York's Upper West Side for petty theft, running numbers, dealing junk, and passing stolen goods. Finally, having grown tired of prisons, hospitals, and a string of failures, Maher moved to California, determined to straighten out his life. Out of his determination, Delancey Street was born.

Mimi Silbert is co-president of Delancey Street and holds Ph.d. degrees in criminology and psychology from the University of California, Berkeley. She has taught at Berkeley and has served as Director of Institutional Change at San Francisco State University, a program which encourages students to involve themselves in the community. While devoting most of her time to Delancey Street, she is also a Training Consultant to the San Francisco Police Department as well as other law enforcement and corrections agencies around the country. In this interview, Dr. Silbert describes in some detail how Delancey Street residents learn the social survival skills which are essential for their re-entry into society.

Carol Kizziah: What is the major purpose of the Delancey Street program?
Mimi Silbert: Delancey Street is essentially a re-education center. We don't think of the process as rehabilitation. To us it is a matter of mutual restitution. The residents gain the vocational, personal, interpersonal and social skills necessary to make

restitution to the society from which they have taken illegally. In return, Delancey Street tries to extract commitments from the community to provide access to legitimate opportunities from which the majority of residents have been blocked for most of their lives. It is this concept which inspired the choice of the name Delancey Street,[1] rather than a more traditional name like Cry Help. We wanted even our name to reflect the fact that our residents are like immigrants to a particular American way of life in which they have not yet learned to survive.

CK: How is the re-education process accomplished?
MS: Delancey Street residents are receiving both formal and informal education every day, 24 hours a day. The emphasis of the program is on self-help—not just in overcoming drug use and criminal behavior, but in taking control over their own lives. We have a half-hour morning meeting and a one-hour seminar at noon each day. These are self-help seminars which relate to such social skills as how to buy clothes, select materials, eat properly, etc. Many seminars are philosophical in nature and attempt to assist residents to understand the concepts of self-reliance as well as the general theories which underlie all modern thinking. Residents study Darwin, Einstein, Freud and many others. The majority of seminars, however, are aimed at teaching residents how to become experts in navigating their daily lives successfully and within the law—without relying on outside experts.

CK: What specific instruction is included in these survival skill seminars?
MS: Beginning with financial issues, we teach residents how to read, interpret and enter into contracts. We discuss real estate issues—how to rent, buy, etc. Money management is another crucial survival skill. Residents learn everything from how to write checks to making wise investments. In addition to these areas, our New Mexico facility necessitated some changes and additions to our training program. Although there is some overlap in the skills needed for urban and rural living, there are some substantial differences.

CK: Can you elaborate on these differences?
MS: The approach to money management, consumerism, and such business skills as buying and selling is very different in rural areas such as New Mexico. While in urban communities it is essential to be able to decipher legal documents and con-

Seminar on urban survival skills

tracts, rural approaches to buying and selling still approximate the old trading principle where all that is needed to consumate a transaction is your word and a handshake. There is still a great deal of reliance on oral agreements over written agreements. There are certain unspoken and unwritten expectations that govern the rural lifestyle, which, if ignored, can place you in the same kind of jeopardy as signing an illegal contract in the city. So, our New Mexico residents are trained not only in the law, but in how to clarify these unspoken expectations. This is essential—making certain that everyone knows what is expected of them and how to properly fulfill these expectations.

CK: What other instruction is presented in the daily seminars?

MS: Welfare and family law is an area of concern to many of our residents. It is important that they learn their rights and responsibilities with regard to such assistance programs as Aid to Families with Dependent Children. We discuss the function of the social worker and the limits on his or her investigative authority; the financial obligations of mothers and fathers; differences between foster care and adoption, etc. Seminars are offered in the rights of the elderly vis-a-vis nursing homes, social security, etc. We also provide substantial training in mediation skills, so that our residents learn how to handle people and situations in such a way as to avoid getting into trouble. All of our instruction is civil, non-criminal in nature. We maintain absolute rigidity when it comes to criminal issues. The rule is simple—you don't break any laws.

CK: Is your training in the area of mediation applicable to the general population?

MS: Absolutely. I think everyone should learn mediation skills. They are one of the really important general crime-prevention techniques—although we don't teach them as crime prevention. Many disputes ultimately escalate into fights and sometimes into crimes of vengence, even among the general "law-abiding" citizenry. We teach a kind of mini-conflict resolution course which includes learning to recognize when people are in crisis— i.e., how to read non-verbal cues—and then to use this awareness to avoid violence. We teach residents to watch their distance when they are arguing with someone, and how to avoid certain provocative physical stances which are frequently interpreted as hostile, or suggestive of violence. Residents learn to be aware of their own posture and how to break habitual stances to enable them to talk in ways which will defuse violence.

CK: Are residents taught to resolve conflicts after they erupt?

MS: Yes, of course. If in spite of efforts made to avoid provocation you see that the other person and/or you are agitated, you can break the tension by temporarily separating the people, or suggesting a friendly cup of coffee. You have to stop and say, "Look, I'm sorry. I didn't mean for this to escalate. Let's see if there is some way that we can discuss our points of difference without antagonizing one another." We even suggest that if it can't be done verbally, they should each try and write down their grievances, expectations, etc.

CK: I imagine these skills could be used by a woman in discussing, let us say, child custody with her ex-husband.

MS: Right. In fact, we frequently use role-playing techniques in our seminars. Sometimes we recreate landlord/tenant problem situations. Frequently the subject is repossession, i.e., what to do when you've purchased a cheap couch and discover it has no springs. Other common situations involve how to get rid of ex-husbands when they come to your house loaded, or how to cope with children and other members of your family.

While the majority of residents need to learn alternatives to violent and aggressive behavior, there are some who need to learn to be more assertive. We teach them to be assertive rather than aggressive, an important distinction which many do not comprehend at first. Residents must learn to accept that being right does not mean they are necessarily going to win. Frequently it is not an issue of right and wrong. You can be absolutely right about something and still lose everything. We use the trade-off/pay-off system—deciding what you want, what your pay-off is going to be, and then you trade. For example, sometimes you must trade being correct, or loud, or looking good in front of others in order to win your point. Most people learn the art of negotiation without even knowing it. They unconsciously absorb it from their families and in school. But most of our residents are strangers to the art of compromise. They have no idea what it means to negotiate something to get what you want. The concept is really quite alien to them.

CK: Are there other areas of training we have not discussed?

MS: No—I would say that the two critical areas of training are in written and verbal skills. These skills are intrinsic to almost every aspect of our lives. Our residents learn to handle both the rational and irrational contingencies of daily living. After all, what does it matter if the other person was wrong, or drunk, or anything else if, in fact, you end up in trouble and having to hire a lawyer to keep you out of jail?

CK: Does Delancey Street rely at all on outside experts?

MS: Well, our philosophy is that we are people who have never learned to rely on ourselves and so, although we are not hostile to experts, we feel it is critical to learn to take control over our own lives. Most of our residents have rigid enough personalities that once they take control of their own life, they do it across the board. Our training is in no way anti-professional—it is really just a matter of survival for residents to learn how to fend for themselves in society.

---

1. The Foundation takes it name from Delancey Street in New York's Lower East Side where, at the turn of the century, it came to symbolize the self-reliance of Old World immigrants who worked and earned their way into the mainstream of American life.

Carol Kizziah is a freelance consultant in the fields of criminal justice, health and social policies planning. She and Dr. Silbert have worked together over the last seven years on police training projects, victimization studies, jail and prison programming projects, and the development and evaluation of alternative community-based criminal justice programs.

The Legal Right to Be a Father

by Lee Cunningham

The courts are one of the most powerful American institutions dedicated to the perpetuation of the outdated notion that a woman's role is to raise a family and take care of the home, while men are uniformly expected to be providers—that is, to trundle off to work their 40 hours a week and bring home the bacon. This remains true even though the social and economic facts of life have changed radically in the last few years, with a majority of women now working and many fathers happily changing diapers. In short, our conservative judiciary (most of whom are old, male and middle-class) continues, in the majority of cases, to act as if everyone who appears before them is living the American dream, circa 1947.

Hardly a week goes by when one or another of us at Nolo isn't approached by a father, or father's group, asking for help in gaining custody of, or visitation with, their children. Just as collecting child support payments is one of the biggest problems of the majority of divorced mothers, many men feel that law and lawyers have done a completely inadequate job in guaranteeing one of their most basic human rights— the right to be a father. Those of you who have seen the movie "Kramer v. Kramer" will understand a little of what many men have endured. Lee Cunningham is a man who took his own sense of anger and outrage at the legal rules which, after his divorce, frustrated his right to relate to his children, and organized a state-wide father's rights movement in Oregon. Others are doing similar things in other states, and gradually the laws and court procedures that have prevented men from relating to their own children are being changed. While there are a few lawyers who have helped in the effort, father's rights has largely been a people's movement led by such men as Lee Cunningham, who have learned that if they don't help themselves, no one else will do it for them.

There are many old-fashioned people who think that divorce is something that happens only to other people. I was once one of them. Even though I was very dissatisfied with my marriage, my children were my life and I couldn't imagine leaving them.

But as a result of my wife's refusal to relocate so that I could pursue my career, I found myself with no career to pursue. Constantly barraged by her accusation that I was a bum who didn't care to support his family and wouldn't work, I almost believed it. Occasional part-time and temporary work hadn't "cut it" at all, and our life became desperate. After months of futile job-seeking, accompanied by steadily worsening relations at home, my wife demanded that I "get out." Finally, I left. The situation was unbelievable. The brilliant young career man with no job. The great father and loving provider driving away with his clothes strewn over the back seat of the car. The children crying in disbelief that Dad was leaving home.

This was the way I saw my life when my marriage ended. In the five years since I founded the Non Custodial Parents Association (NCAP) in Portland, Oregon, I have seen and talked to four or five hundred men whose lives were much like mine—devastated. Men—the traditional leaders and bastions of our system—become bumbling idiots at the loss of home and children. And once the downhill slide begins, it usually gets worse. Despite good intentions, almost everything these men do compounds the problem. They often move out and abandon their homes, property, and monetary resources for the sake of their children and then find themselves on the street—starting over like teenagers, but with wrinkles and gray hair. Frequently they move toward booze, drugs and some rather strange bedfellows, when what they really want is that old familiar hearth, their children, and their wives.

But there is no going back. They must start their lives anew, whether they are 27 years old or 57. Family men, little league coaches, family campers, home repairmen and stalwart providers all—alone. Inside they still feel like Dad, the family man, but in truth they are now just bachelors, men who neither look, act nor feel free. And where is Mom? Stuck

163

with the responsibility of the kids, a job, legal proceedings, insurance, bills, and a house and car that need repairs.

In my case, I wanted to be sure that the kids had everything they could possibly need, so I gave my wife our home, the older car, the stocks, furnishings and appliances—everything. And even though I was guilty of failing as a provider, I did the best I could and thought that my wife would understand. I also expected the court to grasp my situation. After all, I'd given everything to my family and had nothing more to give. But my wife and the courts didn't see it that way at all. With the assistance of the District Attorney, my wife demanded the court-ordered child support NOW and wanted it IN FULL. In addition, my wife decided to punish me for my inability to keep my support payments current by keeping the children from me and refusing to let me see my oldest child at all.

Divorce, child custody, etc., is suppsed to be resolved in our courts of domestic "justice." Justice? There couldn't be a worse misnomer. Our courts are comprised of legal technicians with no training in family matters, yet who make decisions concerning a major social dilemma. Like any technicians, lawyers and judges are often blinded by their own lingo and procedures. I have found that a courtroom is often a place where legal mumbo-jumbo is what matters and where common sense is irrelevant. I have seen people lose their liberty, money and children while standing helplessly by, not knowing how they could offer a few words in their own defense. Time and time again I have seen the court system operate with a sort of circular craziness, attempting to draw upon itself for nonexistent answers.

The typical solution in child custody disputes is to strap mothers with all of the worries of parenthood and home and to permanently strip fathers of their assets and their roles as loving parents. Judges mumble words like "in the best interests of the children," but mean it in only the most impersonal way. Quite simply, it is a system gone berserk.

Let's look at an example. A college professor I know raised his two infant children himself for five years after his wife left him. He arranged his teaching load so that he could be home when the children returned from school. He joined the P.T.A. and learned to cook, shop and bake. He was active

in Boy Scouts and Girl Scouts. He bought a home. In short, he did everything a model mother and father should do. When the mother returned and petitioned the court for custody, the judge awarded her the children, the home, the car, and 80% of the professor's net income. Although it might be an extreme example, this type of bias against fathers is not unusual.

Fathers are faced daily with the legal theft of their children in the courts. As a consequence, some fathers "steal" their children back "illegally." Although the courts have come to realize that the kidnapping is a problem, they have never acknowledged that their prejudices against fathers are the real problem, and that fathers kidnapping their children is only the result. Court "solutions" to the kidnapping are predictable: get tough, use more muscle with these "criminals," and stack the prisons even deeper.

One such father, a member of our Non Custodial Parents Association, had a two-year-old daughter. On visiting days when this father would go to pick up his daughter, he would usually find her in bed with her mother and the mother's boyfriend. He kept silent about it until he started to see drugs in the house, and a different boyfriend every time he came. Piles of dog excrement, which he finally had to scoop up himself, were all over the house. His ex-wife even began charging him fifty dollars for each visit. He tried to obtain the assistance of lawyers, the Child Services Division, and even the television stations, but to no avail. At last he became wild with grief and, after careful planning, he finally kidnapped his child and fled across the continent. His planning wasn't careful enough, however. He was arrested and thrown into a cell the size of a small bathroom, with no mattress, and a hole in the floor for elimination. This was his punishment for the crime of loving his daughter. And the daughter was restored to the ex-wife—"in the child's own best interest," of course.

The bonds that tie parents to children are often stronger than those they feel toward their own parents, their spouses, or even to themselves. When this bond is broken, men are often reduced to a totally demoralized condition. At the Non Custodial Parents Association, we hear of fathers who have lost their children committing homicide, suicide, rifle snipings, hijackings, courtroom shootings, kidnappings, assaults, and thefts. Yet the courts never acknowledge their part in these tragedies. I am often surprised that so few men commit violent acts. And although the desperate behavior of these few does draw attention to their situation, unfortunately the fathers are viewed by society as "dangerous" and "nuts" and are killed or put away behind bars. If you've ever known a parent who has lost a child through illness or accident, you know that they never completely recover from their loss. Neither do the fathers who have lost custody of their children.

And what of the children? The children think their absent fathers don't care about them anymore, and as a result they often suffer despondency, guilt, anger and grief. Meanwhile, Dad is desperately trying to cram a month's loving and parenting into an 18-hour weekend. And what is worse, many fathers simply give up. They "drop out" or move away. They become "support skippers," flakes, alcoholics, or drug abusers. They don't even utilize the minimal visitation rights they do have. They feel damned if they see their kids and damned if they don't. It is during this period of hopelessness that the really "nutty" fathers succumb to violent or illegal means.

There are cases where the custodial mothers cannot, or do not, take proper care of the children, and

still the fathers are passed over by the courts. They watch as the care of their children is awarded to adoptive or foster parents. Fathers are sometimes deprived of their children because of irregular visitation, or the inability to catch up on support arrearage; the courts forever ignore the fact that it takes time for a newly displaced father to reestablish his emotional and financial stability. The NCAP has seen fathers living in boarding houses, or with parents, on cots at their workplaces, in flophouses, with sisters or brothers or friends, in basements, attics and campers, and even nudist camps. Where does a man go when he no longer has a home, but all of his income still goes toward paying the mortgage so his wife and kids can carry on? So many displaced fathers live in temporary quarters which are deemed unsuitable environments for children to visit, and almost impossible for accommodating overnight stays. The courts consider this to be negligence, but the fact is that if he had the money, a father would buy the Taj Mahal for his children.

Many fathers have the same erroneous idea that I had, that the courts respond to reason. They do not realize that our laws and courts are willfully dedicated to sexual prejudice and that the mother is almost always awarded custody. They don't realize that they can be thrown in jail if they fail to make support payments, even if the failure is because their ex-wives have denied them visitation rights.

In most states, fathers are still obligated to pay, even if they haven't seen their children for 15 years or more, or even if the kids live 3,000 miles away. The court's role is to enforce its own order. In this country, we don't have debtor's prisons except for fathers. A judge finds them "in contempt of court" and off they go to the hoosegow for a little "re-education." The courts often don't care if payments put fathers out of business or lead to a second divorce. If a father feels unfairly treated or deprived of his right to parent, he must pay the money and then fight aggressively in court. Tragically, even if a divorced father eventually wins a judge's sanction, years of a child's life and thousands of dollars in attorney fees are gone.

Despite all that I have just said, I want to emphasize that fathers must not become martyrs to their causes. Every week I hear fathers say that they will go to jail to make their point. But no point can be made from a prison cell. Jails are hell-holes to punish the worst elements of our society. They are numbing, degrading, demoralizing and embittering places. The common mistake made by the men who choose to be martyrs is to think that they are alone. But in my experience, the only way to influence the law and the courts is for fathers to break through their sense of isolation and unite together and fight.

In my own situation, it took more than three years of court wars before the final grim realization came that one of my children was to be permanently wrenched from me, and that I was slowly becoming estranged from the other two. I just couldn't get it through my thick head that justice wouldn't prevail in the end, and there wasn't anything I could do to change it. My God, I thought, there must be hundreds upon hundreds of children and fathers in similar circumstances, victims of court decisions which are, clearly, totally and hopelessly unjust.

After finally getting my own finances a little straightened out, I started an organization for non-custodial parents. I was working ten hours a day and weekends, but I knew that the organization had to be established. In the beginning I put my name on a mailing list for a men's resource center. When they called me, I asked if there was a group that was working for equal domestic court justice for fathers. I was referred to two other interested fathers who cooperated with me in arranging a meeting and announcing it in a local newspaper. Eight people responded and membership steadily increased. Unfortunately, finding regular meeting places and times was a constant problem, as was forming a charter and collecting dues. We soon realized that unless a group is well-organized and its bylaws and direction clear, no end of conflicts and dissatisfaction will occur. So before we could even deal with the issues, we had to spend days, weeks, and months on paperwork and other housekeeping details.

And there were many conflicts. For example, members opposed applying for CETA grants for permanent office space and staff because it would mean government intervention. Dealings with the media were disastrous and egos were constantly bruised. Following a particularly difficult meeting with serious differences of opinion, several of the members convinced me that we should form a separate group.

In attempting to reorganize, we had recurring problems finding appropriate meeting places. In addition, no one was available to routinely answer the phone, send out regular mailings, or chair meetings. I learned that working with damaged family men takes an enormous amount of energy. Displaced fathers are budding bachelors, learning to date, cook, wash, sew, and live alone. It was impossible to get commitments from most of them. Even a reliable mailing list was impossible, because so many of them moved every few months. Often just getting them on the phone was a three-day job. Nevertheless, our efforts were finally rewarded and our new organization was off the ground. In addition, I had finally adjusted my schedule so that I could work one-quarter of the time for myself and three-quarters of the time for the NCAP.

This new "spinoff" organization began to plan and execute some substantial projects. For example, we were able to hammer out a "Blueprint for Domestic Reform" which spelled out a direction for overall legislative and judicial change in Oregon. Finally we had a cohesive statement. We then found a state legislator who was angry over his own child visitation rights and, with a little help from him, wrote a bill which covered many of our areas of concern. We went to the legislature, testified in open hearings, and spent one day lobbying every legislator we could find. The bill passed relatively easily, but in a much watered-down version. Nevertheless, a parent deprived of his or her visitation privileges can now petition a judge to decrease child support if these privileges have been denied. So far, judges have upheld the new law. Unfortunately, the new law has a major weakness—the affluent parent with custody may cynically refuse to accept monetary support in order to deny visitation rights. If this happens, the father (or mother) is back to square one.

Non Custodial Parents Association recommends (and is lobbying for) joint legal custody in almost all cases. Even if joint physical custody cannot be granted, or doesn't make sense in a given situation, joint "legal" custody can be ordered—meaning that physical custody goes to one of the parents, but both have equal standing to make important decisions. This simple legal solution would always provide two legal parents and recognize the right of fathers to continue to have a strong relationship with their kids. In the event of death or emergency, children would automatically go to the custody of a parent rather than to the state.

By this time we were more politically astute. We shared a press conference with the sponsor of a bill which allows joint custody. We advocated the bill as introduced, but used the opportunity to push for a much expanded version. Both the legislator and our group received publicity and the bill passed. As usual, however, not enough men worked on it. Bumbling along, we were lucky the bill passed at all.

We have learned that more people attend our meetings when we have guest speakers. These speakers include candidates for political office, psychologists, attorneys and domestic court counselors. Our speakers seem surprised to find such a large body of men who care about these particular issues; we don't fit their stereotypes.

Another project of ours is an attorney referral service, since there is a great need for good attorneys and we get many requests. At first we referred lawyers who had been recommended by other members. However, none of these referrals worked out well. Unfortunately, we learned this only by seeing attorneys lose the cases of the men we referred to them. We now use a list of five or six attorneys who were referred to us by a humanistic judge — but we still operate on a trial-and-error basis. In our opinion, based on our experience thus far, attorneys are mostly interested in their fees and in protecting the divorce industry. There is a great need for fathers to learn the legal rights and procedures related to problems of custody, so that we won't always have to depend on lawyers.

We have just organized a group called "second wives — second family," for lack of a better name. It is made up of the wives and co-vivants of NCAP members. Many second wives are interested in the children of their husband's or co-vivant's former marriage. For some women, these are the only children in their lives. Others are concerned about their mates' anguish over the loss of their children. Understandably these women are hostile to the idea that their income is included in the support of their husbands' first wives, especially when children from the first marriage are not permitted to participate in the new family. We hope that the women in the new organization will help us with a newsletter, telephone staffing and our research efforts. We know that we will achieve more public validity as a sexually balanced group than as a bunch of disgrun-

tled "chauvinistic" men. We believe that women may be better organized than the men and hope that they will prove to be better delegates to the public — more verbal, and better at follow-up. We also hope that they will give us the credibility to reach out to women's groups. Many women who have chosen to forfeit custody of their children, either for a career or some other reason, also bear a social stigma. We know that bringing women into our movement will help us hold on to our own humanity — we don't hate women, we simply want equal rights to parent our children.

We are now in the early stages of a plan to make public the judicial decision record of judges as they run for re-election. We intend to publicly question judges as to their position regarding our "Blueprint for Domestic Reform" after we have acquired the endorsement of many legislators. The idea is to develop a landslide — or bandwagon — approach and then to affect individual judicial campaigns both positively and negatively, by any means open parental equity for our children?

We have a huge task before us, a social problem that will take years to change. However, if we can pull together locally and nationally, in a decade or so there will be a change of such major proportions that it will affect our whole society enormously for the good. Taking our places as good, loving parents is but one problem in the whole spectrum of the social dilemmas that our country faces, but it is one we can solve. It is within our grasp. What better purpose can we dedicate our lives to than to provide equity for our children?

Lee R. Cunningham is founder of the Fathers Rights Movement in Oregon. He is Public Education Director for Non-Custodial Parents Association of Oregon, Coordinator for National Council of Fathers Rights Organizations, and the 50/50 Legal Defense Fund, 11366 S.E. Fuller Road, Milwaukie, OR 97222. Phone (503) 652-2244, res. 653-1963.

The Non-Profit Gambit:
From Handbook to Corporation

by Ron Nowicki

When we were in the process of putting the People's Law Review *together, we picked up a copy of the* San Francisco Review of Books *and read one of the most convincing reviews of a self-help law book that we had ever seen.* S.F.R.B. *editor Ron Nowicki explained that he knew that* The California Non-Profit Corporation Handbook, *by Anthony Mancuso (Nolo Press) was a good book because he had used it to incorporate the* Review, *and it worked. We couldn't resist a plug like that, so we called Ron and asked him to tell his story in a bit more detail. Here it is.*

The San Francisco Review of Books was founded by a small group of booklovers in 1975 as "a magazine of outlandish opinion serving a fastidious clientele." While the founders were aware that literary magazines aren't moneymakers, they nonetheless held out some vague hope that perhaps, after several years, they might at least have their investments returned. To that end, they formed a legal entity called a Limited Partnership. An attorney's advice at the time was that the magazine was too small to invest the monies necessary to form a for-profit organization. The idea of setting up a non-profit corporation was barely considered.

The *SFRB* managed to survive for five years as a cultural success but a financial disaster. Even though we published exciting materials, finding independent backers was impossible. Finally we turned to foundations and corporations for financial help, but we were always turned down because the *SFRB* lacked tax-exempt status.

The survival of *SFRB* was a minor miracle, and the result of: considerable volunteer labor; several grants from the National Endowment for the Arts; grants from the Coordinating Council of Literary Magazines (CCLM); some matching funds; and a modest amount of advertising and subscription revenues.

No matter what we did, our debts continued to mount, and only an occasional grant prevented creditors from beating down the door. On several occasions, I suggested to the Partnership that we go the non-profit route as an educational organization, but the idea always met with stubborn resistance from several of the partners who were certain that eventually the magazine's fortunes would improve. Besides, they asked, what was to be accomplished by forming a non-profit corporation if we weren't making money anyway? I explained that the main benefits as far as *SFRB* was concerned were not for income tax savings, but the ability to qualify for lower non-profit postage rates, the elimination of taxes from our printing bills, plus several other benefits such as being able to hire a CETA worker and having access to government-surplus materials at a lower rate than commercial companies paid. And perhaps the most important benefit would be that non-profit status would make us eligible to receive grants. But I was still unable to budge the partners.

In 1978, I hired an experienced fundraiser who had raised money for such diverse Bay Area projects as the Gay Switchboard, the Save the Goodman Building Fund (the Goodman Building is a performing arts cooperative building in San Francisco), and a peace march. The fundraiser agreed to work for us on a commission basis. Although his methods were rather unorthodox, I knew he was hard at work soliciting funds because the reponses to his letters came through my office. But all the responses except one were negative. It was all very discouraging because, in most cases, the rejections were based on the fact that the granting corporation or foundation only contributed to non-profit, tax-exempt organizations. One private foundation did respond with a modest gift, and several individuals gave small amounts, but it hardly seemed worth the effort.

On one occasion, an officer of a Palo Alto–based

foundation came to the *SFRB* office to observe our operation. While he was excited by what he saw and praised the magazine highly, he reluctantly turned us down, again on the basis that his board of directors refused to contribute to organizations that were not tax-exempt. It was then that I decided to form my own non-profit organization, leaving the magazine as a partnership. The corporation would be utilized in an umbrella fashion, and would be an entity through which money could be loaned or given to the magazine.

I had known attorney Fay Stender for some time, and although her reputation was not that of a business lawyer, I knew that she had formed a non-profit organization for her Prisoners' Defense Fund. I discussed the situation with her, told her my plans, and we agreed that she would do the necessary research and draw up papers for a corporation for a nominal fee. The name of the corporation was to be Friends of Literature. Fay warned me, though, that if more work was required beyond the basics, she would feel obliged to charge her regular fee.

As it turned out, Fay was able to do the research and have the corporation papers drawn up without problem, resulting in minimal costs (less than $100). However, there was still the problem of getting the papers through the various government agencies in Sacramento. Several people I knew, including my fund-raising friend, told me anecdotes about others who'd "walked" their papers through the Secretary of State's office and the Franchise Tax Board in one day. It was at this juncture, in 1978, that Fay decided to run for the presidency of the State Bar Association. It was also at this time that, because of intervening personal and financial considerations, I suspended publication of the *SFRB*. However, I continued to be interested in getting non-profit for *SFRB* and Fay referred me to an attorney who specialized in helping non-profit organizations for a "reasonable" fee.

A meeting was arranged with the new attorney. With papers in hand, I went to his office, confident that my goal was near completion. My confidence was quickly shaken when he quoted a fee that was completely out of the question. Although his hourly rate was low, he more than made up for it with "extra" fees. At that point, I was completely discouraged. I couldn't support the magazine without forming a non-profit corporation, and I couldn't

afford the legal fees necessary to form one.

But thanks to a CCLM grant (which does not require tax-exempt status), and some modest income from ad revenues, the SFRB surfaced again in early 1979. However, we weren't functioning long before I had to set aside the day-to-day problems of running the magazine to again consider the drastic measures that had to be taken if we were to survive. The problem seemed more urgent than ever because we were now receiving submissions from such writers as Herbert Gold, Kay Boyle, and Raymond Carver. Furthermore, our subscription count was slowly going up, with many requests from libraries for copies of the SFRB. It seemed that, once again, we might have to suspend publication until we found another source of funding. By this time, I clearly understood that, my partners' views notwithstanding, we weren't going to survive as a supposedly profit-making enterprise. The usual tightening-the-belt actions were taken. We did smaller press runs, substituted newsprint stock for quality paper, etc. And then, I came upon a possible way out of the dilemma—a review copy of a book titled *The California Non-Profit Corporation Handbook* by

Anthony Mancuso, and published by Nolo Press. Perhaps this is an example of what Dr. Jung called "meaningful coincidence." I have never believed in omens that predict the future, but I don't believe in giving up easily either. No sooner did I have the book out of its wrapper, than I decided to resume efforts to form a non-profit corporation. There was now no need to seek out an attorney. Instead, I would rely on the *Handbook* to help me get the job done.

I opened the book to the sections that were the most relevant to the type of organization I wanted. Then I went back and read the book from cover to cover, comparing the information it contained with the papers that Fay Stender, who had since been badly injured in a tragic assassination attempt, had drafted for me. As time had elapsed since the original papers were prepared, changes had to be made. Using the *Handbook* as a guide, I was able to draw up the application. Needless to say, being able to complete the application myself, without additional advice or input from a professional, gave me a great deal of satisfaction.

My next step was to phone the California Secretary of State's office in Sacramento to see if the name I'd originally reserved for the corporation — Friends of Literature — was still available; it was. (By the way, I found that many of my questions could be answered simply by phoning either the Secretary of State or the Franchise Tax Board. The clerks with whom I spoke were friendly and helpful.) Again, after double-checking my work with the Handbook, I felt that I had finally collected all the necessary documents, information and fees to be able to make my non-profit corporation a reality.

But as is so often the case, my job wasn't as easy as I had hoped. I had prepared the *SFRB* papers under the law which was in effect before 1980. When I arrived at the Secretary of State's office, a clerk informed me that the Articles would have to be re-done in accordance with the new regulations.[1] That meant a trip back to San Francisco to do the bloody thing all over again. But once again, fate intervened on my behalf. The friend who'd accompanied me to Sacramento knew someone in town who had an office complete with typewriters and photocopy machine — so off we went. With a copy of the new regulations in hand, I again went

through the application, revising and retyping as needed, while my friend made copies of each sheet. After a couple of hours, we took the non-profit application back to the Secretary of State, where, after about 20 minutes of waiting, a clerk reviewed our application, informed us that everything was in order and that we would be hearing from them soon.

Within two weeks of the trip to Sacramento, I received a letter from the Secretary of State, stating that the Articles had been approved, and that we would be receiving our tax exemption within 30 to 60 days. It looked like we were home free.

Then, several weeks later, I received a short questionnaire from the Franchise Board, asking for further information about my proposed organization. I tried to be cautious in my response and frankly, I wasn't sure how to answer some of the queries. Because they had to do with our specific future plans, I couldn't go to the *Handbook* for the answers, but I felt that if I erred on the conservative side, perhaps things wouldn't go too badly. Unfortunately, they did.

One small statement on the question of sharing copyrights — i.e., possible revenues — with writers, snagged me. Within a week after returning the form to Sacramento, I received a two-page, single-spaced letter from the Franchise Tax Board, the gist of which was that the request for tax-exempt status had been denied because of my incorrect response to the question of sharing copyrights. The letter also informed me that there was no such thing as an appeal, but that the Board would review any additional materials submitted, or answer any questions. For a moment, I was really ready to flip. My long-cherished goal of getting my non-profit corporation on file had been achieved, but *SFRB* was being denied tax-exempt status, which was really the purpose of making the application.

After much anxious pacing, I phoned the Franchise Tax Board and asked very directly what had to be done to rectify the situation. The auditor to whom I spoke was very amiable, and when I suggested that our Board of Directors would meet and revise the offending clause in our proposal, he replied that as soon as he received written confirmation of such an action, he would be glad to grant us tax-exempt status. And the rest, as they say, is history. We revised the clause, sent off another statement to the Franchise Board, and shortly thereafter, Friends of Literature was granted tax-exempt status. As of this writing, we are waiting to hear from the Federal Government on our application for federal tax-exemption. In the meantime, I have submitted applications for funding to four foundations, two of which have already returned favorable responses. I have a hopeful feeling that we have finally turned the corner and can get back to the business of publishing the best literary magazine in California.

1. Editor's note: As of January 1, 1980, California made several changes in its non-profit corporations law. Author Nowicki was using the first edition of the *California Non-Profit Corporations Handbook* which didn't include the changes. The second edition, which is up-to-date, has since been published.

★★★

Ron Nowicki is the editor of the San Francisco Review of Books, *an excellent monthly paper headquartered at 1111 Kearny Street, San Francisco (above Enrico's Cafe and down the street from City Lights Books).*

Law Collectives
by Paul Harris

Not every lawyer is trying to make a lot of money in a hurry by practicing law in the traditional manner. There are many attorneys practicing in areas such as poverty law, consumer, environmental or labor law who are doing excellent, dedicated work. Unfortunately, when one leaves these social cause areas, it becomes harder to find concerned, altruistic practitioners. Therefore, it's particularly interesting to find lawyers who are delivering a full range of traditional legal services in a creative and enthusiastic way. And it becomes more interesting when the effort to accomplish this involves everyone in the law office—lawyers and non-lawyers alike—in decision-making. As Paul Harris explains, this non-elitist way of practicing law in the community is going on in many law collectives across the United States. It's refreshing to find some lawyers who are a genuine part of the people's law revolution.

"Equal pay!" "Equal decision-making power!"— slogans shouted by lawyers like Lenin and Fidel Castro. Now law communes and collectives are attempting to make these slogans a daily reality within their own firms. In practice this means that salaries are equal among all active members of the firm whether they be lawyers, legal workers (paraprofessionals), law students or secretaries. Equal policy-making power is also shared by all members of the collectives.

Law collectives began in the late '60s and were viewed by some of our jaded brethren as an experiment doomed to failure. We can now say that the experiment is over, and is successful. The San Francisco Community Law Collective has celebrated its tenth anniversary, while collectives in Los Angeles, Seattle and Santa Fe are into their ninth year of existence. There are between 30 and 40 law collectives spread throughout the country, from Little Rock to New Haven, Syracuse to Portland. Some of the offices use the names of the members, others are called by such titles as the Echo Park Community Law Office (L.A.), the Feminist Law Collective (D.C.), the Fruitvale Law Collective (Oakland), and the now dissolved "Bar Sinister." The firms vary in size and composition. The firm of Kaplan & Horwich in Richmond, California consists of eight women; the firm of Smith, Kaplan, Witney, Sona & Salmi consists of four men and four women. The offices are usually one-third to one-half legal workers.

While most of the collectives are still made up of white radicals, there has been a strong move to racial integration. Also, as more Third World law students graduate from law school, the potential for multi-racial firms develops. Presently the office of Romero, Paz, Rodriguez & Sonora in Los Angeles is the largest bilingual collective servicing primarily the "Raza" community, and is viewed as a model for minority law students who are planning to build their own collectives.

The collectives vary in their specialties and in the nature of the income-producing cases they handle, from criminal law to labor law to family law. Bachmann, Weltchek & Powers stress community organizing; the Souther Illinois Law Collective received a grant to do prison law; some firms have built a personal injury base, while others supplement their income by law teaching jobs.

All of the collectives are committed to using their abilities to bring about fundamental social change. Many of the collectives have produced the lawyers and legal workers who have been involved in the major political cases of the seventies. They have also provided significant leadership in the National Lawyers Guild, the radical alternative to the American Bar Association.

Law collectives grew out of a fusion of socialist theory and New Left lifestyle. Since we professed the belief that all those who join together in production should share equally in the remuneration, it seemed ironic, if not hypocritical, to organize law firms in which salaries were not equal.

The reality of the practice of law is that most lawyers are men, and most secretaries are women. Often the lawyers are white, while the clerical staff may be composed largely of minorities. Therefore, the objective fact is that almost all law offices are tied to sexism and racism. A pleasant working situation with relatively high salaries does not change these facts; it only makes them more subtle and palatable.

Law collectives make a conscious decision to struggle against elitism and to demystify the legal system. By working in a collective, by training community people to be legal workers, by encouraging and accepting criticism, lawyers become more effective people's advocates.

In law school, students are given the fundamentals and philosophy of the priesthood. The lawyer accepts and even relishes his role as interpreter of the dogma and the rituals of the Law. He begins to cultivate that mystique which says to his clients that only the lawyer-priest can adequately understand the law, and only he can lead them safely through its web. Behind this facade of "professionalism" the lawyer unconsciously perpetuates his monopoly of the mystery of the law.

The political result of this alienation is a feeling of powerlessness. The powerlessness of the client is increased by his dependence on the attorney. If the lawyer is not around at the crucial time or does not succeed in court, then the client is thrown back on his inadequately developed self-resources, and he often flounders and fails. Consequently, the attorney who is insensitive to his priestlike role may be actually retarding the development of power in his clients.

At times the professional aspirations of the lawyers even conflict with the good political sense of others in the collective. An example of this is when one office had the opportunity to represent professional criminals in a big conspiracy prosecution. Initially, the lawyers wanted to take the case. There was a lot of media attention; many of the other lawyers were excellent practitioners; the legal issues raised significant constitutional questions; and the fee was assured because it was a court-appointed case.

At the weekly collective meeting, one of the minority law students raised the criticism that it would be bad for the office's reputation in the community to represent overtly racist clients. One of the legal workers pointed out that a six-month trial might be exciting and even educative for the two lawyers, but would put a great deal of work pressure on the rest of the people in the collective.

After further investigation of the case, the client's involvement, and two more office meetings, the collective decided not to take the appointment. Although there was still some hesitation at the time from the lawyers, in retrospect everyone agreed it was absolutely the correct decision.

A critical task in demystifying the law is the work

of the "layperson," more properly described as a "legal worker." In traditional law firms, legal workers are not allowed to take part as equals in "management" decisions. In law collectives, all members decide on how much salary to pay, whom to hire, how the office is set up and how to structure the workload.

When collectives meet to decide their political priorities, legal workers have as much input and decision-making power as the lawyer. The following example from the history of the San Francisco Community Collective shows the significant role a legal worker can play in this process. When President Nixon closed the U.S.–Mexican border to marijuana traffic, heroin flooded into San Francisco's Mission community at low prices. The Community Law Collective, based in the Mission district, set up internal office education meetings on the role drugs play in ghetto neighborhoods. These meetings were led by a woman legal worker who had researched this topic and could help bring a political understanding to the other members. Another legal worker had grown up in the Mission and had a close relative who was an addict. Her insights were extremely valuable to the ultimate policy decision made by the collective. Three basic decisions resulted from the educationals—all of which directly lowered the fee-generating power of the law office.

The first policy was that the lawyers would not represent heroin dealers who were not themselves addicts. The second policy was that one legal worker was freed to spend 90% of her time organizing a drug research project focusing on the dangers and false promises of methadone maintenance programs. The third decision was to defend a young Latino charged with assaulting a policeman. This case was taken on a no-fee basis because the defendant was active in a Mission community-based drug abuse group. These policies, spearheaded by the legal workers, led to the collective's participation in a successful community-based anti-heroin movement.

Legal workers can also do tasks usually viewed as solely for the lawyer. With proper training, many legal workers are capable of writing basic civil complaints. They can do all of the probate, bankruptcy and dissolution cases except the actual court appearances. In welfare and unemployment cases, they can represent the client in the administrative hearings. Of course, the legal worker must work under the responsible supervision of a lawyer, or else the individual and the office are subject to violation of laws against the unauthorized practice of law.

In fact, the legal profession has maintained a well-kept secret. This secret is that for years women secretaries have been doing almost all the legal work in the above areas, while the lawyer meets with the client, goes to court, takes a vastly unequal share of the fee and takes all the credit. It is a goal of law collectives to pierce this veil of elitism and mysticism and to redistribute the profits.

Legal workers can also participate in the once sacred area of "trials." They can do investigation, work with witnesses, write memos and sit at counsel table. In areas such as jury selection, handling of witnesses, preparing voir dire, and similar "legal strategy," non-lawyers can and do lend insight and energy. A number of legal workers in the National Lawyers Guild are part of the National Jury Project which has provided invaluable aid to lawyers in many of the major political cases of the last ten years.

Law collectives are not utopian experiments based on naive romanticism. They have proven they can provide excellent legal representation for their clients. At the same time they provide a model of people attempting to work in non-sexist, non-racist, non-capitalist ways. The result of this equal, cooperative process has been greater commitment by all persons involved. It has allowed collectives to handle complex, high-pressure cases, and to reach the high quality of performance to which they have dedicated themselves. Whether law collectives continue to exist and grow, or fall as casualties, will depend largely on their members' deep commitment and on the desire and sustained efforts of future attorneys and legal workers to create new and more humanistic forms of practice.

★★★★★★★★★★★★★★★★★★★★★★★★★★★★★★★★★★★★★★

Paul Harris is a founding member of the San Francisco Community Law Collective and a former president of the National Lawyers Guild. He teaches trial litigation at New College of Law in San Francisco, and enjoys the enviable distinction of being one of the few (if not the only) lawyers to ever include a real juggling act in a criminal trial.

Hunting Queers with the Vice Squad (or Peephole Law)

by Charles Sherman

Criminal law is one area where people are often too frightened or intimidated to represent themselves. After all, if you lose— you really lose! And most of us assume that a person is more likely to get off, or cop a light sentence, if he or she has dedicated representation by a knowledgeable criminal lawyer. But most of the time this isn't the case. Since no one —least of all the state—can afford to provide trials to even a small fraction of criminal defendants, a semi-corrupt, but cheaper, system is substituted. The police are encouraged to overcharge defendants—for example, to charge them with resisting arrest, assaulting an officer and possession of a concealed weapon, in addition to possession of marijuana. Then the "plea-bargaining" starts. The state offers the defendant a "good deal" —they will drop charges on the first three offenses in exchange for a guilty plea on the fourth. Alternatively, if the defendant doesn't take the deal, and insists instead on a trial, the District Attorney will go all out to convict him on all four charges. Defense lawyers all too often participate in this system by forming a sort of partnership with the prosecution. They collect a healthy fee up front from a scared criminal defendant and then participate in the plea bargaining process. When the inevitable deal is offered, they act as if they have won a great victory for their client and advise him or her to plead guilty to the lesser offense.

What does all of this mean, if you or a friend or family member find yourself charged with a criminal offense? At the very least, it should encourage you to want to understand how the criminal law system really works, as opposed to how it works on TV. There may be a reason to pay a criminal defense lawyer a lot of money to represent you, but if you do, you should be very sure that he or she is going to get a better result than you could get on your own by accepting a plea bargain. But enough lecturing— Ed Sherman's tragi-comic story says it better than we can. Read on.

Fall, 1965
Long Beach, California

I was working for Evelle Younger as one of his 240 Deputy District Attorneys in Los Angeles County. I had been a lawyer for only a few months, so I was only allowed to handle the easy preliminary hearings. A "prelim" is the routine first step in a felony prosecution, and while there is plenty that a good lawyer can do, none of it calls for courtroom dramatics. Yet, to my surprise, here I was, in an ordinary, open-and-shut prelim, with a noted defense attorney carrying on as if there were cameras on him instead of just the judge's bored gaze.

Counsel was on his feet again, interrupting my witness with yet another technical objection, waving his hands and intoning some long speech. He was a shrewd and capable man, known respectfully as the "Old Fox." All the more reason to wonder what he was up to. It was a flashy show, but there was no point to it, and at the end his client was, inevitably, bound over to Superior Court for further proceedings.

The defendant was a neatly dressed young man, sitting calmly at the defense table, looking grimly pleased by the grand performance of his attorney. Being a layperson, it was unlikely that he understood the technicalities of the proceedings, but he did have eyes and ears. A courtroom proceeding is in many ways like a Balinese temple dance; it is highly formal and stylized, being based upon a vast and intricate set of rules and assumptions which are not at all apparent. If you are not thoroughly immersed in the subject, you haven't a hope of

---

NOTE: Use of the term "queer" is not intended as disrespect to gay people. It is used only because it is the term that was used by the people at the time and place of this story. All characters in this piece are fictional and no resemblance to actual people, living or dead, is intended.

understanding what it's all about. In fact, a surprising number of attorneys are fairly lost in court, so how was the defendant to know that all the noise was to no particular end?

This nice young man was charged with oral copulation in a public bathroom, having been caught in the act very early one morning, a couple of weeks ago, by myself and my witness, officer Norman of the vice squad.

Officer Norman caught lots of nice young men licking no-no's in dark bathrooms. That was his specialty and his assignment. Faithfully, just like a good house-cat bringing home its prey, he would bring in two to five "couples" each and every week. He had to testify at preliminary hearings against all of these men, and for the rare case that actually went to trial, he would mount the stand a second time. He was a very experienced witness. Most policemen are; it's part of the job and they are usually trained at it.

But Officer Norman was an especially devastating witness, more so even than most other officers. Clever, articulate, handsome, sincere and cool—he was the all-American male pitted against perversion and evil, at time-and-a-half for hours spent in court. He was absolutely dangerous to the defense on cross-examination. Looking earnest and honest, just trying to be helpful, you know, he could make any defense attorney very, very sorry for having asked Norman anything at all. He could turn any answer to his own advantage and he would forever keep bringing up before judge and jury the image of the defendant in the sordid act with which he had been charged:

"Officer Norman, could you tell the court at just what time after the arrest did you first advise the defendant of his constitutional rights?" (Attorneys are notorious defilers of syntax.)

"Gee, sir, as soon as I could; it smelled pretty bad in there by the toilet, so I got the defendant up off of his knees, and got his pants pulled up and zipped, and outside into some fresh air, so I would say it was less than three minutes from the time I saw your defendant with Mister Johnson's penis in his mouth that I told him his rights."

Better not to have asked.

Better never to ask Norman anything. He knew all of the defenses, all of the tricks and traps.

Norman was always way ahead of any attorney. In a way it was beautiful to watch. It made my job as prosecutor a cinch, and it had something of the fascination of watching the kill, as when, with quiet grace, a cat stalks and grabs an innocent mouse.

Norman did have something of the naturally cruel air of a cat about him. It was mostly an undercurrent, quite intangible, and it took a while to notice. But even from the first case, I couldn't help noticing how much satisfaction he had from his work. Pretty soon, I began to notice other things, like how many defendants wore bruises as souvenirs of their arrest, and how so many of them were angry and forever glaring silently at Norman who, cat-like, sat smug and pleased and paid them no mind at all. I didn't form any conclusions, but I became interested in these cases and began to talk to my office mates about them.

Somehow Norman found me out. He confronted me one day.

"Say, Mr. Sherman, could I talk with you privately out in the hall after court?"

"Sure." How could I say no? I wanted to, because in some inexpressible way, I was a little afraid of Norman. He was so damn Aryan and military—a softspoken niceness overlaying cold steel, contempt and, possibly, malice. Something about him reminded my stomach and diaphragm of the tough little kids who used to lord it over the playground in my grammar school. He had a compact athletic body, blond crew cut, blue eyes, lean face, and full, sensual lips. He straddled that indefinable line between handsome and ugly, having the better of it by just a hair.

In the hallway, after that day's prelim, he approached me with Officer Strake, a quiet and competent policeman who was Norman's usual sidekick on the queer hunts. Norman looked at me directly and came straight to the point:

"We heard that you're suspicious about the way we make our busts—is this true?"

Damn! I was in no way ready to deal with this. Now I was the mouse, almost hypnotized by the cold, blue-eyed stare. Trapped! Unable to meet the glare, I looked around and said, "Oh well, I don't know, where did you hear a thing like that?" Stall for time. Think!

"It doesn't matter. Say, I don't mean to put you

on the spot or anything, but we thought it would be a good idea if you could come along with us on our beat one night and see how we work. Then you could see what we're dealing with out there."

Reprieve! A sticky situation turns into an adventure. "Hell, yes! I'd love to go."

So this is how a clean-cut, naive young lad like myself came to round out his education by creeping around smelly bathrooms in the dead of night, peering into toilet stalls in earnest search of the elusive public cocksucker.

★★★

It was a comfort to know that we were armed, as we went about our sneaking and peeping. The two officers were each lightly, but effectively, armed with a pistol, a mean little blackjack, handcuffs, and police badges, all cleverly concealed under casual attire. I was armed with a heady sense of adventure, cleverly concealed under a straight face. But far more important, we were all armed with the full force and authority of THE LAW. As official representatives of the will of the people of the State of California, we were sanctioned to lurk around the toilet stalls to catch and punish those who would interfere with the right of a male citizen to take an unmolested leak some dark night on the beach.

The particular law which Officer Norman so energetically enforced was California Penal Code Section 288(a), which, prior to 1975, made it a felony punishable by several years in prison for any person, anywhere, under any circumstances, to put his or her mouth upon the sexual organ of another person (oral copulation). Penal Code Section 286 made the act of sodomy (anal copulation) a felony, but it seemed to be much more rare amongst our cases.

In 1975, California once again showed itself to be a progressive state by repealing the laws against oral copulation and sodomy as they apply to consenting adults, leaving the felony restriction only where a minor, or force, is involved. As of 1980, about 20 states are in accord. However, some of you may be interested to know that it is still unlawful in California to seduce a previously chaste female with promises of marriage, so watch your step.

In my town, the sexual laws were enforced almost entirely against homosexual males. This could have been because most vice squad officers hated queers, but more likely it was because the queers were the only ones that regularly committed these offenses in public restrooms.

Even in 1965, when it was more or less open season on queers, an arrest against consenting adults in a private place was all but unheard of because of the obvious extreme difficulty in obtaining the right evidence. In order to gain a felony conviction on a charge of oral copulation or sodomy, someone had to testify to actually seeing the penis of one person in the oral or anal aperture of another, and this called for some very tricky police voyeurism indeed. But the arrest record of these two showed that they were up to the challenge, and I was now invited to see them in action for myself.

★★★

"The night I joined the queer hunt. . . ." What an unbeatable opening line that is!

It was Friday night, so after my work in court I went out to my car and changed into casual clothes and sneakers. I had been especially warned to wear sneakers. I have always owned and worn sneakers, but this was the first time I was actually going to sneak around in them. Slipping them on gave me goose-bumps, just thinking about why I was wearing them.

My excitement was premature, however, since we were not going to start hunting queers until closing

time for the bars—somewhere around 1 a.m. Meanwhile, it was part of the vice-squad job to keep tabs on the downtown night spots, so I tagged along as Norman and Strake went from bar to bar, hanging around, laughing with the regulars, taking free drinks and solicitous treatment wherever they went (it pays to be nice to the fuzz, you know). Strake stayed quietly in the background, but Norman walked tall and accepted the deference shown him by the bar folks. From time to time he would drift into a corner for a private flirt, in grinning whispers, with some pretty bar girl or other. As he was said to be married, I just naturally assumed that this, too, was part of his job.

At last it got to be about 1 a.m. and time to start the nightly hunt. More coffee, try to wake up. First we went down to the amusement park to check out some bathrooms. We would sneak silently through the entrance, sticking to the shadows cast by the garish neon lights outside, and cautiously slither a head around a corner. All clear. Then we would tiptoe over to the toilet stalls, get down on hands and knees for a peek under the partitions. I assume that if we had seen four or more feet in any one stall, instead of the permitted two, we might have hung around; but in fact, we saw no feet at all in either of the two bathrooms we snuck through—they were empty. I felt like an idiot. What an undignified, slimy business.

Half an hour later we were about three miles up the beach, checking a bathroom near the fishing pier. There was no action there either, but I was getting lots of background about the problem. Every bathroom we went into was grossly marked and disfigured by years of "queer" activity. The most noticeable custom redecoration was the lighting—there wasn't any. The bulbs were smashed faster than they could be replaced, because some people preferred it dark in there. But wherever light did glimmer in from outside, you could see that all the walls and surfaces were covered, and covered over again, with scrawled outbursts, invitations, names and crude drawings. Every wooden toilet partition had peepholes punched through here and there, and most had at least one larger hole, about 2 inches in diameter, cut crudely through, probably with pocket knives. When I looked puzzled at this, Norman explained. First the queers on the toilets would look through the peepholes at each other, then maybe

one would wiggle a finger or pass a note through one of the larger holes. Then, if some anonymous agreement were reached, one would put his penis through the hole and the other would suck it. Most enlightening, no?

Our next stop was about halfway back to town where the coast road is high on a bluff overlooking broad beaches and the harbor. This is a very classy part of town. A long stairway leads down the cliff face to the beach below, and at the bottom there is a pretty little wooden building which houses the public bathroom. The head of the stairs was lit with a dim circle of yellow light cast by an undersized streetlight. In spite of the fact that it was well after 3 a.m., there were several men loitering around—a few on the stairs and some more at the bottom, near the entrance to the bathroom. No smiles, no talking—they just stared at us and at each other, smoking cigarettes in a tight, nervous way.

As we went down the stairs, one man casually, almost accidently, let his hand drift over and brush against the front of Norman's pants at the fly. I tensed, expecting an explosive reaction, but Norman just ignored him and passed on by, going toward the head, down into increasing darkness.

Norman said that he gets groped a lot, and I could well believe it. There is something about his appearance and manner which encourages certain queers to try him. I think this is because he looks a little like one of the tough-boy queers—the sultry type, all leather and dark scowls—and he does seem to possess a kind of repressed effeminate quality. At any rate, he is very attractive to some of them, and in his line of work, he gets lots of exposure.

Norman could have busted the guy that touched him for lewd conduct or loitering near a public bathroom. But this is only misdemeanor stuff and Norman always prefers the bigger game, the felonies, like oral or anal copulation. He's proud of some of his trophies, like the bank manager he caught in an act of bathroom sodomy the year before, or the schoolteacher. Anyway, if there's no action downstairs, he can always come back up and look for this guy, the groper.

When we go into the bathroom, it is utterly black; I can't see my own hand, even when I'm nearly poking it in my eye. Now and then a man drags on his cigarette and that very tiny little glow is all the light I have to find a place safely out of the way, over by a wash basin. He drags again and I can vaguely see dark forms of men standing all around. Later, some fool lights a cigarette and nearly blinds everyone with his paper match that comes across like a flare. The place is packed! There is a man on each of the four toilets, a man standing at each of the four urinals, and several more just standing around, maybe a dozen in all besides us secret agents.

Twenty or thirty minutes go by in dark silence, like a month in the morgue. Everybody is in exactly the same position, and nothing is happening, absolutely nothing. I wonder what these guys do for fun? Or maybe this is it? God, what a way to spend an evening. I think maybe one guy over at the urinal is masturbating. He's been shaking something for a long damn time. Who cares? I am very tired and this is very, very boring. I guess Norman and Strake get bored, too, because we leave this place, passing more of those weird zombies on the way up the stairs. The groper has gone.

We drive back to the amusement park and walk over to the alley that runs behind the main midway. There we set up a stake-out on a dim and dingy little doorway which, if you feed it a dime, will admit you into a 6 × 8-foot room which just happens to contain what is in all probability the most absolutely famous bathroom in all of California, and probably the whole United States, including Alaska and Hawaii.

***

Possibly it has never occurred to you that a bathroom could be famous, but to tens of thousands of lawyers, judges, policemen, professors and students, this little shithole has been a cornucopia of case law, an important beacon and a major refinement of the legal rules governing police (mis)conduct in their relentless pursuit of criminals.

A few years before our hunt, the Long Beach police, in their program to patrol restroom recreation, had noticed a lot of activity at this particular amusement park pay toilet. So had the owners of the building, who agreed to let the police set observation pipes through the roof (notice the wonderful Freudian imagery) through which they could, at will, observe people on the pots directly below. Eventually, the patience of the police peepers paid off when they spied two men in an act of sodomy, whereupon they ran down and arrested them. One of the men, Mr. Bielicki, was so sorely burned at the sneaky way

he was busted that he appealed his conviction all the way up to the California Supreme Court, which, several years and thousands of dollars later, set him free because his arrest was achieved through illegal police conduct. The law had been broken on both sides of that pipe.

Both the federal and the California constitutions protect the citizen against "unreasonable searches and seizures," which has been interpreted to mean that police cannot search a private place without good cause to think that a crime, or evidence of one, is to be found. They cannot engage in general or exploratory searches, also known as "fishing expeditions," just hoping to run across evidence of something. In Bielicki's case, where the police spied on the public on the pot, eyeing the innocent and guilty alike, they were in violation of the law, and the police are not allowed to break the law to catch a criminal.

The main point of the Bielicki case is about police spying on private places, but nothing disqualifies them from observing what any member of the public can observe. If people choose to break the law in their own bedroom, but leave the blinds open on a window in full view of a public street, there is no reason why a policeman can't look in, just like you or I can. The police were quick to observe that the Bielicki bathroom was unique in that it had the pay-lock on the entry door instead of on the toilet stalls, as is usual. This led them to conclude that the inside of that bathroom was a public place, since anyone with a dime could walk in. Since the toilet stalls would still be considered private, their doors "just happened" to disappear one day, rendering them no longer private. The window to the famous little bathroom now becomes highly important.

One wall of the room was pretty much taken up by a four-foot-square window. It was a steel casement job with four 18 × 20-inch panels in it. The glass "just happened" to be completely broken out of it, so three of the four panes were covered with plywood, leaving the upper right pane completely open and uncovered. There "just happened" to be several nail holes in the plywood at about eye-level, through which someone standing in the alley could peep, getting a commanding view of most of the room, looking directly into the two toilet stalls opposite, about six feet away. The sill of this window was about 44 inches off the ground, so the open panel was just a bit above head height. The bathroom was on a corner, with the window on the alleyway and the dime-lock door opening onto a dim lane which connected the alley with the amusement park midway about 100 feet away.

★★★

When we arrived on the scene, Norman and Strake tiptoes up to the window. The peepholes were, as usual, filled with little wads of toilet paper stuck on from the inside. Strake quickly cleared one with a small nail he had in his pocket, applied his eye to the hole and said, "Empty!" They both cleaned out their favorite holes to perfection, and then we retired about 100 feet down the alley. We hid ourselves behind a wooden signboard where we waited all hunkered down in the filth and litter, shivering a little in the damp air, talking only briefly in whispers. We kept watch on the bathroom through cracks in the boards. My body was stiff and aching and I was punchy from lack of sleep.

"Pssst, Strake," goes Norman, "you got a dime?"

"No, I don't think so, just the nail; I forgot about the dime."

"Oh, shit! What about you, Sherman?"

My hand was already fumbling in my pocket. "Yeah, I got one for each of you . . . here."

"Thanks. I'd hate to have to bust down the door again. It pisses the owners off real bad."

"Hey, be quiet, you guys! Here somes someone."

"Where? Oh, yeah, I see him. Hmmmm, I don't recognize him, do you, Strake?" Strake shakes his head. "Keep back, Sherman, don't let him see you. Quiet now, let's see what he does."

I get a look just in time to see the back of some man going into the bathroom. A few seconds later, Norman takes off, motioning us to stay put as he advances on rapid little tippy-toe steps up to his peephole, elbows held high. I strangle down a laugh because he looks ridiculous, and though he's done it several times this night, I haven't got used to it yet. Strake, grinning like he agrees with me, whispers that Norman will check the guy out and see what he's doing. Norman is all hunched over now, with his eye screwed up to the peephole, one hand up to hold us in position. Suddenly, like a cat, he leaps up and back, turning in the air. He darts behind a small post and presses his back up against the wall, hiding in a shadow. Corny, just like on TV, and now I'm really choking on laughs. The man emerges and

walks down the lane to the midway. Norman shrugs and strolls back.

About 20 minutes later Norman says, "Hey, Strake, just lookey-here who's coming." I'm miserable with cold and fatigue and I don't care who's coming. Fuck it, let's go home.

Strake is still on the job, though. He peers through a crack and studies the approaching figure. "Oh, yeah. We busted him before. What the hell's his name? I forget."

A slender, medium-tall man in his early thirties is standing in front of the bathroom door. He has reddish hair and patchy shadows on his face cast by the flow of dim light over his rough complexion. He stands there for at least five full minutes, looking around casually at nothing, then he goes in. This time we wait several minutes before Norman slips over to see what's happening. He returns and whispers that the guy is sitting on the pot, pants up, just hanging out. In other seven or ten minutes we see a dumpy man, not much over 20, come wandering up the alley, moving slowly and with obviously false nonchalance, craning his head around, looking here and there into the dark shadows and whistling quietly, tunelessly. He has curly brown hair, tight on his small head, narrow rounded shoulders which slope out to a puffy waist hanging softly over his belt, the whole of it balanced on spindly ankles and small feet. He looks like a shmoo that's been on a crash diet. He stands in front of the bathroom for a while, just looking around, then he goes in.

The door barely closes before Norman is off like a flash, on tippy-toes, making over to his peephole. A few minutes have passed when, without looking up, he waves us over to him. We sneak over to his side and stand there watching Norman watching the room. I stare at soggy cigarette butts, broken glass, dry vomit stains on the concrete. It stinks here. This whole goddamn scene stinks.

Suddenly, Norman straightens up, gets a knee up on the window ledge, and with Strake helping by pushing up on his ass, he gets his head into the open window panel over our heads. Now I understand— he has to actually see the penis in the mouth to make a felony out of this. Looking through the peephole all he can see is the kid's back. So in he goes, head and neck first, then one shoulder, then the other, all the time with Strake pushing on his ass, stuffing him into that dark mouth of a window like a big duplication of the act going on inside. It's little in that room and Norman's torso must be filling a big part of it, because all that's outside is his legs. His body is resting quietly now, everything's completely silent. There's just the distant sounds of a city that's mostly asleep and the ocean making little lapping sounds on the beach.

"Police! You're both under arrest!" Norman's voice shatters the silence.

Instantly the scene bursts into action. Strake leaps around in two giant steps to the door, dimes it, jumps into the room with me on his heels and hauls the regular up off the pot, pulling at his arms, turning him to get the cuffs on. The kid is huddled over in the corner, shaking, his face screwed up in shock and anguish. His fly is open, but there's nothing sticking out. Norman is in now, leaping at the kid, his arms outstretched.

Dear God, can you imagine those two guys in that dark room, completely absorbed in what they are doing; the only sound is their own breathing and maybe a soft liquid licking noise, and their own blood pounding in their ears, and silently a big, dark form slides overhead, unnoticed, a military face with cold eyes hanging right there in the air, less than 12 inches over the kid's shoulder, and suddenly a voice booms in their ears, "You're under arrest!" Jesus!

The kid is thrashing around in the corner, crying, sobbing, while Norman tries to grab a wrist. He's wailing, "Ohhhhhhh, no! No! Nooooo! Ohhhh, God!" Norman has one wrist hard up behind his back and the kid is beating his head on the wall, crying, gurgling, sliding down towards the floor. Norman is not quite brutal, but hard and firm, cutting the kid no slack. His eyes gleam and I wonder if my presence is holding him back any. He hauls the kid up, who is still sobbing, but limp now, babbling out of control.

"My Mom! They'll throw me out of the Navy! She'll find out! Arghhh, God! No! Noooo! No!" Norman has one cuff on and he's dragging at the other wrist. "Why did I do it? I've never done it before! Oh, God, I'm sorry, I'm sorry, I'm sorry. My Mom'll die, it'll kill her! Ohhhh, no! Oh, God! Please, please, please, no! Don't!" Norman's eyes shine. The kid is incoherent, blubbering. There's snot on his face, running down from his nose and lips. Norman is behind him with both wrists in cuffs

and he leans over and talks softly into his ear while the kid keeps babbling — Norman is advising him of his constitutional rights.

"You're under arrest for violation of Penal Code Section 288(a); you do not have to make any statement at this time; you have a right to talk to an attorney before you say anything; anything you say now can be used against you in court."

The kid is still crying and pleading. "I didn't mean to do it, I've never done it before. Oh, no, God, I'm sorry. I'll never get a job . . . the Navy . . . oh, please, I'm sorry."

The regular is just standing there, completely cool, not particularly upset so much as resigned. He's older, more in control of himself, and he's been through it before. He and Strake just stand there and watch the kid, waiting for him to quiet down. Pretty soon he's just snuffling and sobbing. Norman goes right to work on him, having already satisfied the legal requirement of advising him of his rights.

"You let this man suck on your penis, didn't you."

The kid nods, says, "Yeah." His head is hung way down, and he's swaying unevenly.

"He had his mouth on your penis, didn't he?"

"Uh-huh."

"Why'd you let him do it?"

The kid's voice raises hoarsely in one last wail and cry, "I don't know, oh, God, I don't know, I don't know. I've never done it before . . . girl's don't . . . I can't, I mean I was horny and. . . . Oh, God, I don't want to live anymore; I'm sorry, please . . . ." and his voice trails off into sobs.

Norman had his complete confession.

★★★

We drove the kid and the regular over to the police station, down underground to the lock-up and into the booking cell. I hung around for the routine booking procedures. Even under these circumstances, the regular had a nice, easy air about him. I instinctively liked him, so I sat next to him and told him who I was and why I was there. We chatted a bit. The kid was lost in a cloud of gloom so thick you could hardly see him. The desk sergeant was filling out arrest reports and booking forms, and started on the regular.

"Name?"

"Dave Dewby."

"Full name, yer full name fer Chrissake!"

"Richard David Dewby, III."

"Residence address?"

"Well, care of Harrison's Marina, I guess. I live on a boat over in San Pedro harbor."

"What's your occupation, fella?" He's shaking his ballpoint, trying to get it to flow better.

"I'm an organ repairman."

The sergeant looked up, eyeing him with a squint. The word "organ" worried him (goddam perverts, ya never know about them). "You mean musical instruments?"

"That's right."

"You fix' em?"

"Right."

Satisfied, he went back to his paperwork. An idea flashed into my mind, so I turned to Dave and said, "Let me guess, now. I bet you don't work on electric organs at all. I bet you only work on pipe organs, don't you?"

He grinned up at me. "How did you know?"

"Just a guess. Listen, Dave, here's something I can't guess about, I can't figure it out: you've been around some, and you know these cops are out hunting every night. If you meet somebody, like this kid here, and take them home to your boat or a room or someplace private, why there's no chance in hell anybody would ever bother you. Why do it in the public bathroom? Why not go someplace private?"

He sat there for a minute thinking it over, then shrugged his shoulders over his handcuffed hands, crossed and resting in his lap. He looked over at me, shaking his head helplessly. "I don't know, I really don't . . . no kicks that way I guess. It just wouldn't be the same."

Pretty soon business was finished and they led him away and I left.

★★★

Every now and then over the next few months I would see Dave again, out on the street, at a magazine stand, in some store. He'd always smile and wave, sometimes we'd say hello, nice day, and so on. I always felt a little embarrassed at my part in what had been a very unfriendly act against him, so it seemed to me. He, on the other hand, didn't seem to think anything of it, he held no grudges. He was a very nice guy.

I saw the kid again, too. He went out and hired the Old Fox to represent him, so I saw him at the prelim a few weeks later. The Old Fox gave him a very spirited performance at the prelim, which is what I was describing at the very beginning of this tale. The difference between what happened to the regular and to the kid after the arrest is very informative about the way The Law works—not the letter of the law, but the practice of it.

You couldn't blame the kid for being scared and trying to get the best help he could afford, or, in this case, much better than he could afford. After all, not only was this his first and only arrest, but he was facing the possibility of a big fine and years in prison. When you're in bad enough trouble, then who knows, maybe if you pray enough and pay enough, you just might win somehow. Maybe a good attorney could pull him out of this horror. Chances are he didn't even know the worst of what he was up against—the provisions of the Sexual Offender's Registration Act.

The Sexual Offender's Registration Act is an interstate compact, which means that many states have substantially the same law and they all cooperate in its use and enforcement. It also means that if anyone is convicted of any kind of sexual misconduct, from simple indecent exposure to violent rape, then for the rest of his life, wherever he goes, that person must register with the local police as a convicted sexual offender. Until the day he dies, he must make it his first order of business in any new community to go into the police station, walk up to the desk and register. It's a lifetime sentence.

It is an attorney's duty to outline for a client just what legal penalties and problems he is facing, so we can be sure the Old Fox told the kid all about it in complete and emphatic detail. If the kid wasn't scared going into that office, he was for sure good and scared when he came out.

Fear is no doubt what drove the kid in over his head to hire the best talent he could get. The Old Fox was, in fact, an excellent attorney. Also expensive. I would guess that he probably charged at least $1,000 as an initial retainer, and this was, don't forget, in 1965. The Old Fox was a Rich Old Fox. But for the kid, it was a desperate necessity to have someone that he believed in to help him through this, give him a chance. It would be worth it at any

price.

Here's a few facts which the Old Fox probably omitted to mention to the kid:

Long Beach had lots of queer action; always had and always will. Hundreds of them were arrested and convicted each year, many thousands over a few years. Every time any convicted queer moved and registered somewhere, the police there would routinely fire off an inquiry to the Clerk's office in Long Beach. It didn't take the clerks long to figure out that they were faced with a threat of serious proportions. Soon they would be swamped and buried under mountains of paperwork. All of their time would be taken up just keeping the world informed about the queers we had busted. Word got over to the judges who, for the most part, were open-minded enough to regard these bathroom perverts as more of a harmless nuisance than a dangerous threat. They came up with a brilliant plan based on humane principles (and self-interest) which would serve the law and at the same time avoid its ultimate consequences—the holy grail for every legal talent.

In every unaggravated case (nonviolent, no minors) where a queer was found guilty by plea or by trial, they would impose a routine and uniform penalty of some time in jail, sentence suspended; one year of informal probation (no supervision, no reporting, no cost to the County); and a fine of $300, payable over the year of probation. If the fine was paid and no serious crimes committed during that year, the case would be reopened, defendant's plea of guilty would be vacated and a plea of not guilty would be entered, then the case would be dismissed! Under this sublimely clever system a guilty defendant paid his fine, paid his bail, paid his attorney and thus paid his dues and respects to the law, but in the end he was never convicted of anything at all. No need to register. No burden upon the clerks. Could Solomon have done any better?

So the Old Fox put on a dynamic, energetic and in every way impressive (though meaningless) preliminary hearing. Next he probably let the kid dangle for a few days or weeks of anxious waiting, then he would call him in for a conference.

"Listen, kid, I've gone over your file and the police reports and the transcripts of the hearing very thoroughly. A trial in this case is going to cost you another $2–3,000, and frankly, on these facts, I don't think you have a very good chance." He never had a chance from the beginning. "You could run a technical defense—Jesus, that damn bathroom goes up on appeal more often than appellate judges go to the bathroom—but that could cost you as much as $8–10,000."

He lets this news sink in, until the kid says, "But what am I going to do, my God. . . ."

"Well, look, I was talking to a friend of mine in the D.A.'s office, and I think we can work out a good deal for you. Listen. . . . ." Then he tells him how if he pleads guilty they can work it so all he gets is a $300 fine and a year of probation without even any supervision, just keep clean, and then after a year of being good he can get the whole thing dismissed so there won't be any record or anything, maybe just a small additional attorney's fee. That's the best part, the magic words . . . no record! The kid jumps at it, and he's really grateful. What a relief! Boy, it's sure worth it, having a good attorney, no matter what it costs.

The regular just went in on his own a few days after he was busted, pleaded guilty and paid his fine. His case was finished before the kid even got into court.

Charles "Ed" Sherman is the founder of Nolo Press and the author of several self-help law books, including the most famous of all— How To Do Your Own Divorce in California, *a pioneering work which has sold over 275,000 copies. Ed has also written several excellent books on hydroponic gardening, including* Hydro-Story: The Complete Manual of Hydroponic Gardening *(Nolo Press).*

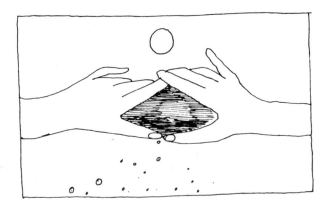

Learning to Fish:
Teaching Law in High School
by Tom Goldstein

Several years ago, some of us here at Nolo decided that something should be done about the general failure of California high schools to teach practical legal skills. How could our society make a dent in legal illiteracy, we thought, if our schools didn't even teach kids the basics of landlord-tenant, domestic relations, consumer and business law? Armed with little more than our convictions, we approached members of the Los Angeles Times editorial staff with the idea that they should join with us to push for legal education in the public schools. It was all an eye-opening disappointment. Everyone treated us politely, proceeded to tell us why our ideas were impractical, and swept us out of their offices. Nothing was accomplished except to remind us that dealing with large, established institutions is usually a waste of creative energy. Eventually—perhaps ten years after people have independently discovered the need—they will catch up with current thinking, but it's a waste of time to expect them to innovate.

As a society we need to provide more—and more creative—law teaching in our high schools. No one can ever hope to represent themselves if they are ignorant of how our laws and dispute resolution systems work. As Tom Goldstein points out, democracy will prosper only if citizens understand how it works.

Education in the law is an absolute necessity, though I wish that it were not.

Our society was founded on liberal beliefs which included an acceptance of "natural" or "positive" law—the idea that all men recognize and respect natural equality. The original dream was that all men would, and could, freely contract with each other and that no intervention by the state would be necessary. If and when disputes occurred, a jury of twelve would hear evidence and arrive at a verdict on the basis of fairness, much as councils of elders in tribal societies. Education would be properly tied

to moral lessons intended to produce a consensus as to what constituted fairness.

As our society grew into an urban and mechanized state, we lost much of this liberal spirit, just as we lost many of our other natural sensations. It became easier to write rules and create programs for social and economic interaction than to mediate disputes as they arose. In the attempt to institutionalize fairness, freedom suffered.

The rules that we have evolved can transform the simplest transactions into bureaucratic nightmares. Whereas the 19th-century farmer built his home and barn as he saw fit, his 20th-century counterpart must file an environmental impact report, take out building permits, hire licensed contractors and build to specifications which are unrelated to his needs or concerns. The urban homeowner will find that the legal complexity of constructing a backyard shed costs more in time and money than the construction itself.

The businessman of the 19th century looked to his banker for guidance. His 20th-century counterpart requires legal assistance from an attorney specializing in tax law, an accountant familiar with mandatory insurance programs, plus a host of other quasi-legal specialists. Where the 19th-century youth group could gather at the local church for a dance, today's youth must incorporate, and report to two governments, before they can rent a hall. The conditions which must be met before those same youths can be legally employed to mow a lawn or babysit often price them out of the labor market.

It seems that law has grown geometrically and the population arithmetically. The moral homilies of the 19th-century legal education were not sufficient tools for coping with 20th-century legal complexity, yet it is only within the last two decades that the curriculum in public schools has shown any recognition of this fact. And the limited changes which have been made would probably not have come

about had it not been for the moral dilemmas produced by the Vietnam War and the activism of the 1960s.

At the beginning of the 1960s, the social studies curriculum of the public schools was based on the idea that a teacher was a "culture transmitter." Part of his or her responsibility was to pass on to students the legacy of the Constitution and the Bill of Rights. This task became increasingly difficult, hypocritical, and finally impossible as civil rights workers were beaten, jailed, and assassinated in a land where equality was supposed to be an established fact. Students themselves were getting caught up in the contradictions. Student leaders were being muzzled and arrested as they protested U.S. involvement in Vietnam at the same time that teacher and text spoke of freedom of speech. The military drafted 18- and 19-year-old students into the army before they could vote, while their history books stated that involuntary servitude had ended with the Civil War.

Clearly, the discrepancy between the values that the culture-transmitting teacher was espousing and the values of the society the student was experiencing had to be addressed. In a wave of demonstrations, teach-ins, armbands and leafleting, the question of relevance in education came directly to the doors of boards of education throughout the country.

The issues that the schools had to confront went far beyond the immediate questions of the draft and racism. The entire question of the rights and responsibilities of students, as well as their preparation for entering society, was on the table. While students were not without their adult advocates, it was student energy and student initiative that led to curriculum review. In the process, students learned the legal game. It became clear that there was an "establishment," and that it was white, male, and over thirty. It also became clear that the necessary curriculum was one that would afford our youth opportunities to learn to cope with the entire establishment, and not just the draft. The rights which were won as a result of student struggle became the foundation for new struggles to win additional rights.

When the rebellion quieted, students in many school systems had succeeded in creating separate courses in "constitutional law," "juvenile rights," "street law," "civil rights," and other similar areas and/or won inclusion of special legal rights units in traditional civics courses. But as so often happens, as soon as the goal of infusing relevance into the classroom was attained, the world turned and its focus and needs changed. The war in Vietnam was over; the 18-year-old had the vote; and the backlash against compensatory civil rights programs had taken root. Students felt more repressed by their economic precariousness than by direct political pressure. Burning issues of the 60s became boring classroom fodder for the 70s.

What does the future look like to the student of the 80s? For a very large group of students, education is a carrot/stick affair, with jobs and unemployment hanging fore and aft. MegAmerica has no time or energy to consider the individual and his unique talents, at least not until he or she has been pressure-cooked and rolled through twelve, sixteen, eighteen, and twenty years of school. Even where academic achievement is high, the student still has no guarantee that his or her education will guarantee a living. Not surprisingly, the authoritarian structure of the educational system tends to seed its successors and terminate the insurgents.

Moreover, the classroom teacher is as much a victim as a perpetrator of this system. He or she is closest to students' anxieties over academic achievement and career placement. Stress levels in many classrooms are so high that drug and alcohol abuse are inevitable as escapes. The teacher must deal with the desperation of those who are struggling to keep pace, the anger and frustration of those who are falling behind, as well as the apathy of those who have given up entirely.

With this picture in mind, and with a view to evolving a long-range plan for reasonable education in good citizenship, the primary goal must be to overcome the defeated feelings of the sullen majority by teaching them tools that will enable them to cope confidently with crisis situations. Then, after this has been accomplished, we can devise courses in which these tools can be applied to the specific issues which the student will confront after graduation.

The familiar adage, "Give a man a fish and feed him for a day; teach a man to fish and feed him for a lifetime," hints at the nature of the change that is needed. The students who advocated and fought for reform in the 60s and early 70s learned to "fish," but the courses which they subsequently created were only "fish for a day." Why? Because the specific information taught in these courses did not provide students with an approach to deal with the many other legal problems which they would encounter in the future. In other words, their mistake was to

concentrate on immediate survival information, rather than to teach long-term, problem-solving techniques. For example, a typical inclusion in today's curriculum is a course which details the legal limits of parental, school, and police authority. This sort of course may convey some useful information, but it gives the student no basis to deal with a landlord, a credit-card company, a building inspection, or the hundreds of other conflict-laden situations which he or she is sure to face.

I believe that in order for any real changes to occur in students' ability to relate to our legal system, courses must be devised that do more than list rights and responsibilities. We must design courses that address legal issues in a way which stimulates students to be self-confident in coping with authority. In short, we must teach them to fish.

Many of the courses in the 70s took students into the "real world." A day in court, a ride with a police officer, a visit to a school board, a city council meeting, and literally hundreds of other law-related activities were integral parts of curriculum courses. There was, and still is, great value to this approach, if for no other reason than to counterbalance the world of "Kojak" and "Perry Mason." However, most of what has been tried is superficial. Students aren't really involved in the world of courts and government, but are only given a quick glimpse into its surface structures. To provide a richer and more profound learning experience, community resource volunteers, who are now used infrequently with large groups of students, should be asked to work, instead, with individual students. Apprenticeships and internships based on individual adult/student pairings would help in developing the confidence which students so often lack. For example, a student with an interest in design might be assigned to explore the reason for a large downtown store being denied the right to expand, in an instance where expansion would involve tearing down a two-hundred-year-old building. Optimally, the student would be assisted by a friendly member of the City Planning Department.

As a former high-school teacher who stopped teaching in large part because of the vapidness and dishonesty inherent in our present law-related curriculum, I feel strongly that we can teach students to fish—in the sense of the adage—by instilling in them the confidence to confront and creatively cope with society, and the experience and research ability to make the best use of their own resources.

A good beginning would be to allow the classroom teacher to help students understand and deal with student problems as they, themselves, perceive them. As simple as that appears, few teachers—tenured or not—feel free enough to work in this area because it usually means a challenge to a "higher" school authority. It is one thing to teach the Constitution, and quite another to teach kids their search and seizure rights so that they can protect their marijuana stashes. In a word, academic freedom must precede any other consideration.

Likewise, teachers who a few years ago were thrown, without preparation, into the role of legal authority, must get competent training. This is beginning to happen as community links are created and lawyers, for example, are drafted into teaching workshops for instructors. Colleges and universities are also now offering practical law course to both full-time and extension students. Law schools are making student aides available to junior and senior high schools. The materials, prepared by attorneys and law professors, are being modified and improved through experience based on classroom use.

Perhaps the most relevant workshop for citizenship in our junior and senior high schools is student government. It must be revitalized. Unfortunately, the majority of student government organizations are currently monitored (if not out-and-out controlled) by a school administrator who ensures that they don't do anything "radical" or even "controversial." Of more benefit to the organization would be the presence of a government teacher in an advisory role, but with no authority to censor the student organization.

We need to use student government to provide American youth with practical training so they can more easily make the transition from "rule" by parent and school to self-rule as creative adults. A good analogy is Europe's former African and Asian colonies. Instead of being provided with the proper

assistance to help them achieve a smooth transition to nationhood, the colonies were oppressed and systematically denied the necessary skills for creative independence. To encourage students to participate in self-government, we must not be afraid to support the students' rebellious tendencies. The idea, then, is to foster student independence with the reasonable assumption that experience with freedom as teenagers will help produce powerful and responsible adults. In short, we must live the Bill of Rights in the schoolyard and not just teach them as a textbook abstraction.

Descriptions of the "American Dream" are usually stated in terms of the material objects that represent individual wealth and security. Yet those who have bought into that dream still feel threatened and insecure in this modern society of over-extended credit, multi-national corporations, and corrupt government. I believe we need to restate the dream in terms of mutual trust, respect for the individual and his rights, and government responsive to the society. A social studies curriculum employing these goals can use materials new or old. The strengthening of academic freedom, the revitalization of student government, and individual problem-solving, are all important parts of the process. Children learn through their everyday experiences. Let us transform our schools into desirable and viable environments. Schools should not reflect the ills of our society; rather, they should provide a model for a better society.

Tom Goldstein taught in the San Francisco Bay Area public schools from 1967 through 1979, resigning his last position in protest over the use of undercover police on the high-school campus. His constitutional law and economics courses were integrated with a student-created non-profit recycling corporation, taking students into the real world of business and law. He resides in Berkeley with his three children.

190

A Story of a "Jail-House Lawyer" and Helpful Suggestions Nunc Pro Tunc for Prisoners and Others

by William Gilday

In the midst of putting together materials for the People's Law Review I ran across an article in the Christian Science Monitor about a new wave of do-it-yourself prison law. In this article, William "Lefty" Gilday was described as one of the foremost jail-house lawyers in the country. As I was on my way to Massachusetts (where Lefty is incarcerated) I decided to stop by the Norfolk Correctional Institution and see if he would be willing to write an article about his experiences. Sitting in the waiting area I didn't know what to expect, but as soon as he walked in, the room lit up with smiles and a chorus of "Hi Lefty, thanks for taking care of that divorce matter!" and "Lefty, could I talk to you soon about my appeal?" Twenty-five years in prison notwithstanding, Lefty turned out to be one of the most articulate, charming and intelligent men I've ever met. Within prison walls, Lefty has done more than most of us leading free lives on the outside. He has been instrumental in bringing about a wide range of major prison reform and has handled hundreds of individual prisoners' civil and appellate cases. Here is the story of a remarkable man. [T.I., Ed.]

My name is William Gilday (a/k/a Harry Rapkin—rhymes with napkin) and I am presently serving three life sentences in the Commonwealth of Massachusetts—one of which is a first-degree life without parole (originally a death sentence which was reduced to life). To date, I have been incarcerated nearly a quarter of a century in prisons in Massachusetts and elsewhere.

Let me say at the outset that I did not commit the crime for which I am serving my sentence, even though a jury of my so-called peers determined that I am guilty. Notwithstanding the United States government's position that there are no political prisoners in the United States, I am a political prisoner in the truest sense of the word. However, it must also be said that I was not always politically motivated—for years my profession was that of "thief," witnessed by the fact that at 50 years of age I have, according to social security records, only earned approximately $15,000. During my lifetime I have owned a half-million-dollar electrical contracting business, a luxurious 14-room colonial salt-box home, put kids through college, played professional baseball, served in the military, worked as a seaman, mercenary, arms dealer, and coal miner. You name

it and I've done it.

I was first sentenced, in 1955, to the infamous Walpole State Prison here in Massachusetts for the crime of armed robbery. I was hit with ten to twelve years (in prison parlance this is called "a bit"), but was paroled in four years. In 1962 I returned for violation of parole, was released, and then found guilty of holding up a convicted bookmaker in Haverhill, Massachusetts, in 1963.

After a 22-day trial, I was sentenced to 15 to 25 years at Walpole State Prison. It was during the next seven and one-half years that I became interested in the law and also in furthering my formal education. At the outset of this "bit," I decided that if I were going to be a professional "thief," then I had better become a professional in every sense of the word—not just at stealing, but knowing the law as well. So I began the "case book" method of studying law, and read every legal decision I could lay my hands on. At the same time, I became the "jail-house" lawyer for the 600 other cons in the joint.

The murderous Boston Gang War, in which over 100 people were killed, took place in the 1960s. For the gang members inside, I was the only "jail-house" lawyer. Right at the start I made it clear that if any shit came down with respect to my taking sides, then I would simply not do any legal work for anyone. Thus I was able to function effectively as the inside attorney for both sides, the only problem being to schedule appointments so that members of the different sides did not run into each other.

I learned criminal and constitutional law through experience. During the early and middle 1960s, doing legal work for others was very dangerous. All prisons had rules against assisting inmates with legal work and most wouldn't even allow an inmate to have law books for his own use. If you were caught, you ran the risk of "solitary confinement." In short, getting caught doing "jail-house" law bought you a one-way ticket to the hole.

In order to overcome this obstacle, one had to be somewhat sneaky. First I would type out the letter, writ, brief, motion, etc. on regular paper. Next I would sit down with the person I was helping and make him copy it word for word and return the original. Finally, the original would be destroyed. Formats had to be continually altered so that a reader wouldn't realize that all the writs were coming from the same person. One learned very quickly to use style and dialect in such a way that it appeared that the person sending in the legal document had done it himself. (This has stood me in good stead because a few years ago, while taking a college-level law class, I wrote 11 term papers for 11 different people—including my own—and not one of them was picked up.) Oh, I should also mention that prison officials were so antagonistic to "jail-house" lawyering at one time that even the possession of a legal pad could lead to disciplinary action. I quickly learned that a writ, motion, etc. could be written on anything at all and would be accepted for filing by the courts. Many times I've successfully filed writs on state-issue toilet paper.

In the past decade, the ground rules by which "jail-house" lawyers operate have changed. Now, the judicial system in the United States has recognized the absolute right of a prisoner to file suits on his own behalf. But it was only a short 15 years ago that one federal court ruled: "... prisons are not intended, nor should they be permitted, to serve the purpose of providing inmates with information about methods of securing release therefrom." A

new era dawned with respect to not only prisoners' rights but access to the courts, with the decision of the United States Supreme Court in *Johnson v. Avery*, 393 U.S. 483, 89 S. Ct. 747, 21 L. ED. 2d 718 (1969).

In *Johnson v. Avery*, the Supreme Court held that it was the constitutional right of a prisoner to have access to the courts, including the right to receive assistance from someone with training in the law— including other inmates. Briefly, it overturned a State of Tennessee prison regulation that forbade inmates to "advise, assist or otherwise aid another prisoner" in the preparation of legal materials. As Mr. Justice Fortas wrote for the Court:

> Unless and until the state provides some reasonable alternative to assist inmates in the preparation of petitions for post-conviction relief, it may not validly enforce regulations . . . barring inmates from furnishing such assistance to other inmates.

In short, the Court held that unless the state provided outside lawyers, then "jail-house" lawyers had to be allowed to practice. However, until 1977 there were still continuous battles as to what restrictions —if any—prison administrators could impose in inmates seeking access to courts. The final and decisive blow to prison administrators came with *Bounds v. Smith*, 97 S. Ct. 1491 (1977). This case arose in North Carolina and the Court held that in order for inmates to have "effective access to the courts," prison systems across the country were required to make available the knowledge necessary to bring a lawsuit to any court. The decision gave the states two options: they could either provide outside lawyers to assist indigent inmates, or they could establish adequate law libraries. Since law libraries are cheaper than lawyers, this option was uniformly chosen. (Prior to the *Bounds* case, I had filed a similar suit here in Massachusetss, in 1972.)

The Department of Correction, seeing that they were fighting a losing battle, signed a "consent decree" that provided law libraries to the five major Massachusetts prisons (we now have a $50,000 law library here at Norfolk State Prison) as well as comparable law libraries in the other state institutions. While it hasn't been done in Massachusetts yet, many states, and some federal "joints," have put "jail-house" lawyers to work as law clerks. I am the Chief Law Librarian here at Norfolk prison and work alongside five other law librarians. We are open seven days a week (a minimum of 55 hours). The law library is staffed by two men at all times, and upwards of about 200 inmates use the library or seek advice each week. (There are 700 inmates at Norfolk.) Further, the staff of the law library offers law classes beginning with "Basic Criminal Law" and continuing through "Advanced Criminal Law." The idea is to educate inmates about the legal process and their rights as prisoners. However, a person can only be spoon-fed just so far, and then the burden of deepening their understanding is on that person. I would estimate that perhaps five percent of our students actually become anywhere from good to excellent in their studies—but everyone who takes the course at least gets some basic information about our legal process and inmate rights.

The court decisions which established the rights of inmates to bring suits and liberated the "jail-house" lawyer resulted in a flood of inmate petitions. In the year ending June 30, 1979, more than 25,000 petitions, or writs, were filed by inmates in the federal courts. That is 43.8% more than in 1970, and approximately eight times as many as

were filed in 1960. The state courts, as well, have watched their dockets swell with *pro se* or *in propria persona* (for himself) suits filed by indigent and incarcerated inmates, many of them prepared by "jail-house" lawyers. Most of these petitions, motions, writs, etc., seek to overturn original convictions or have a direct appeal. But some of the legal suits filed by inmates directly challenge the entire prison system, and ask that it—or part of it—be declared unconstitutional. It should be noted that suits filed along these lines have been successful in well over a dozen states, including Mississippi, Rhode Island, New Hampshire, Tennessee, and Arkansas. A third type of legal activity is now developing in the area of civil litigations (i.e., probate, adoption, divorce, etc.). This is exciting, and it allows many "jail-house" lawyers to expand their practice from the traditional constitutional, penal and criminal fields to areas of the law not previously explored.

It is generally lamented that a large majority of *pro se* lawsuits are frivolous, or so poorly written that they are summarily tossed out of court. However, there are the handful of inmates who through sheer perseverance or will power have taught themselves to be good and effective lawyers—better than the average lawyer on the outside. (I certainly consider this to be true of myself—but then "jail-house" lawyers, like *all* lawyers, are notorious for their egos.) Over the years I have been successful in freeing or obtaining new trials for over 100 prisoners who had no other legal recourse. I was also instrumental in setting forth some civil rights and other significant precedents. Some of these cases include:

Gilday v. Scafati, 428 F. 2d 1027 (1970), which set new constitutional standards on the use of prior convictions to impeach the credibility of a criminal defendant when he elects to testify in his own defense and when the prior records were obtained by denying the defendant the right to counsel in the prior proceeding.

Gilday v. Boone et al., which is still pending, seeking injunctive relief for destruction of legal materials, opening legal mail and denying prisoners access to legal materials.

Stone v. Boone et al., which resulted in a consent decree installing complete law libraries in every prison in the Commonwealth of Massachusetts.

Gilday v. Dukakis et al. (still pending), also known as the Norfolk Prison Fire Escape Suit, which seeks to have it declared "cruel and unusual" punishment to hold prisoners in a building that has no means of egress in case of fire. This suit has already resulted in the removal of dangerous foam-type mattresses from Norfolk and all other state prisons; further, one million dollars has been appropriated by the state legislature to upgrade fire safety at Norfolk.

Ramos et al. v. Norfolk Board of Voter Registration, which won the Massachusetts prisoners the right to vote.

Gilday v. Hall et al., absolute right to have legal visits from law students, para-legals and attorneys (injunction issued).

Gilday v. Commonwealth, right of indigent prisoner to have free copy of transcripts for use in collateral attacks.

Commonwealth v. Gilday (my present convictions), challenging prosecutorial misconduct, in particular the dangerously pervasive practice of convincing or coercing one defendant to testify against another in exchange for freedom or reduced

EPILOG: THE LAWYERS PUT UP A TERRIFIC BATTLE WHICH TOOK TWO YEARS AND $6000.00. FIONA GOT MOST OF THE BONUS. HANK GOT A LOAN TO PAY HIS ATTORNEY. THEY SPLIT THE BEER CAN COLLECTION. HANK AND FIONA, UNFORTUNATLY BECAME BITTER ENEMIES FIGHTING OVER FRED. TRAGICALLY, THE NEIGHBOR'S CAT GOT FRED THE DAY HANK WAS AWARDED HIS CUSTODY.

sentence, especially where a specific request is made and there is a deliberate concealing of the "deal" itself and any prior contradictory statements by the co-defendant turned informant.

Even though the majority of *pro se* suits are frivolous and are tossed out of court, they serve two very important purposes: they teach the would-be "jail-house" lawyer, by process of trial and error, where he went wrong, and more important, they tie up not only the courts themselves but the entire judicial process. It is my hope that this increased taxpayer cost and the congestion of the legal system will eventually result in the system's being totally revamped. It should be noted that the system itself is dependent upon making "deals," or "plea-bargaining." If every defendant insisted upon his constitutional right to a jury trial, then the entire judicial system of this country would collapse in a matter of months. A good "jail-house" lawyer can arrange a court appearance for any client, have writs issued, have an answer filed, and even get past a motion to dismiss. I am not saying that I can win every case, but at this stage I can take a case from absolutely nothing — even a case that doesn't exist — and enter it into a court, thereby tying up the system. (One difference between a lawyer on the street and one on the inside is that the courts and the system can punish — via disciplinary action or disbarment — the outside lawyer, but what is a six-month "contempt" citation against a person serving life? What can they do to you — put you in jail?)

Don't be fooled into believing that the legal system in this country is fair. Actually, it is pretty much a game, and one in which a lot of people get hurt — up to and including being murdered. If you learn the game well enough, you may not obtain "justice," but you might get yourself out of jail.

In carrying out my practice, I follow a few simple rules:

1. I don't charge or accept any fee for my services.

2. I never advise a person if he/she should appeal or not, but simply lay out all the facts and insist that they make their own decisions.

3. I never recommend or tout any particular lawyer to an inmate, although I will give my opinion if asked, and then the person meets with the lawyer and makes whatever arrangements he or she wishes to.

4. I never take a "kickback" from an attorney, although if I've worked with him on cases, I might ask him to handle a case *pro bono* for a needy prisoner.

5. I never promise to get anyone out of prison or tell him that he has an absolute winner. There is no such thing. I've seen cases that looked like sure winners lose in court, and sure losers get reversed. I explain everything to the inmate and advise him to give it his best shot.

6. I don't handle rape or child-molesting cases, but will make referrals to other lawyers. I admit to being biased in this area and reserve my right not to involve myself in these cases.

A few words to the would-be "jail-house" lawyer, or anyone interested in the law. First, a "jail-house" lawyer who tells people that he will absolutely get them out of prison is full of shit. There are no guarantees. Second, it is naive for inmates to expect justice from the system. The so-called criminal justice system is not designed to deliver justice, but to put certain people in prison. Third, there is no mystery to law. All it takes is a logical mind and some study. The legal establishment would like everyone to believe that a person needs a law school education to understand law, but this writer has seen enough lawyers who are coming out of law schools these days to know better. In a three-year law school, the student takes one course in criminal law and perhaps two courses in constitutional law, but receives no practical training in criminal law at all. Fourth, it is sometimes easier than you think to beat an Assistant District Attorney or Assistant Attorney General for two reasons: because he or she is so overcome with cases that there simply isn't time to handle yours as well, and because he or she is often a young kid, just a year or two out of law school, who may be bright and ambitious, but who simply doesn't have sufficient practical experience.

Most prison administrators will state that the filing of suits by *pro se* indigent prisoners is not a hardship for them, but the fact remains that they have had to hire extra staff members to handle the volume of materials presently being filed. The argument of most prison officials is that they recognize the problems within the prison system and want to correct them, but they can't get sufficient money appropriated from their respective legislatures; however, prisoners have learned that the federal courts can order the state to supply sufficient money to correct abuses (i.e., overcrowding, medical care, prison conditions, etc.). Thus a suit is needed under the Civil Rights Act—§ 1983—to accomplish what should have been done in the first place. I think that most "jail-house" lawyers would agree that they are ignored so long as they limit activities to challenging their own or someone else's conviction. But lawsuits against prison officials are not looked upon kindly and retaliation may result (i.e., transfer, segregation, harrassment, etc.). Therefore, I suggest that any person who files a suit against either prison officials or a prison system set forth in his or her complaint the following prayer:

> That this Court preliminarily and permanently enjoin and restrain defendants, and each of them, and their subordinates, delegates, employees, representatives, agents, successors, assignees and any other person acting in concert therewith, from punishing, penalizing or in any other way disciplining plaintiff inmates for filing or prosecuting this action; and that no custodial transfer to a more restrictive custody status be effected without filing notice and reasons therefor with this Court.

Toni Ihara of Nolo Press suggested that you might be interested in the mundane details of a "jail-house" lawyer's life. My typical day is as follows. I come into the law library about 7:45 a.m. My shift is Monday through Friday mornings, and Thursday and Saturday nights. I open the place up, put the coffee pot on and get ready for the day's activities. I usually have until about 8:15 a.m. before the first person arrives with a major problem (ranging anywhere from needing a sample letter, to dealing with a disciplinary ticket, to questions concerning when his brief will be ready to be filed). I then stay in the law library until 9:30 to 10:00 a.m., at which time I leave the other fellow in charge and I go to the resident council office or to my housing unit to make some legal phone calls (mostly for others who want me to call their lawyers or the courts). After about half an hour on the phone, I'm back at my desk. Almost always as I walk through the library door, I'm greeted with "where have you been—there have been ten guys here looking for you." Needless to say, if it's important they will return. I never go looking for cases, since I always have more clients than I can handle.

I stay in the law library until 11:50 a.m., when it is time to return to the housing unit for the second major count of the day, and lunch. After lunch I catch the noon news and then go to the hospital for my ulcer medication (ulcers are common among lawyers). Even the days that I'm not scheduled to work, I usually return to the law library—sometimes to work on a divorce or some other action or to prepare a letter or petition. In the afternoon I'm in and out of the law library until about 4:00 p.m.—unless I'm in my room resting or taking a college course. At 4:50 p.m. there's another major count, and then dinner. At 5:30 p.m. the all-clear gong sounds and I go back to the law library, providing I don't have any other meetings or groups to attend.

Throughout the day I am continually being asked for legal advice, and I must admit that at times it gets somewhat tiresome. Sometimes it seems as if everyone has a problem and they all think that it can be solved legally. I try my best to answer if I can. If I don't know the answer, then I'll say so up front and try to research it. Another thing is that I always tell the truth—even if the answer is the opposite of what the person wants to hear. I've found it's always better to tell someone exactly where they stand. There are many lawyers, of course, who make it a practice of telling people only what they want to hear—not what the facts are. This is true not only of people doing law inside the prison, but on the outside as well. The fact of the matter is that a lot of outside attorneys will promise a client anything, take his or her money, and then when things go wrong, blame it on the judge or some other circumstance beyond his or her control. This situation is not unique to prison or criminal law, but is perpetuated by members of the bar in all areas of practice—particularly in divorce cases. For example, two people can be in complete agreement that they should get a divorce—they settle the property issues themselves and ordinarily the divorce itself would be a very simple procedure. But let a lawyer find out that there is some money involved, and then it gets to be more complicated in a hurry. In my experience it's not unusual that by the time the lawyers get through with a simple divorce action, both parties have lost nearly all their money, and the lawyers have made a bundle.

After dinner I usually stay in the law library doing legal work that I have set aside during the day, and at 9:00 p.m. I return to my housing unit and bring my legal papers with me. Usually I work till around 1:00 a.m. before going off to sleep. I try to spend most of the weekend working on briefs and other motions or petitions; letters are done during the day, as is most of my research, not only for my own case but for other cases as well.

Perhaps an illustration of a very recent case I assisted with will give a clearer picture of the value of "jail-house" lawyers. In early 1976 a young black man by the name of Joe A. was sentenced in Massachusetts for the crime of first-degree murder (a life sentence without possibility of parole). Joe was a functional illiterate with an I.Q. of 52, but he gave the impression of understanding what was going on. In any event, he was accused of killing a woman in the city of Boston and, because of his mental condition, he gave in to a police suggestion that if he confessed to the crime, then his brother (who actually did the killing) would be set free and he himself would be allowed to go home after giving his statement. So Joe gave an inculpatory statement. He was assigned a private, court-appointed attorney (who was known to the writer to simply act *pro forma* on behalf of his appointed clients, but to be extremely fast in submitting his bill to the court for payment). The trial took 11 days; Joe was found guilty and sent to Walpole State Prison for life. Subsequently, he was transferred to Norfolk State Prison, where I met him. I asked Joe if he had a direct appeal pending. He told me that he thought so. I got his indictment number (after he had already served a year in prison), wrote for and obtained the docket entries to find out the status of his appeal. Yes, you guessed it, the court-appointed attorney had not even protected his appeal rights; Joe had no appeal pending and was doomed to serve a minimum of 20 years before being able to seek commutation.

Upon receiving this information, I immediately filed a petition for a writ of error and an assignment of errors seeking to have his one and only direct appeal reinstated (in Massachusetts one has to file a Claim of Appeal within 20 days from the verdict and sentence). At the same time, I sent a letter to the Massachusetts Board of Bar Overseers requesting that they look into the matter because this was about

the tenth man whom this court-appointed attorney had abandoned. The attorney responded to the complaint by stating that after an 11-day jury trial, at the conclusion of which his client went to prison for life, without parole, he spoke to Joe in the holding area (an hour after the verdict and sentence). He claimed that Joe told him he didn't want an appeal (after the lawyer told him that there were absolutely no grounds to raise an appeal). Joe told me that he never even saw the lawyer at this time, and I believe him. I countered to the Board that even if one conceded that the American system of justice is excellent (and of course I really don't believe this), it was extremely doubtful that Joe received a fair trial with no possible grounds to appeal.

I persuaded a young woman attorney who had just passed the bar to accept the appointment of the court if it was offered to her. She agreed, and a motion for appointment of counsel was filed, asking that she be specifically appointed. The court granted the motion after many hassles, noting especially that trial counsel was experienced and if he said there were no grounds for appeal then he was probably right. A trial transcript was requested, granted, and then the writ of error was argued. The Massachusetts Supreme Judicial Court, two years after the original conviction, ordered that Joe's appellate rights be reinstated. This new attorney then argued the direct appeal (it took another year) and subsequently the full bench of the Supreme Judicial Court reversed the conviction and ordered a new trial. Appellate counsel, not being that familiar with trial work, asked me if I could contact one of my former lawyers to handle the matter at the new trial. I did this, and he agreed to accept an appointment. So I filed another motion for the appointment of named counsel for trial and it was granted. The only real evidence against Joe was his inculpatory statement. New trial counsel then moved to suppress the statement on two grounds: that Joe did not have the mental capacity to understand the *Miranda* warnings, and that he was arrested illegally, and thus any statements he made were unlawfully obtained. The pre-trial motion was filed, argued and granted on both grounds. The new attorney requested that Joe be tested to determine his mental capacity, and the expert opinion was that with a second-grade education and a limited mental capacity, Joe didn't have the ability to understand what was going on when he was arrested. Since Joe couldn't make the bail for the new trial, he was remanded to County Jail to await his new trial. Less than a week later we had him transferred back to Norfolk so I could work with him.

A year after the motion suppressing the inculpatory statement was approved, the District Attorney's Office dismissed the charges against Joe and he was free. That was great, of course, but don't forget that Joe lost over four years out of his life simply because he had no education, was black, and had a lawyer who didn't care and who abandoned him. I am pleased to say that Joe is a "born-again" Christian who is doing very well on the outside. I only mention this particular case to show how vital a role the "jail-house" lawyer can play in the lives of inmates.

It is no simple task being a "jail-house" lawyer. Indeed, it's a lot of headaches. When all is said and done, you've only assisted a fellow inmate to get out of prison when he shouldn't have been there in the first place. And as I have indicated, I personally don't believe in the American judicial system. It has become a complicated game in which the best player (or actor) wins. Perhaps I've helped some guilty people get out of jail, but the fact remains that

they never received a "fair and impartial" trial in the first place. One continually hears law enforcement people complain about how they are handcuffed by new restrictive decisions and how the guilty go free because of "technicalities." But the truth is that if the whole system has become a game, then law enforcement people have made the rules. If they played the game correctly instead of taking so many short cuts—getting people to perjure themselves, faking evidence, etc.—then when they did put a person into prison, there wouldn't be ways to get him or her out. It's when law enforcement officials cheat that they allow a "jail-house" lawyer to expose them. "Jail-house" lawyers are here to stay and the criminal justice system had better look out!

William M. Gilday, Jr. is a magna cum laude *graduate of Boston University. Although he spends most of his energy working to secure civil rights and judicial relief for himself and fellow prisoners, he still finds time to learn Italian and pitch for and manage the prison baseball team.*

PART IV

Dispute Resolution Through Mediation

Dispute resolution programs deal with conflicts through a mediation process. They allow people opportunities to vent their feelings and frustrations—and possibly find satisfactory resolutions—without lawyers, without time restrictions, and without blame. The mediator or panel does not *impose* a settlement. The programs are run by a court, an agency, or a neighborhood center.

Dispute resolution programs may hold the key to a better way of handling conflicts or they may prove to be merely another adjunct of the traditional court system with no real improvement in the administration of justice. Here we review several programs, and comment on their effectiveness.

Litigation is a machine which
you go into as a pig and come out
as a sausage.
—*Ambrose Bierce*

Mediation—Dispute Resolution Programs[1]

There was a time when people actually fought their own battles. Nobles in the English Middle Ages donned their coats of armor, clambered onto their steeds, set their lances in forward position, and charged. But it didn't take long for the less spirited to realize that it wasn't always worth getting injured or killed to take a stand. Perhaps it would be better to pay someone else to do the fighting.

So, knights were sent to represent the disputants. They wore their noble's colors—in the hope that God would not recognize that the knight was an ersatz rider. But eventually these legendary champions also decided that the glamour and glory weren't worth it.

Rather than find someone else, the nobles removed the disputes from the field to the feudal or king's courts. Somehow in the transition, though, no one thought of returning the dispute to the original disputants. Instead, representatives continued to be intricately involved in the dispute and its resolution. These representatives were lawyers. And from that time on, lawyers have tried to ensure that no one considers the alternatives.[2]

Dispute resolution programs not only consider alternatives, they actually put them into practice. During the past five years, they have created programs where people can settle their own disputes without lawyers, outside the confines of the court system, and without the stigmas of "winner-loser" and "innocence-guilt."

How does it work? Different programs handle the process differently.[3] But generally, an independent third party or panel listens to all sides of the conflict and then assists the participants to reach a satisfactory solution. Most programs have either one or two mediators; a few use panels of three to five. Where there is more than one mediator, the program staff will try to ensure that the mediators in some way reflect the characteristics of the disputants—age, sex, race, etc. For example, if the disputants are a man and a woman, the two mediators would also be a man and a woman.

The resolution of the conflict comes from the disputants—the mediator only encourages dialogue and assists in seeking the resolutions. A mediator does not impose a solution; an *arbitrator* does. And in most cases, the idea of an arbitrator is inconsistent with the concept of the mediation program. A few programs do, however, use a combination of mediation and arbitration.

Mediation has never been intended to substitute for the traditional justice system. Certainly, many kinds of complex cases are better suited to a more formal setting. But there are many more which do not belong in the courts in the first place. Many problems involving families, adolescents, couples, school incidents, tenants and landlords, employees and employers, merchants and consumers, dogs, neighborhood misdemeanors, etc., often seem much more appropriate for mediation than for an antagonistic adversary court proceeding. It is precisely these "minor" disputes which, when left unresolved, erupt into far more serious consequences.

There are basically three kinds of dispute resolution programs: those involved with the justice system, those set up by agencies, and those run by the community or neighborhood served.[4] Referrals can be made by any number of groups or individuals, including the police, the court, local prosecutors, social and community welfare agencies, churches, community clubs, neighbors, and of course, the participants themselves.

When a referral is received, the usual procedure is for program staff to meet with the disputants individually to see whether a settlement could be reached without a hearing; whether the dispute is appropriate for the program; or whether the problem should be referred immediately to a social agency. Where a hearing seems suitable, the disputants are invited to appear at once. In two out of three situations, the disputants will agree to participate.

Mediation hearings are often held in the evening. They are informal—coffee may be served, and the discussion is in common, everyday language. Disputants are given as much time as needed to express feelings and frustrations, which is often more important than the resolution itself. Hearings may last from one hour to five or six hours.

Dialogue between the disputants is encouraged, though some programs emphasize this aspect more than others. More than one-half of the programs use shuttle diplomacy. That is, after the disputants have expressed their "concerns," the mediators separate the parties and meet with each privately. The purpose is to find out exactly what a disputant will accept. A minority of the programs keep the disputants together throughout, feeling that a mediator shouldn't be privileged to any information not available to the other party.

The resolution fashioned by the disputants with the assistance of the mediators allows for creative solutions to the dispute, solutions where no one is "blamed." For example, a TV store owner might agree to fix a new, defective TV after the purchaser agreed to pay for half of the repairs, conceding that his children might have been a little rough with the set. These resolutions are much more likely to be satisfactory than those imposed by a court. Referrals may also be made to social service and community organizations (family, job placement, etc.) where further counseling and support may assist in preventing the problem from recurring.

The resolution is written and signed by the disputants. Many agreements involving traditional property-type disputes would probably be enforced by a court of law, while others—for example, those involving conduct—would probably not be. But even if a resolution is not court-enforced, it is usually just as, or more, effective because the resolution was chiseled out by the parties themselves, not imposed upon them.

One of the disputes we mediated involved three neighbors—Jarrett, Peterson and Holliday. Holliday, whose home was in the middle, owned a dog which was relieving itself in the "common" backyard. (Dog problems are very common in dispute resolution hearings.) The resultant odors and other familiar liabilities (flies, dirty shoes, etc.) created a definite nuisance to the neighbors. All three neighbors liked one another, but Jarrett and Peterson felt that since Holliday was very sensitive, it might be better to have the problem mediated by an independent third party.

* *

The night of the hearing, Jarrett phoned to say that he had to work late, but that he would accept whatever settlement was made by Peterson and Holliday.

Fifteen minutes into the hearing, Holliday offered to get rid of his dog. But the mediators held him off. First, it is not a good idea to consider a resolution until each person has had a full opportunity to express his/her side of the problem. A premature settlement may not release the frustrations—leading to the possibility of a more serious situation later on. Second, it was possible that a less extreme solution could be found—one that Holliday would really prefer.

After each disputant completed his explanation, Peterson suggested that Holliday move the doghouse to the back of the lot—so it would not be adjacent to either neighbor's house. Holliday agreed; but it was obvious that he wasn't very happy about it. With prompting from the mediators, he admitted that he was worried. He worked at night and had bought the dog for protection for his wife and daughters. If the doghouse were moved back, perhaps the dog wouldn't hear an intruder.

So discussion continued.

It was finally agreed that the doghouse would be moved back, but the dog would stay in the main house until Holliday came home. Holliday agreed to purchase a specific kind of fly catcher, which he would keep on his property. He also consented to clean up his yard each morning and evening. The parties then signed the agreement.

Sometimes the problem first raised by the disputants turns out to be only a cover for another—quite separate—problem. Perhaps the reason the neighbor complained about the loud all-night parties next door was not because he was being kept up all night, but rather because he wasn't invited. This would probably never be admitted in a courtroom, but in a well-supervised mediation session, the neighbor may feel enough trust and confidence in the mediators to come to grips with the essential dispute.

The process does not end when a resolution is reached and an agreement is signed. The staff will follow up by contacting the parties again—from one week to two months after the hearing. There may be as many as two or three contacts if necessary.

Program coordinators claim that their rate of

success (measured by the low number of returning cases) is high — usually around 90%. Of course, it is possible that some cases don't return because they go to court the next time.

Mediators are rarely lawyers. [5] Sometimes they are social workers or law students, though programs encourage community people with no particular background to serve. The mediators are trained in conflict resolution techniques. Training sessions are usually 20 to 40 hours, and include skills in making people comfortable, getting them to talk, and in ferreting out satisfactory agreements.

Mediation has met with serious criticism. Some people feel that low-income disputants are often at a distinct disadvantage. In disputes between people of unequal footing—a merchant and a consumer, a landlord and a tenant, an employer and employee, or in criminal matters — there is a tendency to reach agreements which maintain the unequal footing of the disputants. Settlements may be subtly imposed rather than agreed upon. Some legal services lawyers, for example, argue that in a formal law proceeding, the person with less power is afforded a better chance of reaching a fair settlement. They feel that the law, both substantive and procedural, can possibly even up the match, and that there is usually a chance of appeal. Other advocates for the indigent may be wary about the mediation situation, but they would argue that a poor disputant couldn't be treated any worse than he already is in court.

There is also the problem that, in criminal matters, a person may unintentionally incriminate him/herself during a dispute resolution hearing. Though the hearings are meant to be confidential, it is conceivable that someone at the hearing may breach the confidentiality later on.

The materials we have included in this part are meant to be an introduction to several mediation programs — showing what mediation is, and how it works in dispute resolution. Later we review in depth the San Francisco Community Board Program, which many people consider to be one of the more innovative mediation programs. A listing of dispute resolution programs around the country is found at the end of this section.

---

1. A majority of the programs use the term "mediation" in their title. Others use "dispute resolution," "dispute settlement," "conflict resolution," and the like. In describing these kinds of programs, we've decided to use both mediation and dispute resolution interchangeably.

2. See Ann Strick's article on the history of law in the first part of this book.

3. For more information on different approaches, see *Neighborhood Justice Centers, An Analysis of Potential Models*. Office of Development, Testing, Dissemination, LEAA, U.S. Department of Justice, Washington, D.C. 20531.

4. In an article following this section, Paul Wahrhaftig, of the Grassroots Dispute Resolution Clearinghouse, describes the differences.

5. You might like to compare this article with the article written by Gary Friedman on personal mediation — where some lawyers are earning their living as professional mediators (see Part I). Also, this is reminiscent of the "lay judge" system described in Katherine Galvin's article on Cuba.

The Urban Court

The Dorchester Court was formerly named the Urban Court, and is one of the oldest mediation programs in the country. It is located in the Dorchester community of Boston, one of the most financially and racially integrated neighborhoods of that city. Though intimately connected with the court system, its offices are situated in a storefront, two blocks from the Dorchester District Court, in the heart of the community. Referrals come largely from the district court, a few from the police, and fewer still from the community (usually people who have used the court before). A majority of the cases are criminal, such as petty theft, assault and battery.

The program is voluntary. People who are referred to it can refuse to participate and elect to go through the regular court system. But since this kind of program is designed to ease the burden on the traditional courts and funnel off the "less serious" cases (problems which are not in their critical stage yet, but which, if left unresolved, are bound to be seen at a later date), there is probably a subtle pressure on the criminal defendant to go through this program. And of course, he or she would certainly benefit should a satisfactory resolution be reached, since the Dorchester Court mediation approach bypasses the concept of guilt, and the agreement will probably be more creative than any the district court would impose.

There are 40 mediators, ranging in age from 16 to 60. All are members of the Dorchester community. They work on a "when-needed" basis and receive $7.50 per session. They have been trained (40 hours) by the staff, who are also members of the community. No lawyers are used in the program.

Two mediators sit at each hearing. After listening to each disputant, the mediators caucus alone, considering several resolutions. Next, they separate the parties and hold private discussions with each. They may suggest hypothetical solutions to draw the parties out on what sorts of resolutions they might accept. If no solution is possible through the mediation process, the dispute will be sent back to the Dorchester District Court (assuming, of course, that they were referred from the Court initially). Other cases may be referred to outside public and private agencies. Where an agreement is reached, it is written up and signed by the parties, and filed with the court (if it is a court matter). For example, the agreement may include participation in an alcohol, drug, or psychological counseling program, or the participants may be directed to others who can help them find housing and/or employment.

There is a 90-day waiting period after the agreement is reached and filed with the court. If at the end of the period things are worked out, the criminal case is dismissed from the Court. If a problem has arisen, the case can go to trial or return for another mediation session. Similar programs have recently been set up in other Massachusetts counties.

The program is located at 506-A Washington Street, Dorchester, MA 02124, phone (617) 825-2700.

Neighborhood Justice Centers

The United States Justice Department Law Enforcement Assistance Administration (LEAA) sponsors three "Neighborhood Justice Centers" in Atlanta, Kansas City, and Los Angeles. All three programs are tied into the local court system, though the Los Angeles program actively seeks community involvement and input. Referrals to the program come from the local prosecutors, police, social agencies, the community, and some self-referrals.

The Atlanta "NJC" is a private non-profit corporation with a heavy concentration of legal people sitting on its board. The Kansas City program is under the auspices of the city's Community Services Department. The Los Angeles center is sponsored by the Los Angeles County Bar Association and is in the Venice–Mar Vista area.

The Neighborhood Justice Center programs are located at:

Atlanta:
1118 Euclid Ave., N.E.
Atlanta, GA 30307
(404) 523-8236

Kansas City:
American Bank Building Suite 305
One West Armor
Kansas City, MO 64111
(816) 274-1895

Los Angeles:
(Venice–
Mar Vista)
1527 Venice Blvd.
Venice, CA 90291
(213) 390-7666

Using Volunteers
Interview with Edith B. Prim

The following interview with Edith Prim, Deputy Director of the Atlanta program, is reprinted with permission from the "Mooter"—the Journal of the Grassroots Citizen Dispute Resolution Clearinghouse in Pittsburgh.

Edith Prim is Deputy Director of the Atlanta Neighborhood Justice Center where she has built a reputation for skillfully using volunteers in many phases of the program.

Mooter: Most of our readers are familiar with the three Neighborhood Justice Centers as government funded Justice Department backed experiments in dispute resolution. Could you give us a little background on the volume of cases you are handling and similar problems that relate to your use of volunteers?
Prim: The Atlanta NJC is housed in a neighborhood location in the Southeastern part of the city. It receives cases from about eighteen referral sources, but the bulk of our cases come from all over the city and are running now at a level of two to three

hundred cases a month. In one month we mediated over one hundred cases. We have a staff of five, a Director, Deputy Director, two intake people and a secretary. If we tried to get by with just the intake staff we would go bananas.

Mooter: How many volunteers do you use and for what roles?

Prim: I have had twenty to twenty-five volunteers in the past twenty months. They haven't all worked at the same time. We have maybe three or four working now and we are recruiting for the Fall trying to get seven or eight more.

Primarily we use volunteers on intake here at the center. Our two intake staff could not do it all because intake is very time consuming. They must telephone the respondents, send out letters to confirm the dates a day or two before the hearing. At intake they do things like conciliation. We call it a conciliation when we don't have a mediation hearing; like the volunteer calls up the landlord and he says to ask the lady to come up to this office and he will work it out. Then the lady calls us back three days later and says, "The landlord did it. I appreciate it." We will follow it up. A volunteer can do that just as well if not better than I because they are not jaundiced. They are in one day a week or so. They enjoy all these crazy people calling up, while we who are here everyday don't.

We also have them in three courts, a City Court known as Police Court, the State Court in the small claims section, and the Magistrates Court.

Mooter: One of the arguments I hear against putting volunteers in court is that you need consistent staff people there. Court folks don't relate to a consistently fluctuating bunch of volunteers.

Prim: That's a bunch of bull. Honest to God. The whole thing is related to how well you as a staff member go down and relate to those people in court. I've spent a lot of time going down there watching what is going on, going in and talking with them. I didn't talk about legal things all the time. I talked about the Falcons, (our football team). You don't go down there like gangbusters, burn your bra and say you have a terrible system. You say I've got a service. We want to help but we don't want to be in the way. Might I study the system? Might I ask you if this would work? Could we try it for a week or two?

My volunteers stand three feet from the small

claims intake clerk. The volunteer never says to a complainant, "Talk to me and don't talk to him." Complainants always talk to the intake clerk first who will immediately say, "Look, I'll be glad to do this, but why don't you take it to the Neighborhood Justice Center over there. Talk to this man here, and if you don't want to do what they want, come back three feet and stepover here and I'll file a claim."

I think another thing is that the volunteers have got to be aware they represent the Neighborhood Justice Center. They don't go down there and wear blue jeans that haven't been washed since 1970. That might be fine in some cities but not in this one.

Mooter: So you are saying that the fact that there is a different face behind the desk is not a barrier to using volunteers. Where do you recruit your volunteers?

Prim: We get them from public service announcements on the radio, filing notices at the law school, through Volunteer Atlanta, which is sort of a coordinating agency, and through the Junior League and the Council of Jewish Women. We get them from all walks of life. They do not fall into any one category racially or economically.

We use interns from the Urban Corps. I don't know what it is called up your way. It works through colleges. There is federal money which people can use to work to go to college. They intern at an agency that is related to their major. We have had Urban Corps volunteers since the beginning. We pay something like 35% of their hourly rate. For an undergraduate that is about $3.00 an hour. For law students, about $4.50.

To me the critical question to ask in selecting volunteers is, "What's in it for you?" You are going to have a happier, more productive volunteer if that person can see it as a means to an end for him. That may mean a law student who wants to know more about law. Therefore they do intake for you. You do have to be careful with that because your volunteers can't practice their 'skills' of adversarial combat with your clients. You have to make them understand this. I had to do that with one of my volunteers.

To me the secret of having effective volunteers is to get people to see something of value in it for them whether it is skills that might be marketable like mediation. Maybe they were a social worker in 1945 and haven't worked since. They want to get back into the working world. Maybe they simply want to get out for three hours a week. That is fine. Those are all good reasons for being involved in the program.

Along this line, we have told people who have volunteered for us that next time we train mediators, everybody wants to be mediators basically, we will put them in front of everybody else. We have something like a hundred people on the waiting list. We do that because it is an incentive. We get a much better mediator too in the sense they understand the project, the people and all of that.

Mooter: Doesn't the whole system depend on consistency? How do you make sure that volunteers actually show up?

Prim: You set it down as a given. You say that we need people from 10—1 on Wednesday or Monday or Friday from 1–4. When can you go? "I can go every Monday at 1:00." "OK, fine, be sure to pick up your files. It is fine if you can't go one Monday if you have got a conflict or a child is sick. Please let us know. If you let us know, then we will cover it."

If you find that two Mondays go along you let them go or switch them around. You don't get intimidated by volunteers. Therefore the volunteers that stick with you know you mean business and know you need their help, and will have much greater respect and interest in the program.

Mooter: It sounds to me like some expenses are involved.

Prim: Yes; we have money from the government to pay our volunteers. I would see if there is a way in which you can get some organization like the Junior League or League of Women Voters or some organization that is into volunteers to give the center a small grant of a couple of thousand dollars to help you with volunteers. You could say it is to pay parking and mileage or something like that. Maybe you could cover the costs of your Urban Interns. We pay a maximum of $10.00 per day. But a small center where the distances are shorter and has free parking might not need that high a price tag.

I think the bottom line is you have to approach the volunteer program as just another part of your business. Our centers are businesses even though they are not in the business of making money. You have to manage them like you would something that is there to make money. It is the same management system that needs to be in place. Let people know what they are to do. Give them meaningful tasks to do. Have them responsible to somebody and be sure that you have your act together, and make sure they know as much about the program as you do. With the money so up in the air for everybody, who knows what next year will bring? We have to look forward to less and less money being available. At the same time that you have less money available, your program is building. Good use of volunteers is an answer.

The kinds of cases a particular mediation program would hear depends upon its orientation. One program may shy away from domestic problems, another may require that the disputants have some personal or business relationship, thus rejecting random criminal situations, a third may rely largely on referrals from a court which will likely include many minor crimes, and a fourth might require that all the parties live in a particular neighborhood. The Los Angeles Neighborhood Justice Center recently published statistics on the kinds of cases they actually mediate. We thought it would be helpful to include them and give you some idea of the actual breakdown of one particular program. Notice that more than 50% of the cases are consumer/merchant or tenant/landlord.

Neighborhood Justice Center of Venice & Mar Vista

1527 Venice Boulevard • Venice, California 90291 • (213) 390-7666

Cumulative Statistics – 14 Months
April 1978 – May 1979

Phone calls and Walk-ins	4,337
Referrals to other organizations	1,829
Cases opened (mediatable disputes)	853
Mediations	237
Telephone Conciliations	106

Referral sources for cases opened
46%	Self Referrals
17	Judges
12	City Attorney and Small Claims Court Clerk
8	Police
8	Community Agencies
4	Legal Aid
3	Government Agencies
2	Other

Types of Cases
29%	Consumer/Merchant
24	Tenant/Landlord
12	Neighbor/Neighbor
11	Domestic Settlements
6	Employer/Employee
5	Friends
3	Intra-Family
10	Other

A Public Service Project of the Los Angeles County Bar Association

Mediation Summary

Case No: 78-046-AUG
Mediation Coordinator: Karen Gilmore
Mediator: Daniele LeCroy
Observer: Karen Gilmore

Initiator: Marsha S.
Respondent: Bill S.
Initial Contact Date: 8/27/78
Mediation Date: 8/27/78
Approximate Length of Mediation: 3 hours

Intake: Marsha S. and her 19-year-old son, Bill S., live together in the same house. Mrs. S. discovered $20 missing from its hiding place in her home on June 23, 1978. She found $40 more missing on August 25, 1978. Mrs. S. asked her son about the missing money on August 25, 1978. He denied taking the money. Bill has been paying his mother $100 rent sinced he moved in with her in January, 1978. Bill had an agreement with her to pay $130 starting July 19, 1978. He became employed two months ago and has refused to pay the extra $30. His rent was again due on August 19, 1978 and he did not pay it. Mrs. S. wants him to pay the $130 rent on time each month or she wants him to move out. She is also convinced that her son took her money and wants him to admit to it.

Mediation: Information obtained during mediation: Bill S. denied taking his mother's money and stated that she must have misplaced the money, that she's misplaced money before. He also stated that he would not pay the increase in rent unless he would get something in exchange for the increase in rent. He seemed to have a lot of resentment from the past toward his mother. Bill offered his own solution to the rent problem. He would pay the rent increase, plus $5, if he could trade rooms with the French exchange student renting the front bedroom from Mrs. S.

Agreement: Mrs. S. agreed to give the front bedroom to her son, Bill. Bill agreed to move into the front bedroom by September 7 or before and pay $135 per month thereafter. He also agreed to prorate the back rent due from August 19, 1978, at the rate of $3 per day until he is moved into the new bedroom, changing the rent due date to that day. Mrs. S. agreed to call the Mediation Coordinator regarding referral for family counseling. Bill S. and Mrs. S. agreed to see a family counselor to work on their relationship.

Follow-up: Mrs. S. spoke to the Mediation Coordinator on October 2, 1978 and asked for a referral to a family counseling agency. The Mediation Coordinator referred her to Family Services of Santa Monica. Mrs. S. stated how pleased she was with the agreement that was reached between her son and herself and that she wanted to give the Neighborhood Justice Center a token of appreciation. She stated she has contacted a friend of hers who is a sculptor and he will donate his time and materials to sculpt a piece of work for NJC. Mrs. S. also did an interview for Public Service Radio describing the mediation process and her reaction to it.

Portland's Neighborhood Mediation Project

An example of an agency-connected program is the Neighborhood Mediation Project sponsored by the Metropolitan Human Relations Commission in Portland, Oregon. It was formerly funded by CETA, but now relies on the city's general funds, which has resulted in a reduction of the number of offices from three to one. There are two paid staff members and 15 volunteers.

When a complaint comes into the office, a staff person visits the complainant and talks to him/her. This step is called "conciliation," and often the problem is settled then.

If it is not, a mediation hearing is arranged. Three panelists act as mediators. Where the dispute is resolved (and most are), a staff member follows-up 30 days later. If no resolution is reached, or if the staff finds that mediation is inappropriate (it will not hear domestic cases), the disputants will be given information on public and private agencies, or perhaps even a court referral, which might be more appropriate.

The following are some observations made by Elaine Walsh, former coordinator for the Portland program. Her insight into disputes applies not only to the Portland program, but to any dispute resolution program. This piece is taken from the "Rap Sheet," a publication of the Portland Police Association. Permission was given by its editor, Jim Fleming, who interviewed Ms. Walsh.

The project is located at:

Corbett Building, Rm. 312
430 S.W. Morrison Street
Portland, OR 97204
(503) 248-4187

I found Ms. Walsh to have quite a remarkable insight into the ingredients that go to make up a neighborhood dispute. "In longstanding disputes," she told us, "there has probably never been a time when the opposing sides sat down and talked with one another. A key thing in our approach is a staff member going out and listening to both sides.

"In talking to the mediator, it will often be a contest for each side to see who can appear to be the most righteous. They get into seeing who can sound the most reasonable. It's a game in which each side tries to set up the other.

"When a third party enters, it is someone who is getting information from both sides. He becomes someone who has more information about the situation than either side had alone. This in itself changes things.

"There will be 15 things in dispute to start out with, but after some discussion it gets down to one or two.

"In mediating, we always talk about there being some things that are negotiable, some things they can agree upon. It's what can be agreed upon that's going to be the bottom line.

"We always let the person know what our limitations are. We let him know that we are legally obligated to reveal any illegal activities to the authorities."

Ms. Walsh said her office is aware of the severe limitations put upon the police in their efforts to settle neighborhood disputes. When the police car shows up at the scene it is evidence that one party is escalating the fight: "You called the cops on me!"

Calling the police also means that who is right and who is wrong is going to become more important than ever. There is also an expectation that the police are there to punish the offenders. "I pay my taxes, and you are supposed to protect me from people like this!"

Each party tries to draw the police into his side of the contest. The party who called the police believes he has the right to their power to reinforce his position.

It is important, Ms. Walsh feels, that the police know as much as possible about the mediation services. Information literature has been prepared to distribute to officers and mediation staff members try to go to roll calls and to neighborhood meetings where the police are also present.

How do the police feel about dispute resolution programs as a method of settling neighborhood conflicts? Here is another part of that article by Jim Fleming, editor of the "Rap Sheet."

Every police officer has a "least favorite" kind of call. For some it's the family beef, for others it's the drunk down and out.

My least favorite call was the neighborhood disturbance. I knew that whatever kind of nastiness was going on at that particular time was going to be the result of a longstanding feud. It was not going to be the simple "protagonist-victim" cast of characters waiting at the address the radio had give me.

It was going to be two warring clans, several generations of people on both sides. Often the combatting groups would augment their forces with the family dogs. Dogs always seemed to play a big part in neighborhood disturbances, sometimes as cause of the disputes and sometimes as just enthusiastic participants.

Every neighborhood disturbance has a long history, and one of the purposes in calling a police officer is to be able to detail this history to him. It's a story of long-suffered abuses afflicted by one side on the other. The officer is expected to sort out truth from fiction from all the stories told him, come to a quick decision as to which side is in the wrong and haul all the members of that family off to jail.

What the officer really does is look for the quickest exit. He knows there is nothing he can do to help them. No law has been violated that he can arrest anybody for. As soon as he can get the dog to let go of his leg, he hops back in his cruiser and splits, with a few parting words out the window about seeing the DA in the morning.

He has escaped this time, but he knows he will be back. He also knows that eventually, on one of his trips back, the combatants will have reached a point of physical violence as a way of settling their differences. A law has been violated. He can now "take action."

A Time to Question Direction

by Paul Wahrhaftig

Paul Wahrhaftig, Director of the Grassroots Citizen Dispute Resolution Center in Pittsburgh, has written several articles on the three basic kinds of dispute resolution programs. He argues that the community model is the most effective vehicle to help us move away from the traditional justice system, and toward a truly new approach to settling disputes.

This article was taken from the Fall/Winter 1979 issue of "Perspective," a journal of the Crime and Justice Foundation in Boston, Massachusetts, and reprinted with Paul's permission.

In this article I will focus on what appears to be one of the most fundamental but seldom articulated questions. If indeed there is a gap in our society's ability to problemsolve, who or what institution ought best fill that gap? That is a political question. It might be analyzed by asking whose ends are served by successfully operating a mediation center.

I suggest two propositions based upon our current knowledge of dispute processing. First, it is possible for almost any institution to run a successful dispute resolution program using informal techniques. The center will attract and satisfy its participants. There may be structural barriers that make it harder for one institution to do it than another, but the possibility still exists.

Second, as a rule, a group or an organization that successfully operates any program benefits from having done so. At a minimum that organization is seen as more legitimate for having performed a new service successfully. Patronage or employment power is increased. Further, the processes of the program will usually be defined in a way that promotes the parent organization's goals.

If my first proposition is right, that any institution can run a mediation program, then the more important direction to focus on is the political consequences of program sponsorship. To date, program sponsorship has roughly fallen in three categories: justice system sponsored, non-profit agency sponsored, and neighborhood or community based agency or association sponsored.

Justice system sponsored models exist today as adjuncts of police, prosecutors, and courts. Some, as the court sponsored Urban Court, have used a storefront model. Lay community mediators have handled a respectable number of cases. However, beyond settling of individual disputes, how has the community been changed? The answer is very little. People with problems look to the court as the legitimate resource. It may have new informal procedures and a comfortable setting, but it still is the court's property. True, where lay mediators are used community people may have been trained in new mediation skills which could be useful in their community. However, access to these new resources is mainly limited to court storefront intake process. Thus, the model retains the political status quo—the existing judicial system is legitimated as the primary source of aid in filling the gap in dispute processing.

Further, as an example of how ownership of a program can distort it to serve the ends of a host agency, Felstiner and Williams in their critique of a court-owned model described an interesting case. It involved an assault between a respondent and complainant. In the hearing it appeared that the witness rather than the complainant was deeply involved and perhaps was the key to the problem. Yet, the mediators made no attempt to incorporate the third party into the agreement. He was seen only as a "witness." The authors conclude that one reason for not involving the witness more fully is that as far as the court in its structure and record keeping functions is concerned, the papers have been filed by a specific complainant against a specific respondent. The involvement of a third person is structurally irrelevant and that orientation eventually seeps through the mediators.

Agency Model

A number of programs are run by large, privately funded (or often LEAA funded), non-profit agencies. The American Arbitration Association and the Institute for Mediation and Conflict Resolution are the two giants. Others, such as the Community Mediation Center in Suffolk County, New York, are local independent agencies. This model is championed because the independent agency has more openness, commitment, and flexibility than the government, which is seen as riddled with patronage, bureaucratic inertia, and a vested interest in maintaining the status quo. Hence, agencies are more comfortable experimenting, using volunteers, and fighting for their program's integrity.

The flexibility is encouraging. However, is this freedom from bureaucratic inertia an attribute of agencies in general? Or is it an attribute of agencies involved in doing exciting new things? One might look carefully at old-time, stable, United Way–funded agencies and particularly those that are doing well-established tasks. Are they significantly more open and experimental than government agencies? If not, then to the extent we assure funding stability and orderly development of private-agency mediation programs, do we not assure that they become bureaucratized and sluggish?

Further, from a political perspective, how have agency-run programs changed the way people perceive their options for problem solving? Instead of turning to government for help, the person on the street learns to look to the private agency sector. Some external bureaucracy is still seen as the influential resource to go to in time of trouble.

Community Based Models

The most conscious effort at this kind of organizing is the Community Boards Program in San Francisco. They see their role as not only helping individuals problem solve but also increasing their community's resources for handling broader social problems. Through community based, door-to-door organizing in two neighborhoods, a structure was built for the Boards so they are not seen as a product of an outside agency but a community institution. It is neighbors who are running it, solving problems, and demonstrating that they are an effective resource. Mediator-panelists and community people

learn from problem solving in open sessions. Their observations can be discussed and generalized, thereby becoming the base for community-wide attempts to solve more generic community problems. For example, in a case I observed concerning problems arising after a home was burned down and vacated, it appeared that many fires had taken place in that tract. Panelists learned that wiring was substandard in all the tract houses. They then could make the connection that fires were not just individual accidents but a generic problem of the neighborhood. Homeowners associations were questioned, some were present at the hearing, and the suggestion was made that there is a role for community organizations to play in this situation. At least they could notify all homeowners of the hidden defects and possibly could organize further action.

Thus Community Boards has a political perspective of bringing people together with their neighbors to solve immediate problems and to move on towards more general or long range ones. However, the program to date is dependent upon generous foundation support. The present model requires extensive staffing. What will happen when the foundation money runs out? Can one rely on neighbors when they are not backed by a foundation? Are we really empowering neighbors or foundations? Can the government take over to subsidize the program as might be possible under bills currently before the U. S. Congress and State Legislatures of New York and California? Or will government funding with all of its reporting and accounting requirements lead to the same kind of agency bureaucratic inertia that turns community people off?

It may be that by the time funding has run out not only will neighborhood people be trained in mediation techniques but a community-owned network for reaching them will be in place. That infra-structure, if solidly built, could conceivably survive the funding loss and continue as an indigenous part of community life.

A variant on the Community Boards model that tries to avoid the "ultimate funding dilemma" is the Community Association for Mediation (CAM) in Pittsburgh, Pa. A local black woman identified people in her community who are already seen as problem solvers; thus she involved some block club leaders, agency para-professionals, some mothers, and the like. They met at her house and discussed new conflict resolution skills. They defined a useful training program and carried it out themselves with donated services from professionals where needed. They have no center, no records, no fancy intake processing since people seek out the mediators in their existing roles as elders or trouble shooters, and no outside funding. The members return to their original positions as problem solvers but with two important changes. First, their skills are enhanced. Second, they are now part of a network of like-minded community problem solvers who meet together informally to share their successes and problems. As in Community Boards, these neighbors are increasing their prestige and position as problem solvers. Through their get-togethers they are able to share information and generalize from their problems. Their network includes ties to most social action groups and agencies in the neighborhood. Thus, generalized problems can be presented to the appropriate community organization for action.

CAM seems to be telling us that the pioneers have shown the need for the utility of new dispute processing procedures, but they have not demonstrated that a formal, funded project is *the* answer. Possibly the most productive direction to move is towards building mediation into existing community networks and strengthening those networks. If CAM can continue in this informally structured format, change will be taking place. Indigenous leadership structures will have been enhanced through the process of settling disputes.

Conclusion

In this article I have tried to raise questions about the direction in which the dispute resolution movement is going. Project organizers should avoid the easy route of carbon copying existing "successful" programs. Rather, they should critically re-examine every stage of the dispute solving process. Careful attention should be paid to the political significance of the potential program structure. What segment of our society needs strengthening through the operation of a mediation program? It is not too early to try to project ten years into the future to try to predict in what way, if at all, the society served will be different as a result of a dispute resolving program having been organized today.

Community Board Program

* *

One of the chief criticisms leveled against agency and justice programs is that by their dependence upon a court or agency for their identity, structure, and organization, they do not provide a true community alternative to the resolution of conflicts. Their interest in diverting cases from the overburdened courts if often more important than full community input and control.

A program which has moved to reinterpret the traditional system of resolving conflicts into the needs of the community is the Community Board Program in San Francisco. It has set up shop in two adjoining neighborhoods in the city — Bernal Heights and Visitacion Valley — and hears disputes from only those areas. The program is funded by local and national foundations, and is often considered a model for others to follow.

There are many aspects of the CBP which make it unique — one of which its director, Raymond Shonholtz, repeatedly emphasizes is preventive justice.

> One crime in America is that no one does anything until someone is hurt or killed. Law enforcement responds only to hostile acts. There is no place to take frustrations or conflicts before violence occurs. A justice system for the problems and conflicts of everyday life is nonexistent.
>
> Many people say that prevention has little value because it cannot be measured. What can be measured are the costs of not having prevention.

To carry out this design, the Communty Board Program doesn't wait until people come to it. It employs four full-time caseworkers to seek out "problems of ordinary life." They may learn of a problem from community organizations, churches, schools, block clubs, social service agencies, police, neighbors, and the participants themselves. The caseworkers then contact the disputants and see whether the conflict may be worked out on its own. If not, the parties are urged to come to a hearing.

At the hearing, the immediate disputants aren't necessarily the only participants. Other people who may be affected by the outcome, or who had an effect on the situation, would also be invited to attend. In one example, a teenage girl assaulted another at school. Both girls belonged to gangs. So 12 of the girls came to the hearing in the hope of resolving the year-long feud.

Another emphasis of the Community Board Program is revitalizing the neighborhood. Shonholtz (who prefers to use the broader term of "conflict resolution," rather than mediation or dispute resolution) envisions the building of a broad base of education, leadership, identity, communication, and information network in the neighborhood. He feels that the future lies there.

The CBP sees conflict resolution as a distinct alternative to the traditional justice system. While the former stresses participation and conciliation, the latter stresses antagonism. The traditional system will perpetuate the hostility which may possibly lead to further hostilities. Conflict resolution deals with this hostility in its belief that the venting of frustrations is more important than reaching a particular resolution.

In fact, conflict resolution is not only an alternative to the traditional justice system, but also the everyday method of handling disputes — that of calling the police or threatening to sue, or perhaps taking physical action.

Another word they emphasize is "accessibility." Conflict resolution can provide an increased access to justice by lowering costs, increasing time of the hearing, shortening the distance to travel to the hearing, and providing approachability of the mediators. With this background, we'll quickly review the other highlights of the program.

If the caseworkers cannot obtain a resolution when they first interview the disputants, they prepare a list of "concerns," rather than facts. Before the hearing, they meet with the panel to prepare them on the situation. There are usually five, but at least three, panelists at a hearing. They are paid $10 each month, and usually stay on for a year. A panelist will probably serve at one or two hearings a month. Panelists for specific hearings are selected on the basis of race, sex, age and any other factor that may help the disputants feel at ease.

There is no caucusing by the panel during the hearing; nor is there any shuttle diplomacy. The parties are kept together throughout the session, and after the initial phase, where they explain their sides, they are encouraged to talk with one another rather than with the panel.

If an agreement is reached, it is signed by the disputants. The caseworkers follow-up about one week later, with a second follow-up one month later.

Community Board Program offices are located at:

Central Office:	149 Ninth Street
	San Francisco, CA 94103
	(415) 552-1250
Bernal Heights Office	907 Cortland Ave.
	San Francisco, CA 94110
	(415) 285-4688
Visitacion Valley Office	161 Leland Ave.
	San Francisco, CA 94134
	(415) 239-6100

★ How the Community Board Program Works ★

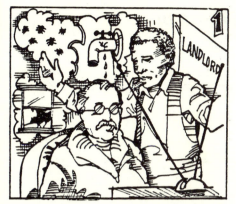

There is a conflict in the neighborhood. Someone contacts the Community Board Program.

Staff interviews everyone involved.

If everyone agrees to attend, staff sets up hearing.

Panel hearing takes place.

In most cases, people reach an agreement.

Staff and panelist follow up to see how the agreement is working.

Community Board Program
Case Resolution Diagram

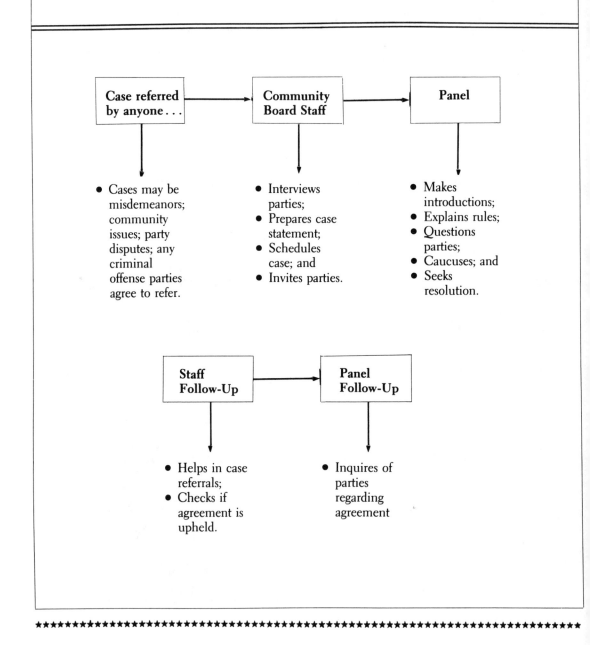

Case referred by anyone...

- Cases may be misdemeanors; community issues; party disputes; any criminal offense parties agree to refer.

Community Board Staff

- Interviews parties;
- Prepares case statement;
- Schedules case; and
- Invites parties.

Panel

- Makes introductions;
- Explains rules;
- Questions parties;
- Caucuses; and
- Seeks resolution.

Staff Follow-Up

- Helps in case referrals;
- Checks if agreement is upheld.

Panel Follow-Up

- Inquires of parties regarding agreement

★★★

Three first-offense minors, ages 9, 10, and 12, had twice broken into an elementary school. The second time, a window had been broken and a pumpkin and some pencils and crayons were stolen from one of the classrooms. Witnesses to the break-in reported it to the school's principal. She then phoned the police. The city's juvenile probation intake unit, reluctant to see such young children with a criminal record, referred the case to the Visitacion Valley Community Board.

The principal, the boys, and their parents, attended a community board meeting. During the two-hour session, the board heard all sides of the issue and met privately with the boys.

Panelists helped the youngsters decide what responsibilities they should take for their actions. The boys volunteered to apologize to the principal, the teacher and the students of the class where they'd stolen the items. The panel, parents, and principal accepted this as a workable solution. The principal thought the boys should also pay for repairing the broken window ($24) by working with the janitor, half an hour each day for 32 days, at 50¢ per half-hour. A work schedule, agreed to by the youngsters and their parents, was outlined.

The day after the meeting, one of the boys' parents phoned the Community Board's office to say that her son could not work the schedule as planned. She wanted to rearrange his work time. If this had been a court case, the valid reason given may well have been used as a "legitimate" excuse for not doing the work.

The principal, impressed with the Community Board's concern, said that she planned to handle similar school incidents by phoning Community Boards before contacting police.

Panel Training

★ ══ ★

The panelists in the Community Board Program are trained by former panelists. Many of them were at one time disputants at a hearing—which is how they got involved in the program. The staff also actively solicits members of the community to take the training and become panelists. Ray Shonholtz feels strongly that leadership qualities are often formed here.

The training sessions are held for three weeks, with meetings one weekday night and all day Saturday, totaling approximately 30 hours. There is very little lecturing; most of the training is in role-playing. About 40 people were trained in the Spring of 1980.

The Community Board Program

Hearing Summary

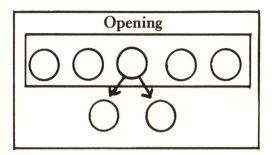

What: The panel welcomes people formally and explains the nature of the hearing and the ground rules.
How:
1) Panel welcomes everyone.
2) Everyone introduces self.
3) Chairperson makes opening remarks.
4) Panelist reads staff report.

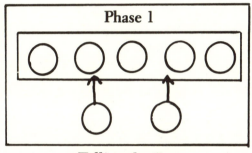

Telling the Story

What: The panel helps the people define the problem and express how they feel about it.
How:
1) Ask complainer to define briefly the problem as he/she sees it, express feelings about it.
2) Ask complainee to define briefly the problem as he/she sees it, express feelings about it.
3) Ask questions that clarify and focus the issues and allow people to get in touch with their feelings. Use active listening skills.
4) Summarize the main concerns of each person.

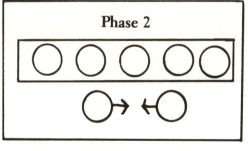

Understanding Each Other

What: The panel helps each person understand how the other experiences the problem.
How:
1) Make a transition statement.
2) Select one issue (concern) and encourage the people to talk about it and help them stay focused.
3) Facilitate the conversation between the people.

Hearing Summary (cont'd)

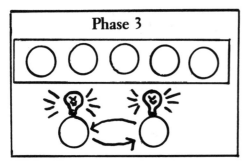

Sharing Responsibility

What: The panel helps the people share responsibility for the problem.
How:
1) Make a transition statement.
2) Facilitate the conversation between the people.

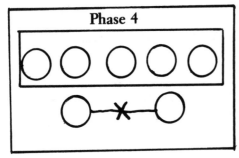

Agreeing

What: The panel helps the people reach an agreeable solution to the problem.
How:
1) Make a transition statement.
2) Ask each person in turn what he/she thinks a fair solution to each issue would be.
3) Ask questions and use other active listening techniques to help the people work out an agreement.
4) Summarize all points of the agreement.
5) Write up the agreement.

Closing

What: The panel finalizes the agreement between the people and the community. The panel and staff review the hearing.
How:
1) Read the written agreement to the people for confirmation.
2) If appropriate, identify possible "outs."
3) People and chairperson sign the agreement.
4) Make closing remarks and congratulate the parties.
5) Review the hearing.

Resolution Agreement

On _____ , the people whose signatures appear below met with the Panel of the Community Board Program. With the assistance of the Panel, they reached the following agreement:

Person 1, _____ , agrees to:

_____

_____

_____

_____

_____

_____

_____

Person 2, _____ , agrees to:

_____

_____

_____

_____

_____

_____

We make the above Agreement, appreciating that it is fair, represents a satisfactory resolution of the issues between us, and supports the Community's values.

Person 1: _____   Person 2: _____

Chairperson: _____   Date: _____

The Community Board Program

Bernal Heights Office
907 Cortland Avenue
San Francisco, CA 94110
(415) 285-4688

Central Office
149 Ninth Street
San Francisco, CA 94103
(415) 552-1251

Visitacion Valley Office
161 Leland Avenue
San Francisco, CA 94134
(415) 239-6100

An Interview with Ray Shonholtz of the
San Francisco Community Board

Many people consider all dispute resolution programs as fundamentally the same, whether they are run by courts, agencies, or neighborhoods. In the following interview, Ray Shonholtz, head of the San Francisco Community Board Program, erodes that impression. He notes that there are marked differences, differences which cannot be glossed over as merely being variations on the same theme. Ray sees very little, if any, future in court or agency models. He feels that only neighborhood run programs can really provide a true alternative to the present-day justice system.

Question: How would you describe the conflict resolution programs?

RS: There are basically two different models—the "agency mediation" model, and what I refer to as the "neighborhood conciliation" model. In the agency model, the program is striving to reduce the caseload of a particular agency or agencies. Normally, it's the prosecutor's office, sometimes the police department, sometimes the court system. The programs that most come to mind on that side are the In titute for Mediation and Conflict Resolution in New York, and the Boston Urban Court [Dorchester] Program. The Institute relates to the prosecutor's office, although it originally started in relation to the Police Department. The Boston Urban Court Program relates primarily to court referrals or court caseloads. Then you have the experiments that the Department of Justice has done in the last 18 to 24 months [the LEAA-funded programs]. The federal effort in Kansas City relates to the Police Department. The one in Atlanta relates to the prosecutor's and court's offices. The one in Los Angeles tried very hard to be similar to us, but they had an orientation mostly posed by the Justice Department, as well as a very limited amount of resources, and there was a serious question of whether they could really do it with the approach they were taking. But they have tried very hard to be a neighborhood-oriented program.

The agency model does not look to a fundamental critique of the justice system. It merely says that the justice system is too busy, has too many cases, and somebody else ought to handle some of those that are easier to deal with and which don't seem to require formal proceedings. But what you really find is that these programs rarely, in fact, reduce agency caseloads. They are experiencing, as best I can see, the same history that we are familiar with in diversion programs, which are mostly run by the probation departments. Ten years ago, diversion was going to save the justice system. What you were really going to do is take cases out of the various agencies and courts and divert them to community restitution programs and various social agencies. Well, if you look at that closely, what you find is that 1) the agency's caseload is not reduced, 2) the agency staff is not reduced, and 3) the quality of the work that's actually being done in relation to the mandate or charge of the agency raises, I think, some serious questions.

Question: Why aren't the caseloads reduced?

RS: Because of the manner in which the referral process works in the mediation programs that are using the agency model. It's similar to the diversion project—somebody has to review them. You're really talking about "after-the-fact" cases. By that I mean that after the hearing you still have the police interview, the police investigation, the police complaint and report. You still have the probation department on the juvenile side or the prosecutor on the adult side, reviewing those reports. Now, somebody along the way may say, and usually it's the probation department or the prosecutor, that a case ought to be diverted to the mediation program. It is still screened, baked, cooked and processed before it gets there, so that the likelihood of actually reducing a caseload—rather, actually reducing the paid staff of the agency—has not happened. I don't know if anybody's documented that at all.

There is also a political-budget consideration. No agency is seriously going to give a mediation program so many cases that it would jeopardize its own budget standing. They talk about these programs in terms of them being an aid, but if you look at the number of cases being moved from the agency or the court to the component program, you find that they represent a very, very small percentage of the cases.

It also doesn't work very well. This is the other area in which there needs to be a lot more research. The best that has been done so far is some of the work by Bill Felstiner. Bill observed a couple of cases that were handled by IMCR-trained mediators for the Boston Urban Court Program. What you find in that agency model situation is that often the parties before the mediator, or in the Boston case, two mediators, are not all of the parties to the dispute. And that captures, I think, one of the fundamental problems with the limitation of the agency critique. The agency model puts blinders on a case, just like the legal system does, and assumes that because the legal system has captured one person and labeled that person a defendant or complainant, it has the whole subject matter before it in the body of that person or persons. And that is commonly not the case. There are many other people who have direct concerns and can influence a particular problem positively or negatively, who are not before the court's jurisdiction or the prosecutor's power. There's no outreach done on any of these cases. That's a serious limitation to the quality of the work that needs to be done. The opportunity for the conflict to be genuinely resolved, or equally important, for the level of hostilities during the dispute-handling to be lowered, is not realistically going to happen.

Now, in the neighborhood programs, what you're really trying to do is reach the problem before it's referred to the agency. You want to let the neighborhood perform as broad a range of activities of prevention and reduction of hostilities during the dispute-handling as possible. If you build conflict resolution in the neighborhood, what you're really doing is training peacemakers in the neighborhood. You are essentially transferring the functions that were once performed by ministers, grocery store owners, school counselors, the "beat cop"—people whom everyone knew about.

Institution-building is what we're really trying to do at the neighborhood level by bringing people with skills together to work on common problems. Which means the kind of problems they can best work on are problems that are at the lowest level, at the threshhold level, not when somebody's shot another person, or they're so angry that's what they want to do. That's really what we're all about. We're talking about leadership training and skill-development in the neighborhood, particularly in the low-income neighborhoods that often have a dearth of leadership people. We're talking about bringing in skilled trainers in the areas of conciliation, peace-making, running meetings and leadership. So, in a really short period of time, we have in each of these neighborhoods a sizable group of people who have never before been asked to do anything and are now asked to do a lot. And, in addition, we are training them. We're probably one of the very few programs in the United States that's actually sharing skills and training people to handle problems in neighborhoods.

Question: How does neighborhood conciliation differ from agency mediation in its handling of a dispute?

RS: In the mediation model, there is enormous pressure on the mediator to work at a resolution because that's what success is for a mediator. Success is getting the person to say "I'll take X even though I didn't get Y." There's the tradeoff. It's like horse-trading, and that's what he or she is trained to do. Success is getting a compromise that will work.

Well, I think that there are real problems with that whole process. The issue for neighborhoods is not conflict resolution. That is secondary. The primary issue for neighborhoods is honoring conflict; that is to say, that it's okay if people have conflicts. It's not necessary for the parties to kiss each other and walk away feeling that they're the nicest people in the wehole world and that they've just had this terrible misunderstanding. We've had hearings where the parties say, "The hell with you! I don't agree with you, and I don't like you." The best way to reduce hostilities during the dispute-handling process is to make certain you've honored people who have a conflict. The fastest way to generate tension and serious injury and property damage is to ignore the conflict or to assume that you can just paste it over. That's why it's better to say to the Gay community and the Hispanic community, "You have basic cultural differences here. You all live in the same 18 square blocks. Now, you can do two or three things. You can lock your doors and go out in groups. You can carry clubs. You can mark out the turf and ghettoize yourself. These eight blocks are Gay and no Hispanic is going to come in, and these eight blocks are Hispanic and no Gay is going to come in or we'll club him." You can do those things or you can say, "Listen, maybe we need some different rules here. We do have a disagreement; we're not going to agree."

One of the things we say to panelists at the end of panel training is that their success is not the resolution of the case. If they get resolution of a conflict, that is great, wonderful. But their primary work is getting the parties to talk to each other. The primary statement to make to a trainer is to let these people make certain that when they leave the room, regardless if they leave in accord or disagreement, they've heard one another. If you do that, you have now reduced the level of hostility during this dispute to the point that these people, even if they don't like one another, won't shoot one another. And that is why I say the neighborhood model means a conciliation approach. It doesn't need the formality of mediation.

Then finally, I think the neighborhood program offers neighborhoods something that agencies have been fighting, both consciously and unconsciously, for a long time—providing information. The only way neighborhoods can begin to take care of themselves is if they have more information about what the hell's happening in their neighborhood. Conflict resolution is an outstanding way of getting information—and a lot of it—fairly quickly.

Question: What future is there for these programs?

RS: Agencies have been able to squander public resources and grow because there's been a liberal tax dollar and a complacent citizenry which essentially wants to be taken care of. There's no longer a liberal tax dollar and there's an annoyed citizenry. People are going to have to decide whether they are going to assert their own individual and neighborhood responsibility and take care of things that are appropriately theirs and not pass the buck and be dependent on agencies, or whether they're just going to set up bars in front of their windows and doors and turn up radios and TVs and just shut up.

Most people, in fact, know what's happening. They might not be able to put it into professional gobbledy-gook, but they understand the issues of credibility and trust which are the fundamental issues for public institutions. The only other avenue to deal with the social problems, really, is to go back to the neighborhood.

Let's take an example. A judge costs the county $50,000 in salary, plus a courtroom, clerks, and all the attendants, etc. Well, if you took the judge's salary at $50,000 and gave it to a neighborhood program, the result would be astounding. What a judge can do for $50,000 and what a neighborhood can do for that same amount of money! You can train one or two hundred people for 25 to 30 thousand dollars to have their own neighborhood forum, to have their own system that the volunteers run in exchange for getting good quality training. You train people to be peacemakers in their own neighborhood. They understand the problems in their own neighborhoods. They can better understand what the issues are on a very basic level for them, and what kind of social resources they need. And that information does not get locked up in the agency, but becomes a reality in the neighborhood. So, for 50 or 60 thousand dollars, you can do an enormous amount. We need to translate the economy back into the neighborhood. We need to say to the agency that they can do some of the work, but not nearly as much as they think they should do. Because they are professionals they can do some things well. But there are some things they cannot do as well—because people won't bring their problems to the agency.

Only neighborhoods can provide the resources and volunteers. The correct public policy over time, the future direction for the '80s for neighborhoods, needs to be the translation of tax dollars in this manner—that the government provides sufficient funds for training and coordination of volunteers.

This directory first appeared in the Fall 1979 and Winter 1980 issues of the "Mooter," a Quarterly Journal of the Grassroots Citizen Dispute Resolution Clearinghouse. The "Mooter" is an excellent source for anyone interested in keeping up with the latest developments. Each issue examines one area of conflict resolution; the Fall 1979 issue explored the use of two kinds of resource people — lawyers and volunteers; the Winter 1980 issue compared conflict resolution efforts in the community to those in industry, prisons, and on the international scene. Book reviews and resource materials are also included.

The "Mooter" is published by the American Friends Service Committee, 4401 Fifth Avenue, Pittsburgh, PA 15213. An annual subscription is $5. Also of interest, although somewhat more oriented to lawyers, is "Dispute Resolution," published by the A.B.A. Special Committee on Resolution of Minor Disputes, 1800 M Street, N.W., Washington, D.C. 20036.

Note: *Though mediation programs exist in nearly every major city, the programs do not necessarily cover the entire metropolitan area. Some programs are localized to particular communities or neighborhoods.*

A Directory of Dispute Resolution Programs and Resources

We have compiled here a listing of programs with which the Clearinghouse has been in contact. Most of the listings are based on responses to a recent survey circulated by *The Mooter*. The list is far from complete, but we have tried to put in all the community-based efforts we know about plus some which may not be well-known. Generally programs based in and controlled by prosecutors' offices and courts are omitted.

If your program is left out, please send us the information and we will put it in an update in the next issue.

Projects are listed by region. Within the region they are listed alphabetically by state and city.

EASTERN REGION

Community Dispute Settlement Program of Delaware
2010 Woodbrook Drive
Wilmington, Delaware 19810
302-654-6711
Contact: Ann Heaton
Sponsor: Quakers
Description: Mediate family, neighborhood and youth disputes using volunteer mediators.
Operating Status: Planning
Trained By: Friends Suburban Project

Community Mediation Center
1470 Irving St., N.W.
Washington, D.C. 20010
202-483-7010
Contact: Barbara May
Sponsor: Metropolitan Ministry With Women
Funding Source: Presbyterian Church
Description: Community-based to provide forum for dispute resolution.
Operating Status: Planning
Training Capacity: No

Citizens' Complaint Center
Superior Court Building B
5th & F Street, N.W.
Washington, D.C. 20001
202-724-7579
Contact: Noel Brennan
Sponsor: Center for Community Justice
Description: Community volunteers mediate disputes involving family members, landlord/tenant, neighbors, employer/employee, etc.
Operating Status: Operational
Trained By: CCJ, IMCR
Training Capacity: Yes

Urban Court Program
506 A Washington Street
Dorchester, Mass. 02124
617-825-2700

Contact: Kathy Grant or Della Rice
Sponsor: Dorchester Municipal Court
Funding Source: LEAA
Description: Trained community residents mediate cases referred by court, police and community. Community Advisory Board but administratively responsible to court. Also victim services and disposition panels (trained community residents make alternative sentencing recommendations).
Operating Status: Fully operational
Trained By: IMCR
Training Capacity: Yes

Cambridge Dispute Settlement Center
99 Bishop Allen Drive
Cambridge, Mass. 02139
617-876-5257
Contact: Keven Virgilio or Clorae Prince
Sponsor: Community Crime Preventip Prog.
Description: Trained community residents mediate consumer-merchant, tenant-landlord, juvenile and family disputes referred by the community. Beginning target population is Cambridge-Riverside neighborhood of Cambridge.
Funding Source: LEAA
Operating Status: Planning
Training Capacity: No

Center for Collaborative Planning and Community Service
12 Cottage Street
Watertown, Mass. 02172
617-924-0914
Contact: Bill Lincoln
Sponsor: Independent— formerly American Arbitration Association
Funding Source: Seeking local support
Description: Develop new models for dispute resolution, train community people in advocate negotiation, collaborating with other groups.
Training Capacity: Yes

Mediation Program
88 N. Main Street
Concord, N.H. 03301
603-271-2605
Contact: Felicity Lavelle
Sponsor: Concord District Court and State Supreme Court, Judicial Planning
Funding Source: LEAA
Description: Alternative to court for family and neighborhood disputes, referrals from court, police, local agencies and walk-ins. Mediation contracts enforceable by court. Mediators are all volunteers.
Operating Status: Fully operational
Trained By: Mediators, trainers and consultants —

Dorchester, MA
Training Capacity: Yes

Albany Dispute Mediation Program
727 Madison Avenue
Albany, N.Y. 12208
518-436-4958
Contact: Lou Fiscarelli
Sponsor: Albany Friends Meeting and Anchor Association, Inc.
Funding Source: CETA, New York Yearly Meeting and Black Development Fund
Description: Community dispute settlement program designed to provide trained, neutral, third-party mediators to aid in the resolution of interpersonal conflicts. Free, confidential, etc.
Operating Status: Fully operational
Trained By: Friends Suburban Project and Schenectady Community Dispute Settlement
Training Capacity: Yes

Community Mediaton Center
356 Middle Country Road
Coram, N.Y. 11727
516-736-2626
Contact: Robert Saperstein
Sponsor: Originally YMCA — Now independent corp.
Funding Source: LEAA, foundations, United Way, industry
Description: Mediation of disputes in suburban Suffolk County. Centralized intake with decentralized hearing sites. Governed by Board including justice personnel and citizens, some of which are blue ribbon. Lay mediators. Intake primarily from criminal justice system.
Operating Status: Fully operational
Trained By: IMCR
Training Capacity: Yes

IMCR Dispute Center, Brooklyn
50 Court Street, Room 904
Brooklyn, N.Y. 11201
212-577-7700
Contact: Don Alf
Funding Source: LEAA
Sponsor: Institute for Mediation and Conflict Resolution
Description: Citizens mediate/arbitrate disputes referred from courts. Vera Institute of Justice staff located in courts help screen cases where "prior relationship" indicated. Centralized hearings for Brooklyn.
Operating Status: Fully operational
Trained By: IMCR

IMCR Dispute Center, Manhattan
425 West 144th Street
New York, N.Y. 10031
212-690-5700

Contact: William Madison
Sponsor: IMCR
Funding Source: New York City, Criminal Justice Coordinating Council
Description: Community panels mediate/arbitrate disputes referred from various levels of criminal justice system.
Operating Status: Fully operational
Trained By: IMCR
Training Capacity: Yes

Nassau County Citizen Dispute Center
585 Steward Ave., Suite 302
Garden City, N.Y. 11530
516-222-1660
Contact: Rick Klenbanoff
Sponsor: American Arbitration Assoc.
Funding Source: LEAA
Description: Hearing in office, lay mediators reflecting broad community. Referrals from crim. justice system. Emphasis on police referrals. Use med./arb.
Trained By: AAA
Training Capacity: Yes

Neighborhood Justice Project
300 Lake Street, Second floor
Lake Street Presbyterian Church
Elmira, N.Y. 14901
607-734-3338
Contact: Bill Darling
Sponsor: Offender Aid and Restoration (OAR)
Funding Source: LEAA
Description: CDR and Victim Assistance Components. CDR one to use volunteers. Currently cases come mainly from neighborhood associations and social service. Seek to increase criminal justice referrals.
Operating Status: Currently staff is mediating. Volunteers to be trained in January and will take over that function.
Trained By: Team Associates, Ohio, U.S. Dept. of Justice, Community Relations Service, Phila. Regional Office

Center for Dispute Settlement
36 W. Main St., Suite 495
Rochester, N.Y. 14614
716-546-5110
Contact: Andrew Thomas
Sponsor: Independent (formerly AAA)
Funding Source: LEAA, CETA, Court, foundations and fees
Description: Provide mediation/arbitration and other dispute resolution services in Western New York area.
Trained By: AAA
Training Capacity: Yes

Community Dispute Settlement
35 State Street
Troy, N.Y. 12180
518-274-5920
Contact: Don Pangburn
Sponsor: United Urban Ministry
Funding Source: Foundations and Church sources
Description: Lay mediators recruited from community. Referrals from courts, probation and other community agencies.
Operating Status: Fully operational
Trained By: Anita Baker, Schenectady CDS

Community Dispute Settlement Service
Box 462
Concordville, PA 19331
215-459-4770
Contact: Eileen Stief, Johanna Mattheus
Funding Source: Philadelphia Yearly Meeting (Quakers) and $5.00 fees from clients
Description: Suburban-rural setting. Central telephone intake with mediation taking place as near the parties' community as possible. Lay mediators. Referrals from District Justice, police, lawyers, agencies, citizens. Youth and family cases heard frequently.
Trained By: AAA, supplemented by many workshops
Training Capacity: Available to consult on organizing and training

Neighborhood Dispute Settlement of Greater Harrisburg
315 Peffer Street
Harrisburg, PA 17102
717-233-3072
Contact: Joe Davis—717-783-8088
Sponsor: Hgb. Human Relations Commission
Funding Source: Human Relations Com. of Hgb., and Human Relations Council of Hgb.
Description: Citizen mediators to do interpersonal disputes
Operating Status: Planning
Trained By: Community Dispute Services, Concordville, PA (Friends Suburban Project)
Training Capacity: No

Community Association for Mediation
511 Junilla Street
Pittsburgh, PA 15219
412-682-6813 (evenings)
Contact: Gloria Patterson
Sponsor: Independent
Funding Source: Totally volunteer
Description: Grass-roots based. Builds mediation capability into existing community organizational network. Trains and follows up with staff of existing organizations.

Trained By: Local community trainers using existing local back-up resources

Community for Neighborhood Justice
207 Butler Avenue
Providence, R.I. 02906
407-274-6384
Sponsor: Independent
Funding Source: Searching
Description: Citizen group organizing center ideas and options. Public education.
Operating Status: Planning
Training Capacity: Yes

SOUTHERN REGION

Community Dispute Settlement Program
14 E. Washington St., Suite 402
Orlando, Fla. 32801
305-420-3700
Contact: Thomas Barron
Sponsor: Orlando County Bar Association
Funding Source: Bar Assoc. and court
Description: Mediation of interpersonal disputes by volunteer attorneys. Referrals primarily from criminal justice system with some walk-ins.
Operating Status: Fully operational

Florida Assoc. for Dispute Resolution
c/o Citizen Dispute Settlement Program
13th Judicial Circuit of Fla.
Hillsborough County Court House
Tampa, Fla. 33062
813-272-5642
Contact: Richard D. Muga
Description: The eleven C.D. Settlement programs in Florida have banded together in an association. Since all but the Orlando one, listed here, are court-sponsored and use professional mediators, they are not individually listed in this directory. They can be contacted, however, through the Association.

Neighborhood Justice Program
316 Princess Street
New Hanover County Court House
Wilmington, N.C. 28401
919-343-8281
Contact: Jerry Powell
Sponsor: Offender Aid & Restoration (OAR)

Funding Source: LEAA — space donated by county
Description: Mediate disputes, primarily from criminal justice system. Staff mediators to be replaced by volunteers to be trained in January. Hearings held in office conference room or in neighborhood where appropriate.
Trained By: Team Associates and Community Relations Service of U.S. Justice Department

Neighborhood Justice Center of Atlanta, Inc.
1118 Euclid Ave., N.E.
Atlanta, GA 30307
404-523-8236
Contact: Linwood R. Slaton, Jr.
Sponsor: Independent corp., dominated by court and lawyers
Funding Source: LEAA
Description: Neighborhood office but city-wide jurisdiction. Lay mediators handle cases referred primarily by courts.
Operating Status: Fully operational
Trained By: AAA and local sources
Training Capacity: Available to train and consult in developing a program

Administrative Office of the Courts — Pretrial Service Agency
403 Wapping Street
Frankfort, KY 40601
502-564-7486
Contact: John Hendricks and Stephen Wheeler
Funding Source: LEAA
Description: Mediation program in Louisville and Lexington, Kentucky. Mediation and Diversion Program in our Northern Kentucky urban area.
Operating Status: Fully operational
Trained By: Technical Assistance from Pretrial Services Resource Center, Washington, D.C.
Training Capacity: Yes

Dispute Settlement Center, Inc.
105 N. Columbia St., P.O. Box 464
Chapel Hill, N.C. 27514
919-929-8800
Contact: Scott Bradley
Funding Source: N.C. grant and United Fund
Description: Mediation, usually using two mediators. Cases are referred from District Court, Social Services, local police or by phoning directly for help.
Operating Status: Fully operational
Trained By: Community Relations Service, U.S. Dept. of Justice
Training Capacity: No

CENTRAL REGION

Dispute Services
Oklahoma State University
Stillwater, OK 74074
405-624-6025
Contact: Bob Helm
Sponsor: Oklahoma State University
Funding Source: Project of Dept. of Psychology at
Oklahoma State Univ.
Description: Mediation/arbitration offered to faculty/
students/staff of Oklahoma State Univ. Services furnished
by faculty and graduate students in the Dept. of Psychol-
ogy. Project also does social psychological research into
the interpersonal dispute resolution processes.
Operating Status: Fully operational
Trained By: Kansas City Neighborhood Justice Center
Training Capacity: Yes

Neighborhood Justice of Chicago
7657 N. Broadway
Chicago, Ill. 60640
312-782-7348
Contact: John Payton or Joe Gatlin
Sponsor: Chicago Bar Association
Funding Source: Foundations
Description: Setting up justice center in Uptown-Edge-
water. Twelve mediators to be trained in initial training —
working with two-tier mediation — arbitration model.
Operating Status: Planning
Trained By: AAA
Training Capacity: No

American Arbitration Association
City National Bank Bldg., Suite 1234
Detroit, Mich. 48226
313-964-2525
Contact: Mary A. Bedidian
Funding Source: Private individuals, fees, law firms,
union organizations, libraries, employer organizations,
corporations, local government
Description: Conciliation/mediation/arbitration of com-
munity and family disputes.
Operating Status: Fully operational
Trained By: AAA
Training Capacity: Yes

Kalamazoo Citizen Dispute Resolution Center
1331 Race Street
Kalamazoo, MI 49001
616-382-0916

Contact: Ruth Copps
Sponsor: Independent corp.
Funding Source: Private donations, foundations, Friends
Meeting, VISTA coordinator
Description: Community-based program located in a
Neighborhood Center using mediation/arbitration to settle
neighborhood disputes.
Operating Status: Fully operational
Trained By: AAA
Training Capacity: Yes

Kansas City Neighborhood Justice Center
American Bank Bldg., Suite 305
One West Armor
Kansas City, MO 64111
816-274-1895
Contact: Maurice Macey
Sponsor: Community Services Dept. of Kansas City
Funding Source: LEAA
Description: Referrals from prosecutor, police and com-
munity are brought before citizen mediators for resolu-
tion. Centralized location for city-wide jurisdiction.
Operating Status: Fully operational
Trained By: IMCR—AAA
Training Capacity: yes

Community Dispute Settlement Program
215 Euclid Avenue, Room 930
Cleveland, Ohio 44104
216-241-4741
Contact: Earl C. Brown
Funding Source: Local government
Description: Mediation/arbitration of cases referred from
criminal justice system and community. Lay mediators.
Operating Status: Fully operational
Trained By: AAA
Training Capacity: Yes

Community Dispute Settlement Program
177 S. Broadway St., Room 438
Akron, Ohio 44308
216-762-8636
Contact: Earl C. Brown
Sponsor: American Arbitration Assoc.
Funding Source: Local government
Description: Mediation/arbitration of cases primarily
referred by criminal justice system as well as community.
Lay mediators. Also a juvenile component.
Operating Status: Fully operational
Trained By: AAA
Training Capacity: Yes

WESTERN REGION

Community Boards Program
149 Ninth Street
San Francisco, CA 94103
415-552-1250
Contact: Raymond Shonholtz
Sponsor: Independent corp.
Funding Source: Private foundations
Description: Community empowerment model. Boards
located in four neighborhoods developed through a com-
munity organizing-like process. Mediators selected by the
neighborhood hear cases and help decide policy. Open
hearings. Referrals primarily from neighborhood.
Operating Status: Fully operational
Trained By: Local sources
Training Capacity: Some information available on
program

Community Dispute Services
445 Bush Street
San Francisco, CA 94108
415-434-2200
Contact: Deborah Todd
Sponsor: AAA
Funding Source: Junior League of San Francisco
Description: Mediation/arbitration program dealing with
minor criminal disputes only—upon direct referral from
the court.
Operating Status: Fully operational
Training Capacity: No

**Neighborhood Mediation and Conciliation Services
of Santa Clara County**
County Government Center, East Wing
70 W. Hedding Street
San Jose, CA 95110
408-299-3953
Contact: Chuck Foley
Sponsor: Santa Clara County Human Relations
Commission
Funding Source: County, CETA
Description: County-wide jurisdiction. Cases processed
from central office where most hearings are held, though
if preferred can hold hearings in 10 neighborhood
locations. Subcommittee of HRC serves as advisory
committee. Lay mediators.
Operating Status: Fully operational
Trained By: Chuck Foley
Training Capacity: Yes

Rental Information & Mediation Service (RIMS)
301 Center Street
Santa Cruz, CA 95060
408-425-1001 or 688-2003
Contact: Joan Fuhry
Sponsor: YWCA
Funding Source: CETA, HUD
Description: Providing information to tenants and land-
lords on laws. Distributing literature, workshops, encour-
aging fair rental practices and training mediators to aid in
dispute resolution.
Operating Status: Fully operational
Trained By: RIMS
Training Capacity: Yes

Santa Cruz Co. Consumer Affairs
Alternative Dispute Resolution Program
701 Ocean Street, Room 240
Santa Cruz, CA 95060
408-425-2054
Contact: Kathie Mabie-Klass
Sponsor: Santa Cruz County
Funding Source: General County Funds
Description: Med./Arb. of consumer and neighborhood
disputes. Consumer complaints plus referrals from district
attorney. Volunteer mediators.
Operating Status: Fully operational
Training Capacity: No

Neighborhood Justice Center of Venice–Mar Vista
1527 Venice Blvd.
Venice, CA 90291
213-390-7666
Contact: Joel Edleman
Sponsor: L.A. County Bar
Funding Source: LEAA
Description: Walk-in and community referred cases.
Mediation only—stress on being non-coercive and not
tied to courts. Advisory board consists of majority from
community, remainder from L.A. Bar.
Trained By: AAA—local resources

Custody Mediation Project
Univ. of Denver—Dept. of Sociology
Denver, Colo. 80208
303-753-3208
Contact: Jessica Pearson
Sponsor: Univ. of Denver
Funding Source: Foundations
Description: Mediate custody and visitation disputes of
divorcing or divorced couples. Lawyers and health
specialists mediate. No charge.

Landlord/Tenant Mediation Project
144 West Colfax Avenue, Room 302
Denver, Colo. 80202

303-575-3171
Contact: Lynn Smith—Wendy Downie
Sponsor: Denver Com. on Community Relations, Colo.
Bar Assoc.
Funding Source: ACTION
Description: Mediate/conciliate landlord/tenant disputes
in City and County of Denver.
Operating Status: Fully operational
Training Capacity: Yes

Conciliation Services
310 E. Cedar Avenue
Denver, Colo. 80209
303-722-5705
Contact: Richard Everetts
Sponsor: Independent
Funding Source: Fees
Description: Mediation of private or public disputes, also
public sponsor and help train government programs,
landlord/tenant mediation.
Operating Status: Fully operational
Trained By: Richard Everetts
Training Capacity: Yes

Neighborhood Mediation Project
Corbett Building, Room 312
430 S.W. Morrison St.
Portland, Oregon 97204
503-248-4187
Contact: Elaine Walsh
Sponsor: Metro. Human Relations Com.
Funding Source: City Council, CETA
Description: Mediation of minor neighborhood com-
plaints. Lay mediators.
Operating Status: Fully operational
Trained By: Chuck Foley

Neutral Ground
P.O. Box 1222
Walla Walla, Washington 99362
509-522-0399
Contact: Daniel N. Clark
Sponsor: Independent
Funding Source: Fees and Church seed money
Description: Mediation and (if necessary) arbitration of
legal and other disputes as an alternative to judicial pro-
ceedings. Including family, commercial, professional, etc.
Operating Status: Fully operational
Trained By: Local and nationally known trainers
Training Capacity: Yes

Community Mediation Service
c/o Univ. of Hawaii at Manoa
Dept. of Political Science
2424 Maile Way
Honolulu, Hawaii 96822

Sponsor: Univ. of Hawaii, Poli. Sci. Dept.
Funding Source: None
Description: Three-person panels. Referrals from Prose-
cutor, legal aid, other agencies and general community.
Representative mediators from multi-racial community.
Operating Status: Operational
Trained By: IMCR

OTHER COUNTRIES

Community Justice Centers Experiment
c/o M. Lizier, Attorney General's Dept.
Goodsell Bldg., Chefley Square
Sydney 2000, New South Wales
Australia
Contact: Mariella Lizier
Sponsor: Attorney General's Dept., NSW
Funding Source: State government and Law Foundation
of NSW
Description: Three pilot centers to begin in late 1980

Community Mediation Service
50 Kent Avenue
Kitchener, Ontario N2G 3R1
519-745-4417
Contact: Dave Worth
Sponsor: Mennonite Central Committee (Ontario)
Funding Source: Private individuals—seeking other
sources
Description: Community-based, locally initiated media-
tion service—referrals from police and social services.
Civil and "pre-" criminal situations.
Operating Status: Pilot stage

North End Diversion & Neighborhood Justice Project
P.O. Box 1235
Halifax North P.O.
Halifax, N.S. B3K 5H4
902-422-1761
Contact: Sandra Lyth
Funding Source: Federal Ministry of Solicitor General
Description: Depends on community referrals—none
from police or prosecutor. Early concentration on shop-
lifting cases.

RESOURCES

American Arbitration Association
140 W. 51st Street
New York, N.Y. 10020
212-977-2080
Contact: Robert Coulson
Sponsor: Independent
Funding Source: Varied
Description: Sponsors CDS programs in Cleveland, Rochester, Nassau County, San Francisco. Performs arbitration at many levels.
Training Capacity: Yes

American Bar Association
Special Committee on Resolution of Minor Disputes
1800 M Street, N.W.
Washington, D.C. 20036
202-331-2200
Description: Clearinghouse for dispute resolution. Quarterly Information Update publication available free from above address.

Center for Community Justice
918 16th St., N.W.
Washington, D.C. 20006
202-296-2565
Contact: Linda Singer
Funding Source: LEAA, foundations, NIC
Description: Design, train, operate and evaluate non-judicial methods of dispute resolution in prisons, schools, hospitals, community.
Operating Status: Fully operational
Training Capacity: Yes

Community Relations Service
U.S. Department of Justice
550 Eleventh Street, N.W.
Washington, D.C. 20530
(Check regional listings in telephone book under U.S. Government)
202-739-4002
Description: Experience in mediation of large community disputes. May be helpful in designing and implementing training and in locating community resources. Services available free. (Availability seems to depend on interest and work schedule of the person you contact.)

Grassroots Citizen Dispute Resolution Clearinghouse
4401 Fifth Avenue
Pittsburgh, PA 15213
412-621-3050

Contact: Paul Wahrhaftig
Sponsor: American Friends Service Committee
Description: Resource to community groups organizing dispute resolution programs. Emphasis on community empowerment. Publishes literature, consults on program design, holds workshops.

Institute for Mediation and Conflict Resolution (IMCR)
49 East 68th Street
New York, N.Y. 10021
212-628-1010
Contact: George Nicolau
Description: Pioneer in training community people in mediation/arbitration skills and particularly for citizen dispute resolution programs.

Mediation Institute of California
P.O. Box 26490
San Jose, CA 95159
408-248-4154
Contact: Chuck Foley
Sponsor: Independent
Funding Source: Consultant and Training fees
Description: Provides training in all forms of mediation (rental, marital, criminal, civil, etc.). Sets up programs for staff, volunteers, government agencies. Provides mediation, arbitration, conciliation, interpersonal negotiations.
Operating Status: Fully operational
Trained By: IMCR & AAA
Training Capacity: Yes

Mennonite Conciliation Service
21 S. 12th Street
Akron, PA 17501
717-859-1151
Contact: Ron Kraybill
Sponsor: Mennonite Central Committee
Funding Source: Churches
Description: Provide training, coordination and clearinghouse services for church-sponsored mediation projects operating in local communities.
Operating Status: Planning
Training Capacity: Maybe as of Jan. 1980

National Criminal Justice Reference Service
Box 6000
Rockville, MD 20850
202-862-2900
Description: Computerized bibliography on criminal justice in general. Circulates publications (usually LEAA funded). Ask for information on Neighborhood Justice Centers and they will send you relevant annotated bibliographies and tell you how to keep up-to-date on information on this subject.

★★★★★★★★★★★★★★★★★★★★★★★★★★★★★★★★★

National Peace Academy Campaign
1625 I Street, N.W., Suite 123
Washington, D.C. 20003
202-466-7670
Contact: Milton C. Mapes, Jr.
Sponsor: Independent
Funding Source: Private individuals and membership fees
Description: Public education on non-litigational and non-force conflict resolution skills and lobbying for a national center for training and research in conflict resolution.
Operating Status: Fully operational
Training Capacity: Yes

RESOLVE, Center for Environmental Conflict Resolution
360 Bryant Street
Palo Alto, CA 94301
415-329-1525
Contact: Richard Livermore
Funding Source: Private individuals, corporations, foundations and government contracts occasionally
Description: Develop alternative conflict resolution strategies for environmental disputes.
Operating Status: Fully operational
Trained By: Experience, Interaction Associates, schooling
Training Capacity: No

PART V

Legal Information Programs

Do you have a legal problem but cannot afford to pay $50 or more an hour to a lawyer? If you are within their income guidelines (which are very low), you could go to legal services. Otherwise, privately-run legal clinics advertise less expensive services, especially in the areas of wills, divorce, bankruptcy, and consumer problems. But even these "low-priced" clinics can charge many hundreds of dollars for a case. It is possible, and even likely, that if you were more familiar with the law, you could handle the problem yourself. But where do you go to learn the necessary basic law and procedures?

Legal information programs may be one source. These are usually community groups and organizations which provide free legal information and materials in specific areas of the law. Of course, not all areas of law will be covered at a location convenient to you, but the area in which you have a problem may be. The staffs of these programs are generally informed and concerned people — not elitist lawyers. Their aim is to encourage you to "do it yourself." If you do need a lawyer, they can help you find a conscientious one. Legal information programs are an important contribution to any community. We explore them in some detail in this section.

One day Brother Fox caught Brother Goose and tied him to a tree.

"I'm going to eat you, Bro' Goose," he said, "you've been stealing my meat."

"But I don't even eat meat," Bro' Goose protested.

"Tell that to the judge and jury," said Bro' Fox.

"Who's gonna be the judge?" asked Bro' Goose.

"A fox," answered Bro' Fox.

"And who's gonna be the jury?" Bro' Goose inquired.

"They all gonna be foxes," said Bro' Fox, grinning so all his teeth showed.

"Guess my goose is cooked," said Brother Goose.

—*An Afro-American folktale*

Legal Information Programs

A woman we know had a relatively simple tenant-landlord problem. She had moved out of her apartment, leaving the place in immaculate condition. She phoned the landlord and asked for return for her $200 security deposit. He told her that it was "nonrefundable." She contacted an acquaintance—a lawyer who wasn't practicing. He told her that under California law, no deposit may be categorized as "nonrefundable." A landlord may only keep an amount necessary to cover actual damage and required cleaning. The lawyer suggested that she file a small claims court action against her landlord.

A while later, a mutual friend told the lawyer that the woman had decided not to take the advice. After all, how accurate could it be from a lawyer who wasn't practicing?

"Maybe you should have charged her fifty bucks," the friend quipped. "Then she would have believed you."

Alas. Too many people still believe that practicing lawyers are the true founts of legal information, and that the more they charge, the more they know. But for those who are willing to put aside this nonsense, there is an alternative. And that is what this section is about.

Before you rush out to see a lawyer, check first to see if there is a group or organization in your community which provides free or low-cost legal self-help information in the area in which you are interested. Do you have a problem with your landlord? There may be a tenants' rights group near you. Need counseling on how to stop your husband from returning to your home to abuse you and the children? There is probably a battered women's service close by. Worried about copyright protection for your paintings? An arts and the law organization could help out.

In most parts of the country there are legal programs for several different types of legal problems. The people who work there are not likely to be lawyers,[1] but they have been trained to deal with specific issues and probably know more about the field than most lawyers. It's their specialty (and really, folks, law isn't that difficult).

Not surprisingly, the local state bar associations do not look kindly at non-lawyers giving out legal information. Laws in every state forbid the "practicing of law without a license." For example, district attorneys have been known to hound groups which prepare divorce papers for you to file in court. But though people who work in the programs cannot act as personal legal counsel, they can legally provide you with general information on the law, and inform you of the options you may have. They can also assist you in filling out court forms to request specific remedies, e.g., obtaining a protection order to stop a man from abusing a woman. Many programs are also staffed with paralegals and law students who can represent you at administrative hearings pertaining to government benefits such as unemployment insurance, food stamps, public housing, or social security. But often the legal information you receive from these services is sufficient to determine the course of action

If you do decide to consult an attorney, many legal advice programs keep a list of knowledgeable attorneys who will be particularly sensitive to your problem. Some of the well-funded programs also hire staff counsel who are available at no fee to people who qualify under specific income guidelines.

How do you find a legal information program? You may be able to locate one through a local consumer organization, legal services program, a Public Interest Research Group (PIRG), city hall, or a social service program or agency.

This section will review several kinds of programs now operating around the country.[2] To our surprise (and disappointment) we found fewer programs than we expected. Those which do exist are primarily in major metropolitan centers. The legal information offered tends to be limited to a dozen or so areas. Obviously, much of the reason that there aren't more programs is a lack of funding. In a few select legal fields, such as legal information programs for the elderly, the government offers some financial assistance. A small number of foundation grants are available for other areas. But for the most part, programs rely heavily on volunteers and user contributions.

We know we have missed many important programs in doing our research. Because most groups are poorly financed and cannot afford to do much publicity, they are not easy to find. Also, some programs make it their policy to keep a low profile so as not to antagonize the local bar association. Nevertheless, this selection of programs is representative. If we have missed you, please let us know so that we won't do it again.

We have chosen three areas of focus — tenants, battered women, and artists. Discussion of these areas is followed by a short selection of interesting programs in other areas of the country. We hope all of this material will inspire you to work with people in your community to establish similar (and new) kinds of programs.

---

1. In this section we do not deal with traditional legal aid or legal services programs which are primarily staffed by lawyers as a part of a federally-funded effort to provide legal help to low-income people.

2. We are only concerned with programs which provide *legal* information. There are many more social service and health programs in this country — but those are outside the scope of this book.

Tenant Organizations

Until the 1960s, landlord-tenant law was an anachronism, a throwback to the agrarian society of the 18th century. The law was based on the theory that the tenant was really renting the land and the dwelling was incidental. The tenant was considered a jack-of-all-trades and was expected to make the repairs.

Of course, as the industrial revolution brought people off the farm and into the cities, the new tenants weren't leasing land but were renting dwelling spaces. Nor were they capable of repairing the more sophisticated plumbing, electrical, and heating systems built into the tenements. But the law purposely ignored reality. In contrast to contract theory, wherein one party's duty to fulfill his or her obligation is dependent on the other party's performance, the principles which applied to lease agreements worked entirely in favor of one party—the landlord. Even if the landlord didn't repair the broken toilet, leaking roof, or hot water heater, the tenant was still obligated to pay the rent, as these obligations were independent of each other. Some states allowed the tenant to use the rent to make the repairs, but this was a sparse remedy. The amount of the repair was limited by the law to usually one month's rent and the deduction could only be taken once a year. Other states allowed a tenant to break a lease and move out if conditions were so bad that he or she could no longer live there. This was called "constructive evictions" but it wasn't really a solution if a shortage of decent and affordable housing forced the tenant to move to yet another substandard place.

In the late 60s and early 70s, a tenant movement began to emerge with strength. With the assistance of committed lawyers, tenants were able to establish in the courts a theory of "warranty of habitability" which is implied in any lease agreement—both oral and written—for residential property. Much like the warranty of merchantability, which provides that when a consumer buys a car, stereo, or couch, he or she is guaranteed that the item will do what it is supposed to do, so a tenant is guaranteed that the dwelling for which he or she pays rent will be in conformity with the minimum health and safety requirements of the state and local housing codes. And if it is not—if there is no hot water, if there is a gaping hole in the floor, if rats scurry through the kid's room—the tenant can refuse to pay all or part of the rent until the landlord lives up to his or her end of the bargain, which is to make the repairs. Some states have actually established formulas for determining how much the dwelling is really worth in a defective condition. Such a theory makes perfect sense—you pay for what you get—yet it took more than 200 years to arrive. The warranty of habitability theory, if recognized by your state, may be incorporated into a statute of rent withholding or rent abatement, or it may be established as a common law precedent because of a court decision, or both. (A list of states which have recognized the warranty of habitability follows this article.)

Another important development for tenants which has reached some areas of the country is rent control. Rent control is not a new phenomenon (ancient Romans had rent control). In this country, nearly every major city was subject to rent and evictions controls from 1942 to 1953. In the late 1960s and early 1970s (and more recently in California), a new wave of organizing for rent control emerged. Rent control usually provides some protection for the tenant from unfair rent hikes and evictions without just cause. It also allows landlords to make a profit which is fair. Rent control measures are often linked to housing shortage situations which are becoming increasingly acute as apartments are converted to condominiums and new housing construction is limited by a depressed economy.

Rent control may be enacted in basically three ways; local ordinance, state statute, and state-enabling legislation. States which have or had some kind of rent control laws, either local or state-wide, include Alaska, California, Connecticut, Maine, Maryland, Massachusetts, New Jersey, New York, and Washington, D.C. Rent control can come and go more quickly than we tenants like to admit, so be sure to check with city hall to see if your town has it.

Other laws which have been passed in many states include protections for tenants from evictions without just cause, condominum conversions, illegal lock-outs and utility shut-offs, withholding security deposits, lead poisoning, discrimination, retaliatory actions, and unfair leases. Some tenants are trying to establish a legal precedent in the courts for the tort of "slumlordism" for which tenants could be awarded damages if they suffered emotional distress as a result of unsafe or unhealthy conditions maintained by the landlord.

The legal rights and protections which tenants have gained are a direct result of the momentum in tenant organizing. The Tenant Movement really had its beginnings in the urban areas of the East Coast. Tenant activist Jessie Gray's well-publicized Harlem rent strike in 1964 (when he delivered a rat to the mayor's office) was among the first tenant activities. New York, New Jersey, and Massachusetts tenant unions became some of the largest and most effective in the country. Since the 1960s, the tenant union movement has swept across the nation, although its strength is uneven. Many gains on the East Coast, especially in rent control, have been cut back and a good number of tenants' groups find themselves in a defensive posture with a less powerful membership. On the other hand, areas in the midwest, southwest, and west are experiencing new surges of tenant activity.

Tenants can be organized into state groups, city groups, by neighborhood, landlord, or building. These tenant organizations can act in numerous ways — counseling by phone or person, advocating in the courtroom or at the local rent control board, educating, publishing newspapers, books, and pamphlets, and lobbying. Some tenant unions also attempt to link up housing with other struggles in their communities.

Many groups are under-financed and must rely on the voluntary commitment and energy of its members. Sometimes there are splits in leadership and membership because of politics or personality. It is also discouraging and debilitating for tenant groups to wage efforts against landlord/business groups which are highly financed and relentless in their attacks. But regardless, new tenant groups are emerging all the time.

In this part we'll describe a few of the present programs, and follow with a listing of tenant groups around the country. The list isn't complete — many groups are so local in their activities that people will never hear of them. If you cannot find a tenant organization in your area, we suggest you contact your local legal aid or legal services office to see whether they know of one. You could also write to The National Housing and Economic Development Law Project, 2150 Shattuck Avenue, Berkeley, CA 94704. They keep abreast of the latest tenant legislation and court decisions around the country and may know of a tenancy advocacy group in your area.

List of States Which Have Recognized the Doctrine of Implied Warranty of Habitability

Alaska: *Alaska Stat.*, §§34.03, 34.03.160, 34.03.180 (1974)

Arizona: *Ariz. Rev. Stat. Ann.*, §§33-1324 and 33-1361 (1974)

California: *Cal. Civ. Code*, §§1941, 1942 (West 1974); and *Green v. Superior Court*, 10 Cal. 3d 616, 517 P. 2d 1168 (1974)

Connecticut: *Conn. Gen. Stat. Ann.*, §§47-24, *et seq.* (1960); and *Todd v. May*, 6 Conn. Cir. Ct. 731, 316 A. 2d 793 (1973)

Delaware: *Del. Code Ann.*, tit. 25, §5303 (1974)

District of Columbia: *Javins v. First National Realty Corp.*, 428 F. 2d 1071 (D.C. Cir.), *cert. denied*, 400 U.S. 925 (1970)

Florida: *Fla. Stat. Ann.*, §§83.51, 83.56 (1973)

Georgia: *Ga. Code Ann.*, tit. 61, chs. 111-112; *Gevens v. Gray*, 126 Ga. App. 309, 190 S.E. 2d 607 (1972); and *Stack v. Harris*, 111 Ga. 149 (1906)

Hawaii: *Hawaii Rev. Stat.*, §521-42 (Supp. 1974); and *Lemle v. Breeden*, 51 Hawaii 426, 462 P. 2d 470 (1969)

Idaho: *Idaho Code*, §6-316 (H.B. No. 34, 1977)

Illinois: *Jack Spring, Inc. v. Little*, 50 Ill. 2d 351, 280 N.E. 2d 208 (1972)

Iowa: Iowa House File 2,244, §15 (June 1978); and *Mease v. Fox*, 200 N.W. 2d 791 (1972)

Kansas: *Steele v. Latimer*, 214 Kan. 329, 521 P. 2d 304 (1974)

Kentucky: *Ky. Rev. Stat. Ann*, §§383.595, 383.625 (Supp. 1974) (Lafayette and Jefferson counties only)

Maine: *Me. Rev. Stat. Ann.*, tit. 14, §6021 (Supp. 1974)

Maryland: *Md. Real Prop. Code Ann.*, §8-211 (Cum. Supp. 1975), superseded in their respective jurisdictions by *Baltimore City Public Local Laws*, §§9-9, 9-10, 9-14.1 (eff. July 1, 1971), and *Montgomery County Code, Fair Landlord-Tenant Relations*, ch. 93A (Nov. 21, 1972)

Massachusetts: *Mass. Gen. Laws Ann.*, ch. 239, §8A (Supp. 1974); and *Boston Housing Authority v. Hemingway*, 293 N.E. 2d 831 (1973)

Michigan: *Mich. Comp. Laws Ann.*, §554.139 (Supp. 1974); and *Rome v. Walker*, 38 Mich. App. 458, 196 N.W. 2d 850 (1972)

Minnesota: *Minn. Stat.*, §504.18 (1974), applied in *Fritz v. Warthen*, 298 Minn. 54, 213 N.W. 2d 339 (1973)

Missouri: *King v. Moorehead*, 495 S.W. 2d 65 (1973)

Montana:	*Mont. Rev. Codes Ann.*, §§42-420 and 42-426 (1977)
Nebraska:	*Neb. Rev. Stat.*, §§76-1419, 76-1425, *et seq.* (Cum. Supp. 1974)
Nevada:	*Nev. Rev. Stat.*, tit. 10, §118A.290 (1970) (but note that the act does not protect tenants whose landlord owns fewer than seven units)
New Hampshire:	*Kline v. Burns*, 111 N.H. 87, 297 A.2d 248 (1971)
New Jersey:	*Marini v. Ireland*, 56 N.J. 130, 265 A.2d 526 (1970)
New Mexico:	*N.M. Stat.*, §§70-7-1, *et seq.* (1975)
New York:	*N.Y. Real Prop. Law*, §§235-b (McKinney 1975), N.Y. Acts 875
North Carolina:	1977-78 N.C. Sess. Laws, ch. 770 (N.C. Gen. Stat., ch. 42, art. V)
North Dakota:	*N.D. Cent.Code*, §47-16-13.1, *et seq.* (1977)
Ohio:	*Ohio Rev. Code Ann.*, §§5321.04, 5321.07 (Page Supp. 1974)
Oklahoma:	*Okla. Stat. Ann.*, tit. 41, §118 (1978)
Oregon:	*Ore. Rev. Stat.*, §§91.770, 91.800-.815 (1974); *L & M Investment Co. v. Morrison*, 236 Or. 397, 594 P.2d 1238 (1980)
Pennsylvania:	*Pugh v. Holmes*, 405 A.2d 897 (Pa. 1979); also *Commonwealth v. Monumental Properties, Inc.*, 329 A.2d 812 (Pa. 1974)
Tennessee:	*Tenn. Code Ann.*, §§53-5501, *et seq.* (Cum. Supp. 1974) (applies to major cities only)
Texas:	H.B. No. 1773 (1979); *Kamarath v. Bennett*, No. B-6821 (Sup. Ct., April 12, 1978), ___ S.W.2d ___ (Tex. 1978)
Vermont:	*Vt. Stat. Ann.*, tit. 12, §4859 (1972)
Virginia:	*Va. Code Ann.*, §§55-248.13, 55-248.25 (Cum. Supp. 1975)
Washington:	*Wash. Rev. Code Ann.*, §59.18.060 (Supp. 1974), enacted after judicial implication of warranty of habitability in *Foisy v. Wyman*, 83 Wash.2d 22, 515 P.2d 160 (1973)
West Virginia:	H.B. 1368 (passed March 11, 1978, eff. June 11, 1978) (sets out landlord obligations but does not provide remedy for breach); *Teller v. McCoy*, 253 S.E.2d 114 (W.Va. 1978)
Wisconsin:	*Pines v. Perssion*, 14 Wis.2d 590, 111 N.W.2d 409 (1961); *but see, Posnanski v. Hood*, 46 Wis.2d 172, 174 N.W.2d 528 (1970).

Tenant Action Group

A primary purpose of the Tenant Action Group (TAG) in Philadelphia is to encourage self-help tenant action. TAG prefers to educate and assist tenants in groups, though it will counsel individuals. However, it will not negotiate with a landlord on behalf of a tenant since this "fosters dependency."

Training sessions for tenants are held three times a week in cooperation with the Community Legal Services (CLS) Program. Classes are held on eviction defenses and other tenants' rights. Cases involving clinic-trained tenants in Municipal Court are monitored by TAG and CLS. They check on the responsiveness of the court to tenant self-representation. We've included in this section the instruction outlines to their classes.

One of TAG's activities is the implementation of legislation (a "Tenants' Bill of Rights") which guarantees reasonable rents, fair leases, repairs, and an end to discrimination against families, single parents, and public assistance recipients.

Tenant Action Group publishes a monthly news-letter, pamphlets, and information sheets, and assists fledgling tenant unions. Funding is tight and although some members pay dues, TAG relies largely on volunteers, especially college students who sometimes receive credit for their participation.

TAG has been in existence since 1975. Its constituents are predominantly lower income tenants. TAG is not involved with public housing concerns.

Their office is open 9 to 5, Monday through Friday.

1411 Walnut St., Suite 826
Philadelphia, PA 19102
(215) 563-5402

With all the variations around the country, it would be difficult to say that any one program is a prototype of a tenant organization. But the Tenant Action Group is a useful model of a low-budgeted, non-government financed program actively involved in community work. The following material describes TAG's community education program, clinics, and court monitoring project.

Introduction to the Community Education
Program on Tenants Rights

The Tenant Action Group and Community Legal Services are initiating an innovative approach to the delivery of services to individual, as well as groups of tenants. The program consists of a continuing series of group training sessions where tenants will be given the information and skills to handle their own housing problems, and will de-emphasize individual tenant services.

The Tenant Action Group has found that repeatedly solving the same problems for individual tenants rarely helps anyone other than the individual tenant, and does not even prevent the same problem from arising again for that same individual. Moreover, this type of service delivery has virtually no impact upon the legal and political systems which can create such housing problems. It is TAG's belief that the current landlord/tenant law often fails to protect tenants, and the only way to effect change is through the education of groups of tenants who can assert their rights and insist upon the expansion of those rights.

Thus, the Tenant Action Group, in conjunction with Community Legal Services, has developed a continuing series of training, educational and organizational programs structured to develop a broader consciousness among tenants. This program will expose tenants to others with the same problems, maximize individual strengths by giving tenants the tools to solve their own problems, and provide an opportunity to educate large groups of people about the politics and economics of housing.

We will, of course, continue to encounter individuals who need substantial support in solving their housing problems. Our Community Education Program is designed to provide for the needs of tenants who are physically or emotionally unable to resolve their problems without the assistance of individual legal representation. In addition, individual legal representation will be provided in situations where required by court procedure.

Referral Procedures for Community Education Program

When tenants contact Community Legal Services, the Community Education Program will be explained in terms of the advantages of self-representation:

1. the education and possibility of later use by the tenant and/or friends of the tenant;

2. tenants have the same chance of victory at hearings regardless of the presence of an attorney, and in many cases there is the possibility of a better verdict if the client appears without an attorney;

3. the recognition that problems faced by tenants are collective, not isolated instances, and that TAG seeks collective resolution;

4. Municipal Court and the Fair Housing Commission are designed for lay persons; appeals from Municipal Court do not rely upon the record established at the hearing.

An intake sheet will be prepared identifying the tenant, landlord, nature of the problem, source of income, etc. The form will also include the clinic to which tenant has been referred, and instructions given to the tenant to prepare for the meeting. The form will be in duplicate; one for retention at CLS and one for transmittal to TAG. Referral forms will be transmitted to TAG on a daily basis by CLS staff.

If it appears to the C.L.S. staff person that the tenant cannot participate in the program due to: language barrier; incarceration; hospitalization; physical disability restricting travel; infirmity of an elderly person; blindness; deafness; or mental disability; s/he would not be referred to TAG. An appointment would be made for the tenant at C.L.S.

Requests for assistance in organizing tenant councils, or providing training to neighborhood organizations and social service agencies, will be referred to TAG to schedule on-site visits, rather than referring such groups to clinics.

Tenants who contact CLS and have hearing dates

before the next scheduled clinic will be instructed to attend the hearing; they will be advised to seek a continuance to allow for better preparation. If a continuance is not granted, each tenant will be instructed to make his or her best common sense argument; agree to no settlement unless certain of the terms and acceptability; to remain in court to insure that the settlement is recorded properly; to understand the judgment, and to attend an Appeal Clinic after the hearing.

Tenants will receive follow-up phone calls to remind them of clinic appointments.

Tenants who contact TAG initially will be similarly screened as to the appropriateness of clinic appointments or CLS individual representation.

Follow-up After Attendance at Clinics

Tenants who attend clinics will be urged to attend on a regular basis, understanding that their problem cannot be resolved within a week (in most cases), and that they might gain more understanding by attending more sessions. To the extent possible, we will help tenants plan strategies in weekly steps.

Every tenant who attends a clinic will have a file including the initial referral form, interview form, and Xeroxed copies of all relevant documents. The files will be maintained at the TAG office and filed alphabetically.

Tenants who attend clinics and call for more information at a later date will receive such information over the telephone from TAG staff if the problem is of an emergency nature, or a simple need for clarification. In other cases, tenants will be asked to return to another clinic to receive more information. The contents of all telephone conversations will be recorded in the file by TAG staff. Tenants will not have to speak to the staff trainer who was present at the clinic they attended in order to receive such assistance. Information in the files will be transferred to CLS if the tenant is referred for individual representation at a later date.

Evaluation and Monitoring of Court Hearings

An integral part of the Community Education Program will be a constant monitoring of Municipal Court's performance in response to tenant self-representation. Monitors supplied by CLS and TAG will daily observe every stage of the Court process for

every case involving clinic-trained tenants. In addition, a number of non-trained cases will also be observed, including cases where tenants are both represented and not represented by counsel.

Monitors will report their observations as to the following matters, among others: judicial conduct; willingness of the Court to listen to specific legal arguments and evidence; Court's action on defenses presented; results of negotiated settlements; effectiveness of tenant's presentation; total number of defaults entered.

In order to emphasize the self-help nature of the program, the Court Monitor will not get involved in actual case resolution; the limited role of the Court Monitor will be explicitly outlined to clinic participants.

How to Make Agreements

When you go to Court, you will see that many cases aren't argued before the Judge, but end up as agreements. There is a lot of pressure on tenants to make agreements, but you are not required to agree to anything.

If your landlord or his lawyer approaches you to make an agreement, make sure that you understand everything before you agree to anything.

If your landlord or his lawyer isn't convinced by the fairness of your case, try to put things into terms they might understand—time, money and aggravation.

For example, the landlord may be willing to give up back rent to avoid the hassle of trying to collect it. Maybe the landlord wants to get you out in order to get another tenant. Perhaps you can get extra time or repairs if the landlord thinks it will stop you from appealing.

If you want to make an agreement, be sure you are completely satisfied with it. Once the Judge has been told the agreement, you're stuck with it. Agreements cannot be appealed.

If you do reach an agreement, do not leave until you have been before the Judge. If you leave, you will be stuck with whatever the landlord or his lawyer tells the Judge. You may also want to have the agreement put into writing, and a copy of it given to the Judge.

Some lawyers will try to make you think they are on your side and tell you that they'll take care of everything. However, the lawyer has been hired by your landlord, and will do what the landlord wants.

REMEMBER:

1. Don't agree to anything you don't understand.
2. Don't agree to anything you can't live with.
3. Don't leave court until you've been before the Judge.

★★★

Metropolitan Council on Housing

The Metropolitan Council on Housing in New York City is one of the largest and best organized tenant groups in the country. Its central office is located in midtown Manhattan; nine neighborhood branches are scattered throughout the city. Membership dues, small contributions, and grassroots fund-raising finance its operations. They receive no government funding.

Met Council advises tenants and negotiates with landlords. They hold workshops like "Taking the Offensive with your Landlord," "Co-op Conversion —How It Hurts You and Tenants All Over the City," and "Rehab Rip-offs" once a month. Volunteers are also active in lobbying with the state legislature and the city council.

Met Council's ultimate goal is to "place all housing in the public domain, under tenant control, financed by direct allocations of government funds." Their book, *Housing in the Public Domain: The Only Solution*, by Peter K. Hawley, explains the strategy to achieve this goal. Hawley elucidates why a housing shortage exists, how landlords make lots of money with minimum investment, how tenant-controlled housing would work, and what sources of funding are necessary to its success. The book is available for $3.50 from Met Council.

They also publish "Tenant," a monthly newspaper carrying the motto "Housing For People Not Profit," which contains well-written articles and exposes of illegal actions of particular landlords. It is written for an educated readership; some of the articles are duplicated in Spanish. Met Council also prints pamphlets and information sheets.

The central office is at:
24 West 30th Street
New York, NY 10001
(212) 725-4800
Hours: 1:30 to 6:00 p.m., Monday through Friday

The neighborhood offices are usually open only one or two days a week, often in the evenings.

The following article appeared in the December, 1979 issue of "Tenant." Permission to reprint was given by Met Council.

Coops/condos fought across nation

★★★★★

Start with an acute housing shortage. Add inflation and the lack of new building for moderate and low income tenants. Add accelerated deterioration of existing housing, and last, but certainly not least, the greed and machinations of the real estate industry. What do you get? *Co-op fever and condo-MANIA.* The whole country is plagued with it.

Co-op and condominium conversions exacerbate problems that add up to a dilemma for all citizens other than the wealthy. Tenants are required to buy their homes at inflated prices, though technically in a co-op they are buying shares in a corporation which are allocated to their apartment, and in a condo they buy the apartment as one would buy a home. (For more background on co-op conversions in New York City see April and September 1979 issues of Tenant.)

As a result, rental housing is removed from the market, therefore raising the price of the smaller number of apartments (same demand, decreased supply). The ability of speculators and developers to make more money through conversions discourages new building and proper maintenance of existing apartments.

Tenants Fight Back

What is being done about this MANIA? Tenant groups across the country are pressing for real solutions which must be legislative. There is much proposed legislation on co-op and condominium conversion. Surely, strong laws are needed to prevent the housing situation from worsening, and to protect tenants from further displacement.

The most extensive legislative proposal so far has been introduced into Congress by Representative Benjamin S. Rosenthal from Queens. *The Condominium Co-operative Conversion Moratorium Act of 1979* calls for a three year moratorium nationwide, during which time a presidential commission would study problems related to conversions and presumably report its findings. Other aspects of this bill would require up to $400 relocation assistance to tenants, prohibit federal block grants to areas not restricting conversions, and treat profit from conversions as ordinary income, which is taxed more heavily than it is now as capital gains.

Some Victories

At this time, moratoriums halting conversions exist temporarily in Seattle and Philadelphia. Hartford, Connecticut has passed a moratorium that lasts only until next April, which exempts apartments that have their own heating systems. Furthermore, a permit is now required to convert in Cambridge, Massachusetts, and in nearby Brookline, evictions as a result of conversion by developers or apartment owners are prohibited. In New Jersey, tenants must be given a three-year notice before conversion can take place.

Chicago and New York City have the highest rates of conversion in the country (Chicago 40,000 units in the last two years, 30,000 projected for 1979; New York City 30,000 units in the last two years, 34,000 or more projected). In Chicago, tenants who choose not to purchase a condominium can never be sure that their new apartment won't go condo a month after they move in. This is not too far from what happens in some neighborhoods in New York, even though in New York City there are complicated laws regarding conversion procedures. These laws do not actually protect tenants though, unless they organize and use them to stop conversion altogether. One bill in the New York State legislature, the *Weprin-Padavan Bill*, would outlaw evictions and necessitate 35% of the tenants buying in order for there to be a co-op.

In cities with rent controls, landlords are using conversions as a way to get around the "limited profits" of rent controls. Once a rental unit is vacated in a co-oped building in New York, rent controls no longer apply.

In a country where there are now two million co-op and condo units, 90% of which did not exist in 1970, it is obvious that comprehensive legislation must be enacted. At the very least, this should include no evictions for non-purchasing tenants with continuation of all applicable rent controls, strong protections with penalties against harassment for non-purchasers, and no sales of occupied apartments!

by Claudia Mansbach

Austin Tenants' Council

The Austin (Texas) Tenants' Council is basically set up to provide individual counseling to tenants. The council publishes materials on basic tenant information, including how to get the landlord to make repairs, getting back security deposits, and dealing with evictions. It also sponsors workshops.

The program is funded by the City of Austin, Housing and Community Development Funds, and CETA funds. It began in 1972, and is a charter member of the newly-formed Texas Tenants' Union.

1619 East First Street
Austin, Texas 78702
(512) 474-1961
Hours: 9 to 5, Monday through Friday

Rental Repair Assistance Program

The Austin Tenants' Council began a new and different program January 1, 1979. It is designed to help low-income renters and their landlords find ways to repair their rental property without rents being raised and the tenants having to move (or be evicted).

We plan to spend the next year (mainly in the East 1st and Rosewood neighborhoods):

1. Counseling tenants about their rights to repairs.

2. Helping tenants work out repair problems with their landlords.

3. Helping housing agencies with the coordination of rental property repair programs.

4. Informing landlords about resources available to them in repairing their rental property.

5. Writing and giving out information about ways to repair.

6. Holding workshops.

7. Working with Advisory Boards and tenant and neighborhood groups to plan programs to repair rental property.

8. Writing lease agreements with tenants and landlords that are fair to both parties.

9. Finding ways that tenants can help do repairs so that rents do not go up.

Why are we starting this program?

Because ⅔ of the substandard property in Austin is occupied by renters;

Because too many people think it is not possible or necessary to keep rent property in good repair;

Because we want to help improve neighborhoods without tenants having to move.

For information on tenants' rights to repairs, our new flyer, "The Austin Housing Code" is available at:

The Rosewood and Rosewood-Zaragosa Neighborhood Centers;

The Govalle, Oak Springs and Carver libraries; and

The Austin Tenants' Council.

Tenant Resource Center

The Tenant Resource Center provides counseling and information on landlord/tenant matters to anyone who requests the service. They also have a number of booklets available, a well as leaflets, slide shows, videotapes, and a newsletter. The TRC serves the mid-Michigan area primarily. In 1979, they aided 10,000 people.

The Michigan Tenants Rights Coalition is a group of pro-tenant organizations and individuals from all over the state of Michigan.

Tenant Resource Center
855 Grove St.
East Lansing, MI 48823
(517) 337-2728
Hotline: 337-9795

Michigan Tenants Rights Coalition
590 Hollister Building
106 W. Allegan
Lansing, MI 48933
(517) 487-6001

CHAIN

CHAIN—California Housing Action and Information Network, is a relatively new organization designed to increase communication and information among the diverse tenant groups around the state. It serves in the capacity of a citizens' lobby of tenants and middle-income homeowners, and acts as a counter-thrust to big landlord interests such as the California Housing Council and the California Association of Realtors. Like New York's Metropolitan Council on Housing, it employs the logo "Housing for People, not Profit."

CHAIN publishes a monthly informative newsletter keeping abreast of state legislative, local city and county actions and court decisions affecting renters and homeowners.

There are several addresses for CHAIN contacts:

Northern California: 2647 E. 14th St.
Oakland, CA 94601
(415) 533-1470

Los Angeles: 2936 W. 8th St.
Los Angeles, CA 90005
(213) 381-5139

Sacramento: 1107 Ninth St., #910
Sacramento, CA 95814
(916) 448-2544

Shelterforce

Shelterforce is an outstanding quarterly journal for housing activists and community organizers. It contains "how-to" articles, political analysis, developments in tenant activities around the country, the most recent housing cases and legislation, as well as publications and events.

Subscription price is $5.00 for 6 issues.

Shelterforce
380 Main St.
East Orange, NJ 07018

Complete set of 12 back issues for $11.00

single issues are $1.25

Issue 5

Ann Arbor Rent Strike: Tenant group wins the right to be the sole bargaining agent for tenants. **Negotiating With Your Landlord, Part II. Tenant Organizations Cop Community Development Funds: Housing Allowance and Section 8:** Two new federal housing programs to aid the poor. **How to Build a Permanent Tenant Union, Part I: Book Review on Small Is Beautiful.**

Issue 6

Coop City Rent Strike Settled: Editorials on the Housing Movement and Elections; **Negotiating With Your Landlord Part III: Hills Vs. Gautreaux**—Will this Supreme Court decision result in more low income housing? **Rent Strike or Tenant Union?** How to build a permanent organization. **Housing in China.**

Issue 7

A Special Issue on Rent Control: Report of tenants across the country fighting for rent control. **Rent Control and the Experts: Latest Rent Control Study: Editorial on Building a National Housing Movement:** The creation of National Federation of tenant and housing organization.

Issue 9

New York Tenants Organize Statewide: An Exchange of Views on Community Control vs. Opening the Suburbs: **The Rise and Fall of Tenants First:** A once powerful statewide tenant union. **Building a Tenant Union:** How tenant unions can defend against legal action and even use them to their advantage. **Using the Media Part 2:** How to use newspapers, radio and T.V.

Issue 10

International Hotel: The tale of a nine-year old fight to save the hotel for its tenants. **Using The Media:** How community groups can get access to free radio and T.V. time. **Sweat Equity and Homesteading:** Will they work? **Squatters Movement in Mexico:** Report on the Progress of Housing Organizations in 14 Cities.

Issue 11

Urban Renewal: How you can stop private developers and government agencies from destroying your neighborhood. **The National Rental Housing Council:** This well-financed real estate group has been formed to attack rent control in the U.S. **Building a Tenant Union;** How to sustain your organization after the initial excitement has died down.

Issue 12

SPECIAL ISSUE! The City Crisis—Who's to Blame?: Written by Frances Fox Piven. **Carter's Urban Programs:** How community groups can use them. **Will Carter's Plan Work?:** An analysis. **Towards a Better Urban Policy. Urban Policy Reading List.**

Issue 13

Arson for Profit: How one community group has successfully tackled the problem of arson in buildings. **Community Reinvestment Act:** A new tool to fight urban decay. **Proposition 13. Tips for Organizers on Community Control.**

Issue 14

Strategies for Organizing: Review of Piven and Cloward's Poor Peoples Movements. **Developing Political Clout. Neighborhood Redevelopment Fights:** Community groups in Cleveland and Newark fight to save their neighborhoods. **The Economics of Housing:** Exchange Value vs. Use Value.

Issue 15

Rent Control Battles Across the Country. Is Rent Control Legal? Neighborhood Control: Alternatives to Gentrification and Abandonment. **Community Development Corporations:** City Owned, Tenant Managed. **Monitoring Landlord Tenant Court:** New Jersey Judge Ousted.

Issue 16

Special Issue on Inflation and Housing: How to Fight Back at the National, State, and Local Level. **Is Rent Control Legal? Part 2:** Tying Repairs to Rent Increases. **Housing Problems That Women Face. Condominium Conversion:** Washington, D.C. Study on Displacement.

Issue 17

The Fuel Passalong: Landlords Bypass Rent Control. **National Committee for Rent Controls. Community Organizing:** How to Mobilize, Win and Stay Together. **Neighborhood Platform Convention. National Tenants' Organization.**

Canada's Rentalsman

We thought we'd include a rather novel approach that several cities and provinces in Canada have adopted for landlord-tenant problems. They've established a "Rentalsman" (perhaps we can convince them to change it to "rentalsperson")—a sort of ombudsperson, an officer with exclusive jurisdiction over landlord-tenant matters including security deposits, termination of tenancies, and repairs.

When disputes arise, the Rentalsman, through telephone contacts, personal interviews, counseling and mediation, will try to reach a resolution. If none is reached, s/he can make a decision and order compliance. The parties may appeal under certain circumstances to a court. But if they do not, they can be fined for disobeying the Rentalsman's order.

In 1979, the Office of the Rentalsman in British Columbia opened 17,200 case files, received 242,304 telephone inquiries, was visited by 13,428 people, and carried out 2,886 inspections. In addition to a Senior Deputy, the Rentalsman has four deputy rentalsmen, and some 34 officers supported by investigative, clerical, and administrative staff. The office has been successful in reaching satisfactory resolutions. Tony Dibley, Executive Assistant to the Rentalsman in B.C. wrote to us that:

> Lacking the respect and dignity traditionally accorded to a court, the Rentalsman's Officer draws heavily in his day-to-day contact with landlords and tenants on his reserves of tolerance and patience, frequently having adversaries before him in an atmosphere of antagonism, charged with emotions. Fortunately, I am pleased to say that the situations a Rentalsman's Officer faces vary considerably and in the variety, there can be found relief and occasionally, in retrospect, humor.

The Rentalsman also promotes a series of education programs for landlord and tenant organizations, conducts radio shows, and, on occasion, prepares articles for magazines.

The Rentalsman Office in British Columbia publishes a booklet called "Getting in on the Act," which is intended to give tenants and landlords a general understanding of the law.

The Office of the Rentalsman in British Columbia is located at:

525 Seymour St.
Vancouver, B.C. V6B 3H7
(604) 689-0811

Tenant/Housing Advocacy Groups

California
Housing Action Project
Barlow House, #109
Humboldt State University
Arcata, CA 95521

National Housing Law Project
2150 Shattuck Ave., #300
Berkeley, CA 94704

Cotati Citizens Alliance
8196 El Rancho
Cotati, CA 94928

Housing Project of Foundation for National
Progress
6529 Trigo, #8
Isla Vista, CA 93017

Long Beach Housing Action Association
2625 East 3rd St., #24
Long Beach, CA 90814

Oakland Tenants Union
2647 E. 14th St.
Oakland, CA 94601

Rent Control Alliance Housing Action Project
P.O. Box 2166
Santa Barbara, CA 93120

Santa Cruz Housing Action Committee
110 Pine Place, #1
Santa Cruz, CA 95060

San Francisco Tenants Union
558 Capp St.
San Francisco, CA 94110

California Housing Action and Information
Network
2647 E. 14th St.
Oakland, CA 94601
2936 W. 8th St.
Los Angeles, CA 90005
1107 Ninth St., #910
Sacramento, CA 95814

District of Columbia
City-Wide Housing Foundation
1419 V Street, N.W.
Washington, D.C. 20009

David Jones
Diffusion Project Center for the Study of Responsive
Law
P.O. Box 19367
Washington, D.C. 20036

Metropolitan Washington Planning & Housing
Association
1225 "K" Street, N.W.
Washington, D.C. 20005

University Legal Services
324 "H" Street, N.E.
Washington, D.C. 20002

Washington Inner City Self-Help
1459 Columbia Road, N.W.
Washington, D.C. 20009

Florida
Florida Organization for Housing and Renters
Rights
c/o Dade Consumers Fighting Inflation
P.O. Box 341164
Coral Gables, FL 33134

Illinois
Lake View Citizens Council
3245 N. Sheffield
Chicago, IL 60657

Rogers Park Tenants Committee
1545 Morse Avenue
Chicago, IL 60626

Champaign-Urbana Tenants Union
298 Illinois Union
Urbana, Illinois

Louisiana
City-Wide Housing Coalition of New Orleans

1802 Orleans St.
New Orleans, LA 70116

Maryland
PIRG Tenant Project
University of Maryland
3110 Main Dining Hall
College Park, MD 20742

Massachusetts
Symphony Tenants Organizing Project
58 Burbank St.
Boston, MA 02215

Back Bay/Beacon Hill Tenants Union
P.O. Box 86 — Astor Station
Boston, MA 02123

City Life
670 Center Street
Jamaica Plain, MA 02130

Cambridge Tenants Organization
161 Columbia Street
Cambridge, MA 02139

Somerville Tenants Union
38 Union Square
Somerville, MA 02143

Michigan
Ann Arbor Tenants Union
4109 Michigan Union
Ann Arbor, MI 48104

United Community Housing Coalition
47 East Adams, 2nd Floor
Detroit, MI 48226

Michigan Tenants Rights Coalition
c/o Tenants Resource Center
855 Grove St.
East Lansing, MI 48923

Tenants Resource Center
855 Grove Street
East Lansing, MI 48923

Poverty Peoples Alliance
1318 Cherry Street
Saginaw, MI 48601

Saginaw Neighborhoods INC
P.O. Box 775
Saginaw, MI 48606

Minnesota
St. Paul Tenants Union
500 Laurel Ave.
St. Paul, MN 55102

New Jersey
Shelterforce
380 Main St.
East Orange, NJ 07018

Fort Lee Tenants Association
P.O. Box 311
Fort Lee, NJ 07024

New Jersey Tenants Organization
P.O. Box 1142
(442 Main Street)
Fort Lee, NJ 07024

Newark Tenants Organization
944 Broad Street
Newark, NJ 07102

New Mexico
New Mexico P.I.R.G.
P.O. Box 4564
Albuquerque, NM 87106

New York
United Tenants of Albany
65 Columbia Street
Albany, NY 12210

Opportunities for Broome
56-58 Whitney Avenue
Binghamton, NY 13905

Fordham Bedford Community Coalition
290 E. 196th St.
Bronx, NY 10458

Caring Community
20 Washington Square
New York, NY 10011

Harlem Restoration Project, Inc.
525 W. 125th St.
New York, NY 10027

In Rem Tenants
P.O. Box 2015 A.P.O.
New York, NY 10001

Met. Council on Housing
24 W. 30th St.
New York, NY 10003

Mitchell-Lama Council
Room 612, 799 Broadway
New York, NY 10001

New York State Tenant and Neighborhood
    Coalition
198 Broadway
New York, NY 10038

Peoples Housing Network
198 Broadway, Rm. 100
New York, NY 10038

Westside Tenants Union
155 W. 72nd St., Rm. 605
New York, NY 10025

Westsiders United
525 W. 125th St.
New York, NY 10027

Ohio
Columbus Tenants Union
5 W. Northwood
Columbus, OH 43202

Oregon
Oregon State Tenants
P.O. Box 7224

3000 Market St., #416
Salem, OR 97301

Portland Tenants Union
834 S.E. Ash
Portland, OR 97214

Pennsylvania
Housing Council of the Action Alliance of Senior
  Citizens
401 N. Broad St.
Philadelphia, PA 19108

Tenant Action Group
1411 Walnut St.
Philadelphia, PA 19102

Texas
Austin Tenants Council
1619 East First St.
Austin, TX 78702

East Dallas Tenants/Small Homeowners Alliance
107 N. Colette
Dallas, TX 75214

Texas Tenants Union
P.O. Box 221
Ft. Worth, TX 76101

Wisconsin
Madison Tenants Union
1045 E. Dayton St.
Madison, WI 53703

National
National Tenants Organization
348 W. 121st St.
New York, NY 10027

National Lawyers Guild
National Housing Task Force
853 Broadway, #1705
New York, NY 10003

With thanks to:
Taffy Castro
Tony Dibley
Eva Gladstein
Mark Goldowitz
Lynn Greenberg
Bob Marrero
Susan Silberstein
Jim Simons
Michael Yates

Battered Women Programs

F.B.I. statistics reflect the shattering fact that a woman is abused every 18 seconds. In Boston, 70% of all assault victims in the city hospitals' emergency rooms are battered women.[1] Of 274 women surveyed in Hartford, Connecticut, 45% had been kicked, beaten, or abused by their husbands, 28% were beaten with weapons or other objects, and suffered broken bones, and 40% of their children had also been beaten.[2] There are an estimated 28 million battered women in the United States—more than half the married women in the country.[3]

There are a variety of reasons why women take such abuse. They may be financially dependent on the man and without income and skills that would enable them to find a job. Or if the woman has children, she may worry about how she can support them. On the other hand, if she leaves her children behind, the man has the leverage for her return. Many women are emotionally dependent and without supportive relatives and sympathetic friends. They find themselves incapable of making the break. Women may also fear that if they leave the abusers and are later found, they will be killed by them. Furthermore, many women were battered as children and therefore have accepted their abuse as a part of the human condition. These women have long ago suffered a loss of self-confidence which deters them from breaking away.

For many years, women (and men) have been attempting to convince the state courts and legislatures to recognize the seriousness of this problem. Presently, at least 27 states have laws which provide civil protection or restraining orders for battered women. These laws make provisions for a judge to order the man to move out, stop abusing her, and/or avoid all contact with her. The judge may also award custody, support payments, and damages to the woman for injuries suffered. In addition, the man may be required to attend counseling sessions. In many states, the orders may be issued within a few hours after application and often people are permitted to file the papers without lawyers.

Of course, if the police and the courts are ignorant or refuse to enforce the orders, the existence of any abuse protection law makes little difference. In Memphis, Tennessee, for example, despite the fact that over 200 women filed for protection orders during the first year the law went into effect, only one order was issued.

On the other hand, in Toledo, Ohio, at least 90% of 150 petitions filed during a six-month period after the law went into effect resulted in removing the abuser from his victim. Protection orders were generally issued within one and one-half hours after the woman filed her petition, and within 15 minutes after a hearing was completed. Nearly all the cases were handled without the assistance of a lawyer.

However, fees, whether for filing and service of papers (usually between $20 and $50) or for attorneys, can discourage a woman from filing for a protection order. Even though courts, in theory, can waive some fees when a women is indigent, and legal services are similarly available, many judges and legal services programs determine indigency and eligibility on the basis of family income—which naturally includes the husband's.

The effectiveness of the law is also reduced when it does not provide for court hearings at night and on weekends. Unless the woman can obtain the order quickly, she has minimum opportunity of preventing the abuser from returning and beating her again.

Battered woman programs usually offer two basic services. One is a shelter, an actual place where women and sometimes their children may stay for a period up to several months. The cost is minimal—perhaps a couple dollars a day including food. Often retroactive payments can be made after the woman has obtained employment. The location of the shelter is not made public in order to protect the women from their abusers. The programs also act as service providers. Many programs counsel women in legal, medical, welfare, and job skills, as well as providing housing information. Several of the programs use paralegals who assist women with their petitions for protection orders and other legal remedies. They may also accompany women through the court system, giving support at court hearings, as well as representation at administrative hearings for public benefits or public housing.

Some battered women programs work closely with legal services programs by utilizing their staff—lawyers and paralegals—and their resources. Others encourage the woman to represent themselves (appear "in pro per" or "pro se"), or with one of their lay advocates. The choice depends in part upon whether the state's law of filing for a protection order

has been simplified so that a woman can do it herself without an attorney.

In this section, we'll review the legal remedies available to battered women, describe a few well-established programs, and note some strategies. We'll then close with a list of coalitions and programs around the country.

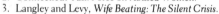

1. Betsy Warrior, *Wifebeating*.
2. Connecticut Task Force on Abused Women.
3. Langley and Levy, *Wife Beating: The Silent Crisis*.

1838

There are a few national resource centers which serve as back-up on issues of domestic violence. One is the National Center for Women and Family Law which was recently set up as a support center by the Legal Services Corporation. The Center has a library of documents which is very useful for efforts in litigation and legislation. They also try to keep tabs on what is occurring across the country on issues of domestic violence.

> 799 Broadway, Room 402
> New York, NY 10003
> (212) 674-8200

The second is the Center for Women Policy Studies which has a Family Violence Resource Center. The Resource Center provides information and direct assistance to programs and individuals in areas including battered women, child sexual abuse, social and health services, and the criminal justice process. Its library holds extensive materials on family violence and is open to the public. They will answer questions by phone, mail, or in person.

The Center for Women Policy Studies also publishes a montly newsletter—"Response." It is an excellent review of current and emerging domestic violence issues.

> 2000 P Street, N.W., Suite 508
> Washington, D.C. 20036
> (202) 872-1770

The following discussion on the legal remedies available to women was prepared by the Center for Women Policy Studies.

Legal Help for Battered Women
by Lisa G. Lerman

During the last few years, almost every state has made new legal remedies available to abused women. State laws have been passed which strengthen both civil protection and criminal penalties. Advocates for battered women are working with police, prosecutors, legal services lawyers, judges, and others to encourage active enforcement of the laws.

Availability of these tools varies from state to state. The following decription of legal rememdies for battered women does not explain which remedies are available in each state. Instead it outlines the most effective of the recent developments in the laws affecting battered women, and describes some problems encountered in implementing the new laws.

CIVIL REMEDIES
Several forms of civil relief are available to battered women. These include:
- Protection Order
- Temporary Restraining Order
- Peace Bond
- Divorce or Separation
- Child Custody and Visitation Rights
- Alimony and Child Support
- Money Damages for Personal Injury

Protection Order
What is a Protection Order?
A protection order (also called a restraining order) is an order from a civil court to an abuser to require him to change his conduct. It can last for a period of up to one year. Depending on the state law, the court may order the defendant:
- To refrain from abuse of any household member.
- To leave the victim alone.
- To move out of a residence shared with the victim even if the title or lease is in the abuser's name. The abuser may be required to make rent or mortgage payments even if he has been evicted.
- To provide alternate housing for the victim.
- To pay for the support of the victim and/or of minor children in her custody.
- To attend a counseling program aimed to stop violence and/or alcohol or drug abuse. Both the abuser and the victim may be ordered to partici-

pate in counseling.

- To pay the victim a sum of money for medical expenses, lost wages, moving expenses, property damage, court costs, or attorney's fees.

Also, temporary custody of minors may be awarded to the victim, and visitation rights of the abuser may be established.

Who Can Get a Protection Order?

While rules differ from state to state, many states will issue a protection order on behalf of anyone abused by a spouse, former spouse, family member, household member, or former household member. Some states will only issue a protection order to a woman married to her abuser; in others, protection orders are available only to married women who have filed for separation or divorce.

How Can a Victim of Abuse Get a Protection Order?

A protection order may be obtained by filing a petition in the court which has authority to issue it. It is useful but not necessary for a victim to be represented by a lawyer when she files a petition. In some cities there are clinics which assist victims in writing their petitions.

When a petition is filed, the court schedules a hearing, usually within two weeks of the date of filing. The abuser is notified of the hearing and asked to appear. The hearing is held before a judge or a magistrate; there is no jury. Both parties have an opportunity to testify as to why an order should or should not be issued.

Some form of protection order is available in nearly every state. To find out which court issues protection orders in a particular community, and where she can get assistance in filing a petition, a victim of abuse should call a local shelter, women's organization, legal services office, police department, or a clerk of a local court.

What Type of Abuse Must Be Shown to Get a Protection Order?

"Abuse" for which a protection order is available may include:

- An act causing physical injury, e.g., hitting, shoving, use of a weapon;
- An attempt to cause physical injury, e.g., raising a fist, pointing a gun;

- A threat to cause physical injury, e.g., saying "I'm going to beat you up;"
- Sexual abuse of a spouse or of her children.

How Are Protection Orders Enforced?

Violation of a protection order is often treated as contempt of court,[1] punishable by a jail sentence (up to six months), a fine (up to $500), or both, or a term of probation. An abuser released on probation may be required to attend counseling sessions, to avoid contact with the victim, to refrain from abuse, etc. The abuser must report to a probation officer, who is responsible for making sure that the abuser does what the order says.

Many states allow a police officer to make an arrest without first obtaining a warrant if he believes that a protection order has been violated. In some places, warrantless arrest is allowed even if the officer did not witness the abuse and even if there are no visible injuries.

Temporary Order of Protection

A temporary order of protection (also called a temporary restraining order) is an emergency protection order, which may be issued within a few hours or a few days of the time it is requested. In most states, the temporary order is available to the same categories of victims as a regular protection order; in most places the same relief is available under temporary order, and the procedure for enforcement is the same. A temporary order is different from a protection order in the way it is obtained, the period of time it stays in effect, and the conduct or circumstances which must be proven to get one.

A temporary order:

- May be issued *ex parte* (after a hearing at which the victim is present but not the abuser). This means the victim can obtain the order the same day that she files the petition.
- May be available at night or on weekends from a magistrate's court, when the civil or family court is closed.
- Remains in effect until a full hearing can be held (usually within two weeks) or until the regular courts re-open the next weekday morning.
- May be issued if "immediate and present danger of abuse" is shown. This usually includes visible injury or threat of serious physical injury.

Peace Bond

A peace bond is an order to an abuser to refrain from abuse and to deposit a sum of money with the court which is not refunded to the abuser if the order is violated. (This procedure is similar to posting bail). In some states the peace bond is simply a warning to the abuser, and posting of bond is not required. This remedy has traditionally been used by the courts in lieu of measures with more "teeth."

Peace bonds are often ineffective, since the victim cannot get the abuser arrested when an order is violated. She must go back to court and request a hearing to determine whether the order has been violated. If she wins, the abuser will lose the money he deposited.

Divorce and Separation

Many beaten women terminate their relationships with abusive husbands by filing for separation or divorce. While filing for divorce may not stop the violence, it can be an an important step for a woman seeking to get away from an abusive relationship. Some abusers, however, become more violent when victims separate from them. It may be important for a victim to get a protection order when she starts divorce or separation proceedings. In some states divorce is granted if one party is shown to be at fault, and in those states "cruelty" is one ground for divorce.

When a separation or divorce is granted, the court may grant custody of children to one parent and may decide a property settlement. One party may be ordered to provide financial support to his or her spouse and children, and property owned by either party may be awarded to the other or divided.

Personal Injury (Tort)

In some states a victim of domestic abuse may sue her mate to obtain a court order that he must pay for any injury to her or her property. This type of lawsuit is like a criminal charge of assault and battery, false imprisonment, etc., except that it is brought by the victim and not by the state. This remedy has not yet been widely used, although battered women have won awards of money damages in at least a few cases.

A tort suit may be useful where the abuser has money or property and/or where there are large hospital bills, attorney's fees, property damage, or lost wages. Damages may also be awarded for pain and suffering. Traditionally, husbands and wives were not allowed to sue each other, but the rule of interspousal immunity has been abolished in the majority of the states for intentional injuries. The disadvantages of this type of lawsuit are that it may take years to resolve, and attorney's fees can be very high. Some lawyers will accept a contingency fee in tort cases. This means that if the lawsuit is successful, the lawyer will be paid a percentage (usually one third) of the money damages awarded. If the claim fails, the lawyer does not get paid.

CRIMINAL PROSECUTION

Spouse abuse is a crime. Every state has laws prohibiting physical assault; these may be enforced against abusers where there has been any physical violence or any threat of physical violence. Some states have enacted laws that make spouse abuse a separate criminal offense.

In the past, spouse abuse was treated as a family

1870

matter, and criminal law was rarely enforced against wife-beaters. Recently, however, several prosecutors' offices have initiated programs to increase prosecution of domestic abuse.

What Action May Be Prosecuted Under Criminal Law?

Conduct which may violate state criminal law, which may be the basis of a criminal complaint includes:

- Hitting, slapping, shoving, or other physical assault;
- Sexual assault, rape, or attempted rape;
- Harassment or threat of physical assault;
- Any act causing the death of another;
- Destruction of private property belonging to another;
- Kidnapping or confining another against his or her will;
- Violation of the terms of a protection order.

How Can a Battered Woman Get the State to File Criminal Charges?

There are two ways in which a criminal action against an abuser may be started:

- When the police make an *arrest* after being called for assistance.
- When the victim goes to the prosecutor's office[2] or to an intake unit in criminal or family court to file a *private criminal complaint.*

Arrest

In many cases the police must obtain a warrant from a judge or magistrate before making an arrest. This means that the arrest cannot always be made when the police are called to a residence. The police must go to the courthouse or police station to request a warrant, and must sometimes wait a few hours to get the request processed.

Each state has different rules about when a warrant is required. Generally, warrantless arrest is permitted where there has been a serious assault and there are visible injuries (a felony), or where the officer witnessed the abuse (a misdemeanor). In some states, if the victim makes a statement that she has been abused, then warrantless arrest is permitted, even if she was not seriously injured. Many states allow warrantless arrest where the victim has a

protection order and the police officer thinks that the order has been violated.

After an arrest is made a criminal charge is filed. In some places charges are filed by the police; in other places the police send a report to the prosecutor's office, and the prosecutor files charges.

Private Criminal Complaint

A victim of domestic abuse may file a criminal complaint if the police were not called after the abuse occurred, or if they were called, but failed to appear or did not make an arrest. A complaint is a paper filed with the court which describes the abusive incident. After a complaint is filed, the prosecutor's office will conduct an investigation and decide whether charges should be filed. If charges are filed, the court will issue a warrant for the arrest of the abuser.

What Can a Prosecutor Do Besides Filing Criminal Charges?

In many cases it is inappropriate to file charges because the evidence is insufficient to make conviction likely or because the victim has no interest in prosecution. In these cases the prosecutor can take informal action to assist the victim in stopping the abuse. Below are samples of such informal action:

Information and Referrals: The prosecutor can advise the victim of her legal and other options. After determining which of these options the victim wishes to pursue, the prosecutor can refer her to another legal or social service agency.

Warning Letter: The prosecutor can send a letter to the abuser to notify him that a complaint has been made that he has abused a member of his family, that such conduct is against the law, and that further violence will be prosecuted.

Meeting With Abuser: The prosecutor may request that the abuser come to the prosecutor's office to discuss the alleged conduct. At the meeting he may be informed of the seriousness of the conduct charged and of the potential consequences of further abuse.

Office Hearing: The prosecutor may meet with both the victim and the abuser in the office to discuss the complaint and gather further evidence. Sometimes the purpose of this meeting is to make it easier for the parties to talk to each other about the violence.

What Can a Criminal Court Do After a Charge Has Been Filed?

The arrest of the abuser and the filing of the criminal charge begins the process of prosecution. The next step is to hold an arraignment or bail hearing, at which the abuser is required to submit a sum of money to the court to insure that he will reappear for his trial. Other conduct may be required as a condition of release from jail, such as participation in counseling, avoiding contact with the victim, or terminating the abuse. If the terms are violated, the abuser may be returned to custody until the charge is disposed of.

The filing of a criminal charge does not necessarily mean that there will be a trial. The charge may be disposed of in any of the following ways:

Pretrial Diversion, or Deferred Prosecution: Prosecution may be postponed after charges are filed, in cases where injuries are not severe and the abuser is a first offender. An order is issued in those cases requiring counseling, no contact with the victim, departure from a shared residence, and/or cessation of the abuse. The prosecutor is responsible for making sure that the abuser complies with the order. If the abuser does so, then the charges will be dropped. If he violates the order, prosecution will be resumed. Deferred prosecution programs have different names, such as adjournment in contemplation of dismissal (ACD) and accelerated rehabilitative disposition (ARD).

Plea Bargaining: In most criminal cases the prosecutor, the defense attorney, and the defendant (the person charged with a crime) make a deal in which the defendant agrees to plead guilty to charges and the prosecutor agrees to request a less severe penalty than would be imposed if the defendant were convicted by a court. The process of making deals to avoid trial is called plea bargaining.

Plea bargaining of spouse abuse cases usually results in a sentence of a period of probation. During probation the abuser may be required to attend counseling, to move out of a shared residence, to stay away from the victim, and/or to refrain from abuse. A probation officer is supposed to stay in touch with the abuser and make sure that he does not violate the probation order. If the abuser violated the terms of probation, e.g., by beating his wife again, he may be put in jail without a trial on the charges. By pleading guilty, he has agreed to his own conviction.

Trial: If the abuser pleads innocent, he will be tried on the offenses charged. If convicted, he may be jailed, fined, or placed on probation. Jail sentences are rarely imposed in domestic assault cases, and are almost never longer than one year. Where a victim of abuse is required to testify at a trial, she may be able to get help from either the prosecutor's office or from another agency. She may need someone to go to hearings with her, or to explain the court system to her. She may need child care while she goes to court. She may need assistance in getting housing, public benefits, a divorce, or a protection order. If no one in the prosecutor's office can help, then they or a local shelter or women's group can tell her where to go for help.

CHOOSING A REMEDY

In many states, a battered woman can use any of the remedies described, or she may want to use more than one. For example, a protection order is often useful to a woman who files criminal charges against her husband. In deciding what action to take it is important to find out what the victim wants from the court. Most victims want to end the violence. Some may also want to punish the abuser, to get help for him, to end the relationship, or all of these. The remedy chosen must depend on which of the remedies available in the state best corresponds to the desires of the victim.

Information about the legal remedies available to battered women may be obtained from a local shelter or hotline, from a legal services office or the bar association, or from any victim/witness assistance program or women's organization. These will be listed in the yellow pages under attorneys, city government, women, human services, etc.

Legal action is only one of many options available to battered women. Other action in addition to or instead of getting help from the courts may be more successful. A victim of abuse may need immediate medical care. She may elect to spend time in a shelter or to stay with relatives or friends. She may eventually move to a new residence or a new city.

She may wish to get help from a minister or a counselor in a mental health or family service agency. In the process of recovering from an abusive situation, stopping the abuse and recovering from the trauma are only the first step. A victim may need career counseling or job training. She may need to apply for AFDC or food stamps. Combined with other nonlegal assistance, the remedies provided by the courts may give a victim of abuse the strength re-

quired to change or terminate a violent relationship.

---

1. Contempt of court is the term used to describe any violation of a court order.
2. The prosecutor will be listed in the phone book in a section listing government offices. It may be called the Office of the District Attorney, City Attorney, City Solicitor, Attorney General or United States Attorney.

1910

Massachusetts Coalition of Battered Women Service Groups

★ ══ ★

The Massachusetts Coalition, which includes both shelter and service providers, is one of the most ambitious programs for battered women in the country. Shelters house a battered woman up to several months, and provide counseling in legal, medical, welfare, housing, and job skills. Lay advocates on the staff of service providers assist a woman in filing for a protection order or for any other legal remedy. Emphasis is on self-help rather than reliance on an attorney.

Recently, the coalition published an easy-to-follow booklet, *Women's Guide to the Abuse Prevention Act,* which explains how the new act has simplified the paperwork and court procedures. Under the new law, any woman can file for temporary restraining order without an attorney and with-

out paying filing fees (though the constable can charge $20 for serving the papers on the abuser). Other available civil and criminal options in Massachusetts are also described step-by-step. Sample forms (filled out), an appendix of state support groups, and a list of definitions are included. The manual is available from the Coalition.

The Coalition also runs an Educational/Training Project funded by the Community Services Administration. It provides skill-sharing and training for member groups and others who offer direct services for women in crisis. The training covers legal, media, counseling and advocacy skills.

120 Boylston Street
Boston, MA 02116
(617) 426-8492

Pennsylvania Coalition Against Domestic Violence

If you're interested in coordinating a state-wide coalition or becoming a service provider or shelter, you will find the people at the Pennsylvania Coalition to be helpful contacts. They are a well-organized, relatively well-financed organization composed of 35 groups and hotlines and 16 domestic shelters. In 1978, 25,000 women and 14,000 children were served by the Coalition.

The central office in Harrisburg works to educate the public to the problems of battered women, trains police to be sensitive to these issues, informs state trial courts on the rights of women, provides technical asistance to attorneys and interested groups, and lobbies the state legislature for strong protective legislation. PCADV also distributes a manual for lobbyists—*State Domestic Violence Laws and How to Pass Them*, by Julie E. Hamos. Thanks in large part to the Coalition's efforts, the Pennsylvania Protection from Abuse Act is a model piece of legislation.

The Coalition works closely with legal services offices and utilizes paralegals. Funding for this network of providers and shelters comes from the National Law Enforcement Agency, the Levinson Foundation, Pennsylvania Commission on Crime and Delinquency, and the Community Services Administration.

One of the Coalition's publications describes its history. We've decided to reprint it here to give you an idea of the breadth of the organization. Maybe it will be of assistance to people wishing to develop a program in their state or locale.

2405 N. Front Street
Harrisburg, PA 17110
(717) 233-6030
1-800-692-7445

History of the Coalition

In the Commonwealth of Pennsylvania during early 1976, there were only six Domestic Violence Programs in operation with several other groups in various stages of development. Women working in the area of domestic violence met while lobbying and testifying for the Protection from Abuse Act.

One of these women, Jean Hurd, the Director of the Lancaster Shelter, sent out invitations to the women she had met and the groups she had heard about to attend a meeting in October, 1976, for the purpose of discussing where to go with the issue of domestic violence. Approximately 25 women from across the state attended that meeting and discovered that they were not alone in their fight against domestic violence. The meeting brought a commitment from those women to continue to meet for support, sharing, and developing strategies for obtaining funding.

The first official meeting of the Coalition was held one month later and brought together 50 women statewide representing a variety of grass roots groups. Each organization had their own philosophies, values, and methods for dealing with the problem, yet all believed that fighting domestic violence and providing quality services to victims must be their priorities.

During that meeting, these women wrote and agreed upon the purpose of the Coalition:

Purpose

1. To eliminate domestic abuse of women and their dependent children in the Commonwealth of Pennsylvania.

2. To provide services to the victims of domestic violence; services to be provided by member organizations shall include crisis telephone counseling, and/or temporary shelter for the victim and her dependent children, and/or peer and professional

counseling, and/or assistance in obtaining community resources, and/or help in acquiring employment skills, and/or work referral.

3. To expose the roots of domestic violence in the institutionalized sub-servience of women in this culture.

4. To provide quality services statewide and to expand service such that every victim of domestic violence in the Commonwealth may obtain immediate, comprehensive service locally.

5. To do any and all lawful activities which may be necessary, useful, or desireable, for the furtherance, accomplishment, fostering, or attainment of the foregoing purposes, either directly or indirectly, and either alone or in conjunction or cooperation with others, whether such others may be persons or organizations of any kind or nature, such as corporations, firms, associations, trusts, institutions, foundations, or governmental bureaus, departments, or agencies.

They also wrote and agreed upon the goals of the Coalition:

Goals

1. To coordinate the sharing of skills, information, and resources among members; and

2. To obtain information and conduct research, studies, and analyses of domestic violence in the Commonwealth of Pennsylvania, to document the extent and character of the problem of domestic violence in the Commonwealth, and the larger culture, as well as prepare and publish reports as to any and all matters that may be of use in eliminating domestic violence in the Commonwealth; and

3. To conduct educational and other efforts to inform the residents of the Commonwealth about the extent and character of domestic violence in this Commonwealth and the larger culture; and

4. To expand membership so that all geographical areas of the Commonwealth are represented in the Corporation; and

5. To conduct educational and other efforts to inform the victims of domestic violence of their legal rights and remedies; and

6. To conduct educational and other efforts to encourage the victims of domestic violence to utilize the service provided by member organizations; and

7. To conduct educational and other efforts to inform legislators, police, courts, social service organizations and mental health agencies of the multiple needs of women who are victims of domestic violence; and

8. To engage in activities to develop and expand resources and service where few or none presently exist; and

9. To engage in any and all other activities which will directly or indirectly contribute to the elimination of domestic violence and in the interim to provide service for victims thereof.

They developed the eligibility for membership which supported "grass roots" participation.

Membership

1. There shall be only one class of members of this Corporation. And there shall be no limitation on the maximum number of members the Corporation may have at any one time. Membership is available only to organizations.

2. Eligibility. In order to be eligible for membership in the Corporation, an organization must:

a. Be autonomous and self-governing.

b. Be governed by women.

c. Be committed to

1) Providing services to the victims of domestic violence.

2) Exposing the roots of violence in the institutionalized sub-servience of women in this culture; and

3) Providing quality service statewide through cooperative non-competitive means.

d. Operate its principal place of business in the Commonwealth of Pennsylvania.

During the early years, the Coalition offered its members support, information, and assistance in dealing with all areas of starting and operating programs for victims.

Coalition members have helped each other write proposals and applications for funding. They have given each other ideas on where to obtain funding and how to approach sources.

Members have assisted and supported each other in dealing with program development and conflict resolution.

Members have come together to learn new skills in order to provide better service to their clients.

Members have given each other emotional support in their fight against domestic violence.

While struggling to finance and operate their own programs, members also lobbied on both the State and Federal level for funding and new legislation.

All of this was done with only contributions from the members and memberships.

Finally, in March, 1978, the Coalition obtained a grant from the Levinson Foundation for the purpose of hiring an Executive Director: Susan Bienemann. Sue worked for funding for an office and staff. The Coalition office opened in Harrisburg in September, 1978; and by the end of November, all staff were hired.

The Coalition continues to work toward their goals and support their members.

1923

La Casa de Las Madres

The Legal Committee of La Casa de las Madres in San Francisco, in conjunction with the San Francisco Commission on the Status of Women, prepared a manual on the *Legal Rights of Battered Women*. This handbook is chock-full of basic legal and practical information. The first part explains how to deal with the justice system—the police, district attorney, and the court. The second part covers divorce, spearation, child custody, and money problems. Tactics on coping with harassment from men with whom one is not having a relationship (ex-husbands, ex-boyfriends, casual acquaintances) are also included.

Unfortunately, parts of the manual are outdated. But the information and strategy section on dealing with the police are still exceptionally useful, and would apply to almost any situation around the country. In addition to the manual, La Casa has also developed a paralegal advocate program. A lay advocate is trained to assist women in obtaining restraining orders and other legal remedies as well as accompanying the woman to any court or administrative hearing (such as welfare or immigration).

P.O. Box 15147
San Francisco, CA 94115
(415) 585-4100 (business)
(415) 585-2844 (crisis)

La Casa has given us permission to reprint the following material from their manual:

In general, we've found it's best to take a friend with you when you deal with any part of the legal system. Especially when you're upset, someone else with you can remember to ask questions and can help present your story.

One thing our experience has shown us is that our society doesn't really think it's wrong for men to abuse, harass, intimidate or control women, and our laws and legal system really show it. If you've tried to use the legal system to protect yourself, you've already experienced the disappointment, discouragement and even hostility that's there on every level. Until we live in a society that really respects women and all people we can expect little help or support from our institutions, including the legal system; but we're convinced we must continue to demand it.

(We want to say clearly that we don't think men are the enemy. Men are abused and degraded in this society too—especially poor, old and non-white men.)

We use the legal system because it's all we have right now. We stop short of doing things we think are totally wrong—like deporting men or committing them to mental hospitals. In the name of helping battered women, we don't want to become partners with groups trying to build more prisons, restore the death penalty or stir up racist hysteria. We try to work the legal system to protect battered women and change society's ideas about violence against women; but we also try and stay clear about what the bigger, more long term, picture is. We want women to be safer now, AND we want a better society for everybody in the future.

THE CRIMINAL JUSTICE SYSTEM

If your husband or boyfriend is beating, threatening or harassing you, he is committing a crime. You have the right to call the police to protect you or to arrest him. The following sections will describe how to use the police.

The Police

There are no magic tricks to getting the police to come when you need them or getting them to help you once they arrive; but it may be helpful if we outline generally what the police can do if you're in immediate danger, if you're being beaten or harassed by a man you live with, or if you're being hurt by someone you don't live with.

Calling the Police

Small towns have just one police station which people from all parts of the town go to and call when they need help. Big cities have a main police station (with offices for investigators, detectives, police complaints, jail) and smaller neighborhood stations

for day to day business and problems. If you live in a city with neighborhood or district stations that is where you should call or go to for help.

If you're in immediate danger when you call the police, tell them that you are in danger and need their help immediately. If the man is drunk or on drugs, if he has a gun, knife or club, if he has hurt you before, or if you're afraid for yourself or your children, let the police know about it on the phone. Try to explain your situation clearly and quickly. It won't help to exaggerate or misstate what is happening; this will make the police suspicious of everything else you say and could make them very uncooperative.

If the police don't come in a few minutes, call them again or call the shelter in your area—they can often help get a police response by calling and saying how urgent the situation is.

When the Police Arrive

Try to talk to the officers alone. They will often separate you and the man and talk to each of you. The police don't need to know about your relationship. They DO need to know about your injuries and what has happened to you.

If you want to leave the house, the police can stay while you get together a few things for yourself and your children. If the man is the father of your children, the police don't have to let you take the children with you if the man objects; but sometimes they will. The police may drive you to a nearby hospital or police station or other safe place. Check with them before you leave to see if they'll give you a ride; otherwise, use the time they're there to call a friend or a cab. If you have time, get your important papers together—these might include birth certificates for your children, medi-cal cards, food stamp ID cards, check book, insurance policies, charge cards, deeds, social security cards, etc.

Arrest and Citizen's Arrest

If you want your attacker arrested, this can happen in several ways. If the police see the man hurting you they can arrest him. If you are hurt very badly (bleeding, broken bones), they can arrest him even though they didn't see him injure you if it looks like he did it, if you say he did it or if he admits he did it.

If the police don't see the man hurt you and you

are not visibly badly injured, they can't arrest him on their own; you must ask for a citizen's arrest. To make a citizen's arrest you must tell the police:

1. That a crime has been comitted. (Do this by describing what happened.)
2. Who your attacker was.
3. That you want to make a citizen's arrest and that you are willing to sign a citizen's arrest card.

You can make a citizen's arrest for either a felony or a misdemeanor.[1] Also, remember that besides assault and battery, the man can be arrested for disturbing the peace or trespassing if he doesn't live with you.

If your attacker has left the house before the police arrive, you cannot make a citizen's arrest, but you should make sure that a police report is made and file a complaint the next day. Go to the police and ask where to go to file a complaint. Filing a complaint is the first step in getting an arrest warrant issued and having the man picked up by the police and either held or ordered to come to court.

Citation

If the police do not want to arrest your attacker, there is a third procedure in addition to police arrest and citizen's arrest called a "citation". A citation is like a traffic ticket—the police fill out a form that says your attacker must appear in court on a certain date. A citation is much less serious than an arrest because your attacker doesn't have to be taken away from the house in order for the police to give him a citation; the police can decide, however, to take the man away and give him a citation at the police station.

After Arrest

You must be aware that once your attacker has been arrested and taken to the police station, it is likely that he will be out again in a short period of time. If he has money for bail, he will be released on bail within a few hours; if he has no money for bail, but has friends and relatives who will vouch for him, he may be released without having to post any bail on his "own recognizance" (O.R.). To be released on O.R., he must promise to appear in court on a certain date for a formal hearing. Of course the more serious your injuries and the more serious the charges against him, the less likely it is that he will

be released soon. It is important to understand that it is possible, and even likely, that your attacker will return to your home even after he has been arrested. So act fast.

If the Police Won't Help

Although there are lots of things the police CAN do to help you, they often don't do anything. They consider arrest the most serious step that can be taken and are often unwilling to do it. Particularly in situations involving domestic violence, the police are often afraid to interfere (police are injured and killed on this type of call more than any other); the police may side with the man or try to talk to him for a few minutes and then leave. If you are sure you want the man arrested, you have the right to insist that he be arrested. If the police won't help you, take down their names and badge numbers—they must give them to you. You can call the police station while the officers are still at your home and complain that they won't help you. You can also call the shelter in your area; they can sometimes talk to the police and convince them to take some action. If the police still won't do anything, use the minutes they are there to safely leave the house. If they don't arrest the man now, you may still be able to get him arrested and to press charges aainst him later.

The Police Report

The police report of this incident is your proof that it happened. When dealing with anyone from the DA to welfare workers, if you don't have a police report, an incident might as well have never happened. Even if you don't want to press charges or have the man arrested now, you may want to do something at a later time and you will need a police report to do anything. Remember that criminal and civil suits depend on police reports.

Just because the police come to your home or take your attacker out for a walk around the block is no guarantee that they have written a report about what happened. They don't have to write up every call that they take. You can only be sure a report is written if you see it or if the man is arrested. If the police don't write out the report at your house, arrange to go to the police station with them or the next day to make sure it gets done. Ask for the number of the police report; then you can ask for it by number; also you know they're really going to make a report if they give it a number.

If you are attacked and don't call the police, you can still make a report later. Go to the station nearest your home. Try and go within 24 hours of the incident. This deadline is set up by the police because they feel that if you wait any longer than a day to report the attack that you're probably not serious about doing anything about it. Also, it is difficult for the police to investigate an old crime.

Make sure the report is complete; if you have injuries, if the house is busted up, if the man was drunk or had a weapon, if any witnesses saw or heard him breaking in or hurting you—all of this information needs to be in the report. You can also

ask the police to take pictures of your injuries or the damage to the house, or you can take pictures yourself.

Once the police report is finished, you can get a copy of it. (You have to pay for it—a few dollars.) Especially if you are leaving the area, you should get a copy of each police report—you can use them to back up your story when you need to tell people in other places what happened to you.

---

1. A felony is a serious crime punishable by imprisonment in a state prison; a misdemeanor is less serious and is punishable by a fine or county jail term of less than one year.

1946

Obtaining a protection order need not be complicated. Any abuse prevention law should provide an easy mechanism for women to do it without an attorney. Ohio is one state which provides for a

one-page petition that is simple to fill out. We've included a copy here in the hope that advocacy groups in states with more complex requirements will act to modify them.

IN THE COURT OF COMMON PLEAS, LUCAS COUNTY, OHIO
DIVISION OF DOMESTIC RELATIONS

_____
          Petitioner   :   DV NO. _____

-vs-   :   P E T I T I O N

_____   :
          Respondent   :

                    : : : :

    Now comes the petitioner, being first duly sworn, and states that the following facts herein set forth are true:

That the respondent attempted to cause or recklessly caused bodily injury to
_____ ;

That the respondent placed petitioner (_____) by the threat of force in fear of imminent physical harm;

That the respondent committed an act with respect to child(ren) _____
_____ That would result in child(ren) being abused pursuant to R.C.2151.031;
*   *   *   *   *   *   *   *   *   *   *   *
That the incident causing the filing of this petition occurred on ____/____/____..
That the respondent(describe what happened)_____
_____
_____
_____
_____ .

That the respondent and petitioner(_____) do – did reside together
at _____ .
   Number   Street   City or Township   State   Zip Code

That they last resided together at the above address on ____/____/____ ;

That the respondent and petitioner(_____) are (spouses-living together
as spouses – other_____ .

    THAT THE PETITIONER(_____) IS IN IMMEDIATE AND PRESENT DANGER
OF DOMESTIC VIOLENCE FROM THE RESPONDENT, AND THAT THE RELIEF REQUESTED IS NECESSARY
TO PROTECT HIM FROM IRREPARABLE HARM.

WHEREFORE, petitioner respectfully requests the Court for protective relief AND for an
immediate hearing of his/her petition.

  ☐ Enjoin the respondent to refrain from abusing, beating or assaulting petitioner
(_____);

  ☐ Grant exclusive possession of the residence to petitioner by evicting respondent;

  ☐ Restore possession of the residence to petitioner (_____);

  ☐ Award custody of minor child(ren) to petitioner, award visitation and companion-
ship of said child(ren) to respondent;
NAME(S)_____ AGE_____ _____ _____
_____ AGE_____ _____ _____
_____ AGE_____ _____ _____

  ☐ Require respondent to maintain support because respondent has a duty to support,
or because respondent customarily provides support, or because respondent contributes to support of petitioner (_____); AFFIDAVIT OF SUPPORT MUST
BE ATTACHED or prepared prior to full hearing;

  ☐ Require respondent to seek counselling;

  ☐ Enjoin respondent from entering the residence-school-business-or place or employment of petitioner(_____);
ALL PURSUANT TO OHIO REVISED CODE SECTION 3113.31.

                                 _____
                                 PETITIONER
Sworn to before me and signed in my presence this ____ day of _____ 19___ .
                                 CLERK OF COURTS

The following list of state coalitions and/or contacts on domestic violence is provided by the National Coalition Against Domestic Violence, P.O. Box 32423, Washington, D.C. 20007. Not all the organizations listed here are members of NCADV.

State Coalitions/Contacts Working Against Domestic Violence

Region I

CT: CT Task Force on Abused Women
148 Orange Street
New Haven, CT 06510
203-562-1816

MA: MA Coalition of Battered Women Service Groups
120 Boylston
Boston, MA 02116

NH: NH Social Welfare Council
20 S. Main Street
Concord, NH 03301

RI: RI Council on Domestic Violence
185 Meeting Street, #205
Providence, RI 02912

VT: VT Coalition on Family Violence
Box 21
Eden Mills, VT 05653

Region II

NJ: NJ Coalition for Battered Women
P.O. Box 1127
Elizabeth, NJ 07207

NY: Volunteers Against Violence Technical Assistance Project
15 Rutherford Place
New York, NY 10003

Region III

MD: The House of Ruth
P.O. Box 7276
Baltimore, MD 21218
301-889-6679

PA: PA Coalition Against Domestic Violence
2405 N. Front Street
Harrisburg, PA 17110

Region IV

FL: Spouse Abuse, Inc.
1102 W. Carlton Ct.
Leesburg, FL 32748

GA: President's Council on Domestic Violence
136 Grady Avenue, Apt. D-2
Athens, GA 30601

NC: Task Force on Battered Women
Council on the Status of Women
526 N. Wilmington Street
Raleigh, NC 27604

TN: YWCA Domestic Violence Program
1608 Woodmont Blvd.
Nashville, TN 37215

Region V

IL: IL Coalition Against Domestic Violence
842 S. Second Street, #2
Springfield, IL 62704
217-789-2830

IN: IN Coalition on Domestic Violence/Wife Abuse
3314 Tara Lane
Indianapolis, IN 46224
317-293-9574

MI: MI Coalition Against Domestic Violence
YWCA, 211 S. Rose Street
Kalamazoo, MI 49007

MN: Domestic Abuse Project
2445 Park Avenue South
Minneapolis, MN

OH: Action for Battered Women in Ohio
P.O. Box 15673
Columbus, OH 43215

WI: Task Force on Battered Women
1228 W. Mitchell St.
Milwaukee, WI 53204

Region VI

NM: Albuquerque Shelter for Victims of Domestic Violence
P.O. Box 6472
Albuquerque, NM 87197

TX: Houston Area Women's Center
P.O. Box 20186
Room E401
Houston, TX 77025

AR: Advocates for Battered Women
P.O. Box 1954
Little Rock, AR 72203

LA: Baton Rouge Battered Women's Program
P.O. Box 2133
Baton Rouge, LA 70821

OK: OK Coalition on Domestic Violence
P.O. Box 474
Norman, OK 73070

Region VII

IA: Dept. Social Services
Domestic Violence Project
Hoover State Office Building
Des Moines, IA 50319

NE: NE Task Force on Domestic Violence
930 Manchester Drive
Lincoln, NE 68530

KS: KS Association of Domestic Violence
Programs
Box 1883
Topeka, KS 66601

MO: Adult Abuse Remedies Coalition
607 N. Grand
St. Louis, MO 63103

Region VIII

CO: Women in Crisis
5250 Marshall Street
Arvada, CO 80003

MT: MT State Task Force on Domestic Violence
3251 4th Avenue South
Great Falls, MT 59405

SD: SD Coalition Against Domestic Violence
Box 500
Eagle Butte, SD 57625

ND: Abused Women's Resource Closet
219 N. 7th St.
Bismarck, ND 58501

UT: Coalition for Aid to Battered Women
322 E. 3rd Street
Salt Lake City, UT 84111

WY: Self-Help Center
1515 Burlington
Casper, WY 82601

Region IX

AZ: Tucson Center for Women and Children
419 S. Stone Avenue
Tucson, AZ 86701

CA: Haven House
P.O. Box 2051
Fairfield, CA 94533

Western States Shelter Network
870 Market Street, Suite 1161
San Francisco, CA 94102

Region X

AK: AWARE, Inc.
P.O. Box 809
Juneau, AK 99802

ID: ID Network to Stop Violence Against
Women
P.O. Box 624
Rupert, ID 83350

OR: OR Coalition Against Domestic Violence
3214 S.E. Holgate
Portland, OR 97202

WA: Domestic Violence Research Bank
Room 327, Cleveland Hall
Washington State University
Pullman, WA 99164

With thanks to:
Chris Butler
Stover Clark
Debbie Clifford
Lisa Lerman
Nancy Lorenz
Dianne Pellicori
Rhonda Pistro
Myrna Poblete

Legal Assistance for Artists

Burt Reynolds may get five million dollars to make a picture, but the average annual income for an actor is only $7,500, for an actress around $4,500. And for many struggling dramatists, even that is pretty good. Other artists do little better, and many do worse.

When an artist finally does get a break—a writer sells a story, a painter finds a gallery to show his/her work, a potter sells sets of bowls to a large shop—how does he or she determine which arrangements are most beneficial? Should the artist assume that the buyer is trustworthy and knowledgeable? Will the artist be getting full copyright protection and the standard trade rights to income? Who explains the laws to the artist? If the artist does find an attorney to help, how can he or she be certain that the attorney is really familiar with the area?

In major metropolitan areas, groups have been established to provide legal (and often accounting and tax) assistance to all kinds of artists—musicians, painters, photographers, printmakers, craftworkers, filmmakers, dancers, and composers, to name a few. Their legal concerns would likely include copy-right, contracts, non-profit corporations, and their rights regarding their work/living spaces (lofts).

Few of the program staff members themselves advise artists—whether over the phone or in person. Instead, they act as a clearinghouse for referrals to lawyers who know the field. A couple of the programs provide free legal counsel; the majority refer the artist and then leave the attorney and client to work out their own fee arrangements. Several also hold workshops for artists and lawyers.

The best sourcebook that we found in the area is *Law and the Arts*, published by the Chicago Lawyers for the Creative Arts and edited by Tem Horwitz. (We have included an excerpt, "Writers and the Law," which appears in the first part of our book.) The Chicago book also includes legal information pertaining to the performing, film, video, and visual arts, as well as real estate, financial management, and non-profit corporations.

The following material describes several arts/law programs. We'll conclude with a list of programs around the country.

276

Lawyers for the Creative Arts

★ ━━━ ★

This Chicago program is one of the best. Lawyers for the Creative Arts (LCA) has assisted over 5,000 artists and groups since it began in 1972. It is one of the few programs to provide free legal assistance by volunteer attorneys.

LCA sponsors educational seminars for both artists and lawyers; organizes a speaker's program for colleges and art schools to alert students of potential problems; provides accounting services and business and financial counseling (including taxes, real estate, fund-raising, management consulting, and labor negotiation) to artists and art groups; and maintains a library of model contracts, books and pamphlets. They also act as consultants to similar programs around the country, and have assisted in establishing at least a dozen such art/law groups. In addition to the resource book, *Law and the Arts* (noted above), LCA publishes pamphlets and information sheets.

Although the Illinois Arts Council has been its principal source of funding, Lawyers for the Creative Arts is now trying to increase its share of contributions from corporations, foundations, individuals, and volunteer attorneys.

    111 N. Wabash
    Chicago, IL 60602
    (312) 263-6989

The following is reprinted, with permission, from an information sheet published by LCA:

Lawyers for the Creative Arts

The need for a program of legal, business, and accounting assistance to artists and art groups has resulted from several relatively recent developments. Most important, there has been a significant increase in public interest in the arts. This increased interest has created not only greater business opportunities for artists but also a need for more business sophistication and information relating to the protection of the artists' rights. While need for this basic information has always been present, neither institutions training artists nor the legal community have made it available as part of any organized curricula

or program of assistance. The result has been confusion, inconsistency, anxiety, and hit-or-miss type of career progression for emerging artists who do not understand the nuances of the copyright and tax laws and the meaning of the contracts into which they are entering.

While there is growing government support for artists, most of these governmental organizations have specific requirements for receiving assistance. The Illinois Arts Council, for instance, only provides substantial assistance for not-for-profit organizations. The Chicago Alliance for the Performing Arts which initiated a voucher program to assist performing arts groups in 1976, requires that members attain IRS Section 501(c)(3) tax-exempt status before they can participate. Most corporate and private foundations also require tax-exempt status before grants will be given, and private donors usually condition their gift on the ability to claim a charitable contribution. Emerging groups, therefore, who find that outside support is essential but do not have the resources to pay for the necessary legal assistance to incorporate and gain tax exemption, have been able to rely on the LCA. Thereafter groups and individuals are assisted with their tax, contractual, zoning and corporate problems.

Lawyers for the Creative Arts was organized in 1972 because the needs outlined above were not being met elsewhere.

The Programs of Lawyers for the Creative Arts
A. Legal Services

To date LCA has aided over 5,000 artists and arts goups. The dollar amount of services contributed by our volunteers is over $1 million. The range of artists we have assisted is broad and includes theatre, dance and other performing arts groups, symphony orchestras, commercial artists, poets and poetry groups, writers, craft groups, acting schools and workshops, art galleries, painters, sculptors, musicians, photographers, cartoonists, prison and ex-prison artists, mural painters, an Indian art and artifacts museum, puppeteers, radio-theatre groups, composers, women's art groups, children's art groups, actors, film script writers, producers, and others. The type of assistance is limited to art-related problems and includes incorporating and attaining tax-exempt status for groups, obtaining monies due, helping repossess art works or portfolios on loan or exhibit, preventing unfair use of copyrighted material, and advising on tax, contracts, housing and lease problems, insurance, management, art works in estates, prison artists' legal problems, form preparation, and other legal problems. Some examples of our work are these:

An artist's work was photographed and unauthorized plates were made from which prints were produced and sold. LCA obtained the plates and recovered damages for the artist for copyright infringement.

A gallery improperly holding the work of an artist and refusing to account for sales was forced to return the work at its expense.

A performer, whose oral contract to perform at a local club was terminated by the club's owner, was able to collect the full amount owing to him through LCA representation.

A beginning filmmaker with no money was able to proceed with production based upon a deferred income joint venture between himself and the technical and performing crews which was drawn up by LCA.

A young photographer, working on a book, obtained advice on copyright, publishing, consent agreements and tax planning.

A not-for-profit music center unable to understand the maze of municipal codes and licensing requirements obtained property authorization to operate through LCA representation.

At present LCA has over 160 volunteer attorneys with expertise in virtually every area of the law.

Volunteer Lawyers for the Arts

Since 1969, this New York program has provided free legal services by volunteer attorneys in art-related matters to artists with a yearly family income under $7,500. People with higher incomes can take advantage of a payment plan. Free legal assistance is also given to arts organizations with annual budgets below $100,000.

Usually, there is a two to three week wait for an appointment, but one-half hour consultations are available for people who walk in off the street. The only workshops conducted by Volunteer Lawyers for the Arts are about non-profit corporations. However, they run periodic conferences for art groups around the country where such topics as "Artist Housing and Loft Living" and "Emerging Issues in Art Law" are discussed.

In addition, they publish pamphlets on non-profit corporations, law for the visual artist, artist housing, and income taxes. The program also keeps a library of model forms and sample contracts.

Funding is from the National Endowment of the Arts, New York State Council on the Arts, individuals, and foundations.

36 West 44th St.
New York, New York 10036
(212) 575-1150
Hours: 9–5 Monday through Friday

(There are branch offices in other New York cities —Glen Falls, Buffalo, Albany, Huntington, Rochester, Oneonta, Poughkeepsie.)

Bay Area Lawyers for the Arts

Besides referring artists to lawyers and conducting workshops, Bay Area Lawyers for the Arts (BALA) issues a bi-monthly newsletter called, "The Working Arts." It features technical and general articles on art/law matters and includes a calendar of events. They also publish books on taxes, contracts, and legal guides for dancers, musicians, and independent publishers.

Presently, BALA is establishing a mediation project designed to help resolve arts-related conflicts.

This group's funding breaks down as follows: 25% private foundation grants, 15% state and federal, and 60% from its own activities, which include referral service fees, publications sales, training and workshop registrations.

Fort Mason Center, Building 310
San Francisco, CA 94123
(415) 775-7200
Hours: 10–5 Monday through Friday

The Artists Foundation

The Artists Foundation in Boston provides a statewide referral service called "Lawyers for the Arts." Fees are flexible, and barter arrangements are often worked out. The foundation holds workshops in law, business, and marketing, and has a non-circulating library.

In addition to the "Lawyers for the Arts," the foundation participate in two other projects—a fellowship program which provides seventy (70) $3,500 grants to Massachusetts artists, and an artist-in-residence program in schools and communities (including museums, hospitals, prisons, libraries, and factories).

100 Boylston Street
Boston, MA 02116
(617) 482-8100

Directory of Legal Resources for Artists

★ ★

San Francisco
Bay Area Lawyers for the Arts
Bldg. 310
Ft. Mason Center
San Francisco, CA 94123

California
Advocates for the Arts
Law School, Room 2467C
University of California
Los Angeles, CA 90024
(213) 825-3309 or 825-4841

Connecticut
Connecticut Commission on the Arts
340 Capitol Avenue
Hartford, CT 06106
(203) 566-4770

Georgia
Georgia Volunteer Lawyers for the Arts, Inc.
c/o Alston, Miller & Gaines
1200 C&S National Bank Building
Atlanta, GA 30303
(404) 588-0300

Illinois
Lawyers for the Creative Arts
111 North Wabash
Chicago, IL 60602
(312) 263-6989

Massachusetts
Lawyers for the Arts
Massachusetts Council for the Arts and Humanities
Boston, MA
(617) 723-3851

Minnesota
Affiliated Arts Agencies
Butler Square Number 349
100 North Sixth Street
Minneapolis, MN 55403
(612) 338-1158

New Jersey
Cultural Law Committee
New Jersey State Bar Association

Trenton, NJ 08608
(201) 232-2323

New York
Albany League of the Arts, Inc.
135 Washington Avenue
Albany, NY 12210
(518) 449-5380

Arts Development Services
237 Main Street
Buffalo, NY 14203
(716) 856-7520

115 Maple Street
Glens Falls, NY 12801
(518) 793-6631

Huntington Area Arts Council, Inc.
12 New Street
Huntington, NY 11743
(516) 271-8423

Volunteer Lawyers for the Arts
36 West 44th Street
New York, NY 10036
(212) 575-1150

Upper Catskill Community Council of the Arts,
   Inc.
101 Old Milne Library
State University College
Oneonta, NY 13820
(607) 432-2070

Dutchess County Arts Council
Cunneen-Hackett Cultural Center
9 Vassar Street
Poughkeepsie, NY 12601
(914) 454-3222

Arts Council of Rochester, Inc.
930 East Avenue
Rochester, NY 14607
(716) 442-0570

Ohio
Volunteer Lawyers for the Arts
c/o Cleveland Area Arts Council

108 The Arcade
Cleveland, OH 44114
(216) 781-0045

Oregon
Leonard Buff
Assistant Professor of Law
Lewis and Clark College
Northwestern School of Law
Portland, OR 97219
(503) 244-1181

Pennsylvania
Ned Donohue, Esq.
3400 Centre Square West
1500 Market Street
Philadelphia, PA 19102
(215) 972-3539

Texas
Steinberg, Generes, Luerssen & Vogelson
2200 Fidelity Union Tower
Dallas, TX 75201
(214) 748-9312

Washington
Washington Volunteers for the Arts
University of Puget Sound Law School
55 Tacoma Way
Tacoma, WA 98402
(206) 756-3327

Washington, D.C.
Charles B. Rutenberg, Esq.
Arent, Fox, Kintner, Plotkin & Kahn
Federal Bar Building
1815 H Street, N.W.
Washington, D.C. 20006
(202) 347-8500

With thanks to:
Lisa Cohen
Tem Horowitz

Programs for Senior Citizens

For centuries Asian countries have respected and even venerated the elders of the society. Until recently, Western society barely acknowledged our elders' existence, much less respected them. But lately, strong pressure from our older citizens has forced us to make some amends. Programs for senior citizens are now available in many communities. We'll mention three of them.

Legal Assistance for Senior Adults

LASA, Inc. has two components—a legal advice and counsel unit, and a non-legal advocacy unit. A staff attorney assists low-income seniors for free, and people with higher incomes are referred to outside attorneys, where payments are made on a sliding income scale. The non-legal advocacy side handles government benefits and administrative agency matters. They also assist on consumer problems of concern to the elderly, like health insurance and home repairs.

5311 Johnson Drive
Mission, KS 66205
(913) 677-1211

Legal Counsel for the Elderly

Specially trained senior volunteers under the supervision of lawyers assist the elderly residents of Washington, D.C. in obtaining their full share of public benefit programs [Social Security, Supplemental Security Income (SSI), Medicare and Medicaid, Food Stamps, Meals-on-Wheels]. The volunteer will counsel the client, negotiate on his/her behalf, and act as an advocate at an administrative hearing. They also inform clients on wills and other probate matters. Should a lawyer be necessary, the elderly person must meet specific income guidelines. The program is funded by the District of Columbia Office on Aging and the Legal Services Corporation and is duplicated in many other cities.

1016 16th St., N.W., 6th Floor
Washington, D.C. 20036
(202) 234-0970

SIRC Senior Legal Centers

SIRC senior legal centers exist in Chico, Oakland, Red Bluff, and Redding. This program for senior citizens is designed to provide legal advice and assistance through staff attorneys and paralegals. It also presents workshops and provides written materials and booklets on areas of concern to seniors, such as wills and insurance.

Senior Information & Referral Center
2nd St. and Normal
P.O. Box 3583
Chico, CA 95927

. . . And More Self-Help Programs

★★★

Center for Independent Living: The Disability Law Resource Center

The United Nations has designated 1981 as the year of the disabled. In recognition of this designation, the British Broadcasting Corporation (BBC) is producing an hour-long documentary on facilities and centers for the disabled around the world. Fifteen minutes of the program are devoted to the Center for Independent Living (CIL) in Berkeley, California which the producers feel to be "the most forward-looking" in the world. CIL's legal arm is the Disability Law Resource Center (DLRC).

DLRC divides itself into two units—a legal services unit and an advocacy unit. Legal services will assist for free those people who meet the income guidelines. They file both individual and class action suits against those who discriminate against the handicapped and disabled. For those people who do not meet the income eligibility requirement, DLRC provides a lawyer-referral service. Counseling on handling a small claims court action is free.

The advocacy unit handles problems involving public assistance and government-benefit programs for anyone, regardless of income. The Center currently has on its staff five lay advocates who represent clients at administrative hearings and in negotiations with the agencies.

CIL also has several other legal programs. The Education for the Handicapped Project employs paralegals to represent clients at school hearings where the mainstreaming of the child (i.e., placing the child in a class with "normal" children) is in issue.

Training and technical assistance on the rights of access to all public buildings and buildings constructed with government funds is provided in CIL's 504 project (named after the federal statutory provi-

sion number).

The Center also employs two lay advocates to act as ombudspersons for California Department of Rehabilitation matters.

> 2539 Telegraph Avenue
> Berkeley, CA 94704
> CIL: (415) 841-3900
> (415) 840-3101 (teletype)

> DLRC: (415) 548-4274
> (415) 548-4282
> (teletype for the deaf)

People's Law School

People's Law School is not a law school in the traditional sense that people attend classes to become a lawyer. However, they do a fine job of educating people on their legal rights. People's Law School has published a dozen or more pamphlets which are all inexpensive. The topics include, "How to Use a Law Library," "Legal First Aid," and "Take the Offensive: A Guide to Small Claims Court." Two are also translated into Spanish—"It's Your Body"

and "Getting Unemployment Insurance." Several of these are reviewed in the Book Review Section.

People's Law School also holds workshops and provides information and referrals to callers and drop-ins. They are associated with the Lawyers Guild, a progressive national lawyers organization.

558 Capp Street
San Francisco, CA 94110
(415) 285-5069

Bar Association Tapes

Several state bar associations, alone or in conjunction with local attorney general offices, have a library of tapes describing basic legal information. You merely phone in and ask to hear a tape on a particular subject. Tapes usually last from one to

five minutes. Subjects may include bankruptcy, divorce, food stamps, social security, small claims court procedure, tenant problems and credit. Boston has a library of 250 tapes which may be heard 24 hours a day.

We must admit that at first we were skeptical. We doubted that the tapes would provide helpful or dependable information. We cannot vouch for them all, but we did listen to a few in Boston and were pleasantly surprised. They were found to be slow-paced, easy to understand, and reasonably detailed. References were also given to related tapes and to other agency resources, with phone numbers.

Three tape libraries of which we are aware are:

Consumer Phone: Boston, MA
(617) 894-8030
Tel-Law: Kansas City, MO
(816) 753-4706
Tel-Law: San Mateo, CA
(415) 345-4822

Consumer Action Lines

Have a consumer problem and don't know where to turn? Local radio and television stations and newspapers often promote a consumer action line. Call them up and tell them your problem. They may direct you to the appropriate agency, organization, or person, or they may even contact the other party directly for you. Because of their community influence and power (there's always the threat of publicizing the issue) they can often get results, or at least open new lines of communication. They can act to smooth out ruffled feathers and get people to rethink their positions.

If you do not know of a consumer action line in your metropolitan area, just call a local station or paper. They're always receptive to news.

Automobile Owners Action Council

AOAC is a non-profit membership organization of Washington, D.C. motor vehicle owners. When a member has a vehicle-related complaint against an auto dealer, repair shop, service station, finance company, or insurance company, the council will investigate and attempt to resolve it. If AOAC cannot resolve the dispute satisfactorily, it will take further steps. These may include assistance in taking the case to Small Claims Court, filing the complaint with an agency, or obtaining legal help.

The council represents itself as an automobile consumers' union. It will also assist members in filing insurance claims, finding dependable repair shops, and purchasing a vehicle. There is a staff of investigators, researchers, and educators. Basic membership is $25.

1411 K Street, N.W.
Washington, D.C. 20005
(202) 638-5550

Pro Per Collective

Pro Per was one of the first groups in the country to set up a program to help people do it themselves— "in one's own behalf." They hold workshops, counsel people on how to file small claims court cases, and direct people to helpful books and pamphlets. Lately they have been having funding problems,

requiring them to limit their emphasis to welfare, unemployment insurance, and tenant matters. The staff was CETA-funded but now is volunteer.

477 15th Street, Rm. 200
Oakland, CA 94612
(415) 834-3051

★

With thanks to:
Oda Van Cranenburgh
Jay Jackson

PART VI
Self-Help Law:
The Tools to Do the Job

In this section, we review the best self-help law materials we have been able to find. Because of space, we have had to focus on a few books in each legal area. Sadly, we found that a lot of what's available in the people's law field is either mediocre or out-of-date, and there was little point in reviewing it. We also found a dearth of resources, good or bad, in some areas. Incidentally, we include publication dates where possible and again remind you that in many areas of the law, old information is usually bad information.

This is a good time to confess to a few biases, since it's easier to set them out and let you make allowances for them than it is for us to change. First, we tend to like our own "Nolo Press" books. While they have generally been recognized as being of good quality, it is only fair that you know that we have a financial interest in their success. So any time you see a symbol like this: be alerted that we are reviewing material on which at least one of us has worked. Second, we have a strong bias toward good regional books (as opposed to national ones). Many laws vary from state to state, and a good regional book almost always gives more detailed information than a book that is trying to cover all 50 states. Third, we have included a number of "general" law books which are not "how-to-do-it" manuals. We did this simply because one or another of us liked the book. Fourth, in organizing the material by subject heading, we have had to be somewhat arbitrary. So if you don't find ▶

what you need right off, be a little patient and look through all the material. For example, a woman wanting information on her legal rights after a divorce will find help under the "Rights of Women" heading, but also will want to check "Marriage & Divorce." Last, despite conscientious efforts, we surely missed a number of good books, especially regional ones published by non-profit organizations and not easily available to the book trade. If we left you out, we apologize. Please do put us on your mailing list (Nolo Press, 950 Parker St., Berkeley, CA 94710) so we can include you in our next edition.

★★★

291

Always remember that you were an attorney once. Not too long ago you were out there trying to make a living in the same vineyards. The black robe doesn't change things. You're the same guy as you were back then.

Remarks made at Special Orientation Program for New Judges as reported in the San Francisco Examiner 4/27/80

I. Civil Suits and Law in General

★ A. Basic Law and Litigation

How to Handle Your Own Lawsuit
Jerome S. Rice
1979; 238p; $5.95
Contemporary Books Inc.
180 N. Michigan Ave.
Chicago, IL 60601

This book is best suited for the non-lawyer who wishes to represent him/herself as plaintiff or defendant in "medium-sized" lawsuits too large for Small Claims Court but too small to make hiring a $75/hour lawyer worthwhile.

Unlike many self-representation manuals, this book does not gloss over the procedural and technical aspects — forms and motions — but instead provides very helpful examples of the all-important pretrial steps in a lawsuit. For those who are not too sure about handling an entire civil lawsuit from start to finish without a lawyer, the book shows how to proceed without a lawyer up until the case gets too complex, then how to ask the lawyer selected questions or how to turn the case over to him/her in an organized form. This beats dropping everything in the lawyer's lap in the beginning and incurring $2,000 in fees for a $3,000 case. NOTE: This book is not recommended for use when representing yourself in big-money personal injury cases!!

●

In this chapter, you will learn how to prepare the first formal documents that pertain to your case. Often, they are the first things your opposing lawyer or your opponent encounters reflecting your lawsuit. In all likelihood, they will be the first things His Honor, the judge who presides over your case, will see. Since you want to put your best foot forward, your pleadings must be good. In this chapter, I have included examples to be used as models for your pleadings. Above all, your objective in drafting pleadings should be clarity of communication. The best advice I can give you in this regard is: *Use plain and simple English and be brief.* This is no place for complex, convoluted

sentences. It is the place for the shorter, Anglo-Saxon word, rather than the more flowery, Latin-derived equivalent.

Cluing into Legal Research
by Peter Jan Honigsberg
1979; 145p; $7.95
Golden Rain Press
P.O. Box 5458
Berkeley, CA 94705

Have you ever read an article dealing in some way with one or more legal principles, and when the "authority" for a particular proposition was cited, wondered what the heck "3 Cal. 3d 507, 90 Cal. Rptr. 729 (1970)" means? How often have you suspected that it was all part of a mysterious secret code designed by lawyers to keep everyone else baffled, befuddled, and willing to pay (lawyers) to figure it all out? Well, here's good news! The little blurb of secret code above means "in California, a landlord can't evict a tenant for complaining about substandard housing conditions." Now, how does one get from the secret code to the plain English translation? This is what is explained in great detail in this book — the secrets of how lawyers and legal workers conduct legal research to find out "what the law is" in a particular situation.

This is a complete guide for understanding the organization of the legal materials that lawyers use. If you are typical in that you've allowed yourself to be intimidated by the formal and mysterious trappings of our legal system, this book will help you.

●

This book will take you step by step through the legal research process. You will learn how to find a federal or state case, statute, constitutional provision, administrative regulation or decision. You will understand how the reporter system works, how and when to use a legal treatise, law review article, law digest, or legal encyclopedia. You will learn where and how to look for the most recent cases and laws on the subject.

We will describe the court systems, state and federal, and how they are connected. You will see how "precedent" underlines case decisions and how one court's decision can affect other courts. We will show you how the laws passed by state legislatures and Congress and the administrative regulations issued by state and federal agencies are woven together with the cases decided by state and federal judges to establish the law.

The Complete Layman's Guide to the Law
by John Paul Hanna
1974; 513p; $15.95
Prentice-Hall, Inc.
Englewood Cliffs, N.J.

This well-organized book is suitable for use as both a structured reference as well as an easy to read introduction to law for the layperson. Its usefulness as a reference text is heightened by the thorough table of contents and a very good index. Though not by any means a do-it-yourself manual, the focus of this book is to give the information necessary to begin researching your legal problem or at least to make it easier for you to talk with (and avoid being snowed by) your lawyer.

•

A *complaint* is one of a number of legal documents that are collectively referred to as *pleadings*. A complaint names the *plaintiff* and the *defendant*, and has the title of the court in which it is to be filed on its first page. The body of the complaint sets forth the facts upon which your cause of action is based. Complaints are normally drafted by lawyers for their clients, and are filed with the clerk of the court having jurisdiction over the subject matter of the law suit. If planning to file your own case, see the chart on page ii to get an idea of the different courts that exist, and then seek help from the clerk of your local court in deciding which court is the proper one to hear your case. A filing fee must be paid to the clerk when the complaint is filed. The original copy goes into a new file which the clerk sets up under a new number. All later pleadings filed with the clerk that are connected with that action will be stamped with that same number and filed in that same file. This file becomes a public record and is open to inspection.

Your Introduction to Law
by George Gordon
   Coughlin
1975, 1979; 310p; $3.95
Harper and Row
10 E. 53rd Street
New York, NY 10022

While nowhere nearly as well laid out as Hanna's Complete Guide to the Law, *this book is still worth buying if you're interested in an inexpensive paperback (rather than a hard-bound basic reference manual) that is easily read and contains a thorough introduction to the law in simple nontechnical language.*

This is not a do-it-yourself law book since the number of topics covered necessitate less than full treatment on any subject. The book is lacking in areas (such as landlord-tenant law) that have undergone rapid change in the four years between the 1974 and 1979 editions. The only difference in the new edition is a new chapter on consumer protection. There are also problems as a result of the New York author's regional biases — e.g. devoting one short paragraph to explain many Western states' systems of marital "community property" ownership, whereas three pages are devoted to outdated common-law suits for "breach of promise (to marry)," "alienation of affection," etc. But the book is still a good one, particularly in areas of the law that have remained basically unchanged for several hundred years (e.g. the mysteries of title to real estate).

•

Marketable Title
No deed or mortgage should ever be accepted unless the title to the property has been properly examined and the purchaser has been advised by his attorney that when he gets the deed he will have good and marketable title to the property. The title should also be examined for restrictions which might limit the uses to which the property might be put.

In some communities, lawyers or abstract companies make title searches which indicate the validity or invalidity of titles to real property. In other communities the purchaser of real estate buys a title insurance policy to protect himself against loss in the case of faulty title.

Legal Action –
A Layman's Guide
by Edward F. Dolan, Jr.
1972; 299p; $5.95
Contemporary Books, Inc.
180 N. Michigan Avenue
Chicago, IL 60601

This is a very down-to-earth book which speaks in everyday terminology. It is divided into three parts: 1. an explanation about lawsuits in general; 2. summaries of the laws of "torts" (negligence, assault, slander, etc.), contracts, consumer protection, and property; and 3. a description of what it is like to be a party to a lawsuit in the courtroom, using the hypothetical situation of the reader having just been injured in an auto accident.

Unfortunately, family, marriage, and divorce law is conspicuously absent, but otherwise it is a pretty informative and easy-to-read book.

●

Appellate courts hear appeals for the overturning of decisions made by trial courts. The appeals are made by the losing party in a civil lawsuit or the defendant in a criminal action when either feels that the trial court made some error in the law or committed some injustice in the hearing of his case. Appeals may be made for both jury and nonjury cases. They must be made within a certain time following the trial; the time varies among the states but generally runs from 60 to 90 days.

The party that makes the appeal is the *appellant*. He notifies the other side of his action with a *notice of appeal*, and then places with the appellate court a *record of appeal* and a *memorandum of law*. The record of appeal contains all the papers in the case, from the summons, complaint, and answer to the most important document of all — the *transcript* of the trial, which is a verbatim record of the trial made during its course by the court reporter. In the memorandum of law the appellant points out the legal reasons why he feels a mistake was made or an injustice was done in his case.

Everything You've Always Wanted to Know About the Law – But Couldn't Afford to Ask
by Edward E. Colby
1972; 429p; $2.95
Major Books
21335 Roscoe Blvd.
Canoga Park, CA 91304

This book is more "human" than any general primer or introduction to law that I have reviewed thus far.

Although the 1972 publication date renders it a little out-of-date for the rapidly-changing areas of the law, such as landlord-tenant relations and living together unmarried, it's as thorough as a small paperback can be (429 pages of small print might suggest that).

The thoroughness of Colby's treatment can be seen in the number and variety of subjects he discusses in his chapter on wills:

●

Definitions
Who Can Make a Will?
Can a Will Be Changed?
Must a Will Give Property Away?

Form of a Will
Must a Lawyer Be Hired to Prepare a Will?
What Happens if a Part of a Will Is Invalid?
Who May Inherit?
Formal Requirements of a Will
Will Witnesses and Appearance in Probate Court
Must a Will Be in Writing?
Must a Will Be Typewritten?
Where Do You Sign a Will (don't laugh – there have been hundreds of suits over this!)

Paralegal's Litigation Handbook
by Carole A. Bruno
1980; 544p; $27.50
Institute for Business
   Planning, Inc.
IBP Plaza
Englewood Cliffs, New
   Jersey 07632

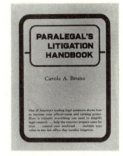

Written from a traditional "paralegal as assistant to lawyer" perspective, this is not a tool for revolutionizing the American legal system. The author, a professional paralegal for nine years, does not envision the possibility of "paralegals in lieu of lawyers" and to a disturbing degree assumes paralegals to be women and lawyers to be men. Despite its limited vision, it accomplishes what it sets out to do with thoroughness, organization and clarity. It is the complete litigation reader for not only the beginning paralegal, but also for the recent law school graduate, interested layperson, or someone representing him or herself in court. It provides comprehensive techniques and procedures for the handling of all aspects of litigation — legal research, pre-trial investigation, pleadings, discovery, motions, settlements and the securing and enforcing of judgments. Because it is designed as a "how-to" manual for the practicing paralegal, it is chock full of sample letters, forms, worksheets, charts and tables, with tips on how to organize a more efficient office and filing system. Certain aspects and levels of complexity within this book will not be of interest to a layperson, but as a whole, it provides a good overview of a court case in all its technicalities.

★ B. Law Dictionaries

The Dictionary of
Practical Law
by Charles F. Hemphill, Jr.
and Phyllis D. Hemphill
1979; 231p; $4.95
Prentice-Hall, Inc.
Englewood Cliffs, NJ 07632

*This is the best of both
worlds—a plain-talking
law dictionary in non-lawyers' language, coupled with
thorough definitions useful
to the law student, para-
legal, or lawyer—all in a 5/8" thick paperback! Of
the five different law dictionaries purporting to make
that all-intimidating "lawyer-lingo" understandable
to ordinary folks, this is by far the best one.*

•

de·mur·rer. A pleading by a party in a legal action,
alleging that the pleadings of the opposite party are not
sufficient to show a cause of action that will stand up in
court. The *demurrer* does not admit the truth of the facts
alleged by the other party. The *demurrer* says, in effect,
"even if your facts were true, they do not contain the
essential elements or legal requirements that would be
necessary to spell out a case against me—therefore, you
should not be allowed to proceed further." Put in other
words, the *demurrer* says, "There are certain basic facts
and elements of law that must be alleged in order to constitute a lawsuit. Some of these are missing from your
pleadings, and the case should therefore be dismissed."

Paralegal's Encyclopedic Dictionary
by Valera Grapp
1979; 584p; $24.95
Prentice-Hall, Inc.
Englewood Cliffs, NJ

*This serious, hardbound dictionary stands halfway
between exalted lawyers' tomes such as Black's* Law
Dictionary *and those written solely for laypersons.
Nevertheless, the definitions are written mostly in
plain English and should be understandable to most.
Recommended for paralegals, litigious nonlawyers
and others who think law is fun.*

•

RES IPSA LOQUITUR
A doctrine of law applied in a TORT action. It is an
INFERENCE which can be rebutted by EVIDENCE.
Because some accidents are of the type which in them-

selves indicate negligence by the opposing PARTY,
usually the DEFENDANT, and because NEGLI-
GENCE would be difficult to prove because the instrument causing the injury was under the *exclusive control* of
the defendant, the JURY is allowed to infer from the
accident itself and the circumstances surrounding it that
the defendant was negligent—even though PLAINTIFF
cannot prove just how he was negligent. Just a few
examples of where the COURT will allow the *doctrine of
res ipsa loquitur* to apply are: restaurant customer injured
by foreign object in food; passenger injured in an unex-
plained airplane crash; railroad passenger injured when
train derails or has a crash with another train owned by the
same railroad; patient in hospital injured during an operation;

The Law Dic·tion·ary
(Also called Cochran's
Law Lexicon, 5th Ed.)
by W. C. Cochran (who
wrote the first edition in
1888 – this is an updated
edition, needless to say!)
Revised by Wesley
Gilmer, Jr.
1977; 429p; Write for price.
Anderson Publishing
Company
646 Main St.
Cincinatti, OH 45201

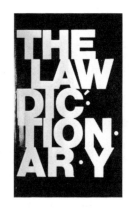

*This is a nice, compact-sized little dictionary (4" ×
6½" × 1") which, more than most of the other
dictionaries we looked at, has all the ancient and
mysterious Latin babblings such as* Clausulae
inconsuete semper inducunt suspicionem, *or
"unusual clauses always excite suspicion." The
complexity of explanations in this dictionary, in
terms of its understandability, is about midway
between a layperson's dictionary (which this is not)
and one for law students. This one is good for 1) law
students, 2) paralegals, and 3) people whose hobby is
to read lots of obsolete Latin phrases.*

•

Adultery, the voluntary sexual intercourse of a married
person with someone other than his spouse. It was not an
indictable offense at common law, but was left to the
ecclesiastical courts for punishment. It is made punishable
by fine and imprisonment by the statutes of most of the
states, and is a generally recognized ground for an absolute
divorce.

Law Dictionary
by Steven H. Gifis
1975; 227p; $3.75
Barron's Educational
    Series, Inc.
113 Crossways Park Drive
Woodbury, NY 11797

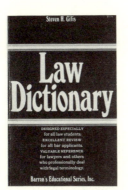

*While a little bit technical
and admittedly designed for
law students, this dictionary
is still understandable by the
layperson.*

•

FORNICATION   generally, sexual intercourse of two
unmarried persons of different sexes, which is punished as
a **misdemeanor** by statute in some states. 10 A. 727, 731.
In some states, it refers to illicit sexual intercourse between
a man, whether married or single, and an unmarried
woman. See 425 S.W. 2d 183, 188. 175 N.E. 661, 662.
In some states, illicit intercourse can be fornication for the
party who is not married, and **adultery** for the party who
is married. See 23 N.E. 747, 748. It is not a **common law**
crime and is not part of modern penal codes. See Model
Penal Code Art. 213. Compare **cohabitation**.

C.   Small Claims Court

**Everybody's Guide to
Small Claims Court**
by Ralph Warner
50 State Edition published
    by:
Addison-Wesley Publishing
    Co.
Trade Sales
Reading, MA 01867
1980; 240p; $11.95 (hard
    cover); $6.95 (paperback)
California Edition
    published by:
Nolo Press
950 Parker St.
Berkeley, CA 94710
1980 (Rev. Ed.); 210p; $6.95

*This is quite simply the best book ever published on
doing your own Small Claims action. It's all here —
from plotting your strategy and preparing your
evidence and witnesses, to arguing in court and
collecting when you win. Warner is thorough and
funny and makes the process of doing your own case
seem like great fun.*

Before you even start thinking about going to court — any
court — you must answer a basic question. Do I have a
good case?

Many mornings I have sat in Small Claims Court and
watched people competently and carefully present hopeless cases. Why hopeless? Usually because the plaintiffs
overlooked one of the most basic facts of litigation. Before
you can collect for a loss you have suffered, you must
show that the other party caused you to suffer the loss. Put
into legal slang, this means that you must show that there
is "liability." Obvious, you say. Perhaps it is to you, but
apparently not to lots of others.

Here is what often seems to happen. People focus on
their own loss — the amount of money that they are out as
a result of whatever incident occurred. They think that,
because they have been damaged, they must have a right
of recovery against someone. But the fact that a loss has
occurred isn't enough to make a winning case. You must
also prove that the person you are suing is legally responsible to compensate you for the loss. Often doing this is
easy and obvious and sometimes it is neither.

How do you establish that another person owes you
money? Or put another way, how do you establish "liability"? Normally, you must establish at least one of the
following three things. There are a number of technical
legal defenses to all of these approaches, but for now, let's
just look at the general theories.

1.   That a valid contract (written, oral or implied) has
been broken by the person you are suing and that, as a
result, you have suffered money damages (see A below);

2.   That the intentional behavior of the person you are
suing has caused you to suffer money damages (see B
below);

3.   That the negligent behavior of the person you are
suing has caused you to suffer money damages (see B
below).

Small Claims Court – A National Examination
by John C. Ruhnka & Steven Weller
1978; 219p; Write for price.
National Center for State Courts
300 Newport Ave.
Williamsburg, VA 23185

*Rather than a do-it-yourself handbook for the lay-
person, this book is a very readable and interesting
comparison of selected and diverse small claims court
systems across the country. It is written for lawyers,
students and laypersons interested in the variations
within this "informal" dispute resolution from state
to state. A few interesting findings are that attorney
representation in Small Claims Court doesn't help
much — nor does one's income, education, or race
make much difference in contested small claims cases.
The study suggests that to better the system,
the use of lawyers and the injection of "legalistic"
intricacies of procedure, particularly transferring the
case to a "formal" court, should be disallowed. One
of the key findings is that many people suing or being
sued in Small Claims Court still tend to be at a
disadvantage because of the unavailability or inade-
quacy of any assistance.*

*This is an excellent book for developing a sense of
perspective necessary for intelligently analyzing one's
own local courts with a view toward making suggestions for more streamlined, informal, and inexpen-
sively obtained justice.*

How to Sue in Washington State Small Claims Court and Collect
by Mark and Betsy Kelly
1979; 112p; $6.95
Peanut Butter Publishing
Peanut Butter Towers
2733 4th Avenue S.
Seattle, WA 98134

*This is strictly a one-state book, but presents every-
thing you need to know about suing and collecting in
Small Claims in so thorough a manner— with none
of the legalese that invariably creeps into a book
written by a lawyer, because the authors, happily,
aren't lawyers— that it's a perfect pattern for state-
specific books to follow. The biggest problem with
Small Claims Court, though, is that while it's fairly
easy (in most states) to sue on a valid claim and win
your case, collecting the money from a defendant
who can't or won't pay is quite something else again.
This is where a naïve plantiff finds out that our*

*wonderful small claims system isn't all it's cracked
up to be. This book fills a vacuum; its focus is on how
to collect, with about 80 pages of forms and straightforward instructions.*

●

The True Dead Beat
This is the guy who is impervious to the forces you can
bring to bear on him to pay up because he has nothing to
lose. If he causes an auto accident, he will not only not
have any liability insurance, he may have no driver's
license. (He lost it because he didn't have insurance the
last time he was in a wreck.) This winner is not just temporarily out of work. He never has worked much. He owns
nothing but debts. If you want to, you can get in line with
his other creditors. However, your outlook is rather bleak.

Remember if the fellow usually has a job, he doesn't fit
the description. You have up to six years to collect. He'll
be back to work before then.

Small Claims Court – Guide for Washington (State)
by Donald D. Stuart
1979; 144p; $4.50
Self-Counsel Press Inc.
1303 N. Northgate Way
Seattle, WA 98133

*This short book is a very
helpful guide to the use of
Small Claims Court in the
state of Washington.
Although somewhat more of
a brief procedural outline
rather than a strategy book for types of claims, it will
acquaint the uninitiated with what to expect in
Small Claims Court so that he/she will be less
mystified or confused with the procedure. One of the
most helpful aspects of this book is that, unlike many
others which ramble on for pages and pages of
nothing but text, here numerous examples of forms
and sample letters are provided.*

●

Despite how wrong the defendant's conduct may have
been there is no basis of a lawsuit without a showing of
losses. A contractor may have delayed completion of the
remodeling job on your dining room and thus inconven-
ienced you greatly, but without a showing that you suffered some financial loss, there is nothing you can sue for.

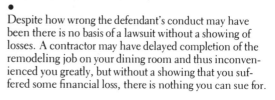

The Layman's Guide to Small Claims Court (British Columbia)
by Patrick Good
1974; 115p; $2.95
International Self-Counsel Press, Ltd.
306 West 25th Street
North Vancouver, B.C. (Canada)

This "bare-bones" outline of do-it-yourself legal procedure in Small Claims Court is also "dry as a bone." (The writing style is somewhat stuffy and formal, though easy to understand.) But once past that, it's a very thorough set of instructions on how to proceed in Small Claims Court in British Columbia, with emphasis on suing rather than defending. This is a plaintiff's book. Unlike many Small Claims manuals, this one thoroughly explores typical problem areas that are all too often glossed over, such as: properly naming the person or business you're suing, subpoenaing witnesses, and trial preparation. The entire Small Claims procedure from the plaintiff's point of view is explained in easy-to-understand language.

II. Family Law

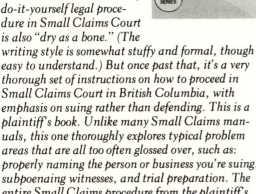

★ A. Living Together

The Living Together Kit (Second Edition)
by Ralph Warner & Toni Ihara
Nolo Press
950 Parker St.
Berkeley, CA 94710
1978, 1979; 200p; $8.95
8½" × 11" with tear-out contracts
Fawcett Crest Books

Box C730
524 Myrtle Avenue
Brooklyn, NY 11205
1978, 1979; 315p; $2.50
4" × 6" pocket book size

This is the most comprehensive book on law for unmarried couples we have seen to date. Warner and Ihara present thorough practical information on the practical aspects of living together, including the Marvin *case, designing your own contract, buying a house, children, wills, etc. The Living Together Kit has been praised by everyone, from* New West, People, *and* Ms. *magazines to academic law reviews. If you're living with a friend, you will benefit greatly from reading this cheerful, no-nonsense guide. If you want tear-out agreements, get the Nolo book. If you don't care, get the cheaper Fawcett version.*

●

We can't do much to change the legal system, but we can and do show you how existing rules can be used to sow the seeds of future understanding. Just as medicine need not be all pills and knives, law can be approached in a positive, conflict-avoiding way. We will show you that legal rules need not be incompatible with your best instincts and that law can be used creatively to minimize the possibility that your relationship will end in paranoia and bitterness.

Like it or not, there are many rules and regulations that apply to unmarried couples. You may ignore them for a time, but they are unlikely to ignore you. Once the rules are understood, the two of you will want to do some talking: to decide together how you and the rules can connect in a positive way. Then it will be typewriter time. We provide you with sample written agreements — living together contracts, real property agreements, wills, paternity statements, etc. It is up to you to adapt these samples to your needs. We advise you to write things down, not because we believe that most people are untrustworthy, but because we know from experience that over time, memories tend to blur. We ask you to make a small leap of faith and believe us when we tell you that sensible written agreements can do much to increase trust and harmony and that they are best made when you think that you will never need them, not when storm warnings are flying.

Marital and Non-Marital Contracts

edited by Joan Krauskopf
1979; 96p; $12.00
American Bar Association
Order Billing 513
1155 East 60th Street
Chicago, IL 60637

This small book consists of a series of essays on the use of contracts in marriage and living together situations. It isn't as comprehensive or as useful as The Living Together Kit *for unmarried couples, but does include some useful sample marriage contracts that aren't easily available elsewhere. It's unfortunate that the American Bar Association doesn't publish more comprehensive volumes to make law accessible to the general public.*

★ B. Marriage and Divorce

The People's Guide to California Marriage and Divorce Law

by Ralph Warner and Toni Ihara
1979; 235p; $6.95
Nolo Press
950 Parker St.
Berkeley, CA 94710

Hey, you Easterners! Ever wondered about all the mysteries of the so-called "community property" system? No other law book for laypersons has ever explained in such lucid and easily-understood detail how community property works. (By the way, the other community property states are Louisiana, Texas, New Mexico, Arizona, Nevada, Washington, and Idaho.) The same is true for the chapter on wills; it's all summed up brilliantly in one chapter and includes the effect of the community property system on inheritance. But that's not all this book is about. It's a positive-looking little paperback that guides you along the steps involved in buying a home (including the mysteries of that other form of ownership everyone's heard of but knows little about—joint tenancy), what legally constitutes a marriage (there is no "common-law marriage" in California, but you

can get married without a marriage license!), child custody (including the popular new creature called "joint custody"), and adoption and guardianship.

•

The community property system which we use in California is rooted in a property scheme devised by the nomadic Visogoths. The Visogoths brought it to Spain when they swept through Southern Europe in the 7th century A.D. It found its way to the New World via the explorers from Spain and eventually spread to those territories in the United States which were originally settled by Mexican colonists. The community property system is somewhat of an oddity in the American legal tradition as most of our law follows the English common law scheme. But if it is an oddity, it is a fair one. Among many simple cultures where the division of labor between husband and wife was substantially equal (usually equally back-breaking), the community property concept arose to reflect the equally shared ownership and possession of property acquired through their joint efforts. It is much more a people's system than the male-dominated property tradition of England. In England, at least among the propertied classes, the wife was viewed as a decoration, a mere possession of the husband, and as such could have no equal claim to his estate.

Structured Mediation in Divorce Settlement

by O. J. Coogler
1978; 204p; Write for price.
Lexington Books
D.C. Heath & Company
Lexington, MA

This publisher has a catalogue listing a number of interesting books, but despite our best efforts at persuasion, they wouldn't send us review copies. (We got this one at the library.) Write them for a catalogue.

We're all too familiar with the divorce that starts out "amicably"—both the husband and wife realize the marriage is long past saved, and both want to look for greener pastures elsewhere. They decide to file for divorce, and unless there is no-fault, pro se divorce, one of them goes to a lawyer. The lawyer sees his/her duty as getting as much for his/her client as is possible; this often means taking the other spouse for everything she or he has. When this happens, that other spouse goes to a lawyer, and the sylized legal battle begins. The once amicable divorce now becomes a battle of intimidation and coercion, with roles played by hired guns. The lawyers "save" your estate from each other's client—and keep it for themselves.

Isn't there a better, more humane way to deal with divorce? Yes, says the author. The procedure utilizes trained mediators to explore areas of agreement and not to decide in favor of either party on a specific point. Marital property rights are discussed, first by objectively identifying community or other marital property and starting from a 50-50 division. If there is reason to depart from the 50-50 concept (e.g., if a jointly used automobile was a gift from the husband's parents to him), the discussion begins there. Advisory attorneys who have been retrained to avoid thinking in purely adversarial terms are utilized to draft property settlement and support agreements. The overall atmosphere is one of cooperation rather than coercion and hostility. If the divorcing spouses start out willing to part on friendly terms, this procedure is designed to reinforce that attitude, rather than to destroy it in the manner that the American adversary system can (and frequently does).

•

The objective of the temporary settlement agreement (Appendix FMA-G, Form FMA 777), is to stabilize the relationship between the parties during the time they are in mediation. They will then be able to work toward a permanent settlement with a minimum of controversy over financial and other arrangements. Only the standard items which need to be agreed upon are indicated by blanks in the temporary agreement. These are such matters as child support, spousal maintenance, mortgage or rent payments on the house or apartment, custody and visitation, joint assets, and joint charge accounts.

In helping the couple work out the support items of the temporary agreement, they should be reassured that any agreement reached does not set a precedent for the permanent agreement. *The purpose of the temporary agreement is simply to maintain the status quo during mediation.* Even though the couple will have already worked on their budgets, detailed consideration of items is not needed in reaching a temporary agreement. But it is important that the dependent spouse know what support will be provided and the supporting spouse know what payments he or she will be expected to make.

Economics of Divorce
edited by Family Law
  Section of the American
  Bar Association
1978; 153p; Write for price.
American Bar Association
Order Billing 513
1155 E. 60th St.
Chicago, IL 60637

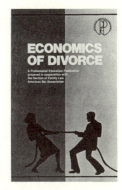

This is not a "do-it-yourself" book (and it only barely begins to touch our concept of People's Law), but a collection of seven essays — good ones. We include it in these reviews because much interest is focused on the emergence of the recent concept of "no-fault" divorce (the kind easily done without an attorney) as compared to the old "fault" types (as in Illinois and Pennsylvania), and the "mixed ground" states which have both. Community property states are compared to common-law "equitable distribution" states as well. Other interesting topics are the effect of divorce on a will and estate planning. This is a very readable and interesting collection of theories and studies.

Marriage and Family Law in Washington (State)
by Adam Kline
1979; 187p; $4.50
Self-Counsel Press Inc.
1303 N. Northgate Way
Seattle, WA 98133

Like the California Marriage and Divorce Law *book by Nolo, this book deals straightforwardly with the legal elements of a valid marriage, living together (with sample living together contracts), joint tenancy and community property ownership, separation and divorce (with more sample written agreements), and child support and alimony. Although there is not enough discussion on the way marriage affects taxes and insurance, this is one of the best books on Washington (State) marriage law.*

•

In the United States, and particularly in Washington, common-law marriage has had little legal recognition. This is now beginning to change as we realize that recognition is not necessarily approval and that the people in such a union do need the protection of the law.

The basic difference between the formal marriage and the common-law relationship has been that the parties in the former have legal status (and an associated bundle of rights and obligations) while those in the latter have not.

The Fighter's Guide to Divorce

by Robert Blackwell
1979; 221p; $4.95
Contemporary Books, Inc.
180 N. Michigan Avenue
Chicago, IL 60601

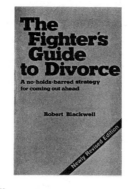

Illinois is one of those few infamous states which has stubbornly refused to adopt "no-fault" divorce laws. In Illinois, it seems one must air out one's dirty laundry in public, showing one's spouse to be a dirty, drunken, adulterous, beastly, rotten swine. Other states sharing this dubious distinction are Pennsylvania and South Dakota. But almost all the states that have adopted the new "no-fault" divorce statutes (based on a mere showing of "irreconcilable differences" or "irremedial breakdown") decided to still keep the old "fault" grounds just in case. Therefore, although the author's experience is in Illinois, this is not a single-state book. It is written from a male perspective for the divorcing father who faces the likely prospect of seeing a bored judge award his former wife custody of the children (fathers face a tremendous burden trying to overcome the sexist bias in favor of women) and possibly half his take-home pay as child support.

•

Don't assume your mate is neither bent on vengeance nor smitten with greed. When the time comes for settlement, it will be a dog-eat-dog battle to determine who gets the larger share of the spoils — you, your spouse or the lawyers. Unless you have protected yourself — particularly if

you are the husband — you may leave divorce court destitute, with all of your assets and much of your future income committed to your ex-mate. Very likely you will remain responsible for all past obligations and for the accumulated fees of your lawyer and your wife's, even though her income and assets are greater than yours. The lawyer's fees alone may be considerable. A friend of mine is now in court, defending himself in a suit brought by a divorce lawyer who is demanding a fee of nearly $30,000 — and he lost the case!

C. Adoption ★

Adoption Guide for Oregon

by Patricia Clark, Katharine English, & Rebecca Swanson
1978; 113p; $15.95
Parting, Inc.
1915 N.E. Everett
Portland, OR 97232

It makes us a little sad that it is state law which governs adoptions; if federal law did, this excellent book would have been written for the entire country. For lucky Oregon residents, however, this is a good guide to the legal aspects of all adoptions, including stepparent adoptions, and a comprehensive set of instructions and forms to cover nearly any contingency in do-it-yourself stepparent adoptions. The form-filling instructions are simple, complete and even visually aesthetic. There are separate sets of forms for the following circumstances:

1. When you have the other natural parent's consent.

2. Whereabouts of the natural parents is unknown.

3. Identity of the biological father is not known.

4. Deceased other natural parent.

5. Adult stepchild adoptions.

•

By law, a child can have only one set of parents — one mother and one father. Adoption is the means which the law has given us for substituting one parent or set of parents for another parent or set of parents.

Legally, this means that the rights of the biological parents are "terminated," or ended forever. The parent whose rights have been terminated no longer has any legal relationship to the child. That parent is treated, legally, as though s/he is a stranger to the child. The NEW parent then becomes the LEGAL parent, and assumes all the rights and duties of a natural parent.

How to Adopt Your Stepchild in California
by Frank Zagone
1979; 142p; $10.00
Nolo Press
950 Parker Street
Berkeley, CA 94710

What if a child is born out of wedlock? What if there's a "presumed" father? What if a missing parent has failed to visit or pay support? What if the missing parent surfaces after you've filed, won't sign a consent form, but is unlikely to hire a lawyer and contest? All these contingencies are thoroughly explained, along with how to draft the forms to reflect the situation. The book also includes information on obtaining the consent of the natural parent and conducting an "abandonment" proceeding, if necessary. Note: This book does not cover private and agency adoptions—only stepparent adoptions.

•

The adoption removes forever all the legal rights and duties of the absent parent with respect to the adopted child. The absent parent loses the legal right to visit the child and to exercise any parental authority over the child. All other parental rights are lost.

On the other side of the legal coin, the absent parent of an adopted child is legally released from child support obligations and any other parental duties toward the child including "relative responsibility" laws (this law requires that parents and grown offspring try to help support one another should either become indigent and require public assistance).

Adoption – The Grafted Tree
by Laurie Wishard and
   William Wishard
1979; 197p; $6.95
Cragmont Publications
China Basin Building
161 Berry St., Suite 6410
San Francisco, CA 94107

The two authors listed above are not husband and wife who have shared the joys of adoption. William is an attorney who married Laurie's mother and legally adopted Laurie who is now grown and a social worker. The combination of a lawyer-adopting parent and his social worker-adopted child make for most sensitive and informative reading.

The authors depict adoption as both a legal and an emotional process, with much more emphasis on the latter. One section deals with the "problem" for which adoptive parents might well prepare themselves—the time the adopted child seeks to discover his/her biological parents or "roots."

D.   Do-It-Yourself Divorce ★

How to Do Your Own Divorce in California
by Charles E. Sherman
1980 (Eighth Edition);
   140p; $8.95
Nolo Press
950 Parker St.
Berkeley, CA 94710

This book was one of the pioneering works of the modern self-help law movement. Self-published by author Sherman in 1971, from his Berkeley, California home, it has now sold over 275,000 copies in California and has been widely copied in other states. When this book was published, pro per or pro se divorces were almost unheard of. Today, almost as many people represent themselves in California as hire lawyers. Using the most conservative of estimates, this one book has saved Californians 80 million dollars. Now you know why Sherman has been attacked by California bar associations and had to endure a California State Bar Association proceeding that almost resulted in his losing his license to practice law.

•

This book cannot teach you the whole of the complex and difficult law of property, but it may be sufficient for your purposes if you know a few generalities:

Community Property—Community property is that which belongs to both spouses. Generally speaking, it is that which you and your spouse earned and accumulated during the term of your marriage. This includes the negative property—bills—which either you or your spouse incurred up to the time of separation. Don't forget about any accumulated vacation pay, retirement funds and paid in equity in life insurance policies which may have been accumulated during the marriage.

Separate Property—Separate property is that which belongs to one spouse only, and is, generally speaking, property which was acquired before the marriage, or which at ANY time came directly to just one spouse by gift or inheritance. After the separation, the earnings, accumulations and bills of each spouse are separate.

Separate property can be changed into community property by agreement or intention of the owner-spouse. Similarly, community can be changed to the separate property of one spouse, but this takes the intention or agreement of both spouses, since both are owners of the community property. The agreement need not be in writing, and can even, in some cases, be inferred from conduct. A written agreement is required, however, to change the separate property of one spouse into separate property of the other.

How to Do Your Own Divorce in Texas
by Charles Sherman and Jim Simons
1980; $9.95
Addison-Wesley
Trade Sales
Reading, MA 01867

This book is basically the same as Sherman's How to Do Your Own Divorce in California, *but completely rewritten for Texas law. It is an excellent book.*

How to Get Your Own Divorce in Connecticut
by Michael Avery, Diane Polen, and Sarah D. Eldrich
1978; 39p plus supplements; $4.00 (supplement for divorces involving children, $2.50)
Pro Se Divorce Group
148 Orange Street
New Haven, CT 06510

This Connecticut do-it-yourself divorce kit contains detailed instructions with sample forms for uncontested "no-fault" divorces.

The booklet is divided into three sections, the first section containing both general information about self-help divorce, plus specific instructions for simple, uncontested divorces where no children are involved. Since the Connecticut no-fault procedure is more difficult when children are involved, and requires full cooperation of both spouses in order to work, the authors recommend that an attorney be hired when there are children. For those who refuse to be intimidated, however, the second section, for those with children, is provided. The third section is for those on welfare who have children.

The step-by-step instructions are very thorough and are easy for the non-attorney to use.

•

In October, 1973, the Connecticut legislature rewrote the divorce law and introduced the concept of 'no-fault divorce' in this state for the first time. In fact, the word

'divorce' was changed to 'dissolution of marriage'. Under the new law, neither party has to be at fault and neither party wins or loses as under the old law. Dissolutions can now be granted whenever a marriage has 'broken down irretrievably'. In short, that phrase can simply mean that the two people don't get along anymore; neither spouse has to be guilty of cruelty or infidelity. Because of the introduction of 'irretrievable breakdown', it is now quite simple to obtain a dissolution of your marriage. If one party says the marriage has broken down, then it has. To obtain a 'no-fault' dissolution in Connecticut, one party must have been a resident of the State for one year before the date of the hearing (not the date of filing).

Parting – A Handbook for Self-Help Divorce in Oregon
by Katherine English and Julie McFarlane
1979; 200p; $15.95
Parting, Inc.
1915 N.E. Everett
Portland, OR 96232

This was the best Oregon divorce guide we found. It deals somewhat uniquely and extensively with issues a woman must consider in deciding whether to ask for child custody, support, and/or alimony. Other self-help divorce books are written with the erroneous assumption that both spouses are on equal financial terms. This book was written solely for women, but that doesn't mean that men can't use it when they file for divorce. All necessary forms are included.

•

Recent legislation has been passed to hopefully put an end to a pattern in American divorces that has gone like this:

Woman marries man. Woman works full time to put man through medical school. Woman stays home raising three children while husband sets up practice and begins to prosper. Man divorces woman—she doesn't interest him anymore. She has no professional skills. She goes to work again as a waitress or secretary and works a second shift as a mother, cook and housekeeper. The court has awarded her child support and possibly some spousal support, the total of which is only enough for her to survive on, and certainly not enough to allow her to get the kind of education that would give her a better income. The result is that even though both partners have worked equally hard during the marriage, the husband emerges from the divorce in a much better financial position than the wife.

Do Your Own No-Fault Divorce (Massachusetts)
by Katherine Triantafillou
1979; 54p; Write for price
Portia Press
104 Charles St., Box 108
Boston, MA 02114

Attorney Triantafillou has written this complete handbook for those of you in Massachusetts who have "separated your personal property ages ago, have no children or real estate, don't want to file joint income tax returns or carry each other on your insurance policies, and have no obligations to pay off each other's loans or debts."

In short, if you and your spouse are in agreement on everything and have already decided to proceed the no-fault route, this is the book for you. It is well-written, detailed, and contains samples of all the necessary forms, with detailed instructions.

●

There are six forms you will have to be familiar with and fill out to obtain a no-fault divorce, and two which you potentially may encounter. These are: (1) Complaint for Divorce; (2) Financial Statement; (3) Dissolution Agreement or Separation Agreement; (4) Affidavit of Irretrievable Breakdown; (5) Domestic Relations Summons; (6) Certificate of Divorce Absolute; (7) Military Affidavit; (8) Appearance.

I will explain each one, but you will also find a small sample copy in the Appendix. All of these forms are available free of charge at the Probate Court, except for the Separation Agreement and Affidavit of Irretrievable Breakdown.

Do Your Own Divorce in Maine
by Divorce Reform, Inc.
1978; 93p; $7.00
Divorce Reform, Inc.
Cobblesmith Publishing
Freeport, ME 04032

Maine is somewhat new to the concept of no-fault divorces, and the usual "fault" divorce concept ("cruel and abusive treatment") still seems to be favored. This book explains both fault and no-fault divorce. Sample forms are included, but the forms themselves aren't provided.

The book is in pamphlet form and very little is mentioned about marital property rights. The emphasis is on divorce procedures.

Do Your Own Divorce in North Carolina
by Michael H. McGee
1978; 104p; $7.00
Cobblesmith Publishing
Patterson's Wheeltrack
Freeport, ME 04032

North Carolina, like Maine, has both "fault" and "no-fault" divorces. But there is a catch—no "mental cruelty," "indignities," etc., are listed in the "fault" grounds. Spouses must prove something really serious, like adultery, impotence, unnatural sex acts with others, commission of serious crime, insanity, etc. The difficulty with the North Carolina "no-fault" law is that the spouses must have separated for a year before filing. Examples of forms are provided, but not the forms themselves. Special instructions are given for obtaining temporary support if needed during the one year. This book is simple and straightforward.

State of Washington: So You Want a Divorce – How to Do It Yourself
by Daniel W. Giboney
1973; $6.95
Spokane Valley Herald
Opportunity, WA
available from:
Daniel W. Giboney
S. ·176 Stevens St.
Spokane, WA 99204

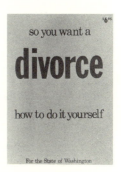

This is one of the books inspired by the California do-it-yourself book. It includes both examples and tear-out forms for Washington state. Although fairly thorough in its sample forms, the explanatory text (on which Washington law applies, etc.) is somewhat lacking in organization.

★★ Other Do-It-Yourself Divorce Books

Divorce Guide for Washington
by G. Daniels
1977; 75p; $4.95
Self-Counsel Press
1303 N. Northgate Way
Seattle, WA 98133

Divorce Guide for Oregon
by Kristena A. LaMar
1977; 119p; $6.95
Self-Counsel Press
1303 N. Northgate Way
Seattle, WA 98133

Divorce in the Washington Metropolitan Area – District of Columbia, Maryland, and Virginia
by Women's Legal Defense Fund
1980; 50p; $2.00
Women's Legal Defense Fund
1010 Vermont Avenue N.W. #210
Washington, D.C. 20005

★ E.   Spousal Support, Child Support and Custody

How to Collect Your Child Support and Alimony (California)
by Eileen Luboff and
Constance Posner
1977; 196p; $7.95
Nolo Press
950 Parker St.
Berkeley, CA 94710

The title of this book is modest indeed, but it is an important contribution to a pervasive problem in our society — men who fail to meet their moral and legal obligations to their ex-wives and their children who are so often left without adequate resources. The book is a guide for women who need to collect court-ordered alimony and child support. It is also useful for anyone who has obtained a court judgment against a fleeing or hiding "debtor" who won't pay. The best chapter is the first on "skip tracing" — that is, tracing where the delinquent husband or debtor "skipped off" to. Motor vehicles, voter registration, military pension

records, and a host of other public and private records can all be used to find the "skip's" new address. If the deadbeat is found but still refuses to pay, he can be forced to appear in court in a contempt hearing and testify to the amount and whereabouts of his assets.

●

Every person who operates a motor vehicle within the state must be licensed and issued a number, commonly known as a driver's license number. The Driver's License Section of the Department of Motor Vehicles keeps many records, including the current addresses of licensees and their vehicle code violations. For a relatively small fee the D.M.V. will mail you information about your former husband's address and driving record. If the information is not up to date, you will at least receive the number and expiration date of his driver's license. In that case, wait 90 days after his birthday in the year of expiration and try again. It takes the Department of Motor Vehicles at least 90 days to process new addresses when received with license renewals. This is an excellent way to find a person's address.

After the Divorce (California Edition): How to Modify Custody, Support and Visitation Orders
by Joe Matthews
1980; $15.00
Nolo Press
950 Parker St.
Berkeley, CA 94710

This book picks up where How to Do Your Own Divorce in California *leaves off. It is a detailed guide which explains how a Californian who already has a divorce decree can modify custody, visitation and support orders. With inflation making most support orders obsolete, and new "joint custody" laws giving men more rights to participate in the parenting of their children, many formerly married couples are facing the necessity of modifying their divorce decrees. The author shows how divorced spouses can do the whole job themselves, cheaply and easily. This book is primarily for people who agree on the details of the proposed divorce decree changes, but also contains helpful information for those who are not yet in accord with each other. All the forms and instructions are in the book.*

Fathers, Husbands and Lovers – Legal Rights & Responsibilities

by Stanford N. Katz and
    Monroe L. Inker
1979; 318p; $15.00
American Bar Association
Order Billing 513
1155 E. 60th St.
Chicago, IL 60637

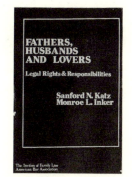

This is a series of essays on subjects which include the value of homemaker's services when unmarried couples separate, alimony orders following short-term marriages, women abuse, termination of the parental rights of the unwed father, etc. It's somewhat academic and a bit dry, but at the same time it is a fascinating collection if you are interested in this fast changing area of domestic law.

•

The law of custody also serves to illustrate how the law adapts and changes in reaction to changing values which achieve consensus or a near consensus. It is not surprising that the common law preference for the father was secure as long as feudalism flourished but disintegrated with the advent of the industrial revolution, nor that the tender years doctrine lost its luster at a time when sex discrimination was "bad form" if not unconstitutional. Eventually the law adapts to social change. The unique thing some of us have learned from the women's movement, if not beforehand, is that sexual stereotyping should be taboo in modern society.

Making Fathers Pay – The Enforcement of Child Support

by David L. Chambers
1979; 365p; $25.00
University of Chicago Press
5801 S. Ellis Avenue
Chicago, IL 60637

This is not precisely a self-help law book but more a sociological analysis of child support collection in Michigan. It's an excellent book, sensitive both to the plight of mothers trying to raise children without adequate resources and to fathers who are "jailed" as part of a modern day system of debtor's prisons (which does seem to get fathers to pay

support, but at an incredible social cost). To increase child support payments at lower social cost, Chambers advocates a national system of compulsory deductions from the wages of non-custodial parents who earn more than enough for their own subsistence. I recommend this book to anyone concerned with this problem.

F.   Name Change ★

Change Your Name (California)

by David Loeb
1979; 102p; $7.95
Nolo Press
950 Parker St.
Berkeley, CA 94710

This little exercise applies to anyone in the United States or Canada. Do you want to change your name legally? Wanna do it right now? Close your eyes and think to yourself, "My name is _____; from now on I will use only that name." Presto! If you really meant it, and you use that new name exclusively from here on in, that's it. You don't have to go to court.

A change of name by the "usage" method is just as legal as going to court. When women marry and use their husband's last name, their name is changed only because they use it; nothing requires them to adopt it. In fact, a newly married man can just as legally adopt his wife's last name; this was sometimes done in merrye olde England when the wife's family name was more prominent. So, why do people go to court to change their name?

Generally it's because having the court approve your name change is frequently easier than convincing the bureaucracies that a "usage" name change is legal. (See the article on "Name Change".)

This book deals at length with the problems faced by women (married v. birth names, establishing credit under their birth names, etc.), birth certificate amendments and reissues (only in rare cases — adoption, typographical error, and sex-change operations), and practical considerations (getting the rest of the world to accept your new name). The book is complete with name-change papers for single adults, children (the "usage" option is not available to children), and married couples or families.

•

Invariably, the first question that women ask me about name change is "Does the law require a woman to take her husband's last name?" The answer is "No." *There is no law in California which requires a woman to assume her husband's name upon marriage.*

Since there is no law requiring a woman to take her husband's last name, how does it happen? If you think about how a woman voluntarily starts using her husband's last name when she marries, it is obvious that she is changing her name by the Usage method. The marriage itself does not contain any legal order changing her name. Instead, what happens is that the woman automatically starts using her husband's last name as her own in all her business and personal affairs. Thus, simply by Usage, it becomes her new legal name. In this particular case of name change by Usage, there is no hassle in getting people to accept the new name you have adopted. It is an understood and expected change, made with a smile and maybe even "congratulations."

Names and Name Change Information for Washington Area Women (D.C., Md., Va., Fifth Edition)
by the Women's Legal Defense Fund
1978; 25p; $3.00
Women's Legal Defense Fund
1010 Vermont Avenue, N.W., Suite 210
Washington, D.C. 20005

This pamphlet contains useful information for women in Washington D.C., Maryland, and Virginia, who are interested in the law of name changes as it applies to them—women who want to retain their birth names after marriage, or to re-assume their birth names after divorce or while married.

The substantive law is covered fairly well and the book contains instructions for name-change court petitions for the three jurisdictions.

•

In Virginia, state Attorney General Andrew F. Miller cited the *Stuart* case with approval and opined that the law of Virginia followed the English common law rule that "a married woman is entitled, but not compelled, to assume her husband's surname as her own." (Letter of June 6, 1973 to Jean S. Mahan, Secretary, State Board of Elections.) It should be cautioned, however, that Attorney General Miller also expressed the opinion "that any public use by a married woman of her husband's surname after her marriage would have the effect of changing her name, as a matter of law, to that of her husband" and that return to her married name could only be accomplished through a court procedure. The Virginia Supreme Court recently reversed a lower courts' denial of two married women's petitions for name changes back to their birth names. *In*

Re Strikwerda, 220 S.E.2d 245 (1975). In that decision the court discusses the common law and notes "Under the common law a person is free to adopt any name if it is not done for a fraudulent purpose or an infringement upon the rights of others."

III.   The Home

A.   Tenants' Rights ★

The Rights of Tenants (An ACLU Handbook)
by Richard E. Blumberg and James R. Grow
1978; 192p; $1.95
Avon Books
250 W. 55th Street
New York, NY 10019

This book is unbelievable! The differences in landlord-tenant law from state to state are more extensive than in any other branch of law. A national book would logically have to trade off detailed accuracy for broader geographical scope. But this book comes very close to giving both detail and accuracy, in addition to depicting the statutes of tenant-landlord law state by state.

The law has finally recognized an obligation on the part of the landlord to maintain the premises in decent, safe, sanitary, and "habitable" condition. The major breakthrough came in Judge Skelly Wright's precedent-setting opinion in the case of *Javins* v. *First National Realty Corp.*, where, for the first time, the court recognized this "implied warranty of habitability." It does not take a great legal mind to understand the reasoning of the court. A tenant living in a fifth-floor apartment is not interested in the rental of a parcel of land, as was the agrarian tenant, but rather is seeking a package of goods and services which includes heat, hot water, plumbing, electricity, and a roof without leaks. The landlord-tenant relationship should therefore be governed by the more flexible law of contracts, instead of the restrictive law of property.

California Tenants' Handbook (Fifth Edition)
by Myron Moskovitz, Ralph
    Warner, & Charles
    Sherman
1980; 203p; $6.95
Nolo Press
950 Parker St.
Berkeley, CA 94710

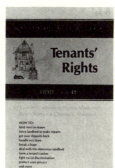

*Landlords have associations,
lobbyists, lawyers and legislators to protect their interests, while tenants have few
comparable resources. This book is designed to
change this imbalance in California. This straight-
talking book (now in its fifth edition and — like most
of us — getting fatter each year) combines a discussion of the real-life aspects of renting with the legal
protections of renters.*

*It begins with general information on the land-
lord's outlook on rental property as an investment,
and moves on to the nitty-gritty of techniques for
looking for a place, negotiating terms, dealing with
roommate hassles, and buying insurance. Also discussed are getting deposits returned, breaking a
lease, getting repairs made, using small claims court,
dealing with an unscrupulous landlord, forming a
tenants union, preventing condominium conversions, etc. It contains sample letters and agreements
as well as a "Fair-to-Tenants" lease and rental
agreement.*

*The best "legal" aspect of the book, though, is the
basic directions for defending against eviction lawsuits in California, including sample legal forms.*

•

In order for a landlord to win an unlawful detainer action
to evict a tenant he *must* start by serving the tenant with a
written notice. Landlords usually know how to make and
serve notices properly. If a landlord does it wrong, your
remedy is to raise the defect as a technical basis. You then
gain time, as the landlord will have to start all over again.
This is a very strong point with which you or your lawyer
can bargain for other concessions.

Below is a brief summary of the technical rules regarding notice and service:

i. 3-day notices. If you are late with your rent in any
amount, the landlord can serve you with a written notice
to either pay up within three days *or* get out. The notice
must describe the premises in question and state the
amount of rent due. It must give the tenant the choice of
paying or leaving. This means that if the tenant pays the

amount demanded within three days, then the notice is
satisfied and is of no further meaning. Three day notices
can also be given for other specific breaches of lease or
rental agreements (i.e., loud parties or pets prohibited by
the agreement). In each case the notice must specify the
fault and demand its correction within three days as an
alternative to moving out.

Texas Tenants Handbook
by Jim Simons, Myron Moskovitz, and Ralph
    Warner
1980;250p; $6.95
Addison-Wesley Publishing Co.
Trade Sales
Reading, MA 01867

*This book replicates the understandable and
valuable California Tenants Handbook. We highly
recommend this book for all Texas tenants.*

Legal Tactics: Handbook for Massachusetts Tenants (Third Edition)
by National Lawyers Guild, Cambridge Tenants'
    Organization, and Somerville Tenants Union
1980; 250p; $5.00
Massachusetts Chapter of the National Lawyers
    Guild
120 Boylston Street
Boston, MA 02116

*The best of both worlds seems to be combined here.
While the book is an easily-read, down-to-earth survival manual for dealing with Massachusetts landlords, references are made throughout to detailed
footnotes of law for advocates and others who want to
learn as much as possible about landlord-tenant
law. This third edition is completely updated to
include all the latest changes in the law, including
the new state sanitary code. New sections include
material on public and subsidized housing, utilities,
suing the landlords (rather than defensively asserting
your rights and waiting for him to sue you), and an
expanded chapter on tenant organizing. The appendix includes the compete text of all applicable laws
and sample pleadings. This is an excellent and
understandable explanation of housing law for
tenants, tenant organizers, and tenant advocates.*

•

Your landlord is obligated to return your security deposit
within thirty days from the day you move out. He may
deduct from the security deposit the following: (1) any
unpaid rent unless the rent was validly withheld, for

example, due to health code violations, (2) any unpaid increase in real estate taxes for which you are responsible under a valid tax escalator clause; and (3) a reasonable amount to repair damage caused by you (including members of your family and guests). These are the only deductions he may make. If the landlord deducts money for repairs, within the thirty days, he must give you an itemized list of *damages*, describing in detail the kind of damages, and the repairs necessary. This list must be sworn to by the landlord or his agent. He must also provide evidence of the actual cost of such repairs by written receipt or other document. The landlord *cannot* deduct for damages listed on the statement of condition that he gave to you when you moved in, or for any damages listed by you and given to the landlord. The landlord *cannot* deduct for "reasonable wear and tear."

California Eviction Defense Manual

by Myron Moskovitz, Peter J. Honigsberg, David G.
  Finkelstein
1971; 389p (supplements are published annually);
  $40.00
Continuing Education of the Bar
2150 Shattuck Ave.
Berkeley, CA 94704

Although this legal treatise is best suited to an advocate defending a tenant from an eviction proceeding in the California courts, it can also be used by a tenant defending him/herself. It is somewhat technical, however.

California eviction ("unlawful detainer") procedure is blatantly tilted toward the landlord and against the tenant, and the use of this book can help tilt it back a bit in the tenants' direction.

This manual is designed to assist the tenant's attorney in defending an unlawful detainer action (eviction proceeding). It is not a treatise on the whole spectrum of legal rights of landlords and tenants in California. Nor is it a complete in-depth exposition of California procedural law. This manual takes the attorney through the unlawful detainer case step-by-step, explaining the necessary procedural steps and ones he might invoke if he wishes. We describe some substantive law to make him aware of certain defenses, and some procedural law that will enable him to understand generally how to handle his case, stressing procedural issues that are likely to arise.

Everything California Tenants Need to Know about Getting Back Their Security Deposits

by David W. Brown
1979; 14p (staple bound); $1.50;
Distributed by:
Nolo Press
950 Parker St.
Berkeley, CA 94710

This little publication contains the most thorough information on the subject of getting back security deposits (cleaning, damage, last month's rent, etc.). Anyone particularly concerned with this area of law will want to get it as a supplement to the California Tenants Handbook *(reviewed above).*

•

Making a Formal Demand

It is a prerequisite to filing a small claims court action that you make a demand on the person, partnership, association, or corporation for payment of the amount in dispute. While this need not be done in writing, it is advisable that you do so because 1) it will show the landlord that you mean business, and 2) your copy of the letter can be shown to the judge to show that you made a good-faith attempt to first settle the matter out of court. You need not send the letter by certified or registered mail, but you might consider doing so to see if it will be refused by the landlord. If he refuses to sign for the letter, you may be able to claim that this shows bad faith, entitling you to punitive damages. You will also know whether you will be able to later use certified mail to have the papers served.

Tenant's Tactics (Ohio)

by the Columbus Tenants' Union
1978; 55p; Write for price
Columbus Tenants Union
82 E. 16th Avenue
Columbus, OH 43201

Consider the following scenario. Tenants in a 100-unit apartment get a 40% rent increase. Some move out, while others stay and fight. They organize a tenant's union for starters, but the landlord refuses even to meet with them. Not only that, but two weeks later, one of the organizers receives a 30-day eviction notice for "violating the terms of your rental agreement by having an unauthorized pet" (known and accepted by the landlord for the two years prior). What can they do?

This booklet will raise your political consciousness while painlessly teaching you tenant's rights in Ohio. Discrimination and retaliation by landlords, legal evictions, getting substandard housing fixed, getting back security deposits, and tenant organizing are all covered in this valuable pamphlet.

●

Changes and Rent Increases in a Month-to-Month Agreement

Under this kind of agreement, a landlord can raise the rent any amount, change any rules, or ask you to leave, simply by following the proper procedure. The law says that the proper procedure involves giving the tenant a thirty day written notice on the day rent is due to take effect on the next rent day. A currently successful interpretation of the law says that the notice *must* be in writing. This notice gives you the chance to move if you don't like the change.

The landlord can make any of these changes for almost any reason (for exceptions see p. 5). This means that every month, your rental situation is in the power of the landlord — *completely.*

Tenants' Rights: A Guide for Washington State

by Barbara A. Isenhour,
　James E. Fearn, Jr., and
　Steve Fredrickson
1977; 130p; $5.95
University of Washington
　Press
Seattle, WA

The law of landlord and tenant is so vastly different from state to state that few generalizations, if any, can ever be made about the status of the law in the United States. This is exemplified by New Jersey, with its well-organized statewide tenants' union and progressive laws — including rent control in over 100 cities, in contrast to Mississippi and Texas where it is legal to lock out the tenant, turn off the utilities, invade his/her privacy, and even go in and take the tenant's property in order to satisfy owed rent.

From this lack of uniformity comes some hope — the Uniform Residential Landlord and Tenant Act (URLTA). This law was drafted by the National Conference of Commissioners on Uniform State Laws with the intent of removing some of the absurdities of urban landlord-tenant law that are derived from thousand-year-old feudal concepts. URLTA has only been adopted in thirteen states, and even these thirteen states have modifications and loopholes, due to the landlords' lobbies.

One of the eight URLTA states is Washington, and this book explains how Washington's URLTA relates to its tenants. The best chapters deal with what to do about needed repairs, how to get deposits back, and how to defend against evictions — legal and illegal. Included are sample letters to the landlord, sample legal forms for eviction actions and the complete text of Washington's URLTA.

●

Although many landlords are interested in maintaining their buildings and are willing to make necessary repairs promptly, you should know your rights when dealing with a reluctant landlord. Hopefully, you will be able to get repairs made with just a telephone call or conversation with your landlord. Not all landlords expect or insist on formal written notices requesting repairs. Before you can take any action against an uncooperative landlord, however, a *written* notice to repair is usually required. There may also be a fairly long waiting period after the written notice is given before you can take any action. The length of the notice period depends on the seriousness of the problem. The sooner you give written notice the better.

You have a number of alternatives if your landlord fails or refuses to make required repairs. The alternatives include:

1. Deducting repair costs from your rent;
2. Suing your landlord;
3. Getting your landlord to agree to arbitration;
4. Reporting your landlord to the local building department or health department;
5. Moving out;
6. Withholding rent.

Landlord/Tenant Relations for Oregon

by Michael H. Marcus
1977; 243p; $5.50
Self-Counsel Press, Inc.
1303 N. Northgate Way
Seattle, WA 98133

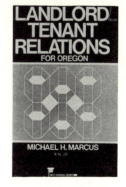

This book is a fairly thorough outline of tenants' rights under the Oregon version of the Uniform Residential Landlord and Tenant Act (currently enacted in ten states). Although a good deal of the book is devoted to tenant's remedies and defenses against unlawful evictions in court, there is still not enough information presented on that topic to inform a tenant how to proceed without

a lawyer, though sample forms are provided. On the other hand, it does present a well-done outline of substantive landlord/tenant law.

•

1. The retaliatory eviction defense

The retaliatory eviction section of the Landlord and Tenant Act is designed to protect tenants against evictions which are motivated by a landlord's desire to get back at a tenant for asserting his or her rights — or to get rid of a tenant to avoid responsibilities imposed on the landlord by the act.

Section 91.865 provides that a landlord may not retaliate by increasing rent, decreasing services, or by bringing or threatening to bring an eviction action after a tenant has:

(a) complained to an appropriate code enforcement agency concerning a code violation "materially affecting health and safety,"

(b) complained to the landlord "of a violation under ORS 91.770" (the major habitability section of the act), or

(c) organized or joined a tenants' union or similar organization.

Subject to the limitations discussed below, if your landlord violates this section you have a right to recover up to twice your actual damages or twice your monthly rent, whichever is greater. You can seek this kind of recovery either in the eviction action or in a separate action. Your damages may include emotional distress.

Chicago Tenants' Handbook

by Ed Sacks
1978; 308p; $4.95
Harper & Row
10 East 53rd St.
New York, NY 10022

This book is basically an indictment of the city of Chicago — its agencies, inspectors, judges, and landlords. It's most likely very true, but also discouraging reading. •

The book can be useful to most urban tenants, but it is by and large a Chicagoan tenants book. Topics of universal applicability include checking out an apartment, helpful hints about moving, explanations of heating and plumbing systems, and organizing a tenants union.

The legal discussions, unfortunately, lack organization and detail. However, an extensive appendix which includes summaries of the Illinois tenant/ landlord statutes, Chicago Building Code Ordinance, and a clause-by-clause analysis of landlord leases is useful.

•

Roaches are the subject of songs, books, jokes, and long conversations. Franz Kafka has died and gone to heaven. He is no longer a beetle and these are not his cousins. Kill them dead, as the ad goes. Oh yes, you can get rid of the roaches, but to do so requires dedication.

First, the roach needs water. Water can be found in the bathroom and kitchen. Water can be found as moist condensation on the outside of the cold water pipes running in the walls. Find where all the pipes — hot, cold, sewer, gas, and conduit — come into the apartment. Seal the wall around them with grout of Sinkloid spackling mix.

Inspect all the sinks, tubs, drains, and so forth for leaking water. Tighten up loose connections and have the landlord repair anything else, including dripping faucets.

Control of roaches will now be in three steps: Clean out and empty all your kitchen cabinets, bathroom shelves, and any other dark hiding places you have seen roaches. Roaches eat soap powder, glue, paper, and other nonfood stuffs, as well as people food. Roaches are found where people live because people bring these delicacies with them. Empty your shelves, wash them, and dry them. Be sure you leave no trace of soap or paper lint. Do not, I repeat, do not put liners on your shelves until after the roaches are purged.

Everything replaced in storage should be wrapped in plastic. Nothing should be accessible to the beasties for about three months.

B.   Landlords' Responsibilities ★

Landlording

by Leigh Robinson
1980; 245p; $15.00
Express Press
P.O. Box 1373
Richmond, CA 94802

Formerly a do-it-yourself legal eviction kit combined with a comprehensive business manual for small and conscientious landlords, the 1980 edition now concentrates only on the latter.

This is a comprehensive guide with detailed information on maintenance, advertising and finding good tenants, in addition to the business aspects. A new chapter, "Getting Problem Tenants Out," deals with the psychological weapons that can be used to get a bad tenant to peacefully leave without his vindictively demolishing the property. "Keeping Good Tenants" is also a very useful chapter.

•

Offer to redecorate their dwelling if it hasn't been done in three or more years and the place is beginning to look shabby. All too frequently good tenants feel compelled to move because their landlord or landlady expects them to tolerate living in a dwelling which needs new linoleum in the bathroom, paint in the living room, drapes in the bedroom, and carpeting in the hallway. When they decide not to tolerate such conditions any longer and they move away to a dwelling which has been completely redecorated by a new landlord or landlady, their former landlord or landlady is forced not only to redecorate but to lose rent while the place is vacant and then to bear the expense and suffer though the process of finding new tenants who will be as good as the old ones. That former landlord or landlady would actually have saved money by redecorating to keep the good old tenants instead of redecorating to attract new ones. You cannot afford to be oblivious to the condition of your vacant rentals.

IV. Rights of Consumers

A. Consumer Protection

Getting What You Deserve
by Stephen A. Newman & Nancy Kramer
1979; 328p; $8.95
Doubleday & Co., Inc.
Garden City, NY

This is an excellent tome covering almost any and everything in the way of consumer awareness. In fact, it is the best book yet on this topic that we have read. The book begins with a vigorous attack on that which induces us all to become consumers in the first place—advertising, its deceptions, its use on children, and its subliminal effects on our choice of products. Also included are the following:

—How to read fine print, illegal and unreadable contract clauses, and how to get out of some contracts (e.g., you can cancel a door-to-door sales contract within a three-day cooling-off period).

—How to complain effectively. How to write complaint letters that are easily read, to the point,

and most likely to get results.

—Tricks of the trade with new and used car dealers.

—Con games: the bank examiner swindle, "pigeon drop", etc.

—Common door to door frauds: how to avoid being taken in—and if you are taken in, how to undo the contract.

—Funeral: common methods by which the funeral industry takes advantage of folks when they're most vulnerable. Sensible alternatives to the traditional funeral.

—Health club and dance studio frauds.

—And much more.

•

. . . it is unlikely that fraud blossomed in the Middle Ages. Merchants and traders dealt within very limited geographic bounds, with those they knew and who knew them. Sharp practices were soon discovered and known throughout the community. The medieval Church, with its considerable authority, condemned deceit and declared its motivating force, avarice, a deadly sin. At the large mercantile fairs, where groups of merchants exhibited their wares and sold to strangers, weights and measures were carefully taken and the ethical character of trade was strictly enforced by official rules.

When market towns replaced fairs as the focus of trade and commerce, strict regulation of merchandise quality and price prevailed. Violators received direct, swift, and public punishment. Cheats might be ignominiously paraded through the streets with trumpets blaring, or have their heads and hands locked in the public pillory for all to see (while their goods were burned at their feet), or be banished from the community for a year and a day. Exposure to public scorn and ridicule served to deter those tempted to give less than fair value and decent wares to their customers.

As business expanded in size and influence, the modes of trade became more impersonal and less responsive to local standards of fairness. The warning *caveat emptor*—buyer beware—began to be heard in the seventeenth century. Despite the Latin words, the phrase did not originate in ancient Rome, nor was it a legal term. It was merely a common-sense warning that, when dealing with rogues and strangers you might never see again, you had better be very careful. Some pretentious person, probably a medieval lawyer, translated the advice into Latin.

Unfortunately for the consuming public, eighteenth- and nineteenth-century English and American courts took this simple adage and elevated it into an exalted legal doctrine. The seller who misrepresented wares suddenly had a legal defense: the deceived buyer should have ignored the seller's words and independently sought out the truth.

The New Consumer Survival-Kit
by Richard George
1978; 345p; $8.95
Little, Brown and Company
34 Beacon St.
Boston, MA 02106

*The uniqueness of this fine
book is due to the fact that
each chapter was originally
a television script (now
revised, of course) for the
Public Broadcasting Service
program "Consumer Survival Kit." One of the best
points of this book is its fine organization of concise
information on numerous topics. The contents look
something like this:*

HOUSING *(buying a house, home improvements
and repairs, weatherproofing, home security —
including an interview with a burglar!)*
AUTOS *(new, used, repairs and body work, tires)*
HEALTH *((family doctors, over-the-counter and
prescription drugs), eye care (glasses, contact lenses),
hearing aids, dental care, weight control, insurance,
nutrition, nursing homes))*
MONEY *(managing it, all about banks, credit,
investments, land frauds, jobs)*
PLANNING *(life insurance, wills and estates,
retirement, funerals)*
SHOPPING *(the great miscellaneous, weddings,
supermarkets, buying for babies, appliances, TV and
stereo, cosmetics, hair care, wine, plants, lawn
supplies)*
SETTLING DIFFERENCES *(complaining,
small claims courts, about lawyers, divorce)*
*Each sub-category listed above is divided into even
more subcategories, so you can swiftly zero in on the
information you need to deal with a problem.*

•

Resealing your driveway. A workman appears at your door,
and says he has enough materials left over from another
job to reseal your driveway at a bargain price. Usually, the
sealing consists of a once-over spraying of machine oil or
black paint that washes away a few weeks later. Proper
sealing of a driveway should take two men several hours.
An asphalt emulsion should be used, and the surface
should last more than a year.

A Consumer's Arsenal
by John Dorfman
1976; 270p; $3.95
Praeger Publishers, Inc.
111 Fourth Avenue
New York, NY 10003

*The major usefulness of this book is that it contains
vast and well-organized lists of public and private
agencies, including branch offices, mailing addresses,
and telephone numbers. The agencies include all
consumer organizations for the 50 states and major
cities, branch offices of the Federal Trade Commission, industry groups that purport to "police" their
member business, and major manufacturers. It also
introduces the consumer to the art of complaining
effectively through a strategy of escalation.*

Young Consumers (available in student edition and teachers manual)
by Linda Riekes & Sally M. Ackerly
1980; 124p; $4.75
West Publishing Co.
170 Old Country Road
Mineola, NY 11501

*Would you think it possible to teach elementary
school children about consumer fraud, warranties,
credit cards, small claims court, labeling laws, and
"bait-and-switch" tactics? Not being elementary
school children ourselves, we can't tell you if it's
perfectly suited, but we can tell you that this book is
entertaining to read and look at (grandiose eye-
catching illustrations in red, blue, and brown). The
sections on contracts, credit cards, and warranties
are especially informative without seeming complex.
(If you think that's an easy chore, just try explaining
all about offer, acceptance, counter-offer, etc. to a
10-year old.) The book is organized into 36 lessons.*

•

The words in this list are often found in ads.

free	magic
brand new	offer
sensational	compare
reduced	latest
improved	popular
bargain	modern
sale	miracle
easy	soothing
suddenly	remarkable
amazing	unbelievable
current	

To learn to be careful about appeal words do these things:

1. Give another word or words having a similar meaning for each of the words listed above.

2. Why do you think these words are used so often in ads? Can you think of other words you often see in ads?

3. Think of a product you like very much. Write an ad about it in one or two sentences. Use as many words from the above list as you can.

4. Look through newspaper or magazines to find ads which use these words or other emotional appeal words. From the ads you collect, add to this list of emotional appeal words. Discuss the ads you bring in. Do *you* think they are effective in persuading people to buy? Why? Why not?

B. Access to Government Information and Its Access to Yours

How to Use the Freedom of Information Act (FOIA)
by L.G. Sherick
1978; 138p; $3.50
Arco Publishing Co.
219 Park Avenue South
New York, NY 10003

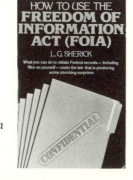

The Freedom of Information Act was signed into law by Lyndon B. Johnson on July 4, 1966. There have been few laws passed which are so fundamental to our maintenance of an open society. Our constitution and the Bill of Rights worked well enough in the days when the enemy was crazy old George the Third, but they appear to have less relevance when pitted against those alphabet-soup monsters spawned by the 20th century marriage of bureaucracy and technology. The FBIs, CIAs, IRSs and HUDs of this world thrive on secrecy. After prying open their file cabinets, we are only beginning to discover the enormity of the harm they have inflicted on the citizens of this and other countries. This little book is an instruction kit on how to use the crowbar. And it's a good job as far as it goes, but unfortunately, that's not far enough. The book is seriously flawed by not including material on what happens if your request for information is denied.

•

Freedom of Information requests and cases abound throughout the Federal bureaucracy. Did you know that it was under the Act that the FBI was forced to open its files on the assassinations of President John F. Kennedy, Robert Kennedy and the Reverend Martin Luther King, Jr.? Dossiers on Ezra Pound, Alger Hiss and the Rosenbergs also surfaced via FOIA. The disclosure that the Nixon White House instigated Internal Revenue Service investigations of social action groups on the left and in the black community was caused by FOIA requests. The alarming news of FBI counter-intelligence activities against "radical" organizations was pried loose with lawsuits under the Act. All this and much more is the result of concerned citizens exercising their rights to knowledge of the governments' activities and demanding accountability.

Getting Your Government Files
by Grand Jury Project/National Lawyers Guild
25¢
Grand Jury Project
National Lawyers Guild
853 Broadway
New York, NY 10003

This is a short and simple guide to getting your files under the Freedom of Information Act.

Privacy: How to Protect What's Left of It
by Robert Ellis Smith
1980; 338p; $4.95
Anchor Press/Doubleday
Garden City, New York

Since the dawn of the electronic age, information has become easier and easier to store and our personal lives have become less and less our own. Smith very graphically demonstrates to us that since the birth of the computer, every institution in society has access to our "private" information with the push of a button. There are ways to resist and combat such easy access and the dire consequences that can ensue. Smith outlines "what you can do" at the end of each topic he discusses. Those topics include records held by the bank, consumer credit bureaus, schools, physicians, pyschiatrists and hospitals, insurance companies, and the FBI and other government agencies. The book also explains how the new technology — in the form of computers, electronic surveillance, finger-

printing and lie detectors — affects our rights. In addition, issues of physical privacy, in sexual matters and in the work place and community, plus psychological privacy, are presented.

This is an extremely important and very upsetting book, and should be read by everyone.

★ C.   All About Credit and Bankruptcy

Credit Where Credit Is Due
by Glen Walker
1979; 198p; $4.95
Brownstone Books
Holt, Rinehart, & Winston
New York, NY

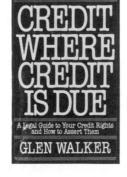

What is the difference between a store's price tag stating "Price: $100. 5% discount if paid by cash or check" and one stating "Price: $95. 5¼% surcharge if paid by credit card"? (Merchants would like to do this because banks typically charge them 5% "commission" on bank credit card purchases.) With both price tags you pay $95 if you pay by cash or check and $100 if you use a credit card. The first appears to be a discount payment by cash or check, the second a surcharge for credit card use. A credit card purchaser might flinch at the "5¼% surcharge" but happily pay the $100 price without the 5% cash discount, when the effect is identical. The difference is that the "discount" is legal while the "surcharge" isn't.

That's one of the many little revelations dealt with in an enlightened fashion here. The book carefully explains to the average consumer the law of credit cards, truth-in-lending, discrimination and credit, credit bureaus and collection agencies.

•

The law is Chapter 4 of the Truth-in-Lending Act, better known as the Fair Credit Billing Act (FCBA). It was passed in 1974 and became effective on October 28, 1975.

Essentially, the FCBA is intended to provide an orderly procedure for correcting billing errors where credit-card or open-end credit purchases are involved (as discussed earlier, that includes practically everything except a fixed, one-time extension of a loan). In general, the law requires the following.

Notification   The creditor must notify you of your rights

under the act and tell you where to send any billing complaint or inquiry you may have. The law requires him to send a "notice of credit billing rights" at least twice a year.

Your Complaint   To take advantage of the law, you must give the creditor *written notice* of your question or complaint within sixty days of the bill he sends you. Until the matter is settled, you don't have to pay the amount in dispute, *but you do have to pay any amount you're not disputing.*

The Creditor's Response   First, he has to acknowledge your complaint within thirty days. Second, he has to investigate and let you know whether you're right or wrong within ninety days of receiving your complaint. Meanwhile, the creditor is prohibited from dunning you for the disputed amount or turning that amount over to a collection agency. If he reports the matter to a credit bureau, he has to explain that the bill is being disputed and later he has to notify the credit bureau how the dispute has been resolved.

Credit and Borrowing
— in New York
— in Illinois
— in Florida
— in Texas
by William R. Wishard
1978; 270p; $6.95
Cragmont Publications
P.O. Box 27496
San Francisco, CA 94127

After Credit Where Credit Is Due, *these are excellent books on the rights of persons owing money. They certainly are the best state-wide books on credit. Since much of credit law is federal, billpayers in states other than New York, Illinois, Florida, or Texas could use most of the information contained herein if nothing else were available in their states.*

Well explained are the differences between secured and unsecured debts, credit card problems and how to correct them, bankruptcy, and how to deal with bill collectors.

•

One of the most important things you must do when you file bankruptcy, and one of the matters in which you must be the most careful, is that of listing all of your *assets* (everything you own). This includes personal possessions, wages, money, bank accounts, etc. Where the amount of your assets is sufficient, the bankruptcy court will use some of them to pay off some of your creditors (never mind which ones, the court will figure that out). Nevertheless, the bankruptcy laws are such that you may keep any necessary things, and these are called *exempt assets* by the court and are extremely important to you.

California Debtors' Handbook (Third Edition)

by Peter Jan Honigsberg and
    Ralph Warner
1979; 177p; $5.95
Nolo Press
950 Parker Street
Berkeley, CA 94710

If you're the type to cringe when the creditor or collection agency threatens to "go right out and garnish your wages next week," this book explains that:

1) It will take them at least 6 weeks to do it— they have to sue you and get a court judgment first;

2) You can delay the process even longer by negotiating, filing responding papers to the lawsuit;

3) Even if they get a court judgment against you, your property and paycheck might be legally non-seizable;

4) You can probably get them to settle for 75¢ (or maybe even 50¢) on the dollar.

Also covered are credit ratings, car repossessions, and a brief introduction to what bankruptcy can and can't do for you. Once you've read this book, you might be able to deal with one of those 7:30 A.M. collection agency phone calls like this:

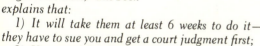

BC: Hello, Mr. "S," I am calling about your charge account. It's overdue.
S: Yes, I know.
BC: Well, when can we expect a payment?
S: Not for another month or two.
BC: I'm sorry but we cannot accept that.
S: Well, there's nothing else I can do. We just don't have any money right now and won't have any next month.
BC: What is the problem, Mr. "S"?
S: It's personal and I would rather not talk about it.
BC: You realize that your credit rating will fall because of this.
S: Yes, I know, but I have no interest in buying more things on credit.
BC: And that it will hinder you from getting credit at other places.
S: Yes, but I just don't have any money right now and I am tired of paying high interest anyway.

BC: We can also attach your wages.
S: Yes, but not until you get a judgment and that takes time.
BC: Why, we have a battery of lawyers and can send them to court in fifteen minutes.
S: Yes, but you still must serve me with papers, have a trial, and get a judgment before you can attach. This takes 30 days from the time you serve me with the papers which you have not done yet.
BC: You think you're so smart. Why, we can call your employer.
S: Yes, but you can only do it once.
BC: How did you know that? Oh (mumble, mumble), but once is enough anyway.
S: And besides you don't know who my employer is.
BC: Oh, we have ways of finding out.
S: And besides he wouldn't care.
    Click—the bill collector hung up.

The Credit Game—How Women Can Win It
Women's Legal Defense Fund, Inc.
1010 Vermont Ave., N.W. #210
Washington, D.C. 20005
1975; 19p; $2.00

This is a useful little booklet that explains in simple, realistic terms how women can get credit and how they can reverse a denial of credit. The booklet has some across-the-board practical advice and discussion of federal laws, but it is primarily aimed at residents of D.C., Maryland, and Virginia.

•

Credit in your own name is established when it is based on your own earnings or property and the account is listed under your own name, with your own individual account number. When applying for credit in your own name, if married:

—give your own name, i.e. Mary Jones, not Mrs. David Jones

—write "not applicable" (n/a) in appropriate blanks requesting your husband's name and credit references.

Remember you will then be judged on your credit history and income alone. If you need your husband's income and history in order to qualify for that loan or account you will have to list it. Both parties will have to sign the application and will be held legally liable for the resulting loan or account. You can, however, still be the primary account-holder. Your husband can sign as authorized user and back-up guarantor.

Bankruptcy: Do It Yourself
by Janice Kosel
50-state edition by
Addison-Wesley Publishing Co.
Reading, MASS
1980; 180p; $11.95
California edition by
Nolo Press
950 Parker Street
Berkeley, CA 94710
1980; 176p; $12.00

*Doing your own bankruptcy is not extremely diffi-
cult, but neither is it a simple task. First you have to
know whether your situation calls for the drastic step
of bankruptcy. Then you have to know what you can
keep: "exempt" property v. "nonexempt" property;
"secured" v. "unsecured" debts (is there a mortgage
or "lien" on property?), federal v. state exemptions,
etc. This book clearly lays it all out. It also includes a
"flow chart" which asks a series of yes-or-no questions
to help with your individual situation. For those trying to decide between the list of federal and state laws
of exempt property, a well-organized Appendix gives
each state's list of exempt property.*

*This book is complete with three copies of all neces-
sary forms—one sample filled out, one with detailed
instructions blocked out on it, and one for you to fill
out.*

•

A "secured" debt is created when you make a written
promise (usually in the form of a printed security agreement) that, if you do not pay, the creditor can take some
particular item of your property—either the item you
purchased or perhaps another item you pledged. Examples
of merchandise where secured debts are common include
motor vehicles, major appliances, expensive jewelry and
furniture. Most secured debts are dischargeable in bankruptcy—that is, they will vanish after bankruptcy. But
they are different from unsecured debts where there is no
written security agreement. *Sometimes,* in exchange for
wiping out a secured debt, you must either return the
secured item to the creditor, or, if you want to keep the
item, you must pay for it. Notice that I used the word
"sometimes." That means we'll have to divide secured
debts into two types.

Type A. The secured creditor sold you the property or
loaned you the money to buy it.

You must be ready to lose the secured property as part of
having the debt wiped out in bankruptcy—unless, of
course, you want to pay for it. According to law, after
bankruptcy you must pay the secured creditor either the
amount of the debt or the present value of the property—

whichever is less—in order to keep the property you
pledged.

Type B. The secured creditor loaned you money and
got you to pledge property that you already owned as
security.

You can get the debt wiped out and are free to keep the
property after bankruptcy—without paying any more for
it.

How To Do A Bankruptcy (California Edition)
by Harry Ellis Rogers
1978; 160p; $8.95 (1980
   edition to be published)
Self-Help Publications
26339 Monte Verde
Carmel-by-the-Sea, CA
   93923

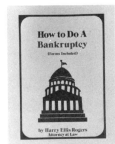

*A person filing for bank-
ruptcy can choose whether
federal or state law is to gov-
ern what "exempt" property she or he gets to keep.
Some state law exempts property more generously
than federal law. This book is California-oriented
and includes tear-out forms, with a second set
adapted for people who either own their businesses
and are going bankrupt, or who want to declare
bankruptcy for their corporation or partnership.*

•

C. The Proceedings
The "petitioner in bankruptcy" (you) completes several
legal forms. These are sent to the Federal Court in your
area. On these forms, you must list all people to whom
you owe money. The Federal Court then sends official
notice to all of these creditors of your request to have these
debts *"discharged"* (forgiven). Your creditors are also
ordered in this notice to not seek payment from you anymore. Your creditors are given a time and date to appear at
your court hearing and make inquiries of you regarding
your eligibility for bankruptcy. This is called a "First
Meeting of Creditors." This will probably be the only time
you'll have to make a court appearance.

Credit Law and Bankruptcy Handbook

Washington edition by Seth
    Armstrong 146p
Oregon edition by Richard
    A. Slottee 142p
1977; $3.95
Self-Counsel Press, Inc.
1303 N. Northgate Way
Seattle, WA 98133

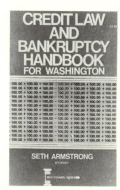

*While not as comprehensive
as* Credit Where Credit Is
Due, *these state-wide editions are worth mentioning.
The Washington edition seems a little more pro-
consumer than does the Oregon edition. They are
more explanatory (outlining aspects of major types of
credit: retail installment plans, bank cards, seller
account cards, loan sharks and finance companies,
etc.) than problem oriented. The "how-to" aspect
(correcting billing errors, finding out what's in your
credit file, etc.) is less emphasized.*

    *Still, these books are an informative introduction
for those who are curious or confused about the many
ingenious devices, plans, and interesting schemes
creditors use.*

Protect Your Home With A Declaration of Homestead

by Ralph Warner, Charles
    Sherman, and Toni Ihara
1978; 77p; $4.95
Nolo Press
950 Parker St.
Berkeley, CA 94710

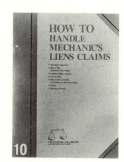

*A "homestead," as referred
to in this book, has nothing
to do with pioneers in TV
westerns filing claim to free
federal land. Instead, it concerns the way homeowners (in California) can prevent creditors with a
court judgment against the homeowner from taking
away the home. If the difference in amount is less
than $40,000 between the selling price of your home
and the outstanding balance you owe; if you're head
of a household or over age 65; or if the difference is
less than $25,000 and you are single, you can protect
your home. Even if the amount is more, you can take
steps to protect your home.*

    *If you file a "Declaration of Homestead" with the
County Recorder's office, it only costs $3.00. This
book explains homesteading and how to fill out the
included forms. It also contains discussion on topics
like residency requirements, effects on credit ratings,
and how homesteading interplays with divorce,
death, and bankruptcy.*

How To Handle Mechanic's Lien Claims

by John C. Howell
1979; 105p; $14.95
Citizen's Law Library, Suc.
6 West Loudon St.
P.O. Box 1745
Leesbury, VA 22075

*Consider the following. You
hire a contractor to build an
addition to your house. The
work is done satisfactorily,
and you pay the contractor the full amount. (And
you are lucky, indeed, if there are no snags up to
now; but just for the sake of example, we'll say there
aren't.) Unfortunately, the contractor didn't pay his
subcontractors or workers, and they go after . . . you!
They file "mechanics liens" which will "cloud the
title" on your property, causing difficulty when you
want to sell it.*

    *Or, you're a carpenter who was hired to frame up a
bedroom addition. You frame it up and the owner
refuses to pay. Furthermore, even if you sue him, he
doesn't have any property except the house to attach
in order to satisfy a judgment. How can you collect?*

    *This book tells everything you want to know from
the points of view of home-owners, contractors,
material suppliers, and workers.*

•

The statutes may or may not confer the right to a lien
upon "mechanics" as such, and where they do, the lien is
not limited to "mechanics," but applies to mechanics
"and others." Normally the lien is conferred upon specifically designated persons, persons in specific occupations,
or persons doing particular kinds of work or furnishing
materials for particularly described purposes. The use of
the term "mechanic" should not mislead you. Contractors, subcontractors, laborers, materialmen, and other
"persons" doing work or furnishing materials may have a
lien. Actually, the term is of historical significance, and
we are reluctant to change the terminology because that,
too, could lead to some confusion. The lien is a statutory
extension or development of the common law "mechanics

lien," that is, the possessory lien of artisans, tradesmen, mechanics, and laborers, on personal property. What we still call a "mechanic's lien" is sometimes referred to as a "contractor's lien," "subcontractor's lien," often a "materialman's lien," a "laborer's lien," and sometimes just a "lien."

Fight Wage Garnishment
by People's Law School
1979; 12p; $1.00
People's Law School
558 Capp St.
San Francisco, CA 94110

This is a brief but well-written pamphlet for those of you who live in California, have been sued and lost (or "defaulted") and as a result, your paychecks are being "garnished" (snatched from your employer) by a creditor. Even though you might really ower the money, you can file a paper with the court to request a hearing with a judge, and at the hearing ask that the garnishment be stopped because of your obvious need to support yourself and your family. This pamphlet tells you how to do just that.

●

Garnishment
Payments from the government, such as welfare, unemployment, disability, social security and workers' compensation can't be garnished at all. If you work for the federal government, your wages can't be garnished. Here's the procedure your employer goes through if you work in private employment. First, your creditor files papers with the sheriff in the county where you work. The sheriff then goes to your employer and finds out how much "disposable wages" you have earned but haven't yet been paid. It is standard procedure for the debtor to pay the sheriff's travelling fee to the employer's place of business. The fee varies but is somewhere between $5 and $15 a trip. If you are an employee of the state, county or city government, the procedure differs somewhat but your defense is the same.

V.   Rights of . . .

A.   Workers ★

The Rights of Union Members (An A.C.L.U. Handbook)
by Clyde W. Summers and Robert J. Rabin
1979; 208p; $2.25
Avon Books
250 West 55th St.
New York, NY 10019

Like the other American Civil Liberties Union handbooks, the format of this useful book is done in question-and-answer style. We found the subject matter to be of particular value since we could find no other widely distributed publication that deals with rights of workers who are already union members. Actually, we couldn't find anything about the rights of non-union workers either in regular bookstores.

This guide discusses the rights of union members within their union, including rights of democratic processes and rights of fair representation by the union. In addition, other rights which extend to non-union workers are covered. These include general rights of freedom of association, freedom to choose which political causes they will support, and even whether workers are required to belong to a union. Sadly, there are many topics of interest to workers that are not covered, such as the provisions of the Occupation Safety and Health Act; but as a general framework within which union members can understand their rights, this book is very helpful. Detailed footnotes and selected statutory references are also included.

●

How is the duty of fair representation defined?
The Supreme Court has provided some general guidelines to help define the duty of fair representation. In one of the earliest cases, *Steele* v. *Louisville RR.*, involving a charge that a railroad union had discriminated against black employees whom it represented, the Court held that the statutory bargaining agent must exercise its power on behalf of all employees in the bargaining unit "without hostile discrimination, fairly, impartially and in good faith." Under this test it was quite clear that the union could not negotiate different benefits for different groups of employees on the basis of their race.

More than twenty years later, in the landmark case of *Vaca* v. *Sipes*, the Supreme Court elaborated upon the duty of fair representation. An employee who had been discharged because of poor health claimed that the union had improperly refused to take his case to arbitration. While the Court held that an individual has no absolute right to have his grievance taken to arbitration, the language of the decision expanded the union's obligation of fair representation in processing grievances. The Court held that in addition to its obligation to process the grievance in good faith and without discrimination, the union "may not arbitrarily ignore a meritorious grievance or process it in a perfunctory fashion." In subsequent cases the lower courts have tended to concentrate on the portion of the *Vaca* test prohibiting "arbitrary" conduct by the union; some courts have also applied the language condemning "perfunctory" handling of a grievance, although, as we shall see, courts have been reluctant to find a breach of fair representation under this test unless the union's carelessness is quite extreme.

Organizing and the Law

by Stephen I. Schlossberg and Frederick E.
    Sherman
1971; 304p; $5.50
Bureau of National Affairs
1231 25th St. N.W.
Washington, D.C. 20037

Labor law can be an intimidating phenomenon to a union organizer. When can meetings be held? leaflets be distributed? elections be called? With a caveat of the 1971 copyright date, this is considered the most useful and complete guidebook for the lay union organizer. In simplified terms, the authors explain the National Labor Relations Act, employer unfair labor practices, union unfair labor practices, recognition without elections, NLRB case procedures, bargaining units, and much more.

The Rights of Government Employees (An A.C.L.U. Handbook)

by Robert O'Neil
1978; 176p; $1.75
Avon Books
250 West 55th St.
New York, NY 10019

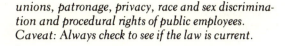

The development of a meaningful body of public employment law is a recent and evolving phenomenon. This guide, almost three years old, is a useful starting point to discover the current state of the legal rights of government employees. Topics covered are public employment and individual rights, initial qualifications for public employment, freedom of speech,

unions, patronage, privacy, race and sex discrimination and procedural rights of public employees. Caveat: Always check to see if the law is current.

•

May a person be denied public employment for homosexual conduct?

The answer, again, is that it depends on the situation. On the one hand, increasing numbers of state and local civil rights laws include "sex orientation" among grounds on which discrimination is forbidden. Such provisions forbid denial of employment to homosexuals or dismissal of persons because they are homosexual. Some government agencies, including the New York City Civil Service System, and the police departments of Los Angeles and Washington State, have removed historic bars against the hiring of homosexuals. The federal Civil Service Commission has recently taken similar action, which we will explore below.

Where such laws and policies do not exist, however, the answer is quite uncertain. The California Supreme Court and several federal courts have ruled in favor of dismissed homosexuals, either on constitutional or statutory grounds. The California Supreme Court has, in fact, quite recently reaffirmed its *Morrison* holding in the case of a teacher actually arrested but not convicted for homosexual solicitation. Since the conduct in *Morrison* was not technically criminal, much less the subject of an arrest, some doubt remained about the scope of that decision. The California court has now reaffirmed that such a transgression simply does not constitute "immoral conduct" nor evidence "unfitness to teach."

The constitutional claim of the homosexual employee has, however, recently become attenuated. In spring 1976, the Supreme Court sustained the Virginia sodomy law by summarily affirming a lower court ruling, thus implicitly rejecting the claim that sexual relations between consenting adults fall within a constitutionally protected zone of privacy. This holding appears to remove the major premise of the several decisions that have struck down homosexual disabilities on constitutional grounds. The Supreme Court later refused to review two cases in which lower courts — the federal court of appeals in California and the Supreme Court of Washington — had sustained the disqualification of employees solely on the basis of admitted homosexual relations. When in the fall of 1977 the Court simply declined to review the Washington case involving a Tacoma school teacher, front page headlines implied that the Justices had in fact affirmed the substance of the lower decisions. Such an impression is clearly incorrect; the Supreme Court has consistently avoided reaching the merits of this highly sensitive and divisive issue.

Labor Contracts Handbook
by National Lawyers Guild
1979; $1.00
NLG National Labor Committee
c/o Mark Stern
11 Meridian Street
East Boston, MA 02128

This handy little booklet is useful for both organized and unorganized workers in determining what important items should be included in labor contracts, and an explanation of the laws which govern labor contracts.

Bargaining for Equality
by Women's Labor Project of the National Lawyers
   Guild
1980; 150p; Write for price
NLG Women's Labor Project
c/o Corrine Rafferty
1230 Broadway, #2
San Francisco, CA 94109

This handy guidebook addresses workplace problems of particular interest to women, e.g., sexual harassment, comparable worth, flex-time, child care, affirmative action, sex discrimination, etc.

Although primarily aimed at women union members, this book is also useful to unorganized women. It sets out individual legal remedies and collective bargaining solutions as well as suggestions for forcing unions to be responsive and to adeqately represent women's issues. Also included are sample contract clauses.

Unemployment Rights of Washington Workers
by the NLG Unemployment Representation Clinic
1980; $1.50
Unemployment Representation Clinic
National Lawyers Guild
1205 Smith Tower
Seattle, WA 98104

Clearly written, this is a comprehensive handbook for workers in Washington state, elucidating their rights to obtain unemployment insurance.

★ **B.   Women**

Women's Rights and the Law
by Barbara A. Brown, Ann E. Freedman, Harriet
   N. Katz, Alice M. Price, with Hazel Greenberg
1977; 432p; $10.95

This book is the most comprehensive assessment of the potential impact of Equal Rights Amendment on the legal system that we have seen. Every crucial area of the law which has potential to undergo change is discussed in terms of background, impact of the ERA, policy recommendations and state reform efforts. As a reference book to evaluate likely changes of laws, we highly recommend it as clear, concise and complete. In addition, model laws drawn from states that now have ERA's are reviewed, as well as the merits and shortcomings of other laws.

**The Women's Guide to
Legal Rights**
by Jane Shay Lynch & Sara
   Lyn Smith
1979; 125p; $5.95
Contemporary Books, Inc.
180 N. Michigan Av.
Chicago, IL 60601

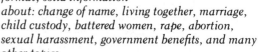

Fairly light but interesting reading, this book avoids legalese and clearly provides, in question-and-answer format, solid information about: change of name, living together, marriage, child custody, battered women, rape, abortion, sexual harassment, government benefits, and many other topics.

There are a couple of problems, however. First, we spotted a few inaccuracies. It is not, as the authors maintain, illegal to live together unmarried in most states, and sexual morality laws are no longer as widespread as they indicate; also, minor stepchildren can not acquire their stepfather's last name through mere usage. Second, the authors are over-reliant on Illinois case law to make their points. Nevertheless, it is a good, easily readable introduction to the problems faced by women at home and on the job.

●

My mother is a displaced homemaker. She says she's unemployable because she has no job history. But she's always been treasurer of ORT, coordinator of community fundraisers, even the head of the PTA. Don't these skills deserve legal recognition?

   Yes, and they do receive it! The United States Civil Service Commission now recognizes volunteer experience as being equivalent to paid employment history. Plus, displaced homemaker centers have resources to advise the mature job-seeker about how to translate that experience — how to emphasize and describe various skills she's acquired and used as a volunteer — when she interviews for a paying job.

Nearly half the states have — or soon will have — employment guidelines for state employees to recognize and evaluate volunteer experience.

Some private businesses are formally beginning to recognize the management skills and organizational talent it takes to run a blood drive, a synagogue film festival, or a hospital auxiliary shop; so the dynamo who's done these kinds of things need not check "none" in the employment application space for "work history"!

What Every Woman Needs to Know About the Law

by Martha Pomroy
1980; 416p; $14.95
Doubleday Co.
Garden City, New York

This is an excellent compilation of topics in the law that relate to women: family, working, housing, money, civil rights, rape, battered women, dealing with government agencies, consumerism, crime and punishment, and how to manage an attorney, to name a few.

The book, although not totally self-help, contains lists of occurrences when, in the author's (a woman attorney) opinion, an attorney should be consulted. Pomroy takes a very practical approach to the extensive catalogue of issues which she presents.

Getting Ours: A Handbook on Women's Legal Rights in Oregon

1978; 78p; $1.50
Community Law Project
1628 S.E. Ankeny
Portland, OR 97214

This handbook is a very well-written and fairly complete compendium of useful information for women in Oregon concerning their legal rights. Topics include health, housing, credit, employment discrimination, education discrimination, unemployment compensation, daycare, public assistance, workers' compensation, older women, marriage, marital contracts, divorce, separation and annulment, out-of-wedlock children, lesbian custody, parents' rights and the Children's Service Division, battered women, civil commitment, rape, and prostitution. The information is presented in a prac-

tical way and encourages women to exercise their rights both as individuals and collectively.

•

The Children's Services Division (CSD) is a statewide public social service agency, a part of the Oregon Department of Human Resources. It is the agency given responsibility for children whose families are not providing the conditions expected by society, such as a safe home. There are many areas where the best course of action for a child is not clear. The result is that CSD interferes in the private lives of some parents, most often poor and single women. Sometimes the agency misjudges and fails to interfere enough to protect the child. In either case, parents should know their rights to use or not use CSD services, and how to protect themselves from losing their rights unnecessarily.

CSD is the agency which usually gets custody of children made wards of the court. CSD has responsibility, subject to juvenile court review, for deciding where and for how long such children will be placed. CSD also recommends to the court whether parents' rights to their children should be terminated. The court and CSD may have different opinions. Sometimes a CSD caseworker will be your advocate in court, and other times will make recommendations you want the court to reject. However, usually the court and CSD work together for what they agree is the child's best interests.

CSD also provides social services to aid children in difficulty. These include counseling, foster care, and adoption.

The 11th National Conference on Women and the Law Sourcebook

by 11th Nat'l Conference on
    Women & the Law
1980; 368p; Write for price
Women's Association
Golden Gate University School of Law
536 Mission Street
San Francisco, CA 94105

We had originally decided not to review sourcebooks, but this is such a valuable collection of well-written essays and informative outlines on various aspects of women's rights law, that we had to include it. A few of the topics covered are sexual harassment on the job and in the classroom, the effect of the women's rights struggles on domestic law issues, battered women, and special problems faced by minority women. One hundred and fifty-eight subjects are broken down into categories of: education, economic independence, health care, housing, employment, lesbian law, older women, violence against women, and criminal law.

This book is not exclusively for women. Many of these issues are of equal importance to men, such as tenants' rights, politics of health care delivery systems, the Freedom of Information Act, and others.

•

B. If, for pregnancy-related reasons, an employee is unable to perform the functions of her job, does the employer have to provide her an alternative job?

Title VII:

1. An employer is required to treat an employee temporarily unable to perform the functions of her job because of her pregnancy-related condition in the same manner as it treats other temporarily disabled employees, whether by providing modified tasks, alternative assignments, disability leaves, leaves without pay, etc. For example, a woman's primary job function may be the operation of a machine, and, incidental to that function, she may carry materials to and from the machine. If other employees temporarily unable to lift are relieved of these functions, pregnant employees also unable to lift must be relieved of the function. (Q & A #5).

2. Yes in general, unless an employer can show a business necessity preventing such assignment, because such a rule, even if neutral on its face, has an adverse impact on women. *Griggs, supra.*

But see *Harriss v. Pan Am.*, 437 F. Supp. 413 (N.D. Cal. 1977) (not required because ground employees are represented by a different union than flight attendants); *Roller v. City of San Mateo*, 399 F. Supp. 358 (N.D. Cal. 1975) (no consideration of business necessity rule).

Women's Action Almanac: A Complete Resource Guide
by the Women's Action Alliance
1979; 432p; $7.95
William Morrow & Company
105 Madison Avenue
New York, NY 10016

This is an excellent reference book which touches upon almost every issue of special interest to women, including legal rights. For each topic there is a brief discussion with listings of organizations and resources. It also includes comprehensive listings of women's bookstores, women's centers, and a directory of national women's organizations.

Old Boys New Women: The Politics of Sex Discrimination
by Joan Abramson
1979; 255p; $8.95
Prager Publishers
383 Madison Avenue
New York, NY 10017

Joan Abramson approaches the legal aspects of sex discrimination from the viewpoint of a journalist and makes some remarkable discoveries in an area of the law which has seen little progress and considerable regression. The author cites six case studies which illustrate the human dimension of sex discrimination. In addition, she traces the history of enforcement and investigates the politics of the court, as well as government anti-discrimination agencies. Though her focus is limited to professional employment, her perceptive analysis conveys an accurate impression of what women can expect when combatting all forms of sex discrimination.

•

Of all the federal antidiscrimination agencies, none produces more ambivalence in the minds of observers than the Equal Employment Opportunity Commission. Columnist James Kilpatrick, generally considered an opponent of strong government enforcement, recently called the agency "plainly the worst—the most maddening, the most arrogant, the most inefficient and the least effective" of all antidiscrimination agencies (1979). Proponents of enforcement found the comment amusing, but not because it was totally wrong. Kilpatrick, they insist, would find EEOC the most maddening because it has in fact been more sincerely engaged in the effort of enforcing the law. Other agencies have been less maddening, from the standpoint of the employer, because they have interfered less. Proponents would also—sadly—disagree that the agency has been the most inefficient and the least effective. For inefficient and ineffective as EEOC has been, it has nonetheless been miles ahead of the other antidiscrimination agencies.

Employment Discrimination Laws: A Handbook
The Women's Legal Defense Fund, Inc.
1010 Vermont Avenue, N.W., Suite 210
Washington, D.C. 20005
32p; $2.00

This manual sets forth the coverage and procedural requirements of the five major federal laws and local statutes of the District of Columbia, Maryland, and Virginia, which prohibit employment discrimination. The information is presented in a very limited way and is useful only as a starting point for workers in D.C., Maryland, and Virginia.

Reproductive Freedom: A Speaker's Handbook on Abortion and Sterilization Abuse
by National Lawyers Guild
1978; $2.75

Anti-Sexism Committee
National Lawyers Guild
853 Broadway, 17th Floor
New York, NY 10003

This is a complete guide to both political and legal issues pertaining to reproductive rights, both nationally and internationally. A valuable resource list and bibliography is also included.

Sexual Harassment of Working Women
by Catherine A. MacKinnon
1979; 312p; $5.95
Yale University Press
92A Yale Station
New Haven, CT 06520

One of the greatest (and least talked about) indignities to which working women are subjected on the job is "sexual harassment," succinctly defined as "the unwanted imposition of sexual requirements in the context of a relationship of unequal power." This may involve anything from an "innocent" attempt at flirtation by a male supervisor directed at his female subordinate to the blatantly exploitative and crude "put out or get out." There are varying degrees along this continuum as well as differing varieties, for example, continual sexual pressure by male customers or by co-workers of more or less equal rank.

The book is written by a feminist attorney whose purpose is to convey that sexual harassment is a specialized form of sex discrimination under the 1964 Civil Rights Act and sometimes — where a government employee is involved — under the 14th Amendment of the U.S. Constitution.

•

Far from being simply individual and personal, sexual harassment is integral and crucial to a social context in which women, as a group, are allocated a disproportionately small share of wealth, power, and advantages compared with men as a group. When women work outside the home, they typically occupy jobs that are low on the ladder of financial reward and personal satisfaction independent of their aspirations, preparation, or potential. Often they are shunted to dead-end "women's jobs." In this context, the problem of sexual harassment is revealed as both a manifestation and perpetuation of the socially disadvantaged status of women. A man in a position of authority, whether a supervisor or a teacher, uses his hierarchically superordinate role to place conditions of sexual compliance on his female subordinate's access to the benefits of her job or her educational program. The necessity of dealing with sexual pressures that are, by virtue of the man's position and actions, bound up with the woman's desired goal (getting a job, doing a job, getting an education) burdens and restricts her access to the means of survival, security, and achievement. In a society in which women as a group are at a comparative disadvantage to men, the negative impact that sexual harassment has on the maintenance or improvement of women's position contributes to the continuation of their socially inferior condition. Viewed in such a light, sexual harassment can be seen as the kind of sex discrimination which Title VII and Title IX were intended to redress.

Sexual Shakedown: The Sexual Harassment of Women on the Job
by Lin Farley
1978; 288p; $2.50
Warner Books
P.O. Box 690
New York, NY 10019

This publication reflects the emerging awareness of the widespread problem of sexual harassment. The legal sections in the book discuss the few cases on the issue and remedies available by detailing the stories of the victims. These stories illustrate the limitations of the law in attempting to find solutions in a society which is still not committed to the full equality and dignity of women.

•

After three months without incident Monge applied to fill an opening on a press machine at $2.79 per hour. She testified that her foreman told her that if she wanted the job she would have to be "nice." She got the job and testified that the foreman then asked her to go out with him, which she refused to do. The machine was subsequently shut down, and she was placed on a lower-paying machine at $1.99 per hour. At the same time she had all overtime removed, although no one else did, and she was informed that if she needed overtime she could clean the washrooms and sweep the floors. She did this and testified that the foreman ridiculed her as she performed these tasks. Shortly after this the foreman fired her (at 2 a.m.). After complaining to the union she was reinstated with a warning.

Stopping Wife Abuse: A Guide to the Emotional, Psychological and Legal Implications for the Abused Woman and Those Helping Her
by Jennifer Baker Fleming
1979; 532p; $8.95
Anchor Press/Doubleday
Garden City, NY

To date, this is clearly the best work on a topic that defies easy explanations and simple solutions. With much thought and research, the author thoroughly but concisely deals with the layers of complexity of the problem facing both the abused woman and those who help her. The lengthy legal section describes the major forms of assistance and protection currently offered by the legal system. Subsections include the differences between civil and criminal law; peace bonds; private criminal complaints; police response; police training; diversion; community mediation; advocates and the criminal justice system; courts; and federal legislation.

It likewise presents an exhaustive survey of experiences, studies, and ideas on how to best use the available programs and services and work toward establishing better ones. Fifty pages of programs providing services to battered women are included. For the abused woman and her advocates, this is a vital guide.

•

Ultimately, the legal system does not create and enforce a new social order but reflects and enforces community norms and values. While advocates must press for structural changes in the legal system to make it easier for women to process their complaints and prosecute their abusers, the success of these reforms depends upon their integration into a community-wide and nationwide campaign of public education about the extent and cost of violence against women. Wife abuse will cease being a major law-enforcement and criminal-justice problem when it is no longer a socially acceptable institution. And it will not become socially unacceptable until the entire society is committed to real equality for women, and sexism is universally understood to be the name of a dangerous social disease that poisons individual relationships as well as the quality of life in the community.

Women in Transition: A Feminist Handbook on Separation and Divorce
by Women in Transition, Inc.
1975; 537p; $8.95
Charles Scribner's Sons
New York, NY

The Women in Transition program began in Philadelphia in 1971 and has since been a model for similar projects throughout the country. The program was implemented to provide survival skills and emotional support to women who were separated, divorced, and/or single parents. One of their projects was a self-help divorce clinic. The book is the story of their ideas, experiences, insights, suggestions, failures, and successes. It has been a tremendously useful and valuable resource for individuals and groups who are likewise attempting to meet the many needs of separated and divorced women and single mothers.

•

Your group has to decide for itself what to focus on. Our only concrete recommendation is to *start small*. You can always expand when you get the resources and energy. Some groups which are operating programs for women in transition are focusing on emergency housing for women who need temporary places to stay until they get their lives organized. Some groups aren't interested in providing ongoing services but have come together just to write a supplement for this book in their own area. Other groups are providing legal services, and still other groups are working on the money problems of women in transition—welfare, job training, and employment counseling. Most of these projects provide some sort of discussion groups along with whatever special services they offer, since one of the best ways to help women through a crisis period is to provide a place for them to meet and talk with other women in similar situations.

Annual Report
My Sister's Place
Task Force on Abused Women
July 1978—June 1979
Women's Legal Defense Fund
1010 Vermont Avenue, N.W., #210
Washington, D.C. 20005

We include this rather unorthodox piece in our reviews because we saw it as being of practical interest to those who wish to know the nuts-and-bolts of setting up a shelter for battered women. Besides a history of the task force and description of its projects, the report includes information on budget and fundraising.

C.   Racial Minorities

The Rights of Racial Minorities (An A.C.L.U. Handbook)
by E. Richard Larson and Laughlin McDonald
1980; 253p; $1.95
Avon Books
250 W. 55th St.
New York, NY 10019

Since Brown v. Board of Education *in 1954, the state of the law has expanded to afford extensive protections to national minorities. Nevertheless, in the wake of* Bakke, *these protections are gradually being eroded, and those protections that have not been cut back are not vigorously enforced. But they do exist. And there are agencies responsible for their enforcement. It is with much satisfaction, therefore, that we welcome this recent edition to the A.C.L.U.'s series of handbooks dealing with the rights of people. Other sources on this topic which we encountered at regular bookstores, though informative, were primarily in the nature of sociology, political science or history. This handbook concerns the law.*

In question-and-answer format, the legal rights of the individual are examined in the areas of employment, housing, accomodations, federally-assisted programs, education, voting, and the administration of civil and criminal laws. A valuable addition in this book to the regular A.C.L.U. format, are the appendices: legal resources for racial minorities who need legal assistance; and federal agencies responsible for enforcing the rights of racial minorities.

•

Is it *unconstitutional* for government agencies to provide assistance to organizations engaged in discrimination?

Yes. It is unconstitutional under the Fourteenth Amendment for a state government, and unconstitutional under the Fifth Amendment for the federal government, to provide assistance to entities that discriminate. There are, however, several problems in enforcing the law. First, provision of assistance is unconstitutional only if it can be proved that the government is knowingly and intentionally assisting discrimination. Second, the only effective means of terminating the unconstitutional assistance is through a lawsuit against the government.

Is it *unlawful* for federal government agencies to provide assistance to organizations or institutions engaged in discrimination?

Yes. It generally is unlawful under a variety of federal laws for agencies of the federal government to provide assistance to entities that discriminate. The theory behind

this principle was explained by President John Kennedy in 1963: "Simple justice requires that public funds to which all taxpayers of all races contribute, not be spent in any fashion which encourages, entrenches, subsidizes or results in racial discrimination."

Equality on the Job: A Working Person's Guide to Affirmative Action
by the Affirmative Action Coalition of Washington, D.C.
1979; 115p; $3.00
Center for Law and Social Policy
1751 "N" Street, N.W.
Washington, D.C. 20036
Affirmative Action Coordinating Center
126 W. 119th Street
New York, NY 10026
(800) 223-0655

In discussing affirmative action, the metaphor of the shackled runner is often used. In essence, it would be extremely difficult, if not impossible, for a runner whose legs had been chained since birth to compete successfully with runners who had not been so impaired. In order to have a truly fair and competitive race, therefore, the formerly shackled runner should be allowed preferential treatment by being allowed to have a head start. That is really what affirmative action is about — programs of preferential treatment for impairments due to economic disadvantages.

It is no secret that at the bottom of the economic rung are people who have been victims of racism. As long as opportunities are color-coded, and as long as there exist sharp racial differences in life expectancy, medical care, income, job categories, education, and political power, affirmative action programs will be indentified with race.

However, but for life expectancy, every category mentioned above applies to the status of women in this society as well. The fact that women make 59 cents to a man's dollar and the fact that the job market is as sex-segregated as ever is evidence that opportunities are sex-coded as well.

This excellent little book not only details the history of discrimination against black Americans, women, and national minorities, but it also explains the necessity and evolvement of affirmative action programs. In addition, it includes discussion of the current state of law, including the Bakke *and* Weber *cases. It explains pragmatically how to determine if your employer has an affirmative action plan, how to evaluate it, and how to enforce it.*

The Bakke Case: The Politics of Inequality
by Joel Dreyfuss and
   Charles Lawrence III
1979; 278p; $3.95
Harcourt Brace Jovanovich,
   Inc.
757 Third Avenue
New York, NY 10017

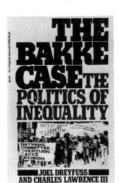

The Bakke *case has been continuously referred to as "perhaps the most important Supreme Court decision since* Brown v. Board of Education." *Allan Bakke, a white man who was denied entrance to the University of California at Davis Medical School, brought suit, alleging "reverse discrimination." The issue of affirmative action programs had been evaded by the Supreme Court before its decision in* Bakke *in 1978. But even in the* Bakke *decision, the court relied on what the authors term "a gentlemanly solution." Although the Court upheld affirmative action programs in the most narrow way, they also ordered the admission of Bakke to medical school.*

This is a fascinating account of the legal melodrama played out in one of the most controversial Supreme Court decisions of our time.

●

The Court had failed to address itself to the issues at the core of the national debate provoked by Bakke. By their silence, the justices who took the Stevens position alleging a violation of Title VI had sidestepped the serious questions raised about the meaning of race and the scope of racial problems still existing in the United States. And because of Justice Powell's concern about responding to the most immediate political pressures, he too had written an opinion that had avoided any clear position on the nature of the Constitution's commitment to resolving the American Dilemma of race and equality. Only the four justices who had joined the Brennan opinion had seen fit to confront the reality that a history of American racism had left the country divided by race and opportunity. The question of the meaning of the equal protection clause could not be answered without a decision on what equality meant. Did the Constitution require a maintenance of the existing inequities of opportunity, or did it require a fundamental readjustment of those opportunities?

Ultimately the greatest impact of the Court's decision would be outside the bounds of the laws it had handed down. Americans had looked to this respected and still-hallowed institution for guidance on a difficult and troubling issue. The justices had been aware of the most

melodramatic aspects of the case and had done their best to sidestep the most obvious pitfalls by refusing to entangle themselves in semantic problems such as "goals," "quotas," and "qualifications." After all, one reason the Court had maintained its aura in a time of growing mistrust of government was its very cautious approach to jurisprudence. Even the favorite term of the meritocrats and journalists, *reverse discrimination*, was referred to only once in the massive opinions, and Justice Powell took care to wrap it in quotation marks.

Simple Justice
by Richard Kluger
1977; 822p; $6.95
Vintage Books/Random House
400 Hahn Rd.
Westminster, MD 21157

In the same genre as The Bakke Case, *Richard Kluger presents us with a most interesting discussion of how law was used in the Civil Rights Movement through an analysis of* Brown v. Board of Education. *The book is as moving and enthralling as any novel, but infinitely more valuable.*

D.   The Poor ★

You will not discover a plethora of books in this section. There are a number of reasons for this. The "rights" of the poor are virtually dependent on the whims of the legislators who decide, when devising a budget, which programs remain and which are eliminated, in addition to the "budget-minded" bureaucrats who erode benefits within remaining programs. The "law," then, is constantly changing to reflect their actions, and thus self-help books ar often out of date as soon as they are published. A second reason is that self-help or informational books are most often written and published by community groups or legal services programs and may not be widely available. If you are interested in information about your rights in relationship to a government-funded program, you should call your local legal services office and ask if they have any written information and if they don't, who does. We also list here the major support centers funded by the Legal Services Corporation, who very often publish educational materials.

★ Specialized Litigation and Support Centers

Center for Law & Education
6 Appian Way, Gutman Library, 3rd Fl.
Cambridge, MA 02138
(617) 495-4666

Center on Social Welfare Policy & Law
95 Madison Ave., 7th Floor
New York, NY 10016
(212) 679-3709
821 Fifteenth St., NW, Suite 638
Washington, DC 20005
(202) 347-5615

Food Research and Action Center (FRAC)
2011 Eye St., NW, Suite 700
Washington, DC 20006
(202) 452-8250

Handicapped People's Legal Support Unit
373 Park Ave., S., 7th Fl.
New York, NY 10016

Indian Law Backup Center, Native American Rights Fund
1506 Broadway
Boulder, CO 80302
(303) 447-8760

Mental Disability Legal Resource Center
ABA, 1800 M St., NW
Washington, DC 20036
(202) 331-2240

Migrant Legal Action Program
806 Fifteenth St., NW, Suite 600
Washington, DC 20005
(202) 347-5100

National Center for Youth Law
3701 Lindell Boulevard
St. Louis, MO 63108
(314) 533-8868
693 Mission St., 6th Fl.
San Francisco, CA 94105
(415) 543-3307

National Consumer Law Center
11 Beacon St.
Boston, MA 02108
(617) 523-8010

National Economic Development Law Project
2150 Shattuck Ave., Suite 300
Berkeley, CA 94704
(415) 548-2600

National Employment Law Project
475 Riverside Dr.
New York, NY 10027
(212) 870-2121

National Health Law Program
2401 Main St.
Santa Monica, CA 90405
(213) 392-4811

National Housing Law Project
2150 Shattuck Ave., Suite 300
Berkeley, CA 94704
(415) 548-9400
East: 1016 Sixteenth St., NW, Suite 800
Washington, DC 20036
(202) 659-0050
(Service calls should be directed to the Berkeley office.)

National Legal Aid and Defender Association
2100 M St., NW, Suite 601
Washington, DC 20037
(202) 452-0620

National Paralegal Institute
2000 P St., NW, Suite 600
Washington, DC 20036
(202) 872-0655

National Senior Citizens Law Center
1636 W. 8th St., Suite 201
Los Angeles, CA 90017
(213) 388-1381
East: 1200 15th St., NW, Suite 500
Washington, DC 20005
(202) 872-1404

National Social Science and Law Project
1990 M St., NW
Washington, DC 20036
(202) 223-4541

SSI: A Handbook for Advocates

by Massachusetts Law Reform Institute and Office
    for Children of the Commonwealth of
    Massachusetts
Massachusetts Office for Children
120 Boylston Street
Boston, MA 02116
Published in ring-bound notebook form.
Revised in 1980

*SSI stands for Supplemental Security Income. SSI is
a federal cash assistance program administered by
the Social Security Administration for people who
cannot work because of age or because of a substantial impairment — physical or psychological. Appli-
cants must also demonstrate that they need the
money.*

*The laws and regulations which govern SSI are
among the most obscure and complex. This handbook, originally written for paralegals, is the best
and most up-to-date publication on the subject. It is
clearly written in non-legalese and thoroughly covers
every aspect of SSI law. We highly recommend it.*

The Rights of the Poor

by Sylvia Law (An A.C.L.U. Handbook)
1975; $1.25
Avon Books
250 West 55th St.
New York, NY 10019

*We are not reviewing this particular book because the
copyright date indicates it is out of date. However, a
revised edition should be issued sometime at the end
of 1980. We anticipate that it will be a very useful
publication.*

★ E.   Gays

A Legal Guide for Gay & Lesbian Couples

by Hayden Curry and Denis Clifford
1980; $10.95
Addison-Wesley Publishing Co.
Trade Sales
Reading, MA 01867

*This book is particularly timely. For years the legal
establishment pretended that gay/lesbian couples
had no legal rights. In the last few years this has
changed radically, as the right of gay/lesbian couples
to exist has become recognized. Now, regulations are
profuse, and there's much confusion over joint*

*ownership, living together agreements, children of
former marriages, wills, etc. The authors deal with
all of these areas and many more. Curry and Clifford
haven't produced a long essay on abstract legal
rights, but a book full of nitty-gritty agreements,
letters, wills, separation agreements, etc. In Part
Two of the* People's Law Review, *you will find an
article excerpted from* A Legal Guide for Gay and
Lesbian Couples. *Here's another from this highly
recommended book.*

•

No one likes to look forward to the day when they will
depart this vale of tears, and actually, making plans for
that inevitable time seems dull, even macabre. However,
whether you are gay or lesbian, single or coupled, rich or
poor, a little practical planning insures that your property
will be distributed as *you* choose, with the least cost, and
will also immensely ease the burdens of those who must
tidy up your affairs. Because state death laws do not recognize gay or lesbian "marriages," or friendships, paying
attention to your estate is particularly important. If you die
without making a will, or using other legal means for the
disposition of your property, the distribution of your property will be determined by your state's "intestacy" laws.
Those laws require that *all* of your property pass to certain
specified blood relations. We've heard quite a few horror
stories of disaster befalling a surviving lover when his or
her deceased lover's family suddenly swoop down to claim
all the deceased person's property.

A Gay Parents' Legal Guide to Child Custody

by the NLG Anti-Sexism Committee
Anti-Sexism Committee of the
    San Francisco National
    Lawyers's Guild
558 Capp Street
San Francisco, CA 94110
1980 revised edition; 44p; $2.00

*This is a truly excellent little pamphlet on the polit-
ical, personal, and legal aspects of gay custody. In
very simplified terms, the whole complex court process in a custody battle is explained, always with
attention to the particular issues of gay parents.*

*In addition, the pamphlet includes areas which
may necessitate personal decisions by parents and
how those decisions will affect a legal custody battle.*

•

Peer relationships play an important part in any child's
life. Children, like adults, don't like to be outsiders or to
be made fun of by their peers. Have you considered the
consequences of publicity from a trial where your sexuality
is at issue? Will this publicity have a detrimental affect on

your child? If so, have you thought about ways to help your child to deal with this situation?

For example, many of us have also grown up in areas where we were in some way different from our neighbors, be it racially, economically or religiously. Think about ways you can explain to your child that "different" isn't wrong or bad. Will your child understand this? Is s/he confident enough about her/himself and her/his relationship with you to understand and feel comfortable with being "different?" Does your child have enough personal and emotional support from his/her relationship with you to have the strength to be "different?"

Gay Parent Support Packet
by National Gay Task Force
$2.00
National Gay Task Force
80 Fifth Avenue
New York, NY 10011

This is an extremely useful packet of information pertaining to custody of children by gay parents. The packet includes statements from psychiatrists and psychologists, lists of resource organizations, pertinent articles, synopses of gay custody cases, lists of gay parents organizations, tips on expert testimony, and a list of psychiatric and psychological literature.

F.   The Disabled

The Rights of Physically Handicapped People (An A.C.L.U. Handbook)
by Kent Hull
1979; 256p; $2.25
Avon Books
250 W. 55th St.
New York City, NY 10019
Reviewer: Susan Shapiro, of
    the Disability Law
    Resource Center of the
    Center for Independent
    Living

This book is an introduction to the area for those with little or no knowledge of civil rights law as it pertains to physically disabled people. It deals almost exclusively with federal law, touching only slightly on relevant state laws, of which there are many. The author has attempted to provide a basic overview of the current developments in disability civil rights law — and since the law is constantly in flux, this is a difficult task. While not the definitive guide to the

rights of disabled people, this book is a good starting point. Its publication is extremely important as evidence of recognition by the ACLU that physically disabled people, as a class, have long been denied a basic civil right — the right to use and take part in the world around them.

A word of warning for the reader: the author presupposes knowledge and understanding of the federal regulatory, legislative, and judicial systems. Laypeople without some understanding of these systems may find the book difficult to use. Also, the book is written in a question-and-answer format that starts to sound rather stilted after one has read it for a while.

•

Has the problem of stereotypes about handicapped persons impeded their achievement of equal rights?

Yes. There is evidence that opinions about handicapped persons by nonhandicapped persons are formulated more on the basis of categorical judgments about the class to which handicapped persons belong than on the basis of the characteristics of individual handicapped persons. A report by an international group of experts convened by the United Nations to study the problem of architectural barriers to handicapped persons concluded that the "social barriers we have evolved and accepted against those who vary more than a certain degree from what we have been conditioned to regard as normal" were as serious as the physical barriers. The panel concluded: "More people have been forced into limited lives and made to suffer by these manmade obstacles than by any specific physical or mental disability."

Handbook of Employment Rights of the Handicapped
by Anne Marie Hermann and Lucinda Walker
1978; 86p; Write for price
Regional Rehabilitation Research Institute
1828 "L" Street N.W., Suite 704
Washington, DC 20036

"It is usually not easy for anyone to find a job or to remain employed. However, if you are a person with a physical or mental handicap, you may have a more difficult time finding and advancing in employment. You may have already experienced an employer's refusing to hire you or to promote you, regardless of your abilities or training, solely because of your handicap. Such actions by employers may violate Federal law, and it usually depends on you to make certain that such laws are enforced. The purpose of this handbook is to examine an employer's obliga-

*tions under Federal law in order to inform you of
certain employment rights which you have and to
suggest what steps you may take to protect those
rights. These suggestions include what you might do
personally, as well as what you can do through legal
action, to force employers to comply."*

Know Your Rights: A Handbook for Disabled Californians (Second Edition)

1978; 60p; $2.00
Published by:
Disability Law Resource
   Center of the Center for
   Independent Living
2539 Telegraph Ave.
Berkeley, CA 94704

*This recently updated
booklet should be in the library of every disabled
Californian and everyone else who is concerned with
the legal and civil rights of persons with disabilities.
The purpose of the handbook is to explain these rights
in non-technical terms. Both state and federal laws
are discussed, as well as some general information on
how to recognize and remedy incidents of disability-
based discrimination.*

●

Federal Law. Section 504 of the Rehabilitation Act of
1973 is by far the most significant piece of federal legislation enacted on behalf of the rights of the disabled in
recent years. This one-sentence prohibition against disability-based discrimination states that "no otherwise qualified handicapped individual in the United States . . . shall,
solely by reason of his [or her] handicap, be excluded from
the participation in, be denied the benefits of, or be
subjected to discrimination under any program or activity
receiving federal financial assistance".

Access – Newsletter of the Disability Resource Center of the Center for Independent Living

4 to 8 page tabloid
6 issues (one year) $4.00
Center for Independent Living
2539 Telegraph Ave.
Berkeley, CA 94704

*This is an excellent little newspaper that summarizes
all the latest of interest in the field of disability law.
We have seen nothing else that keeps on top of legislation, law suits, conferences, and administrative
regulation changes nearly so well.*

A Service Providers Guide to Federal Disability Law

by Lloyd Burton, Jr.
1979; 200p; $19.50
Published in ring binder to allow for updates
Disability Law Resource Center of the Center for
   Independent Living
2539 Telegraph Ave.
Berkeley, CA 94704

*The most sophisticated CIL publication we have
seen, this is still carefully designed for use by
non-lawyers as well as attorneys. In this regard, it
provides introductory material which gives the non-
lawyer enough background on how the legal system
works, so that she or he can deal with the rest of the
material. This book is not recommended for people
with a casual interest in disability law ("Access" is
better for that purpose). It is, however, a must for
anyone with a continuing need to work with federal
disability laws and regulations.*

●

A history of epilepsy was also the issue in *Duran v. City of
Tampa*, in which an applicant for the position of policeman with the City of Tampa who had met all the entrance
requirements was denied employment because of a record
of epileptic seizures as a child. Although he had not had
any seizures since childhood and was not medically
defined as epileptic, employment was nonetheless denied.
In finding that the City was guilty of disability-based
discrimination, the court relied on the definition of disability found in the Rehabilitation Act, which includes:
   "...any person who has a physical or mental impairment which substantially limits one or more of such
person's major life activities, (b) has a record of such
impairment, or (c) is regarded as having such an
impairment."
   The court found in its earlier hearing on the case that
the "plaintiff clearly fits within the definition of handicapped in category (c)". In its final decision, the court
ordered the City to examine the plaintiff, and not use his
history of epilepsy as a criterion; if plaintiff passed, he was
to be employed as a policeman and awarded back pay to
the date of his original application (less actual wages
earned since), and awarded seniority rights as of the
original application date as well.

G.   Youth

Student and Youth Organizing
by John Schaller and Mark Chesler
1977; 97p; $3.00
Youth Liberation Press
2007 Washtenaw Avenue
Ann Arbor, MI 48104

The usefulness of this book is not restricted to youth — the organizing techniques discussed are applicable to community organizing in general. Topics include how not to be co-opted into "proper channels," like student council, etc., how to build a successful power base, fund-raising, putting together flyers, newspapers, posters, etc., non-violent but "threatening" demonstrations (picketing, guerilla theater, walk-outs), and more.

•

Any strategy you use, whether it is consciously planned or not, will call for using several specific tactics. These tactics can be divided into several categories, which overlap each other in several respects.

First are those that aim to *build a power base* among students and others in the community, including parents, sympathetic educators, and political groups. These tactics include leafleting, education programs, and meetings with various groups. The assumption here is that change will come only if students can present demands forcibly.

Second are tactics that directly *threaten the people in power.* These include demonstrations, picketing, guerilla theater, and legal suits. The assumption behind these tactics is that you have to threaten the power of those who are currently running the school system before they will consider changing anything.

Third are tactics that *appeal to the good will of people,* and to their desire to serve and educate students. These tactics include the appeal of grievance, some forms of petitioning, and discussions with friendly educators. The assumption here is that administrators really want to meet student needs and do things that students feel are important. Unfortunately, that assumption is wrong 90 percent of the time, but it doesn't hurt to maintain cordial relationships with administrators — as long as you aren't coopted.

Young People and the Law
by Diana Autlin
1978; 45p; $2.50
Youth Liberation Press
2007 Washtenaw Avenue
Ann Arbor, MI 48104

Within this great nation of ours, there are designated localities where citizens who are considered quite sane and have committed no crime must obtain government approval before circulating literature, assembling in groups, making speeches, and where personal belongings can be searched without warrants or probable cause. These citizens have no choice about submitting to a restriction of their rights — both the government and the Supreme Court agree that it is mandatory. And almost every American has served a "stretch" there — including you! Or didn't you ever attend public school?

Actually, the situation is not as bad as it once was. For example, there are now limits on the types of censorship that school authorities can exercise; freedom of assembly can be denied only in extreme cases; and a "due process" hearing must be granted to any student before "corporal punishment" can be administered. High school authoritarianism, however, is just one of the many topics relating to the rights of young people that is covered in this book. Other topics include availability of birth control and abortion without parental consent, the limits of parental authority, making and breaking contracts, rights of juvenile court, and legal remedies when rights of young people are violated. This straight-talking pamphlet can be helpful to those seriously interested in young people's rights. It also contains numerous footnotes and an excellent list of cases and statutes.

H.   The Elderly ★

Rights of the Elderly and Retired
by William R. Wishard
1978; 240p; $5.95
Cragmont Publications
P.O. Box 27496
San Francisco, CA 94127

One area where our country has been grossly negligent is in its treatment of the elderly. An elderly parent who looks to his or her children for love and support is often regarded as excess baggage and consigned to live in a sparsely furnished, rented room and is left to battle inflation and frequent rent increases on his or her own, despite a fixed income.

Limited though it may be, the government does

*provide some assistance to the elderly and retired —
social security, supplemental security income (SSI),
disability benefits, medical care, publicly-subsidized
housing, and other privately-supported federal,
state, and local programs. This book explains in
understandable language the eligibility requirements
for these programs and what benefits their recipients
are entitled to receive.*

*Other topics covered are age discrimination, debt
problems, taxes, wills, housing problems, how to
select a good retirement community, and much
more.*

●

There are two separate parts to Medicare health insurance. The *hospital insurance* part (sometimes called Part A) provides limited coverage for inpatient hospital care, post-hospital care, and home health care services.

The *medical insurance* part of medicare coverage (sometimes called Part B) provides for limited coverage of certain services of doctors, hospital outpatient services, and other forms of medical treatment, and the costs of medical equipment and supplies.

The Rights of Older Persons (An A.C.L.U. Handbook)
by Robert N. Brown
1979; 436p; $2.50
Avon Books
250 West 55th St.
New York, NY 10019

*Published in 1979, this is one of the most current and
complete handbooks for the elderly. It answers, with
a fair amount of detail, common questions that arise
about employment discrimination, pension and
retirement benefits, social security, health care and
taxes. It is written in a straightforward, comprehensible style and is liberally sprinkled with legal citations. There are appendices which include lists of
services and social security computation tables on a
nationwide basis.*

●

When is a widow entitled to benefits?
A widow who is 60 or older, or is between 50 and 60 and is disabled, will receive monthly survivors' benefits if her husband was fully insured at his death. A surviving divorced wife who meets these requirements, is now unmarried, and was married to the individual at least 10 years, also is eligible for widow's benefits. To be considered a widow by the SSA (Social Security Administration), you must have been married to a deceased widower for at least nine months, or have borne him a child or have

adopted his child. A widow also may be eligible for mother's insurance benefits. If her husband died fully or currently insured, and if she is unmarried and is caring for the deceased husband's child, she is eligible for mother's insurance benefits. A woman entitled to widow's benefits will receive between 82½ and 100% of her husband's basic monthly benefits, while a woman entitled to mother's insurance benefits will receive about 75% of her husband's basic monthly benefits.

Retirement in the Pacific Northwest
by Virginia Diegel & Henry
    S. Hunnisett
1978; 253p; $4.95
Self-Counsel Press, Inc.
1303 N. Northgate Way
Seattle, WA 98133

Although not quite as comprehensive as Rights of the
Elderly and Retired, *this
book makes up for the slight
sacrifice in legal depth with
a caring introduction to the social and psychological
ramifications of transferring from an active workaday world to retirement in the Pacific Northwest.
Sections include estimating retirement income,
social security, other government benefits, retirement
homes, annuities, and life insurance.*

●

(g) In Washington the present property tax program allows complete exemption of all special levies for senior citizens 62 and over or disabled homeowners if household income is less than $5,000.

(h) There is credit available for the elderly on Oregon income tax. If you are an Oregon resident or part-year resident, 65 or over, you may be able to claim a credit against your state income tax. To qualify, you and/or your spouse must have received over $600 of earned income (wages, etc., or annuities or pensions) during each of any of the 10 years before 1976. (The years did not have to follow in order.) If you are a surviving widow or widower and have not remarried, you can use the earned income of your deceased spouse in figuring whether you meet this test, even if you had no earned income. You can also add your deceased spouse's earned income to yours to figure whether you qualify.

I. Aliens

Immigration Law and Defense

by The Immigration Project
  of the National Lawyers
  Guild
1980; 550p; $55.00
Clark Boardman Co., Ltd.
435 Hudson St.
New York, NY 10014

This excellent lawyer's and paralegal's reference manual contains a thorough up-to-date summary of statutory and case law in the area of immigration. The emphasis is on defense of a person threatened with deportation and topics include obtaining visas and legal permanent residence, legal grounds for deportation, deportation hearing procedures, and administrative and court remedies and appeals, plus a chapter on citizenship and naturalization. Also included are more than 50 Immigration and Naturalization Service forms.

●

Procedure at the Hearing. At the opening of the hearing the immigration judge will determine whether an interpreter is needed, *see* §7.17, *infra*, and whether a trial attorney should be utilized to present the government's case. 8 C.F.R. §242.16(c). In practice, a trial attorney is assigned to every case according to the last three numbers of the respondent's immigration file number. However, if an agreement is reached before the hearing between the INS trial attorney and the respondent (e.g., respondent agrees to admit deportability and only wants voluntary departure), the trial attorney may or may not appear at the hearing, *see* 8 C.F.R. §§242.9(b) and 242.16(b).

"The special inquiry officer shall advise the respondent of his right to representation, at no expense to the Government, by counsel of his own choice authorized to practice if the proceedings require him to state then and there whether he desires representation." 8 C.F.R. §242 16(a).

Immigrating to the U.S.A.

by Dan P. Danilov
1978; 168p; $7.95
International Self-Counsel
  Press, Ltd.
1303 N. Northgate Way
Seattle, WA 98133

Author Dan Danilov immigrated to the U.S. from China in 1947. For the past 21 years he has been a lawyer specializing in immigration law. This little book is good introductory material, although I would like it better if it weren't so dry and lawyerly. It deals with student visas, preference categories, deportation, requirements for foreign medical graduates, quotas, etc. As an added bonus, it contains forms with complete instructions for their use.

Again, we add our caveat. Even though 1978 may seem to be a recent copyright date, the laws and regulations concerning immigration change rapidly.

Immigration Law and Procedure

by Charles Gordon, Ellen Gittel Gordon and Harry
  N. Rosenfield
1980; 7 volumes; $300.00
Matthew Bender
235 E. 45th St.
New York, NY 10017

We include the above because it is the immigration attorney's bible. Every form, every statute, every regulation, every case is included. In fact, three of the seven volumes contain primary source material and may be the easiest place for a non-lawyer to research and find immigration laws.

★ J. Trees (and Other Living Things)

Should Trees Have Standing?
by Christopher D. Stone
1974; 102p; $3.75
William Kaufman, Inc.
One First Street
Los Altos, CA 94022

Should Trees Have Standing?
TOWARD LEGAL RIGHTS
FOR NATURAL OBJECTS
Christopher D. Stone

The question is "should trees, etc. have standing to sue for an injunction to stop their own destruction?" Actually, the real question is whether private individuals having no direct connection with an about-to-be-destroyed environment (they don't own the property or reside nearby) be allowed to sue to stop the despoilers?

The 1972 case of Sierra Club v. Morton posed this question. The Sierra Club, a statewide California conservationist group, sued the Secretary of the Interior to stop a monstrous ski resort development on National Park land. Without getting to the merits of the environmentalists' argument, the U.S. Supreme Court ruled that the development could go ahead because the Sierra Club had no "standing" to sue—it couldn't show the court that it would suffer "sufficient harm" to justify bringing suit. (Never mind that the environment suffered the harm.)

The author presents a convincing argument that dispels the "lack of standing" barrier to class action suits on behalf of citizens who are concerned with the environment.

•

On a parity of reasoning, we should have a system in which, when a friend of a natural object perceives it to be endangered, he can apply to a court for the creation of a guardianship. Perhaps we already have the machinery to do so. California law, for example, defines an incompetent as "any person, whether insane or not, who by reason of old age, disease, weakness of mind, or other cause, is unable, unassisted, properly to manage and take care of himself or his property, and by reason thereof is likely to be deceived or imposed upon by artful or designing persons." Of course, to urge a court that an endangered river is "a person" under this provision will call for lawyers as bold and imaginative as those who convinced the Supreme Court that a railroad corporation was a "person" under the fourteenth amendment, a constitutional provi-

sion theretofore generally thought of as designed to secure the rights of freedmen. (As this article was going to press, Professor Byrn of Fordham petitioned the New York Supreme Court to appoint him legal guardian for an unrelated foetus scheduled for abortion so as to enable him to bring a class action on behalf of all foetuses similarly situated in New York City's 18 municipal hospitals. Judge Holtzman granted the petition of guardianship.) If such an argument based on present statutes should fail, special environmental legislation could be enacted along traditional guardianship lines. Such provisions could provide for guardianship both in the instance of public natural objects and also, perhaps with slightly different standards, in the instance of natural objects on "private" land.

Law and the Environment
by Pauline Cusak, Ginny Point and Lynn
    Hjartarson
1979; 174p; Write for price
Ecology Action Center
Dalhousie University
Halifax, Nova Scotia, Canada B3H 3J5

This is an odd and wonderful book—an attempt to teach environmental law to high school students, using narrative and dialogue, and with Chief Justice No-See Sun as the head honcho of the Supreme Court of Nature. The authors take on both science (evolution, food chains, symbiosis, nuclear energy, the carbon cycle, etc.) and the environmental laws of Canada generally, and Nova Scotia in particular. It is an ambitious task; the numerous details tend to overwhelm the reader so that it's not always easy to remember that the purpose of the book is to give students an overview of environmental law. Still, even with its problems, this is the most creative law book for kids we have seen, and one that anyone writing and teaching in the field will want to study closely. The authors have brought a sense of happiness and fun to this task that is totally absent from the typical textbook. A draft was used for the purposes of this review, and it may well be that the final product will be simpler and easier to use.

Solar Law Reporter
by Solar Energy Research
Institute
Published bimonthly at
$12/year and available
through:
U.S. Government Printing
Office
Washington, D.C. 20402

*This publication provides a
good summary of the law
and legal institutions as
they affect the development*
of solar energy and is particularly valuable in reviewing the latest state and public agency (TVA, etc.)
innovations. Anyone working in the solar area will
want to subscribe.

●

Santa Barbara Requires Solar Water Heating
Santa Barbara County, California, has followed San
Diego County's lead in requiring solar water heaters in
new homes in areas without natural gas service [1 Solar L.
Rep. 10 (1979)].

The Santa Barbara ordinance (No. 3115), adopted September 17, states: "No permit shall be issued by the
administrative authority for a new residential building in
the unincorporated area of Santa Barbara County not
being served by pipeline natural gas unless said building
includes the use of a solar energy system as the primary
means of heating water."

Santa Barbara County previously (July 30, 1979)
ordered that new outdoor swimming pools and existing
unheated pools could be heated only with a solar system as
the primary source of energy.

A San Diego ordinance which went into effect on
October 1 was the first in the country to require solar water
heaters in new housing. It covers unincorporated areas not
served by natural gas. Beginning October 1, 1980, it will
cover areas with natural gas service.

Shutdown! Nuclear Power on Trial
1979; 191p; $4.95
The Book Publishing
Company
156 Drakes Lane
Summertown, TN 38483

*This is a trial transcript.
Lawyers will tell you that
reading trial transcripts
(usually while searching for
that all-elusive "reversible*
error") is a boring task. Not so here. In Honicker v.
Nuclear Regulatory Commission, *Mrs. Jeannine
Honicker, a Nashville businesswoman whose daughter nearly died of leukemia (a radiation-caused
disease), brought suit for revocation of a license
granted for a reactor in nearby Hartsville. The issue
she posed to the court was whether nuclear power
significantly affects human health. Although the
court sidestepped the issue by ruling that it didn't
have the authority to stop the nuclear power industry
in Tennessee, it took very interesting testimony from
scientific experts in the fields of biology and radiation
physics.*

*One of the major questions testified to was whether
there exists a minimum "threshold" level of radiation
exposure below which there is zero risk of radiation-
caused disease, or whether lower radiation levels still
cause disease but merely have a more limited effect
(e.g., killing fewer people over a long term than a
larger dose would.) This is a valuable and frightening explanation of the effects of radiation.*

*For a more comprehensive edited treatise on
1) medical principles, 2) the nuclear fuel cycle and
how it works, and 3) the applicable law, the Book
Publishing Company also published* A Lawsuit to
End Atomic Power—Honicker v. Henrie *(1978;
160p; $5.00).*

●

Q. Could you tell us briefly what is radiation?
A. Radiation is one form of energy. We have radiation
ranging in wave length all the way from very long wave
length to very short wave length, and the types of radiation
we are concerned about here are those of very short wave
length in the form of X-rays and gamma rays; and in
addition these can be generated by machines, for example,
X-ray generators, or they can come from natural and
man-made substances.

In addition to that form of radiation, we have particles
that can be emitted by radioactive substances such as electrons, which we call either beta rays or positrons.

We have alpha particles which are charged nuclei of
helium.

These are all forms of radiation; either waves in nature
or particles. Actually the waves are also regarded as partic-
ulate for some purposes.

Q. Okay. How does radiation affect living organisms?
A. In general, ionizing radiation affects living organisms
in a destructive manner. It causes, as it goes through the
cells of living organisms, the ripping away of electrons
from the molecules or atoms in which they are present and
thus altering those atoms and molecules to some other
form.

In addition to ripping away electrons from atoms and molecules, it can often displace electrons from one energy state in the molecule to another. All of these have the effect of altering the naturally occurring substances in a biological organism.

VI.   Criminal Law

★ A.   Rights and Wrongs in the Criminal Process

Legal First Aid for Today's High Society
by Kenneth L. Weiss and David J. Kurland
1979; 212p; Write for price
Legal First Aid, Inc.
Box 5202
Clearwater, FL

This is one of the very few thorough and informative books we could find on the subject of the way the Constitutional guarantees against "unreasonable searches and seizures" relate to police "busts" for drug-related offenses. Not one of those narrow, bare-bones outlines, this is a concise and thorough textbook on areas of criminal law such as evidence the police cannot use, confessions, searches of home and automobile—with and without a warrant—and searches of the individual. This book is, in fact, so well written, that it comes close to being a passable textbook for a course in the criminal procedure aspects of constitutional law.

•

Once the person realizes that he is under arrest, he is so nervous and upset that he can barely remember his name. A thousand thoughts run through his head. While he is wondering what is going to become of him and his future, the officer is reading his rights to him. He may not even hear them; then the officer finally says, "Okay, are you ready to talk now?"

You may feel a compulsion to speak in order to get your guilt off your chest. It acts like a purgative. No longer able to keep it inside, you feel that by telling all, it will cleanse your soul. The only thing it will do is dig your grave deeper.

The most common reason that an individual talks at this stage is the misguided belief that he will be able to talk himself out of a situation that he has created. Unfortunately, the practical effect is just the opposite. Instead of extricating himself, he implicates himself further. As a general rule, anythings that you say or do after the time you are arrested, aside from being respectful to the officer's authority, will further contribute to your conviction.

You and the Police
by N. Robert Stoll
1978; 118p; $3.50
Self-Counsel Press, Inc.
1303 N. Northgate Way
Seattle, WA 98133

Can police maliciously arrest, beat, bludgeon and jail an innocent person without probable cause, and then charge "resisting arrest"? Sure they can—they have the guns—and besides, they can back one another with all sorts of lies. Such are the vagaries of the real world. Ahhh, but in theory. . . .

And that's what this book is all about—the "theory," explained clearly and simply. It is an excellent introduction to criminal procedure, beginning from the moment the police officer begins to contemplate detaining you or making a search, the legalities of the arrest, confessions and admissions, seeing a lawyer, bail, pretrial proceedings, trial, and sentencing. Also covered are drug and weapons laws, juvenile law, and civil and criminal complaints against the police.

The format is bare-bones and straightforward. For example, the following:

•

C. When Can There Be a Search Without a Warrant?

Although, under both federal and state constitutions, police may not make "unreasonable" searches or seizures and must have search warrants before they can search citizens' homes or property, there are three major exceptions to this rule:

a. There is no "search" and no need for a warrant if the incriminating evidence that is seized is in plain view of the police officer.

b. No warrant is necessary if the citizen being searched consents to the search or seizure.

c. No warrant is required if there are so-called "exigent" (special) circumstances. (We shall discuss these on page 4.)

The Defendant's Rights Today

by David Fellman
1976; 446p; $20.00
University of Wisconsin
   Press
Box 1379
Madison, WI 53701

This is an excellent, albeit a little out-dated, scholarly treatise by a political scientist on every conceivable problem area in criminal procedure. Arrest procedures, preliminary hearings, right to bail, speedy trial, cross-examination, habeas corpus writs, jury trials and bias, attorneys, searches, and more is covered. This is an outstanding text for undergraduate criminal justice or constitutional law students, or as a supplemental text for first year criminal procedure law students.

Your Rights and the Criminal Justice System

by People's Law School of San Francisco
1977; 20p; 50¢
People's Law School
558 Capp Street
San Francisco, CA 94110

This 20-page pamphlet is easy to read, with non-technical language on your rights vis-à-vis questioning or arrest by the police, whether on the street, in your car, or at home. Helpful information is included on whether to plea-bargain or go to trial, and how to communicate with your lawyer. Prudently, the pamphlet does not attempt to discuss what you should do at trial, leaving that to you and your lawyer.

•

Your Rights on the Streets

1. Obviously suspicious behavior on the streets invites police attention.
2. If the police ask you, you are required to identify yourself.
3. If they ask you, account for your presence.
4. The police can legally pat you down for weapons. Unless they feel an object that could be a weapon, they cannot go through your pockets without arresting you first. If you are carrying a nonconcealed weapon, the police can check to see if it is legal and unloaded.
5. Whether you are arrested or not, you have the right to remain silent, you have the right to consult with a lawyer. Never confess to anything. Whatever you say will be used against you later, so — *Don't talk!*
6. If the police continue to question you, ask, "am I under arrest?"
7. If they say no, but continue to ask questions, say, "I have nothing to say until I speak to my lawyer." Remember, even if you don't have a lawyer, if you are arrested, the court will appoint one for you.
8. If the police say yes, you are arrested, ask "What are the charges?" They are required to tell you.
9. The police may legally search you if you are arrested. If you are not under arrest and they search you, say "I do not consent to a search." Be sure to say it loud enough so that witnesses present will hear.
10. The police are required to identify themselves. Remember if they do this or not.
11. Remember everything that happens. Stay cool, don't instigate the police. Don't talk or sign anything. Get badge numbers of police involved.
12. If there are people around, tell them you want them as witnesses. Give them your name and someone to contact. The police are not allowed to prevent you from getting witnesses. Remember if they do and tell your lawyer. If you are witnessing an arrest, don't obstruct the police or this will subject you to arrest.

Jury Work — Systematic Techniques

by National Jury Project
1979; ringbound for updates; 298p; $40 (discounts available)
available at

1419 Broadway, #530
Oakland, CA 94612

310 4th Avenue South, #700
Minneapolis, MN 55415

P.O. Box 675
Brookline Village, MA 02147

1531 Healey Bldg.
57 Forsyth St., N.W.
Atlanta, GA 30303

This manual is an excellent guide for attorneys and defense committees in building strategy for all phases of jury selection.

The National Jury Project was founded in 1975 by legal people and social scientists who were involved in political trials in the early 70's and wanted to focus on developing a strategy for jury selection. Their casework has involved the American Indian Movement, rights of gay people, labor struggles, death penalty work, and women's self-defense.

The manual contains discussion in the areas of

case analyses, juror evaluation, community analysis, voir dire, preemptory challenges, and much more. Sample motions and forms are also included.

•

Community activists are likely to be familiar with the composition, attitudes and events in their communities because of the work they do or the activities they are involved in. They can include tenant organizers, union organizers or shop stewards, local politicians, people who work in local planning offices, PTA activists, club officers, clergy and others.

It is often a good idea to interview community activists early in the interviewing process. They can be most helpful in differentiating groups or neighborhoods within the community and providing overviews of attitudes and opinions on issues of community interest. They are also a good source for names of other people who are familiar with different neighborhoods, organizations or workplaces.

It is equally important to interview people who are not community leaders or activists but who represent a *cross-section* of the types of people who are likely to hear the case. The tabulations which were done to identify the composition of a typical jury panel can be used as a guide to deciding which groups in the population should be represented among those interviewed.

★★ Other Books of Interest for the Advocate

Police Misconduct Litigation Manual (with updates)
by National Lawyers Guild
1979; $35.00
National Lawyers Guild
1427 Walnut Street
Philadelphia, PA 19102

Comprehensive materials for legal people on aspects of filing suits against police misconduct.

Raising and Litigating Electronic Surveillance Claims and Cases
by NLG Special Projects Staff, 1977
1978; Write for price
Lake Law Books
142 McAllister
San Francisco, CA

Includes chapters on making motions, challenging court-ordered surveillance and national security surveillance.

The Rights of Ex-Offenders (An A.C.L.U. Handbook)
by David Rudenstine
1979; 240p; $1.95
Avon Books
250 West 55th Street
New York, NY 10019

What are an ex-offender's rights in the areas of employment and occupational licensing? Can an ex-offender vote? Change his or her name? These questions and others of practical and academic concern are answered in this inexpensive publication of the ACLU. It not only sets out what employment, domestic, property and citizenship rights exist for ex-offenders, but also how they can be exercised and in some cases, regained. Included in the back is a list of state and national organizations that give job assistance to ex-offenders.

Anti-Nuclear Power: *Pro Se Handbook*
by the National Lawyers Guild
1980; Write for price
Anti-Nuke National Project
Massachusetts Chapter of National Lawyers Guild
120 Boylston St.
Boston, MA 02116

This pamphlet explains in easy terms the issues which confront people when facing arraignments and trial after arrest at anti-nuke demonstrations.

Will the Circle Be Unbroken: A People's Guide to Grand Juries and FBI Harassment

You, Your Rights and the FBI
by the National Lawyers Guild
1977; Write for prices
Grand Jury Project
National Lawyers Guild
853 Broadway
New York, NY 10003

These informative pamphlets explain both how to deal with the FBI as well as what the grand jury process entails.

► B.   Traffic Ticket Defense

How to Avoid and Beat Traffic Tickets
by "Lawyer 'S' " (anonymous)
1977; 52p; $2.95
Good Life Press (Charing Cross Publishing
   Company)
658 Bonnie Brae Street
Los Angeles, CA 90057

*This book is full of practical "nuts-and-bolts" infor-mation on how to avoid and beat traffic tickets —
just like the title says. The chapter, "Gamesmanship,
How to Beat the Ticket Without a Trial," discusses
tactics like demanding trial in a distant city, delay-ing the case until the time during which you must be
tried expires, and other wonderful little gems. Sam-ple forms for certain procedural techniques (such as
disqualifying a bad judge, demanding a transfer of
the case to a distant city) are included.*

*The basic trial preparation techniques are well
stated, although cross-examination of the police
officer is glossed over — apparently the attorney-author decided that cross-examination is just for
"experts." The best chapter is "The Highway is Part
of the Courtroom" — an essential guide for preparing
your case from the very second you see the flashing
red light in your rearview mirror, rather than being
embarrassed and goaded into incriminating yourself
on the spot when the officer stops you.*

*One caution — the procedural aspects of this book
are heavily California-oriented, and will often not
apply to other states. Except for the chapters on
what-to-do-when-the-cop-stops-you, and trial prepa-ration, there's not too much else that's applicable
outside of California.*

The Ticket Book
by Ron Dornsife
1978; 467p; $6.95
The Ticket Book
P.O. Box 1087
La Jolla, CA 92038

*Although this sometimes reads like a cross between a
high school Driver Ed book and a catalog of elec-tronic toys for the author's fellow traffic cop buddies
to drool over, the sheer volume and number of items
discussed here ensures that some useful information
on "how-to-beat-traffic-tickets" will seep through.
An interesting book to read as you would a novel.*

*The best aspect of the book is that it skillfully
manages the impossible — to explain in about 100*
*pages how radar speed detection systems work with-out being overly technical, but without glossing over
the basic idea.*

*The author is a former San Diego traffic officer,
who has written "thousands" of traffic tickets. Thus,
much of the emphasis of the book is on tactics of
traffic officers in apprehending their victims, where
they like to look for violators, what attracts their
attention, how there really is a "quota system" in
every police department, and what type of equipment
is used.*

*What little space is devoted to actual ticket-fight-ing strategy (72 pages) is pretty well developed, espe-cially the types of cross-examination the person
charged with the offense should ask of the officer at
trial. Unfortunately, the important steps one can
take before trial in order to beat the ticket on a
technicality are completely glossed over. The book is a
"national" book, supposedly applicable in general
terms to every state, thus procedural laws of fighting
the ticket are virtually ignored.*

*The biggest problem with the book, though, is the
author's perspective. His experience as a traffic officer
seems to have given him the idea that the whole
traffic enforcement system is especially designed to
gratify the macho urges of traffic officers, who are
referred to as "hungry bears," and "cowboys" out on
the prowl for violators among the "herds" of autos on
the road. One also gets the impression that Dornsife's
experience in the squad car has resulted in his too
often assuming that the driver of the targeted vehicle
is guilty.*

Fight That Ticket – In Washington (State)
by Charles L. Smith
1977; 73p; $1.95
Self-Counsel Press, Inc.
1303 N. Northgate Way
Seattle, WA 98133

*Although a little thin — 73 pages — this book will be
helpful in heightening the odds that you'll be able to
beat that traffic ticket some overzealous, quota-inspired police officer gave you. The emphasis seems
to be on down-to-earth instructions on how to beat
the ticket — guilty or not — on either a technicality
or by raising the famous issue of "reasonable doubt"
in a traffic court hearing.*

VII.   Business

★ A.   General Business Practices

Small-Time Operator
by Bernard Kamoroff
1976, 1980; 190p; $7.95
Bell Springs Publishing
P.O. Box 640
Laytonville, CA 95454

*I have known Bernard
"Bear" Kamoroff and his
wonderful book for three
years. In that time I have
personally heard hundreds of
small business people praise*
Small-Time Operator *as being a lifesaver. Bear self-
published this all-purpose guide for small business in
1976. Even though he still runs his publishing business out of his house, the book has become a national
bestseller and is now in its 9th printing.* Small-Time
Operator *shows you how to start your own small
business, keep your books, pay your taxes and stay
out of trouble. Need I say more? Note: See Part II of
this book for Bear's article on sole proprietorship,
partnerships, and small corporations, largely excerpted from* Small-Time Operator.

•

Bookkeeping seems to be the one aspect of business that
so many people dread. Columns upon columns of numbers, streams of adding machine tape, balancing the books
(whatever that means), and "I'm a craftsman, not an
accountant." Whenever I try to explain or defend the
paperwork end of business to a new business person, I
always feel I have two strikes against me before I even open
my mouth. But once a person understands why a business
requires a set of ledgers and how these records can be kept
with a minimum of time and effort, the fear vanishes, the
work—somehow—gets done, and you are left with the
satisfaction of seeing the total picture and of having done it
yourself. And that is a nice feeling.

Bookkeeping is an integral part of business, of *your*
business. To attempt a definition, bookkeeping is a system
designed to record, summarize, and analyze your financial activity—your sales, purchases, credit accounts,

cash, payrolls, inventory, equipment. Your "books"—
your ledgers and worksheets—are the bound papers on
which the bookkeeping activity is recorded or "posted."

The Small Business Handbook
by Irving Burstiner
1979; 342p; $10.95
Prentice-Hall
Englewood Cliffs, NJ 07632

*This deceptively thin (its pages—all 342 of them—
are thin enough to make for only ⅝" thickness) tome
has 23 chapters on topics you probably never though
about before—management of prices, product development, production and promotion, improving efficiency in a manufacturing plant or wholesale, retail,
or service business.*

*Legal and tax considerations are not neglected in
favor of these topics, however; pluses and minuses for
sole proprietorships, partnerships, and small corporations are discussed. One might summarize by stating
that sole proprietorships are simple but expose the
owner to liability; partnerships allow pooling of
resources and making for disagreement and dissen-
sion; corporations allow for limited liability and
pooling of resources but sometimes face double taxation (dividends are taxed first as corporate profits
then as individual income) and over-regulation.
Sample income tax forms for partnerships and corporations are included.*

Business Law – An
Introduction
by Lowell B. Howard
1965; 590p; $6.50
Barron's Educational
   Series, Inc.
113 Crossways Park Drive
Woodbury, NY 11797

*The 1965 copyright date on
this book almost made us
toss it in the "NO" box until
we read it and realized that
business law (with the major
exception of consumer law) hasn't changed much in
the past 15 years. The most informative sections are
the ones on:*

*1. the workings of the American state and federal
court systems; and*

*2. basic contract law—offer, acceptance, consid-
eration, non-validity.*

Also discussed are the meanings, advantages, and disadvantages of doing business as a partnership or corporation. The emphasis is on commercial transactions between business people rather than retail dealings. It is well-written and understandable.

•

Implied In Fact Contracts. An implied in fact contract is one inferred from the circumstances or acts of the parties. These indicia of an intention to contract may exist in combination with the words of the parties, where the words alone would be insufficient to create an express contract.

There is no generic difference between an express contract and one implied from the acts of the parties; both are true contracts and rest upon the mutual assent of the parties along with the other essential elements of a contract.

Generally when one person requests a stranger to render services without any express agreement to pay for such services, a promise to pay the reasonable value of such services is implied. The resulting contract in such a case would be an implied in fact contract. The circumstances and relationship of the parties must not suggest that the parties intended that the services were to be rendered gratuitously, as is generally the case where close relatives render services for one another.

What You Should Know About Contracts
by Robert A. Farmer
1979; 189p; $3.95
Cornerstone Library
Simon & Schuster Bldg.
1230 Avenue of the Americas
New York, NY 10020

If your friend orally offers you $400 for your beat-up Buick and you agree, what happens if she or he doesn't come through with the money?
Do you still have a valid contract? Can you make your ex-friend pay you the $100 difference between his/her $400 offer and the $300 you got for it from someone else? Contrary to what most people think, contracts don't always have to be in writing. That, and more, is explained here in full.

Although somewhat dry (as contract law invariably is), this book is a well-organized, concise, no-nonsense approach to contract law — without the scholarly humdrum breakdown of "the law of third party beneficiary contract actions in the 51 jurisdictions." The book discusses the essential elements of a contract (legal parties, offer, acceptance), whether

contracts must be in writing, breaking contracts, and "defenses" to their enforcement.

"The Law" is clearly laid out for easy review by law students, business people and consumers. Both the "common law" of contracts and the Uniform Commercial Code (UCC) are covered.

•

As a general rule, the offeror can revoke his offer at any time before the offeree's acceptance. Revocation of an offer occurs when the offeror decides to revoke the offer and the offeror's change of mind is committed to the offeree. The revocation does not become effective until it is communicated to the offeree, and thus if the offeree makes an acceptance before learning of the revocation, a valid contract is formed. For example, suppose you offer to sell your house to your cousin Tom, but before Tom accepts, you put a revocation in the mail; an hour later you receive Tom's acceptance by telegram. As long as your letter of revocation did not reach Tom before he sent his acceptance, a valid contract has been formed.

Usually, a revocation will take place when the offeror informs the offeree that he no longer wishes to make a contract. However, a revocation can also occur if the offeree learns from a third party that the offeror has revoked his offer. Thus, if Bill offers to sell a book to Harry, and Harry later learns from George that Bill has revoked his offer, Harry cannot make an acceptance to purchase the book. The only question at issue is the trustworthiness and validity of the source of information, which must be reasonably reliable. Hence, if George is a reasonably reliable person, then Bill's offer to Harry has been revoked.

How to Prepare Building and Construction Contracts
by John C. Howell
1979; 125p; $14.95
Citizen's Law Library, Inc.
6 West Laudoun Street
P.O. Box 1745
Leesbury, VA 20075

One of the most complex legal arrangements, rife with traps for the unwary, is with the contractor to whom you entrust your home for improvement. This book presents a thorough introduction to basic contract law, in addition to topics such as soliciting bids, correction of work, supplying of materials, bonds, delays. Contract law is pretty much the same in all states, with only minor variations, so the book is useful nationally.

The best aspect, though, is the multitude of sample forms to cover almost any sort of anticipated problem or contingency.

●

Judges, lawyers, law students, professors and others spend an inordinate amount of time working, debating and arguing about contracts. It is easy to give a legal definition of a contract, but the problem arises in determining whether a transaction comes within the definition. A textbook definition is that a contract is a promise, or set of promises, for breach of which the law gives a remedy, or for the performance of which the law in some way recognizes a duty. This is a little like saying a contract is a "contract" or a contract is a "valid agreement." The textbooks usually proceed to explain the essential elements of a contract, which are:
1. A valid offer
2. An acceptance of the offer
3. Valid consideration
4. Legal capacity of the respective parties
5. Legal subject matter
6. A writing, if required by law (Statute of Frauds).

Dictionary of Economics and Business

by Erwin Esser Nemmers
1979; 523p; 95¢
Littlefield, Adams & Co.
81 Adams Drive
Totowa, NJ 07512

This is not a do-it-yourself law book in any sense, but since economics, business, and law are inextricably intertwined, we decided to throw in this unique dictionary. It is useful to serious students of economics and people who want to know about economics and who are not intimidated by graphs and equations. Yet enough terms are explained in simple language, without mathematics, to make the purchase worthwhile even to those who are intimidated.

●

absolute priority. The right of senior creditors and stockholders to be paid in full before any junior issues receive anything. For example, if there are $500,000 in assets, $100,000 in bonds, $500,000 in preferred stock, and $500,000 in common stock, the bondholders are paid in full, the preferred stockholders get 80 cents on the dollar, and the common stockholders nothing. Cf. *relative priority.*

B.   Incorporation ★

How to Form Your Own California Corporation
by Anthony Mancuso
1980; 182p; $15.00
Nolo Press
950 Parker St.
Berkeley, CA 94710

Incorporating yourself or your business is not a long, complicated procedure. This book tells you how to form a "close" corporation having ten or fewer stockholders. This step-by-step guide is both well-written and well-organized. Each main topic is broken down into topics and subtopics to the point where only one or two short paragraphs are needed to explain things such as: sole proprietorships, partnerships, "foreign" vs. domestic, stock vs. non-stock, and "close" corporations. Since the 1977 amendments, the incorporation procedure consists mainly of filling in the blanks of standardized forms, all of which are included as tear-out forms in the back of the book, along with by-laws and articles of incorporation.

●

California classifies corporations in several, sometimes overlapping, ways. The first classification is "domestic" versus "foreign." A domestic corporation is one which is formed under the laws of California by filing Articles of Incorporation with the California Secretary of State. A corporation which is formed in another state, even if it is physically present and is doing business in this state, is a foreign corporation.

California also classifies corporations as "stock" or "non-stock." A stock corporation is simply one which is authorized by its Articles of Incorporation to issue shares of stock. A non-stock corporation is any corporation not so authorized.

In addition to these general classifications, the Corporations Code recognizes the existence of certain special kinds of corporations (divisions of these larger groupings, such as professional, close, non-profit, or cooperative corporations). There are special provisions and rules relating to each of these sub-groups. Let's review some of them briefly before we deal in detail with the subject of this book — the small profit corporation known as the close corporation.

How to Form Your Own Texas Corporation

by Jim Simons and Anthony Mancuso
1980; $14.95
Addison-Wesley Publishing Co.
Trade Sales
Reading, MA 01867

This book is the Texas sister to the California book above. Highly recommended.

The California Non-Profit Corporation Handbook (Second Edition)

by Anthony Mancuso
1980; 248p; $15.00
Nolo Press
950 Parker St.
Berkeley, CA 94710

This is a remarkable book. Any California non-profit organization that wants to incorporate under §501(c)(3) of the Internal Revenue Code (charities, religions, scientific, literary, educational, etc.) will find everything it needs here. Not only are sample articles, by-laws, and minutes of the first meeting included, among other items, but the book contains all sorts of practical information such as the ins and outs of choosing a name, non-profit mailing rates, and filing tax returns after you are organized.

But perhaps the most valuable aspect of this handbook involves getting your federal tax exemption under §501(c)(3). This is the reason that most groups, whether they are involved in art, social services, education, medicine, or the environment, wish to set up a non-profit corporation in the first place. The federal tax information — complete with instructions on filling out the forms — is good in all 50 states.

•

Interest in forming nonprofit corporations is on the increase. All sorts of groups, from artists, musicians and dancers to people active in education, health, ethnic and other community services, women's rights and dozens of other concerns, wish to operate as nonprofit corporations. Often the reason for doing this is simple — being organized as a nonprofit corporation is commonly a requirement for obtaining funds from government agencies and private foundations. Obtaining grants, however, is not the only reason to incorporate. There are also important federal and state tax exemptions available to the nonprofit

corporation as well as significant (20–50%) tax deductions available to people who make contributions to nonprofit groups.

In addition to funding source requirements and tax benefits, there are several other important reasons why people choose to set up nonprofit corporations. Perhaps the most important is limited liability. The nonprofit corporation normally protects its directors, officers and members from personal liability for claims brought against the corporation. This means that lawsuits can only reach the assets of the corporation, not the bank accounts, houses, or other property owned by the individuals who manage, belong to, or work for the corporation. Many incorporators of nonprofit corporations also feel that the act of setting up a corporation is itself beneficial. Why? Because the act of organizing the corporation serves as a convenient means of focusing on and dealing with initial and ongoing business details, and because the existence of the corporation gives the group increased standing in the community.

How to Form Your Own Corporation Without a Lawyer for Under $50.00

by Ted Nicholas
1978; 109p; $14.95

How to Form Your Own Professional Corporation

by Ted Nicholas
1977; 106p; $19.95
Enterprise Publishing
    Company
Suite 501 Beneficial Bldg.
Market Street
Wilmington, DE 19801

The main reason we're reviewing the first book is that it's so well-known that to omit it may be construed as an oversight. But, in fact, we consider it to be of limited use. The author's main point is that when you've decided that the corporate way of doing business (with its advantages of limited liability, separate legal entity, facility in raising capital, and taxation) is appropriate for you, the best state in which to incorporate is Delaware. This book contains by-laws, articles of incorporation, and other forms necessary to set up your business as a Delaware corporation. If you really want to incorporate in Delaware, buy this book.

Incorporating in Delaware, however, is not always the panacea the author would have you believe. It's true that Delaware is the easiest state in which to incorporate, but if your Delaware corporation does business in a state which was not thrilled that you forsook it in an attempted tax dodge (few are), you may wind up with very few of the advantages you would have otherwise obtained if you had incorporated there in the first place. For example, in California (and many other states), if your Delaware (or other out-of-state) corporation is considered to be doing any business at all in California, it must "qualify" to exist as a corporation in California, and you must pay filing fees and taxes as though it were incorporated in California.

A companion book is How to Form Your Own Professional Corporation, *for lawyers, accountants, doctors, dentists, etc., who for liability or tax reasons wish to incorporate their practices. Since all states closely regulate such professions, the corporation must be incorporated in the state where the practice is located. Here the author realizes this and does not foolishly suggest Delaware as a state of incorporation. So this is meant as a "national" book appropriate for professional practitioners in any state. As in many such "national" books, however, the depth of information, sample forms, and details about incorporating (which vary from state to state) are quickly glossed over.*

Still, some useful information is conveyed in both books — the basic ideas behind incorporating, federal tax treatment, what by-laws and articles of incorporation should look like, issuing stock, and more.

Incorporation & Business Guide for Washington
by Harold B. Coe
1978; 115p; $9.95

Incorporation & Business Guide for Oregon
by Magar E. Magar
1978; 114p; $9.95
Note: Necessary forms must
   be ordered separately for
   $6.95 per set.
Self-Counsel Press
1303 N. Northgate Way
Seattle, WA 98133

These two books are nearly identical, though adapted for each particular state. The five basic methods of carrying on a business are discussed clearly: sole proprietorship, general partnership, limited partnership, joint venture, and corporation. Each one has

its own special advantages and disadvantages in terms of simplicity, taxes, and liability of individuals for business debts. Once past preliminaries, realities such as corporate by-laws, minutes, stock, workers' compensation, business licenses, and tax withholding are covered in enough detail to aid you in launching your business.

•

This section will explain the formation, nature, characteristics, rights, obligations and dissolution of general partnerships. Limited partnerships and joint ventures will be discussed in the next section.

A partnership is defined as an association of two or more persons who operate a business for profit. Like a proprietorship, a partnership is not a separate legal entity apart from its partners or members. It is an association of two or more persons who have agreed to engage in a business venture.

A general partnership is created by an agreement that can be oral, written, or implied.

A general partnership agreement is not required by law to be in writing and it may simply be an oral understanding (that is sometimes evidenced by a handshake) followed by performance of the terms of the understanding. However it is *strongly recommended* that the agreement of the partners be put into writing and signed by all partners.

Legal Guide for Corporate Officers & Directors
by John C. Howell
1980; 150p; $14.95
Citizens' Law Library
P.O. Box 1745
Leesburg, VA 22075

There are several books on forming your own corporation; however, there is little material in most of these (with the exception of How to Form Your Own California Corporation *which is fairly thorough) about the rights and responsibilities of corporate officers and directors. Many people think that serving as a director is an honor and something that involves little work and no potential liability. This is simply not true — at least, as far as liability is concerned. Courts are more and more often holding directors to strict standards of accountability, both for their actions and failures to act.*

This book explains the duties, responsibilities, obligations, and potential liabilities that ensue from positions of corporate officers and directors.

•

During the past few years, the exposure to legal liability for directors and officers who buy and sell the company's stock and who may have possession of "inside information" not available to the investing public, have been dramatic in their expanding numbers, and in the amounts involved. Class actions instituted by many plaintiffs seeking return of profits allegedly made as a result of inside information are becoming common. These risks can be avoided if you know what to look out for and know how to make the right moves at the right time.

C.   Art and Technology

The Business of Art: A Comprehensive Guide to Business Practices for Artists
by Diane Cochrane
1978; 256p; $12.50
Watson-Guptill
    Publications
1515 Broadway
New York, NY 10036

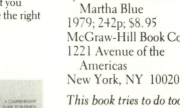

Artists tend often to be careless about business details when they start their careers.
Then, after being burned a few times by sharpies who are more than happy to take advantage of their naïveté, they often become paranoid and overly fearful that everyone is going to take advantage of them. Happily, there is a reasonable middle ground where common sense and common law come together and the artist has the information needed to make sound business decisions. This book is a good place to begin. It covers commission agreements, advances and stipends, contracts, consignment sales, co-op galleries, insurance taxes and much more.

•

How do I write commissions into an agreement?
A sales commission clause might state:
The gallery shall receive the following sales commission:
    (a) _____% of the agreed sales price for works in the following medium: _____;
    (b) _____% of the agreed sales price for works in the following medium: _____;
    (c) _____% of the amount paid for studio sales made directly by the artist.

Making it Legal: A Law Primer for the Craftmaker, Visual Artist and Writer
by Marion Davidson &
    Martha Blue
1979; 242p; $8.95
McGraw-Hill Book Co.
1221 Avenue of the
    Americas
New York, NY 10020

This book tries to do too much and doesn't quite succeed. Still, it is valuable and helpful, especially for the craftmaker running his or her own small business. If it is read with Small-Time Operator, *it can provide the legal and practical tools necessary for a craftmaker to stay out of trouble. We are not aware of any other book that does as well in this area. However, we do not recommend it for the writer or visual artist, as there are more comprehensive publications available, several of which we review here.*

•

If you are selling fiber or fur products like wool hangings, tie-dyed scarves, handwoven pillows, batik shirts, quilts, fur jackets, wool hats, and so on, the federal laws governing the labeling of textiles concern you. Although individual artists and craftmakers seldom are prosecuted for violation of these laws, some of your works could well be covered by the labeling requirements contained in these laws.

At first reading, these labeling requirements look like a lot of trouble. But federal requirements aside, many in the fiber field routinely do inform their customers concerning the fiber content as an integral part of the creation and sale of handmade fiberwork. In addition to notifying your customers of exactly what they are getting, the fiber-content information also helps with the care of the textile.

The major federal laws and regulations in the textile area are the Wool Products Labeling Act of 1939, the Fur Products Labeling Act, the Textile Fiber Products Identification Act, the Flammable Fabrics Act, and the Care Labeling of Textile Wearing Apparel. There is also a Trade Practice Rule on shrinkage of woven cotton yard goods. These laws pretty much cover most people who sell textile, wool, and fur creations and require that these products be labeled with certain information. This section will amplify who and what is covered by these laws and the labeling requirements for each law.

A Writer's Guide to Copyright

by Poets & Writers, Inc.
1979; 60p; $4.95
Poets & Writers, Inc.
201 W. 54th St.
New York, NY 10019

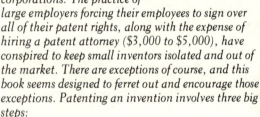

*The law of copyright, like that of patents and income
tax, is one of those wonderful subjects that is uniform
throughout the country. Also, it has become less
complicated since enactment of the "new" 1976
copyright law. Basically, this brief yet thorough
booklet emphasizes that:*

*1. As an author, you're protected as soon as you
create the work.*

*2. Registering a work with the U.S. Copyright
Office is not required, unless you want to*

*a. bring suit against an unauthorized copyright
infringer, or*

b. sell your work or license its publication

*Also included is a chapter on when rights should
be transferred to publishers (should you sell the whole
copyright or just grant limited rights?); when to
register the work with the copyright office, how to
deal with the copyright office (all the forms you'll
need are in the back of the book); renewal (after 28
years); and the new "fair use" doctrine which allows
limited unauthorized copying.*

*This brief book is excellent for the writer who wants
to concentrate on his/her work without having to
read a detailed treatise on law.*

Cartoonists Guild Publications:
Copyright Pamphlet, $3.75
Syndicate Survival Kit, $6.00
Cartoonists Guild Publications
156 West 72nd Street
New York, NY 10023

*The Cartoonists Guild publishes two invaluable
staple-bound pamphlets. One is entitled "An Introduction to the New Copyright Law," and is just
that. The other is entitled "The Syndicate Survival
Kit," and discusses the contracts that the major new
syndicates offer cartoonists, as well as ways that they
can be modified to better protect the cartoonist's legal
rights. Six standard syndicate contracts are reproduced and discussed clause by clause.*

•

The Guild, of course, can only voice its disapproval of past
contracts and make recommendations. Artists themselves
must make the decisions to sign or not to sign. The

temptation to sign a contract, even one as completely and
obviously unfavorable to the artist as any of these, must be
stong indeed. An artist works for many months on an idea
with only one goal in mind — to have it published and
seen by the rest of the world. It's an ego trip that must be
fulfilled, very often *at all costs!*

The syndicates recognize this and prey upon the emotional weaknesses of the artist. He gets fulfilled and the
syndicate gets the gravy.

Only when the strip becomes a valuable property via
success does the artist deal from any sort of power base and
then very often it is too late because he has relinquished
his most valuable asset — ownership of the idea itself. Not
even his talent is recognized as being indispensable.
Someone else may end up doing the feature.

Patent It Yourself

by David Pressman
1979; 210p; $14.95
McGraw-Hill Publishing
    Company
1221 Avenue of the
    Americas
New York, NY 10020

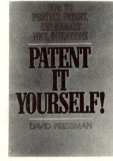

*This is people's law in a field
which is dominated almost
entirely by multi-national
corporations. The practice of
large employers forcing their employees to sign over
all of their patent rights, along with the expense of
hiring a patent attorney ($3,000 to $5,000), have
conspired to keep small inventors isolated and out of
the market. There are exceptions of course, and this
book seems designed to ferret out and encourage those
exceptions. Patenting an invention involves three big
steps:*

1. Keeping meticulous records;

2. Writing down how to manufacture it; and

*3. Writing down the "claims" (why you're claim-
ing your legal 17-year monopoly).*

*Writing down the manufacture procedure is some-
thing most inventors can do with ease, the difficult
parts are the "legalese" of patents — the claims.
Having a new, useful, and "non-obvious" invention,
process, etc., isn't enough. If your claims are over-
broad, the patent is invalid; if too narrow, copiers
can get around them too easily. This book shows you
how to write the claims.*

*The author explains how to decide at the outset
whether market considerations will justify patenting,
and how to market and sell the patent once it's
obtained.*

The book is remarkably "folksy" for a subject as technical as patent law — that mysterious mix of science, engineering and law.

•

Before you make a search for patentability, you must be sure that your invention comprises *patentable subject matter*, that is, something upon which the Patent and Trademark Office will be able to grant a patent, assuming you're the first to come up with it. The patent laws do not allow the PTO to grant patents on everything that is new; only certain categories of inventions can be patented; everything else is considered nonpatentable subject matter.

The categories of patentable subject matter, although only five, are pretty comprehensive. They are:

1. Processes
2. Machines
3. Manufactures
4. Compositions of matter
5. New uses of any of the above four

VIII. Before, When, and After You Die

★ A.   All About Wills, Trusts, Etc.

Planning Your Estate with Wills, Probate, Trusts & Taxes (California)
by Denis Clifford
1980; 239; $15.00
Nolo Press
950 Parker St.
Berkeley, CA 94710

Everything you need to know about federal and California estate and inheritance taxes, wills with numerous sample wills for couples, singles, families with children, etc., probate, gifts and gift taxes, life insurance, joint tenancy and trusts.

Each of the ways to pass on property is explained in down-to-earth language; what it is, how the property is taxed, and how you can pass on your property. This is a well-written book on the whole of "estate planning" — not simply on avoiding probate, or how to draft a will, or death taxes.

Actually, the emphasis is on minimizing probate. In California, the fee an executor and his/her lawyer receives is based on a percentage of the assets transferred through probate usually by a will, but sometimes without. There's no need to include expensive assets like a home in your probate estate — that will just boost these fees. Besides, a home can be transferred to the surviving spouse because it's community property, or it can be owned in joint tenancy; in both these cases, it doesn't go though probate. On the other hand, probate can sometimes be helpful — if that portion of an estate going through probate is small, the percentage fee will also be small and reasonable.

Questions that arise in a community property state like California (and Texas, Louisiana, New Mexico, Arizona, Nevada, Washington, and Idaho) are likewise answered.

Other topics discussed include: practical matters (burial or cremation instructions, funerals, organ donation, etc.), how to best give gifts before death to minimize taxes, and simple "summary probate" for estates under $20,000). The book is complete, clear, and concise.

•

Estate planning covers many problems. The major ones include:

1. Having a practical plan for body disposition;
2. Reducing death taxes as low as possible;
3. Reducing probate costs and fees as low as possible;
4. Providing prompt cash to dependent survivors (usually family); and
5. Transferring the property of your estate to those you want to have it.

The phrase "estate planning" has many meanings. When rich folks' lawyers, accountants, and their ilk talk about "estate planning," they are using one of the many dignified-sounding terms they have invented for that grand old American game of "beat-the-taxman." You may wonder, as I do, why a civilization should set up the rules so that property transferred, or owned, under certain labels and forms is taxed less than if held in other ways. It is rather puzzling, but that's how it works. The Anglo-American legal system has a (warped) genius for protecting property of the wealthy, and that genius has produced many types of "estate planning" to minimize the impact of death taxes. These can often be so esoteric and involved that only a handful of tax lawyers understand them. For example, the nuances of new tax rules governing "generation skipping transfers"—e.g., where wealth is left in "trust" for grandchildren, with the children receiving only the income produced by the trust property—are now being explored and created by properous tax lawyers. Most of these intricacies aren't covered here. Fortunately, however, estate planning can have meaning for average folks too. These are safe and understandable ways for the average person to save substantial sums of momey while passing his or her property in ways that make sense.

Planning Your Estate with Wills, Trusts, & Taxes (Texas)
by Jim Simons and Denis Clifford
1980; $14.95
Addison-Wesley Publishing Company
Trade Sales
Reading, MA 01867

This Texas version of the California book is excellent. We highly recommend it.

How to Avoid Probate
by Norman F. Dacey
1978; 361p; $7.95
Crown Publishers
One Park Avenue
New York, NY 10016

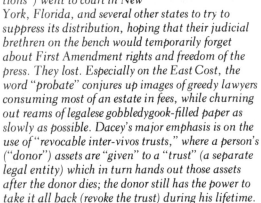

One of the major testaments in support of the effectiveness of this pioneering work is the fact that lawyers' trade associations ("bar associations") went to court in New York, Florida, and several other states to try to suppress its distribution, hoping that their judicial brethren on the bench would temporarily forget about First Amendment rights and freedom of the press. They lost. Especially on the East Cost, the word "probate" conjures up images of greedy lawyers consuming most of an estate in fees, while churning out reams of legalese gobbledygook-filled paper as slowly as possible. Dacey's major emphasis is on the use of "revocable inter-vivos trusts," where a person's ("donor") assets are "given" to a "trust" (a separate legal entity) which in turn hands out those assets after the donor dies; the donor still has the power to take it all back (revoke the trust) during his lifetime.

Although Dacey's method of relying almost exclusively on such trusts to avoid probate really will avoid probate, it will not avoid estate taxes. Also, he virtually ignores other probate-avoiding devices such as joint ownership ("joint tenancy") and "community property" (in community property states: Texas, California, Washington, and others) of husband and wife. Also, little emphasized are the tax advantages of trusts versus other probate-avoidance devices and, in some cases, even probate itself.

Dacey's book is best read as explaining in down-to-earth language many aspects of one useful probate-avoidance device.

Estate Planning: What Anyone Who Owns Anything Must Know
by Peter E. Lippett
1979; 376p; Write for price
Reston Publishing
   Company, Inc.
   (Prentice-Hall)
Reston, VA 22090

This book is a bit complex for those of you who just want to draft your will without studying the subject in depth. But for those of you who want a well-written and easily-read treatise on the subject, this is the one. There is a good index that allows you to find a particular item of interest without reading the whole book.

●

Two or more persons, up to an infinite number, may own property as tenants in common. Each tenant owns an *undivided interest*, which means his own specified percentage of the whole, often based upon his contribution to the purchase of the property. The percentage may be any that is agreed to by the co-tenants, including unequal portions and portions not reflecting investment percentages. The percentages can be large, such as 99%, or minute fractions, as in oil and gas deals or other major investments with many owners, such as .0003487.

The most important point is that this undivided interest is an asset of its owner, and this asset behaves precisely like all of his solely owned property. Thus, an undivided interest in a tenancy in common passes pursuant to the owner's will, or by the laws of intestacy if he leaves no will. It may be sold, leased, given away, or mortgaged to secure a loan and may also be levied upon by creditors or taken in bankruptcy.

Settling and Safeguarding Estates in California Without an Attorney (Seventh Edition)
by Clive Hinckley

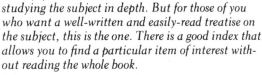

1979; 242p; $8.95
Clive Hinckley
106 East Sunset Drive South
Redlands, CA 92373

We got tired of reading do-it-yourself law books writ-ten for the purpose of eliminating lawyers when the books were written by—you guessed it—lawyers. This is a refreshing change. The author, not an attorney, learned about probate when he was named as an executor in a relative's will. Rather than paying an attorney to do the stylized legal dance of probate with its innumerable but routine forms and court appearances, he struggled along through the procedure himself. (He recommends this only when all the people who stand to inherit are able to get along. If there's a "will contest" or similar legal battle, an attorney is required.) In the "simple" but "uncontested" California estate, the "legal" work entails the executor filling in the blanks on standard-ized legal forms which this book explains.

Although the format of the book is disorganized, muddling through "probate" and death taxes with-out a lawyer will be easier with this book than without.

Estate Planning and Will Writing Guide
by John C. Howell
1979; 179p; $14.95
Citizens' Law Library, Inc.
6 West Loudoun Street
P.O. Box 1745
Leesburg, VA 22075

Are "holographic" (handwritten) wills valid in your state? Do you need to have your will "witnessed?" How many witnesses? Who can be a witness? How is a will revoked?

The best aspect of this book is Part IIIk ("Statutory Provisions of All 50 States Covering Wills...") which provides a state-by-state list of the basics for a valid will—a skeleton of legal requirements.

Also included are sample wills for:
1. *a single person leaving everything to parents,*
2. *a widow(er) leaving everything to children, and*
3. *a married person leaving his/her estate to the other spouse or to the children.*

The most major flaw of the book is the oversimpli-fication of estate planning, even for a small estate.

●

What are the items to be covered in a will? Well, there is no magic formula for what should be in a will, but the usual items, discussed later, include:
1. A statement identifying the testator;
2. Special instructions on payment of debts, or other such items;
3. Burial instructions and other general matters;
4. Appointment of an executor or executrix;
5. General and special disposition of property;
6. Residuary clause; and
7. Attestation clause with signatures and witnesses.

B.   Life Insurance ★

Running Press Glossary of Insurance Language
by Marianne T. Klein
1978; 91p; $2.50
Running Press
38 South 19th Street
Philadelphia, PA 19103

One episode of the former TV series "Night Gallery" portrayed a person who had died and gone to hell. Rather than burning fires, red hot coals, and pitchforks, however, each person's hell was tailored precisely. This person had to spend eternity in a room watching home movies and listen-ing to old 78 RPM records. He was bored to the point of desperation—a true hell indeed.

My hell will no doubt be an endless parade of life insurance salespersons staring me straight in the eye while enthusiastically leading me through the garden of "accelerated options," "cash surrender value," "delay clauses," "dependence period income," and "incidental beneficiaries." Having this insurance lingo dictionary would perhaps make my stay in hell a little less objectionable.

The author states in the preface that "[t]he indus-try is entering an era of policy language simplifica-tion." But until this occurs (if it goes as fast as the legal world toward this goal, we should be there in the year 2580), this glossary will be a useful tool to do battle with a lingo-prone insurance salesman trying to intimidate you.

●

Delay clause. A provision in life insurance policies per-mitting the company to defer granting a loan of the cash value for any purpose besides that of paying the premium. Such deferral is for a stated period of time, usually six months.

IX.   Where We've Been . . .
Where We Could
Be Going

★ A.   Legal History

Law and the Rise of Capitalism
by Michael E. Tigar and Madeleine R. Levy
1977; 346p; $16.00
Monthly Review Press
62 West 14th Street
New York, NY 10011

*The authors trace the rise to power of the bourgeoisie
and the main outlines of bourgeois law; the struggle
between feudal and bourgeois legal ideologies
through the French and English revolutions.*

*The book is designed to be a study of how Marxist
theories of law evolved and in some ways predated the
bourgeoisie's revolt against feudal institutions. On
this level the book doesn't work, since the minute
historical detail overshadows the flow of the theory.
This small criticism shouldn't obscure a much larger
success, however. Quite simply, we found this book
to be the best review of Western law from the eleventh
century to the present that we have ever read. We*

*include a portion of Chapter 2 in Part I of the present
book, but don't let this stop you from reading the
whole thing. It's fascinating.*

The Law of the Land
by Charles Rembar
1980; 447p; $15.00
Simon & Schuster
1230 Avenue of the Americas
New York, NY 10020

*This book differs somewhat from Tigar & Levy's in its
purpose. Where they explore the connection between
the development of the law and the emergence of
capitalism, Rembar is concerned with the evolution
of our present legal system in the United States. He
traces this development from its origins in medieval
England to the present, where he details the most
recent developments in American law. The origins of
trial by jury, the legal profession, and different legal
concepts are explained. This is a fascinating legal
history book and is easier to read than Tigar &
Levy's.*

The Civil Law Tradition
by John Henry Merryman
1969; 172p; $2.95
Stanford University Press
Stanford, CA 94305

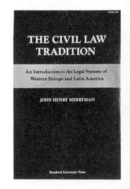

*For the serious student of
comparative legal systems,
this book presents the basic
structures and underlying
philosophies of the "civil
law" system of jurispru-
dence. Civil law is derived
from the Code Napoléon, a
codification of law and legal procedure based on the
ancient Roman Justinian Code, which was based, in
turn, on the Roman "Twelve Tables." The "civil
law" system spread throughout both Europe and the
countries colonized by Europeans. Civil law encom-
passes very extensive systems of codified laws designed
to foresee every possible dispute and relies very little
on "case law."*

*In contrast, the United States' legal system is
based on the "common law" concept of England,
which relies heavily on case law and the interpretation of codified laws by the courts.*

*This is a clearly written and fascinating study of a
system of law with which we Americans are unfamil-*

iar but which governs the societies of most of the world.

●

As in many Utopias, one of the objectives of the Revolution was to make lawyers unnecessary. There was a desire for a legal system that was simple, nontechnical, and straightforward—one in which the professionalism and the tendency toward technicality and complication commonly blamed on lawyers could be avoided. One way to do this was to state the law clearly and in a straightforward fashion, so that the ordinary citizen could read the law and understand what his rights and obligations were, without having to consult lawyers and go to court. Thus the French Civil Code of 1804 was envisioned as a kind of popular book that could be put on the shelf next to the family Bible. It would be a handbook for the citizen, clearly organized and stated in straightforward language, that would allow citizens to determine their legal rights and obligations by themselves.

The emphasis on complete separation of powers, with all lawmaking power lodged in a representative legislature, required that the judiciary be denied lawmaking power. Experience with the prerevolutionary courts had made the French wary of judicial lawmaking disguised as interpretation of laws. Therefore some writers argued that judges should be denied even the power to interpret legislation. (The history of this attitude and its subsequent relaxation are described in Chapter VII.) At the same time, however, the judge had to decide every case that came before him. The premises of secular natural law required that justice be available to all Frenchmen; there could be no area for judicial selection or discretion in the exercise of jurisdiction.

B.   Alternatives and Commentary

Woe Unto You, Lawyers
by Fred Rodell
1939, 1957; 180p; $2.50
Berkley Publishing
    Corporation
200 Madison Avenue
New York, NY 10016

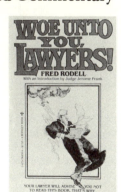

Is it really true, as many a pompous law professor will tell students and laypersons, that "law is a science"? Or is law really a phony pseudo-science replete with jargon and mumbo-jumbo designed to make the simple and logical seem magical and mysterious? As you may have guessed, the author believes the latter. The book was originally written in

1939, at a time when the "nine old men" of the U.S. Supreme Court were doing everything in their power to undermine F.D.R.'s "New Deal." The book was republished in 1957 because of its popularity, but unfortunately does not reflect the two decades which passed in the interim; the "Clayton Act," "Guffey Coal Act," and the "Wagner Labor Act" are all referred to with little explanation for those born after 1940. In this respect, Rodell is almost as guilty as the lawyers whom he derides for their obscure phraseologies.

Overall the book is a good one, complete with humor and biting sarcasm that hits the legal profession where it is most vulnerable—its hypocritical lawyers and intellectually dishonest judges who collude in perpetuating the mystification of the law.

●

But the whole idea of constitutionality and unconstitutionality is so mixed up with notions like patriotism and politics, as well as with the most sacred and complicated of all legal rules, that it deserves and will get full treatment a little later on. The point here is that, after saying part of the Guffey Act was unconstitutional, the judges went on to say that the good part had to be thrown out with the bad part. Not unreasonable perhaps, on the face of it. Not unreasonable until you learn that Congress, foreseeing what the Supreme Court might do with part of the Act, had taken particular pains to write very clearly into the Act that if part of it should be held unconstitutional, the rest of it should go into effect anyway. And so in order to throw out the whole Act, the Court had to reason this way: Part of this law is unconstitutional. The rest is constitutional. Congress said the constitutional part should stand regardless of the rest. But that is not our idea of a proper way of doing things. We do not believe Congress would want to do things in a way that does not seem proper to us, who really know The Law. Therefore, we do not believe Congress meant what it said when it said to let the constitutional part stand. Therefore, we will throw it out along with the unconstitutional part. In the name of The Law.

Verdicts on Lawyers
by Ralph Nader and Mark
    Green
1976; 341p; $4.95
Thomas Y. Crowell Co.
521 Fifth Avenue
New York, NY 10017

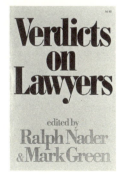

If you've always distrusted the legal profession but found it difficult to pinpoint your reasons, you will be interested to read this book

in which many lawyers — and even judges — who profoundly share your mistrust articulate their reasons.

Read how the American Bar Association voted down 2 to 1 the suggestion that lawyers give 10% of their time to community work; how it handpicks judges; and how its leaders pass through the "revolving door" between private practice and high government positions. Read about the "Ten Worst Judges." And then read "Reflections of a Radical Judge," a judge who is so "radical" that he releases accused shoplifters and drunks without bail while his colleagues are denying bail and forcing these same "offenders" to await trial for months in jail, despite the fact that their ultimate punishment, if any, would not involve incarceration. Be aware that the examples of the conduct of these judges are not aberrant, but on the contrary, are very familiar to any lawyer serving the indigent, and certainly to any poor litigant or defendant.

This collection of essays by thoughtful legal commentators unwilling to accept the status quo without question is a tough and honest attempt to put complex problems in perspective and suggest solutions.

•

The Queens Bar Association submitted a second well-documented petition against Margulies in 1973. Nine lawyers filed sworn statements detailing their humiliations before Margulies. One affidavit said the judge "acts like a maniac." Another attorney swore he witnessed Judge Margulies enter his courtroom at 9:20 a.m. and direct a court officer to move the hands of the clock forward to 9:30 a.m. Then Margulies called the daily calendar, and those lawyers not present had their cases dismissed! And, in February 1974, the Appellate Division censured Margulies — with no public announcement — for the second time.

Injustice for All
by Anne Strick
1978; 282p; $3.95
Penguin Books
625 Madison Avenue
New York, NY 10022

This book is well on its way to becoming a classic, even though it's only three years old. Anne Strick takes on the adversary system and scores a knock-out. We include material from Injustice for All in Part 1 of this book.

This will give you a feeling for her work, but we invite you to sample more in her book, especially her sections demonstrating how the adversary system tends to corrupt the parties to a lawsuit, as well as witnesses and lawyers. Or to restate Anne's observation in the words of Roscoe Pound, the doctrine of contentious procedure " . . . is peculiar to Anglo-American law . . . [it] disfigures our judicial administration at every point, [it] gives to the whole community a false notion of the purpose and end of law. . . . Thus the courts . . . are made agent or abettors of lawlessness."

The Brethren: Inside the Supreme Court
by Bob Woodward and Scott Armstrong
1979; 467p; $13.95
Simon & Schuster
1230 Avenue of the Americas
New York, NY 10020

This book needs no introduction. We include it here because despite its alleged inaccuracies, the over-use of poetic license, and its gossipy format, we believe The Brethren should be required reading for every high-school student. The judiciary, particularly the "Supremes," have perpetuated the dangerous myth that they make decisions according to principles which are ordained by God, and that they are free of bias, prejudice, fear, pressure, or special interests. Thank goodness that Woodward and Armstrong have pierced the veil of secrecy and finally exploded this myth, exposing the pettiness, politics, and prejudices of the "nine old men."

The Client's Handbook (California)
by People's Law School
1979; 16p; $1.00
People's Law School
558 Capp Street
San Francisco, CA 94110

It's a sad fact of life that the resolution of disputes in our society is a cumbersome process which relies upon highly paid gladiators whose dedication appears to be to a "fee up front" rather than to their client's cause.

Lawyers should ideally try to "educate" their clients, keep them diligently informed, and consult with them before making important decisions. Often, however, the "leave it to me" attitude prevails.

The fact is, any lawyer you hire is your employee, and you are the boss. Why should you feel intimidated? Take your lawyer by the horns! Ask him or her about fees, whether it is a fixed, hourly, or contin-

gent fee. Ask that you be sent copies of every legal document filed on your behalf. And how do you tell if you've been had? This pamphlet provides information vital to a successful relationship (from your standpoint) with your lawyer.

●

It's intimidating for many of us to have any contact with an attorney— it often means bad news. And we don't always know how we should act in front of somebody who knows so much more than we do about something that affects our lives directly (our legal problem). There are three basic things to remember when dealing with an attorney: 1) You are the boss; 2) Stay informed about your case; and 3) Keep your lawyer informed about your case.

Wide World of Arbitration: An Anthology
edited by Charlotte Gould and Susan MacKenzie
1978; 211p; Write for price
American Arbitration Association
140 West 51st St.
New York, NY 10020

This isn't really a how-to-do-it book, although many pieces of practical information do crop up throughout the various essays. It is a series of articles about how arbitration can be and is being used to solve just about every type of dispute imaginable. The fields of labor law, commercial law, medical malpractice, personal injury, and many more are treated in detail. At a time when our traditional court system is simply not working, arbitration is the sensible way to resolve disputes at a reasonable cost. People wanting to know more about this area will get their money's worth here.

Afterword

Putting this book together has been a dream here at Nolo Press for at least the last three years. We couldn't do it sooner because, unlike most of our other books, it wasn't possible to do the job with lots of energy and almost no money. To have any hope of bringing all the strands of the self-help law movement together, we needed to gather articles, publications and program information from all over the country. We estimated that to do a thorough job, we would need the creative energy of six people working for six months. As it happened, this was a little on the optimistic side.

But before we get into the details of putting the *Law Review* together, it may be helpful to provide a perspective—that is, to give you a little history on Auntie Nolo and her little book company. The energy that led to Nolo Press can be traced to the late 1960s when Ed Sherman and Ralph Warner were legal aid lawyers in Richmond, California. Like so many other "dropped-out" lawyers who have since come to work with Nolo, they believed then that, if a bunch of energetic young lawyers applied intelligence and energy to doing away with poverty in the U.S., positive change would be forthcoming. You can probably guess—not surprisingly—the rest of that story. Poverty turned out to be more stubborn than our young heroes. After three years of ghetto frustration, they found themselves sitting in a large brown-shingle house in Berkeley, California, burned out with poverty law and trying to learn how

to be hippies. By this time, both were divorced, with kids to support, and neither was either graceful or patient enough to become a waiter. "Ah—," as the man sitting between an erupting volcano and a flooding river said, "what to do?"

Ed supplied the answer, and it bore the title *How to Do Your Own Divorce in California.* Reasoning that recent changes in the California divorce law, including divorce without fault and the substitution of pre-printed forms for typed pleadings, opened the possibility of relatively easy self-divorce, Ed was on his way. Writing out the instructions in the form of a short book wasn't hard, but then came the larger problem—who would publish it? As it turned out, no one would. One publisher after another sang what was to become a familiar song called "It's too dangerous." The second verse usually began with

Ralph Warner and Toni Ihara

Charles Sherman and Trudy Ahlstrom

357

"No one will be stupid enough to buy it," and the chorus ran "A person who represents himself has a fool for a client." Fortunately, Ed was stubborn—he printed the book himself, naming his new enterprise Nolo after Auntie Amanda Nolo, a recluse who lived in a small attic apartment in the old house and kept eight cats.

And there this story might have ended if it hadn't been for the Sacramento County Bar Association. In late 1971, when the little "home-made" divorce book was selling about one hundred copies a month, they called a press conference and warned Californians against using it. Fortunately, it was a slow news day, and the print, voice and film media people spread the warning all over California. For most people it was the first time they had heard of the book, and sales immediately sprinted to 1,000 copies a week. Suddenly the biggest problem was to supply the books.

Finally, Ralph Warner, who had been living with all of this energy, realized that people really were ready for good solid legal information without buying it from a lawyer, and he started working on a book too. Called the *California Tenants' Handbook* (with Sherman and Moskovitz), it was published in 1972 and was also a success, despite the fact that copy had been typed on an uneven twenty-year-old typewriter and printed in purple ink. To date, the *Tenants' Handbook* has sold about 80,000 copies.

So, before they knew it, a couple of dropped-out lawyers were in the book business. The financial end of the business was all a bit of a joke and probably would have stayed that way if there hadn't been rent to pay and groceries to buy. At the beginning, no one knew anything about how books were printed, distributed or sold. In fact, no one even knew how to keep a set of business books until Trudy Ahlstrom arrived in 1973 and proved once again that knowing how to add and subtract goes a long way in any business. And a business it was getting to be. Ralph, along with Ed and new collective member Toni Ihara, a dropped-out anthropologist who joined in 1972 to edit the *Tenants' Handbook*, wrote *Protect Your Home with a Declaration of Homestead* in 1973; in the next year Ralph went on to co-author the *California Debtor's Handbook: Billpayers' Rights* (with Peter Jan Honigsberg) and *Sex, Living Together, and the Law* (with Carmen Massey). And if that wasn't enough, Ed and Ralph, with more than a little help from Trudy and Toni, organized the Wave Project—a series of approximately twenty-five "pro per" divorce offices located throughout the state.

As one book led to another, it became evident that Nolo had developed certain operating principles. They aren't unchangeable, but they do seem to work:

1. Work only on books that are at some level exciting and fun. (Linda Allison's wonderful drawings always helped with the fun part.)

2. Never do a book for the moment—think of the long term and don't let books go out of print.

3. No volunteer workers—everyone should be paid a decent wage (altruism doesn't buy groceries).

4. Don't accept grants (for obvious reasons).

5. Keep materials up-to-date. That means a new edition of each book every two years (at least). But it's worth it, as people eventually come to trust you.

6. Stay independent—don't borrow money or get involved in business deals where someone else

Kathy Galvin & Dave Brown

Keija Kimura and Ralph

gains power to tell you what to do.

7. Don't take any of the above too seriously.

But back to our story. By late 1974, Nolo had divided. Ed Sherman was off in the woods building a house and writing books on hydroponic gardening. Trudy Ahlstrom was running the business end of things from Occidental with Yolanda Gonzalez (books were stored in a barn), and Ralph, Toni, and Keija Kimura were running the editorial and media-promotion end of things from the old brown-shingle house in Berkeley. And so things continued for several years, with new books on such topics as name change, marriage and divorce law, incorpora-tion and non-profit incorporation, and adoption. But gradually things were changing too—more books meant more dealings with printers, graphics, artists and illustrators, and more books meant more need to understand how books are distributed and sold. After six years in the business, Auntie Nolo even subscribed to *Publishers Weekly.*

By 1979, Nolo was finally too big for the old house and moved to an old clock factory on Parker Street. Carol Pladsen, Robyn Samuels and Barbara Hodovan joined the staff, and Auntie Nolo was suddenly employing 11 people (about 8 full-time equivalents). This meant that for the first time it was possible to divide work into small departmental areas rather than relying on everyone to do a bit of everything. In the meantime, Trudy Ahlstrom had turned the Occidental operation into a closely related, but independent, wholesale distributor's business (Nolo Press Distributing).

Then came the Addison-Wesley Publishing Co. and a chance to expand more (scary to be sure). Starting with the notion that California was a big enough market to try and sell to directly, a decision was made to have Addison-Wesley sell Nolo books to the national market (Fawcett-Crest had previously done well with the *Living Together Kit*)as well as to handle any expansion into other states. All of this new energy was so exciting that Ed Sherman was coaxed out of the woods and back into active partici-pation in the business, and prepared a Texas version of *How to Do Your Own Divorce.*

Which brings us finally to the *People's Law Review* and the decision that Nolo Press would produce, and Addison-Wesley would publish, the book under the editorship of Ralph Warner, with Toni Ihara, Peter Jan Honigsberg and David Brown.

Because material would go out of date quickly, an intense work schedule was planned. In December 1979, a start was made, with Dave to handle book reviews, Peter mediation and self-help law pro-grams, and Toni and Ralph the articles in the first three parts of the *Review.* Toni and Dave were dispatched to the east coast, books were collected, articles commissioned, and self-help law programs contacted. Quickly it became apparent that we had taken on more than we could handle. Books were pouring in, authors of articles were calling, manu-scripts arrived, and self-help law programs in Boston, Minneapolis and Dayton had to be con-tacted. Things were a mess at the overcrowded office and tempers were short. Fortunately, at about the time when the 60-hour-per-week work schedule began driving everyone bananas, and mutiny was in the air, Kathy Galvin arrived from Boston, fresh from co-authoring *Legal Tactics: A Handbook for Massachusetts Tenants, 3rd Edition.* With Kathy doing all-purpose editing and Stephanie Harolde just back from Japan doing copy editing and typing seventy hours a week, progress suddenly became apparent. Almost magically, by May 1, 1980 the text was completed—only two weeks late. From there, Toni Ihara and Keija Kimura, working with artists Linda Allison and Hope Winslow, as well as typesetter Steve Murray, turned typed sheets into a book in seven weeks. With a great many sighs of relief all around, the book went to the printer at last.

Nolo Press